THE ENCYCLOPEDIA OF BIBLICAL ERRANCY

C. DENNIS McKINSEY

Prometheus Books

59 John Glenn Drive
Amherst, New York 14228-2197

Published 1995 by Prometheus Books

99 98 .   5 4 3 2

Library of Congress Cataloging-in-Publication Data

McKinsey, C. Dennis
  The encyclopedia of biblical errancy / by C. Dennis McKinsey.
      p.   cm.
  Includes bibliographical references and index.
  ISBN 0-87975-926-7 (hardback)
  1. Bible—Controversial literature. 2. Bible—Criticism, interpretations, etc. I. Title.
BS533.M385   1995
220.6—dc20   94-40048
                                                                   CIP

Printed in the United States of America on acid-free paper.

Table of Contents

5

Preface

This work is the essence of articles that appeared in the monthly newsletter *Biblical Errancy* from January 1983 to July 1993. The periodical, which is subcaptioned "The only national periodical focusing on biblical errors, contradictions, and fallacies while providing a hearing for apologists," was condensed onto twenty-four audio tapes with a sixteen- to twenty-one-page transcript of each. These transcripts, in turn, have been modified to comprise a separate chapter each.

Biblical Errancy grew out of a need to create the most comprehensive and relevant critique of the Bible available in the English-speaking world. Balance is sorely needed. One need only turn on the radio or watch television to see that Americans are receiving an almost totally one-sided presentation of the Bible. They are hearing all of the pros and none of the cons, all of the positives and none of the negatives. Only when people are given both sides of an issue can a truly objective analysis be possible and the danger of mass indoctrination be averted. This book and *Biblical Errancy* teach a kind of Sunday School in reverse by telling people all of the things they should have heard on Sunday morning but didn't. After all, if atheists, agnostics, freethinkers, and humanists don't reveal the contradictions, errors, fallacies and problems in the Bible, who will?

Certainly ministers, priests, and rabbis aren't going to perform that function. That's not what they are paid for. Much of the information contained herein will be reinforced by quotes from biblicists themselves, so I am by no means alone in my observations. Indeed, apologists, even some of a very fundamentalist philosophy, will corroborate many of my observations.

All biblical quotations are from the King James Version of the Bible unless otherwise noted.

Acknowledgments

I would like to gratefully acknowledge the assistance of Dr. John Nernoff III, Ernie Brennaman, and Ben Fuson, who spent many hours proofreading my manuscript. I also thank Douglas Smith whose computer expertise enabled him to create the indexes and a disk of the manuscript compatible with the publisher's programs.

1

The Composition of the Bible

Inerrancy, Canon, Excluded Literature, Authorship, Originals, Variances, Versions, Greek and Hebrew, Interpretation

Inerrancy

The first and most important consideration in any analysis of Scripture is what should be discussed. In light of the fact that the Bible is composed of a wide range of topics, our options are almost too numerous to mention. Some people might want to discuss God and his behavior in the Old Testament, while others would prefer an analysis of biblical prophecies. Still others would no doubt focus on the credentials and behavior of Jesus Christ. All of these are topics of immense importance and will be discussed in subsequent chapters. However, the best place to launch our critique is with the question of inerrancy and all of its ramifications, not only because that underlies the whole question of the Bible's credibility but also because that underpins the focus of our publication. Before turning to whether or not biblical inerrancy is a valid concept, we should first establish beyond any reasonable doubt that there are notable adherents to a belief in biblical infallibility. One could quote any number of prominent spokesmen for Christianity to prove that inerrancy is, in fact, a key element of conservative Christian thought. This is not really a subject of dispute, so one quote from fundamentalist William Arndt's book *Bible Difficulties* should suffice. On page 99 he says, "The Bible itself teaches that it is without error in every respect. When Jesus says in John 10:35 that the Scripture cannot be broken, he is ascribing perfection to our sacred book, not merely to just part of it."

A comment of this nature aptly summarizes the attitude of nearly all fundamentalists. Feeling the Book is God's inerrant word, without errors or imperfections, they proceed from that point onward. There is no need to quote a large number of people to prove the obvious, namely, that millions clearly claim the book is inerrant. However, this book will provide more than enough evidence to prove the opposite is true.

Having established inerrancy as a belief held by many, the question now becomes one of establishing its degree of importance. Just how important is it to have an inerrant Bible? In order to answer this question, let's turn to several books by prominent apologists and see what they have to say in this regard.

In a book entitled *The Battle for the Bible* fundamentalist Harold Lindsell states on page 13, "I regard the subject of this book, that is, biblical inerrancy, to be the most important theological topic of this age."

That is about as concise a quote as one could formulate. For most conservatives inerrancy is *the* major topic because if it collapses, if it is undermined, not only the Bible but Christianity in general is dealt a blow from which recovery is all but impossible.

In a thick volume entitled *Basic Theology* Charles Ryrie, a professor at a well-known conservative bastion in Texas known as Dallas Theological Seminary, states on page 77,

> Can one be a biblicist and deny inerrancy? Not if the Bible teaches its own inerrancy. . . . If the Bible contains some errors, no matter how few or many, how can one be sure that his understanding of Christ is correct? . . . Even if the errors are in supposedly "minor" matters, any error opens the Bible to suspicion on other points that may not be so "minor." If inerrancy falls, other doctrines will fall, too.

This is a valid point that the conservatives make repeatedly and the liberal wing of Christianity would do well to note the truth contained therein. If you don't have an inerrant Bible, you are going to encounter a massive number of problems. And what are some of the difficulties? Ryrie notes that doctrinal questions having to do with basic biblical concepts "may well be effected by denying inerrancy" and he provides a brief list of some of the more prominent examples. *First*, people will tend to deny the historical fall of Adam. If the book is not error-free how can we be sure Adam and Eve really existed? If they did not exist, the whole concept of original sin disappears. *Second*, a denial of inerrancy will undermine belief in the experiences of the prophet Jonah. *Third*, an explaining away of the miracles of both the Old and New Testament could very well materialize. If you deny inerrancy, you begin to question the whole concept of miracles. And if miracles vanish, the Bible itself is brought into question, because if there is any concept central to the Bible it is that of miracles. Without miracles there can be no resurrection, for instance. And without a resurrection, Christianity crumbles. To quote Paul, "Your faith is in vain." *Fourth*, Ryrie says that without inerrancy Mosaic authorship of the Pentateuch will be denied. Conservatives contend very strongly that Moses wrote the first 5 books of the Bible, and if, in fact, he is not the author, it weakens the adherence conservatives would have to the book. *Fifth*, the possibility that there are, in fact, two or more authors of the Book of Isaiah would become more credible. Fundamentalists have always adhered to a strong belief in only one author for the Book of Isaiah, not two and not three. Ryrie states on the next page that, "Inerrancy is a crucial issue," and he concludes by saying, "So inerrancy is not a tempest in a teapot." The validity of the latter comment is shown in the fact that Christianity and the Bible rise and fall on this issue.

In *What You Should Know About Inerrancy*, Ryrie states on page 103,

> No one can predict with total accuracy what doctrinal dominoes may topple after inerrancy falls. Defections do not always follow a logical pattern. Nevertheless, some general predictions can be made as to what may happen when inerrancy goes. . . . It is historical fact that a less than total view of inerrancy has resulted in a denial of some or all of the miracles of the Bible.

As Ryrie states in *Basic Theology*, without inerrancy a belief in miracles is going to be undermined. He continues by saying on pages 103 and 104 of *What You Should Know About Inerrancy*,

> Usually, Old Testament miracles are the first to either be denied outright or explained away as happening naturally rather than supernaturally. Often the attack is directed against the historical events recorded in the first eleven chapters of Genesis. That means that the accounts of creation or of the sin of man or the Flood are denied as being historically and factually true.

It goes without saying that if the creation account goes out the window, then the entire evolution-creation controversy is all but abolished. If Adam and the sin of man are denied, then the whole question of why Jesus died on the cross is brought into doubt, if not actually proven to be useless. And if the Flood is denied, a lot of apologetic scientists are going to be walking around with egg on their faces. Ryrie states, "The direct attack calls them myths with no factual content."

Then Ryrie addresses what he calls the less frontal attacks that approach the problem tangentially: "Less frontally, some try to maintain the truth of the stories while denying the factual and historical content." Then Ryrie strongly implies that this is dishonest exegesis.

They say, for example, that nothing could be more truthful than the fact of sin but, of course, no persons named Adam and Eve ever lived at any time in history or in an actual place called Eden to commit that sin. But by either the direct or less direct routes the result is the same. The events did not happen historically and, therefore, many biblical passages are erroneous."

Later Ryrie notes that if you deny inerrancy you are going to deny the existence of the Egyptian plagues, the Hebraic exodus, and what Moses did with regard to the pharaoh.

Several other scholars have also noted the ramifications of an undermined belief in inerrancy. In *Does Inerrancy Matter?* fundamentalists James Boice and James Packer state on page 8,

Those who undermine the truth of the Bible sometimes claim truthfulness for some parts of the Bible. These would be parts in which God has spoken as opposed to other parts in which only men have spoken. But this position is unsound. People who think like this speak of biblical authority, but at best they have partial biblical authority, since the parts containing error obviously cannot be authoritative. What is worse, they cannot even tell us precisely what parts are from God and therefore truthful and what parts are not from God and therefore are in error. Usually they say it is the "salvation parts," quote, unquote, whatever they are, that are from God. But they do not tell us how to separate these from the non-salvation parts."

A valid criticism of this kind is directed primarily at the liberal wing of Christianity. How do you know what is true when you begin to admit certain parts are false?

In *A Defense of Biblical Infallibility*, apologist Clark Pinnock says on page 18, "The surrender of biblical infallibility would be a disastrous mistake having deadly effects upon the church of God and its theology."

One of the foremost apologetic authorities on the Old Testament, Prof. Gleason Archer, states on page 22 in his book *A Survey of the Old Testament*,

If this written revelation contains mistakes, then it can hardly fulfill its intended purpose, that is, to convey to man in a reliable way the will of God for his salvation. Why is this so? Because a demonstrated mistake in one part gives rise to the possibility that there may be mistakes in other parts of the Bible. If the Bible turns out to be a mixture of truth and error then it becomes a book like any other book.

Again, the question arises, how do you know what is true when you begin to admit certain parts are false? Every book contains some truth, if it is nothing more than the name of the author and publisher. As Harold Lindsell says on page 25 of *The Battle for the Bible*,

I contend that embracing a doctrine of an errant Scripture will lead to disaster down the road. It will result in the loss of missionary outreach. It will quench missionary passion. It will lull congregations to sleep and undermine their belief in the full orbed truth of the Bible.

Anything that results in a loss of missionary outreach, a reduction of missionary passion, and a reduction of belief in the Bible's inerrancy has to be positive. Lindsell concludes by saying, "It will produce spiritual sloth and decay and will finally lead to apostasy," an apostate being one who has gone off the well-worn path of what is supposedly accurate.

A significant problem that has always confronted fundamentalists having to do with their own membership emerges. Some of them have recognized the contradictions and problems within the Bible and tried to leave the ranks, so to speak, by providing a less than inerrant strategy. Needless to say they have been soundly criticized. A good example is provided on page 165 in Lindsell's book. Rather than reading the text a simple summary will suffice. Anybody reasonably well acquainted with the Bible knows that there is a mathematical inaccuracy in 2 Chron. 4:2. In plain language the Bible says that there is a bowl with a diameter of 10 and a circumference of 30, while any reasonably competent high school math student knows that's an impossibility. If pi, which is 3.14, is multiplied times a diameter of 10, the circumference is 31.41, not 30. Apologist Robert Mounce, being a somewhat more practical fundamentalist, says that this can be explained by the fact that people within the biblical narrative lived two or three thousand years ago and the Bible is not supposed to be a book of absolute scientific precision. As one would expect, fundamentalist Lindsell refused to accept this explanation in any way and promptly attacked Mounce by providing an accurate refutation of such a weak rationalization. He states, "To say that 2 and 2 make 5, and then excuse it because it was said 3,000 years ago in a different culture hardly makes good sense."

The world would be far better served if more fundamentalists would follow this advice and cease making preposterous rationalizations such as that developed by Mounce, At least Lindsell is willing to admit that the argument based on cultural differentials is much too weak a reed to lean on. One can't retain intellectual integrity while using ancient culture as an excuse. When it comes to simple mathematical computations, such as that of determining the circumference of a circle, few objective scholars doubt that the people of two or three thousand years ago could come up with a considerably more accurate assessment than 30 being the circumference of a circle with a diameter of 10.

Near the end of his book Lindsell states the following on pages 202 and 203, "Inerrancy is important, but what is equally important is what happens once inerrancy is scrapped." At this point he turns to one of his fellow fundamentalists, Richard Coleman, who advocates a doctrine of what is known as "limited inerrancy" and attacks him. Coleman contends that only parts of the Bible are inerrant and Lindsell says,

> Coleman is advocating limited inerrancy. This term is meaningless, it is nonsense, the sooner we realize this, the sooner we will see the issue of inerrancy in its proper perspective. Once limited inerrancy is accepted, it places the Bible in the same category as every other book that has ever been written. Every book contains in it some things that are true and what is true is inerrant.

Lindsell has a much stronger case than Coleman and continues by saying, "Only two things remain to be determined once you accept limited inerrancy. The first is what proportion of the book is true and what proportion is false. It may be 90 percent false and 10 percent true or it may be 90 percent true and 10 percent false. The second thing that needs to be determined is what parts of the book are true."

In other words, according to Lindsell, you know the percentages. It could be 90 and 10 or 10 and 90, but you don't know which section is the true part. He continues,

> Since the book contains both error and falsehood, of necessity, other criteria outside the book must be brought to bear upon it to determine what is true and what is false. Whatever the source of the other criteria, that becomes the judge of the book in question. Thus, the book, that is the Bible, becomes subordinated to the standard against which its truth is determined and measured. . . . What limited inerrancy means. First it means that something outside of and above the Bible becomes its judge. There is something that is truer and more surer (sic) than Scripture and whatever it is has not been inspired by God. So a noninspired source takes precedence over an inspired Bible. Second, it leaves us in a vacuum without any basis for determining what parts of the Bible tell the truth and what parts do not.

All of Lindsell's comments are true. How could one possibly lend unqualified credence to a book with only limited inerrancy? The very phrase is an absurdity because of its applicability to nearly every book in a library.

Apologist Don Stewart, who often works with Josh McDowell on various apologetic writings, stated on page 63 in *100 Questions People Ask Most About Jesus*, "Once the door opens to the possibility of error in the Scripture, the eventual and logical result is that the entire foundation of the Christian faith will crumble." That is about as succinct a statement as one could devise and puts the entire issue in a nutshell.

By now, the entire question of whether or not inerrancy is important has been covered to a sufficient degree. One can only speculate on what would be required for someone who is not convinced by now.

So we'll conclude the whole question of whether or not inerrancy is important with what is probably the most common defense that apologists make in support of this concept, namely, the alleged substandard qualifications of the people who question the Bible's infallibility. Their honesty, integrity, morality, and intellect are brought into question. In *The Defense of Biblical Infallibility* biblicist Clark Pinnock states on page 19, "It requires an infallible critic to declare at the present state of our knowledge that the Bible contains errors."

In other words, no one can criticize the book until he becomes infallible. Why? Because the book is allegedly infallible and only the infallible can criticize the infallible. The obvious mistake in this defense is that it assumes the very point in dispute. Biblicists are assuming the book is infallible, but have failed to prove as much. And until infallibility becomes evident, one should feel no restraint about criticizing the Bible. If, indeed, the book was infallible then, yes, they would have a case, since fallible men would hardly be justified in criticizing an infallible book. But since the book is light years from infallibility, restraint is inappropriate. Freethinkers are not obligated to refrain from criticizing the book simply because infallibility is imputed by fallible proponents. Apologists have to prove inerrancy and that is something they are incapable of doing.

Lastly, Archer also decries biblical criticism by saying on page 29 in *A Survey of the Old Testament*, "The Bible must sit in judgment upon man; man can never sit in judgment upon the Bible."

He, too, is assuming the very point in dispute. If we can't sit in judgment upon the Bible, then we are conceding the battle before the encounter begins. And critics would have to have taken leave of their senses if they were to concede in any way that the Bible is infallible. Until biblicists substantiate infallibility, freethinkers are completely free to pass judgment on its qualities. And any reasonably objective observer of the world scene would have to concede that it should be judged very critically in light of the fact that it is having such a negative effect upon society in general.

Canon

Having established the importance of inerrancy for an analysis of the Bible and proven beyond any reasonable doubt that the question of whether or not the Bible is infallible is of monumental importance, it is incumbent upon us to turn to the historical formation of the Bible. Before examining the Bible's contents and analyzing such issues as God, Jesus, original sin, prophecy, etc., the historical formation of the Bible and the mechanism by which it was created as well as how that impinges upon and affects the people who believe it today need to be discussed. For if, indeed, the Bible was not divinely created, then what it says is of no more importance than any other book on the shelf.

We'll begin our investigation of this issue by turning to *The Light of Reason*, volume one, a writing that appeared several years ago by Schmuel Golding, the editor of the *Biblical Polemics* newsletter. Golding's synopsis of the process by which the Bible was formed is not only accurate but succinct. On page 23 he says,

> First the NT was not written by any of the disciples of Jesus nor by persons who even lived in that era. . . . When the church fathers compiled the NT in the year 397, they collected all the writings they could find and managed them as they pleased. They decided by vote which of the books out of the collection they had made should be the word of God and which should not. They rejected several, they voted others to be doubtful, and those books which had a majority of votes were voted to be the word of God. Had they voted otherwise, all the people since calling themselves Christians would have believed otherwise. For the belief of the one comes from the vote of the other.

It is important to note the key concept here is that the Bible was put together by a group of men who met, went through a collection of writings, and *chose through voting* those that are to be deemed divinely inspired. Many of them wound up on the cutting room floor. Golding continues,

> Who the people were that did all of this we know little of. They called themselves by the general name of church fathers and this is all the average Christian knows of the matter. . . . Disputes, however, ran high among the people calling themselves Christians not only as to points of doctrine but as to the authenticity of the books.

Although not stated verbatim, the essence of Golding's next paragraph is that when disputes broke out the opposition was often either eliminated or ostracized. Then, he continues by saying,

> Constantine, an unbaptized pagan, convened the Council of Nicea in the year 325 in order to settle these disputes. A major issue was the nature of the deity they worshipped. Based upon their decisions Jesus was changed from man to God in the flesh, the sabbath was changed from Saturday to Sunday, the Passover was changed to Easter . . . and the NT was canonized as a holy book.

In other words, men, rather than a god, composed the Bible. Many Christians, especially Protestants, have great difficulty with any assertion to the effect that men are responsible for the Bible coming into existence. On page 6 in *Answering Christianity's Most Puzzling Questions*, volume one, apologist Richard Sisson states,

In fact, after the death of Jesus a whole flood of books that claimed to be inspired appeared. . . . [D]isputes over which ones were true were so intense that the debate continued for centuries. Finally in the fourth century a group of church leaders called a council and took a vote. The 66 books that comprised our cherished Bible were declared to be Scripture by a vote of 568 to 563.

Although this happens to be basically what occurred, Sisson then proceeds to allege that this is *not* what happened. He states on page 7 that what really occurred is that, "Actually when the council of Hippo in A.D. 393 and the Council of Carthage in A.D. 397, named the 27 books of our NT as authentic, they were simply recognizing the inspiration of those books."

Sisson has managed to highlight the key difference between the Protestant and Catholic positions. The Catholic position is historically more accurate and simply states that the church fathers assembled in a council, went through all the writings that were circulating at that time and chose the ones that were to be deemed divinely inspired. In other words, the church fathers, men, put the book together by a vote. The Protestant position, on the other hand, is that men went through the writings and chose those that were divinely inspired through mere recognition. They had already been made divinely inspired by God prior to their analysis. The difference between the positions is essentially one of recognition versus determination. Catholics say their leaders determined which books were divinely inspired; Protestants say they were divinely inspired by God and later recognized as such. In one case men did it; in the other God supposedly did it.

Theologically speaking, by simply stating that God created the book and men only discovered that fact, the Protestant position is stronger. Historically speaking, however, the Catholic position is much stronger and clearly more accurate. Men merely convened and determined which books were divinely inspired. In *Today's Handbook for Solving Bible Difficulties* apologist David O'Brien on page 41 upholds the Protestant position by contending that although church councils put their stamps of approval on the canon of Scripture, "that canon was in place before they ever thought of meeting to approve it."

Ryrie makes the same point on page 108 in *Basic Theology*: "Remember that the books were inspired when they were written and thus canonical. The church only attested to what was inherently true."

And in *Evidence that Demands a Verdict* apologist Josh McDowell states the same position on page 33: "But the upshot of the Jamnia debates [Jamnia was another council in which the books of the Bible were being determined] was the firm acknowledgment that all these books were holy Scripture."

In other words, the church fathers simply acknowledged, they did not determine the books to be holy Scripture. But McDowell makes the following statement on page 29,

The word "canon" as applied to Scripture means an officially accepted list of books. One thing to keep in mind is that the church did not create the canon or the books included in what we call Scripture. Instead the church recognized that the books were inspired from their inception. . . . We don't know exactly what criteria the early church used to choose the canonical books.

McDowell had just stated that God inspired the canonical books. So how can he say that he does not know the criteria by which they were chosen? The criterion must be that they are God-inspired. An inadvertent contradiction is in evidence.

In essence, although possessed of a more impressive stance theologically, the Protestant position is historically indemonstrable. Historical evidence strongly implies that the books were not canonical but simply deemed as such by a group of influential religious and political figures. The book was put together by a vote; it was not compiled by God and subsequently discovered to be God's work.

Excluded Literature

As stated earlier, quite a few books did not make it into the Bible or what is commonly known as the canon. It might be of interest to note the names of some of these writings. For instance, we find that mentioned in the Old Testament are many books not in the Bible. The Book of the Wars of the Lord is referred to in Num. 21; the Book of Jasher is referred to in Joshua 10:13; the Book of Nathan and Gad is mentioned in First Chronicles and the Book of the Acts of Solomon is mentioned in Second Chronicles. All of these books, as well as many others, did not make it into Scripture, although they are mentioned in the Old Testament. Where they are, no one knows. Why were these books allowed to perish? No one knows. Why were they left out of the Old Testament? Again, no one knows. Another group of books were left out of the New Testament. It is a rather lengthy list in which can be found the following: the Gospel According to the Hebrews, the Gospel Written by Judas Iscariot, the Gospel of Peter, the Gospel of Marcion, the Gospel of Matthias, the Gospel of Eve, and the Gospel of Philip. Besides the Gospels are such writings as the Acts of Peter, the Book of the Judgment by Peter, the Hymn by Christ, the Magical Book by Christ, and the Letter to Peter and Paul by Christ. None of these books survived the cut and all were left on the debating room floor, again, primarily because of politics in the religious realm. All of these books had their advocates and all of them lost.

In *The Bible, the Quran, and Science* Maurice Bucaille, a French Muslim, observes on page 78 that, "Perhaps a hundred gospels were suppressed," which is a rather sizable number to say the least. On the other hand, there are a number of writings that did make it into the Bible, at least the Catholic Bible, and they are commonly known as the Apocrypha. They include such titles as: Tobit, Judith, the Wisdom of Solomon, Baruch, Susanna, Bel and the Dragon, First and Second Maccabees, and a few other books. Scholars have never agreed on whether these books should be considered canonical. It is a question upon which they have always argued and upon which the Christian world today is about evenly divided.

Some of the reasons Protestants give for these books not being included in their version of Scripture are wholly without merit. In *Evidence That Demands a Verdict* Josh McDowell says on page 33, "They abound in historical and geographical inaccuracies and anachronisms."

To that one can only say he must be speaking in jest, because if there is anything that abounds in historical and geographical inaccuracies, it is the Bible as currently constituted. One should have no compunction about challenging anyone to prove that the Apocrypha is any less reliable in that regard than the books that are in the Bible itself.

In *99 Questions People Ask Most About the Bible* apologist Don Stewart states on page 124 that, "The primary reason for not accepting the Apocrypha as Scripture is that there is no claim within the books that they are inspired by God. This is in contrast to the Scriptures, which claim to record the revelation of God." That is a poor rationale, because the Book of Esther doesn't even mention God. Why is it in the Bible?

Another reason given by Stewart is that the Apocrypha contains demonstrable errors. The Apocrypha contains errors! Imagine anyone talking about the Apocrypha as if its counterpart, the Bible, did not contain errors! Stewart's stance is vacuous and over eleven years of *Biblical Errancy* have proven as much.

Another apologist by the name of E. M. Blaiklock, in a book entitled *Jesus Christ, Man or Myth*, refers on page 47 to what he calls "the wildly extravagant stories found in the so-called Apocryphal gospels."

Wildly extravagant! If there is any book that is full of wildly extravagant stories it is the Bible. The miracles alone are about as extravagant as one can imagine. Talking serpents and donkeys, sticks turning into snakes, people rising from the dead. How much more incredible can one become? Extravagance would be a ridiculous reason for keeping the Apocrypha out of the Bible.

Bucaille says on page 77 of *The Bible, the Quran, and Science*,

In the early days of Christianity many writings on Jesus were in circulation. They were not subsequently retained as being worthy of authenticity and the church ordered them to be hidden. Hence their name, the Apocrypha. Some of the texts of these works have been well preserved because they have benefitted from the fact that they were generally valued."

Bucaille goes on to say that, "Some of these apocryphal writings contain imaginary details, a product of popular fantasy." If that doesn't describe the Bible, what does? He concludes by saying,

> Authors of works on the Apocrypha also quote with obvious satisfaction passages which are literally ridiculous. Passages such as these are, however, to be found in all the gospels. One has only to think of the imaginary description of the events that Matthew claims took place at Jesus' death. It is possible to find passages lacking seriousness in all the early writings of Christianity. One must be honest enough to admit this.

So, keeping the Apocrypha out of the Bible because it is full of extravagant claims, ridiculous situations, and popular fantasy is pure political nonsense. These books were kept out of the Bible because they did not have the advocates the other books had. As was stated earlier, religious politics was the prime determinant.

To further substantiate the fact that the Bible was put together by votes and political decisions, some quotations from additional apologetic sources with reference to the councils that occurred back in the days of A.D. 200, 300, and 400 are in order. In a rather voluminous book entitled *The Bible Handbook*, Edward Blair, observes on page 35: "Church councils at Rome in 382, at Hippo in 393, at Carthage in 397, and again at Carthage in 419 fixed the list at those now present in our NT."

Finally, in *Basic Theology*, Ryrie observes on page 109, "It is generally agreed that this church council [the council of Carthage in 397] fixed the limits of the NT canon as including all 27 books as we have them today."

Authorship

Another topic that is often brought up in regard to the formation of the Bible has to do with who wrote what book when. Although this entails an historical discussion and an intensive analysis of a topic of this nature is not warranted at this time, some comments by a few fundamentalist authors are well worth noting. In a book called *Biblical Criticism*, which was compiled by a group of conservative scholars, the following can be found on page 41: "Research into the historical literature has not been successful in determining the authorship of anonymous works such as Samuel, Kings and Chronicles and even questions of dating can not be settled with anything like precision."

In other words, these men are willing to admit that there are books in the Old Testament whose authors are anonymous. We don't know who wrote them or when this occurred. They proceed to make an even more candid admission on page 116 by saying, "Indeed, one of the major problems in any kind of NT criticism is the paucity of Christian or non-Christian evidence outside of the NT itself for the historical and literary background of its writers."

Apologists who claim precise knowledge as to the authorship and date of composition of each book in the Bible are nearly always whistling in the dark. They don't know and, indeed, knowledgeable scholars who are sufficiently honest are often willing to admit that it simply can't be determined and involves a tremendous amount of guessing, estimating, and theorizing. But as was stated earlier, because this whole issue primarily involves a historical discussion and doesn't sufficiently affect peoples' attitudes toward the Bible, we'll move to the next topic— the originals.

Originals

One of the most common defenses employed against those exposing the contradictions, inconsistencies, and inaccuracies within the Bible is that one has to return to the originals. Defenders of the Bible will often admit that modern-day versions such as the Revised Standard, the New American, the New American Standard, and the New International, have contradictions and inconsistencies, but they often declare that if you return to the original manuscripts you will find that the Bible is totally consistent. Unfortunately for its proponents, this theory is wholly without merit. We are by no means the only source for this contention. Oddly enough there is a "King James Only" fundamentalist organization within Christianity itself that takes a position quite similar to ours. One of their writers, Norman Ward, states on page 6 in a book called *Perfected and Perverted,*

> In discussing the text of the Bible the revisionists [those who do not believe the King James is the only Bible] will often use the phrase "According to the Original Greek." This leads one to believe that they have access to the original autograph manuscripts. Nobody today has the original writings themselves. Let me repeat that; the original autographical manuscripts of the NT no longer exist. They were written on perishable material and it is unlikely that they lasted for more than a few years, let alone 19 centuries.

Later Ward states,

> Often the same people who refer you to the original Greek will also refer you to the original Bible. *There was no "original Bible."* At no time did the original autographical manuscripts of the 27 books of the NT ever reside between the covers of one particular book. To say I believe in the verbal, plenary [complete], inspiration of the original Bible is to say you believe in nothing, for no such book ever existed.

Three pages later Ward declares, "Many people have a vague idea that there exists somewhere a single authoritative Greek text from which all translations and versions are made. *This is not true.* What we do have is a collection of what is called manuscript evidence."

As far as the existence of the original autographical manuscripts is concerned, Ward is supported by apologist Don Stewart on page 33 in *99 Questions People Ask Most About the Bible:*

> With rare exceptions, the original autographs of the ancient works have been lost. . . . The science of attempting to reconstruct the text of these documents is known as textual criticism. . . . We do not possess any of the original writings of the Old or New Testament. We are dependent upon copies to reconstruct the text.

On the next page Ward states, "The original manuscripts in which the books of the Bible were written have been lost. Today we do not possess any biblical book in its original form. This is true for the originals of almost all other ancient writings as well." Ward concludes by saying, "We do not have the original autographs of the books of the Bible." So Ward is in full agreement with our earlier analysis of this situation.

On page 51 of *Problem Texts* apologist Peter Ruckman supports Ward's position by saying, "Can anyone produce one or part of one original . . . ? You would not know whether you or anyone else had restored them because you don't have them. The real reason for bragging about the verbal, plenary, inspired originals is *cowardice* and *desertion* in combat." Two pages later Ruckman states, referring to the revisionists, "*None of them had a Bible.* They had what they fondly call 'reliable' and unreliable 'translations' of some 'original manuscripts' that they never saw or read a day in their life."

On the next page, ultrafundamentalist Ruckman alludes to the so-called Christians who "*professed* to believe that an unread, unseen Bible is the word of God." Ruckman's observation is quite appropriate—if you have never seen or read a book, how do you know what it really says? On page 202 Ruckman accurately notes,

> When Rice [a famous fundamentalist preacher and mentor of Jerry Falwell] says that he wrote the most scholarly . . . exhaustive book in print on what the Bible claims for its inspiration . . . he is no more seriously dealing with the Bible than Rev. Ike or Jimmy Swaggart. Rice has never seen the Bible. . . . He has no Bible to go to.

And then Ruckman mentions some other people who have no Bible to go to, either. One of them is J. Vernon McGee, who, he says, "must have it for he tells us the way to learn the Bible is to DISCOVER WHAT THE ORIGINAL SAYS. Wow! Isn't that terrific?" Ruckman continues, "Is there anyone who can do it? No! Has it ever been done in 15 centuries? No! Could you find *the original* if you wanted to? No! Then why say it?" Ruckman concludes, "Well, it's part of the party line."

The truth of his observation can't be ignored. It *is* part of the party line. Concluding in the same vein Ruckman states on page 208,

> We will lay the reader odds of 10 to 1 that he will not obtain *one* clear-cut *statement by any man listed* [the revisionists] that *any* Bible is the infallible word of God. All he will own up to is a collection of manuscripts which he never saw and *which were not a Bible when they were written.* There was no such thing as the Bible when Paul wrote Corinthians and Ephesians.

So what can we deduce from our analysis of the originals? Essentially, it's this: When somebody gives you a book, be it the RSV, the KJV, the NIV, or what have you, all they are doing is giving you a writing that was put together by a group of scholars who read some ancient manuscripts that purportedly are accurate representations of the originals, which no longer exist. That's what you receive when you go to the store to buy a Bible. You cannot obtain a copy of *the Bible*. As one of the scholars who was quoted earlier stated, the book was never assembled within the covers of one particular volume.

In conclusion, we might note a comment by Josh McDowell that is exceedingly inept, to say the least. First some background. Liberal Protestant scholar Julius Wellhausen developed a theory about a hundred years ago that the first four books in the Bible were not composed by Moses but by four different authors he labeled J, E, D, and P. Of course, the fundamentalists of today not only hold that theory in contempt, but attack it whenever possible. While discussing Wellhausen's thesis, McDowell says on page 84 in *Evidence for Faith, Practical Apologetics*, "Now what do we have today? We have four documents. These are four sources. Now realize, no one's ever seen these documents." McDowell completes his final descent into quicksand on page 87. "Would you feel confident about your theory of how the Bible was written if it were based on a set of documents no one had ever seen and an editor no one knows?"

Talk about blind faith! McDowell has the unmitigated temerity to allege that no one has ever seen these documents of Wellhausen, when that is precisely the position of Bible adherents. That is exactly the position of McDowell himself. He criticizes another individual for practicing the same baseless scholarship upon which his philosophy of life rests.

While criticizing the Wellhausen theory, McDowell appears wholly unable to realize he is blowing his own theory, his own philosophy of life, right out of the water because his attack is directly applicable to the Bible. Nobody has ever seen the originals.

Realizing that the subject of biblical reliability is quite uncertain, Harold Lindsell in *The Battle for the Bible* tries one last, desperate gambit. On page 37 he states, "It must be remembered too that those who scoff at the inerrancy of the autographs, because they can't be produced for examination, have no better case arguing for the errancy of the text they cannot produce either. At the worst it is a standoff."

In other words, when all else fails, Lindsell has decided that although he cannot prove that they are inerrant, opponents cannot prove they have errors. Talk about a pathetic approach! As we have so often said in regard to the existence of God, *the burden of proof lies on him who alleges*. It is the Achilles heel of the entire religious/superstitious movement. It is the lethal injection for all supernatural/superstitious thought. The importance of this comment lies in the fact that I am not saying God does not exist; the exponents of rational thought are only asking God's proponents to prove he does. After all, the latter are the ones who brought up the idea. And by the same token, when it comes to the inerrancy of the Book, its advocates are required to provide adequate evidence of the inerrant originals, because certainly everything that comes after them is replete with errors and contradictions. Why on earth anybody would assume the originals have no mistakes, when all of the copies reek with errors and often conflict with one another is beyond comprehension. That is a leap in logic that only the irrational can fathom. Of course, the problem lies in the fact that there is no logic involved.

Variances

We now know what we don't have. We don't have copies of the originals. What, then, do we have? Well, we have thousands of manuscripts that purport to be accurate representations of the originals. The fundamentalist book *Biblical Criticism* states on page 128,

> The originals probably written on papyrus scrolls have all perished. For over 1400 years the NT was copied by hand and the copyists, the scribes, made every conceivable error as well at times intentionally altering the text. Such errors and alterations survived in various ways with a basic tendency to accumulate. Scribes seldom left out anything lest they omit something inspired. There are now in existence, extant, in whole or in part, 5,338 Greek manuscripts as well as hundreds of copies of ancient translations, not counting over 8,000 copies of the Latin Vulgate.

That may lead readers to believe that with that many manuscripts we must know what the original said. No, the more extant manuscripts the greater the problem becomes because no two manuscripts anywhere in existence are exactly alike. In *A General Introduction to the Bible* Norman Geisler states on page 360, "The multiplicity of manuscripts produces a corresponding number of variant readings. For the more manuscripts that are copied, the greater will be the number of copyist errors." On page 252 he states that in the New Testament there are "over 200,000 variants in some 5,000 manuscripts."

In other words, based upon the admission of fundamentalists themselves, don't succumb to the belief that the more manuscripts that are in existence the better the representation of the originals that exists. Far from it. In fact, the more manuscripts that are in existence the more variances and differences between the manuscripts that exist and the more difficult it becomes to reconstruct the originals if, indeed, they ever existed. So, instead of solving the problem, a tremendous number of manuscripts only enhances it. As Geisler states on page 360, "The gross number of variants increases with every new manuscript discovery. . . . To date there are over 200,000 known variants and this figure will no doubt increase in the future as more manuscripts are discovered."

In other words, more manuscripts don't solve the problem; they only compound it. In *The Bible, the Quran, and Science* Bucaille says on page 79, "One might reply that other texts may be used for comparison. But how does one choose between variations that change the meaning?"

On the next page he quotes a book by Oscar Culmann to the effect that sometimes the variations

> are the result of inadvertent flaws. The copier misses a word, leaves it out or conversely he inserts it twice. Or a whole section of a sentence is carelessly omitted because in the manuscript to be copied it appeared between two identical words. Sometimes it is a matter of deliberate corrections. Either the copier has taken the liberty of correcting the text according to his own ideas or he has tried to bring it into line with a parallel text in a more or less skillful attempt to reduce the number of discrepancies.

Culmann is saying, in other words, that they are rewriting the script. He continues,

> As little by little the NT writings broke away from the rest of early Christian literature and came to be regarded as holy Scripture, so the copiers became more and more hesitant about taking the same liberties as their predecessors. They thought they were copying authentic text when in fact they wrote down the variations. Finally, a copier sometimes wrote annotations in the margin to explain an obscure passage. The following copier thinking the sentence he found in the margin had been left out of the passage by his predecessor thought it necessary

to include the margin notes in the text. This process often made the new text even more obscure.

After having quoted Culmann Bucaille concludes on the next page by saying, "All that modern textual criticism can do in this respect is to try to reconstitute a text which has the most likelihood of coming near to the original. In any case, there can be no hope of going back to the original text itself."

In essence, the problem is that even though you may have the original in the manuscripts, it is buried in there somewhere, assuming it's in there at all, and you don't know which one has it. The more manuscripts that are present, the greater the number of variations that are apparent and the less chance of being able to reconstruct what the supposed original said. If you have a verse in which five thousand manuscripts say it says one thing, while four thousand say it says another, why assume the five thousand are more correct than the four thousand? It could be the reverse. In an attempt to allay the fears of true believers that there is no copy of the real Bible, the apologist Geisler states on page 366 in *A General Introduction to the Bible*,

> At first the great multitude of variants would seem to be a liability to the integrity of the Bible text. But just the contrary is true. The larger number of variants supplies at the same time the means of checking on those variants. As strange as it may appear, the corruption of the text provides the means for its own correction.

And, of course, that is absurd. The more variations on a story that are submitted, the less chance one has of reconstructing what really occurred. Geisler is trying to tell us that the greater the number of variants, the greater the possibility of reconstructing the original text when the opposite is true.

In *Reasons Skeptics Should Consider Christianity* apologists McDowell and Stewart team up to state on page 78, "With the abundance of manuscripts, that is, handwritten copies of the NT numbering over 25,000, nothing has been lost in the transmission of the text."

In the first place, even if there were a million copies, how do they know that the original is located somewhere in that million? But even more importantly, they slipped in a rather insidious concept. Notice what they said: "nothing has been lost." That could very well be true. Nothing has been lost. It is in the 25,000 copies, but where? That's being kept surreptitiously behind the scenes. Even if it is contained within, its precise location becomes the central question. Where is it? Which one has it? Do we play a shell game? That's the fallacy in their logic. True, the more texts and manuscripts you have, the greater the chance of having the original. But simultaneously, the chance that you can't find the original increases exponentially. It's lost; it's buried somewhere in a maze of conjecture and the greater the number of manuscripts the less chance you have of finding the real McCoy. That second part is crucial and that's what they want to overlook.

To close out this discussion, we'll return to *Biblical Criticism* and note that the authors say on page 134, "However, the abundance of material is likewise the textual critic's problem, because no two copies are exactly alike, and the greater the number of copies the greater the number of variants among them."

Although this is quite true, it leaves out the third point, the same point omitted by McDowell and Stewart. The greater the number of copies the less chance of finding the original wording. It becomes buried in an ever larger number of choices.

Versions

Because of the above arguments, some apologists have devised an additional strategy of deception, namely, although there are a lot of variances and a great deal of difficulty is involved in reconstructing originals, none of the variances affect a material aspect of the Bible. None of them impinge on a fundamental doctrine of Christianity. On page 44 in *Evidence That Demands a Verdict* McDowell states, "There are some 200,000 variants in the existing manuscripts of the NT . . . but only 50 of these are of great significance." On the next page he states, "No fundamental doctrine of the Christian faith rests on a disputed reading. . . . A careful study of the variants, the different readings, of the various early manuscripts will reveal that none of them affects a single doctrine of Scripture."

In the same vein, McDowell's sidekick Don Stewart states on page 40 in *99 Questions People Ask Most About the Bible*, "Variant readings about which any doubt remains affect no material question of historic fact or of Christian faith and practice."

These statements are ridiculous. One need only turn to the ASV's version of 2 Tim. 3:16 to see a major problem. There are two ways to read the verse. Some versions contend that it says, "All Scripture is given by inspiration of God." That's the version fundamentalists propound. However, the ASV, the NEB, and the Living Bible say, "Every Scripture inspired by God is also profitable for teaching." Notice the latter does *not* say every Scripture is inspired; it says Scripture *that is inspired* is profitable to teach, which clearly implies that other Scripture is not.

This is a fundamental teaching of extreme importance. Indeed, if someone were asked to show where the Bible says that it is the inspired word of God, virtually every apologist in the land would race to 2 Tim. 3:16. That is not only the strongest passage but the one relied upon the most. Clearly scholars are in disagreement as to what it says in the supposed original. Support for our position is provided by Ryrie in *What You Should Know About Inerrancy*. On page 39 he states,

> If someone wishes to reduce the amount of Scripture included in this verse he translates it, all Scripture inspired by God is also profitable. In other words, whatever parts of Scripture that are inspired are profitable but the other uninspired parts are not. Thus, by such a translation only part of the Bible is inspired. Is this translation accurate? The answer is yes. Is such a translation required? The answer is no. Equally correct and preferable is the translation: All Scripture is inspired of God and is profitable.

So anybody alleging there is no material aspect of biblical doctrine affected by conflicting variances is practicing self-deception.

Another example is found in 1 Timothy 6:10. We have all heard the comment, "The love of money is the root of all evil." Notice it says "*the* love" of money is "*the* root" of all evil. That is in the King James and a few other versions. But the NIV says, "For the love of money is a root." It does not say *the* root, it says *a* root, one among several. The quote goes on "of all *kinds* of evil" (not necessarily *all* evil). Another version says, "For the love of money is a root of all evil." And a fourth version that can be found, for instance, in the NWT, says, "For the love of money is a root of all sorts of injurious things." That does not necessarily mean it has to do with evil at all. So we have four different versions of 1 Tim. 6:10, all of which have differences, some small and some large, that go to a material doctrine in the Bible that is of critical importance. In dealing with evil and how it materializes we have these variations.

Other examples are also readily available. One that comes immediately to mind is Mark 16:9–20, in which the problem is not so much over what the verses say as whether or not they should even be in the Bible. The New International Version states as a footnote: "The two most reliable early manuscripts don't even have these verses," even though they are very important. They pertain to the biblical doctrine of taking up serpents and drinking any deadly thing. In light of the fact that many fundamentalist children have died while using these verses, a very important concept is involved. Yet, even people who support the Bible can't agree on whether or not these verses should be included.

This is a topic upon which one could elaborate at great length since examples are in abundance. Clashes among the various manuscripts often go to matters of great importance, not trivia, as apologists would have us believe. Trying to trivialize conflict is another excuse, another ruse, another strategy, devised by the Bible's defenders to give biblicists the impression, the confidence, that they possess the true Word of God. Bible adherents are deceived into believing they don't have to worry, that scholars have brought forth that which came from the horse's mouth so to speak. In point of fact, they have no way of substantiating a guarantee of that kind. They are wishing and hoping while projecting an aura of certainty. It's all front and facade.

Greek and Hebrew

Another strategy of apologists is rather interesting. The Bible's defenders will often say that you have to go back to the original Greek. You have to know Greek and Hebrew. The obvious retort is that if that is true, then why do scholars who know Greek and Hebrew fluently still disagree, often strongly. Because that doesn't solve the dilemma, that's why.

In his *Answers to Questions About the Bible* apologist Robert Mounce asks this very question on page 29: "If a knowledge of the original Greek clears up all questions then why are the experts still arguing?" This question should bother any reasonably objective observer of the Bible and Mounce answers it by saying, "I sympathize with those lay students of Scripture who are from time to time put down by someone who has studied a bit of Greek and settles every argument with the *shibboleth* 'The original Greek says.' " Mounce concludes, "A knowledge of the Greek does not solve all problems."

It certainly doesn't, even among the experts. This Greek question is well addressed in Dr. Peter Ruckman's *Problem Texts*. Known for vituperation and not mincing his words, the President of the Pensacola Bible Institute lays it on the line as well as anybody when he says on page 58,

> One of the standard gimmicks which the stick men set up at the flat joints is that a knowledge of the original Greek is essential to *understand* the NT. This age-old con man's tool has probably put more young men out of the ministry and destroyed the fidelity of more Christian teachers than any other single gimmick. Prevailing opinion is that the NT teaches that without a knowledge of Greek grammar and a knowledge of the Greek text, the hidden riches of the word of God are unavailable to the student. *Since no one has ever produced a chapter or verse of either testament that says anything of the kind or has even given a general hint in that direction*, it is amazing how 5,000 ministerial students fall sucker for that trotline every year and take it in.

Anyone acquainted with the problem and possessed of a modest degree of honesty would agree with Ruckman's observations wholeheartedly. Ruckman follows them up on page 66 with the statement, "You need Greek grammar like a baby kangaroo needs a cradle." On page 438 he says,

> The confidence of the Bible department of Bob Jones University according to the president is to be placed in the *Greek* and the *Hebrew* without saying *which* Greek or which Hebrew or *which* text or which set of manuscripts or *who* interprets

any of them. The expression the *Greek* and the *Hebrew* is as inane a piece of foolishness as ever busted out of a Halloween party. There is no such thing as the *Greek* and the *Hebrew* to put confidence in. *Bob Jones III*, who originally founded the university, knew it when he wrote it.

Well, at least one fundamentalist has managed to burst through the wall of fundamentalist propaganda.

Interpretation

An extremely important topic when discussing the Bible is the question of how to interpret it. Any Bible analyst would be remiss if he failed to provide a reasonably comprehensive explanation of the rules that should be followed while interpreting the Bible. According to Dallas Theological Seminary professor Dwight Pentecost, in his book *Things to Come, A Study in Biblical Eschatology*, "When the plain sense of Scripture makes common sense, seek no other sense; therefore, take every word at its primary, ordinary, usual literal meaning unless the facts of the immediate context studied in the light of related passages and fundamental truths indicate clearly otherwise" (page 42).

In *508 Answers to Bible Questions* M. R. DeHaan writes on page 36, "The Bible should always be taken literally except when the language is plainly symbolic or where it is plainly stated that it is a parable or a type." On page 133 in *Bible Difficulties* William Arndt states, "It must be remembered that a deviation from the literal sense is not justified unless Scripture prescribes such a course." And on page 9 of *The Bible Has the Answer* Henry Morris and Martin Clark affirm the same maxim by saying, "The best rule to follow is to take the Bible literally unless the context clearly requires a symbolic meaning."

All of these men agree on a crucial point: the Bible should always be taken literally unless there is an unmistakably correct reason for doing otherwise. Unbeknownst to many is the fact that we have a view expounded by four fundamentalist writers that is systematically ignored by apologists in general. One place it is ignored is the third chapter of Genesis, almost at the beginning of the Bible. In the story of Adam and Eve, the Serpent talked Eve into violating God's rule not to eat the fruit of the Tree of Knowledge. In the Living Bible the text states, "The Serpent was the craftiest of all creatures the Lord God had made. So the Serpent came to the woman." The woman told the Serpent that they couldn't eat of the forbidden fruit because God had told them not to. And the Serpent says, "None of the fruit in the Garden? God says you must not eat any of it?" And the woman says, "Of course, we may eat it; it is only the fruit from the tree of the center of the Garden that we may not eat. God says we must not eat it or touch it or we will die." And the Serpent says, "That's a lie! You will not die." So the question becomes, Did Adam and Eve die? No, they did not die. Now if we take God's comment literally, they should have died. To extricate themselves from an embarrassing predicament, religionists will say, Well, they died spiritually. But that's not what the book says. It says they will die. Nothing is said about a spiritual death. Fundamentalists love to talk about a literal interpretation until they begin to feel the pinch, at which time they immediately opt for a figurative analysis. They always scrap the literal approach when expediency dictates, while simultaneously denouncing Christian liberals for the same practice. Indeed, this is one of their most common criticisms of liberal Christianity.

On page 9 of *The Bible Has the Answers* Morris and Clark state,

> Whenever a biblical writer uses figurative or poetic language he makes this evident in the context. And the truth intended to be conveyed by the figure is likewise evident in the context. When symbols are used they also are defined and explained either in the immediate context or in other passages of the Bible.

These rules have little to do with reality because the Bible does not make itself clear in many, many instances, especially in figurative or symbolic books such as Daniel, Revelation, and Ezekiel.

To wrap up the question of interpretation, we'll turn to fundamentalist James Sire's book *Scripture Twisting*. Interestingly, the rules Sire lays down for interpreting Scripture are often ignored by fundamentalists. For instance, Sire states in "Misreading Rule #4" that the simplest error is the failure to consider the immediate context of the verse or passage in question. To say this rule is violated routinely, especially in regard to interpreting Old Testament passages and their messianic reliability, is an understatement of the first magnitude. Fundamentalists ignore this maxim en masse. They allege that many Old Testament passages pertain to Jesus Christ when one need only look at the context to see they clearly do not.

In "Misreading Rule #12" Sire says, "Some parts of the Bible are obscure. Puzzling to say the least. Scholars simply don't know what is being said or referred to. Sometimes even when we have considered all the evidence seemingly available in Scripture, there is not enough to satisfy our curiosity or to draw solid conclusions" (page 82). All of these comments are valid. Then Sire says, "The inadequacy of scriptural data, however, has not kept people from speculating."

How true that is! They have let their imaginations run wild. To illustrate his point Sire refers to the giants roaming the earth discussed in the sixth chapter of Genesis. Who these giants are is a matter of conjecture and Sire notes that speculation has run rampant in this matter. Other examples of unleashed imaginations are clearly evident in any discussion of the Book of Revelation and the Book of Daniel. Apologists have gone through the Bible and twisted and distorted verses with reckless abandon. The current social issue of abortion provides another example in which apologists have perverted many verses that have nothing to do with abortion and speculated no end in order to buttress a wholly unbiblical precept.

On page 150 Sire says, "No translation of Scripture is without its problems. Some passages have been notoriously difficult to translate, let alone fully understand." On page 152 he states, "In all matters where Scriptures are vague or silent we should not pronounce that the Bible has the answer." Unfortunately, this rule is violated on a regular basis also. Sire concludes by saying, "Many matters in Scripture are not obvious at all."

To close out our general discussion of the Bible and the process by which it emerged, some additional quotes are not only relevant but either accurate or ridiculous, as the case may be. They pertain to how one should view the Bible's contents. What follows is essentially a grab bag of comments from various apologetic writings. The first is from R. C. Sproul, who perceptively states on page 17 of *Knowing Scripture*, "Absurdities often sound profound because they are incapable of being understood." Sproul continues, "When we hear things we do not understand sometimes we think they are simply too deep or weighty for us to grasp, when in fact they are merely unintelligible statements like one-hand clapping."

Many people who read the Bible assume it to be profound, not realizing that it abounds in contradictions and absurdities. Because the Bible sounds like a fountain of wisdom, readers often tend to demean themselves and feel they are simply incapable of analyzing the book when, in truth, the problem often lies not with them but with the book itself.

Moving from Sproul's accurate assessment, we come to a ridiculous comment with reference to martyrdom made by the apologist Don Stewart on page 72 of *99 Questions People Ask Most About the Bible*: "The final evidence of the truthfulness of the disciples' testimony is that they were martyred for their beliefs." How silly can one be! Many people have died for their beliefs. That certainly does not mean they were truthful, that their beliefs were valid.

And finally, we have a quote from a book entitled *I'm Glad You Asked*, in which the apologists Kenneth Boa and Larry Moody say on page 84, "There have been numerous attempts to burn, ban, and systematically eliminate the Bible, but all have failed."

As far as dishonesty is concerned, that comment is probably the clincher. The burning and the banning has been on the part of those supporting the Bible, not those who are trying to reveal it for what it is. If there has been any persecution it has been by people who are in support of the Book and not by those critical of its validity. That history accounts in large measure for the fact that the Bible is so strong today. An intelligent analyst of the national scene recently made a very observant statement in that regard by saying, "If you think it is hard living as a Christian in this nation, you ought to try living as not one."

In summary, an analysis of the Bible's evolution shows it is not to be trusted from a historical or a textural perspective.

2

"Jesus Christ Is the Answer?"

Twenty-Two Questions About Jesus

Chapter 1 discussed inerrancy, the originals, the Apocrypha, variances, rules for interpreting, and various topics having to do with the historical creation of the Bible. This chapter will focus on the questions and problems that are present in a pamphlet distributed several years ago by *Biblical Errancy* entitled "Jesus Christ Is the Answer?" The title is appropriately followed by a question mark because the title itself is wholly inaccurate. This pamphlet and the pamphlet discussed in chapter 3 ("The Bible is God's Word?") are both composed of some of the best questions one could ever employ while confronting Christianity in general and the Bible in particular. While proceeding down the list and discussing each point, additional information will be brought into the picture as well as some of the responses that apologists often use in opposition to the questions that are posed. Armed with information of this kind, analysts of the Bible will be far better prepared to confront Christians on their own turf. One should always know what lies in the other side's arsenal before engaging in ideological combat.

Before beginning our discussion of each difficulty, we might note the fact that many people do not even realize that problems exist within the Bible. In a book entitled *The Bible, the Quran, and Science*, the French Muslim Bucaille alludes to the fact that many Christians are completely in the dark with respect to the Bible's shortcomings. A good deal of the information that he furnishes to prove his point is quite similar to, if not identical with, that found in *Biblical Errancy*. He begins on page 107 by making the obvious statement, "It is impossible to believe two facts that contradict each other."

Then he proceeds to talk about contradictions within the Bible and says,

"These contradictions, improbabilities, and incompatibilities pass unnoticed by many Christians." They certainly do! One need only go on the radio to be amazed at the number of people who aren't even aware of problems within the Bible. Clearly, ministers, priests, and rabbis don't look upon themselves as agents of biblical criticism or exposure. Rest assured that the poor, misguided human beings sitting out in the pews are certainly not going to hear what is wrong with the book. Instead, they are going to be subjected to a totally one-sided presentation and that is precisely what has been occurring on a regular basis. Bucaille continues by saying, "People are astonished when they discover these contradictions because they have been influenced by their reading of commentaries that provide subtle explanations calculated to reassure them and orchestrated by an apologetic lyricism." In other words, they have been led down the primrose path by a melodious sounding explanation that is often nothing more than a masterpiece of obfuscation. Bucaille then says, "Some very typical examples have been given of the skill employed by certain experts in exegesis in camouflaging what they modestly call 'difficulties.' " Fortunately, Bucaille is one of those astute critics who is able to recognize the subtle use of the word "difficulties" as a smokescreen. While confronting Christians one should notice that they rarely refer to problems within the Bible as contradictions. They are marketed under the euphemisms of "difficulties," "discrepancies," or "problems." Over one hundred years ago the apologist Haley even labeled his book *Alleged Discrepancies in the Bible*. Of course, any reasonably unbiased observer can easily see that they are not just discrepancies but major contradictions in direct conflict with one another.

To move on to the problems that are discussed in the pamphlets, we *first* encounter one of those imbroglios that Trinitarians detest. While on the cross Jesus said in Matt. 27:46, "My God, my God, why hast thou forsaken me?" The obvious question any rational person would have in regard to this comment is: How can Jesus Christ be our savior when he couldn't even save himself? Those aren't the words of a man who is voluntarily dying for our sins; those are the words of a man who can think of a hundred places he would rather be. Christians strongly proclaim that Jesus willingly died for us. If so, then why does he show an obvious displeasure for what is occurring? You don't cry out in agony and desperation when your wishes are being fulfilled. Jesus would use the word "forsaken" only if he felt he had been abandoned. There can be no doubt that the words emanate from a man who does not have the situation under control. Quite the contrary, the words of desperation clearly describe an individual who is not dying willingly for anybody. On page 227 in *The Jew and the Christian Missionary* Jewish scholar Gerald Sigal poignantly states,

> Christian missionaries claim that Jesus came into the world expressly to offer himself as a willing sacrifice to atone for mankind's sins. If that was true, why did he hesitate and pray for the reversal of the fate prescribed for him. Matt.

26:39 says, ". . . going a little way forward, he fell upon his face praying and saying: 'My Father, if it is possible, let this cup pass from me. Yet, not as I will, but as you will.'" Jesus' alleged exclamation: "Yet, not as I will, but as you will," undoubtedly indicates that had it been his choice, he would not have undergone execution. And why did Jesus, the god-man, need an angel to strengthen him in Luke 22:43?

The *second* question goes to the heart of Jesus' character. In Matt. 5:22 he condemns people to hell for calling others "fools" although he engages in the practice himself: in Matt. 23:17 and Luke 11:40 he refers to others as fools. The obvious question then becomes, Shouldn't Jesus be sent to hell too? After all, he did lay down a maxim for all to follow. Or is Jesus to be exempt from morality and allowed to do whatever strikes his fancy? Some apologists try to resolve this problem by alleging that there are different Greek words for "fool" and Jesus did not call people the kind of fool that is referred to in Matt. 5:22. This is not only a case of rationalizing but of blatant inaccuracy and deception. The word "fool" in Matt. 5:22 and the word "fool" in Matt. 23:17 and 19 come from the same Greek word, which is transliterated as "moros." There is no way to employ the "You have to go back to the Greek" approach to escape this dilemma. The problem is there and it's blatant. So the next question becomes, What are we going to do with Jesus?

This is not the only time Jesus engages in either reprehensible behavior or rhetoric. Yet we never hear of him being condemned by others. Perhaps a double standard rules the universe. One law for man, another for God and Jesus. The question then becomes, Who made that standard? If it was God, i.e., Jesus, then Jesus is, in effect, nothing more than a law unto himself. He is above and beyond morality. He can do whatever he desires, whenever he desires to do it. Earthly tyrants are often accused of propounding the same philosophy.

The *third* question will be addressed more extensively in a subsequent chapter and need not be covered in depth here. In essence, it is that there is no writing in all of ancient history outside of the Bible that clearly refers to a man by the name of Jesus of Nazareth. If you want to read writings about Jesus that were written when he roamed the earth, you'll have to confine yourself to the Bible, because there is nothing outside of Scripture that one can use. As one would expect, of course, apologists heatedly deny this contention and refer to some comments by such well-known ancient authors as Josephus, Tacitus, Suetonius, Pliny the Younger, and others. They will trot out passages from some of the greatest figures of ancient literature that supposedly refer to Jesus and his religious activities.

What they neglect to mention, however, are the numerous flaws that surround their arguments and their propensity to employ deception. For instance, biblicists repeatedly denounce their critics for taking verses out of context. If there is any argument that is employed in abundance this is it. But taking verses out of context has always been a hallmark of their own exegesis. As is true with messianic prophecy, in which they scoured the Old Testament for any passage that could be twisted in such a manner as to refer to future events, the biblical have gone through all the writings of the ancient world and twisted every word, every phrase, every paragraph, every comment that could possibly be stretched in such a manner as to be applied to Jesus of Nazareth.

The key word is "stretched." The biblicists have employed the very tactic which they have so heatedly decried in others for so many centuries. For instance, the only passage referred to from Suetonius is found in section 25 of *The Deified Claudius*, which says, "Since the Jews constantly made disturbances at the instigation of Chrestus, he [Emperor Claudius] expelled them from Rome." Apologists overlook the obvious fact that the passage refers to "Chrestus," not Christ. It says Chrestus, C-H-R-E-S-T-U-S. There is no justification for arbitrarily assuming that Christ and Chrestus are identical. Why assume Chrestus is another name for Christ when many people were named Chrestus? Why assume this passage refers to Jesus Christ in particular? Moreover, even if the two words are identical, that in no way proves Jesus ever lived. Greek gods such as Zeus had followers also. Does that mean they really lived? Because people believe in a being is no proof for his existence. Otherwise, God would exist merely because he had an entourage.

Apologists also neglect to mention that even they are desperate for passages to use. There are no books, no chapters and few paragraphs that can even be cited as relevant to the issue. All of the passages to support the existence of Jesus that biblicists mention from ancient literature wouldn't fill much more than a few pages. That's a sorry record, indeed, in light of the fact that there is a sizable body of literature from that era. Isn't it amazing that the savior of the world was all but ignored by everyone but the authors of the New Testament, who were no doubt followers of his, if not his creators? On page 271 in *The Life and Works of Thomas Paine* one of the most distinguished men in American history summarized the entire problem rather well when he said, "There is no history written at the time Jesus Christ is said to have lived that speaks of the existence of such a person, even as a man."

The *fourth* question is a classic and should always be used in any discussion with defenders of the Bible in general and Jesus in particular. In Matt. 12:40 Jesus prophesied that he would be buried three days and three nights as was Jonah in the whale for three days and three nights. Since he died and was buried some time on Friday afternoon and rose sometime Saturday night or Sunday morning, he couldn't have been buried for three days and three nights. To be technical, from Friday afternoon to Saturday night is barely a day and a half. Clearly the prophecy failed.

The contortionistic reasoning apologists have displayed to escape from this problem is truly a sight to behold. Some have even gone so far as to allege that the Crucifixion occurred on Wednesday rather than Friday in direct defiance of the verse that says it occurred on the day before the Sabbath. Every Jew in the land knows that Saturday is the sabbath and the day before Saturday is Friday. So the Crucifixion had to have occurred on Friday. Others have alleged that Jews considered any part of a day to be equal to an entire day. Thus, when one takes into account the fact that the events covered part of Friday, all of Saturday, and part of Sunday, the prophecy of being three days in the grave proved to be true, so they claim.

Of course, in using this argument the biblicists ignore the fact that the prophecy said three days and *three nights*, not just three days. How does one cram three nights into a period from Friday afternoon to Sunday morning? As the Jewish scholar Gerald Sigal said on pages 239–41 in his book *The Jew and the Christian Missionary*,

> While it is true that according to Jewish law part of the day is equivalent to a full day, Matthew's Jesus promised to be buried specifically for three days and three nights. . . . Although Jesus did not have to be buried exactly 72 hours, he did have to be buried at least on parts of three days and three nights. . . . The NT evidence does not add up to three days and three nights as specifically promised by Jesus. Therefore, Jesus did not fulfill his very own prediction.

On page 55 in *508 Answers to Bible Questions*, apologist M. R. DeHaan was asked on what day Christ was crucified, and on what day he arose. His answer: "It is my firm conviction that Christ was crucified on Wednesday, and arose right after sundown on Saturday night, which was the beginning of the first day in the Jewish calendar. In no other way can we account for three days and three nights. 'Good Friday' is an unscriptural tradition only."

Of course, DeHaan is wrong on two counts. First, it may be his conviction, but that's about all. Nothing justifies shifting the Crucifixion from Friday to Wednesday other than the need for some means by which to escape the problem that was originally presented. Second, "Good Friday" is not unscriptural. Quite the contrary, the text clearly states that the Crucifixion occurred on the day before the sabbath. Some apologists have asserted that the sabbath referred to is not the Saturday sabbath but a special sabbath referred to in the Old Testament. This argument will not withstand analysis because of technical reasons having to do with the fact that the sabbaths referred to in the Old Testament all occurred in the seventh month, while the Crucifixion occurred in the first month. Therefore, the sabbath referred to is the normal sabbath, which all Jews know falls on Saturday.

This problem becomes even more impossible for apologists to resolve when one realizes that according to Mark 8:31 Jesus was to rise *after* three days, not *on* the third day. That would mean he had to have arisen sometime after Monday afternoon. Noting this dilemma, the apologist Josh McDowell contends that "on the third day" is synonymous with "after the third day."

Apparently desperation set in. On pages 50 to 51 in his book *Answers to Tough Questions*, McDowell defends this position with the following comment, "If the phrase 'after three days' was not interchangeable with the 'third day,' the Pharisees would have asked for a guard for the fourth day." Well, how does he know they didn't? Just because they asked for three doesn't mean they didn't ask for another. McDowell is making an assumption that is based on nothing in Scripture and is a weak reed to lean on, regardless.

The *fifth* question exposes another failure in the prophetic talent of Jesus. In far too many instances, to use the current vernacular of the adolescent, he just couldn't get it together. In John 13:38 Jesus told Peter, "The cock shall not crow, till thou hast denied me thrice." But one need only read Mark 14:66–68 to see that the cock actually crowed after the first denial, not after the third. The strength of this kind of contradiction lies in the fact that it is so easy to verify and so hard to refute. As is so often said, facts are stubborn things. If one compares what is prophesied in a gospel with what actually occurs in the same gospel, John, for example, the problem usually vanishes. But if gospels are compared with one another, if what is prophesied in John is compared with what actually occurs in Mark, the problem steps forward to reveal its awesome magnitude.

On pages 82 and 83 in *Answers to Tough Questions* apologists McDowell and Stewart say, "A problem that has perplexed many careful students of the Bible concerns the accounts of the denial of Christ by Simon Peter." To resolve the difficulty they say, "Peter, as was his way, probably objected loudly to the idea that he would deny his Lord. Jesus then in turn repeats His earlier prediction, along with a further note that before the cock crows twice Peter will deny Him three times." Use of the word "probably" demonstrates that McDowell and Stewart decided to rewrite the script based on speculation rather than resolve the problem at hand. The prophecy in Mark said nothing about the cock crowing twice. Once was sufficient.

The *sixth* question opens a whole can of worms with regard to the character and integrity of Jesus. Jesus asked a rather simple question in Mark 10:18. "Why callest thou me good? There is none good but one, that is God." Here we have a clear-cut statement by Jesus that he is not perfect, that his character is flawed and that he is not to be considered the model of propriety. We have it from his own mouth. What more could one want? Yet the followers of Jesus contend to the end that he is immaculate and the model of sinless perfection.

Besides the fact that Jesus denied his perfect goodness, we have numerous instances in which he behaved or spoke in a manner that was anything but a model of rectitude. In John 7:8–10 he told some people to go to a feast and that he would not be going. The text states that he later went up, not in public, but in private. In other words, he broke his word. In Matt. 26:18 Jesus told a man to "go into the city to such a man, and say unto him, The Master saith,

My time is at hand; I will keep the passover at thy house with my disciples." Jesus could use a course in etiquette. That's clear. You don't just invite yourself into someone's home. First you receive an invitation. Lastly, Jesus lied to the thief on the cross when he told him that, "Today shalt thou be with me in paradise." How could they have entered paradise that day when Jesus lay in the tomb for three days? On page 241 in *The Jew and the Christian Missionary*, Jewish spokesman Gerald Sigal said in this regard, "There is no end to the inconsistencies, for Luke has Jesus promise the thief . . . that 'today you shall be with me in paradise.' This promise could not be true if one is to believe Mark, who states that Jesus rose on the first day of the week, which was three days later."

The *seventh* question involves one of many conflicts between Jesus and Paul. Jesus said at the end of Matthew, "Go ye therefore, and teach all nations, baptizing them in the name of the Father, the son and the Holy Ghost." But Paul later said in 1 Cor. 1:17 that Christ sent him not to baptize but to preach the gospel. In effect, Paul is saying that Jesus lied. Either that or Paul is rewriting the script and has usurped the leadership of Jesus in Christianity. Several astute observers have noted the clash between Jesus and Paul. In *Androcles and the Lion* the playwright George Bernard Shaw said, "There is not one word of Pauline Christianity in the characteristic utterances of Jesus." And on page 245 of volume 15 in *The Writings of Thomas Jefferson* can be found, "Of this band of dupes and impostors, Paul was the . . . first corruptor of the doctrines of Jesus."

The *eighth* question addresses one of those problems that is systematically ignored and evaded by nearly all apologists. The latter take great delight in going back to the Old Testament to distort and pervert verses that can be related to Jesus in a positive way. Indeed, they have made quite a specialty of this. But they have shied away from or intentionally avoided all verses that could be just as easily applied to the founder of Christianity in a negative way. For example, the New Testament repeatedly refers to Jesus as the son of man. But one need only read the Old Testament to see that the son of man is often referred to in the most uncomplimentary fashion. For instance, Psalms 146:3 states, "Put not your trust in princes, nor in *the son of man* in whom there is no help." Job 25:6 says, "How much less man, that is a worm? and *the son of man*, which is a worm." Notice it refers to the son of man as a worm. One would have less difficulty applying these verses to Jesus than many of the verses that have been deemed forecasters of his presence. Nearly all of the latter are of no relevance. On page 277 in volume 5 of his *Works* the nineteenth-century freethinker Robert Ingersoll spared no words in this regard:

> There is no prophecy in the OT foretelling the coming of Jesus Christ. There is not one word in the OT referring to him in any way—not one word. The only way to prove this is to take your Bible, and wherever you find these words: "That it might be fulfilled" and "which was spoken" turn to the OT and find

what was written, and you will see that it had not the slightest possible reference to the thing recounted in the NT—not the slightest.

On page 269 of volume 9 of *The Life and Works of Thomas Paine* Paine was equally candid in his observations on this matter:

> I have now gone through and examined all the passages which the four books of Matthew, Mark, Luke, and John quote from the OT and call them prophecies of Jesus Christ. When I first sat down to this examination, I expected to find cause for some censure, but little did I expect to find them so utterly destitute of truth, and of all pretensions to it, as I have shown them to be.

Christians have gone through the Old Testament and taken what can be used for purposes of expediency to prove their case and systematically discarded all the rest. When Psalms and Job refer to the son of man as a worm, however, they are intentionally ignored. There is no reason they could not apply to Jesus other than the fact that they would tarnish the image of Christianity's founder.

The *ninth* question is a direct assault upon the doctrine of the Trinity, which has been called the "Great Backdoor" by *Biblical Errancy*. According to Christian theology, Jesus is God. But how could this be true when he repeatedly said he was not God's equal? In John 14:28 Jesus said, "My Father is greater than I"; in John 20:17 he said, "I ascend unto my Father, and your Father; and *to my God*, and your God"; and in John 7:16 he said, "My doctrine is not mine, but his that sent me." Clearly, in every instance Jesus is denying that he is God's equal. Why would anyone who is God's equal say that the Father is greater than himself and that he recognized the Father as his god?

Here we are dealing with the Christian concept of the Trinity, one of the most ludicrous religious ideas ever propounded. Even apologists admit the Trinity is incomprehensible. On page 71 in *Answers to Tough Questions* McDowell and Stewart state that the Bible teaches, "There is one God who has revealed Himself in three persons, the Father, the Son and the Holy Spirit, and these three persons are the one God. Although this is difficult to comprehend, it is nevertheless what the Bible tells us."

It is not difficult to comprehend; it is impossible to fathom. Without going into an involved analysis of the Trinity, let us open our brief comments on this topic by noting the astute observation made by Robert Ingersoll in the last century. On pages 266 and 267 of volume 4 in his *Works* he notes,

> Christ, according to the faith, is the second person in the Trinity, the Father being the first and the Holy Ghost the third. Each of these three persons is God. Christ is his own father and his own son. The Holy Ghost is neither father nor son, but both. The son was begotten by the father, but existed before he

was begotten—just the same before as after. Christ is just as old as his father, and the father is just as young as his son. The Holy Ghost proceeded from the Father and the Son, but was equal to the Father and the Son before he proceeded, that is to say, before he existed, but he is of the same age as the other two. So it is declared that the Father is God, and the Son God and the Holy Ghost God, and these three Gods make one God.

Ingersoll continues later by saying, "According to heavenly subtraction if we take two from three, three are left. The addition is equally peculiar, if we add two to one we have but one. Each one is equal to himself and the other two. . . . Nothing ever was, nothing ever can be more perfectly idiotic and absurd than the dogma of the Trinity." This entire issue and all of the problems associated with such a concept will be outlined in greater detail in a subsequent chapter.

The *tenth* question also focuses on the absurd concept known as the Trinity. The question is: While on the cross Jesus said, "Forgive them father, they know not what they do." To whom was he speaking? Apologists will naturally say, "God." But isn't Jesus God? How can God speak to God if there is only one God? The mental gyrations through which apologists go to escape from this dilemma are truly a sight to behold. They claim there is one God but three persons within God. How can three distinct beings exist within another being? The answer is that they can't. Christians are actually tritheists masquerading as monotheists. They believe in three gods rather than one. The God to which they pay homage is not a being at all but merely a general term, a rubric, encompassing three beings. It's like the words "mankind" or "humanity" or "literature." None of these represents an actual entity, but are merely general titles for a body of actual physical objects or beings. You can't touch a literature but you can touch individual entities within literature. You can touch particular books but you can't touch the general descriptive term literature. You can touch individual human beings but you can't touch humanity as if it were a distinct entity or being. In the same way, the father, the son, and the Holy Ghost are distinct entities or beings, but the general term in which they are united, that is, God, is not a conscious being. It is merely a general term. In effect, Christians don't believe in God at all; they believe in three distinct beings with all the powers one would need to be a god. In other words, they believe in three gods; they are tritheists.

Unfortunately, nearly all Christians have been indoctrinated to think of one God within which exist three distinct persons. If they insist on believing that God is an actual being, rather than merely a general term encompassing three distinct entities, then they are unable to realize that they are believing in four distinct beings: God, the Father, the Son, and the Holy Ghost, four separate entities with four distinct consciousness. Christians then become tetratheists.

The problems accompanying a concept as foolish as the Trinity are almost too numerous to mention. The relationship of Jesus to Mary, for example, becomes almost too absurd to discuss. If he was born of Mary, she was his mother. She "being with child by the Holy Ghost," as is stated in the King James. Father, Son, and Holy Ghost being one, she was his wife. God being the Father of all mankind and God and Christ being one, she was his daughter. She being the daughter of God and Jesus being the son of God, she was also his sister.

Or to take another example; by definition the son must be younger than the father, in which case they could not be equal.

The *eleventh* question goes straight to the character and contradictory teachings of Jesus. In Matt. 15:4 he told people to "Honor thy father and thy mother"; yet, he was one of the first to ignore his own maxim by saying to his mother in John 2:4, "Woman, what have I to do with thee?" Jesus also egregiously violated his maxim in Luke 14:26, where he said, "If any man come to me, and *hate* not his father, and mother, and wife, and children, and brethren, and sisters, yea, and his own life also, he cannot be my disciple." Apologists seek to escape the obvious problem these verses generate by saying that the word "hate" actually means to love less. According to them, it doesn't mean to actually hate someone. But the question is, what does it say? It says "hate," not "love less." If the translators of the verse had meant to say "love less," they could have used those terms. But they chose the word "hate" and that settles the matter. One can't help but be perturbed by the constant apologetic refrain: "That's what it says but that's not what it means." That becomes a rather old, threadbare, hackneyed defense that reaches a point of diminishing returns.

I have often told apologists who constantly use this tactic that they should put aside the King James, the New American Standard, the Revised Standard, and every other well known version of the Bible on the market and, instead, write their own version of the Bible, and send me a copy, which I would be glad to critique. Frankly, I'm becoming rather tired of people telling me that they have a more accurate version of what a particular verse should say. This is the kind of defense that can strain one's patience rather rapidly. Are we going to interpret a verse by how it is written or how biblicists say it should have been written? This kind of defense has to be squashed immediately; otherwise, apologists will be able to run from version to version as expediency dictates and choose the wording they prefer. Before people can even discuss or debate the Bible, there has to be some common ground upon which to operate. There must be just one version of each verse, otherwise chaos will reign. How can people discuss a book upon which there is no agreement as to the words that are on the page? If one version says that the correct word in the Sixth Commandment is "kill," while another version says the correct word is "murder," there is no sense in proceeding until that fundamental conflict is resolved. Until the words are agreed upon, all else is for nought and there is no sense in continuing further.

The *twelfth* question exposes an instance in which Jesus made a comment that is directly contradicted by an event in the Old Testament. In John 3:13

he said that, "No man hath ascended up to heaven but he that came down from heaven, even the Son of man." In other words, Jesus claimed that no man had ascended to heaven prior to himself. But 2 Kings 2:11 clearly states that, "Elijah went up by a whirlwind into heaven" and that occurred long before Jesus was even born. Gen. 5:24 says that, "Enoch walked with God; and he was not; for God took him." Heb. 11:5 says that, "By faith Enoch was translated that he should not see death; and was not found, because God had translated him." Apparently Enoch also went straight to heaven without dying long before Jesus lived. On numerous occasions one can't help but feel that Jesus should have been told to consult the Old Testament before he made some of his more outlandish comments.

Like the fourth and fifth questions, the *thirteenth* question provides additional proof that the prophetic talents of Jesus were far from adequate and he often erred in his prognostications. In Matt. 16:28 Jesus said, "There be some standing here, which shall not taste of death, till they see the Son of man coming in his kingdom." Yet every one of the people he was addressing died, and the Son of man is yet to come in his kingdom. Normally, the more sophisticated defenders of the Bible will try to shift the focus of this problem by quoting similar comments in Luke 21:32 or Mark 13:30, which say, "This generation shall not pass, till all be fulfilled," or "This generation shall not pass till all these things be done," respectively. By stressing the verses in Luke and Mark rather than the more difficult rendition in Matthew, they can concentrate their efforts on perverting the meaning of the word "generation." On page 97 in his book *Essential Christianity* apologist Walter Martin focused on this very problem. He says,

> Another objection raised by critics of Christianity is that Christ said He would return before the generation in which He was living perished from the earth. They cite accounts in both Mark 13:30 and Luke 21:32. Although this appears on the surface to be a formidable argument, a careful study of any good Greek lexicon of the NT will quickly show that the Greek word *genea,* translated "generation" in the aforementioned passages, can refer not only to those living at a specific time but also to those of a specific race—in this instance to the Jews.

Martin continues, "What our Lord was teaching was that the Jews as a nation would not pass from the earth until all of His prophecies had come to pass. The record of history validates our Lord's words. For the Jews have survived despite the Torquemadas, the Hitlers . . . etc."

Several errors are apparent in Martin's train of thought.

First, he conveniently ignores the obvious fact that if the word should have been translated "race" rather than "generation," then scores of scholars are incompetent translators.

Second, can Martin name one place in the entire Bible where the word *genea* is translated as "race" or "Jews" rather than "generation"? Other than to escape an obvious problem, why translate *genea* as "the Jews" in this instance only? Why make an exception in this particular case?

Third, in his *Exhaustive Concordance* the famous scholar James Strong says that *genea* means "age," "generation," "time," "nation." Why assume that the last option, "nation," is the most appropriate word to use?

Fourth, in Mark 8:12 Jesus says, "There shall no sign be given unto this generation." If generation is to be understood as the Jewish people, then the prophecy is clearly erroneous because Jesus said in Matt. 16:4, "A wicked and adulterous generation seeketh after a sign; and there shall no sign be given unto it, *but the sign of the prophet Jonas.*" In other words, by Jesus' own admission they would receive a sign after all—that of the prophet Jonah.

And lastly, Matt. 1:17 refers to fourteen generations and Luke 1:50 states "generation to generation." Would Martin advocate translating the Greek word *genea* as "the Jews" in these instances rather than the word "generation" or "generations"? Hardly, since that would be neither expedient nor coherent.

The *fourteenth* question directly focuses on Jesus' frequent hypocrisy. In Matt. 5:44 Jesus told people to love their enemies and bless them that curse them; but Jesus ignored his own advice by repeatedly denouncing his opposition and calling them names. In Matt. 23:17 he said, "Ye fools and blind." In Matt. 12:34 Jesus called people vipers and in Matt. 23:27 he referred to some people as hypocrites and whited sepulchres. In John 10:8 he went so far as to allege, "All that ever came before me are thieves and robbers." Is that practicing brotherly love? Jesus most assuredly was not above calling others names and has no business denouncing those who do the same. Clearly he preached one thing and practiced another. Blessing and loving others hardly accords with hurling epithets. Although some may defend Jesus on the grounds that his comments are correct, that is irrelevant. The fact is that he advised people to bless them that curse them. To put it bluntly, he was a hypocrite. He didn't even address his own mother in a respectful manner.

The *fifteenth* question discusses an issue that has plagued Christians for centuries. Even many of the staunchest defenders of Jesus are hard pressed to reconcile Matt. 26:52, which says, "All that take up the sword shall perish with the sword," with Matt. 10:34, which says, "I came not to send peace but a sword." If all that take up the sword will perish with the sword, then Jesus, too, should perish. After all, he said that he would send the sword. In Luke 22:36 he said, "He that hath no sword, let him sell his garment, and buy one." If that's not a call to arms, what is?

The *sixteenth* question opens up a Pandora's box that apologists would just as soon remained closed forever—the contradictory genealogies found in Matthew 1 and Luke 3. According to Rom. 1:3 and Acts 2:30 the Messiah must be a physical descendant of David. But how could Jesus meet this requirement when the genealogies in Matthew and Luke show that he descended from David through Joseph, who was not his natural father? Since Jesus was supposedly the product of a virgin birth, he had no natural father. Joseph could not have been his natural father and if Joseph was not his natural father, then the physical chain from David down to Jesus had to have been broken. Apologists have been exceptionally dishonest in their attempts to reconcile this major difficulty.

The most common explanation by the apologists is that the genealogy found in Matthew is that of Joseph, while that in Luke is that of Mary. They contend that the genealogy in Luke retains his physical connection to David through Mary, his natural mother, and the genealogy in Matthew retains his legal claim to the throne of David because Joseph is a physical descendant of David and simultaneously the legal father of Jesus. On page 60 in *Answers to Tough Questions* apologists McDowell and Stewart seek to evade this dilemma by saying,

> At first glance, the impression is created that both accounts are tracing the family line of Jesus through His earthly father Joseph, in which case we would be faced with an obvious contradiction, because Matthew 1:16 indicates Jacob is Joseph's father, while Luke 3:23 tells us that Heli is the father of Joseph. A plausible solution to this difficulty is to understand that Matthew is indeed giving us Joseph's family line, but Luke is tracing the genealogy of Mary. The reason that Mary is not mentioned in Luke 3 is because she has already been designated the mother of Jesus in several instances.

Later they state,

> The purpose of the two genealogies is to demonstrate that Jesus was in the complete sense a descendant of David. Through his foster father, Joseph, He inherited by law the royal line, while through his mother he was a flesh and blood descendant of King David. Thus, Jesus had the proper credentials to the throne of David.

Of course, all of this is pure doubletalk for several reasons. First and most obvious is the fact that Mary isn't even mentioned in the genealogy of Luke. Imagine a genealogy in which the most important person involved isn't even mentioned! There is absolutely nothing in Luke's genealogy that would lead anyone to believe that it is that of Mary. Second, the Bible has no genealogical record of any woman. And there is nothing that would lead one to believe that Mary is an exception. Every name in Luke's genealogy is that of a man, yet we are supposed to believe that the last one is that of a woman.

The *seventeenth* question is direct and obvious and perhaps that is why it has remained relatively obscure. It is so obvious, so simple, that people just haven't taken notice of its presence. Biblicists have heard the contextual verses to this question for most of their lives but never taken time to engage in serious analytical thought.

In essence, the problem is this: Jesus told a man in Mark 8:34, "Whosoever will come after me, let him deny himself, take up his cross and follow me." The obvious question is, what cross? There is no cross to take up. Jesus had not yet died on the cross. The man to whom he was speaking would have had no idea what he was talking about. The cross did not become a Christian symbol until *after* the Crucifixion. So any reference to the cross *before* the Crucifixion would have made no sense to anyone unless they knew the future. Apologists have tried to resolve this difficulty by saying the cross referred to the burdens of being a Christian in general. But that has no validity. Would Jesus refer to a cross other than the one upon which he died? Moreover, apologists are obligated to prove that the cross represented some kind of burden prior to the Crucifixion. Otherwise, what does "take up your cross" mean? It could mean any one of a large number of things. If a cross, other than the one upon which Jesus died, is the object of his attention, then one could follow Jesus by just bearing the trials and tribulations of existence in general. Hindus, Muslims, and Jews could very well be saving themselves by taking up a cross.

The *eighteenth* question exposes the rather pronounced tendency of Jesus to rewrite the Old Testament to his own specifications. In Matt. 5:17–19 he strongly committed himself to upholding the Old Law at all costs by saying,

> Think not that I am come to destroy the law, or the prophets: I am not come to destroy, but to fulfill. For verily, I say unto you, Till heaven and earth pass, one jot or one tittle shall in no wise pass from the law, till all be fulfilled. Whosoever therefore shall break one of these least commandments, and shall teach men so, he shall be called the least in the kingdom of heaven.

Yet Jesus rewrote the Old Law and ignored its tenets on numerous occasions. He denied the dietary laws; he ignored the laws requiring the washing of hands and the sabbath restrictions; he failed to heed laws requiring fasting; he excused an adulteress, and altered the Old Law in several other matters in clear violation of Deut. 4:2, which says, "Ye shall not add unto the word which I command you, neither shall you diminish aught from it, that ye may keep the commandments of the Lord your God."

Jesus not only rewrote the text but added to it. In Mark 10:19 Jesus said, "Thou knowest the commandments, Do not commit adultery, Do not kill, Do not steal, Do not bear false witness. Defraud not, Honour thy father and mother." Do you notice something unusual about this list? There is no Old Testament commandment pertaining to defrauding. Lev. 19:13 says thou shalt not defraud thy neighbor, but it is not among the commandments. It is also interesting to note that Jesus listed only five of the ten commandments. Five were omitted and one was included that wasn't even a commandment. How's that for rewriting the script! Apparently Jesus felt he was above the law and could alter the rules as he deemed necessary.

The *nineteenth* question focuses on the duplicity of Christianity's savior and exposes the deception that is inherent to his character. In Luke 12:4 Jesus took a stance not unlike that of many brave politicians by saying, "Be not afraid of them that kill the body." In other words, display character and fortitude by having the courage and stamina to stand up for your convictions in the face of adversity. Few would deny that that is a noble tenet. Unfortunately Jesus couldn't muster enough strength on several occasions to do anything other than flee to the hinterlands. One need only read several verses to see that he not only didn't have the courage of his convictions, but on several occasions he hid, sneaked, escaped, fled, slinked around, and otherwise operated as a bowl of jelly.

Several of these occurrences are worthy of consideration. John 7:1 says, "After these things Jesus walked in Galilee: for he would not walk in Jewry, because the Jews sought to kill him." John 8:59 says, "Then took they up stones to cast at him: but Jesus hid himself." John 10:39 says, "They sought again to take him: but he escaped out of their hand." Jesus clearly felt that discretion was the better part of valor on many occasions. He was not about to die for the movement and judging from his "My God, my God, why hast thou forsaken me?" comment on the cross, Jesus apparently *never* felt there was any good time to die for the cause. Matt. 12:14–16, John 11:53–54, Matt. 10:23, Mark 1:45, and John 6:15 also clearly show that Jesus often felt it was better to be a live coward than a dead hero.

In fact, except for Stephen and possibly John the Baptist, there is no biblical figure that was willing to die for the cause. Biblicists constantly talk about Christians surrendering their lives willingly in the cause of Jesus Christ. Yet there is no biblical text to that effect and precious little outside the Bible. The willingness of Christians to become martyrs in the cause of Jesus Christ is based far more on Christian mythology than sound history. I can remember attending a meeting several years ago sponsored by a Seventh-Day Adventist church. After enduring a rather protracted discussion of the martyrdom of Peter, Paul, and the Apostles, I had the temerity to ask where that could be found in Scripture. An air of consternation swept through the room followed by some rather feeble attempts to provide evidence of Christian self-sacrifice. When I asked for some biblical confirmation of their long-held, but never examined, beliefs, nothing of substance was forthcoming. Not one person in the audience had really questioned or examined something they had been told all their lives. Examples such as this clearly demonstrate the importance of indoctrination at an early age. If people are given information prior to their ability to critically examine what they hear, a mass of nonsense can slip through the door that would otherwise never be given a second thought.

The *twentieth* question highlights a point of direct conflict between biblical verses. In Luke 23:43 Jesus said to the thief on the cross, "Today shalt thou be with me in paradise." But how could they have been together in paradise that day if Jesus, by his own prophecy, was to lie in the tomb for three days? After all, didn't Jesus say in Matt. 12:40 that just as Jonah was in the belly of the whale for three days and three nights, so would the Son of man be buried for three days and three nights? If Jesus had not remained in the tomb for three days and three nights, he would have exposed his own dishonesty. And if he remained in the tomb as he predicted, then the promise to the thief on the cross had to have been a lie.

This problem also creates a point of contention between Christians themselves when baptism is considered a prerequisite for entrance into heaven. Several years ago I witnessed a debate between a member of the Church of Christ who contended baptism is absolutely essential for salvation and a Baptist who disagreed. The Baptist representative wisely asked how the thief on the cross could have been saved, since Jesus promised him salvation that day without baptism. The Church of Christ spokesman contended that the man had been baptized earlier, a contention for which, of course, there was not a shred of biblical testimony.

When confronted with the thief-on-the-cross problem, another tactic often used by those who claim that baptism is a necessity is to literally rewrite the script by repositioning a comma. The full text of Luke 23:43 in the RSV says, "He [Jesus] said to him, Truly, I say to you, today you will be with me in Paradise." The defenders of the importance of baptism contend the text should read as follows: "Truly, I say to you today, you will be with me in Paradise." In other words, by putting the comma after the word "today," rather than before, readers are led to believe that Jesus was *telling* the man something on that day rather than promising him that he would be *with him in paradise* on that day. The simple relocating of a comma makes all the difference in the world and drastically alters what is being said. Whether the word "today" is attached to the first part of the sentence or the last is crucial. Yet, there is no valid grammatical reason for changing the comma.

The *twenty-first* question addresses a problem that has been asked of Christians for centuries and to which they are yet to devise an adequate response. Briefly stated, the problem is: How can justice be served when an innocent person is executed for the crimes of others? According to Christian mythology Jesus went to the cross willingly to die for the sins of mankind. He voluntarily took upon himself the burdens of us all and earned the undying gratitude of humanity. At least that's the party line. Apologists fail to realize that for Jesus to be executed for our sins makes about as much sense as my son telling a judge that he would accept execution for my crimes. Although a magnanimous gesture, it has nothing to do with justice. What judge would agree with such an absurd arrangement? You don't execute the innocent for the crimes of the guilty, regardless of who agrees to it.

In effect, Christians are saying that their God wants vengeance and doesn't really care who pays the price as long as it's paid. That isn't a god of justice, that's a god obsessed with getting even, a god who wants blood. Somebody has to pay and that's that. No judge in the nation would accept an arrangement in which one person agrees to be executed for the deeds of another. It just isn't done. In effect, every judge in the nation has a greater sense of propriety and fair play than the Christian god. Even the Bible says that you don't punish the children for the sins of their fathers. That's clearly stated in Deut. 24:16. One of the cardinal tenets of Christian theology is founded upon a travesty of justice. We are all unjustly punished for the sin of the first Adam, and now the last Adam, to paraphrase Paul's characterization in 1 Cor. 15:45, is unjustly punished for all of us. In effect, a centerpiece of Christian theology is that two wrongs make a right. We are punished for Adam's deed, which is wrong, and now Jesus is punished for our deeds, which is also wrong. But the deeds of the last Adam corrected the imbalance created by the first Adam. As Paul said in Rom. 5:19, "For as by one man's disobedience many were made sinners, so by the obedience of one shall many be made righteous." Talk about a theology based on injustice! On page 113 in *I'm Glad You Asked* apologist Kenneth Boa addressed this problem by saying,

> God is a righteous judge, and He cannot change His verdict on man's rebellion. What He did do, though, was offer to pay the penalty for us. Now the choice is up to us; we can pay the penalty ourselves, or accept payment of our heavenly Father. The penalty *will* be paid. The only question is, "Who will pay it?"

That last comment can only make one pity someone caught in the Christian web. Thank goodness the American judicial system does not operate on the principle that the penalty *will be paid*, regardless. That would mean someone would have to be executed for every murderer that evaded capture. After all, what did Boa say? The penalty *will be paid*; the only question is who will pay it. A rule of this kind is preposterous because it doesn't take into account the fact that evildoers can't be apprehended in many instances. If one were to say that God always knows their identity, the problem would only be compounded because that would mean an innocent person would die even when the culprit is known. There is no escape. The theology all but blasphemes any god that may exist.

The *last* question, focuses on the indecisiveness of Jesus. In Matt. 15:24 he said, "I am not sent but unto the lost sheep of the house of Israel," but later he told his followers in Matt. 28:19 to "Go ye therefore, and teach all nations." The question that is obviously generated by these conflicting comments is: To whom are they to go, to the Jews only or to everyone? Because the Jews almost universally rejected the message of Jesus Christ, Peter and Paul later propounded the view expressed in Matt. 28:19; namely, the message was to be carried to everyone. If Christians had stayed with the marching orders originally issued in Matt. 15:24, there is little doubt that Christianity would have either died out entirely or remained a relatively obscure Jewish sect with a small following. Only by rewriting the script did Christians manage to forestall being relegated to the world of anonymity. The world of practicality supplanted the world of visionaries. The same message that is found at the end of Matthew is also found at the end of Mark where Jesus says, "Go ye into all the world, and preach the gospel to every creature." If that is not a complete reversal of the message found in earlier passages, such as Matt. 7:6, 10:5-6, 15:26, Mark 7:27, and John 4:22, what is?

Conclusion

We have now not only completed an extensive analysis of the pamphlet *Jesus Christ is the Answer?* but simultaneously illuminated twenty-two of the best questions one could ever employ in the struggle against Christianity in general and Jesus in particular. Every rational person should find them to be a welcome addition to his or her antisuperstition portfolio.

3

"The Bible Is God's Word?"

Twenty-four Questions About the Bible

Chapter 2 discussed the pamphlet issued by *Biblical Errancy* several years ago entitled "Jesus Christ is the Answer?" This chapter will focus on the problems that are present in the other pamphlet distributed several years ago by *Biblical Errancy* entitled "The Bible is God's Word?" The title is appropriately followed by a question mark because the title itself is wholly inaccurate. It is important to concentrate on this pamphlet because it reveals some of the best questions one could ever employ while confronting Christianity in general and the Bible in particular. As each point is discussed additional information will be brought into the picture as well as some of the responses that apologists often use in opposition to the questions that are posed. Armed with information of this kind objective observers will be far better prepared to confront Christians on their own turf. One should always know the composition of the other side's arsenal before engaging in ideological repartee. Having said that, let us turn to the problems that are exposed and proceed down the list.

The *first* question addresses a dilemma that is truly one of the classics. In any debate with Christians this is one of those poignant queries that should always be brought into the fray as soon as possible. It's a humdinger. During radio and television appearances I have never encountered a biblicist with a good explanation. One can easily understand why: there is none. Briefly stated, the problem is this: If you must accept Jesus as your savior in order to be saved, and that's the essence of John 14:6, which says, "I am the way, the truth, and the life, *no* man cometh to the father but by me," what do you do about the billions of beings who died as fetuses and infants, mental deficients, and people who lived in the New World before missionaries arrived? One should not lose sight of the fact that it says "no man." It doesn't say "some men," "most men" or "a few men." It says "*no* man cometh to the father but by me." There are no exceptions and that includes infants and fetuses. For them to accept Jesus would be impossible; so they are condemned to hell because of conditions over which they had no control. Deut. 32:4 says God is just, but where is the justice here?

In addressing the most common apologetic responses to question No. 1, we might first turn to a book entitled *Answers to Tough Questions Skeptics Ask About the Christian Faith* by apologists McDowell and Stewart. On page 129 they say, "No matter where we go or what subject we are speaking on, this question always seems to come up. [The question being: What about those who have never heard?] The Bible is very clear that no one can come to God except through Jesus Christ." Fortunately, they presented the problem in absolutist terms, so there is no needless haggling to be done over the meaning of words. They continue by saying, "Jesus said, 'No one comes to the Father except through me.' The only basis for forgiveness of sin and life everlasting is the way made by Jesus. Many people think this implies that those who have never heard about Jesus will be automatically damned." Obviously that is a safe deduction considering the fact that no alternative was allowed. More than mere implication is involved. It's nothing more than a logical conclusion from a flat-out absolutist statement.

McDowell and Stewart continue, "However, we do not know this is the case." Of course, we do know it is the case in light of the fact that the verse allows no exceptions. They continue, "Although the Scriptures never explicitly teach that someone who has never heard of Jesus can be saved, we do believe that it *infers* this." Note the use of the word "infers." Where is this implied in Scripture? By what rationale are they defending this "inferred" nonsense? Incidentally, "implies" should have been used rather than "infers," since a speaker "implies" while a hearer "infers." They continue, "We do *believe* that every person will have an opportunity to repent. And that God will not exclude anyone because he happened to be born at the wrong place and at the wrong time." Notice the use of the word "believe." In other words, they have no evidence. They merely "believe." Moreover, what does an opportunity to repent have to do with this? That's irrelevant. The question is: Do they believe in Jesus or don't they? Do they accept Jesus and his truth as their savior or don't they? You either accept him or you don't.

From that inglorious beginning McDowell and Stewart move on to a series of ridiculous statements. They realize there is a problem, of course, and state on the next page, "Even though we may not know how he is going to deal with these people specifically, we know that his judgment is going to be fair." Why on earth they would make that judgment in light of God's prior biblical performance is puzzling to say the least. They have no way of knowing that. People who have never heard must be condemned because of verses contending

Jesus is the only way. There is no way to escape that crucial point. On the next page they state, "No one will be condemned for not ever hearing of Jesus Christ," which is patently false! John 14:6 says you have to have heard of Jesus. Exceptions aren't allowed.

Then they state, "Based on the above examples from Scripture, it can be seen that God will fairly judge all mankind—that no one can claim that he or she received an unfair hearing." False again! Near the end of their defense they go to the heart of the matter when they basically confess that they don't have an answer. "Although we may not be able to answer the question about those who have not heard to the satisfaction of everyone," God will provide. That's the essence of their concluding comment. That's nothing more than a wish, a hope, and a prayer and has nothing to do with a biblical, or rational, explanation of anything.

In the book *Science and Christianity* apologist John Callahan makes a much clearer, more concise, and honest statement on this matter. On page 92 he says, "It is true that many innocent people will never hear about Jesus such as those who lived before him, [actually a small percentage given the population explosion], and those who live in remote parts of the world. But again God has done all he can do." What kind of an explanation is that? What did he do? He didn't do anything. Callahan continues by saying, "If the innocent are lost it is the fault of Satan, demons, and other men, but not God." Now if that isn't absurd! What Satan, demons, or other men have to do with the issue one can only speculate. If you are not going to blame the injustice on God, then you have no grounds for blaming it on anyone. You'll have to leave it to the elements or the evolution of natural events.

Actually if one were to analyze John 14:6 closely he would realize missionaries are doing a tremendous *dis*service to people throughout the world by their proselytizing. If people are going to be saved who have *not* heard of Jesus, their welfare is going to be jeopardized once they have heard of him. This particular issue is addressed in a couple of apologetic writings. One of them is called *I'm Glad You Asked* by Kenneth Boa, who states on page 146,

> These concerns have led some people to the conclusion that those who have never heard about Christ will escape the judgment of God. If this is true Christian missionaries are not only wasting their lives but may be doing great harm by preaching the gospel to those who are unaware of Christ, they have brought people from a state of innocence to a state of moral culpability if they do not respond. This would mean that passages such as the Great Commission [at the end of Matthew, in which Jesus tells people to go unto all the world and preach the gospel] make no sense at all. The death and resurrection of Jesus Christ should have been kept a secret.

Boa has correctly assessed the situation. God can't, in all fairness, condemn anyone for failing to heed what they have never heard.

R. C. Sproul addresses the same problem on page 50 in his book *Reason to Believe*. With reference to natives who have never heard he says,

> Since the native is not guilty of this we ought to let him alone. In fact, letting him alone would be the most helpful and redemptive thing we could do for him. If we go to the native and inform him of Christ we place his soul in eternal jeopardy. For now he knows of Christ, and if he refuses to respond to Him he can no longer claim ignorance as an excuse. Hence, the best service we can render is silence.

That is in agreement with Boa's statement that the very existence of Jesus should have been kept a secret, an observation with which all reasonable men would agree.

At any rate, moving from the natives who have never heard, we proceed to another group that presents an equal amount of difficulty for the apologists—infants. What do you do about infants, especially fetuses that die in the womb? In the book called *Answering the Tough Ones* apologist David DeWitt states on page 65, "We admit that it is unusually difficult to find clear biblical teaching about the salvation of infants and the mentally disordered, but we can say this. Biblical evidence indicates that people unable consciously to choose Christ are not held accountable for rejecting him."

To that one can only say: What evidence? Where? There is no biblical text that would justify a comment of that nature. People are interpreting the Bible as they would like it to be, rather than how it is.

In the same vein, we find on page 137 in *508 Answers to Bible Questions* by M. R. DeHaan, "We believe that all babies who die before the age of accountability are saved through the finished work of the Lord Jesus Christ and only as they grow up and reject the offer of salvation are they finally lost." To that one can only reply, What age of accountability? There is nothing in the Bible about an age of accountability. Upon what possible basis do Christians keep alluding to this wholly unbiblical concept? The Bible does not allow for such a construct. Apologists are talking about the Bible as if it were a book permeated with logic, reason, justice, and common sense, when the opposite is true. There is no equivocation about the fact that you have to believe in Jesus to be saved; there *are* no exceptions.

In regard to the same subject, Boa says on page 161 of *I'm Glad You Asked*, "It is evident that infants and the mentally impaired are not held accountable to make a response they are incapable of making." Upon what basis does he say that it is evident? There is nothing evident about it. Any objective analyst of the Bible would not hesitate to challenge biblicists to show where the Bible supports a concept of this kind.

In *Answers to Questions About the Bible* Robert Mounce says on page 173 with respect to babies, "If there is some third alternative, we know nothing of it from Scripture. The specter of a new-born babe suffering eternal punishment is entirely unacceptable in a moral universe." It may be unacceptable from the point of view of a moral universe, but it's certainly not unacceptable from the point of view of Scripture. The Bible does not allow for exceptions.

On the next page Mounce turns to those who have serious mental illnesses and asks how they can accept Jesus by stating, "Two questions are closely related. What of those who are victims of serious mental retardation . . . and never hear the gospel. . . . I would assume that the mentally retarded would fall into the same class as infants." Notice his use of the word "assume." There is no proof. Again, nothing in the Bible allows for an exception.

Returning to *508 Answers*, DeHann readdresses the issue and states on page 185: "It is comforting to know, however, that all children who die before the age of responsibility do go to heaven and none of them are lost." The Bible, in fact, says precisely the opposite.

When you think about going to an eternity of punishment or reward, it is probably fair to say that those who really believe that children are automatically saved would do well to tell their children to engage in dangerous activities so that they might die and forestall any risk to their eternal souls. If people took this seriously, they would be wise to either kill their children or arrange for it to be done by others in order to ensure their entrance into heaven. In this way chance would be eliminated at the outset. After all, you never know what temptations adulthood might bring.

In *Questions Non-Christians Ask* apologist Barry Wood declares on page 100, "Only God knows when a person is ready for the gospel. Some retarded persons never come to the age of accountability and are under God's watchcare just like a little child. It is my understanding that children who die go immediately to be with the Lord." That may be his understanding, but nothing can be found in the Bible to corroborate it. Wood continues by saying they are, "perhaps escorted by guardian angels (See Matthew 18:10) into the presence of the Lord." Whence comes this idea is even more of a mystery. As usual, people are writing their own text to escape obvious dilemmas. If only they were required to cite chapter and verse every time they made statements without biblical support! A requirement of that kind would certainly forestall a mountain of rhetoric.

On page 172 of *Answers to Questions About the Bible* Mounce is probably more honest than any apologist encountered so far. "The Scriptures are remarkably quiet about a lot of things. The fate of children who die at an early age is certainly one of these." Well, thank goodness! Somebody is finally willing to admit the obvious. He continues, "The reluctance to discuss the issue undoubtedly stems from a lack of scriptural passages which speak directly to the issue." Reluctance also lies in the fact that passages deemed relevant to the issue don't say what

Christians want to hear. They provide a theology at variance with what the average Christian would like to propound.

The most common response one will hear with reference to this question is that you have to turn to Romans 1. R. C. Sproul says on pages 50–51 of *Reason to Believe*, "The biblical response to the question of the person who never heard of Christ is found in Romans 1 beginning with verse 18." He then quotes verse 18 and follows this up later by citing verses 19 and 20, which say, "For what can be known about God is plain to them because God has shown it to them. Ever since the creation of the world his invisible nature, namely his eternal power and deity has been clearly perceived in the things that have been made. So *they are without excuse.*"

It is important to note that what Sproul and other apologists have done is to shift the focus. Realizing that everyone can't possibly have heard of Jesus, they deceptively change the requirement to: Did they know about God? And they say, in effect: Everybody knows about God. The common refrain is that according to Romans 1, they are *without excuse.* All people have to do is look at the world because God is evident in everything that exists according to them. Sproul continues,

> Here the apostle gives a description of what theologians call general revelation. . . . First, . . . it is clear and unambiguous. . . . Secondly, we learn that the knowledge gets through and finds its mark. . . . Thirdly, this revelation has been going on since the foundation of the world. . . . Fourthly, it comes by way of creation. . . . And Fifthly, we learn that the revelation is sufficient to render man inexcusable. The passage says, "so they are without excuse." What excuse do you suppose the apostle had in mind? What excuse does general revelation eliminate? Obviously, the excuse eliminated is that of ignorance [of the existence of God].

But that is not the requirement for salvation and critics of the Bible should never allow themselves to be sidetracked by this particular apologetic maneuver. Don't let biblical proponents shift the focus in their favor. You are not saved by believing in God or being aware of God or knowing about God or seeing God through general conditions in the world. According to Christian theology you are saved by believing in Jesus and that is clearly stated in John 14:6, John 3:18, John 3:36, and 1 John 5:12. Jews, Muslims, and a wide assortment of other religious people believe in the existence of God. If we are going to concentrate on the guidelines laid down in Romans 1, then they, too, are saved. If all you have to do is believe in God, then millions of non-Christians will pass through the pearly gates. So Romans 1 is not going to save the day for Christian apologists when the issue of those who have not heard comes onto the scene.

On page 160 in *I'm Glad You Asked* Kenneth Boa states,

Even those who have not heard about Christ have some knowledge about God, sin, and the solution of casting oneself upon the mercy of the one true God. . . . No one is entirely ignorant about the Creator, because, even apart from the special revelation of His Word, He has made himself known to all through general revelation. This includes His external revelation through the creation and his internal revelation through the human heart.

Again, this entire rationale has nothing to do with being saved, and that is clearly stated by fundamentalist professor Charles Ryrie, in his book *Basic Theology.* He states on page 521, and the entire topic will conclude with his synopsis. "Everyone is either saved or lost and anyone [Notice it says anyone] who dies without receiving Christ as his personal savior will be eternally condemned." Therefore, it necessarily follows that babies, the mentally ill, and people who lived in the New World before missionaries arrived could not possibly be saved and are eternally lost because of conditions over which they had absolutely no control. For them to receive Jesus Christ is out of the question.

Let us now move on to the *second* question addressed in the pamphlet: Why are we being punished for Adam's sin. After all, he ate the forbidden fruit, we didn't; it's his problem, not ours, especially in light of Deut. 24:16, which says that the children shall not be punished for the sins of their fathers. This is another one of those questions that should definitely *not* be overlooked when the Bible's defenders appear on the horizon. Apologist Richard Sisson says on page 90 in volume I of *Answering Christianity's Most Puzzling Questions.* "Adam's problem instantly became our problem." The immediate question that should come to the mind of any rational person is: Why? It's his problem not ours. He committed the sin, we didn't. Sisson continues, "He also passed on to all humanity a sin nature," that is, an appetite, a sin disposition, a propensity for sinning.

On the same point, apologist Hal Lindsay states on page 51 in his book *The Liberation of Planet Earth,* "It makes a lot of people angry to hear that something which some far off ancestor did implicates them with such grievous consequences." Of course, that is understandable, since it is absurd on its face. Lindsay continues,

> And I can sympathize with how they feel. But in God's eyes Adam was representative of man, the federal head of the human race. What he did judicially implicated all of his fellow men. If the president of the United States and the Congress declared war on some country today, I would be at war too, even though I might not personally be in favor of it. It makes no difference whether I voted for them or not. What they did would implicate me because they act as my federal head.

The fallacy in this line of reasoning, as for much apologetic literature, lies in the fact that the analogy drawn is invalid. In the first place, you can extract yourself from the situation outlined by doing any one of several things. You could leave the United States; you could do nothing; you could join the other side; or you could be victorious. Why assume you will be punished at all? Quite possibly your side could win. And on the following page Lindsay sinks even deeper into this morass by stating, "If we had been in Adam's shoes the chances are very good that we would have done the same thing he did. God in his great foreknowledge (His omniscience), could see that all men would, indeed, ratify Adam's rebellion in their own behavior."

To an inane comment of this kind one can only say, don't be ridiculous. You don't punish people for what they might have done given the opportunity. They didn't do it, so there is no way of knowing what they would have done under the right conditions. Lindsay is making an assumption for which there is not a shred of evidence.

The question of Adam and original sin is as ludicrous as the following analogous situation. Suppose I were sitting home one evening watching television and the police came and arrested me and I asked them why I was being arrested and they said, "Well, your father out in California just shot and killed someone." When asked what that had to do with me, they said, "Well, he's your father, isn't he?" The fact that he is my father has nothing to do with the situation. He's responsible for his acts and I'm responsible for mine and never the twain shall meet.

Even the Bible supports a more rational position. Deut. 24:16 says that children shall not be punished for the sins of their fathers. In effect, biblicists are abandoned by their own book. Realizing the innate injustice of this concept, apologist Barry Wood tried to salvage the myth on page 99 of his book *Questions Non-Christians Ask* by declaring, "We are not guilty because Adam sinned but because we ourselves sin. Thus, a child is born with a spiritual deadness which shows itself as a selfish tendency. Somewhere in that child's maturation he will intentionally sin."

In other words, we are to believe that although a child has not sinned at the start he will do so later. At the moment he sins he will become guilty and not a moment before. Unfortunately for Wood, this ruse will not hold water because it contradicts Scripture. Wood is trying to escape through the back door by saying people are not sinners until they can and do sin at some point in their development. But all he need do to see the antibiblical aspect of his stance is to read Romans 5:12, in which Paul states, "Wherefore as by one man sin entered the world, and death by sin; so death passed upon all men, for that *all have sinned.*" Notice it says all, everyone, sinned the moment Adam sinned, not later. Psalms 58:3 states, "The wicked are estranged from the womb; they go astray as soon as they be born, speaking lies." In other words, children are sinners from the start, not later on at some age of accountability, or when they can sin. It says *as soon as they be born.* In effect, they are being punished for being born, not for reaching an uncertain point in their maturation process known as the age of accountability when they can and do sin. Moreover, we are also punished by the act of Adam in that he gave us a propensity to sin that we would not otherwise have had.

On page 113 in *I'm Glad You Asked* apologist Kenneth Boa states, "We have established the cause of evil to be the disobedient choice of man." Notice he says "man" and that is clearly false, because it was the choice of "a man" not humanity in general. Mankind did not sin; a man did. Defenders of the book repeatedly try to shift the burden onto the shoulders of all people. Their apologetic writings reek with this subtle alteration in blame.

Finally, to close out this second question we'll turn to a book entitled *So the Bible is Full of Contradictions* by Carl Johnson. On page 19 he is asked how he would reconcile Exod. 20:5, which says, "I the Lord thy God am a jealous God, visiting the iniquity of thy fathers upon the children unto the third and fourth generation," with Ezek. 18:19–20, which says, "The soul that sins, it shall die. The son shall *not* bear [notice it says *not* bear] the iniquity of the father, neither shall the father bear the iniquity of the son."

Johnson's answer is as follows. "These two passages have perplexed many people. One says that God visits the iniquity of the father upon the children; the other says the son shall *not* bear the iniquity of the father. Both statements are true and there is no real contradiction. It is true that God visits the iniquity of the fathers upon the children in that He *permits* the latter to suffer the consequences of the sins of the former." This last sentence is clearly false in that God does not just "permit" it; he causes it. That's a crucial distinction.

Johnson continues by saying, "If a man is a drunkard he bequeaths to his children poverty, shame, poor health, wretchedness, and many times a desire for strong drink." In other words, Johnson claims they are not the cause of the problem although they suffer from it. This analogy is often made to justify the negative influence of Adam upon us all. True, we are sick sometimes because of our parents, even though we had nothing to do with the onset of the original illness. However, the analogy breaks down in the fact that the illness is not something that is pronounced upon one being because of another being's behavior. It is not something that is judicially decided; there is not a conscious effort on the part of one being to punish another being because of a third being's behavior. Illness is simply a state of nature, a natural turn of events. If somebody drives through a traffic light, hitting and killing me, naturally I suffer the consequences of his behavior. I am bearing the results of his actions. But there was no conscious decision on the part of anyone to create what occurred. It had nothing to do with justice and for that reason is not analogous to the doctrine of original sin.

The *third* question in this pamphlet says God created Adam, so Adam must have been perfect. How then could Adam have sinned? Regardless of how much free will he had, if he chose to sin he was not perfect. In the book entitled *Know Why You Believe* apologist Paul Little addresses this very issue. On page 80 he says, "We must never forget that when God created man, he created him perfect. Man was not created evil. He did, however, as a human being, have the ability to disobey or obey God . . . the first man rebelled against God." The logical question in this regard is: How could Adam have rebelled if he was created perfect? Regardless of how much freedom he had, if Adam chose to rebel, that would clearly prove he was not perfect. Apologists do not have an answer to this question because the moment man sinned, he proved he wasn't perfect. If someone tells me they are perfect and immediately sins, that's excellent proof they are not perfect.

In *I'm Glad You Asked* Boa found himself confronting the same predicament. On page 111 he states, "God created the universe without evil and suffering; he also created man perfect. . . . Genesis 3 tells us that man chose to go his own way rather than following God's." If that is true, then Adam was not perfect. How could he have been perfect if he chose not to follow God? He's either perfect or he isn't; there is no in between. Still further Boa states, "The actual origin of evil came about as a result of man, who directed his will away from God and toward his own selfish desires. . . . God told man what to do, but man corrupted himself." How could man have corrupted himself, when Boa just finished saying he was perfect?

This problem highlights a very important rule or caveat one should follow when discussing or debating the Bible with apologists. Try to stay with absolutes as much as possible. The Bible digs itself into a hole when it makes statements dealing with "all," "each," "never," "every," "none," and other statements that allow no exceptions. We have all taken exams and been confronted with true and false statements. Experienced test takers will tell you that statements containing absolute terms are nearly always false. That is very applicable to this particular problem because of the word "perfect." Perfect allows no exceptions or gradations. Therefore, when the Bible uses this word, as it often does, it digs itself into a hole from which escape is impossible. So anyone seeking to engage biblicists in dialogue should go through the Book and find any kind of statement that is absolutist in nature, that allows no exceptions. They are quite abundant and easy to find. Only one exception need then be found to destroy the rule. The coup de grace can then be performed by asking an apologist for an explanation. All that is required is one exception.

Another good example of an absolutist imbroglio is shown in the *fourth* question on our pamphlet. How can Num. 23:19, which says God does not repent, be reconciled with Ex. 32:14, which clearly says he does? In regard to this problem apologist William Arndt states on page 99 of *Does the Bible Contradict Itself?*,

These two passages are often pointed to as being in outright, unqualified disagreement. How can both statements be true that God never repents and that he did repent? . . . The task [of reconciling them] is not so difficult as might seem to be the case. . . . God is frequently spoken of as if he were a being with those emotions, affections, and moods with which we are all familiar, possessing them ourselves. Since God acted as if he had repented of having made man when he sent the Flood [the text does not say he acted *as if*; there is no acting involved, it flatly states that he repented] repentance or change of attitude is ascribed to Him" [it's not ascribed, it's stated in the verse]. "God repented," then, means, God took a course which among men we attribute to repentance" [there's no attribution involved; the text clearly states he repented]. . . . The language in such a case is simply figurative and must not be taken literally.

In chapter 1 we noted the fact that even fundamentalists conveniently abandon the literal interpretation when expediency dictates. They criticize a common practice among liberals which they don't hesitate to invoke themselves.

Arndt concludes by saying, "Lest anyone think that this is a shrewdly invented device for extricating oneself out of a difficult position, let him compare other passages of Scripture," which he then goes on to cite. This is nothing more than another example of an absolutist statement digging a hole into which the Bible and its followers readily stumble. There is no escape from the "God repents" problem; one need only read the verses to see that. It says he repented and no allegorical or figurative meaning can be honestly attributed. That's about all that can be said on that matter. Both repents are derived from the same Hebrew word, so apologists can't play the word game either.

The *fifth* question is: How can 2 Kings 8:26 say Ahaziah began to rule at age twenty-two when 2 Chron. 22:2 says he began to rule at forty-two? I can remember debating this very issue with a Church of Christ minister on a Cincinnati radio station years ago. He thumbed through his book; we cut to a commercial; he still had no answer when we returned. The minister said he would have to look that one up and get back with me later. The host of the program said that was pretty good and asked for another one. In effect, the minister conceded the point. There was no answer and that's why it should be used by all rational people.

One need only read the Bible to notice that the Old Testament is more populated with blatant contradictions than the New Testament. This is especially true with reference to numbers, which can't be debated. These are the kinds of problems that should definitely be brought up when confronting apologists. Of course, biblicists are always trying to find escape hatches. But when they are brought face to face with simple, blatant, straightforward examples of biblical incompatibility, argument becomes nearly hopeless. One of the most critically redeeming features of the Bible is that the Book is horribly repetitious. And in all this repeating the Book constantly gets facts out of synchronization.

The *sixth* is: How can Exod. 33:20, which says no man can see God's face and live, be squared with Gen. 32:30, which says a man saw God's face and his life was preserved? On page 111 in *Does the Bible Contradict Itself?* Arndt addresses essentially the same question, although he uses a different verse in one instance. He does use Gen. 32:30, which states, "Jacob called the name of the place Peniel: for I have seen God face to face, and my life is preserved," but he replaces Exod. 33:20 with John 1:18, which says, "No man hath seen God at any time." On the next page Arndt gives the following explanation for this contradiction:

> It might appear as if these passages were in total disagreement with one another. Yet harmonization is not difficult at all. Jesus tells us that God is a spirit, John 4:24, from which it follows that He cannot be seen. His essence is invisible— that is an unalterable fact. But this invisible and glorious God may grant to man special manifestations of Himself, reflections of His glory.

Although Arndt says "reflections of his glory," the text does not say reflections of anything. It says his face. Arndt changed the words. He continues, "some unmistakable signs of His presence." There are no signs; the verse is talking about God's face. Be it ever so subtle, don't let apologists alter the words that lie before you. Arndt continues, "He may, for the benefit of men, assume a human form and thus become visible to them. Upon beholding these manifestations, men will say that they have seen God." Of course, the real reason they say they have seen God is because that's what the text states. Nothing is said about manifestations of something or other. It clearly says God's face. And then Arndt makes the incredible statement that, "They are justified in saying this although they have not seen that most blessed, omniscient, and all-wise Spirit but merely certain manifestations of Him or the form which He temporarily assumed."

What dissimulation! The text says nothing about his "most blessed, omniscient, all-wise spirit;" it says *his face*. Nothing is said about God's glory or his presence. The two verses clearly contradict each other and trying to turn the issue into one of different manifestations of God is not going to resolve the difficulty. It is nothing more than an apologetic ploy, pure and simple.

This brings us to the *seventh* question in our pamphlet, one we employed during virtually every radio appearance. Rom. 3:23 says, "All have sinned." Please note this is another one of those absolutist statements. All means all. Yet Gen. 6:9, says "Noah was a just man and perfect in his generations." Job 1:1 and Job 1:8 say Job was perfect. The question to be asked here is: How could these men be perfect if all have sinned? The common response to this query is that the word "perfect" should have been translated as "complete," "blameless," or "righteous." But that really doesn't change the difficulty. If they are complete, blameless, or righteous, they are perfect. They are either complete and blameless or they are not complete. If they are incomplete, then they are not complete. And if they are incomplete, they are imperfect. The problem remains, regardless. Changing the word is not going to solve the difficulty. Many apologists love to resort to word games when they find themselves in difficulties of this nature. If they are going to constantly argue with that which can be found in most of the current versions of the Bible on the market, then the only recourse for them is to create their own version of the Bible and send me a copy. On several occasions I have made that very point.

The *eighth* question in our Bible pamphlet is covered rather extensively in the nineteenth and twentieth issues of *Biblical Errancy*. The question is: Did Moses really write the Pentateuch, as fundamentalists claim, or was it penned by others? In light of the fact that the burial of Moses is related in Deut. 34:5–6, one would hardly expect Moses to be the author. How many people have provided a written account of the events surrounding their own funerals? That verse alone is sufficient to bring the whole theory of Mosaic authorship of the Pentateuch into doubt.

The *ninth* question is purely a factual matter of whether or not Solomon had *forty thousand* stalls for his horses, as is said in 1 Kings 4:26, or *four thousand*, as is stated in 2 Chron. 9:25 of the KJV, and whether he had *two thousand* or *three thousand* baths according to 1 Kings 7:26 and 2 Chron. 4:5, respectively. These are purely factual matters that aren't really subject to dispute. The common apologetic defense that somebody copied something incorrectly, is wholly insupportable in light of the fact that the originals no longer exist. How do they know it was copied wrong? The contradiction stands until they can prove otherwise. To attribute nearly every contradiction of this nature to a copyist mistake is wholly insufficient and based on pure conjecture. If the conflict exists in the copies, then it is logical to assume it is present in the originals as well, absent evidence to the contrary. The burden of proof lies on him who alleges. Besides, the apologists can hardly argue copyist errors to explain contradictions, then assert inerrancy in all other parts of the Bible.

The *tenth* question asks how the Resurrection can be of any real importance when so many people rose from the dead before Jesus. The widow of Nain's son rose from the dead, Jairus's daughter rose from the dead, Elisha raised the dead son of a Shunammite, Lazarus rose from the dead, and many others followed suit. And all of these people rose before Jesus. So by the time Jesus rose, rising from the dead was actually a rather common occurrence.

The usual apologetic response one can expect to hear in this regard is that Jesus never died again. All those who preceded him rose from the dead, but they all died again, whereas Jesus did not. At least that's the argument. This is nothing more than another attempt to shift the focus that is so prevalent in apologetic rationalizations. In 1 Cor. 15:14 and 1 Cor. 15:17 Paul clearly states that Christianity lives or dies on the Resurrection. It is the Resurrection that matters, not the fact that Jesus never died again. Moreover, how can biblicists be sure these people died again when the Bible is silent in this regard? They are making an extrabiblical assumption. How do we know they did not go straight to heaven like Elijah in the chariot?

The *eleventh* question concerns another factual contradiction about which there can be little dispute. Was Jehoiachin eighteen years old when he began to reign in Jerusalem and did he reign three months, as is stated in 2 Kings 24:8, or was he eight years old and reigned three months and ten days, as we find in 2 Chron. 36:9? In addition, did Nebuzaradan come to rule Jerusalem on the seventh or the tenth day of the fifth month, as is stated in 2 Kings 25:8 and Jer. 52:12, respectively? Like so many problems the apologists attribute these, too, to copyists' mistakes.

The *twelfth* question in our Bible pamphlet has been a subject of dispute not only between Christians and freethinkers but among Christians themselves. How could Christians correctly adhere to the Sixth Commandment when there is no agreement as to its proper wording? Does it say, Thou shalt not *kill* or Thou shalt not *murder*? Several versions of the Bible such as the King James, the Revised Standard, the New American Bible, the American Standard Bible, the Jerusalem Bible, and the Lamsa Version say "kill" is the correct word to use. On the other hand, the New English Bible, the New American Standard Bible, the New International, the New World Translation, Today's English Version, and the Masoretic Text opt for the word "murder." The word is of crucial importance. Soldiers would avoid combat and police would not be inclined to draw their weapons if they felt that killing was in violation of God's law. On the other hand, if the commandment is only for murder, then a wide assortment of lethal activities would be permissible. In large part this accounts for the fact that newer versions of the Bible are increasingly selecting "murder" rather than "kill" as the word of choice. Political expediency rather than objective scholarship has become more dominant.

The Bible is supposedly a book of scientific precision. Our *thirteenth* question focuses on some of the most glaringly inaccurate scientific comments one could find in any book. How could the Bible be a work of inerrant perfection when the bat is referred to as a bird in Lev. 11:13–19 and some fowl and insects are referred to as creatures with four legs in Lev. 11:20–23. A subsequent chapter will discuss scientific inaccuracies in more detail.

The *fourteenth* question addresses one of the most prominent nonquotes in the entire Bible. A nonquote is defined as a New Testament reference to a non-existent Old Testament passage. New Testament authors often made reference to statements in the Old Testament that, in fact, don't exist. Matt. 27:9–10 refers to a prophecy by Jeremy the Prophet which does not even exist in the Book of Jeremiah. Although some biblicists allege that Matthew is referring to Jeremiah 32:6–9, the facts diverge in too many instances. Matthew says thirty pieces of silver, while Jeremiah says seventeen; Jeremiah says Jeremiah alone bought the field, while Matthew says "they" bought the field; Matthew is discussing blood money that was *not* approved by God, while the money in Jeremiah *was* approved by God. Realizing that there is nothing of relevance in Jeremiah, some apologists have tried to use Zechariah instead. Even if data in a similar account in Zechariah were identical, which they are not, the fact is that Matthew made reference to Jeremiah, not Zechariah.

The *fifteenth* question addresses a problem that should concern all adherents to the Bible *immensely* in light of the fact that the ultimate goal of all Christian activity is to attain heaven. Heaven is supposed to be a perfect place; yet Rev. 12:7 says it experienced a war. How could a war occur in a perfect place and if it happened before why couldn't it occur again? Moreover, why would anyone seek to enter a realm in which war is a possibility, when that is what nearly all people are trying to avoid? This verse deals a death blow to the security that all Christians seek. If *war* is possible in heaven, why wouldn't all other nefarious activities be equally plausible? After all, it would be hard to imagine a war without lying, stealing, cheating, brutality, killing, inhumanity, and all the other activities we have all grown so accustomed to seeing on television and in society at large.

The *sixteenth* question is of special importance to those who seek concrete evidence of biblical deception. The Bible rarely makes statements or comments that open themselves up to immediate scrutiny, testing, and exposure. And very few lend themselves to immediate scientific observation and rebuttal. But a few are available and one of the most prominent can be found in Mark 16:17–18, where believers are told that they can drink any deadly thing and take up serpents without being injured or killed. Because of this text many true believers have suffered the consequences of handling deadly snakes and drinking poisons. In fact, in many instances the courts have had to step in and protect the lives of children who were in danger as a result of such practices.

The text in question provides immediate and obvious evidence of the Bible's duplicity and for that reason many Christians have tried to vitiate its effect by several methods. Some have simply declared that the verses do not belong in the Bible and should be expunged from all versions. They will note, for instance, that they are not in a couple of early key manuscripts. Why this would jeopardize their validity one can only speculate, since much of the Bible is absent from one or another key manuscript. Other biblicists will claim that one should not put the Lord to a test; he should not be tempted. But taking God's word seriously is not an attempt to test the Lord. It is the Bible that is being asked to demonstrate its validity. If the text is valid, why is there so much hesitancy about putting the words to a test? Anyone who is reasonably open-minded knows that the real reason Christians are so defensive on this issue is that the words can't stand the strain. They are patently false and the only escape available is to find some kind of back door through which one can exit. Verses such as those found in Mark 16 are not only invalid but just plain dangerous. Indeed, if taken seriously, lives will be lost. History has demonstrated their lethal nature on numerous occasions. When certain groups claim that the Bible can be dangerous to your health, they aren't just talking through their hat. One should ask the obvious question to those who feel the text is valid. Would you be willing to test the Book's veracity—lay it on the line so to speak? I doubt it!

The *seventeenth* question exposes a direct conflict between Jesus and Paul. Any believer knows that Paul stressed salvation by faith. For him, faith was the ultimate criterion. If you accept Jesus as your savior, heaven is your destiny. If you do not, then Hell is all you can expect. Jesus, on the other hand, did *not* look upon faith as the crucial factor. When asked by a man in Matt. 19:16–18 what he had to do to obtain eternal life, Jesus stated quite clearly that one should adhere to the Ten Commandments. He then proceeded not only to list the commandments but add an additional requirement, namely, love thy neighbor as thyself, which is not even a commandment. For Jesus, salvation was based on works. The performance of good deeds was the primary obligation of all true believers. If Jesus is correct, then the theology of Paul and fundamentalist Christianity will be dealt a blow from which recovery will be all but impossible. Everyone on earth can practice good deeds, good works, and accepting Jesus is no longer a requirement. If good works are all that are obligatory, then people not only don't need Jesus but they don't even need religion or the Bible. That can be done by anyone. Secondly, if faith in Jesus is mandatory, as Paul and John 14:6 claim, then the salvation of all those who lived before Jesus' entry into the world is brought into question. After all, how could people be expected to believe in somebody who is yet to live? Apologist Barry Wood addresses this issue on page 114 in *Questions Non-Christians Ask*:

> How then was Abraham saved if he never heard of Christ? He was saved by faith in the limited "light" that he had. God looked down through the years of history and deposited the blood of His Son Jesus to Abraham's account. All the OT "saints" were saved by faith, and the God who transcends time accounted the cross to their cause.

What a maze of doubletalk! In the first place, what does "limited" light have to do with the issue? Light, especially limited light, does not save; only Jesus does. Light of what? Of God? You are not saved by believing in God. If limited light is all that is required, then Jews should be saved as well. Second, how could all the Old Testament saints be saved by faith? Faith in what? Faith in Jesus, who had not even lived yet? How do you believe in someone who is yet to exist? Abraham and many of the other Old Testament saints lived long before even the messianic prophecies came into existence. So they couldn't have believed in Jesus, even as an expected savior or a being yet to come, let alone one who has already arrived. The issue of whether salvation is to be by faith or works has troubled Christian theologians for centuries.

The Bible is very contradictory on this issue and the Book of James only adds to the confusion by saying that faith without works is dead. If works are mandatory, as James alleges, then Paul is in error. One or the other has made a mistake, and in light of Jesus' position on this matter, Paul appears to be the one in error. Paul made a rather strong attempt to change Christianity into Paulianity and judging by the number of Christians who adhere to a theology of salvation by faith, he appears to have succeeded.

The *eighteenth* question is another one of those straightforward factual problems that biblicists just can't seem to reconcile. One need only read Joshua 15:21–32 in the RSV to see that the number of cities listed is thirty-six, not twenty-nine, as is summarized in the last verse.

The *nineteenth* question highlights one of the more prominent problems within the Bible, especially the Old Testament. Scripture often makes statements that are blatantly false and Eccle. 1:9 in the RSV is a good example. The verse states that, "What has been is what will be, and what has been done is what will be done, there is nothing new under the sun." Nothing new under the sun! We all know that no city had ever suffered atomic attack until 1945 and no one had ever walked on the moon prior to 1969. So there *is* something new under the sun, after all.

The *twentieth* question addresses an issue that is kept under wraps as much as possible by nearly every spokesperson of the Judeo-Christian creed—Scripture's sizable number of offensive passages. When the Bible refers to eating *dung* and drinking *piss* in 2 Kings 18:27, for example (that's the Bible's language not mine), one can't help but wonder how anyone would want to send their children to Sunday School to risk exposure to such trash. A later chapter will expose a far larger number of corrupting comments that are nearly always overlooked in Sunday sermons. How a book with language such as that found in the Bible could be deemed the word of a perfect being is an enigma to say the least.

The *twenty-first* question opens up a sizable can of worms for the typical biblicist. If, in fact, God created everything, as is alleged in Col. 1:16, Eph. 3:9, Rev. 4:11, and John 1:3, then he must have created all the evil that exists. Oddly enough, Isa. 45:7 ("I form the light, and create darkness: I make peace, and create evil: I the Lord do all these things") and Lam. 3:38 ("Is it not from the mouth of the Most High that good and evil come?") concur in that assessment. For that reason *God* should be held responsible for the world's condition. Surely, he shouldn't take credit for just the good things in life. Evil or antisocial behavior is as real as anything else.

A problem of equal perplexity is addressed in the *twenty-second* question. If God is everywhere, as Christians so often assert, if he is omnipresent, as is claimed in Psalms 139:7–11, then how could he constantly move from place to place, as the Bible describes in such verses as Gen. 11:5, Gen. 18:21, and 1 Kings 19:11–12? After all, why would you need to move at all if you are everywhere?

The *twenty-third* question tackles a biblical problem that has troubled both supporters and critics of the Bible for centuries. No matter how many evil deeds someone commits while on earth the number is finite; it is limited. You can only do so much that is wrong in one lifetime. So why should people be subjected to the injustice of an infinite punishment in hell? To say this a case of overkill is a gross understatement, not to mention a gross injustice.

And lastly, the *twenty-fourth* question notes that according to Paul in Acts 20:35 Jesus said, "It is more blessed to give than to receive." The fourteenth question discussed a nonquote and this is another example of same. This alleged statement by Jesus is nowhere to be found in Scripture and is another figment of someone's imagination, in this case, Paul's.

Conclusion

That completes not only an extensive analysis of the pamphlet *The Bible is God's Word?* but twenty-four of the best questions one could ever employ in the struggle against Christianity in general and the Bible in particular. Every rational person should find them to be a welcome addition to his or her antisuperstition portfolio.

4

Contradictions

Numerical, Theological, Chronological, Factual, Philosophical, Ethical

In the previous chapter we discussed the pamphlet issued by *Biblical Errancy* several years ago entitled "The Bible is the Answer?" This chapter will concentrate on the myriad contradictions contained in the Bible and the common apologetic defenses one can expect to hear in response. If there is any aspect in which the Bible is unique among pieces of literature it lies in the number of contradictions it contains. For one to list all of the Bible's inconsistencies would require scores of chapters if not several books. So rather than try to exhaust the topic, we will focus on enough examples to give any objective observer a clear idea of the magnitude of the problem.

The newsletter *Biblical Errancy* is often described as a publication exposing contradictions in the Bible. But that's only partially correct. It also deals with errors and fallacies having to do with a wide variety of subjects. Although contradictions occupy a position of supreme importance, they are by no means the only area of concentration. Every analyst of the Bible should realize that the Book is a veritable miasma of contradictions, inconsistencies, inaccuracies, poor science, bad math, inaccurate geography, immoralities, degenerate heroes, false prophecies, boring repetitions, childish superstitions, silly miracles, and dry-as-dust discourse. But contradictions remain the most obvious, the most potent, the most easily proven, and the most common problem to plague the Book. For that reason we will now focus on some of the more glaring examples. All readers are encouraged to check these contradictions for themselves in the King James Version of the Bible.

One of the most obvious, if not fatal, weaknesses of the Bible lies in its propensity for repetition. Deuteronomy repeats much of Exodus; Chronicles repeats much of Kings and Samuel; Proverbs is repetitious, and the Gospels follow in lockstep. In all of this repeating the Book often fails to maintain consistency. The right hand often doesn't know what the left hand is doing. For example, in identical stories, 1 Kings 5:16 says that *3,300* chief officers were involved, while 2 Chron. 2:18 says it was *3,600* overseers, a difference of 300 people. In another story 1 Kings 4:26 says *40,000* stalls were involved, while the same account in 2 Chron. 9:25 says it was *4,000* stalls.

On page 39 of a book entitled *Does the Bible Contradict Itself?* apologist William Arndt offers the following explanation for the latter conflict. He states, "The old Lutheran theologian Pfeiffer points out that the passage in First Kings deals with the affairs of Solomon at the beginning of his reign, while that in Second Chronicles belongs to the closing verses of the section describing the life and the deeds of the wise king [at the end of his reign]." In essence, Arndt makes an assumption based upon information that is nowhere to be found in the Bible. There is no reason whatever for making a distinction of this nature other than to escape an obvious imbroglio. It would mean that Solomon was far weaker militarily at the end of his reign than at the beginning. And the number of stalls in his possession went from forty thousand to four thousand. Later Arndt says, "If anyone feels that the difficulty is not fully removed by this method, he may assume that a copyist's error has crept into the text, a scribe writing *40,000* instead of *4,000*." In other words, Arndt is just throwing out some rationalizations and you can take your pick. How's that for objective scholarship!

On page 45 of his book *So the Bible Is Full of Contradictions*, Carl Johnson addresses the same problem and says, "The solution to the problem comes when we realize the similarity of the figures *four* and *forty* in the Hebrew and see this as a copyist's error. There are a considerable number of copyists' errors, especially in the Old Testament. I list some of these errors below." At this point he proceeds to provide a sizable number of what are alleged to be copyist errors. Then he says, "Copyists' errors did creep in. But once again we say that these errors were not in the autographs but in the copies, and none of them affects the doctrinal contents of the Bible." But as was shown in the first chapter: How does Johnson know the errors weren't in the autographs? Has he ever seen the autographs? No! Can he prove they ever existed? No! So any reliance upon the supposed inerrant originals is pure speculation. We also noted in chapter 1 that some of the contradictions certainly do create major doctrinal difficulties. Many are by no means benign.

In any event, to move on, 1 Kings 7:26 says *2,000* baths while 2 Chron. 4:5 has *3,000* baths in the same account. Apologist Johnson sought to solve this problem by stating on page 37 of the same book: "There are at least two possible solutions to this. It could be a copyist's error, or it could be that the molten sea ordinarily contained 2,000 baths, but when it was filled to capacity it received and held 3,000 baths. Either way, there is no real contradiction here."

Well, Johnson is wrong on both counts! Does he have any evidence whatever that there is a copyist mistake? No, he does not, and until he does, the contradiction remains. Secondly, the text says nothing about one of the baths being filled to capacity. There is no distinction whatever made between the two baths and both texts have almost precisely the same wording. Apologists constantly rely upon interpolation as a means by which to escape what is otherwise a cul de sac, a dead end. If the text doesn't say what they like, they simply put in words that do. How's that for an out! In this case, for instance, the text says nothing about one bowl being filled to capacity. But that's no problem. Just put it in anyway. Objective scholarship is not one of their more prominent traits.

Moving on, 2 Samuel 8:4 says *700* horsemen, while the same account in 1 Chron. 18:4 says *7,000*. In 2 Kings 8:26 Ahaziah is twenty-two years old when he began to reign, while 2 Chron. 22:2 says he was forty-two. As a fundamentalist minister conceded to me during a radio debate in Cincinnati several years ago, "Obviously he can't be both." On page 45 in *Does the Bible Contradict Itself?* Arndt says in answer to this problem, "That there is disagreement between these two texts, as we read them in our Bible at present, seems to be undeniable." Notice he says "undeniable." He continues,

> In all probability 2 Chron. 22:2 contains a copyist's error . . . and it's not a farfetched assumption that a scribe, in copying Chronicles, through an oversight wrote 42 instead of 22. It is a remarkable proof of the fidelity with which the Jews transmitted the sacred text that they did not dare to change this palpable error which inadvertently had been allowed to slip into the text.

In other words, to go to the heart of the matter and cut through all the verbiage, Arndt admits there is a contradiction and can only think of this copyist-error excuse as a way out.

Ahaziah presents another horrible problem for the Bible's defenders when we compare 2 Kings 8:26 with 2 Chron. 22:2. On page 40 of his book *So the Bible Is Full of Contradictions* apologist Johnson highlights the conflict between these two verses when he says,

> According to the first reference Ahaziah was *22* years old when he began to reign, but the second reference says he was *42*. His father, King Jehoram died when he was forty years of age (2 Chron. 21:20). If the second reference above is correct, King Ahaziah would be two years older than his father.

Succinctly stated, how could a forty-two-year-old man take over from his father, when his father just died at age forty? To say this is a mystery is an understatement.

Johnson concludes, "It is undeniable that there is a seeming contradiction between the two reports. The solution to the problem comes when we realize that this is a copyist's error." Where have we heard this before? In essence, Johnson admits there is a contradiction and again tries to pawn it off on the usual excuse, for which there is not a scintilla of evidence. On the next page he submits the standard proviso, for which there is no corroboration either: "The original manuscripts, the autographs, were, and are, inerrant."

To move on, 2 Samuel 6:23 says Michal had no sons, while 2 Sam. 21:8 says she had five sons. On page 34 in *So the Bible Is Full of Contradictions* Johnson defers to the *Wycliffe Bible Commentary*, which suggests, "Michal raised the five sons of her deceased sister Merab, whom Merab had borne to Adriel." Then Johnson quotes Dr. Robert Jamieson, who also says, "Merab, Michal's sister, was the wife of Adriel (1 Sam. 18:19); but Michal adopted and brought up the boys under her care." The obvious problem with this explanation lies in the fact that it is not backed up by any biblical testimony. The text of 2 Sam. 21:8 specifically says, "The five sons of Michal." Nowhere does it imply, much less state, that they were adopted; moreover, nowhere does the text claim that Merab, Michal's sister, had five sons whom Michal had adopted. So, in effect, we are being asked to ignore a clear statement in Scripture while making two assumptions, neither of which is textually supportable. Are we going to go by what the Bible says or by what its defenders wish it said?

To proceed further, 2 Samuel 24:9 says *800,000* men drew the sword, while the same account in 1 Chron. 21:5 says it was *1,100,000*, a difference of 300,000 men. That can't be attributed to one figure being rounded off. You don't round off 300,000 people. Moreover, the figures are already rounded off to the nearest 100,000.

In other conflicting accounts, 2 Kings 25:8 says the seventh day, while Jer. 52:12 says the tenth day in the same story.

In 1 Kings 9:23 there are *550* chief officers, while the same story in 2 Chron. 8:10 says it was *250* chief officers. In 2 Kings 24:8 Jehoiachin was *eighteen* years old when he began to reign, while 2 Chron. 36:9 says he was *eight* years old. And 2 Kings 24:8 says Jehoiachin reigned *three months,* while 2 Chron. 36:9 says he reigned for *3 months and 10 days.*

One need only read Scripture with a reasonably critical eye to realize that conflicts of this nature are almost too numerous to mention.

Having said that, let us move on to a discussion of how Saul died. There are not two but three versions of this event. The account in 1 Sam. 31:4 says that he killed himself; 2 Sam. 21:12 says that he was killed by a Philistine; and 2 Sam. 1:10 says that he was killed by an Amalekite. Which is it? Was he killed by himself, by a Philistine, or by an Amalekite? On page 33 in *So the Bible Is Full of Contradictions* Johnson says in defense of the Bible,

The probable solution to this problem is that Saul was mortally wounded by the Philistines; he fell upon his sword in order to kill himself but failed to do so. His armorbearer thought he was dead and killed himself. Then the Amalekite came along and Saul asked him to kill him. The Amalekite reported to David, "so I stood upon him and slew him, because I was sure that he could not live after he was fallen." So it was a case of being wounded by the enemy, an attempted suicide, and then being killed by a young Amalekite.

To this one can only say, "What a lot of gobbledygook!" For goodness sake man! What does the text say? In 2 Sam. 21:12 Saul is said to be slain by the Philistines. Specifically, the text states, "When the Philistines had slain Saul in Gilboa." It says *slain*, S-L-A-I-N. In other words, he was dead. D-E-A-D. Nowhere does it say they wounded him. Secondly, nowhere does the text say that Saul failed to kill himself. Quite the contrary, it says in 1 Sam. 31:4–5, "Saul took a sword, and fell upon it. And when his armorbearer saw that Saul was dead, he fell likewise upon his sword." So for Johnson to say that "he fell upon his sword in order to kill himself but failed to do so" is ridiculous. The text clearly says he succeeded. Moreover, the text does not say that the armorbearer *thought* he was dead. It says "his armorbearer *saw* that Saul was dead." There's no "thought" to it. It says he was DEAD. Johnson began his defense by using the phrase "probable solution." His solution isn't even probable. It's pure nonsense.

To proceed further, 2 Sam. 24:9 says that the number of men that drew the sword in Judah were *500,000* men. The identical story found in 1 Chron. 21:5 says the number that drew the sword in Judah were *470,000* men. What kind of rationalization does Arndt give in explanation for this dilemma? He says on page 37 in *Does the Bible Contradict Itself*, "Evidently the account in First Chronicles is more exact than the other. The writer of Second Samuel contents himself with stating the number of warriors in round figures. Here, then, there is no discrepancy." And to that one can only say, "Whom is he kidding?" Of course there is a discrepancy. It's a major discrepancy of 30,000 men. One of them is wrong. Possibly both are wrong. But when one says 500,000 and the other says 470,000, it's beyond question that one of them is erroneous. You don't round off 30,000 men.

Moving on, there is a contradiction between Acts 7:14, which says, "Then sent Joseph, and called his father Jacob to him, and all his kindred, three score and fifteen souls"—that's seventy-five people—and Ex. 1:5, which says, "All the souls that came out of the loins of Jacob were three score and ten souls: for Joseph was in Egypt already"—that's *seventy* people. This discrepancy has baffled scholars for centuries. Were there seventy-five souls or seventy souls that went down into Egypt with Jacob? Gen. 46:27 agrees with the number found in Exodus and says, "All the souls of the house of Jacob, which came into Egypt, were three score and ten." And so does Deut. 10:22. So how many people of Jacob's family went down into Egypt? Was it seventy, as is recorded at three places in the Old Testament, or seventy-five, as is stated in the New Testament? On page 374 in *A General Introduction to the Bible* apologists Norman Geisler and William Nix confront the problem by saying,

> In the Masoretic text it reads that "70" descended into Egypt. This has been a perplexing problem because the New Testament (Acts 7:14) and the Septuagint read "75 souls." This problem has occasioned many ingenious attempts at harmonization, including the counting of 5 grandsons, alleging that Stephen [who was doing the speaking in Acts] was wrong [when he said 75]. . . . Nevertheless, a much simpler explanation is now possible. A fragment of Exodus from Qumran reads "75 souls." It is possible that the Septuagint and Dead Sea fragment preserve the true text. This explanation cannot be considered harmonistic, since it still faces the problem of Genesis 46:27, which says the number was "70."

Geisler and Nix fail to note that it not only doesn't adequately confront the problem presented by Gen. 46:27 but the problem presented by Deut. 10:22 as well. But even more importantly, it proves beyond any doubt that there is a contradiction. To make a long story short, Ex. 1, Gen. 46, and Deut. 10 all say that the number should be seventy, while Acts 7 and the Septuagint, which is the Greek translation of the Old Testament, say the number should be seventy-five. Then, lo and behold, out of nowhere comes a fragment of Exodus from the caves of Qumran that supports the seventy-five in Acts. So, we not only have a contradiction between the Old Testament and New Testament but, judging from extrabiblical data submitted by Geisler and Nix, erroneous figures in the Old Testament as well. Clearly the whole issue is plagued with difficulties.

The next problem concerns Cain and his wife. Many years ago while I was sitting in a cafeteria during lunch hour a devout Christian mentioned a biblical problem that had bothered him immensely. He was never able to figure out where Cain got his wife. The problem is created by Gen. 4:16–17, which says, "Cain went out from the presence of the Lord, and dwelt in the land of Nod, on the east of Eden. And Cain knew his wife; and she conceived, and bare Enoch." Since Adam and Eve had two sons, Cain and Abel, and Cain slew Abel, where did this additional woman come from? That's the issue. Although inadequate for reasons yet to be mentioned, apologist Sidney Collett has a rather abrupt response to this problem on page 237 in his book *All About the Bible*. He says, "It will now be readily seen that there were plenty of women to provide a wife for Cain, who doubtless married one of his sisters . . . or possibly a niece."

Apologists McDowell and Stewart offer the same solution to this problem on page 98 of *Answers to Tough Questions* and in doing so destroy, surprisingly enough, one of the most common apologetic defenses in the process. They state

One of the most frequent questions asked by Christians and non-Christians alike is where did Cain's wife come from. . . . One theory that has been put forth to explain the existence of sufficient numbers of people and Cain's wife is directly contradictory to Scripture and posits a "pre-Adamic" race dwelling in the neighborhood of the Garden of Eden from which Cain could take a wife. This is not a tenable solution, however, for the Scriptures clearly teach that Adam was the first man (1 Cor. 15:45) and his wife, Eve, was "the mother of all living (Gen. 3:20)." [A more viable resolution of the problem lies in the fact that] Gen. 5:4 tells us that Adam had sons and daughters. At first, sons and daughters of Adam and Eve had to marry each other to populate the earth. Cain probably married a sister or niece or grand niece.

Notice that our apologetic friends say "probably" because we all know they are guessing. Their explanation is based on pure speculation and wholly unbiblical data. The only accurate part of their answer lies in their refutation of the pre-Adamic theory; their assertion that there can be no people who lived prior to Adam and Eve because that would be antibiblical is correct.

Unfortunately for McDowell, Stewart, and Collett, a major problem accompanies their explanation. If Cain knew his wife and we are all descendants of that relationship, then we are all the products of incest, if that woman was his sister or niece. In addressing this very issue McDowell and Stewart state, "All this raises the additional question of incest. If incest is scripturally forbidden, according to the Mosaic law, how do we explain all this marrying of siblings?" After going through the rather protracted and secondary issue of genetic deformities, they state, "God forbids incest on moral grounds . . . and after God's ordained family structure stabilized, incest was sin."

In other words, our apologetic friends would have us believe that incest was not immoral until the family structure stabilized. Does that mean morality evolves and incest only became immoral at a certain point in history? That smacks of "situational ethics," which in other cases is the bane fundamentalists are so quick to decry. What is immoral at one time is not immoral at another. Also worthy of note is that McDowell and Stewart surreptitiously slipped in an idea that has no biblical basis whatever—where does the Bible say that Cain and his wife were ever married? Where does it say Cain "married" his wife? Nothing whatsoever is said about marriage in any form. No ceremony of any kind occurs nor are vows exchanged. All the text says is that Eve was formed from a rib of Adam and Cain knew his wife. The latter sounds like a shack-up and the former resembles a chemistry experiment in the tradition of Bela Lugosi and Dr. Frankenstein.

Another problem with the Adam and Eve myth emerges when we compare Gen. 2:17, which says, "In the day that thou eatest thereof thou shalt surely die," with Gen. 5:5, which says Adam lived to be 930 years old. Apologist Carl Johnson confronts this problem directly when he says on page 11 *So the Bible Is Full of Contradictions,*

> In the first verse we are told that Adam would die the very day he ate the forbidden fruit in the Garden of Eden; yet, the second states that he lived until he was 930 years old. "Surely there is a contradiction here," someone says. Not when you understand the meaning of death in the Bible. Adam did die *spiritually* the day he disobeyed God.

The problem with this explanation lies in the fact that nothing is said about a spiritual death. Where does the text say Adam would die spiritually? It says he would die, period. Are we going to allegorize, symbolize, and interpret figuratively every verse that puts the Bible's supporters in a bind?

Another example of fundamentalists interpreting verses in a figurative rather than a literal sense for purposes of expediency appears in explanations for the contradiction between Prov. 3:13, which says, "Happy is the man that findeth wisdom and the man that geteth understanding" and Eccles. 1:18, which says, "For in much wisdom is much grief and he that increaseth knowledge increaseth sorrow." The former says that wisdom brings happiness and the latter says that greater wisdom increases sorrow. So does wisdom bring happiness or grief? You'll never know from the Bible. On page 176 in a famous apologetic writing written over a hundred years ago entitled *Alleged Discrepancies of the Bible,* John Haley provides the following explanation for this conflict: "In the first text 'wisdom' denotes spiritual wisdom, which prepares for and lays hold upon the future life. In the second case, the term implies mere worldly knowledge . . . wisdom limited to the sphere of this life." Pure rationalization is the only appropriate characterization of this defense, because there is no reason whatever for making a distinction of this nature. Not only does the text *not* draw such a demarcation, but it isn't even implied. One could just as easily reverse the situation and say with equal justification that the former is earthly and the latter is spiritual. Two can play that game. As they say: What is sauce for the goose is sauce for the gander.

In several instances we have two or more contradictions in one verse. For instance, 2 Sam. 10:18 says *700* chariots and 40,000 horsemen, while the same account in 1 Chron. 19:18 says *7,000* chariots and 40,000 *footmen.* On page 34 in *Does the Bible Contradict Itself?* Arndt says,

> The difference in the number of chariots is best explained as due to the error of a scribe who . . . could easily write 7,000 instead of 700, or vice versa. With respect to the other divergence between the two passages, the one saying that David slew 40,000 *horsemen,* the other that he slew 40,000 *footmen* in this battle, a simple solution presents itself. These warriors could fight both as cavalry and

as infantry, just as the occasion required. Their status was similar to that of the dragoons a century or two ago.

Arndt fails to realize that what they "could" fight as is irrelevant. The fact is that the text is stating what they are, in fact, fighting as not what they *could* be fighting as. The key word is "could." Anybody could fight as a horseman or a footman, even you, the reader. But the question is not what they could be fighting as, but what they are, in fact, fighting as. That's the issue and that's why the contradiction stands. On page 34 in *So the Bible Is Full of Contradictions* Johnson says in this regard,

> Once again this is a copyist's error. It would be easy for a scribe to write 7,000 for 700, since letters were used as numerals in Hebrew and these letters had a marked resemblance to one another. . . . [Apologist] DeWette wrote of the errors of copyists: They confounded similar letters. Hence, on the supposition that numerical characters were used, we are to explain the difference in numbers.

Again we see the usual gimmick in action—the copyist excuse.

In other instances, contradictions can be found in blocks or groups of anywhere from ten to twenty-five. One of the most prominent examples is the contradiction between Ezra 2 and Neh. 7. In each instance we have a listing of the subclans that returned from the Captivity and the number of people in each. In the King James Version, out of approximately thirty-five subclans listed over half of the numbers are in disagreement. Furthermore, someone doesn't know how to add very well because the totals are in error. Ezra 2:64 says, "The whole congregation together was 42,360," when one can easily see by adding the figures that the total is 29,818. Neh. 7:66 also says, "The whole congregation together was 42,360" when one need only add those figures to see that it's actually 31,089. Ezra erred by 12,542 and Nehemiah erred by 11,271.

As you have probably realized by now, the most common excuse one will hear for the kinds of errors we have noted so far is that a copyist made a mistake. Somebody copied something wrong. Haley, for instance, resorts to this subterfuge repeatedly in his book *Alleged Discrepancies in the Bible*. Of course, the obvious question becomes: How does Haley know something was copied wrong when the alleged originals no longer exist, if they ever did? The answer is that he doesn't. He's guessing, or better yet, whistling in the dark. The Book's defenders love this approach because there is no way it can be definitely checked. The situation mimics the story of the man who says that he literally talked to Jesus this morning in his bedroom, Jesus in the flesh. When asked to provide proof he replies that he has none and you'll have to take his word for it. When asked to repeat the event with others present, he will say that the event was unique and can't be repeated. When asked to provide some tangible evidence, such as a piece of Jesus' garment, he will reply that Jesus took everything with him. When asked to provide some pictures, drawings, or other visual aids, he will say that easels and other equipment were not available. In other words, an alibi will be readily provided for any and every question. The "somebody copied something wrong" explanation falls into the same classification and is nothing more than sophisticated intellectual evasion with a liberal overlay of deception. The contradiction remains until apologists can provide evidence to the contrary.

An example of a simple, direct contradiction that does not involve figures or numbers occurs in James 1:13, which says that God tempts no man, while Gen. 22:1 says God tempted Abraham. On page 15 in *So the Bible Is Full of Contradictions* Johnson says in this regard,

> An understanding of the meaning of the word *tempt* will dispel the seeming contradiction. This word is used in a good sense and in a bad sense. When it's used in a good sense it means to test, to try, to prove. God tested Abraham. . . . When the word *tempt* is used in a bad sense it means to entice a person to do evil. God never tempts man to sin.

Two major fallacies are immediately evident in this rationale. First, there is nothing in the Bible that would justify such a distinction and there is no compelling reason to make it. Second, if God never tempts man to sin, then why is God entreated to "lead us not into temptation but deliver us from evil" in Matt. 6:13? Moreover, Deut. 4:34 says God *does* use temptations to further his ends.

Moving on, in Gen. 37:36 Joseph was sold into captivity by the Midianites, while Gen. 39:1 says it was by the Ishmaelites. According to John 8:14 Jesus' witness is true, while John 5:31 says it's not true. Matt. 1:16 says Joseph's father is "Jacob," while Luke 3:23 says it's "Heli." Jonah 1:17 says that Jonah was in the belly of a fish for three days, while Matt. 12:40 says it was a whale. You don't need to be a marine biologist to know that a whale is not a fish and no fish is a whale. The twelfth verse of Gen. 14 says that Lot was Abraham's nephew, while the fourteenth and sixteenth verses say that he was Abraham's brother. According to 2 Samuel 24:1, which says, "The anger of the Lord was kindled against Israel, and he moved David against them to say, Go, number Israel and Judah," *the Lord* told David to number Israel. Yet the same event in 1 Chron. 21:1 is described this way: "Satan stood up against Israel, and provoked David to number Israel"—alleging that Satan gave the order. A close reading of these two verses could easily lead one to believe that God and Satan are identical.

On page 36 in *So the Bible Is Full of Contradictions* Johnson provides the following explanation for the latter rather poignant embarrassment. "The Lord permitted Satan to encourage David to take the census, so both the Lord and Satan were involved." Later he says, "It was Satan who tempted David, but God permitted Satan to do it." One can't help but conclude that apologists often have trouble reading the Bible and this problem provides vivid proof of same. What does 2 Sam. 24:1 say? It says, "The Lord was kindled and he moved David to number Israel." The text says the Lord, not Satan, moved David. Nowhere does it say the Lord *permitted* Satan to encourage David. Satan is not mentioned at all. The text says the Lord did it directly; he did it himself. When this verse is set alongside 1 Chron. 21:1, which says, "Satan stood up against Israel, and provoked David to number Israel," the contradiction becomes inescapable. One can't help but become very weary with the enormous amount of intellectual dishonesty that is so clearly evident in most apologetic literature. Defenders of the Bible are far more closely allied to the Book and Jesus than they will ever be to truth and objectivity. Defending Jesus and the Bible at all costs are paramount in their thought processes. Their war cry is: Damn the facts; man the barricades.

To move on, Matt. 11 and John 1 expose a direct conflict between Jesus and John the Baptist. In Matt. 11:14 Jesus says John the Baptist is the renewed Elijah, while in John 1:21 John the Baptist says he's not. So who is lying, Jesus or John the Baptist? This is not so much a contradiction as an admission that one of the key New Testament figures is a liar. Logic, along with a reasonable dose of common sense, would lead anyone to the obvious conclusion that Jesus is the guilty culprit, since John the Baptist is in a far better position than anyone else to know who he is. If John the Baptist says he is not the new Elijah, that should settle the matter, and would have done so long ago were it not for the fact that the integrity of the central figure in Christianity is at stake.

According to Acts 1:18 Judas bought a field with the thirty pieces of silver he obtained for turning Jesus in to the authorities, while Matt. 27:3-5 says he returned the money to the priests.

There is also a conflict with respect to how Judas died. Matt. 27:5 says he hanged himself, while Acts 1:18 says he purchased a field with the pieces of silver and as he fell headlong he burst in the midst and his bowels gushed out. The apologists McDowell and Stewart confront the latter issue on page 84 of *Answers to Tough Questions* by stating,

> This question of the manner in which Judas died is one with which we are constantly confronted in our travels. Many people point to the apparent discrepancy in the two accounts as an obviously irreconcilable error. . . . A possible recon-struction would be this: Judas hanged himself on a tree on the edge of a precipice that overlooked the valley of Hinnom. After he hung there for some time, the limb of the tree snapped or the rope gave way and Judas fell down the ledge, mangling his body in the process.

We would only ask the reader to read these verses and ask yourself if this ex-planation is realistic. Realistically, is the contradiction reconcilable in this manner? Although vaguely plausible, does it seem even remotely possible or practical? Does it sound like an honest, unbiased explanation emanating from an objective scholar, or nothing more than pure rationalization and fabrication for purposes of obfuscation?

The repetitious Gospels are especially rich in contradictions because there are not two but four gospel versions covering essentially the same material. Matt. 8:28–31 says there were *two* possessed with devils, while the same story in Luke 8:26–34 and Mark 5:2–14 says there was *one*. Matt. 8:5 says the centurion sent nobody but came alone, while the same account in Luke 7:2–4 says the centurion sent the Jewish elders instead of coming himself. Matt. 20:29–30 says they passed *two* blind men as they departed from Jericho, while Mark 10:46 says they passed *one* blind man. Luke 9:28 says Jesus took Peter, James, and John to a high mountain after eight days, while Matt. 17:1 and Mark 9:2 say it was six days. And according to Mark 6:8–9 the disciples were to take a staff and sandals on their mission, while Matt. 10:9–10 says they were to take *neither*.

The number of factual contradictions of this nature within the Gospels is sizable and a listing of them would encompass more space than we have available. The Gospels also have a large number of chronological contradictions in which the same events are related in two or more gospels but the sequence of activities is out of synchronization. For example, Matt. 4:5–8 says that the devil set Jesus on the pinnacle of the Temple and then took him up unto a high mountain, while Luke 4:5–9 says that the devil first took him to the mountain and *then* to the pinnacle. Matt. 21:12–19 says that Jesus cleaned the temple and then cursed the fig tree, while Mark 11:13–15 says he cursed the fig tree and *then* cleaned the temple. Luke 22:14–21 says that the presence of Jesus' betrayer was revealed *after* the Last Supper, while Matt. 26:21 and Mark 14:18 say it was revealed *during* the Last Supper. Matt. 8:23–27 and 9:9 say that Jesus calmed a storm and later called Matthew, while Luke 5:27–28 and 8:22–25 give the opposite order of events. Matt. 8:1–2 and 14 say the Jesus healed the leper *before* entering Peter's house, while Mark 1:29 and 1:40 say he healed him *after* leaving Peter's house. Matt. 8:28–32 and 10:1–4 say that Jesus caused devils to enter swine and later appointed the Twelve Apostles, while Mark 3:13–19 and 5:1–13 say he appointed the twelve and *later* destroyed the swine. Matt. 8:28–32 and 11:11–14 say that Jesus caused devils to enter swine and later gave tribute to John the Baptist, while Luke 7:24–28 and 8:26–33 say the tribute to John came first. Matt. 5:3–12 and 8:14–15 say that Jesus gave the Sermon on the Mount and later healed Peter's mother-in-law, while Luke 4:38–39 and 6:20–26 say the healing preceded the sermon. And Mark 1:12–13 and 6:17–18 say that Jesus was tempted in the wilderness and later John was arrested, while Luke 3:19-20 and 4:1–13 say the arrest of John preceded the tempting in the wilderness.

These are only a few of the many chronological contradictions that can be found in the Gospels alone. Our listing could be extended significantly but the point has been made. Why on earth the Bible's authors would allow so many blatant contradictions to remain in a supposedly perfect and inerrant book is a question that has bothered both defenders and critics for centuries. The most common explanation given for their presence in the text is that each of the four gospels had a major region pushing for its adoption and in order to satisfy everyone and unify Christendom, an agreement was reached whereby all four were included simultaneously. By that method each of the four areas involved had its favorite version included and pronounced canonical. Political expediency in the religious realm necessitated a theological compromise.

Contradictions of a more philosophical nature are also abundant in the New Testament. For example, John 5:22 says, "The Father judgeth no man, but hath committed all judgment unto the Son," while in John 8:15 and 12:47 Jesus says, "I judge no man." In Matt. 26:52 Jesus tells a disciple that, "All that take the sword shall perish with the sword," while in Luke 22:36 he tells his disciples to buy swords. John 3:35 says that, "The Father loveth the Son, and hath given all things into his hand," while in Matt. 20:23 Jesus denies he has *everything* by saying, "To sit on my right hand, and on my left, is not mine to give." According to Rom. 3:20 and Gal. 2:16 man is justified by faith alone. But James 2:20 and 2:24 say faith alone is insufficient. Works are a necessity.

This contradiction alone has generated as much conflict between Christians themselves as any available. Whether salvation is by works or faith has been a reccurring controversy throughout Christian history and faith has been preferred by most believers.

Deut. 24:16 and Ezek. 18:20 cite Old Testament laws to the effect that children are *not* to be punished for the sins of their parents. Yet, in Exod. 20:5 and 34:7, and Isa. 14:21 God orders children to be punished for the deeds of their parents. On page 20 of *So the Bible Is Full of Contradictions* apologist Johnson says, "Both statements are true and there is no real contradiction. It is true that God visits the iniquity of the fathers upon the children in that He permits the latter to suffer the consequences of the sins of the former."

Permits! Permits! What is this "permits" nonsense? Nothing is said about permitting anyone to do anything. Ex. 20:5 and 34:7 say, "I visit the iniquity." In other words, God causes it. He doesn't just "permit" it. Johnson continues, "If a man is a drunkard, he bequeaths to his children poverty, shame, poor health, wretchedness, and many times a desire for strong drink." Johnson's analogy is invalid because no judgment is involved. There is no conscious decision by someone to punish one being for the deeds of another. It is a mere fortuitous turn of events without any intent or thought being involved that has resulted in children being adversely affected by the sins of their fathers. But when children are *intentionally* punished because of their father's acts, that is an injustice. When an earthquake or a volcano kills one person while leaving his neighbor untouched, we don't say that's an injustice. Acts of nature know nothing of justice or injustice; they just occur, and for someone to consider them unjust is inane.

To move on, Deut. 32:4, Psalms 19:7-8, and James 1:13 say that God is *not* the author of evil. Yet Isa. 45:7, Jer. 18:11, and Ezek. 20:25 say he is. James 5:16 says, "The effectual fervent prayer of a righteous man avails much," while Rom. 3:10 says, "There is none righteous, no, not one." If none are righteous, then why say, "The effectual fervent prayer of a *righteous man*?" There are no righteous men to effect the prayer to begin with. In John 10:30 Jesus says, "I and my Father are one." Yet, according to Matt. 27:46 Jesus cried out on the cross, "My God, my God, why hast thou forsaken me?" That hardly sounds like they are one! It sounds far more like they have a definite difference of opinion as to what should occur. In Mark 1:23-24 a man with an unclean spirit cried out to Jesus, "I know who you are, the Holy One of God" (RSV). Yet, according to 1 John 4:1-2 anyone who confesses that Jesus Christ has come in the flesh is of God. So here we have an unclean spirit confessing that Jesus is of God. According to 1 John 4, therefore, that same spirit must be *of God*. Imagine a perfect God having an unclean spirit or an unclean spirit existing within God! In Matt. 5:34 Jesus tells people not to swear at all; but in Isa. 45:23 God says, "I have sworn by myself. . . . That unto me every knee shall bow." If swearing is wrong, why is God allowed to do it, or is he above morality? And Ex. 20:13 contains the famous commandment of "Thou shalt not kill." Yet, in Ex. 32:27 God tells every man to put his sword by his side and go out from the gate . . . and slay every man his brother, and every man his companion, and every man his neighbor. What happened to "Thou shalt not kill"? Or do we have another instance in which God is above morality and a law unto himself?

Acts 13:39 says that everyone who trusts in Jesus is freed from all guilt and declared righteous, but Matt. 12:31-32 and Mark 3:29 say that anyone who blasphemes the Holy Ghost will never have forgiveness. Blasphemy is an unforgivable sin. So what do you do about someone who commits the unforgivable sin of blaspheming the Holy Ghost but later trusts in Jesus and is thereby freed from all guilt? How can he be forgiven, if he's committed the unforgivable sin? On page 152 in *Does the Bible Contradict Itself?* Arndt offers the following solution to this difficulty:

> It seems that the Gospel promises offering pardon for the sins we commit if we turn to Jesus in true faith are so comprehensive that no sin can be excluded. This latter view is correct. Not a single sin is excluded from the category of those that will be forgiven if the sinner seeks refuge in Jesus. Believe and you are pardoned. But the unpardonable sin which Jesus speaks of has this characteristic, that the one committing it does not, *and will not*, believe in Jesus Christ.

What nonsense! The deceptive aspect of Arndt's explanation lies in the fact that Matthew and Mark do not say that turning to Jesus, seeking refuge in Jesus, or believing in Jesus will guarantee forgiveness. Nothing is said in either about belief in Jesus guaranteeing you an exemption. Matthew and Mark say anyone who blasphemes the Holy Ghost will never have forgiveness and that's that. It doesn't say those who believe in Jesus are exempt. The obligation is laid down clearly and emphatically. No exceptions or provisos are included.

Arndt continues, "The Lord describes the unforgivable sin as blasphemy directed against the Holy Spirit. The Holy Spirit is that Person of the Godhead, that great Force, which converts us. If a person blasphemes this Force and will not let it do and sustain its work in man, he cannot be a believer and hence cannot receive forgiveness of his sins." In other words, according to Arndt, you can be a believer and blaspheme Jesus but you "cannot be a believer" and blaspheme the Holy Spirit, because no true believer would blaspheme the Holy Spirit. Does that make sense considering the fact that Jesus and the Holy Spirit are equal? How could you believe in Jesus and not believe in the Holy Spirit and vice versa? But even more to the point, no such distinction is made in the relevant verses and no such distinction is warranted.

To move on, Prov. 12:22 says, "Lying lips are abomination to the Lord," but 1 Kings 22:23 says, "The Lord hath put a lying spirit into the mouth of all these thy prophets." If God finds lying to be horrible, why does he put lying spirits into the mouths of prophets?

One of the most famous of the Bible's verses is 2 Tim. 3:16, which says all Scripture is inspired. But in 2 Cor. 11:17 Paul says, "That which I speak, I speak it *not after the Lord*, but as it were foolishly, in this confidence of boasting." And in 1 Cor. 7:6 and 7:12 he says, "But I speak this by permission, and not of commandment. . . . But to the rest speak I, not the Lord." So by Paul's own admission, some Scripture is not inspired. He is flatly stating that he is speaking and the Lord is not.

In Matt. 11:28 and 30 Jesus says, "Come unto me, all ye that labor, and are heavy laden, and I will give you rest. . . . For my yoke is easy, and my burden is light." But Heb. 12:6 says, "The Lord disciplines the person He loves and punishes every son whom He receives" (MLB) and in John 16:33 Jesus says, "In the world ye shall have tribulation." So, although the burden of following Jesus is supposed to be light, Christians can expect to be punished, disciplined, and burdened with ordeals.

Job 7:9 says, "He that goeth down to the grave shall come up no more." Notice it says "come up no more." But Isa. 26:19 says, "Thy dead men shall live, together with my dead body shall they arise" and 1 Cor. 15:52 says, "The trumpet shall sound, and the dead shall be raised incorruptible." So, dead men do arise, after all.

Acts 26:23 says that Christ should be the first that should rise from the dead. But Elijah raised a child from the dead long before Jesus (1 Kings 17:17–22) and a dead man came back to life when he was lowered into a grave and touched the bones of Elisha (2 Kings 13:21). In fact, many people rose from the dead before Jesus was resurrected, so how could Jesus be the first to rise from the dead?

John 3:13 says, "No man has ascended up to heaven except he that came down from heaven, even the Son of man which is in heaven." Yet, 2 Kings 2:11 shows that Elijah went up to heaven long before Jesus lived on the earth. So Jesus was not the first man to rise to heaven. Elijah preceded him by centuries.

The text of 1 Cor. 15:50 declares that flesh and blood cannot inherit the kingdom of God, while Heb. 11:5 says that Enoch went to heaven without dying. So his flesh and blood did enter heaven as did Elijah in the chariot.

Eph. 4:26 says, "Be ye angry and sin not: let not the sun go down upon your wrath." Talk about encouraging people to be angry! But earlier we were told in Prov. 22:24 that one should "make no friendship with an angry man: and with a furious man thou shalt not go."

Ex. 20:17 says thou shalt not covet. Isn't that one of the Ten Commandments? Yet 1 Cor. 12:31 says, "Covet earnestly the best gifts." So, are we or are we not to covet?

The text of 1 Cor. 9:24 declares that we should run so that we may obtain, while Rom. 9:16 says, "So then it is not a matter of willing or running, but of God's mercy." So do we run in order to obtain things or do we just sit and wait for God's mercy to grant our desires?

According to Matt. 28:19 the followers of Jesus are to go into all the world to teach and baptize. But how does one reconcile this statement with Paul's comments in 1 Cor. 1:14 and 1:17, which say, "I thank God that I baptized none of you, but Crispus and Gaius . . . for Christ sent me not to baptize, but to preach the gospel"? Paul says he was sent not to baptize, even though that flies in the face of the Great Commission, in which Jesus told people to go unto all the world and baptize.

Gal. 6:2 says that we should bear one another's burdens to fulfill the law of Christ, while three verses later we are told that everyone shall bear his own burden. So who is to bear our burdens?

In Jude 3 Christians are told to earnestly contend for the faith, while Prov. 18:6 says, "A fool's lips enter into contention" and 2 Tim. 2:24 says a servant of the Lord must not strive. Are believers to contend for the faith or aren't they?

One of the most interesting contradictions of a practical nature comes to the fore when we compare 1 John 3:6, which says, "Whosoever abideth in him sinneth not," with 1 John 1:8, which says, "If we say that we have no sin, we deceive ourselves and the truth is not in us." One verse clearly states that if you abide in God you don't sin, while another says that anyone who claims not to sin is a liar. The unavoidable conclusion is that since all Christians are sinners, not one abides in God. While discussing a related issue on page 127 in *Answers to Tough Questions*, apologists McDowell and Stewart make the following misleading comment: "There is a misconception that a Christian is a person who claims that he does not sin, but the truth is that to call oneself a Christian is to admit to being a sinner (1 John 1:5–2:2)." This is not a misconception, because it's biblically based. Our friends need to reread 1 John 5:18 and 1 John 3:9, which say that whosoever is born of God sins not. That's strong evidence that Christians either don't sin, don't abide in God, or don't exist.

Conclusion

Beyond any doubt the number of biblical contradictions available for analysis borders on the incredible. Additional bombs would only make the rubble bounce. More than enough examples have been provided to convince any reasonably open-minded person that the Bible is a fraud.

Proponents of the Book are nothing more than confidence men preying upon the ignorance, troubles, deprivation, and sorrow of their fellow men. A friend of mine once compared clergymen to used car salesmen because both ply their trade through deception and hyperbole. But that's an unfair and invidious comparison because it's little more than a slander of used car salesmen. At least they provide you a product that can be tested. How do you test the existence of heaven or hell? At least car salesmen give you a guarantee, even if it is only for thirty days, that can be enforced by law and relied upon. What guarantee do you have that you will rise from the dead, other than that found in some words in a book? At least you can take your product back to the used car salesman if you are dissatisfied. What do you have from the Bible or Christianity that you can return if you are disgruntled? At least used car salesmen give you something that is tangible and can be immediately examined. What does Christianity or the Bible provide in that category? You can't even take the product out for a test drive. At least you can ask questions of the used car dealer and receive audible replies. When's the last time you heard God speak? At least you can observe the used car salesman's face as his promises unfold. When's the last time you saw God's face? At least a used car salesman can't deny an obvious contradiction between his statement that a car is running fine and the fact that neither of you can get it started.

And lastly, at least the used car salesman gives you something that can be seen as a fraud before it's too late. With the Bible in general and Jesus in particular you never know you have been taken until it is too late and after you have donated substantial amounts of time, effort, self-denial, and wealth. As far as money specifically is concerned, many people have given vast sums of money to their church both before and after their demise. Clergymen have devoted a tremendous amount of time giving people the impression that religious spokesmen are synonymous with the Almighty when it comes to money. When you give to the church, you are giving to God, is the subtle message they seek to convey.

A used car salesmen, on the other hand, doesn't seek to give people the impression that a purchase of his vehicle would be looked upon favorably by the Almighty, in contrast to some television commercials, in which people clothed in religious garb are peddling one product or another.

Summary

In summary and in support of the position that we have maintained throughout, we might quote from one of the most famous of all apologetic works, *Alleged Discrepancies of the Bible* by John Haley. On the first two pages he makes the following admissions.

> No candid and intelligent student of the Bible will deny that it contains numerous "discrepancies," that its statements, taken *prima facie*, frequently conflict with or contradict one another, may safely be presumed. This fact has been more or less recognized by Christian scholars in all ages. . . . That eminent biblical critic, Moses Stuart, whose candor was commensurate with his erudition, acknowledged that "in our present copies of the Scriptures there are some discrepancies between different portions of them, which no learning nor ingenuity can reconcile." To much the same effect, Archbishop Whately observes, "that the apparent contradictions of Scripture *are* numerous . . . is too notorious to need be insisted on."

It is important to note that these are the words of well-known Christians, not atheists, agnostics or opponents of the Bible. But of even greater importance is the fact that these apologists and their colleagues have made little or no effort to make these contradictions and inaccuracies known to the laity at large. Keeping them under wraps as much as possible has clearly been of the highest priority.

To shorten a very long story, those who really know the Book for what it is and what it contains are fully aware of the fact that the Bible is a maze of contradictions, inconsistencies, and inaccuracies. Except for indoctrinated ideologues and propagandists, those who are fully cognizant of the Book's contents don't even argue the point. Why engage in an adventure that is doomed from the outset? Millions of Christians have conceded this fact, which accounts in large part for the division between fundamentalism and liberalism within Christianity.

5

Jesus I

Resurrection, Crucifixion, Ascension, Genealogy, Ancestry, Historicity and Extrabiblical Sources, Pagan Figures

The previous chapter provided a broad overview of the many contradictions that are prevalent in the Bible. This chapter will focus on key aspects of the career of Jesus Christ having to do with his background, history, and existence. That would include such topics as the Resurrection, the genealogies, the Crucifixion, the Ascension, ancestry, and historicity. Did Jesus really exist? Was he a real live human being or a product of folklore and mythology? The topic of greatest importance among those mentioned, as far as the Bible in general and Paul in particular are concerned, as the following quotations clearly attest, is undoubtedly the Resurrection, to which we will now turn our attention.

Resurrection

On page 181 in *Evidence That Demands a Verdict* apologist Josh McDowell quotes H. P. Liddon, who says, "Faith in the resurrection is the very keystone of the arch of Christian faith, and, when it is removed, all must inevitably crumble into ruin." He also quotes Wilbur Smith, who says, "The resurrection of Christ has always been categorically the central tenet, the very citadel, of the Church."

On page 183 Smith says, "If this goes, so must almost everything else that is vital and unique in the Gospel of the Lord Jesus Christ." On page 182 McDowell quotes Michael Green, who says, "Without faith in the resurrection there would be no Christianity at all. . . . Christianity stands or falls with the truth of the resurrection. Once disprove it, and you have disposed of Christianity." On page 183 McDowell quotes the famous Christian historical scholar Philip Schaff, who says, "The resurrection of Christ is therefore emphatically a test question upon which depends the truth or falsehood of the Christian religion. It is either the greatest miracle or the greatest delusion which history records."

On page 105 in his book *Practical Apologetics* McDowell says, "If Jesus Christ was not raised from the dead, then the Christian faith is literally worthless. . . . Everything that Jesus Christ taught, lived, and died for was based upon the resurrection. That's the whole basis of Christianity. The resurrection of Jesus Christ and Christianity stand and fall together." John Wenham follows in the same tradition on page 9 of *The Easter Enigma* when he says, "The resurrection of Jesus has been the spearhead of the Christian case. From it flows belief in the deity of Christ and all other Christian truths." On page xx in *The Battle for the Resurrection* apologist Norman Geisler says, "The Bible declares that the resurrection is the very heart of the gospel (1 Cor. 15:1-3) and is even a condition of salvation (Rom. 10:9). Thus, to tamper with this foundation of faith is to undermine the whole superstructure of Christian truth." On page 26 he states, "Few doctrines are more crucial to Christianity than the bodily resurrection of Christ. It is at the very heart of the gospel (1 Cor. 15:1-5). Without the resurrection there is no salvation (Rom. 10:9) and the whole of Christianity crumbles if it is not true (1 Cor. 15:12-19)." And on page 173 Geisler goes to the bottom line by quoting Paul's comments in 1 Cor. 15:14-19 to the effect that, "If Christ did not rise from the grave, then: (1) Our preaching is useless. (2) Our faith is useless. (3) The apostles are false witnesses. (4) Our faith is vain. (5) We are still in our sins. (6) The dead in Christ are lost. And (7) we are the most pitied of all men (1 Cor. 15:14-19)."

Can one be any more emphatic than that? One can clearly see from all of the above that the Resurrection is definitely a pivotal concept in Christianity. But what is conveniently avoided in this equation is the fact that four major problems accompany this concept, dilemmas that clergymen, biblicists, and other assorted Christians have intentionally kept under wraps or minimized for centuries. And that's understandable in light of the fact that these problems bring the very significance and existence of the concept into question. The lack of sensible answers to these questions and problems exposes the Resurrection to be nothing more than a myth of little import, biblically or otherwise.

First, Why would the Resurrection be of any significance to begin with, when other people rose from the dead before Jesus? In 1 Kings 17:17, 21 and 22 Elijah stretched himself upon a dead child three times and the latter revived; in 1 Sam. 28:7, 11, and 15 Samuel said to Saul, "Why hast thou disquieted me, to bring me up?"; in 2 Kings 4:32, 34 and 35 Elisha raised the dead son of a Shunammite;

in 2 Kings 13:21 the bones of Elisha were touched as a dead man was lowered into a grave and the latter was revived; in Luke 9:28 and 30 Moses and Elijah came back to life at the time of the Transfiguration; in Matt. 27:52–53 the dead saints arose just after the Resurrection; in Matt. 9:18 and 23–25 Jairus's daughter rose from the dead; in Luke 7:11–15 the Nain's Widow's son rose from the dead, and in John 11:43–44 Lazarus rose from the dead. All of these people rose before Jesus did. So by the time Jesus rose, this was actually a rather common occurrence. Rather than being hailed as a fantastic event, common sense would lead one to believe that it would have been greeted with a resounding yawn followed by "So what else can you do?". People not only rose from the dead before Jesus but after him as well. In Acts 9:36–41 Peter raised Tabitha from the dead and in Acts 20:9–10 Paul raised Eutychus. So emerging from the dead is of no real consequence. Paul attributed immense importance to what had actually become a rather bland event.

One of the most common defenses one will hear in response to this question is aptly stated by Frank Colquhoun on page 41 in his book *Hard Questions*. "Accounts of people being raised from the dead are found elsewhere in the Bible, including three by Jesus himself, but in each case they returned to life in a way exactly similar to that of their former life and had subsequently died. They were resuscitated rather than resurrected."

This defense is little more than an act of desperation. The fact is that they were dead, just as Jesus was dead according to Scripture. So if they were resuscitated, then so was he. If he was resurrected, then so were they; there's no difference. Have apologists no decency, no intellectual integrity?

On page 120 in a book entitled *The Case for Jesus the Messiah* televangelist John Ankerberg makes a statement that is even more preposterous. He says, "If Jesus Christ did, in fact, rise from the dead, then one must accept the claims about Himself as being true—that He was in fact God Incarnate (John 5:18, 19:7, Rom. 1:3). No one else of an estimated 100 billion persons who have ever lived in human history has ever risen from the dead." Yet, we have already noted a sizable number of biblical figures who supposedly rose from the dead. They alone are sufficient to refute Ankerberg's claim.

On page 66 in *Answers to Tough Questions* McDowell and Stewart state, "Jesus, in coming back from the dead, established Himself as having the credentials to be God." If that were true, then all those who rose prior to him were God as well.

A *second* major problem with the Resurrection emerges when we compare the accounts of what happened in the four gospels. If we juxtapose the four versions of what occurred after the women's arrival at the tomb on early Saturday night or Sunday morning the problems become all too clear. Some of the most glaring examples are as follows:

1. At what time did the women visit the tomb? Mark 16:2 says at the rising of the sun; John 20:1 says when it was yet dark.

2. Who came? John 20:1 says Mary Magdalene; Matt. 28:1 says Mary Magdalene and the other Mary; Mark 16:1 says Mary Magdalene, Mary the mother of James, and Salome; Luke 24:10 says Mary Magdalene, Joanna, Mary the mother of James, and the other women.

3. Was the tomb open or closed when they arrived? Luke 24:2 says it was open; Matt. 28:1–2 says it was closed.

4. Whom did they see at the tomb? Matt. 28:2 says the angel; Mark 16:5 says a young man; Luke 24:4 says two men; John 20:11–12 says two angels.

5. Were these men/angels inside or outside the tomb? Matt. 28:2 says outside, while Mark 16:5, Luke 24:3–4, and John 20:11–12 say inside.

6. Were they standing or sitting? Luke 24:4 says they were standing; Matt. 28:2, Mark 16:5, and John 20:12 say they were sitting.

As the Jewish scholar Gerald Sigal says on page 242 in his book *The Jew and the Christian Missionary*, "Well, which is it, Mark or Luke, one angel or two, sitting or standing?"

7. Did the women tell the disciples what they had seen? Luke 24:8–9 says yes; Mark 16:8 says no.

8. Did Mary Magdalene know Jesus when he first appeared to her? Matt. 28:9 says yes; John 20:14 says no.

9. Was Mary Magdalene permitted to touch Jesus when he first appeared to her? Matt. 28:9 says yes; John 20:17 says no.

10. And how did the women find out that Jesus had risen? Matt. 28:5–6 says the angel sitting on the outside told them; Mark 16:5–6 says the man who was on the right side, inside the tomb, told them, and Luke 24:5-6 says the two men inside the tomb told them.

Of the more than twenty examples of this kind that are available only ten have been provided here. It should be more than sufficient to make the point. In light of these problems, one can understand why apologist John Wenham was willing to state the views of others on pages 9-11 in his book *The Easter Enigma*.

Now it so happens that the story of Jesus' resurrection is told by five different writers, whose accounts differ from each other to an astonishing degree. So much so that distinguished scholars one after another have said categorically that the five accounts are irreconcilable. Going back to the last century, the great radical, Schmiedel, said: "The gospels . . . exhibit contradictions of the most glaring kind." Reimarus . . . enumerated ten contradictions; but in reality their number is much greater. Even the conservative, Henry Alford, wrote: ". . . I have abandoned all idea of harmonizing throughout."

Coming into this century, P. Gardner-Smith said: "No ingenuity can make the narration of Luke consistent with that of Mark, much less is it possible to reconcile the picture presented by the fourth evangelist with the accounts of any of the synoptic writers. Mutually contradictory narratives cannot all be true. . . . Nothing can be made of a jumble of contradicting statements."

Wenham continues,

E. Brunner says: "The sources contradict one another, and only a 'harmonizing' process which is not too much concerned about truth, could patch up a fairly connected account of the events. . . . Such a dishonest way of dealing with the subject really has nothing to do with 'faith in the Word of God'; it only serves to support the disastrous prejudice that Christian faith is only possible in connection with historical dishonesty." . . . A. M. Ramsey, a relatively conservative writer says, ". . . That we should expect to be able to weave the stories into a chronological and geographical plan seems inconceivable."

With more recent writers the verdict is the same. P. Benoit (1969) says, "I think we have to give up any idea of reconciling John and the synoptics." C. F. Evans speaks of the impression that it is not simply difficult to harmonize these traditions, but quite impossible.

Wenham concludes his recitation of others' comments by stating on page 11, "The most obvious point of difficulty concerns the events of the first Easter morning." The central point to note about Wenham's quotations of others is that all of them emanate from defenders of the Bible, not its vocal critics.

Apologist Carl Johnson adds more fuel to the fire by stating on page 75 of *So the Bible Is Full of Contradictions*, "The infidel, Emil Brunner, said that for anyone to find the record of the resurrection of Christ coherent, he would need to be either ignorant or else less than honest." Dewey Beegle on page 61 in his book *Scripture, Tradition, and Infallibility*, states, "The Biblical passages dealing with the resurrection of Christ swarm with difficulties, some details of which cannot be harmonized."

So, anyone who denies that the Resurrection account is beset with difficulties will have to confront not only commentators such as those represented by *Biblical Errancy* and the freethought movement in general but a wide assortment of Christians and other supporters of the Bible.

A *third* major problem with the Resurrection is that the Bible rules out any possibility of a resurrection of *anybody* to begin with. Many verses conveniently ignored by clergymen and clergywomen clearly rule out any kind of rising from the dead by anyone. Eccle. 3:19–21 in the Revised Standard Version provides the most prominent refutation of any such idea. It states,

For the fate of the sons of men and the fate of beasts is the same; as one dies so dies the other. They all have the same breath, and man has no advantage

> over the beasts; for all is vanity. All go to one place; all are from the dust, and all turn to dust again. Who knows whether the spirit of man goes upward and the spirit of the beast goes down to the earth?

The key elements in this quotation are that: (1) the fate of men and the beasts is the same; (2) man has *no advantage* over the beasts; (3) all go to one place, not two or three; and (4) no one knows if the spirit of man goes upward. Beyond any doubt these verses rule out the existence of heaven, hell, purgatory, or immortality. Otherwise, man would have an advantage over the beasts.

Other verses also obviate any possibility of a resurrection. Job 7:9 says, "He that goeth down to the grave shall come up no more." Eccle. 9:5 says, "For the living know that they shall die: but the dead know not any thing, neither have they any more a reward; for the memory of them is forgotten." That rules out heaven. Isa. 26:14 says, "They are dead, they shall not live; they are deceased, they shall not rise," which rules out any rising from the dead. The text of 1 Tim. 6:15-16 says, "The King of kings, and Lord of lords; who only hath immortality." If only Jesus has immortality, then there can be no real resurrection for anyone.

Many other verses also rule out a resurrection or any possibility of immortality. A significant number of verses obviate, either directly or indirectly, any kind of ascendancy from the dead by mankind, while others prove the opposite. The biblical position on what occurs to someone after death is by no means clear. Verses such as those in Ecclesiastes say that when you are dead you are dead and that's that. There is no more. As is stated at the end of Warner Brothers cartoons, "That's All, Folks."

A *fourth* and final problem with the Resurrection becomes immediately evident when one realizes that it is of no real consequence when compared to other biblical events. How many people came into the world as full-grown adults as did Adam and Eve in Gen. 1:27 and 2:7? Elijah never died at all; he just went straight to heaven in 2 Kings 2:11. According to Gen. 5:22–24, Enoch never died either. He, too, went straight to heaven. In Gen. 18:11 and 21:1–3 Isaac was born to a woman who had passed through menopause, and according to Heb. 7:1–3, Melchisedec had no father, no mother, no beginning, and no end. How's that for grandiose hyperbole! Even Jesus had a father and mother, and many argue from Scripture that he had a beginning as well.

It should also be noted that Jesus did not raise himself from the dead, as many assume. According to Scripture Jesus was raised by someone else. The text is quite clear that God raised him; he did not raise himself. A few of the many verses that prove as much are: Acts 3:15, which says, "And killed the Prince of life, whom God hath raised from the dead"; Acts 13:30, which says, "But God raised him from the dead"; and Acts 5:30, which says, "The God of our fathers raised up Jesus, whom ye slew." So the miracle of the Resurrection was not as spectacular as many contend. Clearly, Jesus wasn't quite the miracle worker he is made out to be.

It should also be noted that an empty tomb does not prove a resurrection really occurred. As apologist Geisler admits on page 37 in *The Battle for the Resurrection*, "The empty tomb in itself does not prove the resurrection of Christ any more than a missing body in a morgue proves someone has resurrected. Neither does an empty tomb plus a series of appearances prove the resurrection. The original body could have disappeared and the appearances could have been of someone else."

Crucifixion

An event closely associated with the Resurrection that is also bountifully endowed with problems is the Crucifixion. The gospels are clearly in disagreement as to precisely what happened prior to, and during, the execution. Twelve conflicts are definitely worthy of note.

First, Matt. 27:28 says the robe put on Jesus was scarlet colored, while Mark 15:17 and John 19:2 say it was *purple*.

Second, John 19:1-2 and 5 say the robe was put on Jesus during his trial, while Matt. 27:26-28 and Mark 15:15-17 say it was put on after Pilate delivered him to be crucified.

Third, Mark 15:25 says Jesus was crucified at the third hour; Luke 23:43-44 says it was before the sixth hour, and John 19:14-16 says it was after the sixth hour.

Fourth, the wording of that which was written on the cross is in dispute. Matt. 27:37 says it was, "This is Jesus the King of the Jews"; Mark 15:26 says it was, "The King of the Jews"; Luke 23:38 says it was, "This is the King of the Jews"; and John 19:19 says it was, "Jesus of Nazareth the King of the Jews." Even if the longest is correct because it encompasses the other three, the others are incorrect because of what they omit.

Fifth, Matt. 27:35, Mark 15:24, and Luke 23:34 say the soldiers at the cross cast lots for the garments of Jesus, while John 19:23-24 says they vied for his coat alone.

Sixth, Matt. 27:48, Luke 23:36, and John 19:29-30 say that Jesus was given vinegar to drink while on the cross; Matt. 27:34 says it was vinegar mingled with gall; and Mark 15:23 says it was wine mingled with myrrh.

Seventh, Mark 15:36 says that when Jesus got the sponge filled with vinegar, the person who actually gave him the sponge said he would see if Elijah would come to his rescue, while Matt. 27:48-49 says Elijah was mentioned by those with the person who gave him the sponge.

Eighth, Luke 23:39–40 says only one of the thieves on the cross reviled Jesus, while Matt. 27:44 and Mark 15:32 say both thieves made comments.

Ninth, Matt. 27:55–56, Mark 15:40, and John 19:25 differ dramatically on the names of the women who were watching the Crucifixion.

Tenth, Matt. 27:55–56, Luke 23:49, and Mark 15:40 say the women observed the Crucifixion from afar, while John 19:25 says they were near the cross.

Eleventh, according to Luke 23:47, after Jesus gave up the ghost the centurion said Jesus was a righteous man, while according to Matt. 27:54 he said Jesus was the Son of God.

And *lastly*, Matt. 27:33, Mark 15:22, and John 19:17 say Jesus was killed at Golgotha, while Luke 23:33 says it was Calvary. Some apologists disputably allege Golgotha is the Hebrew rendering while Calvary is Latin.

Judging from these problems it is clear that there is widespread disagreement as to the precise chain of events surrounding the crucifixion of Jesus and little possibility of harmonization without doing a hatchet job on the text by liberal interpolation and eisogesis.

Another major problem with the Crucifixion pertains to who or what died on the cross. If a man died on the cross, then nothing was accomplished, for a man's death can save no one. If God died on the cross, then we have an impossibility, since God cannot die. So who died? Pseudoprophet Hal Lindsey became entangled in this very problem on page 83 in *The Liberation of Planet Earth* by saying, "What is sin's penalty? Death. Can God die? Obviously not. Therefore the One who would take the penalty for man had to be a true human being as well as truly God."

Lindsey stated emphatically that God cannot die and in the very next sentence said that God did die or at the very least was an integral component of that which died. In no sense can God die. So the question remains: Who or what died on the cross?

While on the subject of dying for a cause, it is altogether appropriate that we should note one of the most prominent pieces of Christian mythology to ever come down the pike. Where does the Bible mention any Christians dying for Christianity, other than Stephen and possibly John the Baptist? Yet, on page 96 of his book *Practical Apologetics* the apologist Josh McDowell lists twelve apostles and the means by which they died for the cause, without providing so much as a shred of biblical support.

Ascension

Besides the Crucifixion, the Ascension is also closely associated with the Resurrection and beset with problems. Luke 24:50–51 says the Ascension occurred at Bethany; Mark 16:14 and 19 say the actual location was a room in Jerusalem, and Acts 1:9–12 says it took place on Mount Olivet. These three could hardly be the same location, although some apologists have alleged as much.

Before leaving the Resurrection, the Ascension, and related subjects, it is important to remember that Judaism had no conception of any messiah dying for the cause. On page 54 in *Answers to Tough Questions* McDowell and Stewart state, "First century Judaism had no concept of a dying and rising Messiah."

One Israeli writer, Shmuel Golding, stated this fact in even more stark terms on page 15 in his book *The Light of Reason*, volume 1: "That God should clothe himself in the body of a man, live nine months in the womb of a woman, suck the breasts and have his diapers changed, is clearly of pagan origin. The Pauline concept of sin, sacrifice, and salvation obtained by belief in a man dying on a cross, does not exist in, and is in no way a fulfillment of, the Hebrew Scriptures."

Genealogy

Moving on from the Resurrection and surrounding events we turn to another subject of crucial importance to the career and qualifications of Jesus, namely, his genealogy. One of the most discussed contradictions in freethought literature is the clash between the genealogies of Jesus found in Matt. 1 and Luke 3. One need only read the text to see that Luke traces the genealogy of Jesus from Jesus back to Adam, while Matthew begins with Abraham and tracks it down to Jesus. Luke lists seventy-seven generations while Matthew has only forty-four. In order to see the problem in proper perspective one need only create a chart listing the names in correct sequence in parallel columns. If horizontal lines are drawn to connect the same names, one can easily see that the lists are almost identical from Abraham to David. However, from David onward there is little similarity, despite the fact that they both conclude with Joseph as the father of Jesus. The major reason for the contradictory names given after David is that the account in Luke traces the genealogy through David's son, Nathan, while that in Matthew traces it through another son, Solomon. This would easily account for the wide divergence in names following David but raises a couple of crucial questions: (1) How could Joseph be descended from two different sons of David? How could two sons of David father two completely different genealogies which merge together with the last two individuals, Joseph and Jesus? And (2) how could Jesus have contradictory genealogies?

Few apologists deny differences are present, so that is not a topic of dispute. The real issue revolves around the common explanation given by most biblicists for two widely different ancestral histories of the same man. Their strategy hinges on a rather simple ploy. They contend that Jesus' genealogy is traced through Joseph in Matthew and Mary in Luke. In other words, the genealogy in Matthew is that of Joseph, while the one in Luke is that of Mary. Unfortunately for apologists, the shortcomings in their rationalization are obvious.

First, Mary's name is nowhere to be found in Luke's genealogy and only arises incidentally in that of Matthew. Imagine a genealogy in which every name is mentioned but that of the person whose lineage is being traced! Both genealogies clearly pertain to Joseph, not Mary.

Second, there is no genealogical record of any woman in the entire Bible. None of the genealogies in either the Old or New Testaments traces the lineage of a woman. Women are never given a position of such importance in the Bible as to merit a genealogy and there is no evidence Luke 3 provides an exception. The superiority granted men in the Bible would forestall any possibility of women being considered equals. Are we to believe that Mary is an exception? According to Num. 1:18, ". . . declared their pedigrees after their families, by the house of their fathers," genealogies were traced through males only.

Third, Joseph's name *is* mentioned in Luke's genealogy and Luke 1:27 and 2:4 show he *was* from the house of David. So one can reasonably conclude that it is his lineage, not Mary's.

Fourth, even if Luke's genealogy were that of Mary, she would be disqualified as a descendant of David because two of her ancestors, Shealtiel and Zerubabbel, were descendants of Jeconias who, according to prophecy, would never have a descendant sitting upon the throne of David (Jer. 22:28–30). Mary would be under the curse of Jeconias.

Fifth, as a woman Mary could never have been qualified to be heir to the throne of David, so she couldn't pass on what she could never possess, even if she was of Davidic descent.

Sixth, according to Old Testament prophecy, the Messiah would be a physical descendant of David (2 Sam. 7:12–13, Psalms 89:3–4, 132:11). Mary appears to have been from the house of Levi, not David, since her cousin, Elisabeth (Luke 1:36) was a daughter of Aaron (Luke 1:5), i.e., from the house of Levi. If Mary was from the house of Aaron, i.e., Levi, how could either genealogy be hers since they relate David's lineage, not Aaron's? Luke 1:27 and 2:4, as we already mentioned, show that Joseph, on the other hand, *was* of Davidic descent.

And *lastly*, according to 1 Chron. 22:9–10 the messiah had to be a descendant of Solomon. However, Luke's genealogy, which is alleged to be that of Mary, is traced through Solomon's brother, Nathan.

The attempt to attribute Luke's genealogy to Mary is one of the more transparent subterfuges employed by dishonest apologists. Desperation set in because they just couldn't think of any other means by which to escape a cacophony. One can easily understand why Bucaille said on page 93 of *The Bible, the Quran, and Science*, "The genealogies of Jesus as they appear in the Gospels may perhaps be the subject that has led Christian commentators to perform their most characteristic feats of dialectic acrobatics, on a par indeed with Luke's and Matthew's imagination."

Another reason for their devious ploy to resolve the contradictory genealogies is that it solves a problem created by the virgin birth. According to prophecy the Messiah must be a *physical* descendant of David. If Jesus' only connection to David is through Joseph, then Jesus couldn't be physically connected to David because the birth was virginal; Joseph was not his biological father. So apologists must attribute one of the genealogies to Mary in order to extend a physical connection from Jesus back to David. Hence, the rationalization. One can only wonder why they didn't apply to Mary the genealogy in Matthew rather than the one in Luke, since one is no more applicable to her than the other.

Ancestry

And finally, Christians should be glad people aren't judged by their ancestry, because if they were Jesus would fail miserably. According to the genealogy in Matt. 1, nearly all of Jesus' ancestors were people who had committed infamous crimes or gross immoralities. Abraham married his sister and seduced her handmaid; Jacob seduced two of his housemaids after committing bigamy; Judah committed incest with his daughter-in-law; David was a polygamist, an adulterer, a robber, and a murderer; and Solomon had a thousand wives and concubines. Other ancestors of Jesus, such as Rehoboam, Abijam, Joram, Ahaziah, Jotham, Ahaz, Manasseh, Amon, and Jehoiachin were little more than monsters of iniquity. It is also interesting to note that only four women are mentioned in Jesus' ancestry. Yet Tamar seduced the father of her late husband; Rahab was a common prostitute; Ruth went to bed with one of her cousins instead of marrying another, and Bathsheba was involved in adultery. In fact, you could even include Eve, since she is supposedly the mother of all humanity and a prime culprit in the fall of mankind. One would hardly be justified in saying that Jesus came from good stock.

Historicity and Extrabiblical Sources

The final topic related to the background and history of Jesus is undoubtedly the question of whether or not he ever lived to begin with—a subject generally known as *historicity*. Was Jesus a historical figure or a product of fantasy? Anyone who has attempted to investigate this question with any degree of objectivity is immediately struck by the absence of extrabiblical information on anyone by the name of Jesus of Nazareth.

Several apologetic writers all but admit as much. On page 31 in *The Bible Has the Answer* apologists Henry Morris and Martin Clark say, "The only real information we have about Christ and His life is in the four Gospels." On page

64 in *Basic Theology* Dallas Theological Professor Charles Ryrie says, "All that we know about the life of Christ appears in the Bible." On page 130 in *99 Questions People Ask Most About the Bible* apologist Don Stewart says, "There are no other first-hand accounts of the life of Christ apart from the four Gospels. All other documents that have survived were written quite some time after the life of Christ."

As the apologist Walter Martin said on April 7, 1989, on his "Bible Answer Man" radio program, "I can tell you right now . . . there are no bona fide documented historical materials about the secret teachings or life of Jesus outside of the New Testament documents. It's fantasy and it has no historical reference whatever."

One could hardly be more emphatic. Stated succinctly, there is almost nothing in all of ancient literature having to do with an individual by the name of Jesus Christ. In fact, scholar Maurice Bucaille noted that there is in fact precious little about the life of Jesus in the Bible itself. On page 58 of *The Bible, the Quran, and Science* Bucaille states, "According to the declaration of the Second Vatican Council, a faithful account of the actions and words of Jesus is to be found in the Gospels; but it is impossible to reconcile this with the existence in the text of contradictions, improbabilities, things which are materially impossible or statements which run contrary to firmly established reality."

In any event, Christian apologists are hard pressed to find any writing of that era that can be related to Jesus Christ. Despite all their efforts, they have been able to scrounge up only enough quotes to fill a couple of pages of written material, showing how desperate the situation is from their perspective. However, there are a handful of writers whom Christians claim made statements in support of a real Jesus, so in order to leave no stone unturned, let's now turn our attention to the quotes that emanate from each.

JOSEPHUS

The first and most famous comment is from the Jewish historian Josephus, who said in nook 18, chapter 3, section 3 of *The Jewish Antiquities*,

> Now there was about this time Jesus, a wise man, if it be lawful to call him a man, for he was a doer of wonderful works, a teacher of such men as receive the truth with pleasure. He drew over to him both many of the Jews, and many of the Gentiles. He was the Christ, and when Pilate, at the suggestion of the principal men among us, had condemned him to the cross, those that loved him at the first did not forsake him; for he appeared to them alive again the third day; as the divine prophets had foretold these and ten thousand other wonderful things concerning him. And the tribe of Christians so named from him are not extinct at this day.

Since this quote is cited by far more apologists than any other, an in-depth exposure of its many flaws is sorely needed. Its most notable inadequacies are as follows:

First, would Josephus, a devout Jew, imply that a man was not a man, that he was divine?

Second, would a devout Jew say that Jesus was the Christ?

Third, would a devout Jew say the messianic prophecies expressly referred to a man at that time?

Fourth, would a devout Jew say that a man did miracles, although Moses might be considered an exception?

Fifth, would a devout Jew claim that a mere man taught the truth?

Sixth, would a devout Jew say Jesus rose from the dead?

Seventh, the passage in question interrupts the narrative. Immediately *before* this passage Josephus tells of an uprising of the Jews, due to a bitter feeling at the conduct of Pilate, and its bloody suppression by the ruling power. The words that immediately *follow* the passage are: "Also about this time another misfortune befell the Jews," and we are told of the expulsion of the Jews from Rome by Tiberius on account of the conduct of some of their compatriots. Josephus was always careful to have a logical connection between his statements. From a rational point of view, Josephus had no occasion, whatever, to put the passage about Jesus in the connection in which we find it. What is the connection between the reference to Jesus and the two narratives within which it is sandwiched? None whatever! That there must be some connection, if Josephus himself wrote the passage, goes without saying.

Eighth, as Joseph McCabe said on page 35 in *Did Jesus Ever Live?*, "The passage is so obviously spurious that it is astonishing to find a single theologian left in our time who accepts it. Most of the passage is rank blasphemy from the Jewish perspective." It was inserted by a later hand and is quite Christian.

Ninth, Josephus nowhere else mentioned the word Christ in any of his works, except in reference to James, the Lord's brother, which will be analyzed shortly.

Tenth, the Arabic translation of this passage is considered by many to be far more accurate. It states,

> At this time there was a wise man who was called Jesus. And his conduct was good, and He was known to be virtuous. And many people from among the Jews and the other nations became his disciples. Pilate condemned Him to be crucified and to die. And those who had become his disciples did not abandon his discipleship. They reported that He had appeared to them three days after his crucifixion and that He was alive; accordingly, He was perhaps the Messiah concerning whom the prophets have recounted wonders.

Note the words "reported" and "perhaps." The differences in the passages are striking.

(a) The first version says he was the Christ, while the Arabic text says *perhaps* he was the Messiah.

(b) The first says he appeared to them alive, again, the third day; the Arabic says, they *reported* that he had so appeared.

(c) The first says he was dispensing truth with pleasure; the Arabic says nothing about dispensing truth.

(d) The Arabic account never implies that he was something other than a mere man.

And (e) the Arabic account says his conduct was good, while the first says he was a "doer of wonderful works," which could be interpreted as miracles.

The differences in these two accounts are critical and bring the validity of the entire passage into doubt.

Eleventh, the works of Josephus are voluminous and exhaustive. They comprise twenty books. Whole pages are devoted to petty robbers and obscure seditious leaders. Nearly forty chapters are devoted to a single king. Yet the great Jesus is dismissed with a dozen doctored lines.

Twelfth, the passage is not found in any early copies of Josephus. It does not appear until *The Ecclesiastical History of Eusebius* came onto the scene in A.D. 320. Eusebius is the same thoroughly dishonest historian who said in chapter 31, book 12, of *Praeparatio Evangelica*, "I have repeated whatever may rebound to the glory, and suppressed all that could tend to the disgrace, of our religion."

Thirteenth, the early Christian fathers were well acquainted with what Josephus wrote. Justin Martyr, Tertullian, Clement of Alexandria, and Origen all would have quoted this passage had it existed. It did not exist during the second and third centuries. Eusebius was the first to use it.

Fourteenth, in the edition of Origen published by the Benedictines it is said that there was no mention of Jesus at all in Josephus before the time of Eusebius.

Fifteenth, the passage is not quoted by Chrysostom, though he often refers to Josephus, and could not have omitted quoting it had it *then* been in the text.

Sixteenth, it is not quoted by Photius, though he has three articles concerning Josephus.

Seventeenth, Photius expressly stated that the historian, Josephus, being a Jew, had not taken the least notice of Christ.

Eighteenth, Justin, Tertullian, Origen, and Cyprian never quoted Josephus as a witness in their controversies with Jews and pagans. Neither Justin in his dialogue with Trypho, the Jew, nor Origen against Celsus ever mentioned this passage. Indeed, Origen, in his work entitled *Contra Celsum*, volume I, page 47, says expressly that Josephus, who had mentioned John the Baptist, did not recognize Jesus as the Messiah. That alone is powerful evidence.

And *lastly*, on page 50 in *The Mythical Jesus* Patrick Campbell notes that the historian Edward Gibbon, author of *The Decline and Fall of the Roman Empire*, considered the passage to be a forgery as do many theologians.

In summary, there is more than enough information to prove the passage is a fraud.

Another, shorter passage from Josephus from book 20, chapter 9, section 1 of *The Jewish Antiquities* states, "So he [Ananus] assembled the sanhedrin of judges, and brought before them the brother of Jesus, who was called Christ, whose name was James, and some others . . . and delivered them to be stoned."

Several problems with this passage are:

First, again, would Josephus, the Jew, say "who was called Christ." This appears to be an interpolation.

Second, "who was called" Christ should actually be interpreted as "the so-called" Christ.

Third, it is extremely doubtful that James is understood by Josephus to be the physical brother of Jesus, since brotherhood might very well mean only that he belonged to the Jesus sect or was one of the brethren.

And *lastly*, many Christian scholars, such as Karl Credner, Emil Schurer, Bernard G. Weiss, and Adolf Julicher, admit the passage is a later interpolation.

TACITUS

The second most famous historian quoted by believers in a real Jesus is the Roman historian Tacitus (A.D. 55–120). After relating what measures were taken by the Roman emperor Nero to lessen the suffering brought about by the great fire at Rome in A.D. 64 and to remove traces of it, Tacitus states on page 44 of volume 15 of his *Annals*,

> But neither the aid of man, nor the liberality of the prince, nor the propitiations of the gods, succeeded in destroying the belief that the fire had been purposely lit. In order to put an end to this rumor, therefore, Nero laid the blame on, and visited with severe punishment those men, hateful for their crimes, whom the people called Christians. He from whom the name was derived, Christus, was put to death by the procurator Pontius Pilate in the reign of Tiberius. But the pernicious superstition, checked for a moment, broke out again, not only in Judea, the native land of the monstrosity, but also in Rome, to which all conceivable horrors and abominations flow from every side, and find supporters. First, therefore, those were arrested who openly confessed; then on their information, a great number [*multitudo ingens*], who were not so much convicted of the fire as of hatred of the human race were arrested also. Ridicule was poured on them as they died; so that, clothed in the skins of beasts, they were torn to pieces by dogs, or crucified, or committed to the flames, and when the sun had gone down they were burned to light up the night. Nero had lent his garden for this spectacle, and gave games in the Circus, mixing with the people in the dress of a charioteer or standing in the chariot. Hence, there was a strong sympathy for them, though they might have been guilty enough to deserve the severest

punishment, on the ground that they were sacrificed, not to the general good, but to the cruelty of one man.

The major reasons this passage is to be considered of no importance are:

First, the worshipers of the sun god Serapis were also called Christians and could be those referred to. Serapis (also called Osiris) had a large following at Rome, especially among the common people.

Second, in no other part of his writings did Tacitus make the least allusion to "Christ" or "Christians."

Third, Tacitus says that the Christians had their denomination from Christ, which could apply to any one of many other so-called Christs who were put to death in Judea, as well as to Christ Jesus.

Fourth, in all the Roman records there is to be found no evidence that Christ was put to death by Pontius Pilate. This passage of Tacitus, if genuine, is the most important evidence in pagan literature. Yet there is no trace of it anywhere in the world before the fifteenth century. How could it have been overlooked for 1,360 years?

Fifth, it is extremely improbable that a special report found by Tacitus was sent to Rome, and incorporated into the records of the Senate, in regard to the death of a Jewish provincial such as Jesus. The execution of a Nazarene carpenter would have been one of the most insignificant events conceivable among the movements of Roman history in those decades; it would have completely disappeared beneath the numerous executions inflicted by the Roman provincial authorities. It would have been one of the most remarkable instances of chance in the world if it had been kept in any report. There is nothing, then, in the records of the Senate. That the founder of Christianity was put to death under Tiberius by the procurator Pontius Pilate must have been discovered by Tacitus in the same archive which, according to Tertullian, also provided the fact that the sun was darkened at midday when Jesus died.

Sixth, most scholars admit that the works of Tacitus have not been preserved with any degree of fidelity.

Seventh, the text says those who were arrested confessed. Confessed to what? That they followed Christ or set the fire? The word *fatebantur*, which means "confessed," refers to the crime of setting fire to Rome. The issue is probably not one of persecuting Christians for what they believed but it was a mere police procedure.

Eighth, the text refers to a great multitude (*multitudo ingens* in Latin), which is opposed to all that we know of the spread of the new faith in Rome at the time. A vast multitude of Christians in A.D. 64? Not likely. There were not more than a few thousand Christians two hundred years later.

Ninth, death by fire was not a form of punishment inflicted at Rome in the time of Nero. It is opposed to the moderate principles on which the accused were then dealt with by the state. The use of Christians as "living torches," as Tacitus describes, and all the other atrocities that were committed against them, have little title to credence, and suggest an imagination exalted by reading stories of later Christian martyrs.

Tenth, the Roman authorities had no reason to inflict special punishment on the new faith. How could the Romans know the concerns of a comparatively small religious sect connected with Judaism and likely appearing to the impartial observer wholly identical to it.

Eleventh, it is inconceivable that the followers of Jesus formed a community in Rome at that time of sufficient importance to attract public attention and the ill-feeling of the people.

Twelfth, some authorities allege that the passage in Tacitus could not have been interpolated because his style of writing could not have been copied. But this argument is without merit since there is no "inimitable" style for the clever forger, and the more unusual, distinctive, and peculiar a style is, like that of Tacitus, the easier it is to imitate.

Thirteenth, Tacitus is assumed to have written this about A.D. 117, about eighty years after the death of Jesus. Hence, Tacitus probably derived his information about Jesus from the Gospels or oral tradition. This is the view of the Frenchman, Jacques Dupuis, who wrote, "Tacitus says what the legend said." Tacitus could in A.D. 117 know of Christ only what reached him from Christian or intermediate circles. He merely reproduced rumors.

Fourteenth, this passage, which would have served Christian writers better than any other writing of Tacitus, is not quoted by any of the Christian Fathers. It is not quoted by Tertullian, though he had read and often quoted the works of Tacitus.

Fifteenth, in the fourth century Eusebius cited all the evidence of Christianity obtained from Jewish and pagan sources, but he makes no mention of Tacitus.

Finally, and most important, what does it matter whether or not Tacitus wrote this passage? He could only have received the information, one hundred years after the time, from people who had told it to others. It doesn't matter, therefore, whether or not the passage is genuine.

More points could be made, but sixteen are more than sufficient for any reasonably objective observer.

SUETONIUS

The third writer Christians cite is the Roman historian Suetonius (A.D. 75–150), who stated in section 25 of *The Deified Claudius*, "Since the Jews constantly made disturbances at the instigation of Chrestus, the Emperor Claudius expelled them from Rome."

Several problems with the passage are immediately evident:

First, the name in the text is not "Christus," but "Chrestus," which by no means is the usual designation of Jesus. Yet Chrestus happens to have been common name, especially among Roman freedmen. Hence, the whole passage may have nothing whatever to do with Christianity.

Second, this passage contains no evidence for the historicity of Jesus, even if we substitute "Christus" for "Chrestus." Christus is merely the Greek-Latin translation of Messiah and the phrase, "at the instigation of Christus," could refer to the messiah generally, and not at all necessarily to the particular messiah, Jesus, as an historical personality.

And *lastly*, Chrestus was not only a familiar personal name, it was also a name of the Egyptian god Serapis or Osiris, who had a large following at Rome, especially among the common people. Hence, "Chrestians" may be either the followers of a man named Chrestus or of Serapis. More discrepancies could be provided but the point has been made.

PLINY THE YOUNGER

We now come to our fourth and final individual, Pliny the Younger (A.D. 62–113), a proconsul of the province of Bithynia in Asia Minor, what is today western Turkey. He wrote a letter to the Emperor Trajan in Rome in A.D. 113 which is also used by apologetic supporters of a belief in an historical Jesus. Pliny said,

> I have laid down this rule in dealing with those who were brought before me for being Christians. I asked whether they were Christians; if they confessed, I asked them a second and a third time, threatening them with punishment; if they persevered, I ordered them to be executed. . . . They assured me that their only crime or error was this, that they were wont to come together on a certain day before it was light, and to sing in turn, among themselves, a hymn to Christ, as to a god, and to bind themselves by an oath—not to do anything that was wicked, that they would commit no theft, robbery, or adultery, nor break their word, nor deny that anything had been entrusted to them when called upon to restore it. . . . I therefore deemed it the more necessary to extract the truth by torture from two slave women whom they call deaconesses. But I found it was nothing but a bad and excessive superstition . . . the sacred rites which had been allowed to lapse [by them] are being performed again, and flesh of sacrificial victims is on sale everywhere, though up till recently scarcely anyone could be found to buy it.

Several problems are immediately apparent with this passage.

First, the letter implies that Bithynia, a large province in western Turkey, had a large Christian population at that time, which is improbable.

Second, if this passage is referring to Christians, then it is also saying that Christians sold the flesh of their sacrificial victims.

Third, the passage proves nothing in regard to the existence of Jesus. It only affirms the existence of Christians.

Fourth, the passage implies Trajan was not acquainted with Christian beliefs and customs even though Christians were quite prominent in his capital, Rome.

Fifth, Roman laws accorded religious liberty to all. Trajan was one of the most tolerant of Roman emperors. Before Constantine arrived on the scene there was not a single law against freedom of thought.

Sixth, the letter is found in only one ancient copy of Pliny the Younger.

And *lastly*, this letter was first quoted by Tertullian and the age immediately preceding Tertullian was notorious for Christian forgeries. For these and other reasons this correspondence was declared by experts to be spurious even at the time of its first publication in the sixteenth century.

More points could be related relative to Pliny the Younger and his quote, but there is no need to belabor the issue. Additional quotes about Jesus from the Talmud could also be addressed, but they are of even less substance.

In light of all these passages one can understand why the apologist James Sire said on page 24 of his work *Scripture Twisting*, "The Bible is the only source of any extensive knowledge about Jesus. References in other sources are too scanty to be useful to one who wants to make Jesus an advocate of his or her philosophy."

Conclusion

In light of what has been said and other biblical and nonbiblical information, what, then, can we conclude from ancient sources about the existence of Jesus Christ?

First, not so much as one single passage purporting to be written within the first fifty years of the Christian era can be produced to show the existence at or before that time of such a person as Jesus of Nazareth.

Second, Renan and others have attempted to write the biography of Jesus but have failed—because no materials for such a work exist.

Third, aside from two forged passages in the works of a Jewish author, two disputed passages in the works of Roman writers, and a few minor comments by other sources, there is nothing to be found that could be related to Jesus Christ.

Fourth, what can Josephus and Tacitus prove? At the most they merely show that at the end of the first century not only Christians but Christian traditions and Christ myths were known at Rome. When Christianity originated, however, and how far it was based on truth, will never be discovered in Josephus or Tacitus.

Fifth, examine Paul's letters and the other epistles of the New Testament and you will find that nowhere in any one of the early Christian documents is there even the slenderest reference to the historical personality of Jesus from which we might infer that the author had a close acquaintance with him. Jesus' life, as described in the Gospels, in all its human detail, seems to have been entirely unknown to these authors. Earlier Christian literature is acquainted with a Jesus god, a god man, a metaphysical spirit, descending from heaven to earth, assuming human form, dying and rising again, but it knows nothing whatever about a merely human Jesus.

And *lastly*, Judea was a Roman province and all of Palestine is intimately associated with Roman history. But the Roman records of that age contain no mention of Christ and his works.

Pagan Figures

Christians refer to the following as mythological figures: Hercules, Osiris, Bacchus, Mithra, Hermes, Prometheus, Perseus, and Horus. According to comments by Patrick Campbell on page 41 of *The Mythical Jesus,* all are pre-Christian sun gods and yet *all* allegedly had gods for fathers and virgins for mothers; had their births announced by stars and celestial music; were born on the solstice around December 25th; had tyrants who tried to kill them in their infancy; met with violent deaths; and rose from the dead. Moreover, nearly all were worshiped by "wise men" and were alleged to have fasted forty days.

Information of this kind is enough to cause any objective observer to pause and think. When the fact that there is precious little outside the Bible that would lead one to believe that the biblical figure known as Jesus Christ ever existed is combined with the fact that there is a considerable body of information showing the similarity between the lives of Jesus and other mythological figures of ancient times, the conclusion is inescapable. Jesus is a mythical figure in the tradition of pagan mythology and almost nothing in all of ancient literature would lead one to believe otherwise. Anyone wanting to believe Jesus lived and walked as a real live human being must do so despite the evidence, not because of it.

6

Jesus II

Credentials, Non-Messiah, Debunked, Incarnation, False Prophet, Virgin Birth, Trinity

The previous chapter provided a broad overview of the background, history and existence of Jesus Christ. This chapter will focus on his credentials, including such topics as false prophecies, inadequate qualifications, the virgin birth, the Trinity, the Holy Ghost, and Jesus debunked. The central question, of course, is whether or not Jesus meets the requirements laid down throughout the Bible as the one who is to be recognized as the messiah, the savior of humanity. Anyone who has reviewed all of the relevant data with any degree of objectivity can only conclude that Jesus most assuredly does not. As can be seen from that which follows, more than enough information is available to rule out any possibility of Jesus being the answer to mankind's problems.

Non-Messiah

Although our analysis could begin with any one of several topics, eight problems having to do with the background of Jesus of Nazareth are deserving of immediate attention.

First, the Bible clearly states that Jesus is from Galilee. Matt. 26:69 says, "Thou also was with Jesus of Galilee," and Luke 22:59 in the Revised Standard Version says, "Certainly this man [Peter] also was with Jesus, for he is a Galilean."

Clearly Jesus was from Galilee. Matt. 21:11 shows that he was also a prophet: "And the multitude said, This is Jesus the prophet of Nazareth of Galilee." Yet on more than one occasion Scripture clearly says that no prophet will come from Galilee. John 7:52 in the RSV says, "Search and you will see that no prophet is to rise from Galilee." John 7:40–42 in the RSV says,

> When they heard these words, some of the people said, "This is really the prophet." Others said, "This is the Christ." But some said, "Is the Christ to come from Galilee? Has not the Scripture said that the Christ is descended from David, and comes from Bethlehem [in Judea, not Galilee], the village where David was?"

In addition, John 1:45–46 in the RSV says that nothing good can come out of Galilee: "We have found him of whom Moses in the law and also the prophets wrote, Jesus of Nazareth. . . . Nathanael said to him, 'Can anything good come out of Nazareth' [which is in Galilee]?"

So, in essence, the Scriptures not only state that Jesus is a prophet from Galilee and no prophet can come from Galilee, but nothing good can come from Galilee.

Second, Jer. 22:28–30 says, "Thus saith the Lord, Write ye this man [Jeconiah] childless, a man who shall not prosper in his days: for no man of his seed shall prosper, sitting upon the throne of David, and ruling any more in Judah." God said that Jeconiah would never have a descendant who sat upon the throne of David, yet the genealogical record in Matt. 1:11 and 1:16 clearly shows that Jesus is one of Jeconiah's descendants. Therefore, Jesus could never sit upon the throne of David. Yet Luke 1:32 says, "He [Jesus] shall be great, and shall be called the Son of the Highest: and the Lord God shall give unto him the throne of his father David," and shows that Jesus must get the throne of David. So, in essence, Jesus *can't* inherit the throne because he is a descendant of Jeconiah, while he *must* receive it because of the Lord's commitment. Several verses show that Jesus is a physical descendant of David and if he were not, he could not be the messiah.

Fundamentalists McDowell and Stewart acknowledge this problem on page 56 in *Answers to Tough Questions* by saying, "According to the prophecy of Jeremiah 22:28–30, there could be no king in Israel who was a descendant of King Jeconiah, and Matthew 1:12 relates that Joseph was from the line of Jeconiah. If Jesus had been fathered by Joseph, He could not rightly inherit the throne of David, since he was a descendant of the cursed line." This is a major reason why apologists try to give people the impression that the genealogy in Luke is that of Mary rather than Joseph. By this subterfuge they hope to maintain the physical connection between David and Jesus.

Third, Matt. 1:11 says that Jesus is a descendant of Coniah or Jeconiah and 1 Chron. 3:16 says that Coniah is a descendant of Jehoiakim. Consequently,

Jesus is a descendant of Jehoiakim. But Jer. 36:30 says, "Therefore thus saith the Lord of Jehoiakim King of Judah; He shall have none to sit upon the throne of David." Thus, by God's command given through Jeremiah, neither Coniah nor his father Jehoiakim could have any progeny sitting upon the throne of David. Yet Jesus was supposedly a descendant of both.

Fourth, Luke 3:31 shows that Nathan was an ancestor of Jesus. But Nathan and all of his descendants were excluded from any claim to the throne of David because Nathan's brother, Solomon, was chosen, instead, to carry on the legacy. This is proven by 1 Chron. 29:1, which says, "David the king said unto all the congregation, Solomon my son, whom alone God hath chosen." Further, 1 Chron. 28:5 says, "Of all my sons (for the Lord has given me many sons), he hath chosen Solomon my son to sit upon the throne of the Kingdom of the Lord over Israel." So we have another reason for Jesus being unqualified for the messiahship— the exclusionary nature of his ancestry and his descent from Nathan.

Fifth, according to prophecy the messiah must be an actual physical descendant of David according to the flesh. Rom. 1:3, Psalms 132:11, Acts 2:30, 2 Tim. 2:8, 2 Sam. 7:12-13, and several other verses can be cited to prove as much. But the physical chain back to David from Joseph in both genealogies was broken because Joseph was not Jesus' physical father; therefore, Jesus couldn't claim the messiahship. The virgin birth destroys the physical connection between Jesus and David.

Sixth, Matt. 20:28 says, "The son of man came not to be ministered unto, but to minister, and to give his life a ransom for many," and shows that Jesus felt he came to minister, not to be ministered unto. But that flies in the face of the Old Testament's presentation of the messiah. According to the Old Testament he was to be served, not serve. Psalms 72:11 says, "Yea, all kings shall fall down before him: all nations shall serve him." Dan. 7:14 says, "All people, nations, and languages, should serve him; his dominion is an everlasting dominion, which shall not pass away." And Dan. 7:27 speaks of a messiah "whose kingdom is an everlasting kingdom, and all dominions shall serve and obey him."

Seventh, according to Scripture Elijah's coming was to precede the messiah's arrival and Jesus said John the Baptist was the predicted Elijah. Two problems immediately arise from this claim: (a) In John 1:21 John the Baptist flatly stated he was not the predicted Elijah, and (b) the arrival of John the Baptist did not usher in the era of love, peace, and prosperity predicted in Luke 1:17 and Mal. 4:5.

Lastly, there are several conflicts between the alleged nature of Jesus and the messiahship:

(a) Nowhere throughout the Old Testament is the power of redeeming from sin and the authority of spiritual salvation attributed to the messiah.

(b) Nowhere does the Old Testament mention the messiah's power and glory in heaven; nowhere does it say the messiah is God.

(c) Nowhere in the Old Testament does God claim to be a man or the son of man. In fact, Num. 23:19 specifically says, "God is not a man, that he should lie."

(d) And lastly, the word "messiah" means "anointed." Yet kings and priests were anointed as signs of distinction and authority on a regular basis throughout the Old Testament. Lev. 4:3 says, "If the priest that is anointed do sin according to the sin of the people." In particular, Isa. 45:1 says, "Thus saith the Lord to his anointed, to Cyrus," and 2 Sam. 23:1 says, "Now these be the last words of David . . . the anointed of the God of Jacob." Does that mean that Cyrus and David can claim the messiahship? The messiahs or anointed of the Old Testament were not immune from sin nor did they claim equality with God. The word "messiah" signifies neither holiness nor godliness.

With that we conclude eight basic *historical* reasons why Jesus is unqualified to be messiah.

Debunked

A *second* major reason Jesus could not be the savior of humanity is that the Old Testament has statements that are seemingly direct denials of Jesus personally. Jesus referred to himself as the "son of man," even though Psalms 146:3 says, "Put not your trust in princes, nor in the son of man, in whom there is no help." And Job 25:6 says, "How much less man, that is a worm? and the son of man, which is a worm." These certainly aren't ringing endorsements of the son of man.

Another verse in the same vein is Nahum 1:11, which says, "There is one come out of thee, that imagineth evil against the Lord, a wicked counsellor." Apologists contend Jesus was called a counsellor in Isa. 9:6, but you can bet this is not one of the Old Testament verses that apologists will apply to him, even though the words are more relevant than those of many other verses that are employed.

Several verses clearly show that nothing pure can emerge from a woman. One need only read Job 14:4 ("Who can bring a clean thing out of an unclean? not one"), Job 25:4 ("how can he be clean that is born of a woman"), and Job 15:14 ("What is man, that he can be clean? Or he that is born of a woman, that he can be righteous"—RSV) to see that Jesus had to have been impure because he emerged from Mary.

Psalms 8:4 says, "What is man that thou art mindful of him, and the son of man that thou dost care for him" (RSV), which could be applied to Jesus but is avoided by apologists because it looks upon the son of man as insignificant. Psalms 37:25 says, "I have not seen the righteous forsaken or his children begging bread." If this is true, then Jesus could not be the righteous because he *was* forsaken by God, and many of his followers, his children if you will, definitely beg for bread.

And lastly, Isa. 42:19 says, "Who is blind, but my servant? or deaf, as my messenger that I sent? who is blind as he that is perfect, and blind as the Lord's servant?" This could more easily be applied to Jesus than most quotations apologists seek to apply to him. After all, to whom can one more aptly apply the word "perfect" or the phrase "my messenger that I sent"? Yet this same messenger is referred to as blind and deaf.

Incarnation

A *third* major reason Jesus couldn't be mankind's savior and God in the flesh is that various biblical verses rule out any possibility of an incarnation. Dan. 2:11 says, "The gods, whose dwelling is not with flesh," and Gen. 6:3 says, "My spirit shall nevermore abide in man, since he too is flesh." Both verses strongly imply that God would never become a man. In a feeble attempt to defend the Incarnation, apologist George Lawlor states on page 105 in his booklet "Almah, Virgin or Young Woman," "Even the eternal almighty God, with all His omnipotence and omniscience, could not know human life by experience without entering human life and living it. He came down and entered into our life in order that He might know by actual experience the problems of human existence."

This is a strange redefining of the scope of omniscience! How absurd! You mean God has to learn; he has to become a human being in order to learn what it's all about? And what about verses saying he will never dwell in flesh?

False Prophet

A *fourth* major factor in this whole question of whether or not Jesus has the requisite credentials to be the messiah relates to his prophetic capabilities. If he is, in fact, God incarnate and the savior of all mankind, then the accuracy of his prophecies should be above reproach and second to none. But any recounting of Jesus' predictions will show that his prophetic batting average is nothing short of pitiful. Some of his most glaring miscalculations include:

First, Jesus predicted in Matt. 12:40, "For as Jonas was three days and three nights in the whale's belly; so shall the Son of man be three days and three nights in the heart of the earth." In other words, just as Jonah was in the belly of the whale for three days and three nights, Jesus would be buried for three days and three nights. As noted earlier, one need only read four verses to see that the prophecy failed miserably. Mark 15:37 and 15:42 show that Jesus died on the day before the sabbath, which would be Friday, while Mark 16:9 and Matt. 28:1 show that Jesus allegedly rose sometime during Saturday night or

Sunday morning. From Friday afternoon to Sunday morning is not three days and three nights. In fact, to be precise, it is barely a day and a half.

Another significant shortcoming within this prophecy is that Jesus did not draw a valid analogy between Jonah and himself when he said "as Jonah was three days and three nights in the whale's belly." Jonah never died in the whale, while Jesus was dead in the tomb. In addition, Jesus was not actually put in the earth, much less the heart of the earth.

A *second* erroneous prophecy is found in John 13:38, where Jesus tells Peter, "Verily, verily, I say unto thee, The cock shall not crow, till thou hast denied me thrice." Jesus clearly told Peter that Peter would not deny him until the rooster had crowed *three* times. Yet, Mark 14:66–68 indicates that the rooster crowed after the first denial, not the third.

Third, while on the cross Jesus said to the thief at his side, "Verily I say unto thee, Today shalt thou be with me in paradise." As noted earlier, (a) Jesus could not have been in heaven with the thief that day because he lay in the tomb for three days, and (b) people saw Jesus walking around on the earth after his crucifixion and he told Mary Magdalene in John 20:17 "Touch me not; for I am not yet ascended to my Father." So how could Jesus have been in heaven with the thief on the first day, when he was walking around on the earth days later saying that he had not yet ascended to his father?

Fourth, in John 10:16 Jesus said, "And they shall hear my voice and there shall be one fold, and one shepherd." However, after nearly two thousand years we have over fifteen hundred separate Christian denominations. That hardly sounds like one fold and one shepherd.

Fifth, in John 2:19 Jesus said, "Destroy this temple and in three days I will raise it up." But numerous verses show that Jesus did not raise himself; he was raised by God. Acts 13:30 says, "God raised him from the dead" and Acts 2:24 says, "Whom God has raised up."

Sixth, according to Mark 8:12, Luke 11:29 and Matt. 12:39, Jesus said, "Why doeth this generation seek after a sign? Verily, I say unto you, There shall no sign be given unto this generation." Yet John 20:30 says, "Many other signs truly did Jesus in the presence of his disciples, which are not written in this book." Acts 2:22 and Mark 16:20 also say Jesus did wonders, signs, and miracles. In fact, Acts 5:12, 6:8, and 8:13 show that the Apostles Stephen and Philip also performed signs for that generation. Jesus' prediction that no sign would be given to that generation is clearly false.

Seventh, in John 12:32 Jesus said, "I, if I be lifted up from the earth, will draw all men unto me." Although he was lifted up according to the biblical account, he is far from having drawn all men to him. In fact, Matt. 20:16 alleges that most men will *not* be drawn to Jesus. It says, "So the last shall be first, and the first last: for many be called, but few chosen." Much of mankind has never even heard Jesus' name.

Eighth, in Mark 10:29-30 Jesus says, "I tell you that anyone who leaves home or brothers or sisters or mother or father or children or land for me and for the gospel, will receive much more in this present age. He will receive a hundred times more houses, brothers, sisters, mothers, children, and lands—and persecutions as well." Several problems accompany these comments: (a) What wealth did the followers of Jesus receive? (b) What houses and lands did they obtain for following Jesus? (c) By promising his followers immense wealth, Jesus engaged in a form of bribery and appealed to greed. (d) And how do you receive retrospective motherhood in wholesale quantities? That would be even more incredible than the virgin birth. This prophecy never materialized in the manner predicted.

A *ninth* inaccurate prophecy is found in Matt. 26:64-65 " 'But I tell all of you: from this time on you will see the Son of Man sitting at the right side of the Almighty and coming on the clouds of heaven.' At this the High Priest tore his clothes and said, 'Blasphemy!' " This prophecy by Jesus clearly failed because the priest died without ever seeing the event that was forecast.

Tenth, in Matt. 28:20 Jesus stated, "I am with you always, even unto the end of the world." But this directly contradicts his comments in Matt. 26:11, which says, "For ye have the poor always with you; but me ye have not always," and in John 7:34, which says, "Ye shall seek me, and shall not find me: and where I am, thither ye cannot come." Isn't it nice to have a friend you can depend on, one who is by your side through thick and thin?

Eleventh, in Matt. 20:19, Mark 10:33-34, and Luke 18:32-33 Jesus predicted that he would be killed by the Gentiles. He said, "shall deliver him to the Gentiles to mock, and to scourge, and to crucify him;." But one need only read John 19:14-18 and 23 to see that Jesus was killed by Roman soldiers *and* the Jews, not Gentiles alone. It states, "It was the preparation of the passover, and about the sixth hour: and he saith unto the Jews, Behold your King! But they cried out, Away with him, away with him, crucify him. . . . Then delivered he him therefore unto them to be crucified. And they took Jesus, and led him away. And he bearing his cross went forth into a place. . . . Where they crucified him. . . . Then the soldiers when they had crucified Jesus," Clearly Jesus erred in predicting he would be killed by Gentiles.

Twelfth, Jesus predicted that he would die in the same manner John the Baptist was killed. Matt. 17:12-13: "Likewise shall also the Son of man suffer of them. Then the disciples understood that he spoke unto them of John the Baptist." But as we know from reading Matt. 14:10, John the Baptist was beheaded in prison, not crucified.

Thirteenth, in Matt. 17:11-13, Jesus said, "Elijah truly shall come first, and restore all things. But I say unto you, That Elijah has come already." From this the disciples understood that he spoke unto them of John the Baptist. But what did John the Baptist restore? Nothing, absolutely nothing!

Fourteenth, in Matt. 27:63 Jesus flatly predicted he would rise after the third day, and Mark 8:31 says, "Jesus began to teach them, that the Son of man must suffer many things, . . . and be killed, and after three days rise again." Both say *after* three days. But in Luke 24:46, Mark 9:31, Matt. 17:23, and several other verses Jesus said he would rise *on the third day*. So which is correct? Would he rise *on* or *after* the third day? Jesus can't even provide his followers with a consistent prediction.

Moreover, we have already shown that both predictions would have to be incorrect if Jesus were going to be in heaven with the thief on the day of his crucifixion, and were in fact incorrect because Jesus actually arose neither on nor after the third day but *before* it.

Fifteenth, in John 10:27-28 Jesus prophesied, "My sheep hear my voice, and I know them, and . . . neither shall any man pluck them out of my hand." And essentially the same comment is repeated in John 18:9, which says, "Of them which thou gavest me have I lost none." So, in both instances, Jesus predicted he would not lose any of his followers. Yet John 17:12 says, "Those that thou gavest me I have kept, and none of them is lost, but the son of perdition." Jesus admits he lost Satan. Matt. 26:56 says, "All the disciples forsook him and fled" and shows he lost disciples. And John 13:21 and 25-27 prove Jesus lost Judas. In them Jesus states, "verily I say unto you, that one of you shall betray me."

Jesus' *sixteenth* erroneous prophecy is found in Matt. 5:17-18, where Jesus says, "Think not that I am come to destroy the Law, or the prophets: I am not come to destroy, but to fulfill. For verily I say unto you, Till heaven and earth pass, one jot or one tittle shall in no wise pass from the Law, till all be fulfilled."

Jesus clearly predicted he would uphold every single aspect of the old Law, until heaven and earth passed away and all was fulfilled. Yet, Jesus altered or ignored the dietary laws in Matt. 15:11 and Mark 7:15, the washing of hands in Luke 11:37-38, the sabbath in John 5:8-11 and Luke 13:10-16, the rules on fasting in Mark 2:18-20, the rules on adultery in John 8:4-11, and the rules on divorce in Matt. 5:32.

Jesus should fear God as much as any man because of Prov. 30:5-6, which says, "Every word of God is pure: he is a shield unto them that put their trust in him. Add thou not unto his words, lest he reprove thee, and thou be found a liar." Rev. 22:18-19 is even more emphatic. It says, "I warn every one who hears the words of the prophecy of this book: if any one adds to them, God will add to him the plagues described in this book, and if any one takes away from the words of the book of this prophecy, God will take away his share in the tree of life" (RSV). Judging by this standard and in light of Jesus' dramatic alteration of the old Law, one can only conclude that our savior isn't even going to make it himself.

Seventeenth, in John 14:12 Jesus made a prediction that is easily disproven. He said, "Verily, verily, I say unto you, He that believeth on me, the works that I do shall he do also; and greater works than these shall he do." What believer has ever done a miracle greater than those performed by Jesus?

Eighteenth, John 14:13–14 says, "Whatever you shall ask in my name, that will I do that the Father may be glorified in the son. If ye shall ask any thing in my name, I will do it." This is one of those predictions that is easily shown to be divorced from reality. Millions of people have made millions of requests in Jesus' name and failed to receive them. This promise or prophecy has failed miserably.

Nineteenth, in Rev. 3:11 Jesus said, "Behold, I come quickly." After two thousand years Jesus is yet to come and by any measure that is hardly "quickly."

Twentieth, one can't help but notice the development of historical events after Jesus said in John 8:12, "I am the light of the world: he that followeth me shall not walk in darkness, but shall have the light of life." Christianity was subsequently adopted by the West and the Western world soon moved from the light of the Roman Empire into the Dark Ages.

And *lastly*, in Matt. 24:35 Jesus says, "Heaven and earth shall pass away, but my words shall not pass away." Yet Eccle. 1:4 in the Old Testament says, "One generation passeth away, and another generation cometh, but the earth abideth forever." So who is the more accurate prophet? The author of Ecclesiastes, who says the earth abides forever, or Jesus who says the earth shall pass away?

In conclusion, all of the above clearly demonstrates that Jesus is wholly inept in the arena of prophetic accuracy. Deut. 18:22 says, "When a prophet speaks in the name of the Lord, if the word does not come to pass or come true, that is a word which the Lord has not spoken; the prophet has spoken it presumptuously, you need not be afraid of him" (RSV). By this criterion Jesus is a false prophet, does not speak in God's name, and certainly could not be God. Biblical testimony alone is sufficient to expose Jesus as a fraud and a charlatan.

Virgin Birth

We now come to the fifth major problem associated with Jesus' credentials, the virgin birth: a topic that has generated an enormous amount of controversy over the centuries. It is among those concepts that are crucial to an adequate understanding of Christianity, one of the stones in the ideological foundation. Yet, like other stones, it is permeated with difficulties and contradictions that need to be exposed. Apologists contend the miraculous nature of the event could only be associated with the birth of a divine being, namely Jesus Christ. For many, its importance is comparable to that of the Resurrection. On page 58 in the booklet "Almah, Virgin or Young Woman" apologist George Lawlor highlights the significance of the doctrine by saying, "The Virgin Birth is an integral part of the Biblical testimony concerning the Lord Jesus Christ. It is thus absolutely essential to the true Christian faith." On page 64 he says,

If the Virgin Birth accounts in Matthew and Luke are fable, invention, legend, and fabrication, to which no credit can be attached, then everything else in those Gospel narratives is equally dubious and untrustworthy. It is upon the truth of these Gospel records that our belief in the Virgin Birth depends. If these cannot be trusted we are left with no real ground for our faith.

Finally, Lawlor states on page 71,

We cannot surrender the Virgin Birth without surrendering every other point of the doctrine of Christ. If we yield to critical pressure in the matter of the Virgin Birth, then our whole doctrinal position is in jeopardy. For one born of human parents by the ordinary procreative process could not possibly have been pre-existent. If Christ was not virgin-born, then He cannot be God, and if He is not God, then He is the greatest impostor the world has ever seen. . . . If He is not the pre-existent Son of God, incarnate in human flesh, but mere man then He is still dead, and could not have risen from the dead as the Scriptures testify. It would have been impossible for His apostles to have seen Him after his death and burial, and His ascension was the creation of their pathological fancy.

On page 56 in *Answers to Tough Questions* McDowell and Stewart state,

Another reason why Jesus needed to be virgin-born was because of His sinless nature. A basic New Testament teaching is that from the day He was born until the day He died, Jesus was without sin. To be a perfect sacrifice, He must Himself be perfect—without sin. Since our race is contaminated with sin, a miraculous entrance into the world would be required, hence the virgin birth.

On page 16 in his work *The Virgin Birth* the apologist Robert Gromacki quotes Professor John F. Walvoord of Dallas Theological Seminary, " 'The incarnation of the Lord Jesus Christ is the central fact of Christianity. Upon it the whole superstructure of Christian theology depends.' A real incarnation requires a literal virgin birth. They are 'two sides of the same coin.' You can't have one without the other." Later Gromacki says on page 96 of the same book, "The Bible believer should not defend the possibility of virgin births within the human race; rather he should argue that virgin births *cannot* happen naturally or artificially and that the only reason why Christ was virgin born was because of the miraculous ministry of the Holy Spirit."

A convincing case for precisely why these apologists feel the virgin birth is so important as to rival the Resurrection is never concretized. But, even more important, what is so miraculous about a virgin birth? *Webster's Dictionary* defines it as a birth in which the mother retains her virginity by having no contact with a male. But this is by no means a miraculous event. An egg can easily be taken from a virgin, be united with a sperm in a test tube and be reinserted into the uterus without any physical contact being involved. Indeed, the parents need never have met. Where is the miracle? Webster defines a miracle as "an event or action that apparently contradicts known scientific laws and is hence thought to be due to supernatural causes, esp., to an act of God." But it's not necessary for God to act in order for a woman to become pregnant even as her virginity remains intact.

Any extended analysis of the virgin birth will expose eight major biblical problems that must be addressed by those who are so foolish as to take the topic seriously:

First, although several verses such as Luke 1:34–35 ("How shall this be, seeing I know not a man?"), Matt. 1:24–25 ("And knew her not till she had brought forth her firstborn son"), and Matt. 1:18 ("Before they came together, she was found with child") corroborate a virgin birth, many verses clearly say either directly or implicitly that Joseph was the *natural* father of Jesus. John 6:42 says, "Is not this Jesus, the son of Joseph . . . ?"; Luke 4:22 says, "Is not this Joseph's son?"; Luke 2:33 says, "His father and his mother marveled"; Luke 2:27 says, "When the parents brought in the child Jesus"; Matt. 13:55 says, "Is not this the carpenter's son?"; and Luke 2:48 says, "His mother said . . . behold, thy father and I have sought thee." Mary refers to Joseph as the father of Jesus, and who is in a better position to know? Moreover, Rom. 1:3, 2 Tim. 2:8, Rom. 9:5, Rev. 22:16, and Acts 13:22–23 show that Jesus had to have been the product of a natural birth. Otherwise, he could not be a physical descendant of David, which is required of the messiah. The messiah must be of Davidic descent, as Acts 2:30, Jer. 23:5, 2 Sam. 7:12–13, Psalms 89:3–4, Psalms 132:11, and Luke 1:32–33 prove beyond any reasonable doubt.

Incidentally, one can't help but wonder how the birth could have been natural, if one of the parents was an un-natural Holy Spirit.

A *second* problem with the virgin birth is that according to the verses already mentioned, as well as Matt. 1:1–16 and Luke 3:23–31, Joseph was a descendant of David and the father of Jesus. But Joseph couldn't be the physical father of Jesus, if Jesus had a virgin birth. If Joseph was *not* the physical father of Jesus, then Jesus couldn't be of David's seed, as is alleged in 2 Tim. 2:8, Acts 13:22–23 and Rev. 22:16. That would forestall any possibility of him being the messiah. Verses previously referred to show that one had to be a physical descendant of David in order to be the messiah.

The necessary conclusion is that Christians must abandon one of two concepts, either the virgin birth or the messiahship of Jesus. They are wholly incompatible. How could Jesus be of Davidic descent "according to the flesh," as is required by Rom. 1:3 and Rom. 9:5, if Joseph was not Jesus' physical father and Jesus emerged from a virgin birth? A virgin birth would destroy the physical chain, the link between generations. If there is a physical link, the virgin birth is destroyed.

A *third* problem arising from the birth of Jesus lies in the fact that the Bible repeatedly says nothing pure can come from a woman. Job 14:4, 15:14, and 25:4 were earlier quoted to this effect. Anyone touching a woman within seven days after she has menstruated is impure, according to Lev. 15:19 in the Old Testament, which says, "When a woman has her regular flow of blood, the impurity of her monthly period will last seven days, and anyone who touches her will be unclean till evening." Lev. 12:1–4 says the same. Mary was purified in Luke 2:22–24 according to an Old Testament law found in Lev. 12:8, which says that turtledoves and pigeons must be brought for purification. Therefore, Mary must have been *impure* when she resumed menstruation, and since it is difficult to see how she could have avoided touching Jesus after his birth, Jesus must have been unclean at one time also. That is a status that is hardly commensurate with being God's equal. Mary was under the curse of original sin like all of us and, thus, was no purer than anyone else. Realizing the problem an impure Mary presents, Catholics tried to resolve this difficulty by proclaiming the Immaculate Conception in 1854. They alleged that Mary, herself, was conceived apart from sin; she was pure. However, instead of being solved, the problem is only removed one step. If this were true, how could Mary's sinful parents produce a pure daughter? Moreover, if Mary was sinless, like Jesus, why did she say in Luke 1:47, "My spirit has rejoiced in God my Savior"? If Mary had been sinless, holy, and the mother of God, why would she need a savior? Only sinners need saviors.

A *fourth* problem with the virgin birth is that it has no real Old Testament support, prophetic or otherwise, because the only prophecy that is supposedly a prognosticator of this momentous event, Isa. 7:14, is fraught with difficulties. In the King James Version, that verse says "Behold, a virgin shall conceive, and bear a son and shall call his name Immanuel." But those who lean on this verse for support conveniently ignore some vital facts.

(a) Christian translators interpreted the Hebrew word *almah,* which means "a young woman" in Hebrew, as "virgin." The actual Hebrew word for virgin is *betulah.* Gen. 24:43 in the RSV and Ex. 2:8 in the KJV show *almah* as meaning "a young woman" or "maid," respectively, not "virgin." Who knows Hebrew better than the Hebrews, and they say in their modern Masoretic text that *almah* should be translated as "maiden," not "virgin," in both Gen. 24:43 and Ex. 2:8. Prov. 30:19 in both the KJV and the RSV say that *almah* should be translated as "maid."

(b) Some translators say "shall conceive" should have been translated as "is with," which is in the present tense and shows it pertains to a woman existing in Isaiah's time, not seven hundred years later. Other critics go even farther and claim "shall conceive" was translated from *harah* which actually means "has conceived." They say *harah* is the Hebrew perfect tense, which represents past completed action in English and is, therefore, referring to a woman who conceived prior to Isaiah.

(c) How could the birth of a child convey any message to Ahaz, if the child was to be born seven hundred years after Ahaz lived?

(d) Except for the reference to the prophecy itself in Matt. 1:23, Jesus was never referred to as Immanuel in the New Testament and has never been called Immanuel except by those who do so in order to fulfill the prophecy.

(e) According to Luke 1:31, he was supposed to be called Jesus, not Immanuel.

(f) And lastly, Jesus could not be the Immanuel discussed by Isaiah, since Immanuel means "God is with us;" whereas Joshua or Jesus means "Yahweh is salvation."

A *fifth* problem with the virgin birth must be faced by Roman Catholics because they maintain that Mary retained her virginity permanently, even after Jesus was born. Yet verses such as Mark 6:3, Luke 2:7, John 2:12, and several others clearly show that Jesus had brothers and sisters. He was only the first of several siblings. Gal. 1:19 says, "Other of the apostles saw I none, save James the Lord's brother," and Matt. 13:55–56 says, "Is not this the carpenter's son? is not his mother called Mary? and his brethren called James, and Joses, and Simon, and Judas? And his sisters, are they not all with us?" Mary could not have remained a virgin unless all of Jesus' brothers and sisters were products of virgin births as well. Matt. 1:25 says Joseph "knew her not till she had brought forth her firstborn son: and he called his name Jesus." The word "till" strongly implies that Joseph had contact with Mary after she brought forth her firstborn. If that were true, then Mary could not have maintained her perpetual virginity. And why say "firstborn" if others did not follow?

Besides these major problems, there are also several ancillary difficulties related to the virgin birth. If Joseph was the natural father of Jesus as some previously mentioned verses allege, then Jesus was illegitimate, since Joseph and Mary were never married, but only engaged at the time. Luke 2:5 in the New International Version says Joseph "went there to register with Mary, who was pledged to be married to him and was expecting a child." This proves Mary and Joseph were engaged at best. To say the Holy Ghost was the father of Jesus is to cover an immorality with an impracticality, and besides, when did Mary ever marry the Holy Ghost?

On page 283 *The Jew and the Christian Missionary*, Gerald Sigal addresses the dilemma by saying,

> Mary, according to the New Testament, did not conceive by her betrothed, Joseph. Therefore, she committed adultery "under law" (Deut. 22:23–24). As a result, the Christian missionary claim that Jesus was born of a woman engaged to a man, yet had God as his father, must be considered to refer to an illegitimate birth. God's law does not allow for Him to seduce a maiden, even through the medium of the Holy Spirit. What would be the worth of a moral code that is violated by God Himself?

Either way Jesus can only be labeled a bastard.

Finally, several figures in the Old Testament had births of an even more miraculous nature. In Gen. 18:10–11 Isaac was born to an aged woman, Sarah, who no longer menstruated, and in 1 Sam. 1:5 and 2:21 Samuel was born to a woman, Hannah, whose womb had been closed by the lord. According to Gen. 1:27 and 2:7 Adam had no father or mother, and according to Heb. 7:3 Melchizedek had no father, mother, or genealogy. Thus, two men and a woman came into the world as full-grown adults which is an accomplishment considerably greater than that of a virgin birth. Eve's birth was not only spectacular but gave rise to a person whose father was also her mate. Jesus never topped that!

Trinity

Our *sixth* and final major topic having a direct bearing on Jesus' credentials is the Trinity, undoubtedly one of the most controversial topics in all of Christianity. The Trinity is defined as the belief that there is one God who has revealed Himself in three persons, the Father, the Son, and the Holy Ghost, and these three persons are the one God. What apologists neglect to mention is the fact that the whole concept is plagued by a multitude of major problems that need to be exposed:

First, one cannot deny that there *are* verses in which Jesus is equated with God by others or by himself. Some of the most prominent examples are John 10:30 ("I and my Father are One"); John 1:1 ("In the beginning was the Word, and the Word was with God, and the Word was God"; John 1:14 ("And the Word was made flesh and dwelt among us"); John 14:9 ("He that hath seen me hath seen the Father"); John 17:22 ("And the glory which thou gavest me I have given them; that they may be one, even as we are one"); Col. 2:9 ("For in him dwelleth all the fulness of the Godhead bodily"); Phil. 2:6 ("Who, being in the form of God, thought it not robbery to be equal with God"); Phil. 2:11 ("That every tongue should confess that Jesus Christ is Lord, to the glory of God the Father"); John 20:28 ("And Thomas answered and said unto him, My Lord and my God"); and Titus 2:13 ("Looking for that blessed hope, and the glorious appearing of the great God and our savior Jesus Christ").

The obvious conclusion to be drawn from all of these verses is that Jesus is God. But what the typical parishioner is not made cognizant of, what is kept from the minds of the flock as much as possible, is the fact that a far larger number of verses clearly show that Jesus did *not* consider himself to be God or God's equal. Some of the most relevant comments in this regard are. Matt. 19:17 ("And he said unto him, Why callest thou me good? there is none good but one, that is God"); John 5:30 ("I seek not mine own will, but the will of the Father which hath sent me"); John 6:38 ("I came down from heaven, not to do mine own will, but the will of him that sent me"); John 14:28 ("My Father is greater than I"); John 7:16 ("My doctrine is not mine, but his that sent me"); 1 Peter 3:22 ("Who is gone into heaven, and is on the right hand of God"); and Matt. 27:46, in which Jesus address God ("My God, my God, why hast thou forsaken me?").

One of the best such quotes is John 20:17, which says, "I ascend unto my Father, and your Father, and to my God and your God." The latter verse, alone, clearly shows that Jesus did not consider himself to be God. The list of passages in this vein could be extended dramatically, but the point has been made. Contrary to some biblical verses, Jesus repeatedly showed that he did not look upon himself as God's equal.

A *second* problem with the Trinity, besides the fact that Jesus often said he was not God's equal, is that the Bible repeatedly says God is one, unique, a unity, a being without equals, divisions, or parts. For example, Deut. 4:35 says, "The Lord he is God; there is none else beside him." How, then, does one reconcile this with previously quoted 1 Peter 3:22, which states that Jesus is "gone into heaven, and is on the right hand of God"? According to the latter Jesus is beside God in heaven. As Gerald Sigal said on page 141 of *The Jew and the Christian Missionary*, "If the second 'lord,' Jesus, is sitting next to the first 'Lord,' the triune godhead or two-thirds of it, or any aggregate of it, he cannot be part of it. That which exists outside of God cannot be God." In other words, you can't sit beside that which you are.

Deut. 4:39 says, "The Lord he is God in heaven above, and upon the earth beneath: there is none else." But there must be something else, when you have three persons within the Trinity. That isn't a unity. Isa. 45:6 says, "There is none beside me. I am the Lord, and there is none else," and 1 Sam. 2:2 says, "There is none holy as the Lord: for there is none beside thee." If these are true then how could Jesus rise to heaven to sit at his right side? The text of 2 Sam. 7:22 reads, "Wherefore thou art great, O Lord God: for there is none like thee." If that were true, then how could Jesus be God down here on earth?

Jewish writers, in particular, strongly oppose any attack upon the unity of God. On pages 125–27 of *The Jew and the Christian Missionary* Sigal says,

> This belief, called the Trinity, is not only diametrically opposed to Jewish belief, but is the very antithesis of the teaching of the Torah, the Prophets, and the Writings concerning the oneness of God . . . this teaching, the result of theological and doctrinal speculation, is not even a pale reflection of what is taught in the Hebrew Bible, the Old Testament. . . . Missionary Christianity manipulates the Scriptures to establish the doctrine of the Trinity. If it had a quaternity [four] to prove, this would be demonstrated just as easily from the biblical text.

A *third* problem with the Trinity is that the Bible repeatedly says that only God can save. Isa. 43:11 says, "I, even I, am the Lord; and beside me there is no savior." Hosea 13:4 says, "Thou shalt know no god but me: for there is no savior beside me." And Psalms 3:8 says, "Salvation belongs to the Lord" (NKJV). How, then, can a being down here on earth be our savior, who is not only separate from God, but repeatedly draws a distinction between himself and God?

A *fourth* problem with the Trinity lies in the fact that a couple of verses say that God could never dwell on the earth. He's far too big for that. 1 Kings 8:27 and 2 Chron. 6:18 say, "Can God indeed dwell with man on the earth? Heaven itself, the highest heaven, cannot contain thee; how much less this house that I have built?" (NEB). They show there is no way the godhead could have dwelt in Jesus bodily.

Then there is a *fifth* problem with the Trinity. God stated in Gen. 6:3 that he would not abide in man or the flesh. He said, "My spirit shall not abide in man for ever, for he is flesh" (RSV). Thus, Jesus could not be both man and God and be so forever, for that would violate this verse.

A *sixth* problem with the Trinity resides in the fact that if Jesus is God, he would be by definition eternal and uncreated. But that flies in the face of verses that clearly show that Jesus was created at some time or other. Col. 1:15 in the RSV speaks of Jesus "who is the image of the invisible God, the first-born of all creation." And Prov. 8:22 says, "The Lord created me at the beginning of his work, the first of his acts of old" (RSV). If Jesus was ever created, regardless of when it occurred, whether before or after the Incarnation, he could not be God. As Gerald Sigal says on page 163 of *The Jew and the Christian Missionary*, "The very fact that Jesus' existence is connected with the beginning of creation nullifies the claim that Jesus is God. What is begotten cannot be eternal, and what is not eternal cannot be equal to God; moreover, that which is created by God cannot be God."

A *seventh* and final problem with the Trinity emerges when we notice several ancillary problems that must be addressed by trinitarians:

(a) By definition, a son must be younger than his father. How, then, could Jesus be equal to the Father?

(b) As was noted earlier, who or what died on the cross? If a man died then nobody is saved, because the death of a man could save no one. If God died on the cross then we have an impossibility. God can not die. If the God/Man died, then we have either an impossibility or an insufficiency.

(c) Jesus is called God by others, but so is the Devil in 2 Cor. 4:4, which says, "In whom the god of this world hath blinded the minds of them which believe not" (KJV).

(d) If the Trinity has validity, then Jesus' relationship to Mary is extremely strange. If he was born of Mary, she was his mother. If she had a child by the Holy Ghost and the Holy Ghost is the equal of Jesus, then she was his wife. If God is the father of all mankind and Jesus is God, then Jesus is the father of all mankind and Mary would be his daughter. And since Mary is the daughter of God and Jesus is the son of god, Mary would have to also be Jesus' sister.

On page 42 in *The Light of Reason*, volume 2, antitrinitarian Shmuel Golding highlighted some of these difficulties rather well by stating,

> To those who believe in a trinity the question must be asked. Is the trinity three persons in one Godhead? Is the trinity three persons all carrying office at the same time? If one believes that the three persons of the trinity are all in office at the same time, e.g., God the Father is in heaven while God the Son is on earth, then this would border on polytheism. And if the trinitarian answers that the trinity is three in one, thus being indivisible, e.g., always together in one Godhead, then surely there must have been a God the Father in heaven, when God the Son was crucified and buried in a tomb; otherwise, who would have resurrected him after three days, and if God came to earth and died, then during the three days that he was dead, who ruled the heavens and the earth? Also if the trinity is indivisible, then Jesus, being also the Holy Ghost, must have had intercourse with his own mother in order to produce himself as the son. And if not, then it is clear that Father, Son, and Holy Ghost, are three separate persons; thus the trinity cannot be a unity in one Godhead.

In 1645 the Englishman John Biddle endangered his life by publishing a document entitled "Twelve Arguments Refuting the Deity of the Holy Spirit." He was imprisoned and Parliament subsequently passed a law that promised death for anyone who denied the Trinity, the divinity of Jesus, or the Holy Spirit. Biddle specialized in logical syllogisms such as,

> He that is distinguished from God is not God. The Holy Spirit is distinguished from God. Therefore, the Holy Spirit is not God. He that is sent by another is not God. The Holy Spirit is sent by God. Therefore the Holy Spirit is not God. He that changes places is not God. The Holy Spirit changes places. Therefore the Holy Spirit is not God.

It is important to note that there is no biblical verse that specifically mentions the Trinity or uses the word Trinity, and many Christian scholars are willing to admit as much. On page 57 in *508 Answers to Bible Questions*, apologist M. R. DeHaan states, "There is no verse in the Bible which says in so many words that God is a 'trinity' consisting of one God and three Persons, but there are enough passages which indicate this very clearly, so that we can form a doctrine of the Trinity on it."

On page 22 in *What You Should Know about Inerrancy* Charles Ryrie says, "It is fair to say that the Bible does not clearly teach the doctrine of the Trinity, if by clearly one means there are proof texts for the doctrine. In fact, there is not even one proof text, if by proof text we mean a verse or passage that 'clearly' states that there is one God who exists in three persons."

Many biblicists are also willing to concede that the very concept of the Trinity is beyond rational comprehension. This refrain from making any real attempt to put the idea within a framework which people can understand. They not only admit there are no proof texts for the doctrine but freely admit that the entire concept is incomprehensible. Support for this assertion is not hard to find. On page 168 in the already cited *508 Answers to Bible Questions*, DeHaan states,

> The Trinity, that is, three persons in one, is a mystery which is revealed in the Bible, but cannot be understood by the human mind. Since man is finite, and God is infinite, this is one of those things which must be accepted by faith, even though it cannot be reasoned out. The Trinity cannot be explained, but it must be believed because the Bible teaches it throughout.

On page 55 of *Basic Theology* Ryrie alleges, "Even with all the discussion and delineation that we attempt in relation to the Trinity, we must acknowledge that it is, in the final analysis, a mystery. We accept all the data as truth even though they go beyond our understanding.

On page 25 in *Essential Christianity* apologist Walter Martin says,

> No man can fully explain the Trinity, though in every age scholars have propounded theories and advanced hypotheses to explore this mysterious Biblical teaching. But despite the worthy efforts of these scholars, the Trinity is still largely incomprehensible to the mind of man. Perhaps the chief reason for this is that the Trinity is a-logical, or beyond logic. It, therefore, cannot be made subject to human reason or logic.

Martin neglects to mention that no one can fully explain the concept because there is nothing to explain. How do you describe an all-black white horse, or a square circle? How can something be a-logical, whatever that means? Something is either logical or illogical. This is the kind of word one would expect to emerge from the apologetic mindset of those who must defend doctrines at all costs. How do you step beyond logic? The answer is: you don't. Certainly the trinity is incomprehensible. And so is a square circle or a two-sided triangle.

On pages 10 and 11 of *Answering Christianity's Most Puzzling Questions*, volume 2, apologist Richard Sisson says, "The doctrine of the triune Godhead may upset the neat, logical order of your mind, but it is taught in the Scriptures. We are not to adjust the Bible to satisfy our sense of logic; we are to adjust our logic to conform to the Scriptures."

A comment of that nature is almost too absurd to warrant a response. One can only imagine the number of people with half-baked, crackpot, superstitious, metaphysical concepts with absolutely no rationality attached whatever saying, "Right on brother. That expresses our sentiments exactly." If logic, reason, and rationality are not going to be our standard, what will be? What other standard is there? Once they are jettisoned, any concept is as valid as any other, no matter how absurd they may sound. Proponents need only say that they are above and beyond human comprehension, that they are "a-logical."

On page 19 in *The Bible Has the Answer* apologists Henry Morris and Martin Clark state, "The mystery of the Trinity is beyond the capacity of our finite and limited minds to comprehend in its fulness. . . . Although beyond the ability of the human mind to comprehend by reason, the tri-une nature of God can easily be understood in the heart by faith."

If reason and proof are not to be our guide, firm believers in *any* absurd concept could make this claim. For one to say that it is to "be understood in the heart by faith" is to rely upon feelings, whim, and intuition, hardly a practical basis for anything! On page 41 in the same book Morris and Clark also state, "The mystery of the divine-human nature of Christ is beyond our finite understanding. . . . The Bible simply presents as fact the great truth that Jesus Christ was both God and man. It does not try to explain how this could be, because it is inexplicable. It must be apprehended on faith alone."

Here, again, we see no attempt to defend the concept rationally. Believers are simply told to dogmatically believe it without understanding, simply because the Bible says so. On pages 112 and 113 of "Almah or Young Woman" apologist George Lawlor makes the same admission. He says,

> All the difficulties and problems surrounding the mystery of the person of Christ will never be solved. The great difficulty is that of understanding how the Lord could have but one personality when he possessed two real natures, divine and human. How can these natures be united in the one Person? This is the "mystery of godliness . . ." (1 Tim. 3:16). There are some matters that are beyond us, which we shall never totally comprehend.

"Totally comprehend"? Most Christians would be happy to be able to comprehend even a minute part of the Trinity. Lawlor concludes, "We must finally fall upon our faces before the mystery of the eternal, almighty god in Christ, having come in flesh, and confess that we cannot explain Him."

"Explain him"!? Any Christian would be happy to even *understand* the Trinity, much less explain it. Talk about blind, unquestioning faith! The concept of the Trinity makes no sense; the apologists admit it makes no sense, but the faithful are to believe it, regardless. The problem lies not in the fact that it can't be understood by the human mind, but that it can't be understood by any mind, period. The very concept is a hopeless muddle of pure fantasy.

Some apologists have tried to apply a veneer of respectability by generating parallels in everyday life. One of the most common is the analogy that is often drawn between the Trinity and the three stages of water, namely, solid, liquid and gas. Just as there are three forms in which water can exist, we are told there are three forms in which God can be manifested. Of course, there is no validity to this comparison whatever because water, unlike the Trinity, does not exist in all three stages simultaneously. On page 55 of *Basic Theology* Ryrie all but admits as much by saying, "No illustration can possibly capture all that is involved in the biblical revelation of the Trinity. Most are, at best, only parallels of a three-in-one idea."

When all parallels and analogies have been destroyed and the press of the wall from behind is growing, biblicists will usually retreat to the "It's a mystery" subterfuge. Every time Christians come to an obligatory concept that is totally irrational, they seek to invoke the subterfuge of "mystery." In truth, there is nothing mysterious about the Trinity. It is nothing more than a blatant impossibility with a heavy overlay of contradiction and irrationality. Logic, reason, common sense, and reality play no role in the equation, whatever.

Conclusion

Apologist McDowell summarized the Jesus predicament as well as anyone on page 107 in *Evidence that Demands a Verdict*: "There needs to be a moral honesty in the above consideration of Jesus as either a liar, a lunatic, or Lord and God."

Well said! Moral honesty *is* sorely needed. The evidence does, indeed, demand a verdict and any reasonably objective person knows which of the three—liar, lunatic, or Lord and God—is most applicable and what that verdict must be.

7

Jesus III

Character, Deceptiveness

In the chapter 5 we discussed the history and background of Jesus Christ, while in the chapter 6 we addressed a wide range of topics concerning his credentials. This chapter will focus on the character and credibility of Jesus. Do his words and deeds exemplify one who is to be the model of sinless perfection for our children to emulate? Needless to say, traits such as honesty, integrity, and sincerity are of crucial importance to anyone claiming to be the savior of mankind. On numerous occasions biblical passages describe Jesus as the very personification of truth and perfection. Some of the more notable biblical comments in this regard are 1 Peter 2:22, which says, "Who did no sin, neither was guile found in his mouth"; 1 John 3:5, which says, "And in him is no sin"; and Eph. 4:21, which says, "As the truth is in Jesus." Many other verses of this nature could be employed, such as 1 John 3:3 and 1 Peter 1:19, so the kind of behavior to be expected from one so exalted is not subject to dispute. Interestingly enough, verses of this kind counteract comments such as those found in Mark 10:18, in which Jesus says, "Why callest thou me good? There is none good but one, that is God."

Nevertheless, Jesus' followers endlessly proclaim his alleged goodness and moral rectitude. On page 120 in *Evidence That Demands a Verdict* McDowell says of Jesus, "He never spoke an improper word, he never committed a wrong action." In the same vein apologist Paul Little says on page 19 of *Know Why You Believe*, "Jesus Christ was sinless. The caliber of his life was such that he was able to challenge his enemies with the question, 'Which of you convicts me of sin?' (John 8:46)" If only a *Biblical Errancy* representative had been present to raise his hand!

129

Present-day followers allege that Jesus was not only sinless but notably lacking in hypocrisy. On page 128 in *Answers to Tough Questions* apologists McDowell and Stewart state, "Christianity stands or falls on the person of Jesus, and Jesus was not a hypocrite. He lived consistently with what He taught, and at the end of his life He challenged those who had lived with Him night and day, for over three years, to point out any hypocrisy in Him." Again, if only an informed individual had been there to point! On page 100 in *Reasons Skeptics Should Consider Christianity* McDowell and Stewart summarized the importance of this whole topic rather well by saying, "Christianity stands or falls on the person of Jesus Christ. If He can be refuted, then the Christian faith also can be refuted."

While being smothered by all the praise of Jesus, true believers are not told that the entire biblical career of man's alleged savior is a veritable miasma of deception, duplicity, hypocrisy, and complicity. Although often the source of euphoric comments, moralistic pronouncements, and grandiloquent rhetoric, Jesus often spoke and behaved in a manner quite distant from that which he espoused. More than a mere incompetent prognosticator, as was noted in the last chapter, Jesus was a hypocrite and a deceiver. More than enough information exists within the Bible to prove that his character and integrity are such as to obviate any possibility of Jesus being the model for, or savior of, humanity. The rest of this chapter will be devoted to an exposition of the overwhelming number of instances in which the true nature of Jesus steps into the light of day. The last chapter discussed approximately twenty false prophecies by him, so there is no need to recount this character weakness. Instead, instances of actual duplicity will be discussed and followed by an even larger number of comments exhibiting verbal deception.

Deceptive Deeds

Jesus carried out a number of deceptive actions.

First, in John 7:8–10 of the RSV Jesus said to some of his followers, "Go to the feast yourselves: I am not going up to this feast, for my time has not yet fully come. So saying he remained in Galilee. But after his brothers had gone up to the feast, then he also went up, not publicly, but in private." Here we have a clear instance in which Jesus lied. He said he was not going up, but later he went up secretly.

Second, in Matt. 5:22 Jesus said, "Whosoever shall say, Thou fool, shall be in danger of hell fire." But Jesus himself called others fools in Matt. 23:17 and 23:19 and Luke 11:40. From Jesus' own words we must conclude that Jesus, too, along with the rest of mankind, is in danger of going to hell.

Third, in Matt. 5:44 Jesus said, "Love your enemies; bless them that curse you, do good to them that hate you." But in Matt. 12:34, 23:15, 17, 19, 27,

33, Luke 11:40, and John 10:8 Jesus called people "fools," "vipers," "serpents," "hypocrites," "whited sepulchres," "thieves," and "blind." Who would equate adjectives of this kind with loving your enemies and doing good to those who hate you? What a hypocrite! Whether true or not, these remarks fly in the face of Jesus' professed belief in loving, blessing, forgiving, and aiding one's enemies.

Fourth, in the Mark 10 a man asked Jesus what he had to do to be saved and Jesus said, "Thou knowest the commandments, Do not commit adultery, Do not kill, Do not steal, Do not bear false witness. Defraud not, Honor thy father and thy mother" (Mark 10:19). That was what the man had to do in order to be saved according to Jesus. Notice anything odd about this list? In the first place, Jesus deleted five of the ten commandments, primarily those related to religious rituals such as honoring the sabbath and avoiding idols; second, he added an obligation that isn't even a commandment—there is nothing in the Old Testament Ten Commandments about "defrauding not." In addition, Jesus directly defied a stern New Testament prohibition against any alteration of the Bible. Rev. 22:19 alleges that if you alter the Bible in any way, you do so at your own peril: "If any one takes away from the words of the book of the prophecy, God will take away his share in the tree of life." And Deut. 12:32 says, "Everything that I command you you shall be careful to do; you shall not add to it or take from it." Both of these warnings were ignored by Jesus, who did not hesitate to alter the old Law as he deemed fit. In effect, Jesus looked upon himself as being above the law. For Jesus to allege that he had created a new commandment is blasphemous from a biblical perspective.

One would be hard-pressed to find a statement more at variance with reality than that found on page 108 in apologist Don Stewart's *101 Questions People Ask Most About the Bible.* Completely oblivious to the New Testament record of Jesus, Stewart says, "Jesus did everything the law required, never once breaking any of its commandments . . . he fulfilled the law." Later, on page 128 in the same book, Stewart says, "Jesus was obeying the law of God up until the end. . . . He honored and obeyed the law throughout his life and he also honored the law while suffering his death." And on page 167 in *All About the Bible* apologist Sidney Collett says, "The whole law was given to the Perfect Man, who perfectly kept it on our behalf."

How can apologists be more in error? Aryeh Kaplan was quite correct when he said on page 56 in his book *The Real Messiah.* "Jesus claimed that he did not intend to change the Laws of Moses. . . . Later on, he himself abrogated some of the laws, while his followers eventually abolished or changed nearly all of them. However, the Torah itself clearly states in many places that its laws are eternal, never to be abolished."

Jesus made a comment in John 13:34 that in two major respects also reveals his attitude, if not contempt, toward the Old Testament. He said, "A new commandment I give unto you, That ye love one another." If Jesus had read Deut.

12:32 and 4:2 with more concern for precision and less for revision, he would have noticed that the old Law was not to be altered or diminished in any respect. *Second*, how can Jesus call "love one another" a new commandment, when he said in Matt. 19:17 and 19:19, "But if thou wilt enter into life, keep the commandments. Thou shalt love thy neighbor as thyself." By Jesus' own admission this was an Old Testament law, so how was it a new commandment? But even more important, where is the commandment that states as much? The answer is, nowhere! There is no such commandment. Lev. 19:18 says, "Thou shalt love thy neighbour as thyself," but that is not among any list of commandments. In summary, Jesus created a new commandment in direct violation of biblical injunctions, later stated the commandment which he created was not really new after all, and then relied on comments found in Lev. 19:18, which are not even among the commandments. Talk about a maze of discombobulation!

Fifth, Matt. 15:1–3 is not only interesting but revealing. The scribes and Pharisees of Jerusalem came to Jesus and said, "Why do your disciples transgress the tradition of the elders? For they do not wash their hands when they eat bread." Jesus responds, "Why do you also transgress the commandment of God by your tradition?" Jesus did not say their criticism was false or deny that his followers transgressed the rules of God. He merely said, "Well, you do it too." By saying, "Why do you *also*," Jesus is not denying the accusation but merely trying to put his accusers on the defensive. Jesus occasionally operated on the principle that the best defense is a good offense.

Sixth, Luke 6:1–4 says, "It came to pass on the second sabbath after the first, that he [Jesus] went through the corn fields; and his disciples plucked the ears of corn, and did eat, rubbing them in their hands. And certain of the Pharisees said unto them, Why do ye that which is not lawful to do on the sabbath days . . . ?" In this instance, Jesus and his disciples not only violated the sabbath by picking ears of corn thereon, but stole property as well. The ears of corn were not theirs to pluck, any more than the Gadarene swine of Luke 8:33 were theirs to destroy.

Seventh, in Luke 12:4 Jesus said, "Be not afraid of them that kill the body and after that have no more that they can do." While Jesus loved to talk about the importance of being bold and courageous, his behavior exposed an attitude that was noticeably lacking in both. Evidence for this is not particularly hard to find. Matt. 12:14–16 says, "Then the Pharisees went out, and held a council against him, how they might destroy him. But when Jesus knew it, he withdrew himself from thence: and great multitudes followed him. . . . And he charged them that they should not make him known." In other words, Jesus wanted his whereabouts kept secret. John 7:1 says, "After these things Jesus walked in Galilee: for he would not walk in Jewry, because the Jews sought to kill him." John 11:53–54 says, "Then from that day forth they took counsel together for to put him to death, Jesus therefore walked no more openly among the Jews; but went thence unto a country near to the wilderness." And John 8:59 says, "Then took they up stones to cast at him: but Jesus hid himself." You don't hide from what you don't fear. One could also consult John 10:39 and 6:15, Matt. 10:23, and Mark 1:45 to see that Jesus in many instances was little more than a scared rabbit, who often felt that discretion was the better part of valor. Courage and bravery were noticeably lacking.

Eighth, in Luke 8:43–45 a woman came up behind Jesus and touched the border of his garment and he said, "Who touched me?" The obvious question that arises in this instance is that if Jesus is God, then why doesn't he know the answer to any question before the query is posed? If Jesus is God, as Christians claim, then he must be aware of all and had to have been practicing deception. How could he not have known who was touching him?

Ninth, in Matt. 5:22 Jesus condemned being angry by saying, "I say to you, that every one who is angry with his brother shall be liable to judgment" (RSV). But in Mark 3:5 Jesus exhibited the very anger that he decried in others: "He looked around at them with anger, grieved at their hardness of heart." Jesus failed to practice what he preached.

Tenth, in Matt. 19:21, Mark 10:21, and Luke 3:11, 11:41, 12:33, 14:33, and 18:22 Jesus told his followers to dispose of all their possessions; yet, he himself owned a house, according to Mark 2:15, which says, "And it came to pass, that, as Jesus sat at meat in his house." Here we have another example of Do as I say, not as I do. Jesus not only owned a house but was bold enough to say in Matt. 8:20, "The foxes have holes, and birds of the air have nests; but the Son of man has nowhere to lay his head" (RSV). What prevarication! Some apologists have tried to allege the home referred to in Mark 2:15 is owned by Levi, but one need only read the comment in context to see that this defense won't stand the light of scrutiny.

Eleventh, according to Matt. 27:46 Jesus said on the cross, "My God, my God, why hast thou forsaken me?" Jesus is supposed to be the savior of humanity, but he can't even save himself. Those aren't the words of a man who is voluntarily dying for the sins of humanity or offering himself willingly as a sacrifice for mankind. Those are the words of a man who can think of a hundred places he'd rather be and most assuredly does not have the situation under control. It should also be noted that if Jesus died willingly, then Jews should not be condemned for having helped him complete his task.

Twelfth, John 18:37 says, "Pilate therefore said unto him, Art thou a King then? Jesus answered, Thou sayest that I am a King. To this end was I born." Apparently, Jesus doesn't know the difference between a question and a statement. Pilate asked a question; he didn't make an accusation. An overly defensive attitude on the part of Jesus is not only quite pronounced in several instances but unjustified.

Thirteenth, in Luke 22:31–33 we are given an excellent example of why prayer is all but worthless. Jesus said, "Simon, Simon, behold, Satan demanded to have you, that he might sift you like wheat, but I have prayed for you that your faith may not fail; and when you have turned again, strengthen your brethren. And he [Simon, otherwise known as Peter] said to him, Lord, I am ready to go with you to prison and to death." Jesus prayed that Peter would not desert him; but one need only read Matt. 14:31, 16:23, and 26:69–70 to see that his prayers were to no avail. Peter denied him after the trial. How can prayers be of value, when even the supplications of God, himself, are of no use? Jesus asked but never received. He prayed for Peter's faith to endure; yet, Peter denied him when the chips were down. The efficacy of prayer is one of those elusive hopes that is held out in a kind of now-you-see-it-now-you-don't fashion.

In Matt. 21:22 Jesus seems to answer all our problems by saying, "And all things, whatsoever ye shall ask in prayer, believing, ye shall receive." John 14:14 holds out the same ephemeral promise by saying, "If ye ask anything in my name, I will do it." But these promises are dashed by much more realistic comments found in Lam. 3:44 and Isa. 1:15. They say, respectively, "Thou [God] hast covered thyself with a cloud, that our prayer should not pass through," and "When ye spread forth your hands, I [God] will hide mine eyes from you: yea, when ye make many prayers, I will not hear." Those who think their prayers are going to be answered on a routine basis have discovered, like millions of Christians, that that is little more than a pipe dream. Millions of believers have prayed to Jesus millions of times only to be met by disappointment and failure. His promise of the universal efficacy of prayer has proven as miserable a sham as his promise of all power to those with faith.

Fourteenth, John 20:17 records Jesus as having said to Mary Magdalene when she met him after the Crucifixion, "Touch me not; for I have not yet ascended to my Father." What a pathetic scene! Mary Magdalene was one of the true disciples of Jesus. In the darkness of the Crucifixion she lingered near and was one of the first to arrive at the sepulcher. Defeat, disaster, disgrace could not conquer her love. And yet, according to this account, the risen Christ told her, "Touch me not." Is that any way to reward the infinite devotion of a loyal follower?

Fifteenth, Jesus told people in Matt. 19:19 to love their neighbors as themselves. Yet Jesus told his mother in John 2:4, "Woman, what have I to do with thee?" Imagine someone talking to his own mother in such a disrespectful manner and addressing her by such an impersonal noun as "woman." Talk about an insolent offspring!

Sixteenth, in Matt. 15:4 Jesus told people to honor their fathers and mothers. Yet in Luke 14:26 he said, "If any man come to me, and hate not his father, and mother, and wife, and children, and brethren, and sisters, yea and his own life also, he cannot be my disciple." How is that for inconsistency! Luke 2:48–49 and Matt. 12:46–50 provide additional instances in which Jesus was rude to his mother. He required traits from others which he failed to exhibit himself. Imagine! The alleged foremost advocate of family values actually told people to hate their parents.

Seventeenth, In Matt. 5:39 Jesus said, "Resist not evil; but whosoever shall smite thee on thy right cheek, turn to him the other also." Yet in Matt. 21:12–13 Jesus went into the temple of God, cast out all them that bought and sold in the temple, and overthrew the tables of the moneychangers. And John 18:22–23 says, "When he [Jesus] had spoken, one of the officers which stood by struck Jesus with the palm of his hand, saying, Answerest thou the high priest so? Jesus answered him, If I have spoken evil, bear witness of the evil: but if well, why smitest thou me?" Jesus was struck during his trial because he engaged in verbal repartee with his prosecutors. In Matt. 10:32–33 he also failed to turn the other cheek and practice forgiveness by saying, "Whoever denies Me before men, him will I also deny before My Father who is in heaven." That more closely resembles carrying a grudge than exercising forgiveness. So, clearly Jesus resisted evil.

Eighteenth, in Matt. 15:28 Jesus told a woman with a sick child who believed in him: "O woman, great is thy faith: be it unto thee even as thou wilt. And her daughter was made whole from that very hour." Although superficially a magnanimous act, Jesus only cured the child as a reward for the mother's faith, not out of a humane concern for the child's welfare. Matt. 18:23 verse shows that Jesus did not respond to her pleas initially, but only later, after she had begged.

Deceptive Statements

Having covered many of Jesus' *deeds,* ranging from questionable to deplorable, we can now concentrate on his large number of *verbal* pronouncements, ranging from doubtful to utterly false.

Nineteenth, one of the most ridiculous comments by Jesus is found in Mark 8:34, where he told some people, "Whosoever will come after me, let him deny himself, and take up his cross, and follow me." The key question that should come to the mind of any astute analyst following a comment of this nature is: What cross? There was no cross to take up. Jesus had not yet died on the cross when that comment was uttered. The people to whom he was speaking would have had no idea what he was talking about unless they knew the future. How can you take up something that is yet to exist? This kind of comment can easily lead to the suspicion that the author of this verse wrote it while the legend of Jesus was being formulated in a later period. While trying to put words into the mouth of Jesus, this author failed to realize that he had mistakenly created a comment that could only have been uttered after the event in question had occurred. One can't help but think of the famous proverb: what tangled web we weave when first we practice to deceive.

Twentieth, in John 3:13 Jesus said, "And no man hath ascended up to heaven, but he that came down from heaven, even the Son of man which is in heaven."

One need only read 2 Kings 2:11, which says, "Elijah went up by a whirlwind into heaven," to conclude that Jesus didn't read the Old Testament very closely. Elijah went up to heaven long before Jesus appeared on the scene. In fact, according to Heb. 11:5 and Gen. 5:24, Enoch duplicated the antics of Elijah and also appears to have beaten Jesus to the pearly gates.

Our *twenty-first* example provides one of the more blatant instances in which Jesus exposed his true character. In Matt. 26:18 he told his followers, "Go into the city to such a man, and say unto him, The Master saith, My time is at hand; I will keep the passover at thy house with my disciples." Talk about rudeness, bad manners, and a callous disregard for the feelings of others! You don't just invite yourself into someone's home. First you receive an invitation. If Jesus can't display anything else, he should at least have felt an obligation to be civil.

Twenty-second, in Mark 9:25–26 Jesus said, "Thou dumb and deaf spirit, I charge thee, come out of him, and enter no more into him. And the spirit cried, and rent him sore, and came out of him." In this case, events clearly show that Jesus erred in two major respects: (a) The spirit could not have been deaf in light of the fact that it heard him and came out. If the spirit were really deaf, as Jesus alleged, then why did it accede to his commands? And (b) the spirit could not have been dumb because it cried out. Mute beings make no noises.

Twenty-third, in Mark 8:35 Jesus said, "For whosoever will save his life shall lose it: but whosoever shall lose his life for my sake and the gospel's, the same shall save it." What gospel? How on earth could Jesus have made this statement, when there was no gospel during his lifetime? The gospel did not come onto the scene until years after the Crucifixion. A comment of this nature exposes either an historical falsehood or a subsequent forgery.

Twenty-fourth, in Rev. 22:16 Jesus is quoted as having said, "I am the root and the offspring of David, and the bright and morning star." How could this statement have any validity in light of the virgin birth? The genealogies in Matt. 1 and Luke 3 trace the ancestry of Jesus back to David through Joseph. But Joseph was not Jesus' physical father. Therefore, as was shown in an earlier chapter, there can be no physical connection between Jesus and David, and without that union Jesus could not be the root and offspring of David.

Twenty-fifth, in John 7:38 Jesus said, "He that believeth on me, as the Scripture hath said, out of his belly shall flow rivers of living water." The problem with this comment lies in the fact that there is no such statement in the Old Testament. Where did "Scripture," i.e., the Old Testament, say this? Although biblicists have tried to rely on Isa. 44:3, Isa. 55:1, Ezek. 47:1, and several other verses for support here, their responses won't stand the strain. One need only read these verses to see that they are inapplicable.

Twenty-sixth, one of the more glaring contradictory aspects of Jesus' teachings arises from his portrayal of his mission. In Matt. 15:24 he says, "I am not sent but unto the lost sheep of the house of Israel." He even told his followers in

Matt. 10:5–6, "Go not into the way of the Gentiles, and into any city of the Samaritans enter ye not. But go rather to the lost sheep of the house of Israel." And in John 4:22 Jesus says, "Salvation is of the Jews." Jesus told his followers to go to the Jews alone, because only Jews were to be saved and only Jews merited attention.

But in the Great Commission at the end of Matthew, Jesus states, "Go ye therefore, and teach all nations, baptizing them in the name of the Father, and of the Son, and of the Holy Ghost." In Mark 16:15 Jesus stated that his followers were to go into all the world and preach the gospel to every creature. Comparable comments are found in Mark 13:10 and Luke 24:47. So obviously Jesus never gave a consistent message to his followers about even to whom they should direct their efforts, let alone what the message should be.

Also worthy of note is that although Jesus told his followers to go to the Jews alone, several biblical verses show that he personally did the opposite. Luke 17:11 says, ."And it came to pass, as he went to Jerusalem, that he passed through the midst of Samaria and Galilee," and John 4:40 says, "So when the Samaritans were come unto him, they besought him that he would tarry with them: and he abode there two days." John 4:3–5 shows that Jesus occasionally told these followers to do one thing while performing the opposite himself.

Twenty-seventh, another major problem with Jesus' mission is also evident to anyone with a reasonably critical eye. In Matt. 10:34 he clearly stated, "Think not that I am come to send peace on earth. I came not to send peace, but a sword." This attitude is further demonstrated by Jesus' comment to his followers in Luke 12:51, "Suppose ye that I am come to give peace on earth? I tell you, Nay, but rather division." In fact, in Luke 22:36 Jesus went so far as to tell his followers that those who have no sword should sell their garments and buy one. If that doesn't sound like a prescription for violence and a negation of the image of Jesus as peacemaker, what does? For Christians to portray Jesus as the quintessential paragon of pacifism is to turn reality on its head. Christians even go so far as to allege that Jesus is the Prince of Peace referred to in Isa. 9:6.

On the other hand, Jesus occasionally did make comments like, "Put up again thy sword into his place: for all they that take the sword shall perish with the sword," and "Blessed are the peacemakers: for they shall be called the children of God," which can be found in Matt. 26:52 and 5:9, respectively. Surely here Jesus is the prince of inconsistency!

The question becomes one of deciding which side of our two-faced friend is the real Jesus and how should his followers behave. Should they take up the sword and fight for the cause, or should they avoid violence at all costs, because those who live by the sword shall die by the sword? Is it any wonder that Christians throughout the world are often at opposite ends of the spectrum when crucial issues of this kind come to the fore? People often think that hundreds of denominations exist throughout the planet because millions of people are reading poorly, interpreting erroneously, or thinking chaotically with respect to Scripture. No, the problem resides not with people but with the inconsistent Book. People aren't the problem, Scripture is. With a book sending so many garbled and mixed messages, is it any wonder that there are over 1,500 separate Christian denominations? You couldn't reliably determine what is to be thought or done, even if you took Scripture seriously and really wanted to be an obedient follower of Jesus.

Twenty-eighth, Jesus told his disciples that following him would be a relatively easy affair. In Matt. 11:29–30, for example, he said, "Take my yoke upon you, and learn of me; . . . and ye shall find rest unto your souls. For my yoke is easy, and my burden is light." Yet several other verses clearly show that his followers could expect to receive treatment that is by no means easy or light. In. Matt. 10:17–18, for example, Jesus told Christians, "Beware of men: for they will deliver you up to the councils, and they will scourge you in their synagogues; And ye shall be brought before governors and kings for my sake, for a testimony against them and the Gentiles." In Matt. 10:22–23 and Luke 21:17 Jesus told them they could expect to be hated for his sake, and in John 16:33 Jesus said, "In the world ye shall have tribulation; but be of good cheer." Comments of the latter variety don't lead one to believe that Christians can expect easy burdens. Quite the contrary, Jesus promised his followers that which many of his current supporters feel does not exist.

Twenty-ninth, with reference to the spreading of Christian teachings, Jesus made one of his most contemptible statements in Mark 7:27 when he said, "Let the children first be filled: for it is not meet to take the children's bread, and to cast it unto the dogs." When read in context one can see that Jesus is putting the welfare of Jews, whom he affectionately refers to as children, above that of Gentiles, whom he is referring to as dogs. We are hearing this from an historical figure whom we are to believe never plays favorites and shuns classism.

Thirtieth, in Matt. 9:13 Jesus appeared to have made a rather profound statement when he said, "I am not come to call the righteous, but sinners to repentance." The problem with this comment lies in the fact that it clashes with Mark 10:18, which says, "Jesus said unto him, Why callest thou me good? there is none good but one, that is, God." If there are none good but God, then there are none righteous but God. If there are none righteous but God, then there are no righteous to call. If there are no righteous to call, then Jesus couldn't have called the righteous, even if he had wanted to. So what does the statement tell us? Nothing. Although superficially profound, realistically, the statement is inane.

Thirty-first, one of the most obvious cases of superficial profundity by our alleged savior is found in Mark 6:10, in which Jesus says, "Wheresoever ye enter into a house, there abide till ye depart thence" (ASV). Now let's don't be ridiculous. What else could you do except remain in a house until you depart from it? There's a third option?

Thirty-second, a simple and clear-cut clash of verses is exposed when we compare John 5:31, in which Jesus says, "If I bear witness of myself, my witness is not true" with John 8:14, in which Jesus says, "Though I bear record of myself, yet my record is true." The obvious question is that if Jesus bears witness of himself, is his witness to be trusted or not? Moreover, how could he possibly be God and state something that is false? How could his witness ever be anything but true?

Thirty-third, in Matt. 5:16 Jesus clearly reveal the importance he attached to letting everyone be aware of one's good deeds by saying, "Let your light shine before men, that they may see your good works." But one chapter later, in Matt. 6:1, Jesus says, "Take heed that ye do not your alms before men, to be seen of them: otherwise, ye have no reward of your Father which is in heaven." So on the one hand you are told to make your good deeds known to all, while on the other you are told to keep them under your hat, if you want to attain heaven. In essence, we are faced with another example of conflicting testimony that could generate schizophrenia!

Thirty-fourth, one of the more glaring conflicts in the teachings of Jesus comes to light when we compare Luke 16:9, which says, "Make to yourselves friends of the mammon of unrighteousness," with Luke 16:13, which says, "You cannot serve God and mammon." Apologists have tried to resolve this inconsistency for centuries and one man's theory is as vacuous as another. If you cannot serve both God and mammon, if you must choose between the two, then it would be foolish to become mammon's friend, as the Bible requires, because that would entail the exclusion of God.

Thirty-fifth, another one of the statements by Jesus that flies in the face of numerous biblical verses is found in Matt. 19:26, which says, "With men this is impossible; but with God all things are possible." If something is impossible for men to do, then why on earth would Jesus have said in Mark 9:23 that, "All things are possible to him that believeth?" Why did he say in John 14:14, "If ye shall ask any thing in my name, I will do it?" And why did he say in Matt. 17:20, "If ye have faith as a grain of mustard seed, ye shall say to this mountain, Remove hence to yonder place; and it shall remove; and nothing shall be impossible unto you?" Notice that the latter verse says nothing, *nothing,* shall be impossible. As a practical matter, the inaccuracy of the latter statement is shown in the fact that nobody, with or without faith, has ever successfully ordered a mountain to move.

The mustard seed verse, in which Jesus says nothing is impossible to those with faith, also clashes with Mark 9:29, which says, "This kind can come forth by nothing, but by prayer and fasting." According to the former only belief is needed to do anything. Now it requires prayer and fasting.

Thirty-sixth, one of Jesus' most repulsive analogies comes to light when Matt. 12:12, in which Jesus says, "How much then is a man better than a sheep?" is compared with other verses of opposite import. Although Jesus allegedly looked upon man as of great importance, verses such as John 10:11, 10:15, 10:26, and 10:27 clearly show that he viewed his followers as sheep or lambs and himself as their shepherd. John 10:14 says, "I am the good shepherd, and know my sheep," and John 10:15 says, "I lay down my life for the sheep." Can you imagine belonging to a movement in which the founder and central figure looks upon you and your compatriots as sheep! How demeaning! How disgusting!

Thirty-seventh, several verses show that Jesus often gave insolent replies, evaded questions, or failed to respond. Relevant verses in this regard are Matt. 27:11 ("The governor asked him, saying, Art thou the King of the Jews? And Jesus said unto him, Thou sayest"), John 18:34 ("Sayest thou this thing of thyself, or did others tell it thee of me?"); John 18:37 ("Pilate therefore said unto him, Are you a king then? Jesus answered, you say rightly that I am a king") (NKJV); and John 19:9 ("And saith unto Jesus, Whence art thou? But Jesus gave him no answer"). One need only read dialogues of this nature to see that Jesus occasionally got what he deserved. If you are going to give insolent answers, then you can expect an appropriate response. Jesus could just as well have answered yes or no and avoided being evasive or rude. Why didn't he show some backbone and openly admit he claimed to be the messiah?

Thirty-eighth, another one of the wholly inconsistent comments by Jesus comes to the fore when we compare John 3:35 and 13:3 and Matt. 28:18, which say, "Jesus came and spoke unto them, saying, All power is given unto me in heaven and in earth" with Matt. 20:23, in which Jesus says, "To sit on my right hand, and on my left, is not mine to give." On the one hand he has all power, while on the other he doesn't even have enough power to tell people where to sit. Jesus can move mountains, but he can't tell people where to repose. How silly! How childish! Situations like this can't help but cause one to wish Christians would follow the advice found in 1 Cor. 13:11 of their own book which says, "When I was a child, I talked like a child, I thought like a child, I reasoned like a child. When I became a man, I put childish ways behind me" (NIV). Although mature chronologically, many Christians have not managed to make the transition intellectually.

Thirty-ninth, Jesus is supposed to be the moral guide for all behavior, but he can't even give mankind consistent rules with respect to the treatment of adultery and divorce. Mark 10:11 says, "Whosoever shall put away his wife and marry another, committeth adultery against her." Note well that if you get rid of your wife for any reason and marry another, you have committed adultery, according to Jesus. But in Matt. 19:9 Jesus says, "Whosoever shall put away his wife, except it be for fornication, and shall marry another, committeth adultery." In other words, Jesus' pronouncement in Matthew allows divorce in cases of fornication, that is, presumably, in cases where the wife has commited adultery, while that in Mark does not.

On page 200 in *The Jew and the Christian Missionary* Gerald Sigal summarized this matter quite well:

Contrary to Matthew's record, which allows only adultery as a reason for divorce, Jesus' words, as recorded by Mark and Luke, do not permit divorce under any circumstances. . . . Paul supports the extremely rigid, legalistic declaration as found in Mark and Luke. He also directly attributes to Jesus this legislation, whose restriction goes beyond the law of divorce as stated in the Law of Moses.

So, again, we ask. Will the real Jesus please stand up and provide the proper teaching for all Christians?

Fortieth, one of the most disappointing promises ever made by Jesus is found in Matt. 28:20, where he says, "I am with you always, even unto the end of the world." Careful observers have no trouble noting that this is nullified by his prior comment in Matt. 26:11, which says, "Ye have the poor always with you; but me ye have not always." Jesus further eliminated his perpetual presence by saying in John 7:34, "You shall seek me, and shall not find me: and where I am, thither ye cannot come." How's that for fulfilling your commitments and standing by your man!

Forty-first, another particularly bothersome comment by Jesus is found in Mark 13:32, where he says, "But of that day and that hour knoweth no man, no, not the angels which are in heaven, neither the Son"; yet, in John 10:30 Jesus has the temerity to say that he and the Father are one. How could he be at one with the Father, i.e., God, when he admits he does not know all? God, by definition, is omniscient. If Jesus does not know something, then he cannot be God.

Forty-second, in Luke 6:37 Jesus said, "Judge not, and ye shall not be judged: condemn not, and ye shall not be condemned," but he later stated in John 7:24 that we were to "judge not according to appearance, but judge righteous judgment." Christians have bounced this one back and forth for centuries. Are we to judge or aren't we?

On page 57 in *Answers to Questions About the Bible* apologist Robert Mounce attempts to resolve this contradiction by stating, "The judging which Jesus speaks against is the habit of censorious and carping criticism." An explanation of this kind is typical of apologetic rationalizations. There is absolutely nothing in Luke 6:37 that would justify such an interpretation. Later Mounce says, "In Matt. 7:1 two things are quite clear: (1) the admonition is directed against that kind of caustic and debilitating criticism which depresses and condemns and (2) the form of the prohibition indicates a continuing habit which must be brought to a halt."

What kind of nonsense is this? There is nothing whatever in the verse that would substantiate a claim of this kind. Even Jesus calls people names and his comments would certainly depress any normal person and make them feel like objects of condemnation. As a practical matter, this command is completely unrealistic, since its implementation would entail the abolishment of all judicial systems. Moreover, we all make hundreds of judgments with respect to others every day of our lives and, in fact, many are not only unavoidable but necessary. Existence would be impossible without them.

Forty-third, in John 8:15 ("I judge no man") Jesus ruled out any possibility of being the judge of mankind, and in John 12:47 he said, "I came not to judge the world, but to save the world." However, according to John 5:22 ("For the Father judgeth no man, but hath committed all judgment unto the Son") and John 9:39 ("For judgment I am come into this world") Jesus *is* to be the supreme arbiter. So which is it? Is Jesus to judge or isn't he? John 5:27, 5:30, and 8:16 also show that when Jesus said he came to judge no man, he couldn't have been more misleading if he had tried.

Forty-fourth, in John 9:5 Jesus said, "As long as I am in the world, I am the light of the world." But while in the world, according to Matt. 5:14, Jesus said to his followers, "Ye are the light of the world." Who, then, is the light of the world? Jesus or his followers?

Forty-fifth, one of the most well-known scientific blunders by Jesus is found in Matt. 13:31–32, where he says, "The kingdom of heaven is like a grain of mustard seed, which a man took, and sowed in his field: Which indeed is the least of all seeds: but when it is grown, it is the greatest among herbs, and becometh a tree, so that the birds of the air come and lodge in the branches thereof." Jesus would do well to shun the science of botany and return to the more nebulous arena of theology for three reasons: (a) A mustard seed is not the least of all seeds, (b) when grown, it is not the greatest among herbs, and (c) a mustard seed does not give rise to a tree.

The importance of this particular problem was highlighted by the apologist Charles Ryrie on page 94 of his book *Inerrancy,* in which he said,

> In His parable of the mustard seed the Lord said that the mustard seed was the smallest of all the seeds. Is that plainly an erroneous statement, since botanically the mustard seed is not the smallest? Before jumping to that conclusion, remember that it was stated by Jesus Christ. If *He* spoke a lie, how could He have been sinless? This is not simply a small factual discrepancy; if the statement is not true, then it proves something about the one who made it, and that becomes a serious doctrinal matter. You cannot separate this history from its doctrinal ramification.

Thank goodness at least one apologist is able to see the true import of this dilemma and doesn't try to pawn it off as nitpicking.

Probably the most famous scientific error by Jesus is found in Matt. 12:40, in which he says, "For as Jonas was three days in the whale's belly." Apparently Jesus hadn't read the Old Testament very closely, or he would have noticed that Jonah 1:17 says, "Now the lord had prepared a great fish to swallow up Jonah. And Jonah was in the belly of the fish three days and three nights." Anyone with even a minimum of biological knowledge knows that a whale is not a fish and a fish is not a whale.

Another scientific blunder is found in John 12:24, where Jesus says, "I say unto you, Except a corn of wheat fall into the ground and die, it abideth alone: but if it die, it bringeth forth much fruit." How could something that has died bring forth anything, much less fruit?

Forty-sixth, one of the most irritating themes throughout the New Testament is the reccurring absence of simple logic. In Mark 9:50 Jesus says, "Salt is good: but if salt have lost his saltness, wherewith will ye season it?" How could salt lose its saltness and still be salt?

This shortcoming is also evident in Matt. 13:12, in which Jesus says, "For whosoever hath, to him shall be given, and he shall have more abundance: but whosoever hath not, from him shall be taken away even that he hath." It doesn't take a great deal of mental astuteness to realize that you can't take something from someone who has nothing. The appropriate Latin phrase is "Ex nihilo nihil fit." From nothing, nothing can come.

One of the most confusing, if not illogical, comments by Jesus is found in John 3:13, where he says, "No man hath ascended up to heaven, but he that came down from heaven, even the Son of man which is in heaven." If this does not generate bewilderment, nothing will. Jesus is the Son of man, and if he is in heaven, then how could he be down here on earth speaking?

A similar problem is created by the sequence of events in Matt. 26:26, which says, "As they were eating, Jesus took bread, and blessed it, and broke it, and gave it to the disciples, and said, Take, eat; this is my body." If the bread Jesus handed them is his body, then there are two bodies of Jesus—the one being handed and the one doing the handing. For many Christians this presents a problem of real significance, because they do not look upon the bread and wine as merely symbolic representations of Jesus. Upon consecration, the bread and wine are turned into Jesus himself, Jesus in the flesh. On page 370 in *Fundamentals of Catholic Dogma* Ludwig Ott defines the Eucharist as "that Sacrament, in which Christ, under the forms of bread and wine, is truly present, with His Body and Blood, in order to offer Himself." On page 373 he states, "The Body and Blood of Jesus Christ are truly, really and substantially present in the Eucharist." On page 384 he reaffirms his stance by saying, "The Body and the Blood of Christ together with His Soul and His Divinity and therefore the Whole Christ are truly present in the Eucharist." And finally, he states on the same page, "The Whole Christ is present with the flesh and blood of Christ."

So for these Christians the problem becomes one of determining how Christ can hand Christ to others, if there is only one Christ.

Forty-seventh, two of the most hypocritical comments by Jesus are found in John 8:50 ("I seek not mine own glory") and Matt. 11:29 ("I am meek and lowly in heart"). They emanated from the same Jesus who said in John 12:23,

"The hour hath come that the Son of man should be glorified." How's that for humility overlaid by mendacity!

Forty-eighth, another one of those false promises by Jesus is found in Matt. 7:7–8, where he says, "Ask, and it shall be given you; seek, and ye shall find; knock, and it shall be opened unto you: For every one that asketh receiveth; and he that seeketh findeth; and to him that knocketh it shall be opened." Yet in John 7:34 ("Ye shall seek me, and shall not find me: and where I am, thither you cannot come") our alleged savior admits that he personally is not available.

In fact, on numerous occasions we are told that even God himself cannot be reached by those seeking, asking, and knocking. In Jer. 11:11 God says, "And though they shall cry unto me, I will not hearken unto them," and in Ezek. 8:18 he says, "Neither will I have pity: and though they cry in mine ears with a loud voice, yet will I not hear them." Isn't it nice for Christians to have someone they can depend on in times of need! It goes without saying that the number of people who have asked, seeked, and knocked in vain approaches the number of leaves on trees.

Forty-ninth, Mark 10:29–30 contains a teaching by Jesus that is not only inaccurate but immoral. Jesus states, "There is no man that hath left house, brethren, or sisters, or father, or mother, or wife, or children, or lands, for my sake, and the gospel's, But he shall receive an hundredfold now in this time, houses, and brethren, and sisters, and mothers, and children, and lands, with persecutions; and in the world to come eternal life." Jesus is promising his followers that the reward for giving up their wealth and following him is even greater wealth. In essence, Jesus is teaching people to obey in order to obtain personal gain, not out of commitment to proper conduct and moral rectitude. Self-aggrandizement is hardly a basis for morality.

Incidentally, we can all understand the possibility of someone receiving a multitude of brothers, sisters, children, and homes, but how do you obtain a multitude of mothers?

Fiftieth, one of the more baffling pronouncements by Jesus is found in Luke 15:7 ("I say unto you that joy shall be in heaven over one sinner that repenteth, more than over ninety and nine just persons, which need no repentance"). How could there be ninety-nine just persons in need of no repentance, when the Bible repeatedly says we are all sinners in need of repentance? In Luke 13:3 and 13:5 Jesus says, for example, "I tell you, Nay, but, ye repent, ye shall all likewise perish."

Fifty-first, one of the more glaring examples of Jesus being unable to provide consistent stories pertains to the question of signs. In Mark 8:11–12 the Pharisees came forth and began to question Jesus, seeking a sign from heaven, even tempting him. Jesus says, "Why doeth this generation seek after a sign? verily I say unto you, There shall no sign be given unto this generation." Notice Jesus says *no* sign, period. But in Matt. 16:4 Jesus says, "A wicked and adulterous generation seeketh a sign; and there shall be given no sign unto it but the sign of the prophet Jonas." First, we are told that *no* sign would be given to that generation; now we are told that there *will be* a sign after all—the sign of the prophet Jonah. So, will there be a sign or won't there? John 20:30 says, "Many other signs truly did Jesus in the presence of his disciples, which are not written in this book," and Acts 2:22 says, "Ye men of Israel, hear these words; Jesus of Nazareth, a man approved of God among you by miracles and wonders and *signs*, which God did by him in the midst of you." So what happened to the promise? Jesus told his generation that no signs would be forthcoming, but later performed the very deeds he had obviated.

Fifty-second, one of the most interesting clashes in the biblical testimony of Jesus Christ concerns his willingness to die on the cross for the sins of mankind. In John 12:27 we hear the standard fare foisted upon all believing Christians that Jesus went to his death willingly. Jesus said, "Now is my soul troubled, What shall I say? Father, save me from this hour: but for this cause I have come to this hour." But that directly clashes with Matt. 27:46, in which Jesus says while hanging on the cross, "My God, my God, why hast thou forsaken me?" Those words project the image of someone who is *un*willing to die for anything.

Fifty-third, one of the more deceptive events in the career of Jesus can be seen when we compare Matt. 9:18 with Matt. 9:24–25. The former says, "While he [Jesus] spake these things unto them, behold there came a certain ruler . . . saying, My daughter is even now dead: but come and lay your thy hand upon her, and she shall live." But six verses later Jesus says to the ruler, "Give place: for the maid is not dead, but sleepeth. And they laughed him to scorn. But when the people were put forth, he went in, and took her by the hand, and the maid arose." The problem with this series of events is that if the maid was really dead, then Jesus told a lie when he said she was only sleeping. If she was not dead, then he did no miracle whatever and deceived those who thought he did.

Fifty-fourth, in Matt. 19:17 Jesus made one of those statements that apologists can try forever to justify, but their efforts are doomed from the beginning. No matter how hard the apologists may try, they won't be able to avoid the full import of Jesus' comment in Mark 10:18 ("Why callest thou me good? there is none good but one, that is, God"). If that isn't a strong statement of committal, nothing is. In effect, Jesus not only denied being perfect, an alleged trait of his that other verses and his followers never tire of extolling, but ruled out any possibility of being God incarnate. Let's face it: if you aren't good, then you aren't perfect. And if you aren't perfect, you aren't God.

Fifty-fifth, one of the more interesting conflicts between Jesus and the Old Testament arises from his comment in Matt. 24:35, "Heaven and earth shall pass away, but my words shall not pass away." Apparently Jesus is not aware of the fact that the Old Testament distinctly said in Eccle. 1:4, "One generation passeth away, and another generation cometh: but the earth abideth forever." Jesus says the earth shall pass away, but Ecclesiastes says it will remain forever. So who is the more accurate prognosticator, Jesus or the author of Ecclesiastes?

Fifty-sixth, another instance in which the knowledge of the Old Testament exhibited by Jesus is less than exemplary comes to light in John 20:9 ("For as yet they knew not the Scripture that he must rise again from the dead"). Since, the "he" to whom this verse refers is allegedly Jesus, the problems that emerge are: (a) Where does the Old Testament say that Jesus must rise from the dead? and (b) the word "again" means that he rose from the dead earlier as well— that he would rise at least twice. Since Jesus allegedly rose from the dead only once, he couldn't be the person under discussion.

Fifty-seventh, while on the topic of Jesus and the OT, his comment in Matt. 4:10 should not be allowed to pass unnoticed either. Jesus said, "Get thee hence, Satan: for it is written, Thou shalt worship the Lord thy God, and him only shalt thou serve." Where can this be found in Scripture? The only verse of real relevance is Deut. 6:13, which says, "Thou shalt fear the Lord thy God, and serve him, and shalt swear by his name." One need only compare the two verses to see that nowhere does Deut. 6:13 say that we should serve God only. The word "only" was a gratuitous insertion by Jesus. Deuteronomy says serve God; it doesn't say serve God only.

Fifty-eighth, in John 5:37 Jesus says, "The Father himself, which hath sent me, hath borne witness of me. Ye have neither heard his voice at any time, nor seen his shape." The latter observation flies in the face of numerous biblical verses that clearly state that people heard God speak on many occasions. Gen. 3:8–10, Ex. 20:22, and Deut. 4:12 are only a few of the verses that could be cited for confirmation. Many comments by Jesus were nothing short of outlandish and display an abysmal ignorance of even the most elementary biblical information. John 5:37 is a prime example.

Fifty-ninth, and lastly, one of the most easily disproven statements by Jesus is found in Mark 16:17–18, where he says, "These signs shall follow them that believe; In my name shall they cast out devils; they shall speak with new tongues; They shall take up serpents; and if they drink any deadly thing, it shall not hurt them." Few Christians are willing to test the validity of these comments by drinking poisons and playing with deadly snakes, although some have paid a price for trying. Because these verses provide one of the few instances in which the validity of the Bible itself can be directly and immediately tested, some of the more sophisticated Christians are submitting historical, textual, and theological arguments for having them expunged from the Bible.

Conclusion

That concludes our voluminous disclosure of the most important figure in biblical history. Although fifty-nine examples were highlighted, nearly two hundred examples of Jesus' failings are available in issues 2, 3, 24, 25, 27, and 28 of *Biblical Errancy*. Anyone who has examined the Bible with even a modicum of intellectual integrity must be willing to admit that more than enough biblical evidence is available to prove beyond any reasonable doubt that the Jesus of biblical fame is certainly not qualified to be our model for morality or mankind's savior.

Before closing, we can't help but relate the following poignant observation by apologist Hal Lindsey addressed to all those who look upon Jesus, not as God, but as the greatest of all moral teachers whom mankind should follow. Quoting from *Mere Christianity* by C. S. Lewis, Lindsey says on pages 86 and 87 of his *The Liberation of Planet Earth*,

> I'm trying to prevent anyone saying the really foolish thing that people often say about Jesus, i.e., *"I'm ready to accept Jesus as a great moral teacher, but I don't accept His claim to be God."* That is the one thing we must not say. A man who was *merely* a man and said the sort of things Jesus said would not be a great moral teacher. He would be either a lunatic—on the level with the man who says he is a poached egg—or else he would be the Devil of Hell. You must make your choice. Either this man was, and is, the Son of God, or else a madman or something worse. You can shut Him up for a fool, you can spit at Him and kill Him as a demon, or you can fall at His feet and call Him Lord and God. But let us not come up with any patronizing nonsense about His being just a great human teacher. He has not left that option open to us. He did not intend to.

Well said! And judging from the material presented in this chapter, as well as the two previous chapters, only one conclusion is open to any objective observer. Jesus was then, and is now, a fraud to all and a savior for none, far closer to lunatic than Lord.

8

Jesus IV

Second Coming and Messianic Age, Messianic Prophecies

Chapter 5 discussed the history and background of Jesus Christ; chapter 6 addressed a wide range of topics having to do with his credentials; chapter 7 focused on his character and integrity. This chapter will analyze the degree to which the messianic prophecies are inapplicable to him. If there is any topic upon which Christian apologists love to rely for their defense of Christianity in general and Jesus in particular, it is the alleged accuracy of what are commonly referred to as the messianic prophecies. Christians constantly refer to the alleged applicability of numerous Old Testament prophecies to Jesus of Nazareth and contend that no one in all of history fulfills these prophecies to the degree that he does. The argument in this regard is well stated by Josh McDowell on page 161 in *Evidence for the Faith, Practical Apologetics*: "For only 48 of these prophecies to be fulfilled in any one individual using the modern science of probability, is one in every 1×10 to the 157th power. That means 157 zeros. . . . No wonder Jesus constantly appealed to prophecy to substantiate his claims."

On page 141 in *Evidence that Demands a Verdict* McDowell reiterated the same argument by saying,

> The apostles throughout the NT appealed to two areas of the life of Jesus of Nazareth to establish His Messiahship. One was the resurrection and the other was fulfilled messianic prophecy. The OT, written over a 1,000 year period, contains several hundred references to the coming Messiah. All of these were fulfilled in Jesus Christ, and they establish a solid confirmation of His credentials as the Messiah.

149

In essence, the argument is that Jesus must be the messiah because only Jesus fulfilled so many of the messianic prophecies.

Lost in the plethora of apologetic hosannahs to Jesus of Nazareth is one central fact; virtually nothing in the entire Old Testament can be applied clearly and unmistakably to Jesus. Nothing of real import in the entire Jewish Bible can be applied with definite precision to events in the life of Christianity's founder. Instead, followers of Jesus have twisted, distorted, and perverted any and all Old Testament verses that could even remotely be applied to him. Historical accuracy and messianic reliability have been of far less importance than establishing Jesus as the embodiment of mankind's savior. On page 37 in *The Real Messiah* Aryeh Kaplan summarized the situation in a manner that can only be described as exemplary by saying,

> The early Christians tried to justify their contention by finding hints of it in the Jewish Scriptures. They went over the entire Bible with a fine tooth comb, looking for any evidence however flimsy, to prove that Jesus was the Messiah, and that their entire logical structure was in accord with ancient Jewish teachings. In many cases, they were not above using verses out of context, changing texts, and even mistranslating them, in order to prove their point. One needs no further evidence than the fact that most modern Christian Bible scholars totally reject almost all the "proofs" of the early Christians. Indeed, some of the best refutations of these "proofs" may be found in contemporary Christian Bible commentaries.

On page 186 in *The Jew and the Christian Missionary* Gerald Sigal stated in the same vein, "The evangelists are endeavoring, time and again, to link their claim to passages in the Hebrew Bible in order to find support for their contention that Jesus is the Messiah and the fulfillment of what the prophets had to say about the Messiah. Yet details large and small abound which show that this is an impossibility."

Second Coming and Messianic Age

Besides twisting, perverting, and distorting Old Testament verses in such a manner as to apply them to Jesus, apologists devised a devious mechanism by which to account for the fact that Jesus obviously did not fulfill many of the most prominent prophecies. Those numerous predictions that he failed to complete during his sojourn on planet earth will, they allege, be fulfilled when he returns a second time. In other words, what Jesus didn't complete during his first appearance will be accomplished the second time around. For utter deception this ploy has no equal. Using that subterfuge, anyone could claim to be the messiah. All they need do is allege that whatever they did not accomplish while on earth this time would be carried out when they return at some indeterminate time in the future.

Anyone who has read the Old Testament with any degree of objectivity knows that there is only one messiah and that is all, and he is going to come once, and that is it. The Second Coming concept is nothing more than a Christian ruse to conceal some blatant shortcomings on the part of Jesus. According to Old Testament prophecies the messiah's arrival would usher in: the end of sin (Ezek. 36:25-27, 33, 37:23-24, Zeph. 3:13, 3:15, Job 3:17, Isa. 60:21, Jer. 50:20); the end of suffering (Isa. 65:19); peace and tranquillity (Isa. 2:4, 9:6, 11:6-9, 65:19, 25, Zech. 9:10, Micah 4:3, Hosea 2:18); one creed and one religion (Isa. 2:2, 14:1, 45:14, 22-24, 52:1, 60:2-6, 14-16, 66:23, Zech. 8:23, 14:9, Psalm 86:9, Mal. 1:11, Joel 3:17, Jer. 31:34); one kingdom and one king (Isa. 11:12, 43:5-6, 60:11-12, Dan. 2:44, 7:27, Ezek. 37:21-22, 39:28, Zech. 14:9); the resurrection of the dead (Isa. 26:19, Dan. 12:2, Deut. 32:39); the abolishment of idolatrous images and false prophets (Isa. 2:18, 42:17, Zeph. 2:11, Psalms 97:7); the gathering of the ten tribes under a Davidic king (Ezek. 37:21-22); the battle between God and Magog (Ezek. 38 and 39); the cleaving of the Mount of Olives (Zech. 14:4); the building of the future temple (Ezek. 40-46); the issuing of living water from the site of the temple (Ezek. 47:1-2); the renewal of the Covenant as sanctification for the Israelites (Ezek. 37:26-28); the going up of the remnant of the nations to Jerusalem to worship (Zech. 14:16); Jerusalem being safely inhabited (Zech. 14:11); the messiah being desired by all nations (Hag. 2:7); the wicked being slain (Isa. 11:4); and a messianic kingdom stretching from sea to sea (Zech. 9:10, Psalm 72:8, Dan. 7:14). Beyond doubt these and similar prophecies are yet to materialize.

On page 7 in *The Real M ssiah* A yeh Kaplan correctly stated, "Jesus could not have been the Messiah. The Prophets predicted a world of peace and love after the Messiah's coming, and this certainly does not exist today." On page 36 Kaplan says, "First of all, the Jews had a tradition, well supported in the teachings of the Prophets, that the Messiah would bring about major changes in the world. The 'spiritual kingdom' [of Jesus Christ] did not in any way fulfill these prophecies. The Jews were furthermore unconvinced by the answer of the 'second coming,' since it is not even hinted at in Biblical literature." On page 71 Kaplan correctly states, "All the prophecies that Jesus did not fulfill the first time are supposed to be taken care of the second time around. However, the Jewish Bible offers absolutely no evidence to support the Christian doctrine of a 'second coming.' . . . All the embarrassing prophecies that he did not fulfill are swept under the rug of a 'second Coming.' " And on page 55 Kaplan encapsulated the entire issue very well: "Nowhere does the Jewish Bible say that the Messiah would come once, be killed, and return again in a 'second coming.' The idea of a second coming is a pure rationalization of Jesus' failure to function in any way as a messiah, or to fulfill any of the prophecies of the Torah or the Prophets. The idea is purely a Christian invention, with no foundation in the Bible." How true! On page 58 in *The Jew and the Christian Missionary* Sigal notes, "Having fulfilled the Law and the Prophets, what is the need for the second advent? If he truly brought about all that was promised concerning the peaceful society the Messiah will bring, as stated in the Law and the Prophets (Isa. 2:1–4; Jer. 23:5–6; Ezek. 34:23–31; Amos 9:13–15), there should be no reason for a second advent."

Succinctly stated, the Second Coming has no basis in the Jewish Bible and numerous scholars have noted as much.

The concept is plagued by another problem as well. The New Testament enunciates many events that are to precede the Christ's arrival. On page 336 in *The Bible Has the Answer* apologists Morris and Clark ask: What are the signs that the return of Christ may be soon? Their response:

> It is not possible to predict the exact time of the second coming of Christ (Mark 13:32). On the other hand, Christ actually commanded us to recognize when His coming was near by saying, "When ye shall see all these things, know that it is near, even at the doors" (Matt. 24:33). A few of these things are . . . : A general decline in morality . . . , A widespread decline in religious faith . . . , A prevalence of a naturalistic evolutionary philosophy in science . . . , A rebellious attitude of most of the younger generation . . . , Conflict between the prosperous and the poor . . . , Rapid rise of anti-Christian leaders and philosophers . . . , Infiltration of false teachers and leaders into Christian churches . . . , Successive world wars, and widespread fear and confusion regarding the world's future.

This list is always trotted out by Christian propagandists at every opportunity. But, notice anything interesting about the events included therein? Except for the first, every sign mentioned has been applicable to every generation and every period in history. When have there not been wars and rumors of wars? When has there not been conflict between the poor and rich? When has there not been a growth in the naturalistic evolutionary philosophy? The entire history of man has been marked by an evolutionary trend away from religion and superstition and toward science and reason. And when has there not been widespread confusion regarding the world's future? As far as a decline in morality is concerned, it has never been very high from the beginning; so it is difficult to see how it could have declined from the bottom.

One can't help but notice a third major problem with the alleged Second Coming. Jesus and his cohorts repeatedly stated that the Second Coming was imminent. In Matt. 10:7 Jesus said, "The Kingdom of heaven is at hand." In Heb. 10:37 Paul said, "For yet a little while, and he that shall come will come, and will not tarry." In James 5:8 James said, "Be ye also patient . . . for the coming of the Lord draweth nigh." In 1 Peter 4:7 Peter said, "But the end of all things is at hand." And in Revelation Jesus said repeatedly, "Behold, I come quickly." Any impartial observer must concede that the failure of anything to arrive after two thousand years does not constitute quickly by any stretch of the imagination. The prophecy collapsed.

Not only is the Second Coming an invalid concept, but several statements by Jesus himself regarding Old Testament messianic comments are fallacious. In John 5:46 Jesus said, "Had ye believed Moses, ye would have believed me: for he wrote of me." In John 5:39 he said, "Search the Scriptures . . . they are they which testify of me." And in Luke 24:44 Jesus said, "All things must be fulfilled, which were written in the law of Moses and in the prophets, and in the psalms, concerning me." Information to be presented later will clearly show that the Old Testament does not testify of Jesus.

Having noted that the Second Coming has no biblical basis and Jesus looked upon himself without any biblical backing as the fulfillment of Him who was prophesied, the question now becomes one of analyzing the prophecies themselves in order to determine the extent to which they are applicable to him. Ultimately, of course, that is the crucial question. Does Jesus fulfill the Old Testament prophecies as he claims, and, if so, to what extent? Upon that question rests the entire superstructure of Jesus' messianic credentials. If the entire panoply of messianic predictions cannot be reliably applied to him, then Jesus, his disciples, and his propagandists are among the greatest bamboozlers of mankind to have ever come out of the woodwork.

Messianic Prophecies

Now that the groundwork has been laid, the only task remaining is that of methodically exposing the degree to which the messianic prophecies could *not* be referring to Jesus of Nazareth. One need only focus upon those of greatest import to reveal the extent to which Jesus is wholly unqualified to claim the messiahship. If those upon which Christians rely the most are invalid, there is little need to analyze every one that has been cited throughout the years. In order to simplify our presentation, we'll address each messianic prophecy in the order in which they would appear if one were to read the Bible from beginning to end. Those that would be encountered are as follows.

The *first* prophecy is Gen. 3:15, which says, "I [God] will put enmity between thee [the evil serpent] and the woman, and between thy seed and her seed [allegedly Jesus]; it shall bruise thy head, and thou shall bruise his heel."

Christians interpret this as meaning a woman [Mary] will give forth a seed [Jesus] who will fight the devil's descendants. But there is no reason to believe the seed referred to in Gen. 3:15 is Jesus specifically. The name "Jesus" is not mentioned. It could just as easily apply to any good person who ever lived— any person who ever fought evil. Moreover, on page 5 in his excellent work *The Jew and the Christian Missionary* Sigal said,

We see that "he will strike at your head, and you will strike at his heel" does not refer to Jesus since he neither stopped the power of Satan "shortly" nor did he abolish sin among his followers as Paul promised. It is, therefore, clear that the Christian missionary interpretation of Genesis 3:15 is yet another Christological dream that may be placed in the category of those prophecies unfulfilled by Jesus and which Christian missionaries hope will be fulfilled in what is called the "second coming."

The *second* prophecy, Gen. 22:18, says, "In thy [Abraham's] seed [which is allegedly Jesus] shall all the nations of the earth be blessed; because thou hast obeyed my voice."

In regard to the blessing of all nations through Abraham's seed, Christians allege that this promise given to Abraham had no reference to Abraham's descendants but only to Jesus, as the preeminent posterity of Abraham. Several problems with this rationalization are readily apparent:

(a) The prior verse clearly shows that no single person is meant; it refers to all of Abraham's posterity by saying, "I will multiply thy seed as the stars of the heaven, and as the sand which is upon the sea shore."

(b) By using the word "descendants," which is plural, instead of "seed," the RSV is conceding that many people rather than one are under discussion. On page 8 in *The Jew and the Christian Missionary* Sigal poignantly stated, "Paul's claim that a single individual is meant by the term 'seed' in Gen. 13:15 and 17:8 is fallacious. Nowhere in the Hebrew Bible do we find the plural of 'seed' used with reference to human descendants. In all instances, the singular term "seed" is used in a plural sense." The point Sigal is making is that the word "seed" refers to many, while the word "seeds" is not used at all.

(c) All the nations of the earth have not been blessed in Abraham, in Jacob, or in their descendants, the Jews.

(d) Even if this did apply to Christianity, it is unfulfilled since most of the earth does not believe in Jesus.

(e) And needless to say, Christianity has not been a blessing to mankind.

The *third* prophecy, Gen. 49:10, is one of those predictions in which apologists place a great deal of stock. It says, "The sceptre shall not depart from Judah, nor a lawgiver from between his feet, until Shiloh come." Christian theology would have us believe that "Shiloh" is Jesus and Judah would not lose the sceptre until he arrived. This explanation is disproven in several ways:

(a) The sceptre did depart from Judah and it happened six years before Jesus was born. If Shiloh is Jesus then this prophecy is false, for the King of Judah (Zedekiah) was carried away captive by Nebuchadnezzar and all the leading Jews were taken away to Babylon. And all of this took place 588 years before the birth of Christ (2 Kings 25:8). On pages 9 and 10 of *The Jew and the Christian Missionary* Sigal says, "The last king from the tribe of Judah, Zedekiah, was taken captive around 586 B.C.E. . . . there was a period of some 600 years, prior to the birth of Jesus, during which the sceptre of leadership had departed from the tribe of Judah. . . . As for Genesis 49:10, there is nothing in it to suggest that it applies to Jesus."

(b) It is not true that the sceptre was wielded by the tribe of Judah at the time Jesus is said to have appeared, since the Jews had submitted to the Romans long before that period.

(c) The Jews had also been in captivity to the Assyrians for 70 years during which it cannot be pretended that a vestige of royalty remained in Judah or in any other of the tribes. The sceptre had to have departed from Judah during that period.

(d) If the sceptre *had* continued all during the pre-Jesus period, then it would have departed nearly fifty years after Jesus' death with the destruction of the second temple. The sceptre did not depart from Judah when the so-called Shiloh (Jesus) came; it happened nearly 50 years after his demise. So, it either occurred 588 years before he was born or 50 years after he died. In either case, it did not happen when Jesus, allegedly Shiloh, came.

(e) Shiloh is not a messiah or a man. Every time "Shiloh" appears in the Old Testament after Genesis 49:10, it is clearly referring to a place, not a man or a person. It was the seat of the national sanctuary before it was moved to Jerusalem and a place where national gatherings took place before Jerusalem was taken by David.

(f) Scholars can't even agree on the correct translation of this verse. Many say that the correct Hebrew translation is: "until he comes to Shiloh," which clearly implies Shiloh is a place, not a person.

(g) And finally, verses 11 and 12 say in regard to the same individual, "He washed his garments in wine; and his clothes in the blood of grapes. His eyes shall be red with wine." How does any of this apply to Jesus?

The *fourth* prophecy, Num. 24:17-19, says, "I shall see him, but not now: I shall behold him, but not nigh: there shall come a Star out of Jacob, and a sceptre shall rise out of Israel, and shall smite the corners of Moab, and destroy the children of Sheth. And Edom shall be a possession. . . . Out of Jacob shall come he that shall have dominion, and shall destroy him that remaineth of the city."

How could this possibly be a messianic prophecy of Jesus as Christians claim? (a) Jesus had no sceptre except a mock one, nor could he be considered a sceptre. (b) Jesus did not smite the corners of Moab or destroy the children of Sheth. Would Jesus be a destroyer? (c) If this passage refers to Jesus, why are the Edomites, Moabites, and those of Sheth singled out as people to be conquered by him? (d) Jesus never had dominion. And (e) when did Jesus destroy "him" or those who remained in the city?

Fifth, Christians contend that Deut. 18:15 is messianic: "The Lord thy God will raise up unto thee a Prophet from the midst of thee, of thy brethren, like unto me; unto him ye shall hearken." Christians also rely on Deut. 18:18 for messianic claims: It says, "I will raise them up a Prophet from among their brethren, like unto thee, and will put my words in his mouth; and he shall speak unto them all that I shall command him."

Of course, Jesus couldn't be the prophet referred to in these comments for several reasons:

(a) God says the prophet will be "like unto me," whereas Jesus is supposed to be God, not like God.

(b) "Unto him you shall hearken" does not apply to Jesus, since the Jews did not follow, but killed him.

(c) This prophecy could apply to any one of hundreds of prophets. Why assume it is Jesus? On page 17 of *The Jew and the Christian Missionary* Sigal states in this regard, "It is claimed by Christian missionaries that these verses constitute a prophetic reference to Jesus. There is absolutely no truth to this contention. The Hebrew noun *navi* or "prophet" is used generically here and does not at all refer to a particular prophet."

The *sixth* prophecy, Deut. 21:23, says, "His body shall not remain all night upon the tree, but thou shalt . . . bury him that day; (for he that is hanged is accursed of God)." This passage is not messianic because: (a) Jesus was crucified, not hanged. (b) How could Jesus be accursed of God? How could the perfect being be accursed? And (c) the prior verse, Deut 21:22, says, "If a man have committed a sin worthy of death, and he be put to death, and thou hang him on a tree." It is pronouncing sentence upon a man who actually committed a sin. This couldn't be referring to Jesus, since his followers claim he was sinless.

The *seventh* prophecy, 2 Sam. 7:12-13, says, "I [God] will set up thy seed [David's] after thee, which shall proceed out of thy bowels, and I will establish his kingdom. He shall build a house for my name, and I will establish the throne of his kingdom for ever."

This is inapplicable to Jesus because (a) Jesus' kingdom is yet to be established at all, much less forever, and (b) the next verse, 2 Sam. 7:14, says, "If he commit iniquity, I will chasten him with the rod of men, and with the stripes of the children of men." This clearly shows that Jesus is not the person being discussed. God would certainly not imply that his perfect son, Jesus, could or would sin and need to be punished.

The *eighth* prophecy, 1 Chron. 17:11-12, is supposedly messianic and says, "It shall come to pass, when thy [David's] days be expired, that thou must go to be with thy fathers, that I will raise up thy seed after thee, which shall be of thy sons; and I will establish his kingdom."

The difficulties with this quotation are (a) The "seed" couldn't be Jesus because the seed was to be a son of David and Jesus was not one of David's sons, he was a distant descendant, and (b) even more importantly, the prophecy says the seed would appear "when thy days be expired" not one thousand years later, when Jesus appeared.

The *ninth* prophecy, Psalms 2:2, says, "The kings of the earth set themselves, and the rulers take counsel together, against . . . his anointed." This is not messianic for two reasons: a) When did the kings of the earth set themselves against Jesus? They knew nothing about him nor did they have any hand in his death. They probably didn't even know he lived or died; and (b) David was the anointed referred to, not Jesus. According to 1 Sam. 16:3 and 16:12–13, David was the chief anointed of Israel by the express command of God.

The *tenth* prophecy, Psalms 2:7, says, "The Lord hath said unto me, Thou art my Son; this day have I begotten thee." The problems with this are: (a) The son referred to is David, not Christ, as 2 Sam. 7:14 shows. The psalmsist, David, is speaking of himself; and (b) the father must be prior in time to the son; otherwise, the words have no meaning. Yet how could Jesus have a less than eternal lifespan, as the word "begotten" implies? How could he be begotten "this day," since that would involve the period after days were created and not the beginning of time?

As Sigal said on page 87 of *The Jew and the Christian Missionary,*

> In the Christian missionary search for biblical proof of the belief in Jesus as the Son of God, proof has often been found where none exists by violating the integrity of the plain meaning of many scriptural passages. Prominent among these is Psalms 2:7, wherein it is stated: "The Lord said to me: 'You are My son. . . .'" Why would God have to inform Jesus, a fellow member of the Trinity, of the exact nature of their relationship? The verse then continues: ". . . this day I have begotten you." If Jesus is God, how can he be begotten?

Eleventh, Psalms 22 also most assuredly does not refer to Jesus, as Christians allege. Verse 22:1 says, "My, God, my God why hast thou forsaken me? why art thou so far from helping me, and from the words of my roaring?" This verse is not messianic for many reasons:

(a) The cry is contrary to Psalms 46:1, which says, "God is our refuge and strength, a very present help in trouble." God certainly was not a refuge or present to help the crucified Jesus.

(b) If this refers to Jesus, did he pray for the salvation of his flesh or his divinity? If his flesh, then his prayers were unanswered. If his divinity, the divine needs no salvation.

(c) Psalms 22:2 says, "I cry in the daytime, but thou hearest not; and in the night season, and am not silent." This is contrary to Isa. 42:2, also said to pertain to Jesus, which says, "He shall not cry nor lift up, nor cause his voice to be heard in the street." Moreover, the sufferings of the speaker in Psalms 22:2 continued for a time. He cried to God for help by day and night in vain, whereas Jesus cried for a short period.

(d) Verse 22:6 says, "But I am a worm (a maggot)." Would Jesus call himself a maggot?

(e) Verse 22:16 says, "They pierced my hands and my feet." Yet, nowhere in the Gospels does it say that the feet of Jesus were pierced or nailed to the cross. Crucified persons did not usually have their feet nailed to the cross. Moreover, many Hebrew scholars say this passage should have been translated as, "They cling like a lion to my hands and feet," and no group ever clung to the hands and feet of Jesus.

(f) In Verse 22:20 the same speaker says, "Deliver my soul from the sword," but Jesus did not die by the sword.

(g) The description of Jesus' distress while facing deadly peril, his worry in prayer, and his desire to be delivered from death and saved alive are unsuitable to Christ, who supposedly gave himself up to death freely. Verse 22:11 says, "Be not far from me; for trouble is near; for there is none to help," and also indicates that if someone had been available to help, Jesus would have gladly agreed to be saved. Jesus' death occurred against his will. How then can Christians say he willed it?

Twelfth, Psalms 9:41 says, "Yea, mine own familiar friend, in whom I trusted, which did eat of my bread, hath lifted up his heel against me." This is said to be a reference by Jesus to Judas, but clearly is not because:

(a) The speaker in Verse 41:4 who is also allegedly Jesus says, "O Lord, be gracious to me; heal me, for I have sinned against thee." Jesus sinned?

(b) The same speaker says Verse 41:11, "I know that thou favorest me, because mine enemy doth not triumph over me." In view of the fact that Jesus' enemies killed and entombed him, it is safe to conclude that they did triumph over him.

Thirteenth, Psalms 72 is judged by apologists to be messianic even though the very first line presents major problems. It says, "Give the king thy judgments, O God, and thy righteousness to the King's son."

The problems are:

(a) If "The King's son" is Jesus, who was the father of Jesus, who was also a King?

(b) If the King is Jesus himself, when did Jesus have a son and when was Jesus a king?

(c) How could Jesus be given righteousness when he already had it? In fact, how could God give Jesus anything when Jesus already had everything because he is God?

(d) Verse 72:4 says, "He shall judge the poor of the people, he shall save the children of the needy, and shall break in pieces the oppressor."

Jesus never judged the poor of the people or saved the children of the needy, and he never broke the oppressor into pieces.

(e) And finally, verses 72:7–8 say, "In his days shall the righteous flourish; and an abundance of peace . . . and He shall have dominion also from sea to sea." The righteous did not flourish in the days of Jesus; there was no peace, and he never ruled from sea to sea.

Fourteenth, one of the most famous of all the messianic prophecies is found in Isaiah 7. Verse 7:14 says, "Behold a virgin shall conceive, and bear a son." Several problems are immediately evident:

(a) Jewish scholars have repeatedly noted that in Hebrew this actually reads: "Behold the young woman is with child and bears a son and calls his name Immanuel." Bible forgers changed *almah* meaning "young woman" to "virgin." The actual Hebrew word for virgin is *betulah.* Ex. 2:8 and Prov. 30:19 show that *almah* means "maid," not "virgin."

(b) It should also be kept in mind that whenever the Bible wants to say "virgin" in a legal context, where precision is necessary, as in Lev. 21:3, Deut. 22:19, 22:28, and Ezek. 44:22, it always uses the word *betulah,* never *almah.* On page 23 in *The Jew and the Christian Missionary* Sigal says,

> The Hebrew word for "virgin" is *betulah.* . . . The word *betulah* is used in an explicit legal sense leaving no question as to its meaning. While *almah* does not define the state of virginity of a woman, *betulah* by contrast does. One would, therefore, reasonably expect that if Isa. 7:14 refers specifically to a virgin, the prophet would have used the technical term *betulah* so as to leave no doubt as to the significance of his words.

(c) Suppose that *almah* did mean "virgin." The verse "a virgin shall conceive" could depict nothing more than a virgin woman conceiving the first time she had intercourse, i.e., a perfectly normal event. Such an interpretation is more reasonable than introducing a radical new doctrine like a virgin birth.

(d) Would God or the Holy Ghost have relations with a betrothed woman (Matt. 1:18), thereby causing her to violate one of His commandments for which one is liable to receive the death penalty according to Deut. 22:23-24?

(e) Christians also changed *harah* from its correct meaning of "has conceived" to "shall conceive." The word *harah* ("conceived") is the Hebrew perfect tense, which in English represents past and completed action. There is not the remotest hint of future time.

(f) The correct translation, "is with child," is in the present tense and shows it pertains to a woman then existing.

(g) Very important is the fact that *nowhere in Isa. 7:14 is the child said to be the messiah.*

(h) Jesus was never called Immanuel except by those who do so in order to fulfill the prophecy, and he was never called Emmanuel in the New Testament except in Matt. 1:23.

(i) This Immanuel is never called the messiah. On page 26 in *The Jew and the Christian Missionary* Sigal says, "Nowhere in the NT do we find that Jesus is called Immanuel." Nowhere in Isaiah does Isaiah call the future Immanuel a Messiah or Jesus Christ the Son of God or Savior or Holy Redeemer. They are never related in any way. All the evidence thus indicates that Immanuel was a different individual from Jesus, since Jesus was never called Immanuel.

(j) Verse 7:15 says, "Butter and honey shall he eat, that he may know to refuse the evil and choose the good." How much sense would it make for Jesus to learn to refuse evil and choose good, and when did Jesus eat butter and honey?

(k) And lastly, the very important verse 7:16 says, "For before the child shall know to refuse the evil, and choose the good, the land that thou abhorrest shall be forsaken of both her kings."

The birth under discussion was to act as a sign to King Ahaz. But how much sense would it make for Ahaz to be concerned with receiving a sign— the birth of Jesus—that would not happen until many centuries after the death of Ahaz? This verse shows that the prophecy could not refer to a future child, but must be referring to a child then conceived, a child then existing, on the way to being born during the time of Ahaz.

The *fifteenth* prophecy, Isa. 9:6, says, "His name shall be called Wonderful, Counsellor, The mighty God, The everlasting Father, The Prince of Peace." Although this allegedly refers to Jesus one should note that:

(a) Nobody calls or called Jesus by the names Wonderful, Counsellor or Everlasting Father. In fact, Jesus is the everlasting *Son,* not *Father.*

(b) How could Jesus be the mighty God, the Everlasting Father, when he, himself, prayed to God?

(c) On page 32 in *The Jew and the Christian Missionary,* Gerald Sigal says,

> The fact remains that Jesus did not literally or figuratively fulfill any of Isaiah's words. A wonderful counselor does not advise his followers that if they have faith they can be agents of destruction as is found in Matt. 21:19–21 and Mark 11:14, 20–23 . . . he does not ask or need to be saved by anyone (Matt. 26:39, Luke 22:42). . . . He who is called the Son of God cannot himself be called the everlasting Father. One cannot play the role of the son and the Father simultaneously; it is an obvious self-contradiction. He who advocates family strife (Matt. 10:34–35, Luke 12:49–53) and killing enemies (Luke 19:27) cannot be called a ruler [or the Prince of Peace].

(d) And finally, verse 9:7 says, "Of the increase of his government and peace there shall be no end." Jesus did not set up a government of peace without end or, indeed, any government.

Sixteenth, probably the most important of all messianic prophecies is found in Isaiah 53. As apologists Boa and Moody said on page 88 of *I'm Glad You Asked,* "The most explicit and powerful of all messianic prophecies is Isa. 52:13 to 53:12." And apologist Paul Little says on page 37 of *Know Why You Believe,*

"Isaiah 52:13 to 53:12 is the most outstanding example of predictive prophecy about Christ. It is full of contingencies which could not be rigged in advance in an attempt to produce fulfillment."

Indeed, if this one cannot withstand scrutiny, what prophecy can? Because Christians view the suffering servant of Isaiah 53 as Jesus and because they attach so much importance to this prophecy, we will examine it at length:

(a) Isa. 52:13, which introduces the prophecy, says, "Behold, my servant shall prosper. He shall be exalted and lifted, and shall be very high." When did Jesus prosper? Not only was his humanity condemned to death in an inglorious manner, but the verse also implies that he was not high and exalted before, which would be contrary to his divinity. In addition, the verse is contrary to Isa. 57:15, another allegedly messianic verse, which says God, i.e., Jesus, is high and exalted continually—it is not a condition he will attain.

(b) Isa. 53:3 says he is despised and rejected by men and Isa. 52:15 says, "Kings shall shut their mouths at him." When did these occur?

(c) Isa. 53:3–7 says, "He was despised," "he has borne," "he was wounded," "he was bruised," "he was oppressed," "he was afflicted," (RSV). These are all past tense verbs showing reference to that which had already occurred. The text is referring to someone or group in the past, not the future.

(d) Isa. 53:4 says, "Yet we did esteem him stricken, smitten of God, and afflicted." But Jesus was smitten by men, not God. And would God smite and afflict his own son?

(e) Isa. 53:5 says, "He was wounded for our transgressions." Yet Jesus was not so much wounded or bruised for our transgressions as he was killed.

(f) Isa. 53:7 says, "He was oppressed . . . yet he opened not his mouth: . . . so he openeth not his mouth." This directly contradicts John 18:21–23 and 33–37 and Matt. 27:46, which show that Jesus not only opened his mouth at his trial but was judged to be so insolent that a guard struck him. As Sigal said on pages 49 and 50 in *The Jew and the Christian Missionary,*

> Far from showing the humility and silence with which Isaiah describes the servant in verse 7, the encounter between the high priest, the elders, and Jesus is highlighted by a vigorous verbal exchange. In addition, Jesus did not show humility and silence during his confrontation with Pilate. At their meeting Jesus is depicted as skillfully defending himself. Jesus at no time humbled himself, but, on the contrary, presented a clever verbal defense.

Sigal later concludes by saying, "Thus, in summation, we may say that contrary to what many Christian missionary theologians would have us believe, Jesus presented a strong defense before the Jewish officials and Pilate. Jesus was not 'dumb' before his accusers, Jewish or Gentile, and it is simply not true to say of Jesus that 'he humbled himself and did not open his mouth.' "

(g) Isa. 53:9 says, "He made his grave with the wicked and with the rich in his death." When was Jesus with the rich in his death and when did he make his grave with the wicked? The outcome of this verse was actually reversed as far as Jesus is concerned. Christ made his grave with the rich by being buried in the sepulchre of the rich Joseph of Arimathaea, and he was with the wicked, the crucified thieves, in his death.

(h) Isa. 53:9 says, "Because he had done no violence," which is contrary to what we know about Jesus from John 2:15, Mark 11:15, and Matt. 21:19. As Sigal notes on page 54 of his work,

> Jesus did commit certain acts of violence. Whip in hand, he attacked the merchants in the Temple area, causing a fracas (Matt. 21:12, Mark 11:15–16, Luke 19:45, John 2:15). He caused the death, by drowning, of a herd of swine by allowing demons to purposely enter their bodies (Matt. 8:32, Mark 5:13, Luke 8:33) and he destroyed a fig tree for not having fruit out of season (Matt. 21:18–21, Mark 11:13–14).

(i) Verse 9 says, "Neither was any deceit in his mouth." Ten solid issues of *Biblical Errancy* (numbers 2, 3, 24, 25, 27, 28, 83, 84, 85, and 86) were devoted to proving precisely the opposite. Deception, hypocrisy, and prevarication were the very stock and trade of much of what Jesus said and did.

(j) Isa. 53:10 says, "It pleased the Lord to bruise him." Would God be pleased to bruise Christ or put him to grief?

(k) Isa. 53:10 says, "He shall see his seed." In the Old Testament "seed" always meant physical descendants and Jesus had no children. If "seed" referred to Jesus' disciples, as some allege, then the prophet should have written "brethren," because "seed" refers to those produced by carnal acts.

(l) Isa. 53:10 says, "He shall prolong his days," but Jesus did not live to an old age. In fact, he died at the relatively young age of thirty-three. Actually Psalms 55:23 could be deemed much more relevant because it says, "Bloody and deceitful men shall not live out half their days." Do we know Jesus lived out half his days?

(m) Isa. 53:10 also says, "The pleasure of the Lord shall prosper in his hand." Jesus has come and gone, yet the world God desires, the pleasure of the Lord, has never come to fruition.

(n) And finally, Isa. 53:12 says, "Therefore will I divide him a portion with the great . . . and he shall divide the spoil with the strong." When did Jesus ever divide a portion with the great or spoils with the strong? Jesus divides spoils? How unbecoming! Would a perfectly good being ever gain spoils, much less divide them? Where does Scripture say Jesus plundered or divided spoils with the strong? In addition, how can the verse imply that Jesus is not strong? That would be contrary to John 17:2, which says he was given power over all flesh.

To abbreviate a long story, more than enough evidence exists to prove that the most important messianic prophecy of all is wholly inapplicable to Jesus Christ. On page 33 in *The Jew and the Christian Missionary* Sigal wisely injects the following important associated difficulty:

> "There shall come forth a shoot out of the stock of Jesse, and a branch out of his roots shall bear fruit" [Isa.11:1]. When the prophet describes the dynamic appearance of the Messiah as "a shoot out of the stock of Jesse," he is portraying the latter's glorious nature from its very inception. This glowing portrayal provides a glaring contrast to the one in Isa. 53:1-2, where the suffering servant, whom the missionaries also identify as Jesus, is portrayed in somber terms. Since both prophecies of Isa. 11:1 and 53:1-2, if they are to apply to Jesus, must refer to his first coming, we are faced with an irreconcilable contradiction, because the two accounts stand in stark contrast to each other. It takes a feat of missionary exegetical acrobatics to harmonize these two prophecies so as to make them appear to be applicable to one individual. . . . Missionaries attempt to solve the problems inherent in their explanation of this chapter by claiming that Jesus appeared the first time to provide a means of salvation for mankind, whereas in the second coming, he will come to judge and rule the world. This, however, is simply not in accord with Isaiah's prophetic message. The Messiah is not portrayed as part of a triune godhead returning to earth as judge and king. . . . Missionaries cannot legitimately dismember this chapter in order to choose those verses which they believe to have been fulfilled in the first coming and leave the remainder to be fulfilled during the second coming. Isaiah 11 is to be taken as a homogeneous unit. There is no evidence to suggest a division within the chapter.

Sigal is utterly correct when he says that Christians can't possibly claim to be objective scholars when they pick and choose the verses they wish to apply to Jesus at a time of their choosing.

Before proceeding to the next distortion it is very important, indeed crucial, to realize that critics of the Bible are often accused of taking verses "out of context," when that is precisely what Christians have done in abundance with the Old Testament, as can clearly be seen from what we have addressed so far and that which is to follow.

Seventeenth, Daniel 9:25–26, which is one of the most famous of all Old Testament predictions, says,

> From the going forth of the commandment to restore and to build Jerusalem unto the Messiah the Prince shall be seven weeks, and threescore and two weeks [sixty-nine weeks total]: the street shall be built again, and the wall, even in troublous times. And after threescore and two weeks [sixty-two weeks] the Messiah shall be cut off, but not for himself: and the people of the prince that shall come shall destroy the city and the sanctuary; and the end thereof shall be with a flood.

In order to make this prophecy applicable to Jesus, apologists have turned each week into seven years rather than seven days, making a total of 483 years (7 × 69). Four hundred and eighty three years were supposed to elapse from the command to rebuild Jerusalem to the coming of Jesus. Many problems accompany the Christian interpretation of Daniel 9.

(a) The word "messiah" is never applied to the expected deliverer of the Israelites in the whole Bible. It is indifferently applied to kings, priests, and prophets, to all who are inducted into their office.

(b) Distortions are employed in order to make the phrase "Messiah the Prince" apply to Jesus, because Jesus was no "prince" or *nagid*. In Hebrew the word *nagid* always denotes a prince or ruler with temporal authority, something Jesus never had.

(c) But even more importantly, the weeks referred to are real weeks of 7 days, not years. Dan. 10:2 shows this quite well by stating, "I Daniel was mourning three full weeks." Would he mourn 21 years? Dan. 10:3 says, "I ate no pleasant bread, neither came flesh nor wine in my mouth ....till three whole weeks are fulfilled." Would he go without eating for 21 years? Dan. 10:4 says, "In the four and twentieth day of the 1st month," in other words the 24th day. Would he talk about the 24th day after just talking about 21 days (3 weeks), if these 3 weeks meant anything other than 21 days, if they meant 21 years, for instance?

(d) The words "week" and "weeks" come from the same Hebrew word that means seven days as we think of the normal day.

(e) The decree of Cyrus to rebuild the temple and Jerusalem in Isa. 44:28 was made in 536 B.C., which is 532 years before the birth of Jesus in 4 B.C., not 483 years. A shortfall of 532 minus 483 or 49 years in this prediction is readily apparent.

(f) It is difficult to understand how Dan. 9:26 could say Jesus would be cut off or die sixty-two weeks after the decree when Dan. 9:25 just stated he would not appear until sixty-nine weeks after the decree was issued.

(g) Jerusalem was not destroyed until A.D. 70, which was approximately forty years after the Messiah was "cut off." If Jesus is the prince that shall come, when did Jesus' people destroy the city and the sanctuary as was predicted?

(h) Dan. 9:26 ends by saying, "And the end thereof shall be with a flood." When was Jerusalem ever destroyed with a flood?

(i) And finally, Daniel 9:26 says, "After threescore and two weeks ["434 years"] shall the Messiah be cut off, but not for himself: and the people of the prince that shall come shall destroy the city and the sanctuary." The problem is: After what? Is it after Cyrus's decree in 536 B.C.? But Jesus died in A.D. 33. If there are 536 years from the decree to Jesus' birth and Jesus lived an additional 33 years, then that would mean there were actually 536 plus 33 or 569 years from the decree to the Crucifixion. The prophecy was 569 minus 434 or 135 years short. If all this is to come to pass after the birth of Jesus, that would mean Jesus would have to have lived for 434 years.

Apologists employ the *eighteenth* prophecy, Hos. 6:2, because of its specificity and apparent applicability to the resurrection of Jesus. It states, "After two days will he revive us: in the third day he will raise us up." In their strong need for Old Testament comments to support the story of Jesus apologists conveniently overlook these facts: (a) The use of the word "us" shows that more than one person is to be raised; it could not refer to Jesus alone. (b) In Matt. 27:63 and Mark 8:31 Jesus said he would rise *after* three days, not *on* the third day. (c) And most importantly, Hos. 6:2 says, "he will raise us;" it does not say he will *be* raised. He is going to do the raising in the third day-he isn't going to *be* raised.

Nineteenth. with the possible exception of Isaiah 7 and 53, Micah 5 ranks at the apex of the messianic pyramid. Verse 5:2 states, "But thou Bethlehem Ephratah, though thou be little among the thousands of Judah, yet out of thee shall he come forth unto me that is to be ruler in Israel, whose goings forth have been from of old, from everlasting." This is *not* a prognostication of Jesus being born in Bethlehem for several reasons:

(a) Depending on the verse invoked, Bethlehem could be either a man or a town. According to 1 Chron. 4:4 Bethlehem is the son of a man named Ephratah. Since it says "Bethlehem Ephratah" rather than "Bethlehem," the man rather than the town is intended.

(b) Thousands of children have been born in Bethlehem but that doesn't give each of them the right to claim to be the Messiah.

(c) Jesus was by no means a ruler in Israel. On the contrary, the people ruled over him as is shown by his death.

(d) And most importantly, Micah 5:6 says, "Thus shall he deliver us from the Assyrian when he cometh into our land." When did Jesus save anyone from the Assyrians? The Assyrian Empire ceased to exist six hundred years before Jesus was even born. Moreover, when did Jesus ever become a military leader? It was the Romans and not the Assyrians who conquered the land of Judea when Jesus lived. And Jesus did not drive out the Romans. On the contrary, they signed the warrant for his execution. Realistically speaking, they drove him out.

Twentieth, Haggai 2:6–7 says, "Thus saith the Lord of hosts; Yet once, it is a little while, and I will shake the heavens, and the earth, and the sea, and the dry land; And I will shake all nations, and the desire of all nations shall come."

(a) If Jesus is the "desire of all nations" as Christians claim, then the universal earthquake that was to precede his coming appears to have passed unnoticed.

(b) Jesus was never the "desire of all nations."

(c) The verse says "a little while" even though the alleged desire appeared over five hundred years after the prophecy.

(d) The Revised Standard Version says "treasures" of all nations, not the "desire" of all nations. Treasures is plural and couldn't refer to a single individual.

The *twenty-first* prophecy, Zech. 6:12, says, "Thus speaketh the Lord of hosts, saying, Behold the man whose name is the Branch; and he shall grow up out of his place, and he shall build the temple of the Lord." (a) Jesus never built the temple of the Lord. (b) When was Jesus ever called "the Branch"? (c) The next verse, Zech. 6:13, says, "He shall bear the glory, And shall sit and rule upon his throne, and he shall be a priest upon his throne." Jesus never had much glory, never sat or ruled on a throne, and was never a priest.

The *twenty-second* prophecy, Zech. 9:9, is supposedly a prediction of Jesus' entry into Jerusalem and says, "Thy king cometh unto thee: he is just, and having salvation: lowly, and riding upon an ass, and upon a colt the foal of an ass." The problems are:

(a) "Having salvation" should have been translated as "having been saved." The Revised Standard Version translated it as "victorious," which is also inapplicable. Jesus was neither saved nor victorious.

(b) This event could not refer to Jesus since according to prophecy it was to occur at the same time as the restoration of Israel and the establishment of peace and happiness, which have never happened to this day.

(c) Actually Zechariah is congratulating his countrymen who are returning from captivity in Babylon to Jerusalem. Zech. 1:16, which says, "I am returned to Jerusalem with mercies," shows that the entry of the Jews into Jerusalem was the subject Zechariah was discussing, not the entry by Jesus nearly seven hundred years later. Zech. 8:7–8 concurs by saying, "I will save my people from the east country, and from the west country; And I will bring them, and they shall dwell in the midst of Jerusalem."

(d) According to Luke 19:30 and Mark 11:2 Jesus made his entry with a colt. No mention is made of an ass.

(e) The next verse, Zech. 9:10, says, "He shall speak peace unto the heathen: and his dominion shall be from sea even to sea, and from the river even to the ends of the earth." Jesus never had a dominion stretching anywhere, let alone to the ends of the earth; he never brought peace to the heathen, and, in fact, he clearly stated in Matt. 10:34 that he came not to bring peace but a sword.

Twenty-third, an important and revealing messianic prophecy is found in Mal. 4:5–6, which says, "I will send you Elijah the prophet before the coming of the great and terrible day of the Lord. And he shall turn the heart of the fathers to the children, and the heart of the children to their fathers."

On pages 83 through 86 in *The Jew and the Christian Missionary,* Sigal effectively summarizes the problems generated by this prophecy by saying,

> Some Christian missionary theologians, realizing that Elijah did not appear prior to the coming of Jesus, put off the event described by the prophet Malachi to the alleged second coming of Jesus. . . . According to Matt. 11:13–14, 17:12 and Mark 9:13, Jesus considered Malachi's prophecies concerning Elijah, the harbinger of the Messiah, as completely fulfilled in John the Baptist. For Jesus, Elijah had come in the person of John the Baptist. . . . Jesus did not say Elijah would

come in the future. . . . His identification of John the Baptist with Elijah is emphatically rejected in John 1:21 by John the Baptist himself. . . . In view of John's emphatic denial of having any connection with Elijah, it becomes obvious that either Jesus or John was in error about the role of the latter. If John was that prophet, in any form, he failed to carry out God's commission to Elijah. The forerunner of the Messiah is expected to usher in an era of perfect peace and harmony between fathers and their children, ending all discord and strife between them. . . . This John the Baptist failed to do. For his part, Jesus explains his own function as the exact opposite . . . for Jesus said, "Do not think that I came to bring peace on earth; . . . I came to set a man against his father, and a daughter against her mother etc. . . ." There is no doubt that Malachi says Elijah is the forerunner of the Messiah. . . . Since Elijah has not come beforehand, we are compelled to conclude that Jesus could not be the Messiah.

In essence, although Jesus said John the Baptist was Elijah, John the Baptist stated emphatically he was not; and he did not usher in the era of perfect peace and harmony that was required. Therefore, since he could not have been the expected Elijah, Jesus could not have been the expected Messiah.

Twenty-fourth, and lastly, in one instance the New Testament relates an Old Testament messianic prophecy that is nonexistent; it's pure fantasy. Matt. 2:23 says, "He came and dwelt in a city called Nazareth: that it might be fulfilled which was spoken by the prophets, He shall be called a Nazarene." As Sigal says on page 191 in his book, "At no point in the Hebrew Scriptures is the Messiah referred to as a Nazarene. . . . Neither can it be said that Matthew is referring to the Messiah as being a Nazarite, for nowhere in the Hebrew Scriptures is it stated that the Messiah will ever take the Nazarite vow. Furthermore, the spellings of the words Nazarite and Nazarene are not the same in Hebrew."

Conclusion

What is the obvious conclusion to be drawn from all of the above? The writings of Paine, Sigal, and Ingersoll provide good synopses and encompass the entire issue of messianic prophecy as well as any. All three had less concern for civility than making their points crystal clear. On pages 289 and 292 of *The Jew and the Christian Missionary* Sigal states,

> No appeal to faith can alter the fact that the Scriptures do not teach what the missionaries preach. . . . Ultimately, one who studies the Scriptures will find that the reason uncritical faith is emphasized so heavily by the Christian missionary movement is because Hebrew Scriptures lack the proof this movement needs for its contentions. Only by a superficial approach to the Scriptures can the missionary movement pretend to justify itself. . . . The missionary's contention that the Hebrew

Scriptures, are the true word of God means that the New Testament can be true only if it agrees with the Hebrew Scriptures. This is demonstrably not the case. The disagreement between these two books is not due to the unbeliever's lack of spiritual insight but lies in their intrinsically contradictory contents.

On page 206 of volume 9 in *The Life and Works of Thomas Paine,* Paine followed in the same current by stating,

> In the following treatise I have examined all the passages in the New Testament, quoted from the Old, and so-called prophecies concerning Jesus Christ, and I find no such thing as a prophecy of any such person, and I deny there are any. . . . I have given chapter and verse for everything I have said, and have not gone out of the books of the Old and New Testament for evidence that the passages are not prophecies of the person called Jesus Christ.

On page 269 of the same volume Paine states,

> The practice which the writers of the books, the gospels, employ is not more false than it is absurd. They state some trifling case of the person they call Jesus Christ, and then cut out a sentence from some passage of the Old Testament and call it a prophecy of that case. But when the words thus cut out are restored to the places they are taken from, and read with the words before and after them, they give the lie to the New Testament.

And to summarize the whole issue we could do no better than to repeat our quote from Robert Ingersoll who said the following on page 277 in volume 5 of his *Works,*

> There is no prophecy in the OT foretelling the coming of Jesus Christ. There is not one word in the OT referring to him in any way—not one word. The only way to prove this is to take your Bible, and wherever you find these words: "That it might be fulfilled" and "which was spoken" turn to the OT and find what was written, and you will see that it had not the slightest possible reference to the thing recounted in the NT—not the slightest.

To the point and well said!

9

The Character of Biblical Figures
God, Patriarchs, Matriarchs, Prophets, Peter

The last four chapters focused on Jesus Christ and all but exhausted the major problems associated with his role in Christianity in general and the Bible in particular. This chapter will concentrate on nearly all the other major heroes in the Bible, which would include such figures as God, the patriarchs, the matriarchs, Peter, and the prophets. Paul will be discussed in a subsequent chapter.

If there is any fact that emerges from the maze of boring data found throughout the Bible, it is the incredible number of instances in which the major figures, the beings whom today's children are taught to admire and respect, exhibit behavior that can only be described as disgusting and appalling. Throughout the Book, especially the Old Testament, one is struck by the number of times in which the good guys are anything but models of rectitude. Generally speaking, they could more easily be classified as mafiosi than saints. Unless a substantial amount of censorship is employed, parents who awaken their children on Sunday morning in order to read about these characters in Sunday School could easily be accused of child abuse. For believers in the Bible to deny the corruption of its central figures would be ridiculous in view of the fact that an overwhelming amount of evidence is available, a fact readily admitted by some of the Book's more open proponents.

On page 233 in *Today's Handbook for Solving Bible Difficulties,* apologist David O'Brien says, "When we read the Bible, we assume that all the great people of Scripture would make wonderful deacons or elders in our American church. But in fact, there's hardly a person in the OT who would even be allowed to join most of our churches without some major modifications in behavior. On page 260 in the same book O'Brien says,

169

Keep in mind the fact that very few of God's chosen instruments were without fault, or even serious sin. Moses was a murderer. David was an adulterer and a murderer. Jacob was a con-man and Abraham was a liar. Jonah was a racist who rebelled at the idea that God would forgive the Assyrians. And what about Peter's impulsiveness and the contentious spirits displayed by James and John?

Well, at least one apologist does not deny the obvious. In answer to fellow Christians who concocted an excuse to account for Noah's drunkenness, O'Brien says on page 185 in the same book, "Nowhere does Scripture teach that fermentation began after the flood or that Noah's drunkenness is the innocent result of drinking what he thought was wholesome grape juice. It does Scripture no honor to invent ways to make offensive events palatable to us when Scripture itself records them and makes no effort to sanitize them." If only more apologists were as open and forthright!

God

Having completed a broad overview of this chapter's contents, the question becomes one of proving that the Bible's heroes are not paragons of propriety but prototypes of perversity. Turning to the characters themselves, the question becomes one of deciding who should receive priority. Who should be exposed first? Undoubtedly the most important figure in the entire Bible is God himself, and for that reason he should be placed in front of the pack. No one has a role comparable to his. The Bible is supposed to be his word, so who would be more qualified to receive top billing? On page 185 in his book O'Brien distinguishes God from all other figures by saying, "The only real hero is God." In the same vein, on page 28 in *Reason to Believe* apologist R. C. Sproul states, "Nowhere do we find God involved in capricious or arbitrary acts of judgment. His wrath is never directed against the innocent. His anger never flows without reason. It is always directed against human rebellion and sin."

Few comments are more at odds with biblical reality because facts prove precisely the opposite. The problem with any description of the biblical God is that his portrayal by the Bible can only be described as horrible. The God of the Bible is one of the most disreputable beings to have ever emerged from the pages of literature. The dossier of his bad acts would put any criminal to shame. People occasionally ask how I can talk about God's Book in this manner. But that assumes the very point at issue. It is not God's Book. If there were a just God somewhere, he would have nothing to do with this book and, indeed, would condemn all those who would be so bold as to attribute it to him. For the benefit of any who may be inclined to doubt the truth of this, I offer a list of the deeds that God commits in various places in the Old Testament. Now, remember, this is supposedly God's book. A detailed listing of chapter and verse is available in Issues 115 through 120 of *Biblical Errancy*:

God created evil. Evil came from the Lord. He deceived and told people to lie. He rewarded liars. He ordered men to become drunk. He rewarded the fool and the transgressor. He delivered a man, Job, into Satan's hands. He caused indecency. He spread dung on people's faces. He ordered stealing. He made false prophecies. He changed his mind. He caused adultery. He ordered the taking of a harlot. He killed people. He ordered the killing of people. He has a temper. He's often jealous. He practiced injustice. He repented. He played favorites. He sanctioned slavery. He degraded deformed people. He punished bastards for being illegitimate. He punished many for the acts of one. He punished children for their fathers' sins. He punished a man for following his orders. He prevented people from hearing his words. He supported human sacrifice. He ordered cannibalism. He demanded virgins as a part of war plunder. He ordered gambling. He required an unbetrothed virgin to marry her seducer. He ordered horses to be hamstrung. He sanctioned the violation of the enemy's women. He sanctioned the beating of slaves to death. He required a woman to marry her rapist. He taught war. He ordered the cooking of food with human feces. He killed the righteous and the wicked. He intentionally gave out bad laws. He excused the sins of prostitutes and adulterers. He excused a murderer and promised him protection. He killed a man who refused to impregnate his sister-in-law. He aided rather than punished a swindler. He doesn't see all. He's indecisive. He discovered a woman's secret parts. He broke up families. He ordered the killing of women and children. He killed over fifty thousand people because a few merely looked into an ark. He gives unlimited, eternal punishment for limited sins. He violated his own laws (such as those against killing, drawing the sword, and tempting). And scripture clearly shows that he operated on a philosophy of "Do as I say, not as I do." Now can you imagine anyone, any being, saying, "Yes, that's my book; that represents me; that's the way I am," especially a supposedly perfect being? One would be challenged to think of any historical figure with a worse record, including Adolf Hitler and Genghis Khan. The Devil comes out of the Bible looking much better than God. You would almost think that the Bible was written by the Devil about God. Robert Ingersoll made a rather cogent remark in this regard on pages 17 and 18 of volume 1 in his *Works*: "In nearly all the theologies, mythologies and religions, the devils have been much more humane and merciful than the gods. No devil ever gave one of his generals an order to kill children and to rip open the bodies of pregnant women."

Having delineated the wide assortment of atrocious deeds committed by God in the Old Testament, we feel obligated to provide some chapter and verse citations for purposes of substantiation. Since far too many references are available for inclusion in this chapter, we will focus on many of the most glaring examples. The following array is more than sufficient to convince any reasonably objective observer that the God of the Old Testament differs drastically from the kind of God Christians would have us believe is ruling the universe.

The *first* charge relating to God creating evil can be found in Isa. 45:7, which says, "I form the light, and create darkness: I make peace, and create evil: I the Lord do all these things." Or one could cite Lam. 3:38, which says in the Revised Standard Version, "Is it not from the mouth of the Most High that good and evil come?" While addressing this problem on page 120 in *Does the Bible Contradict Itself?*, the apologist William Arndt begins by quoting Amos 3:6, which says, "Shall a trumpet be blown in the city and the people not be afraid? Shall there be evil in a city and the Lord hath not done it?" Then Arndt says, "The Amos passage does not allude to moral wrong, but to physical calamities, earthquakes, storms, and the like. . . . By means of them He punishes evildoers."

This common artifice by Arndt and other spokesmen for the Bible won't stand critical analysis because of verses referring to God which clearly show that the word "evil" refers to bad or immoral deeds as distinct from calamities and catastrophes. In Jer. 26:3 God says, "that I may repent of the evil, which I purpose to do unto them because of the evil of their doings" and in Jer. 36:3 God says, "All the evil which I purpose to do unto them; that they may return every man from his evil way; that I may forgive their iniquity and their sin." In every instance in these two verses the word "evil" comes from the Hebrew words *ra* or *roa* which refer to morality, and in both verses evil is counterposed to bad behavior not calamities. If the word "evil" does not have a definite moral quality attached, then why was it placed in opposition to the word "good" in Lam. 3:38? In an attempt to resolve the same problem from another angle Charles Ryrie says on page 209 in *Basic Theology*, "In Isa. 45:7 God is said to create light and darkness, well-being and 'ra.' Some understand this to mean calamities and others, evil. If the latter, then it can only indicate that all things, including evil, are included in the plan of God, though the responsibility for committing sin rests on the creature, not the Creator."

Like most apologists, when the text is distasteful Ryrie just ignores the content and writes his own. Isa. 45:7 says, "I create evil." It does not say it is included within the plan of God but created by others. It says, "*I* create evil," period.

The *second* major reprehensible act by God that merits comment is found in 2 Chron. 18:22 ("The Lord hath put a lying spirit in the mouth of these thy prophets"), Jer. 20:7 ("O Lord, thou hast deceived me, and I was deceived") and 2 Thess. 2:11 ("God sends upon them a strong delusion, to make them believe what is false"). How could the Bible be God's Word, when it portrays the author as a deceiver and a swindler of people?

Third, God not only deceives according to his Book but tells people to lie in direct contradiction to the Ninth Commandment, one of his own creations. In 1 Sam. 16:2 Samuel says, "How can I go? if Saul hear it, he will kill me. And the Lord said, Take an heifer with thee, and say, I am come to sacrifice to the Lord." God is not only aiding and abetting a deception, but deliberately telling a man what lie to use. Samuel is actually going out to meet a son of Jesse and anoint him king, not to sacrifice a heifer.

Fourth, God not only tells people to lie but lied himself in direct contradiction to Titus 1:2, which says God never lies. One of the most blatant examples is found in the story of Adam and Eve. In Gen. 2:17 God says, "But of the tree of the knowledge of good and evil, thou shalt not eat of it: for in the day that thou eatest thereof thou shalt surely die." But several verses later the Serpent says that if Eve eats of it, she "shall not surely die." We all know that Adam and Eve ate the forbidden fruit; yet Gen. 5:5 says, "All the days that Adam lived were 930 years and he died." So clearly Adam did not die on the day that he ate the forbidden fruit. Quite the contrary, he lived to a very old age. The oldest man in the Bible, Methuselah, lived only thirty-nine years longer. It is also important to note that a spiritual explanation won't suffice, for reasons discussed in a prior chapter.

A *fifth* charge pertains to God ordering men to become drunk. Jer. 25:27 says, "Say unto them, Thus saith the Lord of hosts, the God of Israel; Drink ye, and be drunken, and spue, and fall, and rise no more." Alcoholism is a major social evil and now we are to believe that the Almighty contributed to the plague.

A *sixth* charge has to do with God rewarding the fool and the transgressor. Prov. 26:10 says, "The great God that formed all things both rewardeth the fool, and rewardeth transgressors."

It is amazing that any passage in the Bible would claim that God rewards transgressors!

A *seventh* charge is that God is not as all-powerful as is commonly believed. Judges 1:19 says, "The Lord was with Judah; And he drave out the inhabitants of the mountain; but could not drive out the inhabitants of the valley, because they had chariots of iron." One can only conclude from this that the Lord is less than omnipotent.

An *eighth* charge is that God was so disgusting as to spread dung on the faces of people. Mal. 2:3 says, "Behold I will corrupt your seed, and spread dung upon your faces, even the dung of your solemn feasts."

How could one be more revolting?

A *ninth* charge is that God was a false prophet who broke a promise, something that is impossible according to 1 Kings 8:56, which says, "There hath not failed one word of all his good promise, which he promised by the hand of Moses." Yet in Jonah 3:4 God said, "Yet forty days, and Nineveh shall be overthrown." That was clearly a promise, a promise that was repudiated just six verses later, in Jonah 3:10: "God saw their works, that they turned from their evil way; and God repented of the evil, that he had said that he would do unto them; and he did it not." Apologists say that God went back on his word because they turned from their evil ways. But that's of no consequence. He made a promise that was later recanted, and since he knows the future he must have known they would turn from their evil ways.

Another false prophecy by God is found in Gen. 15:13, which says, "God said unto Abram, . . . thy seed shall be a stranger in a land that is not theirs, and shall serve them; and they shall afflict them four hundred years." That land was Egypt. But the Israelites were Egyptian slaves for 430 years, not 400 years, as is shown by Ex. 12:40, which says, "Now the sojourning of the children of Israel, who dwelt in Egypt, was four hundred and thirty years." A perfect God can't provide imperfect figures. Four hundred years is not 430 years.

And a third false prophecy by God is found in Gen. 35:10, wherein God says to Jacob, "Thy name is Jacob; thy name shall not be called any more Jacob, but Israel shall be thy name: and he called his name Israel." So Jacob is no longer to be called Jacob; he is to be called Israel. But eleven chapters later, in Gen. 46:2, we read, "God spake unto Israel in the visions of the night, and said, Jacob, Jacob. And he said, Here am I." The Bible would have us believe that an omniscient God just can't get his act together.

A *tenth* charge is that God caused adultery, according to 2 Sam. 12:11–12, which says, "Thus saith the Lord, Behold, I will raise up evil against thee out of thine own house, and I will take thy wives before thine eyes, and give them unto thy neighbour, and he shall lie with thy wives in the sight of this sun. For thou didst it secretly: but I will do this thing before all Israel, and before the sun."

God not only instigated adultery but caused it to occur in public, before the entire nation of Israel. How appalling!

An *eleventh* charge is that God ordered the taking of a harlot, which can be shown by reading Hosea 1:2: "The Lord said to Hosea, Go, take unto thee a wife of whoredoms and children of whoredoms: for the land hath committed great whoredoms, departing from the Lord." And later in Hos. 3:1–2 the text says, "Then said the Lord unto me, Go yet, love a woman beloved of her friend, yet an adulteress. . . . So I bought her to me for fifteen pieces of silver, and an homer of barley."

So we not only have the Lord telling a man to take a whore for his wife and love an adulteress, but buy a woman with silver and food.

A *twelfth* charge is that God killed people. I was on a radio talk show many years ago when a man called in to challenge me to show where the Bible says that God killed people. Unbeknownst to my detractor, this is one of the most easily proven allegations against God of all those that are available. The Old Testament is replete with instances in which God killed people, both justly and unjustly. Some of the most obvious verses are Num. 16:35 ("There came out a fire from the Lord, and consumed two hundred and fifty men that offered incense"); Deut. 32:39 ("See now that I, even I, am he, and there is no god with me: I kill, and I make alive; I wound and I heal"); 1 Sam. 5:6 ("But the hand of the Lord was heavy upon them of Ashdod, and he destroyed them, and smote them"); and Psalms 135:10 ("Who smote great nations and slew mighty kings"). In fact, Gen. 7:21 ("And all flesh died that moved upon the earth, birds, cattle, beasts, all swarming creatures that swarm upon the earth, and every man) (RSV) shows that God killed almost everything on earth during the flood.

A list of this kind could extend for several pages, so there is no need to belabor the issue. On page 69 in *Answers to Tough Questions* apologist Josh McDowell sought to defend God's behavior by saying,

> The Old Testament contains stories of God's commanding the destruction of Sodom, the annihilation of the Canaanites and many other stories of God's judgment and wrath. . . . God would not have destroyed certain nations except that He is a God of justice and their evil could not go unchecked and condoned. . . . In the case of the Amorites, God gave them hundreds of years to repent, yet they did not (Gen. 15:16). Noah preached 120 years to his generation before the great flood (Gen. 6:3). The proper Old Testament picture is one of a very patient God who gives these people untold opportunities to repent . . . and only when they continually refuse does He judge and punish them for their evil deeds.

None of McDowell's rationalization has any relevance to Scripture because the behavior of the Israelites was as reprehensible as any, yet they were nearly always forgiven, regardless. Why were they treated better than the other tribes? What had they done to qualify as God's chosen people? Like the Amorites, they too, were given hundreds of years and untold opportunities to repent, which they often failed to do. So why weren't they slaughtered rather than being selected as God's chosen people? Several of the Canaanite tribes were destroyed for no apparent reason other than being in the path of the imperialistic Israelites.

A *thirteenth* charge is that God not only killed but ordered killings. In Num. 25:17 he says, "Vex the Midianites, and smite them," and in Ezek. 9:6 he says, "Slay utterly old and young, both maids, and little children, and women." The God of the Old Testament is a bloodthirsty critter of the nth degree. How one reconciles God's record in this respect with his "Thou shalt not kill" commandment is anyone's guess.

A *fourteenth* charge is that God ignored his own advice, submitted in Job 5:2, which says, "For wrath killeth the foolish man, and envy slayeth the silly one." Many verses show that God often exhibited wrath and anger. Deut. 13:17 ("That the Lord may turn from the fierceness of his anger") and Judges 3:8 ("The anger of the Lord was hot against Israel") are prime examples. If wrath kills the foolish man, then God himself should have died on numerous occasions. Other verses such as Deut. 5:9 ("I the Lord thy God am a jealous God") and Nahum 1:2 ("God is jealous, and the Lord revengeth") show that God was often envious and jealous of something or other. If envy slays the silly one, then God should have died long ago.

A *fifteenth* charge pertains to God's claim of omnipresence. Jer. 23:24, which says, "Do not I fill heaven and earth?" and Psalms 139:7–11 allege that God is everywhere. If so, then apologists must account for verses like Gen. 11:5 ("The Lord came down to see the city and the tower, which the children of men builded"); Num. 23:15 ("He said unto Balak, Stand here by thy burnt offering, while I meet the Lord yonder"); and Job 1:12 ("Satan went forth from the presence of the Lord").

Why would God need to come down to see anything when he is already here, and how could anybody leave the presence of a being who is everywhere? In fact, how could God move anywhere, since he's already everywhere? To move at all is to assume that you are not in one place and seek to move from where you are to where you are not. You can not move into an area in which you are already present. Jonah 1:3 says that Jonah fled from the presence of the Lord and Gen. 3:8 says, "Adam and his wife hid themselves from the presence of the Lord God." That must have been quite a trick!

A *sixteenth* charge focuses on one of the most important traits any god should possess—omniscience. God claims to know everything. In fact Prov. 15:3 says, "The eyes of the Lord are in every place, beholding the evil and the good." But how, then, are apologists to account for verses like Gen. 3:9, which says, "The Lord God called to Adam, and said to him, Where art thou?" He doesn't know? The omniscient God lacks knowledge? And 2 Chron. 32:31 says, "God left him, to try him, that he might know all that was in his heart." He doesn't already know? The same question can be asked of Ezek 20:3, which says, "Thus saith the Lord God; Are ye come to inquire of me? As I live, saith the Lord God, I will not be inquired of by you," and of Psalms 14:2, which says, "The Lord looked down from heaven upon the children of men, to see if there were any that did understand, and seek God."

How could he not be aware of the answer? For an all-knowing omniscient being he certainly has to obtain a lot of information.

A *seventeenth* charge pertains to the numerous instances in which the word "repent" is attached to the words and deeds of God. For a being who knows all, including the future, he made a lot of miscalculations and false projections indeed. Ex. 32:14 says, "The Lord repented of the evil which he thought to do unto his people." And 1 Sam. 15:35 says, "The Lord repented that he had made Saul king over Israel." Jer. 42:10 says, "For I repent of the evil that I have done unto you" and Gen. 6:6 says, "It repented the Lord that he had made man on the earth, and it grieved him at his heart." We are supposed to believe that God knows the future yet we are told that God constantly regrets his own behavior. James 1:17 speaks of God as having "no variableness, neither shadow of turning." If there is no shadow of turning with God, then why so much regretting?

An *eighteenth* charge concentrates on justice and fair play. According to Deut. 32:4, God is just and right, even though a mountain of biblical evidence to the contrary is readily available. Some of the most glaring and infamous examples are as follows. Ex. 4:22-23 says, "Thou [Moses] shalt say unto Pharaoh, Thus saith the Lord. Israel is my son, even my firstborn: And I say unto thee, Let my son go, that he may serve me: and if thou refuse to let him go, behold, I will slay thy son, even thy firstborn." Even some of the staunchest Christians choke on this one. Why should the first-born children in Egypt die because of the deeds of a tyrannical ruler?

Num. 14:18 says, "The Lord is long-suffering, and of great mercy . . . visiting the iniquity of the fathers upon the children unto the third and fourth generation." He may be long-suffering, but he's short on justice. Why should descendants be punished for the deeds of their ancestors? The "great mercy" allegedly attached to this whole arrangement is elusive to say the least.

The text of 1 Chron. 21:1 and 21:7 says, "Satan stood up against Israel, and provoked David to number Israel. And God was displeased with this thing; therefore he smote Israel." Because David conducted a census in Israel, the entire nation was punished. That's justice!

One of the most absurd cases of divine injustice is recounted in 1 Sam. 6:19, which says, "He smote the men of Beth-shemesh, because they had looked into the ark of the Lord, even he smote of the people fifth thousand and threescore and ten men [50,070]; and the people lamented, because the Lord had smitten many of the people with a great slaughter." Imagine! God killed more than 50,000 people because some had looked into the Ark of the Covenant which they were glad to see arrive. Since when did curiosity become a capital offense?

Undoubtedly the greatest of all God's injustices is found in Rom. 5:12, which says, "Wherefore, as by one man sin entered into the world, and death by sin; and so death passed upon all men, for that *all* have sinned." Why all of mankind is being punished for the act of one is a question for which biblicists have never devised a rational response. Why are we being punished for what Adam did? After all, he ate the forbidden fruit, we didn't. It's his problem, not ours, especially in light of Deut. 24:16, which says the children shall not be punished for the sins of their fathers. In this instance, even their own book does Christians in.

The *nineteenth* charge has to do with the validity of Deut. 10:17, which says in the Revised Standard Version, "The Lord your God is God of gods and Lord of lords, . . . who is not partial and takes no bribe," and 2 Chron. 19:7, which says, "There is no iniquity with the Lord our God, nor respect of persons, nor taking of gifts."

If God does not play favorites and remains impartial throughout, then how do we account for verses such as Deut. 7:6, which says, "Thou art an holy people unto the Lord thy God: the Lord thy God hath chosen thee to be a special people unto himself, above all people that are upon the face of the earth." Why were the Jews chosen to be God's special people over all others? What had they done to receive this privileged status? Isa. 65:9 says, "I will bring forth a seed out of Jacob, and out of Judah an inheritor of my mountains: and mine elect shall inherit it." "Mine elect"! What is this "mine elect" nonsense that is coming from him whom we are to believe is impartial and no respecter of persons?

Rom. 1:16 says, "I am not ashamed of the gospel of Christ: for it is the power of God unto salvation to every one that believeth; to the Jew first, and also to the Greek." Why do the Jews get first billing if God does not play favorites? And then there is Rom. 9:13 which says, "As it is written, Jacob have I loved, but Esau have I hated." Why was one of these individuals placed over the other? In Isa. 51:16, Isa. 52:6, and Isa. 63:8 we hear from God's own lips the phrase "my people." But isn't all of humanity supposed to be God's children? Jesus adds to the iniquity by saying in Matt. 15:24, "I am not sent but unto the lost sheep of the house of Israel." If that's not playing favorites, what is?

A *twentieth* charge is the easily proven assertion that the biblical God sanctioned slavery, in clear refutation of 2 Cor. 3:17, which says, "Where the spirit of the Lord is, there is Liberty." God directly condones slavery in Deut. 15:17 ("Thou shalt take an awl, and thrust it through his ear unto the door, and he shall be thy servant [Read this as slave] for ever") and Joel 3:8 ("I will sell your sons and your daughters into the hand of the children of Judah, and they shall sell them to the Sabeans, to a people far off: for the Lord hath spoken it").

Of even greater import is 1 Tim. 6:1–2 in the RSV, which says, "Let all who are under the yoke of slavery regard their masters as worthy of all honor, so that the name of God and the teaching may not be defamed. Those who have believing masters must not be disrespectful on the ground that they are brethren; rather they must serve all the better since those who benefit by their service are believers and beloved." Titus 2:9–10 in the Revised Standard Version says, "Bid slaves to be submissive to their masters and to give satisfaction in every respect; they are not to be refractory, nor to pilfer, but to show entire and true fidelity, so that in everything they may adorn the doctrine of God our savior."

And probably as strong as any are Eph. 6:5 and Col. 3:22 which say, "Servants, be obedient to them that are your masters according to the flesh, with fear and trembling." Is it any wonder that the leaders of the South during and prior to the Civil War cited the Bible so often? On pages 316 and 317 in volume 1 of a book entitled *Jefferson Davis,* Dunbar Rowland cites the leader of the Confederacy as having said,

> Let the gentlemen go to Revelation to learn the decree of God—let him go to the Bible and not to the report of the decisions of the courts. I said that slavery was sanctioned in the Bible, authorized, regulated, and recognized from Genesis to Revelation. . . . Slavery existed then in the earliest ages, and among the chosen

people of God; and in Revelation we are told that it shall exist till the end of time shall come. You find it in the Old and New Testaments—in the prophecies, psalms, and the epistles of Paul; you find it recognized—sanctioned everywhere.

Well, whatever his faults may be, Jefferson Davis nailed truth to the wall in this regard.

A *twenty-first* charge is that God punished bastards for being illegitimate. Deut. 23:2 says, "A bastard shall not enter into the congregation of the Lord; even to his tenth generation shall he not enter into the congregation of the Lord." Even the most rudimentary sense of justice dictates that this act should be judged unfair. You don't punish children for the deeds committed by their parents, especially for acts committed before the former were born. You don't blame children for the process by which they entered the world. No one has anything to say about the marital status of his or her parents and no one should be punished because the parental relationship is socially unacceptable.

A *twenty-second* charge is quite egregious in that we have a clear instance in which God supports the repulsive act of human sacrifice for an equally repulsive reason—to buttress his own image and show he is boss. Ezek. 20:26 in the Revised Standard Version says, "I defiled them through their very gifts in making them offer by fire all their first-born, that I might horrify them; I did it that they might know that I am the Lord." Another example is found in Ex. 22:29–30, which says, "Thou shalt not delay to offer the first of thy ripe fruits, and . . . the firstborn of thy sons shalt thou give unto me. Likewise shalt thou do with thine oxen, and with thy sheep." We all know what happened on a regular basis to oxen and sheep in the Old Testament.

Thomas Paine made a perceptive comment relative to this issue on page 295 of volume 9 in *The Life and Works of Thomas Paine*: "Christian authors exclaim against the practice of offering up human sacrifice, which, they say, is done in some countries; and those authors make those exclamations without ever reflecting that their own doctrine of salvation is founded on a human sacrifice. They are saved by the blood of Christ. The Christian religion begins with a dream and ends with a murder."

A *twenty-third* charge would no doubt be considered by many to be even more disgusting than the ordering of human sacrifice. Believe it or not, in several instances, God actually condoned, if not promoted, cannibalism. Jer. 19:9 says, "I will cause them to eat the flesh of their sons and the flesh of their daughters, and they shall eat every one the flesh of his friend." Ezek. 5:10 says, "The fathers shall eat the sons in the midst of thee, and the sons shall eat their fathers; and I will execute judgments in thee." One could also cite Lev. 26:29, which says, "Ye shall eat the flesh of your sons, and the flesh of your daughters shall ye eat." In fact, Jesus himself bestowed a clear aura of approval on cannibalism when in John 6:53–54 he said, "I say to you, Except ye eat the flesh of the

Son of man, and drink his blood, ye have no life in you. Whoso eateth my flesh, and drinketh my blood, hath eternal life." One could also cite Deut. 28:53–57 and Isa. 49:26 for additional evidence that the biblical God resembles one of the more repulsive figures in a Count Dracula movie.

A *twenty-fourth* charge that could be leveled at the God of the Bible is that he promoted gambling. Joshua 14:2 says, "By lot was their inheritance, as the Lord commanded by the hand of Moses." Num. 26:52 says, "The Lord spake unto Moses saying . . . the land shall be divided by lot: according to the names of the tribes of their fathers they shall inherit. According to lot shall the possession thereof be divided between many and few." Num. 26:55–56 repeat this text. Apparently bingo isn't that far out of line after all.

A *twenty-fifth* charge comes under the category of brutality and shows why God could well have been one of the earliest catalysts for the creation of the Society for the Prevention of Cruelty to Animals. Josh 11:6 in the RSV says, "The Lord said to Joshua, . . . you shall hamstring their horses and burn their chariots with fire." According to *Webster's Dictionary,* a horse is hamstrung or crippled by having his leg tendons cut, especially the large tendon above and behind the hock. Talk about cruelty to animals! As inconsistent as it may be, many animal rights advocates enter churches and synagogues to worship a being whose behavior is antithetical to their own cause.

A *twenty-sixth* charge is sickening. According to Deut. 22:28–29, in the New International Version, a woman is required by God to marry her rapist and can never divorce. It says, "If a man happens to meet a virgin who is not pledged to be married and rapes her and they are discovered, he shall pay the girl's father fifty shekels of silver. He must marry the girl, for he has violated her. He can never divorce her as long as he lives."

One can't help wondering what being a virgin has to do with the issue and noticing that the entire problem is approached from the rapist's viewpoint. Notice that the text says he is required to marry her, when that may be no problem for him. What about the victim? Suppose she doesn't want to marry him, which would be a reasonable assumption? Also notice that God's law allows the rapist to buy his way out of criminal penalties. The male chauvinism of the entire situation is further evident in the fact that for exoneration the rapist pays the girl's father rather than the girl herself. Justice would require that she receive any monetary compensation involved, since one can reasonably assume that she experienced more trauma than her father.

A *twenty-seventh* charge has to do with a decidedly gross divine instruction found in Ezek 4:12, which says in the New International Version, "Eat the food as you would a barley cake; bake it in the sight of the people, using human excrement as fuel."

Food cooked in such a manner hardly sounds appetizing. Repulsive would be a more appropriate term.

A *twenty-eighth* charge highlights an injustice associated with one of the most famous of all biblical stories. In the Revised Standard Version Gen. 4:8-15 says, "Cain rose up against his brother Abel, and killed him. . . . And the Lord said, What have you done? . . . When you till the ground, it shall no longer yield to you its strength; you shall be a fugitive and a wanderer on the earth. Cain said to the Lord . . . whoever finds me will slay me. Then the Lord said to him, Not so! If any one slays Cain, vengeance shall be taken on him sevenfold."

Here we have a clear-cut case in which God not only excused a murderer with a nearly innocuous punishment but promised him protection from his enemies in the process. How one squares this with "Thou shalt not kill" and the associated penalties is anyone's guess. Talk about turning justice on its head! And we complain about overly lenient courts releasing convicted criminals because of overcrowded prisons! Just because the Ten Commandments were given to Moses centuries later does not excuse Cain. Then, again, perhaps the Ten Commandments were inoperative prior to Mt. Sinai and situational ethics, which fundamentalists deplore, were in vogue?

A *twenty-ninth* charge reflects more on God than Onan. Gen. 38:9-10 in the RSV says, "Onan knew that the offspring would not be his; so when he went in to his brother's wife he spilled the semen on the ground, lest he should give offspring to his brother. And what he did was displeasing in the sight of the Lord, and he slew him [Onan] also." Morality and common decency would dictate that what the Lord did was far more atrocious than the act of Onan. God actually killed a man because he refused to impregnate a woman to whom he was not even married, his sister-in-law. That's almost too ridiculous to discuss.

A *thirtieth* charge is morally revolting and could lead one to believe that God is a pervert. Isa. 3:17 says, "The Lord will smite with a scab the crown of the head of the daughters of Zion, and *The Lord will discover their secret parts.*" Any God engaged in discovering the private parts of women has a problem.

A *thirty-first* charge is that the biblical god is just plain brutal, if not vicious. Ezek 9:6 has God ordering the slaying of children: "Slay utterly old and young, both maids and little children, and women." In the same tradition 1 Sam. 15:3 says, "Slay both man and woman, infant and suckling."

Let's face it, the biblical God not only had a mean streak but was cold, callous, and inhumane.

A *thirty-second* charge is that God often just can't seem to harmonize penalty and crime. No matter how many bad acts one commits in this world the number is limited; it's finite. Yet Matt. 25:46 says, "These shall go away into everlasting punishment: but the righteous into life eternal." Eternal punishment in Hell for a finite number of acts will never be just, no matter how much rationalizing is employed.

The *thirty-third* and final charge is that God is a hypocrite of the highest order. He says "Thou shalt not kill" but he kills in numerous instances. We are told in 1 John 4:8 and 4:16 that God is love and 1 Cor. 13:4 in the RSV tells us love is not jealous. Yet Deut. 4:24 and many other verses say that God *is* jealous. God condemns adultery in the Ten Commandments, yet Matt. 1:18 says, "When as his [Jesus'] mother Mary was espoused to Joseph, before they came together, she was found with child of the Holy Ghost." The Holy Ghost, which is God, must have done something to impregnate Mary and if that wasn't adultery what was it?

In Lev. 19:18 in the RSV God says, "You shall not take vengeance or bear any grudge against the sons of your own people"; yet we find in Deut. 32:35 this same being saying, "To me belongeth vengeance." In Luke 6:27 people are told, "Love your enemies, do good to them which hate you"; but God certainly didn't practice love toward his enemies, as many verses clearly demonstrate. According to Prov. 6:16 in the Jewish Masoretic text, "There are six things the Lord hateth" and verse 6:19 of the same text says one of these is "he that soweth discord among brethren." Yet in Gen. 11:9 (NIV) we learn, "The Lord confused the language of the whole world." How's that for sowing discord! In Matt. 26:52 we are told by Jesus, "Put up again thy sword into his place: for all they that take the sword shall perish with the sword." But God made an entirely different pledge in Ezek. 21:5, which says, "That all flesh may know that I the Lord have drawn forth my sword out of his sheath: it shall not return any more." That sounds quite definitive no matter how you look at it. In Deut. 6:16 God tells people not to tempt the Lord their God, but Gen. 22:1 says, "God did tempt Abraham." God can tempt but we can't. Job 5:2 says, "Wrath killeth the foolish man, and envy slayeth the silly one," even though Psalms 18:7, Psalms 21:9, Ex. 32:10, and Num. 16:46 clearly show that wrath was one of God's more prominent traits. In 1 John 2:15 God says, "Love not the world, neither the things that are in the world. If any man love the world, the love of the Father is not in him." Yet John 3:16 says, "God so loved the world, that he gave his only begotten son." For someone to give his only begotten son, he must have loved the world immensely. Reconciling this with 1 John 2:15 will require an exercise in mental gymnastics.

In essence, God's policy is Do as I say, not as I do. If it's wrong for us; then it should be wrong for him. Otherwise, we have a being that is above morality. If God kills, lies, cheats, discriminates, and otherwise behaves in a manner that would put the Mafia to shame, that's Okay, he's God. He can do whatever he wants. Anyone who adheres to this philosophy has had his sense of morality, decency, justice, and humaneness warped beyond recognition by the very book that is supposedly preaching the opposite. If something is bad or immoral, it is bad and immoral, period, regardless of who commits the deed. Whether God or not, if Jesus had raped and murdered a woman, that would have been as despicable an act as any ever performed by a common criminal. Many Christians have had their sense of propriety so perverted that they would defend any actions, no matter how detestable, if they emanated from their divine heroes. Christians would do well to take note of the comment on page 198 in *The Age of Reason* by Thomas Paine, who said, "All our ideas of the justice and goodness of God revolt at the impious cruelty of the Bible. It is not a God, just and good, but a devil, under the name of God, that the Bible describes."

Ingersoll made an equally incisive observation on pages 239 and 240 of volume 2 of his *Works* in a section entitled "Some Mistakes of Moses": "A false friend, an unjust judge, a braggart, a hypocrite, a tyrant, sincere in hatred, jealous, vain and revengeful, false in promise, honest in curse, suspicious, ignorant, infamous and hideous—such is the God of the Pentateuch."

That summarizes the entire issue beautifully and puts everything in proper perspective.

The Patriarchs

Next to God, Jesus, and Paul, who will be discussed in a chapter yet to come, the Patriarchs are probably the most important figures in the biblical scheme of things. The leaders and heroes of the Old Testament, people about whom children's stories are so often written, play a very prominent role in the biblical morality play. What is kept from the audience, however, is that nearly all of these patriarchs are some of the most unsavory characters to have ever emerged from the annals of literature. Their careers are riddled with deeds so gross, so immoral, so distasteful that one would wonder why parents would ever want their children to even approach a book in which such critters play a crucial role. This situation has only been finessed by a tremendous amount of censoring and narrowly focusing on the few commendable deeds committed by this illustrious crew. An obligation to expose these demigods of depravity rests upon the shoulders of all those dedicated to truth and morality. And what better way to reveal their nefarious activities than by discussing them in alphabetical order? What follows are summaries of the careers of leading Old Testament biblical figures. Before proceeding, it is important to note that most of these characters are biblical heroes, not villains, whom children are supposed to admire, emulate, and rise on Sunday morning to read about. Citations of chapter and verse are provided for those who may question the veracity of that which follows.

Abraham told his wife to lie in Gen. 12:13 and debauched Hagar, his maidservant, in Gen. 16:4. He sent his maidservant and her child into the wilderness in Gen. 21:14. He lied in Gen. 20:2, and he married his half-sister in Gen. 20:11–12. Absalom ordered the killing of Amnon in 2 Sam. 13:28–29 and had sex in the open in 2 Sam. 16:22.

Amnon raped his sister, Tamar, in 2 Sam. 13:11–14.

Abimelech took a city and killed the inhabitants in Judg. 9:45 and murdered wantonly in Judg. 9:5.

Elijah committed murder in 1 Kings 18:40.

Elisha lied in 2 Kings 2:24, caused two bears to tear to pieces forty-two small boys who mocked his bald head, and told a man to lie in 2 Kings 8:10.

Gideon killed in Judg. 8:16–17, murdered prisoners in Judges 8:21, and committed polygamy in Judg. 8:30.

Isaac lied in Gen. 26:6–7 and attempted to sacrifice his wife to save himself in Gen. 26:9.

Jacob swindled his brother, Esau, out of his birthright (Gen. 25:31–33), cheated and lied to his father, Isaac (Gen. 27:19), and lied to Rachel, his wife (Gen. 29:12).

Jehoida ordered a murder (2 Kings 11:15–16); Jehu killed (2 Kings 9:24), ordered killings (2 Kings 10:25), and practiced lying and deception (2 Kings 10:18–19); Jephthah slaughtered in Judg. 11:33 and killed his own daughter in Judg. 11:39.

Jeremiah lied in Jer. 38:24–27.

Joab killed (2 Sam. 18:14) and David's friend Jonathan killed in 1 Sam. 14:13–14 and lied in 1 Sam. 20:28.

One of the most famous heroes about whom so many tears are shed was Joseph, the same Joseph who deceived his brothers in Gen. 42:7 and committed nepotism in Gen. 47:11.

Joshua killed and slaughtered without letup (Josh. 8:25–28), murdered prisoners (Josh. 8:29), and hamstrung horses (Josh. 11:9).

Laban lied in Gen. 29:15 and deceived in Gen. 29:20–25.

Lot offered his virgin daughters to a mob in Gen. 19:8.

Moses, the Israelite savior about whom movies are made, murdered an Egyptian (Exod. 2:12), ordered the murder of prisoners (Num. 31:17), ordered the keeping of young female prisoners who were virgins (Num. 31:18), led mass killings of women and children (Deut. 2:34), ordered killings (Deut. 13:15), wrote that he was a greater prophet than Jesus (Deut. 34:10), had a son out of wedlock (Exod. 2:21–22), and was kept from entering Canaan by God for four trangressions: unbelief (Num. 20:12), rebellion (Num. 27:12–14), trespassing (Deut. 32:51–52), and rash words (Psalms 106:32–33).

Samson killed (Judg. 14:19), slept with a harlot (Judg. 16:1), and lied to Delilah (Judg. 16:10, 13).

Samuel murdered in 1 Sam. 15:33.

Saul used his daughters as a snare (1 Sam. 18:20–21), ordered gambling (1 Sam. 14:42), killed people (1 Sam. 15:7–8), stripped himself naked and acted unstable (1 Sam. 19:24), admitted he sinned, played the fool and erred (1 Sam. 26:21), gave David's wife to another man (1 Sam. 25:44), and transgressed the laws of God by consulting a medium (1 Chron. 10:13–14).

Solomon ordered a murder (1 Kings 2:25), tried to kill Jeroboam (1 Kings

11:40), enslaved people (1 Kings 9:21), failed to keep God's statutes (1 Kings 11:11), did evil (1 Kings 11:6), and lied to his mother (1 Kings 2:20–25).

And finally, we come to David, who was excluded from our alphabetical sequence because of his exceptionally notorious career. If David wasn't a gangster, there is no such animal. He killed (1 Sam. 18:7), ordered murders (2 Sam. 1:15), ordered prisoners to be killed (2 Sam. 12:29–31), committed unprovoked aggression and mass killing (1 Sam. 27:8–11), gave up seven of Saul's descendants to be killed (2 Sam. 21:1–9), requested that Joab be killed as he lay dying (1 Kings 2:5–6), intentionally arranged for a man to be killed in battle so he could obtain his wife (2 Sam. 11:14–17), displeased the Lord (2 Sam. 11:26–27), impregnated another man's wife (2 Sam. 11:2–5), lied (1 Sam. 21:1–2), told his friend, Jonathan, to lie (1 Sam. 20:5–6), admitted he sinned by taking a census (2 Sam. 24:19), committed extortion (1 Sam. 25:2–8), prophesied incorrectly in his heart (1 Sam. 27:1), sent a spy into a city (2 Sam. 15:36), hamstrung horses (2 Sam. 8:4), locked up ten concubines for life for no apparent reason (2 Sam. 20:3), committed bigamy and polygamy (2 Sam. 3:2–3, 5:13), despised the word of the Lord (2 Sam. 12:9–11), and exposed himself like a pervert (2 Sam. 6:20).

This is the same David of whom the Bible says in 1 Kings 15:5, "David did that which was right in the eyes of the Lord." One can only imagine what any wrong would have been! In Acts 13:22 God says, "I have found David the son of Jesse a man after mine own heart." If so, then God's heart must be made of stone! The text of 1 Sam. 25:28 makes what appears to be the most absurd statement of all. "My Lord [David] fighteth the battles of the Lord, and evil hath not been found in thee all thy days." If David never committed evil, then either there is no such entity as evil or it needs to be redefined. The text of 2 Sam. 19:27 declares, "My lord the King [David] . . . is as an angel of God," and 1 Kings 15:3 says "His [Abijam's] heart was not perfect with the Lord his God, as the heart of David his father"? How preposterous! Can you imagine requiring children to read about the exploits of degenerates like these? Without censorship and selectivity, that could easily fall under the category of child abuse. No wonder Sunday School propaganda narrowly focuses upon such innocuous fables as Adam and Eve, the parting of the Red Sea, Samson and Delilah, and David and Goliath.

In summary, who can conceive of a more unscrupulous, despicable and debauched gang of reprobates than those found in the Old Testament? As Thomas Paine said on page 142 of volume 9 of his *Works,* "It is a history of the times, and a bad history the Old Testament is, and also a history of bad men, and bad actions, abounding with bad examples."

The Matriarchs

God and the patriarchs are not alone in their Old Testament perfidies. It is important to note that males do not have a monopoly on biblical skullduggery. A significant number of biblical matriarchs exhibited behavior that can only be described as revolting. Gen. 31:34–35 shows that Rachel deceived her father. Judges 4:21 describes how Jael murdered Sisera. Michal lied to Saul and Sarah lied in Gen. 18:15. In light of the fact that according to Ruth 3:9 Ruth went to bed with one of her cousins instead of marrying someone else, she could hardly be considered a model of virtue. Tamar seduced the father of her late husband and Rahab was a common prostitute. Bathsheba was an adulteress, since she appears to have gone to David willingly. And the most famous of all Old Testament females, Eve, is portrayed as the primary cause of sin, since Gen. 3:6 says she ate the forbidden fruit and gave it to her husband, who ate also. So men have no corner on the market when it comes to distasteful biblical figures.

The Prophets

Not only are God, the patriarchs, and the matriarchs an odious bunch, but the Bible repeatedly refers to many prophets as disreputable and objectionable characters. Hosea 9:7 in the RSV says, "The prophet is a fool, the man of the spirit is mad, because of your great iniquity and great hatred"; Micah 3:5 says, "Thus saith the Lord concerning the prophets that make my people err"; Lam. 2:14 says, "Your prophets have seen for you false and deceptive visions; they have not exposed your iniquity to restore your fortunes, but have seen for you oracles false and misleading;" 1 Kings 22:23 says, "The Lord hath put a lying spirit in the mouth of all these thy prophets"; Jer. 23:16 says, "Thus saith the Lord of hosts, Hearken not unto the words of the prophets that prophesy unto you: they make you vain: they speak a vision of their own heart, and not out of the mouth of the Lord"; and Ezek. 14:9 says, "If the prophet be deceived when he hath spoken a thing, I the Lord have deceived that prophet."

So, prophets not only lie but are intentionally deceived by God. With verses such as these, one can't help but wonder why Christians put trust in any of the prophets of old. How could you be sure you were not relying upon a prophet the Lord is deceiving? One would surely be treading on thin ice if he put his undivided trust in biblical prophets when the Lord himself says the prophet is a fool, the man of the spirit is mad, and prophets have seen false and deceptive visions. One could never be sure that the prophets upon which he is relying do not fall into the category of those who are deceiving intentionally or being surreptitiously deceived by God.

Peter

It is important to note that the Old Testament has no corner on odious and unsavory persons. Besides Paul, who will be discussed later, and Jesus, whom we have already analyzed, the New Testament's Peter is unquestionably a defective figure with repulsive credentials. This individual, the first pope whom many deem to be such a paragon of virtue that he was canonized as a saint, committed all of the following acts for which chapter and verse are readily available in the issue 5 of *Biblical Errancy*:

Peter denied Jesus three times and lied in the process; he felt the report of the Resurrection was an idle tale and did not believe the women; he was called Satan by Jesus, which is more than enough by itself to disqualify him from anything meritorious. He admitted he was sinful; he was rebuked by Jesus for having little faith; he drew a sword and violently cut off a man's ear; he deceptively and erroneously stated he would never desert Jesus although all others might. He will be denied in heaven because Jesus said in Matt. 10:33, "Whosoever shall deny me before men, him will I also deny before my Father which is in heaven." He wanted to know what was in it for him if he followed Jesus; he cowardly sneaked along behind as they took Jesus to the trial; he entered Samaritan villages in defiance of Jesus' commands in Matt. 10:5; he rebuked Jesus and accused him of making a false statement; he repeatedly failed to stay awake at the Garden of Gethsemane when asked to do so by Jesus; in John 21:20 he asked Jesus who was going to betray him, even though he was present when Jesus exposed his future betrayer at the Last Supper and was present when Judas led the soldiers to Jesus's arrest; he asked for signs to be given to his generation in opposition to what Jesus said should be done in Mark 8:12; he was afraid to eat with converted Christian Gentiles because Jewish legalists were coming and would object; before the entire community he publicly accused Ananias and his wife of lying to God and the Holy Ghost, which frightened them so much that they fell dead; he lied when he said he would stand behind Jesus to the end; he alleged Lot was righteous, despite the fact that Lot offered his virgin daughters to a crowd; and he was rebuked by Paul in Gal. 2:13–14 for not walking according to the gospel.

How's that for a saintly career! And that's the person whom the Catholic Church alleges is of such integrity and stature that Jesus chose him to be the first pope. If he is the rock, the cornerstone of the Catholic Church, then that organization resides on a shaky foundation, indeed.

Conclusion

The obvious conclusion to be drawn from this chapter and those covered earlier is that heroes worthy of emulation are not to be found in Scripture. The following label should be placed on all copies of the Bible. "WARNING: If not appropriately censored, the contents of this book are dangerous to the mental health and moral development of children and adults."

10

Injustice

Original Sin, Evil, Innocents, Suffering, Atonement, Heaven, Exclusivism, Hell, Sexism, Slavery

If there is any topic upon which Christians expect more from their God than any other, it lies in the realm of justice and fair play. Without justice, without rewards and punishments based on deeds, all else is for nought. Who would worship a being that operated on no other basis than whim and capriciousness, and who would venerate a book that portrayed injustice and inequities as standard fare to be expected from the world at large and God in particular?

Indeed, for God and his book to be objects of adulation and respect, one would expect the bad guys to get theirs and the innocent to be exonerated, when all is said and done. If, in the end, good people get little or nothing and evildoers prosper, obtaining all that is desirable in this world as well as that which is expected to come, then Christianity is a cruel joke and Christ is one of the greatest charlatans of all time. Millions of people will have been deceived by one of the shrewdest con-games to have ever come down the chute. They will have devoted their lives to a fantasy, a dream, that is as far from reality as black is from white. The question to be addressed in this chapter is determining the degree to which the God of the Bible is just and merciful and the degree to which the Bible itself propagates a message inclined to foster and promote justice and fair play. Undoubtedly that is one of the most important questions bearing on the Bible's net worth. If it does not promote justice and a sense of impartiality, then it is not only something less than the word of a perfect being, but a book deserving of contempt and condemnation. So the decisive question becomes: What does the record show? Unfortunately, and succinctly stated, it shows a book riddled with injustice and a God dispensing inequities like a farmer tossing seed to the chicks. In the areas of original sin, evil, heaven, hell, innocents, women, slavery, the Atonement, and elsewhere, the biblical record is little short of appalling, and for substantiation each of these topics deserves a thorough examination.

Original Sin

What better place to begin our analysis than by focusing on the injustice associated with the appearance of sin, or what could more accurately be called antisocial behavior. Rom. 5:12 says, "Wherefore as by one man sin entered into the world, and death by sin; and so death passed upon all men, for that all have sinned." On page 49 in his work *Essential Christianity* Walter Martin, the "Bible Answer Man" of radio, says, "In the Adamic fall every area of man's physical, mental, and spiritual capacities were impaired." He follows this up on page 60 by saying, "In the Fall every property of man's physical, moral, and spiritual being suffered the effects of the Adamic transgression."

Beyond doubt this is one of the most preposterous concepts ever generated by the mind of man. The idea that all people are to be punished because of an act of one, a relatively innocuous act at that, borders on the bizarre and is a living refutation of any belief in a biblical God of justice and impartiality. One of the most important questions discussed earlier is: Why are we being punished for Adam's sin? After all, *he* ate the forbidden fruit, we didn't. It is his problem, not ours, especially in light of Deut. 24:16, which says the children shall not be punished for the sins of their fathers.

Yet the entire tenor of the theological concept known as original sin is based upon the punishment of millions for the act of one man, their original father, Adam. So where is the justice? Thomas Paine was quite perceptive when he said on page 333 of his *Theological Works,* "It is said that Adam ate the forbidden fruit, commonly called an apple, and thereby subjected himself and all of his posterity for ever to eternal damnation. This is worse than visiting the sins of the fathers upon the children unto the *third and fourth generations."*

Secondly, Rom. 5:12 says "all have sinned," which is little short of ridiculous in light of the fact that billions of people were yet to exist when that verse emerged. How could that which does not yet exist sin? In addition, Psalms 58:3 says, "The wicked are estranged from the womb: they go astray as soon as they be born, speaking lies." How can babies just out of the womb be morally responsible for anything they may do, and how could they speak anything, much less lies? Yet that is precisely what the verse says. "They go astray as soon as they be born, speaking lies." What foolishness!

And finally, the entire biblical presentation of the process by which original sin came into being is fraught with problems. It is not only unjust but not borne out by the text itself. After Adam and Eve ate the forbidden fruit, curses were heaped on all concerned. Gen. 3:14 says, "The Lord God said to the serpent, 'Because you have done this, cursed are you above all cattle, and above all wild animals; upon your belly you shall go, and dust you shall eat all the days of your life." One should note that these curses on the serpent are of very little practical consequence, although they sound horrific. Besides the fact that it is difficult to imagine how a serpent would have been moving prior to the curse, serpents don't eat dust now. So where is the curse? In addition, Gen. 3:15 in the Revised Standard Version says, "I will put enmity between you and the woman, and between your seed and her seed; he shall bruise your head, and you shall bruise his heel." The "he" could not be Jesus, who will supposedly kill Satan, the Serpent. If it were, why are there sinners among his followers today? Rom. 16:20 says, "The God of peace shall bruise Satan under your feet shortly" and 1 Thess. 2:18 says, "We would have come to you, even I Paul, once and again; but Satan hindered us." Both verses show that even after the death of Jesus, Satan still lived and exercised control over such paragons of virtue as Paul.

But even more important for our purposes is Gen. 3:16 (RSV), in which God is addressing the woman and says, "I will greatly multiply your pain in childbearing; in pain you shall bring forth children." Why should all women endure pain in childbirth because of Eve's behavior? Where's the justice? Moreover, attributing the pains of childbirth to a curse is far from scientific. Another part of verse 3:16 says, "Your desire shall be for your husband." How that is a curse is yet to be determined, although some divorcees may no doubt agree. According to the verse 3:17 God said to Adam, "Cursed is the ground because of you; in toil you shall eat of it all the days of your life"; and the verse 3:18 says, "Thorns and thistles it shall bring forth to you; and you shall eat the plants of the field." But earlier, in Gen. 1:29, God had said, "Behold, I have given you every plant yielding seed which is upon the face of all the earth, and every tree with seed in its fruit; you shall have them for food." In other words, according to Gen. 1:29, the plants of the field had already been bestowed upon man for food. So how was this a curse?

Gen. 3:19 (RSV) says, "In the sweat of your face you shall eat bread till you return to the ground." Yet Gen. 2:5 (KJV), which earlier said, "There was not a man to till the ground," and Gen 2:15, which says, "The Lord God took the man, and put him into the Garden of Eden to dress it and to keep it," show that man was put in the Garden of Eden to work and maintain it. This more closely resembles a blessing of healthful work than idle existence. So, when all is said and done, where is the curse and, more importantly, where is any justice contained within the pronouncements?

Because there is so little of a textual nature to support the concept of original sin, the Jews placed no reliance upon it whatever. Many Jewish scholars contend that from the first curse in Genesis 3 until the end of Malachi's book, amid all the ravings threatening death upon the chosen people, there is not the remotest reference in all the Bible to the snake story, the curse of Adam, the fall of man or the necessity of redemption from "original sin" and the fires of hell. Hell and its vicissitudes are totally nonexistent in the Hebrew scheme of things. All the furies of God are temporal terrors and end with the death of the accused. Jesus never implied his mission was to undo what Adam had done and not one of the gospel writers uttered anything about Adam, the curse, or redemption. To shorten a long story, the concept of original sin is not only patently unjust but biblically unsupportable.

The question of how original sin came on the scene, the injustice associated with same, and the wisdom of having Adam as man's chosen representative was addressed in R. C. Sproul's apologetic work, *Reason to Believe*. On page 96 he states, "It raises the further question of God's holding me responsible for what somebody else did long before I was born. How can a just God do that? Why am I blamed for something I didn't do?" While rationalizing the problem he says on the following page,

> Only once in all of history have I had an infallibly chosen representative. That was in Eden. To be sure, God made the choice for me; but I must face the question: "Was God's infallible choice of my representative a more accurate or less accurate choice than I could or would have made myself?" If we say that God's choice was anything less than a perfect one, we slander His righteousness and only prove the accuracy of His selection.

Sproul's defense is hardly worthy of a response. In the first place, Adam obviously was not "an infallibly chosen representative" because he sinned. And as far as my making the choice is concerned, I couldn't have done any worse than God. God's choice was clearly less than perfect and hardly proves the wisdom of his selection. Sproul is desperately groping in the dark for a straw to grasp.

Evil

On pages 124 through 126 in his book *Reason to Believe* Sproul addresses the question of how evil could ever have come into existence in the first place if a just God were really in charge of the universe. He says,

> These difficulties are why Karl Barth has called the fall of man an "impossible possibility." Why does he make such an utterly absurd statement?. . . . Barth's clever statement of an impossible possibility is not the remark of a stupid man.

The statement is made not to explain the fall but to dramatize the rational problems connected with it. Barth uses startling language to underline the rational difficulty in explaining the fall. Some search for the explanation for Adam's fall within the dimension of the influence of Satan. This approach simply removes the dilemma one step. All the difficulties raised with respect to the "how" of Adam's fall must then be faced with the question of the "how" of Satan's fall. . . . It is not my intent to be the devil's advocate or to lend assistance to those who reject Christianity. . . . I am not trying to give the skeptic more ammunition than he may already have. I am trying to make it clear that the problem is a severe one and one for which I have no adequate solution. I do not know how evil could originate with a good God. I am baffled by it, and it remains a troublesome mystery to me.

On page 132 in his book *Bible Difficulties* William Arndt concedes the same dilemma by stating,

How could evil enter a world, which was good, yea, perfect, when the work of creation was completed? Here we face a mystery baffling to all thinkers, for which we, standing on the Bible, can offer no other explanation than the one given in divine revelation, to wit, that Satan brought sin into the world. If the inquiry is pushed beyond this point and it is asked, how could Satan, who was evidently created a good being, become the enemy of God? we are not able to give a solution. It is a question on which God has not thought it necessary to inform us in His Holy Word.

And that's readily understandable, of course, in light of the fact that there is no solution. It's another one of those "mysteries" injected at crucial points in Christian theology.

Innocents

Another topic bothering those with a conscience is the biblical God's propensity to punish and even kill children for the deeds of their fathers, the same God that is supposed to be such a fountain of justice and mercy. God orders the slaying of children in Ezek. 9:6 by saying, "Slay utterly old and young, both maids and little children, and women." and in 1 Sam. 15:3 he says, "Go and smite Amalek, and utterly destroy all that they have, and spare them not; but slay both man and woman, infant and suckling." Exod. 12:29 says "It came to pass, that at midnight the Lord smote all the firstborn in the land of Egypt, from the firstborn of Pharaoh that sat on his throne unto the firstborn of the captive that was in the dungeon," showing that God occasionally went even further and did the job himself. Exod. 20:5 says, "I the Lord thy God am a jealous

God, visiting the iniquity of the fathers upon the children unto the third and fourth generation of them that hate me." and clearly shows that he was not above being unjust.

The tortuous rationalizations apologists conjure up to justify obvious injustices are nothing short of drivel. A good example is found on page 260 in *The Bible Has the Answer* by apologists Morris and Clark. They state,

> There is really no such thing as the "innocent" suffering. Since "all have sinned and come short of the glory of God" (Rom. 3:23), there is no one who has the right to freedom from God's wrath on the basis of his own innocence. As far as babies are concerned, and others who may be incompetent mentally to distinguish right from wrong, it is clear from both Scripture and universal experience that they are sinners by nature and thus will inevitably become sinners by choice as soon as they are able to do so.

What palaver! In the same vein author Sidney Collett says on page 111 in *All About the Bible,* "In cases where little ones were slain, the mercy of God is even more conspicuous. The strong probability is that, in many cases, these poor little children, having the blood of their wicked parents in their veins, would, had they been allowed to live, have developed their parents' sins; but their early death saved them from so dreadful a future."

Could one devise a more absurd explanation? In rebuttal:

First, God is showing anything but mercy. Killing babies, infants, and children hardly falls under the category of mercy.

Second, you don't execute somebody on an assumption, or what Collett refers to as a "strong probability," that he may commit a crime. The fact is that the person has not committed a crime and punishment cannot be justifiably dispensed until he or she has done so. That's nothing more than common sense. Otherwise, anyone could be imprisoned at any time on the assumption that he was going to engage in criminal activity in the future. In fact, you could even kill people and say that you forestalled crimes they would have committed had they lived.

Third, what is this "blood in the veins" nonsense? Since when are people judged by the kinds of parents they have? I haven't heard of people being condemned for having "bad blood" in years. This is one of those concepts that belongs in the museum of antiquities.

Fourth, if reasoning of this kind were carried to its logical conclusion, we should kill all babies not only to prevent any sins or crimes they may commit in the future but to thwart any possibility of them committing acts that would exclude them from heaven. They should be killed just to be on the safe side. After all, why jeopardize an eternity of bliss for a mere seventy or eighty years of temptation and access to sin?

Suffering

Another problem with the biblical God is his obvious inclination to allow suffering to reign supreme. Why God allows suffering to even exist, much less dominate, is a question that has always bothered Christians and all other believers in a divine being. One can't help but think of the question posed to Robinson Crusoe by his native friend, Friday, during a religious indoctrination session: "Why he not kill Devil?" If God is as merciful, just, and kind as his followers would have us believe, then why doesn't he destroy all sources of evil and suffering? Certainly he has the power. Apologist Frank Colquhoun tangentially addresses this issue when he is asked on page 93 of his work *Hard Questions* why God allows the innocent to suffer. He says in response,

> In honesty we must recognize this problem and admit the great burden of un-deserved suffering due to poverty, malnutrition, disasters, disease, and the self-ishness of people. Nothing is gained by trying to belittle this paradox, that God who is loving and good has placed man in a world where the innocent often suffer. . . . It is beyond our finite minds to understand why God permits tragic suffering which appears to have no possible beneficial result.

Colquhoun conveniently fails to mention, however, that according to the Bible, God does not just *allow* suffering and injustice. He's a primary contributor. It's interesting to note that nearly every time Christians are faced with a dilemma of this nature, they avoid the inevitable conclusion that God is something less than they would wish and retire to the more comfortable, although infinitely less honest, suggestion that the answer is beyond man's limited intelligence and will be provided in the great beyond. Dilemmas of this nature are designated mysteries. The effort to escape unavoidable conclusions can only be called a blatant copout.

Atonement

Closely associated with the travesty of original sin is the injustice of the atonement. Just as it is ridiculous for all of humanity to be punished for the deeds of one man, it is absurd for one man to die on a cross for the misdeeds of all of humanity. It may be a magnanimous gesture, but it has nothing to do with justice. No judge worth his weight in salt would agree to a man being executed for the deeds of others simply because the former agreed to do so. Any god who would accept such an arrangement does not want justice; he just wants blood and doesn't really care who pays the price as long as someone endures the supreme penalty. Basic to all systems of justice is that he who does the crime does the time. Substitutes are not allowed. If that were permissible, rich people could simply pay others to serve their sentence for them. Robert Ingersoll spoke correctly of the Atonement when he said on page 235 of volume 1 in his *Works*, "This doctrine is the consummation of two outrages—forgiving one crime and committing another."

And on page 370 of volume 2 Ingersoll summarized the topic as well as anyone by saying, "The absurdity of the doctrine known as 'The Fall of Man,' gave birth to that other absurdity known as 'The Atonement.' So that now it is insisted that, as we are rightfully charged with the sin of somebody else, we can rightfully be credited with the virtues of another."

Shmuel Golding provides additional evidence that the Atonement, besides being grossly unjust, was wholly invalid. He states on page 32 in volume 2 of his work *The Light of Reason,*

> Another reason why Jesus could not have been an acceptable sacrifice or the lamb of God, besides the fact that different types of sins required different types of sacrifices in the Old Testament, is that he was not burnt on the altar. Sacrifices, sin offerings for unintentional sins and guilt offerings were all burnt . . . and Jesus . . . was not eaten by the priests who must eat all the sacrifices. . . . The Law states that every man's sacrifice had to be perfect and without spot and blemish. . . . Yet the NT tells us that Jesus was smitten, he was spat upon, he had a crown of thorns pushed into his head which rendered him torn, thus not a perfect sacrifice. . . . One cannot tear the Scripture apart. If Jesus was in place of a sin offering, he must fulfill all the requirements of the sin offering. Thus he should have been slaughtered on the altar instead of a Roman cross, perfect instead of wounded, roasted and eaten instead of buried in a tomb.

Golding attacks the importance of blood sacrifice by saying,

> The Scriptures clearly state that blood was *one* way of obtaining an atonement. There are indeed other forms of atonement as seen in Lev. 5:11–13 where it states that *flour* can make atonement for the soul. *Money* can atone for the soul as seen in Exod. 30:15–16; *jewelry* can atone for the soul as seen in Num. 31:50, and in Num. 14:17–20 and in Hos. 14:3 we find that prayer can atone for the soul.

Thus, the statement in Heb. 9:22 (RSV), "Without the shedding of blood there is no forgiveness of sins," is wholly unsupportable from a broader biblical perspective.

The Atonement has other major problems as well, which are highlighted on pages 136 to 138 in *Jesus, A Prophet of Islam* by Muhammad Rahim. The author states,

Briefly speaking, the doctrine of the atonement preaches that man is born in a state of sin because of the first wrong action of Adam, and that Jesus, by his (supposed) crucifixion, atones for this state of sin and all the wrong actions of those who take baptism and follow him. . . . Socianus denied all this . . . and refuted the doctrine of atonement on the following grounds: Christ could not have offered an infinite sacrifice for sins, since Christ, according to the Gospel narration, suffered only for a short time. The most intense suffering for a limited period is as nothing compared with the eternal suffering to which man was liable [i.e., Hell]. If it is said that the suffering is greater in so far as he who suffers it is infinite, so also the power to endure the suffering is greater. But even the suffering of an infinite being cannot take the place of eternal suffering. . . . The doctrine of the atonement was also indirectly disputed by Socianus by his affirming that Jesus was not God, but a man. For there is no way that a man could atone for all the wrong actions of mankind.

This latter comment brings into focus one of the more perplexing problems in Christian theology. Who or what died on the Cross? If God died then we have an impossibility, for God cannot die. If a man died then we have an event of no real import, for the death of a man could not save anybody. As apologist Charles Ryrie says on page 282 in his book *Basic Theology,* "The savior had to be human in order to be able to die, for God does not die, and the Savior had to be God in order to make that death an effective payment for sin."

But this dual nature was roundly attacked by Rahim on page 139 of his book, where he states,

The doctrine of the Trinity was also refuted by Socianus on the grounds that it is not possible for Jesus to have two natures simultaneously. He said that two substances having opposite properties cannot combine into one person, and such properties are mortality and immortality: to have a beginning and to be without a beginning, to be mutable and to be immutable. Again, two natures each of which is apt to constitute a separate person, cannot be huddled into one person. For, instead of one, there, of necessity, arise two persons and consequently they become two Christs, one divine and one human.

In conclusion, apologists Morris and Clark added exaggerated rhetoric to this whole issue by saying on page 260 of *The Bible Has the Answer*: "The Lord Jesus Christ . . . suffered more than anyone else who ever lived." Apparently they are not aware of the agonies associated with being skinned alive, strapped over an anthill, or eaten alive. Crucifixion is not the most painful way to die. Man is considerably more ingenious than that.

Heaven

If there is any area upon which the minds of all Christians are focused and in which justice should flow like waters from a mighty stream, it lies in that realm to which all Christians aspire to ascend, the place commonly known as heaven. Surely in this area more than anywhere else one can expect justice to reign supreme. But unfortunately Christian theology has developed in such a manner as to forestall any possibility of justice denied now being granted later. Many practical problems clearly show that the entire concept is anything but viable and reeks of injustice and partiality. Yet few people have invested sufficient time or effort to soberly critique what a real heaven would entail. Some of the most poignant questions to be addressed with respect to the viability of heaven are the following:

First, if the number of rewards and possessions in heaven are equal, regardless of the number of good deeds committed on earth, won't that create dissension and a feeling among many that heaven is far from what they expected? And if those rewards and possessions are not equal won't that just add to the inequities?

Second, the Bible repeatedly says that people will be rewarded according to their works. For corroboration one could cite Matt. 16:27 ("For the Son of man shall come . . . and then he shall reward every man according to his works"); Rom. 2:5–6 ("The righteous judgment of God; Who will render to every man according to his deeds"); Rev. 22:12 ("My reward is with me, to give every man according as his work shall be"); Psalms 62:12 ("For thou renderest to every man according to his work"); Rev. 20:12 ("And the dead were judged out of those things which were written in the books, according to their works"); and Rev. 20:13 ("And they were judged every man according to their works").

But where does the rewarding occur, since this world is certainly not the locale, and there is no biblical basis for an intermediate stage, such as purgatory? Apparently it occurs in heaven. If so, does that mean some people in heaven will have six Cadillacs while others will have only one or two, figuratively speaking? How rewards will be dispensed and in what form is a very practical question that is rarely addressed. Since some people committed more good deeds on earth than others, some mechanism must exist by which some will receive more rewards than others. As a result, the inequality so evident on earth will continue and no doubt accelerate in heaven.

Which is the true heaven? One in which people receive equal rewards regardless of the number of good acts committed on earth, or one in which rewards are greater for those who generated the larger number of good deeds? The former sounds like injustice in action; the latter sounds like inequality in action and inequality is something with which this world is abundantly endowed. On page 17 in his work *Dr. Rice, Here is my Question,* apologist John R. Rice was asked if all Christians have the same happiness and joy in heaven and he conceded inequities would prevail: "No, 1 Cor. 3:11–15 clearly shows that many Christians

will have little reward or none. . . . Certainly there will be differences in rewards."
That hardly sounds like a realm of eternal bliss!

An ancillary problem of similar import has always plagued the conservative wing of Christianity. By believing that one is saved by faith alone, fundamentalists have managed to box themselves into a corner and discount one of the most important factors in the Christian scheme of justice—Judgment Day. Their dilemma is quite simple. If one is saved by faith alone, then why have a Judgment Day to begin with? Why have what they refer to as the "Great White Throne Judgment," when the decision as to whether you will spend eternity in heaven or hell is consummated on the day you die? If you accepted Jesus at some time in your life, your eternal existence in heaven is assured. If you never accepted Jesus, you are doomed to spend eternity in hell. Deeds are of no importance in this view. All that matters is whether or not you have accepted Jesus as your personal savior. All else is for naught. Consequently, what is there to judge on Judgment Day? The answer is *nothing*. The decision that matters is past. On page 317 in *The Bible Has the Answer* fundamentalists Morris and Clark concede this problem by saying, "Believers will not be judged as to salvation on the day of the last judgment, because Christ has already borne their judgment when He died for them on the cross."

On page 89 in his work *The Future Explored* apologist Tim Weber aptly states,

> For those in Christ, salvation is a present reality and the final judgment has already taken place. . . . One would not normally expect the verdict before the trial (in this case, the last judgment), but that is precisely what has happened. God has already judged the case of those who accept Christ so they are no longer in jeopardy. . . . Christians have eternal life *now*. Salvation is a present possession. Christians have already been tried and found not guilty before the divine bar of justice because of their faith in Jesus Christ.

A *third* issue to be faced with regard to the existence of heaven is whether or not everything in heaven is abundant and free as is commonly believed. The answer is either yes or no, assuming something is there besides people. In either case, how could heaven be synonymous with paradise? Either we would have to work for that which we sought, or we would be given that which we did not earn. The former does not sound that appealing and the latter violates Paul's admonition in 2 Thess. 3:10: "When we were with you, this we commanded you, that if any would not work, neither should he eat."

Moreover, to say our finite number of good deeds on earth earn us infinitely free rewards in heaven is as unjust as to say our finite sins on earth earn us infinite punishment in hell. One iniquity is as horrendous as the other.

Fourth, do you continue to learn in heaven or is your knowledge restricted to that which was learned on earth? If your reservoir of information grows, then how could that occur without interaction with something other than people and how could the mistakes that always accompany the learning process be avoided? If growth does not occur, then aren't unequal levels of awareness eternally fixed?

Fifth, how could heaven be a utopia when every inhabitant will be far from perfect? Even those we love the most have undesirable traits and would have to be changed. Who can think of a person or group with whom they would want to spend an eternity, since everyone who ever lived is far from perfect? If personalities are not altered and perfected in heaven, how will you be kept from encountering unpleasantness from those who earned admittance but are nevertheless displeasing? If people are segregated to avoid this dilemma, you will be alone forever, because everyone displays some disagreeable characteristics.

Sixth, does everyone in heaven have the same degree of intelligence? If not, then aren't unheavenly feelings of inferiority and inadequacy unavoidable, especially in light of the fact that they would be justified?

Seventh, do people reproduce in heaven or is the number anchored forever? If reproduction is prohibited, wouldn't those who wanted children feel they were in something other than heaven? Or is the desire to have children abolished? If the number is allowed to increase, does this occur by the natural procreative process? And if people are *created* in heaven, how could God be just, since they would have been allowed to bypass the earthly test that everyone must surmount in order to attain heaven? People born in heaven would never have accepted Jesus and/or performed good deeds.

Eighth, how will people be recognized in heaven? If everyone has the appearance they died with on earth, won't many be saddled with features they wished to improve or eliminate? Or is the appearance of everyone altered as desired and you are simply told in some manner who is who? Or is the countenance of everyone completely abolished? One can only guess how you would recognize someone who has no appearance whatever. If you die as an infant are you forever an infant in heaven? According to the fundamentalist John R. Rice, there will be no alteration of appearances in heaven whatever, so how you appear now is fixed for all time. On page 16 in *Dr. Rice, Here Is My Question* Rice says, "In heaven not only shall we know those we know on earth, but we shall know others also. No one will need to introduce me to Paul or to David or to Barnabas or to the martyr Stephen or to the sweet Mary!" If no introductions are required, then obviously no major alteration of features will occur.

These are only a few of the many questions that must be addressed by those who take heaven seriously and seek to provide a rationale for its existence. Queries of this nature aren't immaterial because millions of people are literally staking their lives on heaven's existence. Everything they do and say is done with an eye on the final arena, the expected reward, and they should realize that problems as potent as many found throughout the Bible accompany the whole concept.

On page 184 in *508 Answers to Bible Questions* apologist M. R. DeHaan admits that not much is known about Heaven by saying, "There is not much in the Bible concerning conditions in heaven, and we do not know exactly just what all of us will be like when we get there." Exactly? Is DeHaan serious? They don't even know roughly!

Exclusivism

Another massive injustice inherent in Christianity in general and biblical fundamentalism in particular arises from that infamous verse, John 14:6, in which Jesus says, "I am the way, the truth, and the life: no man cometh unto the father, but by me," as well as John 3:18, 3:36, and 1 John 5:12. Each contends beyond any doubt that acceptance of Jesus as one's savior is an absolute requirement for salvation. But what do you do about people who lived in the Western hemisphere before missionaries arrived? What about the billions of beings that die as fetuses, infants, mental deficients, etc.? For them to accept Jesus would be impossible, so they are condemned to Hell because of conditions over which they had no control. Deut. 32:4 says God is just, but where is the justice?

This problem has plagued Christian apologists since time immemorial and on page 185 in *508 Answers to Bible Questions* DeHaan seeks to provide a solution by saying, "All children who die before the age of responsibility go to heaven, and none of them are lost." The obvious problem with this explanation lies in the fact that there is nothing in the Bible about an age of accountability or responsibility. Where DeHaan is getting this nonsense is anyone's guess. It would no doubt be nice from the apologetic viewpoint if such a concept had biblical viability but it does not. The Bible does not allow for exceptions. It does not say all people must accept Jesus, except children, infants, and fetuses. It says "no man," not many men, not most men, not a few men, but *no* man "cometh to the father but by me" (John 14:6). That's about as absolute as one can be. Later, on the same page, DeHaan says, "The Bible does not have much to say concerning the condition of babies in heaven" when, in reality, it does not have much to say about the condition of anyone in heaven, babies or otherwise.

Hell

There is probably no Christian concept upon which more ridicule, scorn, and castigation have been leveled than that of hell. Even many within the Christian community itself have rejected the idea of eternal punishment. Unfortunately for them, the concept is quite sustainable biblically and belief in its existence is obligatory for all true Christians. Once having realized that hell is a valid biblical concept, two major difficulties face the true believer:

First, regardless of how many evil deeds one may have committed in this world, the number is limited. You can only do so much within a lifespan of seventy to a hundred years. Thus, since the number of possible deeds is finite, how can God be just in assigning eternal punishment for them? While confronting this criticism, apologist Charles Ryrie provided the following subterfuge on page 521 of *Basic Theology.* "Others argue that a just God would not give infinite punishment for finite sin. But this ignores that important principle that crime depends on the object against whom it is committed (an infinite God). . . . Striking a post is not as culpable an act as striking a human being. All sin is ultimately against an infinite God and deserves infinite punishment."

What kind of justice is this? One might just as well say that killing the king should be punished far more severely than killing the janitor. In any system worthy of being called just, the nature of the act is of far greater importance than the nature of the one who was wronged. Talk about partiality! This explanation is the very essence of favoritism and its Siamese twin, nepotism. God is not the victim of sin any more than those living in Japan are the victims of murders occurring in New York. God may get offended, but he is not the victim. Ryrie's final comment is preposterous. If "all sin deserves infinite punishment," then someone who did nothing more than steal a pencil or lie about a report card grade throughout his earthly career would warrant eternal punishment. If that is justice, then the word has no relevance and should be expunged from the dictionary.

The second major problem associated with the concept of hell relates to whether or not all punishments in Hell are of equal severity. Do they vary in intensity? For all punishments to be equal would be as unjust as having equal rewards in heaven. Some people deserve far more than others in both rewards and punishments. On the other hand, if punishments vary in severity, then the fires afflicting some must be considerably cooler than those torturing others. On page 178 in *508 Answers to Bible Questions* DeHaan is asked if all the unsaved will receive identical punishments, or will there be degrees of punishment. In response, he says, "Concerning the unsaved receiving the same punishment, the Bible plainly teaches that there will be degrees of punishment, depending upon the light which men and women have had, and rejected while here upon the earth (see Luke 12:47–48 and Rev. 20:12–13)." Four pages earlier DeHaan stated, "There will be as many degrees of punishment in hell, as there will be degrees of reward in heaven."

In the same vein apologists Morris and Clark say on page 317 in *The Bible Has the Answer,* "There will be degrees of punishment in hell, graded in accordance with the individual's degree of guilt. . . . And just as there are degrees of punishment in hell, so there are degrees of reward in heaven." When asked the same question, apologist John R. Rice says on page 18 in *Dr. Rice, Here Is My Question,*

The Bible teaches that . . . Hell is hotter for some people than for others. In Revelation 20:12-13 we are told that the unsaved dead will be judged according to their works. Judgment will be on the basis of what men deserve. People will go to Hell because they deserve to go; some have a worse Hell because they deserve a worse Hell. . . . This teaching that Hell will be more bearable for some than others is found elsewhere in the Bible also. . . . Hell will certainly be hotter for some than for others.

On page 302 in the same book Rice says, "But in Hell there will be a different weight of punishment for people depending on the degree of their sin, the light which they had."

Absent from all of the above is a crucial consideration. How can there be degrees of punishment in a region in which one will spend an eternity? All eternities are of equal duration and no one can have a longer eternity than someone else. Even if someone were to receive far greater pain on a daily basis than someone else, those receiving the lesser amount would never be outdistanced by those receiving the greater suffering. Ultimately, the amount of pain inflicted cannot be unequal, since there is no limit to an eternity. Nevertheless, despite all the problems accompanying the concept of hell, it remains an absolutely indispensable concept in Christianity. As apologist Frank Colquhoun correctly stated on page 75 in his book *Hard Questions,*

When all is said and done, what becomes of the whole Christian faith if hell is found to be fictitious? Then we must say that the biblical warnings about the danger and destructiveness of sin are thoroughly exaggerated and morbid. Then we must say that the agonizing sufferings of Christ were shockingly unnecessary. Then we must say the choice between life and death with which the whole Bible confronts us is a colossal bluff.

Sexism

Another monstrous injustice propagated by the Bible lies in the arena of that which is generally known as male chauvinism or sexism. One need only read the Bible to see that it is a bastion of male supremacy and female subservience. Verses relegating women to an inferior status abound throughout the Old and New Testaments. Indeed, the biblical position assigned to women lies somewhere between that of a slave and a domestic household servant.

More than any other biblical figure, Paul is responsible for Christianity's degradation of women. His epistles abound in sexual inequities and male dominance. Some of the most relevant verses are: 1 Cor. 11:3 ("I would have you know, that the head of every man is Christ; and the head of the woman is the man"); 1 Cor. 11:7-9 ("The woman is the glory of the man. For the man is not of the woman; but the woman of the man. Neither was the man created for the woman; but the woman for the man"); Eph. 5:22–24 ("Wives, submit yourselves unto your own husbands, as unto the Lord. For the husband is the head of the wife, even as Christ is the head of the church . . . as the church is subject unto Christ, so let the wives be to their own husbands in every thing"); Col. 3:18 ("Wives, submit yourselves unto your own husbands, as it is fit in the Lord"); and Rom. 7:2 ("The woman which hath an husband is bound by the law to her husband so long as he liveth").

Paul is not the only New Testament character reeking with male chauvinism. Peter says in 1 Peter 3:1, "Likewise, ye wives, be in subjection to your own husbands." On page 34 in *A Christian Handbook for Defending the Faith* apologist Robert Morey conceded the importance attached to male supremacy by biblical Christianity by saying, "Adam was the head of the family and Eve was submissive to his headship. This structure is what 'ought' to be in every marriage. Thus the Women's Liberation Movement is in open violation of God's creation ordinance of marriage when it denies the man's headship over the woman." On page 241 in *The Bible Has the Answer* apologists Morris and Clark follow in step with Morey by saying, "The wife has no less important or exalted a position than the husband, but hers is not as head of the home. Subjection, in Scripture, does not carry the connotation of inferiority."

Of this final comment one can only say, What nonsense! What pap! If subjection does not carry the connotation of inferiority, then all black horses are not black. A far more honest presentation of this issue is provided by Charles Ryrie on page 205 of *Basic Theology*: "Women will be ruled by men, a necessary hierarchical arrangement for a sinful world. The New Testament does not abrogate this arrangement (1 Cor. 11:3, 14:34, Eph. 5:24–25, Titus 2:3–5, 1 Peter 3:1, 3:5–6)."

Notice that Ryrie says women will be "ruled" by men in a hierarchy. Ryrie readily admits that subjection carries the connotation of being ruled and inferiority, because you only rule over that which is inferior. Ryrie blames this whole arrangement on the deeds of one woman, Eve, an attribution that was earlier shown to be permeated with injustice. As was asked previously, why should all women be blamed for the deeds of one?

Paul not only required women to be in subjection to men but to remain silent like little children. In 1 Cor. 14:34–35 he said, "Let your women keep silent in the churches: for it is not permitted unto them to speak . . . and if they will learn any thing, let them ask their husbands at home: . . . for it is a shame for women to speak in the church." Obviously this verse excludes women from the ministry, and those churches in which women have a role in the clergy are in direct violation of a biblical mandate. On page 236 in *508 Answers to Bible Questions* DeHaan readily concedes the inferior status assigned to women in the churches and seeks to justify the arrangement by saying,

When the assembly is gathered together in a Scriptural way, then a woman's place is one of silence so far as ministry is concerned. . . . Secondly, a woman must not set herself up as an authority in matters of doctrine, like an apostle (1 Tim. 2:12). Thirdly, a woman must not be put in a place of authority in the church. The place of authority is given to the man. This is no slight upon the woman. It is simply recognition of her proper place in nature. It is not a matter of superiority or of inferiority, but it is a matter of order.

Don't be absurd, Mr. DeHaan. Of course it's a matter of superiority and inferiority. Clearly women's proper biblical place is one of inferiority. For one to say that it is "no slight upon the woman" is ludicrous. It most assuredly is.

Paul followed this up in 1 Tim. 2:11–14 by saying, "Let the women learn in silence with all subjection. . . . I suffer not a woman to teach, nor to usurp authority over the man, but to be in silence. For Adam was formed first, then Eve. And Adam was not deceived, but the woman being deceived was in the transgression." Notice how Paul not only assigns women a subordinate role but blames all of them for Eve's transgression, as if Adam were a poor misguided male led by the wiles of an evil female. It is important to note that if women were not allowed to teach, as Paul commanded, havoc would prevail throughout the educational institutions of the this country. The role Paul desires for women is well summarized by his comments in Titus 2:4–5: "Teach the young women to be . . . discreet, chaste, keepers at home, good, obedient to their own husbands."

The New Testament has no corner on the injustice of male supremacy. The Old Testament reeks with comments in support of sexual inequities and injustice. Gen. 3:16 says, "thy desire shall be to thy husband, and he shall rule over thee," and Esther 1:22 says, "That every man should bear rule in his own house." By saying women are just plain filthy, the Old Testament goes even further than the New Testament. As proof, one could cite Job 25:4, which says, "how can he be clean that is born of a woman?" Lev. 12:2 and 5 say, "If a woman have conceived seed, and born a man child: then she shall be unclean 7 days . . . But if when she bear a maid child, then she shall be unclean 14 days." Apparently female babies make women twice as filthy as males. That the Old Testament views women as a source of evil is shown not only by verses attributing the arrival of original sin to Eve's wiles, but also to Eccle. 7:26, which says in the New American Standard Bible, "I discovered more bitter than death the woman whose heart is snares and nets, whose hands are chains. One who is pleasing to God will escape from her, but the sinner will be captured by her."

In light of all the above one can easily understand why Robert Ingersoll says on page 396 of volume 1 in his *Works,*

As long as woman regards the Bible as the charter of her rights, she will be the slave of man. The Bible was not written by a woman. Within its lids there is nothing but humiliation and shame for her. She is regarded as the property of man. She is made to ask forgiveness for becoming a mother. She is as much below her husband as her husband is below Christ. She is not allowed to speak. The gospel is too pure to be spoken by her polluted lips. Women should learn in silence.

And later on page 43 of volume 12 Ingersoll says the Bible "is not the friend of woman. They will find that the writers of that book, for the most part, speak of woman as a poor beast of burden, a serf, a drudge, a kind of necessary evil— as mere property. Surely a book that upholds polygamy is not the friend of wife and mother."

And one can also see why one of the greatest leaders of the women's movement, Elizabeth Cady Stanton, made the following comments with respect to the Bible's negative influence on women:

> The Bible and Church have been the greatest stumbling-blocks in the way of women's emancipation. The religious superstitions of women perpetuate their bondage more than all other adverse influences. I found nothing grand in the history of the Jews nor in the morals inculcated in the Pentateuch. I know of no other book that so fully teaches the subjection and degradation of women.

But George Foote probably encapsulated this entire issue as well as anyone when he said, "It will yet be the proud boast of woman that she never contributed a line to the Bible."

Slavery

A final major biblical topic drenched with injustice is slavery. Beyond any doubt the Bible depicts slavery as an institution sanctioned by God and deserving of support. New Testament citations in this regard are widespread and numerous. Col. 3:22 says, "Servants [read slaves], obey in all things your masters according to the flesh; not with eyeservice, as menpleasers; but in singleness of heart, fearing God." The text of 1 Peter 2:18 says, "Servants, be subject to your masters with all fear; not only to the good and gentle, but also to the froward [unreasonable]." Eph. 6:5-7 says, "Servants, be obedient to them that are your masters according to the flesh, with fear and trembling, in singleness of your heart, as unto Christ; not with eyeservice, as menpleasers; but as the servants of Christ, doing the will of God from the heart; with good will doing service, as to the Lord, and not to men." And finally, Titus 2:9-10 in the Revised Standard Version says, "Bid slaves to be submissive to their masters and to give satisfaction in every respect;

they are not to be refractory, nor to pilfer, but to show entire and true fidelity, so that in everything they may adorn the doctrine of God."

It is important to note how slaves serving their masters is deemed comparable to serving God himself. If that doesn't serve the interests of the slaveowners, nothing will. First Tim. 6:1–6 (RSV) says, "Let all who are under the yoke of slavery regard their masters as worthy of all honor, so that the name of God and the teaching may not be defamed. Those who have believing masters must not be disrespectful on the ground that they are brethren; rather they must serve all the better since those who benefit by their service are believers and beloved." How's that for licking the slaveowners' boots!

Not to be outdone, the Old Testament also bolsters slavery in many instances. Deut. 15:17 says, "Thou shalt take an awl, and thrust it through his ear unto the door, and he shall be thy servant for ever. And also unto thy maidservant thou shalt do likewise." Lev. 25:45–46 says, "Moreover of the children of the strangers that do sojourn among you, of them shall ye buy, and of their families that are with you, which they begat in your land: and they shall be your possession. . . . they shall be your bondmen for ever." And Exod. 21:20–21 in the New International Version says, "If a man beats his male or female slave with a rod and the slave dies as a direct result, he must be punished, but he is not to be punished if the slave gets up after a day or two, since the slave is his property." Note well that these verses in no way attack slavery—they merely formulate rules for its operation. One could also cite Gen. 9:25; Deut. 15:12, 20:10–11, and 28:68; 2 Chron. 12:7–8; and Joel 3:8 for further corroboration. Is it any wonder that the president of the Confederacy during the Civil War, Jefferson Davis, is quoted as making the following statement about slavery on page 286 in volume 1 of *Jefferson Davis* by Dunbar Rowland: "It was established by decree of Almighty God . . . it is sanctioned in the Bible, in both Testaments, from Genesis to Revelation . . . it has existed in all ages, has been found among the people of the highest civilization, and in nations of the highest proficiency in the arts."

As one might suspect, apologists are not without rationalizations to exculpate what can only be described as an injustice of the first magnitude. On page 93 in *I'm Glad You Asked* apologists Kenneth Boa and Larry Moody say,

> Slavery as we now understand it is quite different from the kind of slavery permitted in the Bible. Slaves were to be treated with human dignity and respect (Job 31:13–15) and if their masters violated their basic rights or abused them, they were to be set free (Exod. 21:26–27). . . . Although the NT also allowed for slavery, the epistles make it clear that all believers have an equal standing before the Father (Gal. 3:28).

What kind of reasoning is this? Slavery with a less barbaric face is still slavery, and when Deut. 15:17 says that you can take an awl and thrust it through your slave's ear and make him your servant forever, that hardly comes under the heading of dignity and respect. Secondly, the New Testament did not just "allow" for slavery. The word "allow" is nothing more than a euphemistic veneer for a rotten scene. More than just allowing, the New Testament actively promulgated rules for maintaining slavery. That explains why the following common defense for New Testament slavocracy borders on the bizarre.

On page 123 in *Why I Believe* apologist D. James Kennedy says, "What brought an end to ancient slavery was the Gospel of Jesus Christ!" Is he serious? Where did Jesus in particular, or the Bible in general, denounce slavery? On page 40 in *The Bible Has the Answer* Henry Morris and Martin Clark directly counteract Kennedy by saying Jesus "lived in a time and place where slavery itself was a significant social institution, but He never spoke against it."

Obviously the authors of *The Bible Has the Answers* are more willing to admit the obvious than Kennedy. But they follow this up by saying, "Slavery eventually was abolished through the moral influence of Christianity, not by means of civil disobedience and revolution stirred up by the Christians." How wrong can one be! Slavery was abolished despite the thrust of Christian teachings, not because of them. Christianity, the Bible, the churches, and the clergy were the last to yield to the tide of history, not the first to lead the attack. Mark Twain said it well on page 109 in *Mark Twain and the 3 R's* by Maxwell Geismar:

> There was no place in the land where the seeker could not find some small budding sign of pity for the slave. No place in all the land but one—the pulpit. It yielded at last; it always does. It fought a strong and stubborn fight, and then did what it always does, joined the procession—at the tail end. Slavery fell. The slavery text in the Bible remained; the practice changed; that was all.

Undoubtedly the most candid admission of all, however, is found on page 384 of *Problem Texts* by ultrafundamentalist Peter Ruckman, founder of the Pensacola Bible Institute, who states, "George DeHoff on page 154 in *Alleged Bible Contradictions* . . . tells us that God *abolished* slavery by a process of 'teaching and instructing the people,' which is about as wild a statement as was ever made on commercial TV. *God never abolished slavery a day since it started* (1 Tim. 6:1–3, 1 Cor. 7:21)."

Well! It's nice to know at least one apologist is willing to admit the obvious.

11

Science

Mathematics, False Science, Geography, Flood, Creationism, Biblical Day

Few topics activate biblical critics more than that of biblically based scientific contradictions and inaccuracies. That is readily understandable, in view of the fact that the book is a veritable miasma of poor science, bad math, and inaccurate geography, all with a heavy overlay of mythology and folklore. As one would expect, biblicists assert the opposite, heatedly denying any conflict between science and the Bible.

For example, on page 97 of entitled *Bible Difficulties* William Arndt says,

> If nature, as well as the Bible, is a book given to us by our great God, it follows that there can be no contradiction between the messages they bring to us . . . that they should be in disagreement with each other is unthinkable. If the scientist reads his text correctly, he will not find a statement which is at variance with science when read and interpreted correctly. We hear much nowadays about a conflict between science and the Bible. There is no such conflict . . . a clash between true science and the Bible is out of the question.

One would be hard-pressed to concoct a comment more at variance with reality. Belief in the existence of miracles alone is more than enough to put one in conflict with science. Fully aware of the fact that there are many scientific problems in the Bible, Arndt seeks to cover his grandiose rhetoric by saying, "The Bible is not a textbook on science," This is utterly irrelevant. The issue has nothing to do with whether or not a book can be classified as a textbook.

The question is whether or not the book is correct and, if not, it should avoid scientific pronouncements and evade subjects in which it has poor qualifications. On page 56 in *A General Introduction to the Bible* apologists Norman Geisler and William Nix seek to minimize the scientific errors in the Bible by saying, "The Bible was written to a non-scientific people in a prescientific age, and it is unreasonable for one to say that it is scientifically *incorrect*; it is merely scientifically *imprecise* by modern standards."

"Imprecise"! Where does this "imprecise" nonsense come from? If I add two and two and get five, the teacher does not say I am merely imprecise. She says my answer is wrong and grades accordingly. We are dealing with science, not a game of horseshoes in which proximity counts. How biblicists can defend imprecision in a book written by God is little short of baffling. How could a perfect being create an imperfect book? Interestingly enough, there is at least one fundamentalist who wholly concurs with this observation. On page 15 in *Genesis and Evolution* M. R. DeHaan plastered truth all over the place by saying,

> Frequently we hear well-intentioned, sincere Bible students defend the apparent conflict between the Bible and science by making the following wholly false and erroneous statement: "Well, we must remember the Bible is not a scientific book. That is not its purpose. It was not intended to be scientific, for it is a book of redemption, not science. It deals with salvation and not the sciences . . . and we cannot expect it to be scientifically infallible."

DeHaan then states,

> This is the biggest piece of nonsense ever attempted by well-meaning but shallow-thinking defenders of the Bible. Who is the Author of the Bible? Who is it that speaks with infallible authority in this book? If this Book is not scientifically correct, then the Author of the Book was not scientific. . . . Think that statement through, and you will see the stupidity of such reasoning. Science is the knowledge of matter, natural phenomena, and the study of the physical universe. And He who made all these didn't know science? . . . What foolish drivel is this! He who formed the earth doesn't know geology?. . . . You see what a dangerous, vicious mistake it is to try to defend the Bible by saying it was not intended to be a book of science.

How true! Could one have said it better?

That which is most important, of course, are the problems themselves, because the entire issue revolves around the degree to which they can be verified. If a multitude of scientific, mathematical, and geographical inaccuracies are apparent in the Bible, then all rationalizations fall by the wayside. Let us therefore turn to Scripture and see what it has to offer in this regard.

Mathematics

The first and most obvious area of scientific blunders by biblical authors lies in mathematical miscalculations. Most are little short of pathetic and unworthy of an elementary student doing his homework. The *first* example is 1 Chron. 3:22, which says, "The sons of Shemaiah; Hattush, and Igeal, and Bariah, and Neariah, and Shaphat, six." It does not require a great deal of wisdom to see that the names of five sons are listed, not six.

Second is 1 Chron. 25:3, which says, "The sons of Jeduthun; Gedaliah, and Zeri, and Jeshaiah, and Hashabiah, and Mattithiah, six, under the hands of their father Jeduthun." Again, five names do not total six.

Third, Joshua 15:33–36 in the Revised Standard Version says, "And in the lowland, Eshtaol, Zorah, Ashnah, Zanoah, En-gannim, Tappu-ah, Enam, Jarmuth, Adullam, Socoh, Azekah, Sha-araim, Adithaim, Gederah, Gederothaim: fourteen cities with their villages." One need only count the cities listed to see there are fifteen, not fourteen.

Fourth, probably the most famous mathematical miscalculation, is in 1 Kings 7:23 and 2 Chron. 4:2, which say, "He made a molten sea, ten cubits from the one brim to the other: it was round all about, and its height was five cubits: and a line of thirty cubits did compass it round about." A circle cannot be 10 cubits in diameter and 30 cubits in circumference. Since the circumference of a circle is the diameter times the transcendental number pi, approximately 3.14, the circumference of this "molten sea" must be 31.4 feet, not 30. The Bible erred. On pages 43–45 in *Answers to Questions about the Bible* apologist Robert Mounce provides the following explanation for this blunder. A problem encountered by almost everyone involved in sharing his faith with someone who questions the validity of the Christian faith is the problem of contradictions in Scripture. I can remember the impact of a professor pointing out to our college class the "mathematical error" in 1 Kings 7:23. . . .

> It is true that there are apparent contradictions in the Bible. This fact has caused considerable concern among those who accept the Bible as the Word of God and want to commit themselves wholeheartedly to its teachings. . . . Not every apparent difficulty in Scripture is that simple to understand—obviously the 10 and 30 are round numbers. . . . The responses to this problem have been several. Some have given up in despair and decided that what they can't understand they will leave alone. . . . The Bible is an ancient book and resists being interpreted in a culture not its own.

What drivel! Round numbers or not, the number is incorrect, period. What difference does the culture make? One of Mounce's own fundamentalist compatriots provides a solid refutation of his argument. On page 165 in *The Battle for the Bible* apologist Harold Lindsell says,

The measurements of the molten sea as described in 2 Chron. 4:2 is the second problem that bothers Mounce. Mounce writes the following. . . . "The rough measurements of antiquity do not have to conform to space age requirements. In the culture of that day the measurement was not only adequate, but also inerrant. In our determination of what constitutes an error we must judge the accuracy of Scripture according to the prevailing standards of the time."

Lindsell then proceeds to knock Mounce out of the ring by saying,

I must say that in the culture of that day, or of any day, the figures are wrong if the Scripture is giving us this information the way Dr. Mounce understands it. Two and two make four, and they did in Solomon's time, just as they do in Mounce's time. To say that 2 and 2 make 5 and then excuse it because it was said 3,000 years ago in a different culture hardly makes good sense.

How very true! It is important to note that this criticism was made by a fellow fundamentalist, not the author of *Biblical Errancy.*

The *fifth* mathematical error lies in 1 Chron. 3:19–20, which says, "The sons of Zerubbabel; Meshullam, and Hananiah, and Shelemith their sister: and Hashubah, and Ohel, and Berechiah, and Hasadiah, and Jusha-bhesed, five." How can the total be five when seven males and one female are listed?

Sixth, in summarizing a list of cities, Josh. 15:21–32 says, "The cities belonging to the tribe of the people of Judah in the extreme South toward the boundary of Edom, were Kabzeel, Eder . . . in all, twenty-nine cities, with their villages." Again somebody can't count because thirty-six cities are listed in the text, not twenty-nine.

Seventh, another vexing problem is found in 2 Chron. 21:20 and 22:1, 2, which say, "Thirty and two years old was he [Jehoram] when he began to reign, and he reigned in Jerusalem eight years, and departed without being desired. Howbeit they buried him in the city of David. . . . And the inhabitants of Jerusalem made Ahaziah his youngest son king in his stead. . . . So Ahaziah the son of Jehoram King of Judah reigned. Forty and two years old was Ahaziah when he began to reign."

If Jehoram began to reign at age thirty-two and ruled until his death eight years later, then he died at age forty. Yet, his son took over at the age of forty-two. How could a son, Ahaziah, be two years older than his father, Jehoram?

Eighth, Ezra 1:9–11 says, "This is the number of them: thirty chargers of gold, a thousand chargers of silver, nine and twenty knives, thirty basins of gold, silver basins of a second sort four hundred and ten and other vessels thousand. All the vessels of gold and of silver were five thousand and four hundred." Again, somebody can't add. Thirty + 1,000 + 29 + 30 + 410 + 1,000 totals 2,499, nowhere near 5,400.

Ninth, Josh. 19:2–6 (RSV) says, "They had in their inheritance Beer-sheba, Sheba, Moladah . . . ; 13 cities and their villages." The cities listed numbered fourteen not thirteen. Perhaps the authors had a defective abacus.

Tenth, beginning at Ezra 2:3 and ending at Ezra 2:64 is a listing of the tribes that came back from the captivity and the number of members in each. The same listing begins at Neh. 7:8 and ends at Neh. 7:66. It is important to note that Ezra 2:64 says in summation, "The whole congregation together was 42,360," when one need only add all the congregations together to see that the actual number is 29,818, not 42,360, an error of 12,542. Neh. 7:66 also says the total was 42,360, but the total of the numbers of people it lists is 31,089, making an error of 11,271.

Eleventh and lastly, Num. 3:17 says, "These were the sons of Levi by their names: Gershon, and Kohath, and Merari." Num. 3:22 says, "Those that were numbered of them [Gershonites] . . . were 7,500." Num. 3:27–28 says, "These are the families of the Kohathites . . . 8,600," and Num. 3:33–34 says, "These are the families of the Merari . . . 6,200." When 7,500 is added to 8,600 and 6,200 the total of all three tribes is 22,300. Yet, the summation in Num. 3:39 says, "All that were numbered of the Levites . . . were 22,000." Twenty-two thousand is not 22,300. Either 300 people disappeared during the counting or 300 were counted who didn't exist.

In sum, we can see that the Bible's math wouldn't pass an elementary proficiency exam. For a perfect book, it leaves a lot to be desired.

False Science

A second major area in which the Bible fails miserably concerns the large number of statements that are patently erroneous from a scientific perspective. On numerous occasions the Bible makes statements that have little or nothing to do with scientific accuracy. Some of the most obvious are:

First, Lev. 11:13–19, which says, "These are they which ye shall have in abomination among the *fowls*; they shall not be eaten . . . the eagle, and the ossifrage, and the ospray . . . and the bat."

The final name in the long list of birds, the bat, is, of course, a mammal, not a bird.

Second, Lev. 11:20–21 says, "All fowls that creep, going upon all four, shall be an abomination unto you." Whoever heard of four-legged fowl?

Third, Lev. 11:22–23 says, "Even these of them you may eat; the locust . . . and the beetle . . . and the grasshopper. But all other flying creeping things, which have four feet, shall be an abomination unto you." Whoever heard of four-legged insects? In fact, whoever heard of any four-legged creeping things that fly?

Fourth, Lev. 11:6 says, "And the hare, because he cheweth the cud." Hares never have and never will chew the cud. They are not ruminants like cattle.

Fifth, Deut. 14:7 says, "As the camel, and the hare, and the coney: for they chew the cud, but divide not the hoof." The appropriate term for a hare's foot is not "hoof." And unlike the camel, the hare does divide the "hoof."

Sixth, Gen. 19:26 (RSV) says, "Lot's wife behind him looked back, and she became a pillar of salt." To say that this miracle as well as all other supernatural biblical events violate the most fundamental laws of science is to utter a tautology. All miracles, and the Bible abounds in same, are antiscientific. A miracle is by definition a supernatural or nonnatural event. In reality, it's a complete fiction— not an event at all.

Seventh, Gen. 30:37–39 describes an absurd event in which some cattle delivered some striped calves because they looked at some striped rods. Affairs of this nature are too childish to discuss and would not even be taken seriously were it not for the large number of people who adhere to a book in which they are given credence.

Eighth, 2 Pet. 3:5 says the earth was formed out of water and by means of water. How land is created out of water remains something of a mystery.

Ninth, according to 1 Sam. 2:8 and Job 38, the earth rests on pillars and has foundations, which brings to mind the mythology of Eastern religions.

Tenth, Josh. 10:13 and Hab. 3:11 say, "The sun stood still, and the moon stayed," while 2 Kings 20:11 says the sun went backward 10 degrees on the sundial. Were these events to actually occur (because the earth stopped rotating at its normal speed of 1,000 miles per hour), the results would be catastrophic. If the tremendous centrifugal force that is always present vanished, havoc would reign throughout the planet.

Eleventh, according to Gen. 11:6–9 the languages of the world appeared on the earth in one fell swoop rather than emerging from a long, slow process of human migration and isolation.

Twelfth, John 12:24 says, "Except a corn of wheat fall into the ground and die, it abideth alone: but if it die, it bringeth forth much fruit." How could something that is dead bring forth anything?

Thirteenth, Isa. 11:12 says, "He shall . . . gather together the dispersed of Judah from the four corners of the earth." With verses like this, as well as Deut. 13:7 and 28:64, 1 Sam. 2:10, Job 28:24, and others, one can readily understand why people believed the earth was flat. After all, if the earth has corners, how could the earth be anything other than flat? And if the world was round, how could all the people of the earth see the Son of man coming in the clouds of heaven, as stated Matt. 24:30 and Rev. 1:7?

Fourteenth, Mark 16:18 says, "They shall take up serpents, and if they drink any deadly thing, it shall not hurt them; they shall lay hands on the sick, and they shall recover." Many Christians have paid the supreme penalty because they took this verse to heart. And that's also true of those who failed to visit a doctor because they trusted James 5:13–15, which says, "Is any among you afflicted? let him pray. . . . Is any sick among you? let him call for the elders of the church; . . . And the prayer of faith shall save the sick." If this latter verse had any validity, hospitals and physicians would be relegated to the museums of antiquities.

Fifteenth, Matt. 13:31–32 (RSV) says, "The kingdom of heaven is like a grain of mustard seed which . . . is the smallest of all seeds, but when it has grown it is the greatest of shrubs and becomes a tree."

Many Christians have lost their belief in Jesus because of the inaccuracy of this comment. The mustard seed is not only not the smallest of all seeds, because the orchid seed, for example, is much smaller, but young trees are not shrubs, as the mustard plant is, and shrubs do not grow into trees.

Sixteenth, Deut. 32:11 says, "As an eagle stirreth up her nest, fluttereth over her young, spreadeth abroad her wings, taketh them, and beareth them on her wings." Does anyone know of an eagle that has carried its young on her wings? In fact, does anyone know how this could even be accomplished? Biblicists will no doubt allege this is to be interpreted symbolically but who can say for certain?

Seventeenth, Lev. 13:9–13 in the Revised Standard Version says, "When a man is afflicted with leprosy, he shall be brought to the priest; and the priest shall make an examination, and if there is a white swelling in the skin, which has turned the hair white, and there is quick raw flesh in the swelling, it is chronic leprosy in the skin of his body, and the priest shall pronounce him unclean."

So far so good. That sounds reasonable. But the passage continues, "And if the leprosy breaks out in the skin, so that the leprosy covers all the skin of the diseased person from head to foot, so far as the priest can see, then the priest shall make an examination, and if the leprosy has covered all his body, he shall pronounce him clean of the disease; it has all turned white, and he is clean." That's correct; you read it right. When the leprosy covers all of his body, the leper is clean. We'll relegate that medical analysis to the realm of quackery.

Eighteenth, Luke 1:44 says, "Lo, as soon as the voice of your salutation sounded in mine ears, the babe leaped in my womb for joy."

How's that for scientific precision! A fetus in the womb can not only hear but understand speech.

Nineteenth, 2 Kings 5:27 says, "The leprosy therefoe of Naaman shall cleave to thee, and unto thy seed for ever. And he went out from his presence a leper as white as snow." Full-blown leprosy can be transmitted from one person to another instantly according to this biblical "science." Talk about fantasia!

Twentieth, Lev. 11:21 says, "These may ye eat of every flying creeping thing that goeth upon all four, which have legs above their feet, to leap upon the earth." Again, we are provided with an absurd reference to four-legged animals that fly.

And finally, Gen. 3:16 clearly attributes the pains of childbirth to a curse by saying, "Unto the woman he said, I will greatly multiply thy sorrow and thy conception; in sorrow thou shalt bring forth children." Incidentally, if all births are accompanied by sorrow, then the birth of Jesus would be included as well.

So that is biblical "science." Can you conceive of a more discordant deluge of deceptive delusion! Saddest of all is that most of Christianity's most prominent spokesmen are fully cognizant of these biblical inanities, but have spared no effort to avoid them or minimize their importance. One can readily agree with Maurice Bucaille, who said on pages viii and ix of *The Bible, The Quran, and Science,*

> I did not even have to go beyond the first book, Genesis, to find statements totally out of keeping with the cast-iron facts of modern science. . . . What strikes us today, when we compare biblical contradictions and incompatibilities with well-established scientific data, is how specialists studying the texts either pretend to be unaware of them, or else draw attention to these defects and then try to camouflage them with dialectic acrobatics. . . . Often the attempt to camouflage an improbability or a contradiction, prudishly called a "difficulty," is successful. This explains why so many Christians are unaware of the serious defects contained in the Old Testament and the Gospels.

On page 250 in the same book Bucaille says,

> Contradictions, improbabilities and incompatibilities with modern scientific data may be easily explained in terms of what has just been said above [they abound]. . . . Christians are nevertheless very surprised when they realize this, so great have been the continuous and far-reaching efforts made until now by many official commentators to camouflage the very obvious results of modern studies, under cunning dialectical acrobatics orchestrated by apologetic lyricism.

Bucaille probably said it best on page 39 in the same book: "In other words, if science is useful in confirming the Biblical description, it is invoked, but if it invalidates the latter, reference to it is not permitted."

That's the sum and substance of the whole matter. Why say more?

Geography

Besides science and math, a third area of mental discipline that is all but mangled by biblical pronouncements is geography. The Bible is awash with geographical inaccuracies that appear to have emanated from the minds of those who never ventured further than the city limits. In reading the following prominent examples one would be well-advised to consult an historical atlas of biblical lands for confirmation:

First, Matt. 2:1–2 says, "Behold, there came wise men from the east to

Jerusalem, Saying, where is he that is born King of the Jews? for we have seen his star in the east." Since the wise men were east of Jesus at the time, how could an eastern star have informed them of anything? It would have to have been a star in the west.

Second, Matt. 4:8 says, "Again, the devil taketh him up into an exceedingly high mountain, and sheweth him all the kingdoms of the world." How could anyone see all the kingdoms of our spherical world from one spot?

Third, Matt. 19:1 says, "It came to pass, that when Jesus had finished these sayings, he departed from Galilee, and came into the coasts of Judea beyond the Jordan." Since the Jordan River *is* the eastern boundary of Judea, no "coasts of Judea" could exist beyond it. The coast of Judea *is* the Jordan River.

Fourth, John 12:21 says, "The same came therefore to Philip, which was of Bethsaida of Galilee, and desired him, saying, Sir, we would see Jesus." Bethsaida is in Gaulonitis, not Galilee.

Fifth, Mark 5:1 says, "They came over unto the other side of the sea, into the country of the Gadarenes [or Gerasenes]." How could this have occurred since Gadara and Gerasa are miles from the sea? They do not border it.

Sixth, Matt. 4:12–13 says, "When Jesus had heard that John was cast into prison, he departed into Galilee. Leaving Nazareth, he came and dwelt in Capernaum." Nazareth and Capernaum are both in Galilee. If Jesus left Nazareth and went to Capernaum, he remained in Galilee. How, then, could he have gone to Galilee?

Seventh, Matt. 4:13–15 says, "Leaving Nazareth, he came and dwelt in Capernaum, which is upon the sea coast, in the borders of Zabulon and Nephthalim: That it might be fulfilled which was spoken by Esaias [Isaiah] the prophet, saying, The land of the Zabulon, and the land of the Nephthalim, by way of the sea, beyond Jordan." To comprehend this problem one should definitely consult a map. Zabulon and Naphtali are not beyond the Jordan River or across the Jordan River. They are on the western side of the Jordan, not the eastern side. So they could not be "beyond the Jordan."

Eighth, one of the Bible's most chaotic geographical descriptions is found in Gen. 2:10–14, which says,

> A river went out of Eden to water the garden; and from thence it was parted, and became into four heads. The name of the first is Pison: that is it which compasseth the whole land of Havilah, where there is gold. . . . And the name of the second river is Gihon: the same is it that compasseth the whole land of Ethiopia. And the name of the third river is Hiddekel; that is it which goeth toward the east of Assyria. And the fourth river is Euphrates.

What a cacophany! The geography of all this makes no sense and clearly shows the author of Genesis needs a geography lesson because: (a) There is no

Middle Eastern river that divides and becomes the four rivers mentioned. There is no river flowing out of Eden or the Mesopotamian region that diverges into four rivers; (b) This geographical presentation incorrectly makes the Nile and Euphrates rivers branch from the same river; (c) There is no record of a river called Pison or Pishon in the Mesopotamian region; (d) The land of Havilah, now called Yemen, has no river flowing around it. Indeed, Yemen is a desert region almost totally lacking in streams of any sort; (e) Havilah, i.e., Yemen, is more than 1,200 miles from the Mesopotamian region of Eden. There is no river connecting them, only immense desert; (f) There is no record of any river called Gihon in the Mesopotamian region; (g) There is no river flowing around the land of Ethiopia, least of all one called Gihon; (h) The Hiddekel river, i.e., the Tigris river, does not flow eastward from Assyria. It flows in a southerly direction and slightly eastward; (i) And finally, Eden, Ethiopia, and Havilah (Yemen) are well over a thousand miles apart and are connected by nothing, especially rivers. It sounds as if Eden is the entire Middle East, since Ethiopia and the Euphrates River are linked together.

Ninth, Acts 1:12 says, "Then returned they unto Jerusalem from the mount called Olivet, which is from Jerusalem a sabbath day's journey." This must be false in view of the fact that Olivet, the Mount of Olives, was just outside the wall of Jerusalem near the Temple, hardly a sabbath day's journey.

Tenth, Acts 22:8 says, "I [Paul] answered, Who art thou, Lord? And he said unto me, I am Jesus of Nazareth, whom thou persecutest." Why would Christ be called Jesus of Nazareth when Matt. 2:1 clearly says Jesus was born in Bethlehem, which is far from Nazareth? Moreover, the Jews had every right to reject Jesus as the messiah since he said he was from Nazareth, not Bethlehem. Nazareth is in Galilee and John 7:41–42 says about Galilee, "Shall Christ come out of Galilee? Hath not Scripture said, That Christ cometh from the seed of David, and out of the town of Bethlehem . . . ?" And Bethlehem is in Judea, not Galilee.

Eleventh, Mark 7:31 (RSV) says, "He returned from the region of Tyre, and went through Sidon to the Sea of Galilee, through the region of the Decapolis." It is difficult to visualize someone going from Tyre to the Sea of Galilee by passing through Sidon, especially if he went through the Decapolis en route. Sidon is to the north of Tyre on the Mediterranean Sea, while the Decapolis is to the south of the Sea of Galilee. It would be like going from St. Louis to Washington, D.C., while going north through Milwaukee and south through Atlanta.

Twelfth, Exod. 14:9 says, "The Egyptians pursued after them, with all the horses and chariots of Pharaoh . . . and overtook them encamping by the sea, beside Pi-hahiroth, before Baal-zephon." A few verses later Ex. 14:22 says, "The children of Israel went into the midst of the sea upon the dry ground: and the waters were a wall unto them on their right hand, and on their left." The Bible says the Israelites crossed the Red Sea when they fled Egypt. Yet they crossed at Baal-Zephon, which is more than a hundred miles south of the Red Sea. If anything, they crossed the Gulf of Suez, which really would have been incredible in light of its width and depth.

Thirteenth, 1 Kings 17:3 in the RSV says, "Depart from here and turn eastward, and hide yourself by the brook Cherith, that is east of the Jordan." The brook Cherith is on the *western* side of the Jordan River, according to biblical maps such as those published by the Standard Publishing Company.

Fourteenth, 1 Kings 9:26 says, "King Solomon made a navy of ships in Ezion-geber, which is beside Eloth, on the shore of the Red Sea, in the land of Edom." The problem with this verse is that Ezion-geber is over a hundred miles from the Red Sea and is certainly not on its shore.

Fifteenth, in Josh. 1:3–4 God says to the Israelites, "Every place that the sole of your foot will tread upon, that have I given unto you, as I said unto Moses. From the wilderness and this Lebanon even unto the great river, the river Euphrates . . . shall be your coast." Israelite territory has never extended to the Euphrates River.

We have now come to a final group of geographical verses which refer to fictitious places as if they really existed.

Sixteenth, John 4:5 says, "Then cometh he to a city of Samaria, which is called Sychar, near to the parcel of ground that Jacob gave to his son Joseph." Samaria has never had a city named Sychar.

Seventeenth, John 3:23 says, "John also was baptizing in Aenon near Salim. . . ." Nearly all critics agree that there is no such place as Aenon near Salim.

Eighteenth, John 1:28 says, "These things were done in Bethabara beyond Jordan, where John was baptizing." The word "Bethabara" is a forgery. No site by the name of "Bethabara" is known in history. The Revised Standard Version seeks to evade the problem by using "Bethany" rather than Bethabara. But it is well known that Bethany was a suburb of Jerusalem and was not beyond the Jordan River.

And *finally,* Mark 8:10 says, "He entered into a ship with his disciples, and came into parts of Dalmanutha." Many scholars say there is no such place as "Dalmanutha."

The obvious conclusion to be drawn from all of the above is that biblical geography also leaves a lot to be desired. Accuracy is by no means one of its strong points.

The Flood

Another topic that has always generated a tremendous amount of interest with respect to the scientific accuracy of the Bible is the Flood. Unbeknownst to most believers in this cataclysmic event, the entire account is riddled with scientific impossibilities and improbabilities. Some of the most obvious are:

First, Gen. 6:15 says, "The length of the ark shall be 300 cubits [a cubit equals approximately 1.5 feet], the breadth of it 50 cubits, and the height of it 30 cubits." In other words, the ark would measure 450 feet by 75 feet by 45 feet. It would be impossible to get two of every animal on a boat this small—the food alone would require a whole fleet of arks this size. Moreover, there are over two million species of animals. How could they all have been taken on the ark? There are over half a million separate species of insects alone.

Second, Gen. 6:17 says, "I [God], even I, do bring a flood of waters upon the earth, to destroy all flesh, wherein is the breath of life, from under heaven; and every thing that is in the earth shall die." Problems: (a) How were the fishes and amphibians killed? (b) How were seals, whales, porpoises, sea snakes, dolphins and other marine animals that would relish more water killed?

Third, Gen. 7:8–9 says, "Of clean beasts, and of beasts that are not clean, and of fowls, and of every thing that creepeth upon the earth, There went in two and two unto Noah into the ark, the male and the female, as God had commanded Noah." The problems with this account are: (a) Are we to believe that animals came in voluntarily and just knew when the time had come? (b) How did the animals know where the Ark was located? (c) How did animals that are restricted to certain parts of the earth, such as penguins, pandas, polar bears, koalas, and so on, get to the Ark? (d) How did many of the animals withstand climatic changes? Animals from the polar regions could never have withstood the heat of the Middle East. (e) How were some portions of the ark heated for animals from the tropics and other areas kept cool for animals from the polar regions? (f) How were animals kept from killing their natural prey? (g) Slow animals from other continents, such as snails and sloths, must have started their journey to the ark before the earth was created in order to cover thousands of miles. (h) How did animals from other continents manage to cross the oceans? (i) How did the animals get back to their respective countries? And (j) the vegetation that many animals eat only grows in certain parts of the world. What did these animals eat during their journey and after their arrival? Pandas specialize in bamboo and koalas eat only eucalyptus, for example.

Fourth, Gen. 7:15 says, "They went in unto Noah into the ark, two and two of all flesh, wherein is the breath of life." How did water creatures, such as whales, porpoises, sea snakes, dolphins, and amphibians enter the Ark? Remember, they have the breath of life also. And what about fish? Gills require the breath of life as much as lungs.

Fifth, in the same vein Gen. 7:20 says, "Fifteen cubits upward did the waters prevail; and the mountains were covered." Authentic Egyptian history does not mention a flood even though uninterrupted records were kept from the pharaoh Menes in 3400 B.C. to Darius Ochus in 340 B.C. The Flood allegedly occurred around 2348 B.C.

Sixth, Gen. 8:4 says, "The ark rested in the seventh month, on the seventeenth day of the month, upon the mountains of Ararat." How could one ship rest on several mountains simultaneously? Moreover, Mount Ararat is about 17,000 feet high and intense cold prevails at that altitude. How were animals from the tropics kept from freezing to death?

Seventh, Gen. 8:8 says, Noah "sent forth a dove from him, to see if the waters were abated from off the face of the ground." Why on earth would Noah send out a bird to see what is clearly evident to anyone energetic enough to look outward from the ark's deck?

Eighth, Gen. 8:11 (RSV) says, "The dove came back to him in the evening, and lo, in her mouth a freshly plucked olive leaf." Where would the dove find an olive leaf to "freshly pluck"? After all, the earth had just been submerged for a year and all vegetation must have been killed. God said he would kill everything.

Ninth, after Noah landed and got out of the ark, Gen. 8:20 says, "Noah builded an altar unto the Lord; and took of every clean beast, and of every clean fowl, and offered burnt offerings on the altar." Killing animals of which only two remain seems preposterous.

Tenth, Gen. 7:13 says, "In the selfsame day entered Noah, and Shem, and Ham, and Japheth, the sons of Noah, and Noah's wife, and the three wives of his sons with them, into the ark." If the human race took its rise anew from Noah and his sons, then all the different varieties of men that now people the earth must have developed from that family in the short space of four thousand years. But science proves conclusively that the blue-eyed, fair-haired Swede, the brown-skinned, dark-haired Indian, the yellow-skinned Chinese, and the black-skinned, black-haired blacks, owe their origin to a variety of ancestors that lived a million years before the dawn of written history. On Egyptian monuments dating from a time long before the age of the fabled flood the features of Egyptians, Semites, and blacks may be seen chiseled in stone.

Eleventh, Gen. 8:19 says, "Every beast, every creeping thing, and every fowl, and whatsoever creepeth upon the earth, after their kinds, went forth out of the ark." How were herbivores preserved after leaving the ark? There was no vegetation except such as had been submerged for a year.

Twelfth, how did only eight people feed, water and remove the excrement of what must have been the greatest menagerie in history?

Thirteenth, what did carnivores eat after leaving the ark, since the only animals available for food were those on the ark?

And *lastly,* Gen. 8:3 says, "The waters returned from off the earth continually: and after the end of the 150 days the waters were abated." And the verse 8:13 says, "The waters were dried up from off the earth; and Noah removed the covering of the ark and looked, and, behold, the face of the ground was dry." Where did all the water come from that covered all the earth's mountains, including Mt. Everest (more than 29,000 feet) and where did it go?

In light of all the above, one can readily understand why Arndt concedes the obvious by saying on pages 111 and 112 of *Bible Difficulties,* "In beginning our examination of alleged difficulties in this narrative, let me say that Bible Christians, of course, admit that the account of the Flood contains many features which we have to class as miraculous, that is, as things which we cannot understand." On page 114 in the same book Arndt says, "In Gen. 7:21 we read, 'All flesh died that moved upon the earth, both of fowl and of cattle and of beast and of every creeping thing that creeps upon the earth and every man.' Verses 22 and 23 are similar in content. That here the powers of imagination are baffled we have to admit."

But an even more powerful indictment of belief in the Flood is found on pages 210 and 211 of *A Survey of the Old Testament* by Gleason Archer, one of the most well-known of all fundamentalists and author of the *Encyclopedia of Bible Difficulties.* He states,

> Formidable scientific problems are raised by a universal flood, according to Ramm's summary. Problems such as:
> 1. According to the best estimates, to cover the highest Himalayas would require eight times more water than our planet now possesses.
> 2. The withdrawal of so great a quantity of water constitutes an almost insurmountable problem, for there would be no place to which it could *drain off.* The mechanics of this abatement of water would certainly be difficult, for the atmosphere could not possibly hold that much water in evaporated form, and it is doubtful if any underground cavities in the earth could receive more than a small fraction of this additional volume of water.
> 3. Scarcely any plant life could have survived submersion under salt water for over a year, and the mingling of ocean water with the rain must have resulted in a lethal saline concentration. . . . Practically all marine life would have perished, except those comparatively few organisms which can withstand tremendous pressure, for 90 percent of present marine life is found in the first 50 fathoms. . . .
> 4. Certain areas of the earth's surface show definite evidence of no submersion. . . .
> It cannot be maintained, however, that even a local flood will solve all these scientific difficulties. . . . How could the level have been that high at Ararat without being the same height over the rest of the world?

So the Flood account suffers from gross inadequacies even by apologetic standards. Parenthetically, an important observation on the Flood can also be found on page 286 in Gerald Sigal's *The Jew and the Christian Missionary.* The author quotes 1 Pet. 3:20–21 and then astutely notes,

> The author of the First Epistle of Peter concludes that the great flood recorded in Genesis chapters 6 through 8 is a foreshadowing of the rite of baptism by establishing the analogy that baptism saves the believer as water saved Noah

and his family. However, if we read Genesis correctly, we will quickly discover that Noah and his family were not saved *by* the waters, but *from* the waters. Such careless use of the Hebrew Scriptures obviously proves nothing.

If any Old Testament group was baptized by a flood of water, it was the Egyptian pharaoh's army. In any event, all of the above clearly shows that the Flood belongs in a book of mythology, not science.

Creationism

Undoubtedly one of the most controversial of all biblical excursions into the realm of science involves that located in the Book of Genesis. If there is any subject guaranteed to stir emotions, it can be found in the Bible's presentation of how man and the earth came to be—science versus creationism. Scientific problems associated with this topic are not hard to find. In fact, they become readily apparent to anyone who reads Genesis with a reasonable degree of objectivity and scientific knowledge. The most obvious examples are:

First, Gen. 1:3 says, "God said, Let there be light: and there was light," and Gen. 1:5 says, "The evening and the morning were *the first day.*" So light appeared on the first day. But Gen. 1:14–19 says,

> God said, Let there be lights in the firmament of the heaven to divide the day from the night. . . . And let there be lights in the firmament of the heaven to give light upon the earth: and it was so. And God made two great lights; the greater light to rule the day, and the lesser light to rule the night: he made the stars also. And God set them in the firmament of the heaven to give light upon the earth, And to rule over the day and over the night, and to divide the light from the darkness. . . . And the evening and the morning were the fourth day.

The problem here is that God created light on the first day; yet there were no moon, no sun, no stars until the fourth day. On pages 22 and 23 in *The Bible, the Quran and Science* Maurice Bucaille says in this regard,

> The first description of creation in Genesis is a masterpiece of inaccuracy from a scientific point of view. . . . It is illogical to mention the result (light) on the first day, when the cause of this light was created three days later. Moreover, the fact that the existence of evening and morning is placed on the first day is purely imaginary; the existence of evening and morning as elements of a single day is only conceivable after the creation of the earth and its rotation under the light of its own star, the Sun!

How could it have even been known when the intervening days ended, when there were no moon, sun, stars, or other celestial bodies until the fourth day? How do you distinguish morning from evening until the sun exists?

Second, Gen. 1:11–13 says, "God said, Let the earth bring forth grass, the herb yielding seed, and the fruit tree yielding fruit after his kind. . . . And the earth brought forth grass, and herb yielding seed after his kind, and the tree yielding fruit. . . . And the evening and the morning were the third day." But Gen. 1:16 says, "God made two great lights; the greater light to rule the day, and the lesser light to rule the night: he made the stars also" and is followed by Gen. 1:19, which says, "The evening and the morning were the fourth day."

So we are supposed to believe that vegetation was created on the third day, when no sun for photosynthesis appeared until the fourth day. That's quite a trick! How could plants have survived without the sun, especially if, as some biblicists admit, each of these days involved millions of years. They might have survived for several days of twenty-four hours each, but not for thousands or millions of years. As Bucaille says on page 24 of *The Bible, the Quran and Science,* "What is totally untenable is that a highly organized vegetable kingdom with reproduction by seed could have appeared before the existence of the sun (in Genesis it does not appear until the fourth day), and likewise the establishment of alternating days and nights."

Third, Gen. 1:1 says, "In the beginning God created the heaven and the earth," which is followed by Gen. 1:5, which says, "And the evening and the morning were the first day." But when we read Gen. 1:16, which says, "God made two great lights; the greater light to rule the day, and the lesser light to rule the night; he made the stars also," and Gen. 1:19 which says, "The evening and the morning were the fourth day," we can see a mighty clash between the Bible and science.

According to the Bible the earth was created before the sun, the moon, and the stars. Nearly all scientists would dispute this. As Bucaille says on page 25 of *The Bible, The Quran and Science,* "The Earth and Moon emanated, as we know, from their original star, the Sun. To place the creation of the Sun and Moon after the creation of the Earth is contrary to the most firmly established ideas on the formation of the elements of the Solar System."

Furthermore, scientists say there are many stars whose light takes millions of years to reach the earth. How, then, could they be only six thousand to eight thousand years old, as many biblical Christians claim? If we are only now receiving light that was emitted from a star millions of years ago, then obviously the age of many stars is well beyond eight thousand years.

Fourth, according to Gen. 1:11–13 plant life, such as grass, herbs, and fruit trees, appeared on the earth on the third day. But later, Gen. 1:20–23 says, "God said, Let the waters bring forth abundantly the moving creature that hath life. . . . And God created great whales, and every living creature that moveth, which the waters brought forth abundantly, after their kind. . . . And God blessed them, saying, Be fruitful, and multiply, and fill the waters in the seas. . . . And the evening and the morning were the fifteenth day."

In essence, according to Gen. 1, life existed first on land as plants and later the seas teemed with living creatures. Science, on the other hand, says the sea teemed with animals and vegetable life long before life appeared on land.

Fifth, Gen. 1:21–23 (RSV) says, "God created the great sea monsters and every living creature that moves, with which the waters swarm, according to their kinds, and every winged bird according to its kind. . . . And God blessed them, saying, 'Be fruitful and multiply and fill the waters in the seas, and let birds multiply on the earth.' And there was evening and there was morning, a fifth day." Geological science says that fishes appeared long before the birds. They were not created during the same day or period.

Sixth, Gen. 1:21 says, "God created . . . every winged fowl after his kind." Gen 1:23 dates the event on the fifth day. But Gen. 1:25 says, "God made the beast of the earth . . . and every thing that creepeth upon the earth after his kind," and Gen. 1:31 says, "The evening and the morning were the sixth day." So, according to the Bible, fowl appeared on the fifth day, while creeping animals like reptiles appeared on the sixth day. Science, on the other hand, says reptiles appeared on the earth before the fowl, not after.

Seventh, Gen. 1:24–25 says, "God said, Let the earth bring forth the living creature after his kind, cattle, and creeping thing, and beast of the earth after his kind: and it was so. And God made the beast of the earth after his kind, and cattle after their kind, and every thing that creepeth upon the earth after his kind."

From this one can see that the Bible alleges cattle and other beasts were created during the same period as every thing that creeps on the earth, which would include reptiles. But science says that reptiles were created long before mammals, not simultaneously. While reptiles existed in the Carboniferous Age, mammals did not appear until the close of the Reptilian Age.

Eighth, Gen. 1:20 says, "God said, Let the waters bring forth abundantly the moving creature that hath life, and fowl that may fly above the earth in the open firmament of heaven." Although it may come as a shock to staunch biblicists, birds did not come from water.

Ninth, Gen. 1:27 says, "So God created man in his own image, in the image of God created he him; male and female created he them," and Gen. 1:31 places this event on the sixth day. If Adam was created on the sixth day nearly eight thousand years ago, as Luke 3 would seem to suggest, then nobody lived before 6000 B.C., which would eliminate the existence of Stone Age man and prehistoric creatures.

Tenth, Gen. 1:30 says, "To every beast of the earth, and every fowl of the air, and to every thing that creepeth upon the earth, wherein there is life, I have given every green herb for meat: and it was so." The problem with this lies in the fact that *carnivorous* beasts and fowl do not need or eat green herbs.

Eleventh, one of the most puzzling antiscientific biblical concepts is found in Gen. 1:31, which says, "God saw every thing that he had made." and in Gen. 2:2, which says, "On the seventh day God ended his work." The words "he" and "his" are obvious reference to the male gender and biblicists would be hard-pressed to show how God could be a male without sex organs. An omnipotent Almighty with genitalia would be more unbelievable than visualizing Jesus going to the bathroom. It just would not meld with the conception most people have been given of God in general and Jesus in particular.

Twelfth, Gen. 3:4-5 says, "The serpent said unto the woman, ye shall not surely die: For God doth know that in the day ye eat thereof, then your eyes shall be opened, and ye shall be as gods, knowing good and evil." Reference to a talking serpent is not the kind of information that one would find in a scientifically valid book.

Thirteenth, Gen. 2:19-20 says, "Out of the ground the Lord God formed every beast of the field, and every fowl of the air; and brought them unto Adam to see what he would call them: and whatsoever Adam called every living creature, that was the name thereof."

Environmentally speaking, samples of every living creature could not have been brought to any spot in the Middle East for naming or for any other reason. Many would have died because of climatic changes and other factors. Besides, naming millions of separate species would have taken a tremendously long time. And how could Noah have distinguished and identified extremely small animals such as bacteria and viruses without a microscope?

And *finally,* Gen. 3:14 says, "The Lord God said unto the serpent, Because thou hast done this, thou art cursed above all cattle, and above every beast of the field; upon thy belly shalt thou go, and dust shalt thou eat all the days of thy life." To begin with, science knows of no serpent that eats dust and secondly, if the serpent was a snake or snake-like in form and condemned to crawl upon its belly, how did it move before?

All of the above clearly demonstrates that the account of creation found in the Book of Genesis belongs in a book of folklore and mythology, not science.

Biblical Day

One of the most common defenses touted by devious Christian minds to escape many of the problems we have enumerated so far is to claim that the word "day" in the earliest chapters of Genesis refers to a long period of time encompassing millions of years. This, of course, would allow for such evolutionary contentions as that the earth is billions of years old, dinosaurs lived millions of years ago, and man has been around for a lot longer than eight thousand years. In fact, a wide assortment of clashes between the Bible and science would be resolved by this major concession to reality. The major problem, however, is that this theory just won't stand critical analysis.

First, the word translated as "day" is *yom* in the Hebrew and *hemera* in the Greek. Both mean a definite twenty-four-hour period from sunset to sunset.

Second, the constant reference to evening and morning in Genesis shows that a twenty-four-hour period is under discussion. This is how Jews computed a day. If a day is an era, why are evenings and mornings even mentioned?

Third, Genesis must be referring to actual days, otherwise men who lived hundreds of years, like Adam and Methuselah, would really have lived millions of years. If a day is an era, then a year must be tremendously long and involve hundreds of millions or even billions of years.

Fourth, if a day is an era, then much of the Old Testament becomes chaotic. For example, in each of the following verses the same Hebrew word *yom* is employed: "The flood was forty days upon the earth" (Gen. 7:17);"I fell down before the Lord forty days and forty nights" (Deut. 9:25); and "He [Moses] was there with the Lord 40 days and 40 nights" (Exod. 34:28). If a day is an era, then Moses was with the Lord for a long time, indeed.

Fifth, if each day is an era or epoch involving millions of years, then the seventh day, the sabbath, is tremendously long as well. It certainly doesn't involve a twenty-four-hour period each week, and there is no reason to honor it by resting or going to church on Saturday or Sunday.

Sixth, Adam was created on the sixth day, according to Gen. 1:27 and 1:31. If each day is an epoch involving millions of years, then a tremendous problem arises from Luke 3. The chapter lists seventy-seven generations from Adam to Jesus. If each man in Luke's genealogy had lived to be 200 years old, for example, then Adam would have been created (200 × 77) or 15,400 years before Jesus. Thus, the seventh day or epoch could not have been longer than 15,400 years. Epochs involve millions of years, not a mere 15,400. Moreover, if we attributed 15,400 years to each of the 7 days, then the earth itself would be a mere 15,400 × 7 or 107,800 years old. Yet science contends the earth is billions of years old.

Seventh, if a day means an era, then how are we to interpret the following verses and scores of others? "Six days shalt thou labour and do all thy work: But the seventh day is the sabbath . . . in it thou shalt not do any work. . . . For in six days the Lord made heaven and earth . . . and rested the seventh day." Our seventh day of rest is going to be long, indeed.

Eighth, according to Gen. 1:26 and 1:31 Adam was made on the sixth day. This was followed by the seventh day, which was supposedly thousands or millions of years long, if we are to believe the day/age theoreticians. Following the seventh day Adam fell into sin and was driven from the Garden of Eden. This would mean that Adam lived throughout the thousands or millions of years of the seventh day. But we know this is impossible, since he died at age 930, according to Gen. 5:5.

Ninth, we are plainly told in Gen. 1:16 that God made two great lights; the greater light to rule the day, and the lesser light to rule the night. In other words, the sun rules the day and the moon rules the night. This is obviously time as we know it—time with days that are twenty-four hours long and daylight prevailing about half the time.

And *finally,* each day was divided into nearly equal parts of a dark portion and a light portion. If each part was millions of years in length, how could green plants live through millions of years of darkness?

In essence, only one conclusion is possible. When the Bible speaks of seven days in the first chapter of Genesis, it is referring to seven periods of twenty-four hours each, seven days as we know them. The day/age theory is not viable. Interestingly enough, even the fundamentalist cofounder of the Institute for Creation Research, Henry Morris, strongly agrees with our analysis of this issue. On page 94 in *The Bible Has the Answer* Morris and Martin Clark state,

> The Hebrew word for "day" is *yom.* In the overwhelming preponderance of its occurrences in the Old Testament, however, it means a literal day. . . . Still further, the plural form of the word *yom* (Hebrew: *yamim*) is used over 700 times in the Old Testament and always, without exception refers to literal "days." . . . Not only is the day-age theory unacceptable Scripturally, but it also is grossly in conflict with the geological position with which it attempts to compromise. There are more than 20 serious contradictions between the Biblical order and events of the creative days and the standard geologic history of the earth and its development, even if it were permissible to interpret the "days" as "ages." For example, the Bible teaches that the earth existed before the stars, that it was initially covered by water, that fruit trees appeared before fishes, that plant life preceded the sun, that the first animals created were the whales, that birds were made before insects, that man was made before woman, and many other such things, all of which are explicitly contradicted by historical geologists and paleontologists.

There you have it from a staunch creationist, not a confirmed evolutionist. Professor Charles Ryrie of Dallas Theological Seminary makes essentially the same point on page 185 of his *Basic Theology*:

> The word "day" when used with a numerical adjective in the Pentateuch always indicates a solar day. Why would Genesis 1 be an exception? Indeed this is true for all the uses of "day" with a numeral or ordinal in the entire Old Testament. . . . The qualifying phrase "evening and morning" attached to each of the 6 days of Creation supports the meaning of the days as 24-hour periods . . . evening and morning, each occurring more than 100 times in the Old Testament, are never used to mean anything other than a literal evening and a literal morning, ending or beginning a solar day.

On page 259 in *All About the Bible* apologist Sidney Collett agrees by saying,

Throughout the whole of Scripture the word day is never used to represent a lengthened period when a numeral is connected to it. In such cases days means days and nothing more—whether it be the 150 days of the flood (Gen. 8:3), the 40 days occupied by the spies (Num. 13:25), the 3 days that Jonah was in the belly of the fish (Jon. 1:17), the 40 days during which the Lord was seen after His resurrection (Acts 1:3), or the 6 days in which the Lord made heaven and earth (Exod. 20:11).

On pages 265 and 266 Collett concludes,

If we take the language of the Bible as it stands, it seems impossible to avoid the conclusion that the "days" mentioned in Genesis 1 were nothing more than ordinary days, as we know them, of 24 hours each. The Jews have never regarded them as other than ordinary days. Four things are mentioned in connection with these days—there was *light* and there was *darkness,* there was *evening* and there was *morning*; and I contend that in the absence of any inspired word to the contrary, we are bound by all known phenomena to regard such words as defining natural days as we know them, of 24 hours, one part of which was dark and the other part light. . . . If these days were immense geological periods, what is the meaning of the words "evening" and "morning," "day" and "night"? Indeed, one would reverently ask, what could have been the object of using terms which would only convey one meaning to our minds, and that a wrong one? . . . Moreover, the very order of the expression, "the evening and the morning," and not "morning and evening," as we would write them today, shows again that they were natural days, calculated *exactly as the Jews have ever since calculated them,* for the Jews still reckon their days to *commence from 6 o'clock in the evening.*

And finally, even apologist Josh McDowell gets into the act when he says on page 103 in *Answers to Tough Questions,*

Regarding the meaning of "yom," those who oppose the age-day theory such as myself point out that when "yom" is used with a specific number, in this case six days, it always means a 24-hour day. Examples of this would be the 40 days Moses was on Mt. Sinai and the three days Jonah was inside the fish. . . . More than 700 times in the Old Testament, the plural of "yom" is used and always has a 24-hour day in view. The burden of proof is on those who argue that the word "yom" cannot be understood in its plain and natural sense.

In summation, any reasonably objective observer of the creation story must conclude that the word "day" means a twenty-four-hour period as we know it.

Conclusion

As far as the conflict between science and creationism is concerned, the inanity of the Christian position was well exposed on pages 109 and 110 of Arndt's *Bible Difficulties*: "To all the attacks made upon the account of Creation as presented by Moses, the Christian can reply, in the first place, that the pronouncements of his God on the origin of the world are more important to him than the dicta of scientists."

In other words, my mind is made up; don't confuse me with any facts. I have concluded the Bible is God's word and all evidence to the contrary is to be rejected. Arndt continues, "In the second place, the Christian can draw attention to the obvious fact that none of the critics was present when the universe was created."

What an utterly thoughtless remark in light of the fact that the alleged author of Genesis, Moses, wasn't present either. And Arndt concludes by saying, "When the assertion is made that what Moses relates is utterly inconsistent with the evolution theory, which is widely taught these days, we admit, of course, the justice of this remark."

Based upon what has come to light in this chapter, we can clearly see that the Bible is light years from being a fountain of scientific wisdom and truth. Quite the contrary, more than enough comments are readily available to convince all but the most dogmatic proponents that Scripture is a veritable cornucopia of scientific inaccuracies, falsehoods, and blunders.

12

Belief

False Teachings, Perfection, Prayer, Testing the Bible, Miracles

One of the most interesting and revealing aspects of biblical teachings lies in the degree to which the Bible makes statements that are either so patently false and misleading as to be reprehensible or so amazing as to be bizarre, if not stupefying. Comments of this nature are especially prominent in the five major areas of *False Teachings, Perfection, Prayer, Testing the Bible,* and *Miracles.* Each of these categories warrants comprehensive analysis and exposure.

False Teachings

False teachings are verses so clearly erroneous or absurd on their face that one need not engage in any kind of involved critique to see their flaws. They are prevalent throughout Scripture, but are especially prominent in the Old Testament books of Job, Psalms, Proverbs, and Ecclesiastes and several New Testament books. Among the most prominent examples:

Eccles. 1:9 (RSV) says, "What has been is what will be, and what has been done is what will be done; and there is nothing new under the sun," and Eccles. 3:15 (RSV) says, "That which is, already has been; that which is to be, already has been." So we are told there's nothing new under the sun. Yet how many cities had an atomic bomb dropped on them prior to 1945 and how many people walked on the moon before 1969?

Prov. 19:23 (RSV) says, "The fear of the Lord leads to life; and he who has it rests satisfied; he will not be visited by harm." Millions of Lord-fearing people have been victimized by untold numbers of death-dispensing calamities. This statement has no relevance to reality whatever.

Job 31:3 (RSV) says, "Does not calamity befall the unrighteous, and disaster befall the workers of iniquity?" As a matter of fact, in far too many cases they are plagued by the least amount of adversity. Many experience little or no calamity throughout their lives.

Pss. 146:7–9 (RSV) says, "God executes justice for the oppressed; who gives food to the hungry. The Lord sets the prisoners free; the Lord opens the eyes of the blind. The Lord lifts up those who are bowed down; the Lord loves the righteous. The Lord watches over sojourners, he upholds the widow and the fatherless; but the way of the wicked he brings to ruin." Pss. 147:6 (RSV) says, "The Lord lifts up the downtrodden, he casts the wicked to the ground;" Pss. 145:20 says, "The Lord preserveth all them that love him: but all the wicked will he destroy," And Prov. 11:19 (RSV) says, "He who is steadfast in righteousness will live, but he who pursues evil will die."

What a maze of nonsense! More often than not, precisely the opposite is true. The most corrupt enjoy the highest standard of living, live the longest, and are the least punished.

In Pss. 50:15 (RSV) God says, "Call upon me in the day of trouble: I will deliver thee." Many a dyed-in-the-wool Christian has experienced the deception of this comment.

Prov. 10:3 (RSV) says, "The Lord does not let the righteous go hungry, but he thwarts the craving of the wicked." My goodness! Is the writer serious? The world is awash in good people enduring the pangs of hunger on a daily basis and all too often the wicked obtain what they crave.

Prov. 10:27 (RSV) says, "The fear of the Lord prolongs life, but the years of the wicked will be short." In reality, the years of the wicked often go on interminably and the lives of Lord-fearing people end abruptly.

Prov. 10:30 (RSV) says, "The righteous will never be removed, but the wicked will not dwell in the land." One need only witness the economic migration of the world's poor, who are often the righteous, and the tendency of the wicked to linger around forever, to see the absurdity of this verse.

You don't even have to look at people today to see the falsity of Prov. 12:21 (RSV), which says, "No ill befalls the righteous, but the wicked are filled with trouble." The fate of righteous Job, as shown by Job 2:7, exposes this lie: "So went Satan forth from the presence of the Lord, and smote Job with sore boils from the sole of his foot to his crown."

Eccles. 1:2 and 12:9 say, "Vanity of vanities, says the Preacher, vanity of vanities! All is vanity."

If all is vanity, i.e. worthless, futile, idle, and empty according to the definition to be found in *Webster's Dictionary,* then why are Christians so concerned about reaching Heaven, escaping Hell, converting others, and following what they view as biblical teachings? After all, if all is futile, why bother?

Eccles. 10:19 in the RSV says, "Bread is made for laughter, and wine gladdens life, and money answers everything." That's right, you heard it correctly. "Money answers everything and wine gladdens life." High moral teaching indeed.

In 1 Tim. 4:8 Paul says, "Bodily exercise profiteth little." Of course, this flies in the face of just about every physical conditioning program in the world and every medical opinion bearing on physical fitness.

Prov. 23:13–14 (RSV) says, "Do not withhold discipline from a child; if you beat him with a rod, he will not die." Some children do die from being beaten.

The text continues, "If you beat him with a rod you will save his life from Sheol." The two words "beat" and "rod" as well as the phrase "he will not die" destroy any hope for this verse. It is more a prescription for child abuse than responsible parental discipline. You don't "beat" a child or use a rod while doing so, and you certainly don't use any measures that would bring his or her very existence into question. Prov. 20:30 (RSV) is similarly callous: Blows that wound cleanse away evil; strokes make clean the innermost parts."

Anyone who wounds others in order to cleanse has no business in a position of authority.

Pss. 34:9–10 (RSV) says, "O fear the Lord, you his saints, for those who fear him have no want! The young lions suffer want and hunger; but those who seek the Lord lack no good thing." How far from the truth can a comment be?! More often than not those who seek the Lord are precisely those who lack the most. In fact, millions seek the Lord for exactly that reason. They try everything else and only seek divine intervention after all else has failed.

Pss. 34:16–20 (RSV) says, "The face of the Lord is against evildoers, to cut off the remembrance of them from the earth. When the righteous cry for help, the Lord hears, and delivers them out of all their troubles. The Lord is near to the brokenhearted, and saves the crushed in spirit. Many are the afflictions of the righteous; but the Lord delivers him out of them all. He keeps all his bones; not one of them is broken." Here, again, we have verses that are totally divorced from reality. About the only true comment in this paragraph is that the afflictions of the righteous are many. If the face of the Lord is against evildoers and those crushed in spirit will be saved, it will have to be demonstrated in the next world, because it certainly isn't the case in this one.

Psalms 37:3–5 says, "Trust in the Lord, and do good; so shalt thou dwell in the land, and verily thou shalt be fed. Delight thyself in the Lord and he will give thee the desires of thine heart. Commit thy way unto the Lord, trust also in him, and he will bring it to pass." Just be glad you aren't required to count the number of staunch Christians who failed to receive the desires of their hearts despite following the mandates prescribed.

Ps. 41:1–3 (RSV) is utterly ridiculous and says, "Blessed is he who considers the poor! The Lord delivers him in the day of trouble; the Lord protects him and keeps him alive. . . . The Lord sustains him on his sickbed; in his illness thou healest all his infirmities." Even now, in the 1990s, thousands of church-going people who gave money to the poor are receiving food and clothing from the same churches that earlier received their donations.

Ps. 53:1 says, "The fool hath said in this heart, There is no God. Corrupt are they, and they have done abominable iniquity; there is none that doeth good." This is patently untrue. Talk about being out of touch! Many freethinkers display behavior that is considerably more moral and decent than that shown by many believers in Jesus and the Bible. In fact, under the mistaken notion that they can be excused from their antisocial deeds by confession and repentance, many Christians engage in more antisocial acts than would otherwise be the case.

Ps. 55:22–23 in the NIV says, "Cast your cares on the Lord and he will sustain you; he will never let the righteous fall. But you, O God, will bring down the wicked into the pit of corruption; bloodthirsty and deceitful men will not live out half their days." Eccles. 8:13 (RSV) says, "It will not be well with the wicked, neither will he prolong his days like a shadow, because he does not fear before God." Aside from the fact that the righteous do fall, the wicked and deceitful often live more than twice the number of days they deserve.

Prov. 18:22 (RSV) says, "He who finds a wife finds a good thing, and obtains favor from the Lord." In view of the national divorce rate, many males will no doubt look upon this verse as laughable.

Prov. 19:5 (RSV) ("A false witness will not go unpunished, and he who utters lies will not escape") is one of those verses that will have to be fulfilled in the next world because it is light years from realization in this one.

No doubt many responsible parents would take issue with Prov. 22:6 (RSV), which says, "Train up a child in the way he should go, and when he is old he will not depart from it." If that doesn't clash with the drug scene, nothing will. Thousands of children have gone to drugs despite responsible parental upbringing.

Prov. 28:16 (RSV) says, "A ruler who lacks understanding is a cruel oppressor; but he who hates unjust gain will prolong his days." Anyone who has studied history knows that decent rulers have often died at young ages and failed to prolong their days.

Prov. 26:3 (RSV) ("A whip for the horse, a bridle for the ass, and a rod for the back of fools") is undoubtedly read with relish by those with a violent disposition. In the same tradition Prov. 29:19 (RSV) says, "By mere words a servant is not disciplined, for though he understands, he will not give heed." That is a green light for the physical mistreatment of anyone in a subservient position.

To lighten up, we might turn to Prov. 30:30 (RSV), which says, "The lion, which is the mightiest among beasts and does not turn back before any," and note that elephants would probably find this to be a rather humorous comment.

Eccles. 1:15 (RSV) says, "What is crooked cannot be made straight, and what is lacking cannot be numbered." If society really believed that the crooked can not be made straight, then there would be no need for either repair shops or prisons.

Eccles. 7:3–4 and 7:1 (RSV) are in direct conflict with a primary tenet of good mental health. The former says, "Sorrow is better than laughter, for by sadness of countenance the heart is made glad. The heart of the wise is in the house of mourning; but the heart of fools is in the house of mirth," and the latter says, "A good name is better than precious ointment; and the day of death is better than the day of birth."

One assertion is as inaccurate as the other. Your day of death is better than your day of birth? What an utterly defeatist comment! Sorrow is better than laughter!

A verse that can't help but bring glee to all hedonists is Eccles. 8:15, which says, "Because a man hath no better thing under the sun, than to eat, and to drink, and to be merry." Unfortunately, much of our younger generation appears to have taken this verse to heart. Far too many look upon life as nothing more than a bowl of cherries with a liberal sprinkling of escapism. Serious self-discipline is the last thing on their minds.

Eccles. 9:11 (RSV) says, "I saw that under the sun the race is not to the swift, nor the battle to the strong, nor bread to the wise, nor riches to the intelligent, nor favor to the men of skill; but time and chance happen to them all."

If this verse were true, then nearly everyone would be inclined to adopt that hedonistic philosophy so prominently displayed in the previously noted verse. If time and chance are the primary determinants of life, then why work, why care, why study, why practice, why even think?

Eccles. 10:20 (RSV) says, "Even in your thoughts, do not curse the king, nor in your bedchamber curse the rich; for a bird of the air will carry your voice." Fortunately George Washington either never read this verse or decided to ignore it.

Isa. 48:22 says, "There is no peace, saith the Lord, unto the wicked." It is a sad fact, unfortunately, that the wicked are very often the ones who have the most peace.

Jer. 13:23 in the NIV says, "Can the Ethiopian change his skin or the leopard its spots? Neither can you do good who are accustomed to doing evil." There goes any need for rehabilitation programs. If this verse were true, and facts clearly show the opposite, the government would have wasted millions of dollars in programs to turn people around. Although high, the recidivism rate has never attained 100 percent. Although admittedly far less in number than one would like, there are many successes, which this verse chooses to ignore.

Job 27:13–17 assails the wicked by saying, "This is the portion of a wicked man with God, and the heritage of the oppressors, which they shall receive from the Almighty. If his children be multiplied, it is for the sword: and his offspring shall not be satisfied with bread. . . . Though he heap up silver as the dust, and prepare raiment as the clay; He may prepare it, but the just shall put it on, and the innocent shall divide the silver." If only the latter were true! Thank goodness the former is not! Punishing a man's offspring for his deeds will never be just.

Job 36:11–12 in the NASB berates kings by saying, "If they hear and serve Him [God], They shall end their days in prosperity, And their years in pleasures. But if they do not hear, they shall perish by the sword, And they shall die without knowledge." No doubt many kings who heard and served can laugh at this admonition. Prosperity did not mark the end of their days.

Job 36:13–14 says, "But the hypocrites in heart heap up wrath, they cry not when he binds them. They die in their youth, and their life is among the unclean." Hypocrites die in their youth! Is he kidding? Most seem to live forever.

Ps. 35:10 (RSV) says, "O Lord, who is like thee, thou who deliverest the weak from him who is too strong for him, the weak and needy from him who despoils him?" The inaccuracy of this comment is shown by the number of exploited poor who are compelled to revolt against their strong despoilers in order to alleviate their conditions. Rarely is anything of substance given to the weak and needy.

Ps. 145:16 (RSV) says, "Thou [God] openest thy hand, thou satisfiest the desire of every living thing." This is light years from reality.

Prov. 1:19 (RSV) says, "Such are the ways of all who gain by violence; it takes away the life of its possessors." No doubt many violent aggressors are amused by this verse.

Prov. 11:31 in the NIV says, "If the righteous receive their due on earth, how much more the ungodly and the sinner!" In fact, neither receive their just deserts on earth. That's a big "if" indeed.

Prov. 16:13 (RSV) says, "Righteous lips are the delight of a king, and he loves him who speaks what is right." Many bearers of bad tidings to kings know this to be a farce. On more than one occasion messengers have paid with their lives for telling the truth and politicians have been purged who told constituents the facts of life.

Ps. 129:4 in the NASB says, "The Lord is righteous; He has cut in two the cords of the wicked." Since the verb "has cut" is past tense, when did this occur?

And finally, Prov. 21:7 (RSV) says, "The violence of the wicked will sweep them away, because they refuse to do what is just." Don't be ridiculous. Ruthless, violent, dregs of society have prevailed in profusion.

In conclusion, facts clearly demonstrate that the Bible is replete with comments that fly in the face of the most elementary knowledge of world affairs. It doesn't require a vast amount of wisdom to see that in far too many cases Scripture swims in a sea of imaginings and fantasy, while projecting a mental state not unlike that of one possessed by narcotics.

Perfection

A second area of duplicitous teachings revolves around the subject of perfection and the applicability of perfection to Christians. Some of the most incredible biblical statements can be found under this heading.

One would be hard-pressed, for example, to think of a comment more at variance with reality than 1 John 3:6, which says, "Whosoever abideth in him [Jesus] sinneth not: whosoever sinneth hast not seen him, neither known him." If whoever abides in him does not sin, then nobody abides in him, because all continue to sin. If whoever sins has not seen or known him, then no one has seen or known him, because, most assuredly, all Christians continue to sin. The only way this statement could be made intelligible would be for apologists to admit that no Christians abide in Christ.

The same problem accompanies 1 John 5:18 and 1 John 3:9, which say, "Whosoever is born of God doth not commit sin; his seed remaineth in him: and he cannot sin, because he is born of God." If this statement is true, then no one is born of God, because all continue to sin. Several years ago I was told by a fundamentalist preacher, who was fully cognizant of this verse, that he abides in God because he no longer sinned after accepting Christ. That is almost too ridiculous to discuss because, in effect, he is claiming perfection, which the Bible clearly precludes by such verses as Rom. 3:10 ("There is none righteous, no, not one"), Rom. 3:12 ("There is none that doeth good, no, not one"), Eccles. 7:20 ("There is not a just man upon earth, that doeth good, and sinneth not"), and Rom. 3:23 ("Since all have sinned and fallen short of the glory of God") (RSV). On page 158 in *The Bible Has the Answer* Morris and Clark seek to address the problem presented by 1 John 3:8–9 by saying, "At first glance, this seems to teach sinless perfection for all true believers. Strict attention to the Greek text, however, reveals that John is speaking of repeated or habitual sin. Consequently, this passage could be rendered, 'No one who is born of God practices sin.' "

Two fatal flaws accompany this rationalization. First, nothing is said in the verse about habitual anything. It does not say, he cannot habitually sin. It says "he cannot sin," period. Second, even if the test referred to habitual sinning, Morris and Clark's defense would be useless because all Christians continue to sin after accepting Jesus and they do so continually. They sin not once but many times. Apologist John R. Rice was candid enough to admit as much when he said on page 275 of *Dr. Rice, Here is My Question,* "Too many people who believe in eternal security put all their confidence in the fact that a born-again Christian will hold out to do right. Actually born-again Christians often fall into very serious sins and continue in many sins."

For believers to obtain and retain the perfection is out of the question in light of James 2:10 ("For whosoever shall keep the whole law, and yet offend in one point, he is guilty of all"). Imagine that! If you break even one precept of the old Law, you've broken all of the laws. Because the Ten Commandments are within the old Law, the smallest lie would be comparable to murder. And since everyone has lied at one time or another, everyone, in effect, has not only committed murder but violated the other nine commandments as well. That is not only patently unjust and absurd on its face, but would require perfect behavior which no one can exhibit.

Finally, 1 John 3:8 says, "He that committeth sin is of the devil; for the devil sinneth from the beginning." If that is true, then every Christian is of the Devil and far from perfection, something their opponents have long suspected.

Prayer

Another stupefying aspect of biblical teachings circulates around the whole area of prayer and the efficacy of supplications to a higher being. Here, again, we have statements that are in direct opposition to daily experience in the real world. James 5:13–15 says, "Is any among you afflicted? let him pray. . . . Is any sick among you? let him call the elders of the church; and let them pray over him, anointing him with oil. . . . And the prayer of faith shall save the sick, and the Lord shall raise him up." If that were true, hospitals and physicians would be superfluous. You could just have the elders of the church pray over all those who are ill. But as all knowledgeable people know, many individuals have paid dearly because they trusted this nonsense. They chose clergy over surgery and often paid the supreme penalty for their naivete.

Even more absurd are statements that promise believers the moon if they will only persevere in the faith. Christians are told they will obtain anything they want, for example. Matt. 7:7–8 says, "Ask, and it shall be given you; seek, and ye shall find; knock, and it shall be opened unto you. For every one that asketh receiveth; and he that seeketh findeth; and to him that knocketh it shall be opened." One should carefully note that no strings are attached; accordingly this statement has little relevance to reality.

Equally absurd comments promise the believer powers equal to those of superman, but qualifiers are attached. Matt. 21:21–22, along with Mark 11:23–24, says, "Jesus answered and said unto them, Verily I say unto you, If ye have faith, and doubt not, ye shall not only do this which is done to the fig tree, but also if ye shall say unto this mountain, Be thou removed, and be you cast into the sea; it shall be done. And all things, whatsoever you shall ask in prayer, believing, ye shall receive." Now *as long as you have faith* anything can be done.

Several verses clearly say that you can do anything as long as it is done in Jesus' name. John 14:13–14 says, "Whatsoever ye shall ask in my name, that will I do, that the Father may be glorified in the Son. If ye ask anything in my name, I will do it." And John 16:23–24 says, "Verily, verily, I say unto you,

Whatsoever ye shall ask the Father in my name, he will give it you. Hitherto have ye asked nothing in my name: ask, and ye shall receive, that your joy may be full." And 1 John 3:22 says that you will receive whatever you ask as long as you keep God's commandments. Time after time Christians are told that the world is their oyster as long as they pray, ask with faith, request in Jesus' name, or keep the commandments. Although obligations are attached to most promises, that is by no means true of all.

However, the most obvious refutation of prayer's efficacy is apparent to anyone who has either engaged in prayer or witnessed prayer in action. In virtually every instance prayers go unfulfilled. (Those few that appear to be successful will be discussed later.) And they often fail miserably. Why is this? After all, didn't God's book promise the universe to anyone who would join the faith and ask in the name of Jesus? So what is the problem?

This question has been posed to apologists for centuries and their answers are no better now than they were two thousand years ago. On page 112 in *Hard Questions* apologist Frank Colquhoun explains,

> Here then are two blunt reasons why our prayers don't seem to produce the goods. First, because we don't really ask in faith. That means that we don't believe God *can* answer this particular prayer even though we say it, just in case! Secondly, all too often, as we've already seen, we only ask for things to please ourselves, whether they are good for us or not. God answers the first kind by ignoring it, because frankly it isn't a real prayer at all. And he answers the second by saying "No." So, because men always tend to blame God when things go wrong, we say, "He hasn't answered my prayer" when he certainly has! It's just that he hasn't answered it *our* way.

In other words, according to Colquhoun God answered it and the answer is no. Although this may appear to be a plausible reply, the unmistakable fallacy in his line of reasoning lies in the fact that it conflicts with clear statements in Scripture. Matt. 7:7–8 and Luke 11:9–10 have no provisos, addenda, or restrictions attached. All you have to do is ask, seek, and knock, and it's yours. There is no obligation or requirement to ask for something that does not please ourselves. In fact, why would somebody ask for something that didn't?

Second, whoever heard of a Christian asking something from God while believing God was too weak to respond? Without any evidence Colquhoun is accusing those who fail to have their prayers answered of not believing that God is omnipotent. Colquhoun conveniently ignores all those failed prayers offered by people who do have faith. Is he contending that every unfulfilled prayer emanates from someone who lacks faith in God's powers? That is absurd on its face. On pages 204 and 205 in *The Bible Has the Answer* Morris and Clark responded to the same question: "There are, however, certain conditions to be met before we can rightly expect God to answer our prayers. The first is that there be no unconfessed sin in our lives. If we are deliberately living in disobedience to God's Word, then obviously we cannot expect Him to grant our requests."

Where on earth are they getting this nonsense? What conditions? As we saw earlier, some verses have no conditions whatever and others merely require the supplicant to have faith, keep the commandments, or ask in the name of Jesus. And of that there is certainly no dearth. Nothing is said about "unconfessed sin," although it would no doubt be desirable from an apologetic perspective if there were. Morris and Clark continue by saying,

> No one has a right to pray to God for personal needs if he has ignored God's Son and the tremendous sacrifice He made for us on the cross. . . . We must also be in right relationship with the members of our own family. Another condition for answered prayer is faith that God will keep His Word. . . . Finally, one's purpose in prayer is important. Selfish, covetous prayers obviously are not pleasing to God.

Like Colquhoun, Morris and Clark have not only rewritten and supplemented Scripture to suit their own predilections, but ignored all of the prayers that have gone unanswered even though the requirements they inserted into the text were adhered to. Everyone knows of hardcore Christian believers who failed to have their prayers answered satisfactorily, although they met every requirement attached to prayer by Colquhoun, Morris, and Clark.

Apologists often try to counteract the massive number of disappointments accompanying all of these prayer-related verses by relying on one lone verse, 1 John 5:14, which says, "This is the confidence that we have in him, that, if we ask any thing according to his will, he heareth us." The theory behind employment of this verse is that God will only grant prayers that are submitted according to his will. And since nearly all prayers go unrequited, nearly all prayers aren't offered according to God's will.

Three problems accompany this defense. *First,* there are no reservations or preconditions attached to several of the verses we cited earlier, such as those in Mattew 7 and Luke 11. If one chooses to interpret 1 John 5:14 as having a condition attached, then one has created a contradiction between it on the one hand and Matt. 7:7–8 and Luke 11:9–10, on the other. The latter have no reservations. *Second,* the verse says that if we ask according to God's will he will hear us; it does not say we *must* ask according to his will in order to be heard. If I say a dog is an animal, I am not saying that in order for something to be an animal it must be a dog. The text of 1 John 5:14 says that if I ask something in God's name it will be granted, but that does not mean I *must* ask it in his name in order for it to be granted. And *third,* the verse says prayers will be heard, but that's not equivalent to prayers being answered. "Hearing" does not necessarily mean "answering," "heeding," or "complying."

A few apologists also seek to escape through James 4:3, which says, "Ye ask, and receive not, because ye ask amiss, that ye may consume it upon your lusts." But the third passage is inapplicable to this debate because it does not explain the failure of all those prayers submitted without any lusts being involved. Most assuredly, every failed prayer is not involved in lusts.

Another common response concocted for those who are not biblically informed, but are distressed by the number of ineffective prayers, is that you need to pray more. As incredible as it may be, that is precisely the tack taken by some ministers, priests, and rabbis. According to them, unanswered prayers can be attributed to the fact that you didn't pray enough; you didn't pray hard enough; you didn't say the right prayer; you didn't have the right attitude or frame of mind; you weren't penitent enough; or you lacked sufficient sincerity. In other words, by one rationale or another the distraught supplicant is led to believe that he or she is the problem, not the inefficacy of prayers in general. One would think that after millions of failures, people would get the message.

You would think that sooner or later they would realize that the problem lies not with the ineptitude of the supplicant, but with the insufficiency of prayer itself. It's like telling a drowning man that his problem lies in an inadequate supply of water. One can't help but think of the senior citizen with a very serious ailment who is told to pray by the local minister. She prays but the illness worsens. She is subsequently told to pray some more but the sickness grows even more threatening. Finally the minister tells her to pray without surcease. So she prays so hard her sides hurt, but she dies anyway. Now, what do most religious people conclude from this? They decide that she did not meet one of the prior criteria, while a sane man concludes that prayer is useless.

Prayer also suffers from the malediction of selectivity. People will shout to the housetops about the one prayer that seemed to be answered, while quietly ignoring all those that collapsed. Not only do religious people focus on the few alleged successes while ignoring a myriad of failures, but they fail to see that they have not established a cause and effect relationship between the desired event and the prayer offered. How do you know the prayer caused it? How do you know that it would not have happened regardless? Just because I pray for an event that subsequently occurs does not mean prayer was the catalyst, any more than a loud bang causes a bullet to leave the barrel of the gun. Every time a loud bang occurs a bullet goes out the barrel, but one would be foolish, indeed, to conclude that the bang rather than the ignition of gunpowder caused the bullet to be expelled.

When the subject of selectivity arises, along with the inability of superstitious people to see that reality is sending them a message contrary to that which they wish to hear, one can't help but think of the following story. One day the son of an old farmer came in and said to his father, "One of the ewe lambs is dead."

"Well," said the father, "that's all for the best. Twins never do very well anyhow." The next morning the son reported the death of the other lamb and the old man said, "Well, that's all for the best, the old ewe will now give more wool." The next morning the son said, "The old ewe is dead, too." "Well," replied the old man, "that may be for the best, but I don't see it this morning."

Another major problem with prayers is that the petitioner has taken it upon himself to ask God to alter his thoughts and behavior to fit the needs of an undeserving sinner. Ambrose Bierce described prayer as a request that the laws of the universe be annulled on behalf of a single petitioner confessedly unworthy. In a very real sense, every prayer denotes an attempt to affect, alter, or influence the activities of God. People who pray apparently don't realize that they are giving suggestions or advice to an omniscient being. How is that for an immense display of intellectual pomposity, haughtiness, and conceit! And, yet, these same people will accuse freethinkers of being victims of their own egos.

The words of Thomas Paine on page 44 of *The Age of Reason* summarize this predicament as well as any:

> Mankind finds fault with everything. His selfishness is never satisfied; his ingratitude is never at an end. He directs the Almighty what to do, even in governing the universe. He prays dictatorially. When it is sunshine, he prays for rain, and when it is rain, he prays for sunshine. He follows the same idea in everything that he prays for; for what is the amount of all of his prayers, but an attempt to make the Almighty change his mind, and act otherwise than he does? It is as if he were to say—You, God, know not so well as I.

You would think that those who pray would realize that if God wanted it done that way, he'd do it; if he does not want it done that way, then who are they to suggest otherwise?

Testing the Bible

As powerful as the promises of prayer are, they pale in comparison to six verses that bestow upon those with faith powers that rival those of God himself. Mark 9:23 says, "Jesus said unto him, If thou canst believe, all things are possible to him that believeth." Matt. 17:20 says, "Jesus said unto them. . . . If ye have faith as a grain of mustard seed, ye shall say unto this mountain, Remove hence to yonder place; and it shall remove; and nothing shall be impossible unto you." Nothing! Truly that is the ultimate in allurement. If that doesn't bring in raw recruits ready to sign on Christianity's dotted line, nothing will.

John 14:12 says, "Verily, verily, I say unto you, He that believeth on me, the works that I do shall he do also; and greater works than these shall he do;

because I go unto my Father." You are promised powers more potent than those of Jesus himself. If your deeds can exceed those of Jesus himself then you have attained a role comparable to, or exceeding that of, God Almighty, because Jesus is God. These are the promises made to all those who adopt Jesus Christ as their personal savior and become adherents to the true faith. If this is not the apex of mind control and behavior modification, what is?

Unfortunately, the whole theory comes crashing to the ground when believers become aware of the fact that they can't do any of the acts promised. When they try to implement these promises, as millions have done through the ages, they soon realize they have been victimized by a cruel hoax. They cannot perform deeds exceeding those of Jesus; they cannot move mountains; they cannot do what would normally be impossible. In fact, they cannot do anything that is astounding. Not only do their powers remain unenhanced, but many have paid with their lives to learn they have been duped.

The most famous of all passages promising believers supernatural powers is found in the Book of Mark and provides one of the most readily accessible tests for the Bible's validity. In Mark 16:17–18, Jesus says, "These signs shall follow them that believe; In my name shall they cast out devils; they shall speak with new tongues; they shall take up serpents; and if they drink any deadly thing, it shall not hurt them; they shall lay hands on the sick, and they shall recover."

Even today, Americans are dying because these verses are in the Bible. Unfortunately, all too often children pay the price for their parents' stupidity. Those who choose to put their God-inspired book to the test and really believe they can drink any deadly thing and play with dangerous serpents with impunity are headed toward catastrophe. That's why so many leading Christians are surreptitiously seeking to have the last twelve verses in the Book of Mark expunged from the Bible and many others are claiming these verses are only applicable to the people Jesus addressed at that time.

In responding to the latter defense, Gerald Sigal was completely correct when he said on page 260 of *The Jew and the Christian Missionary,*

> According to this passage, the true Christian can cast out demons, speak with tongues, pick up serpents, drink any deadly thing, and heal the sick. These are promises made by Jesus to all the faithful, not only of his generation, but of all generations. The Christian, his Messiah informs him, possesses the ability to bring all of these miraculous deeds to pass. The formula for success is simple: "Believe!" . . . But can the Christian actually perform these miraculous deeds? No, of course not! Yet everyone who believes Jesus is the true Messiah has been guaranteed by Jesus the power to cast out demons, speak in tongues, pick up serpents, drink anything deadly, and heal the sick.

The verses in Mark 16 provide one of the most readily available disproofs of that fraud known as the Bible. No con man wants his scheme or product exposed to the public eye, but the Book of Mark fosters just such exposure by providing one of the few places where the Bible's validity can be immediately tested.

The number of sick people upon whom hands have been laid in a misguided and futile attempt to heal the sick by trusting in the Bible's reliability is astronomical. Faith-healers and adherents to the Mark 16 and James 5 are nothing more than charlatans preying upon those who have either tried all else or can afford nothing else. After all, most people don't pray when they are on their knees but when they are on their backs. George Bernard Shaw correctly stated, "Common people don't pray, my lord; they only beg."

Miracles

The most preposterous biblical statements for those unacquainted with the intricacies of textual analysis lie in the category of miracles or supernatural events. For millions of people the whole idea of sticks turning into serpents (Exod. 7:10), a serpent and donkey talking (Gen. 3:4–5 and Num. 22:28–30, respectively), iron floating (2 Kings 6:5–6), a women turning into a pillar of salt (Gen. 19:26), the sun standing still (Josh. 10:13), and people rising from the dead (Matt. 27:52), for example, are as far from the realm of possibility as black is from white. Little do these people realize that their rejection of miracles and the supernatural in general is simultaneously a rejection of the validity of the Bible itself. If all miracles were excluded from the Bible, the book would be dealt a crushing blow from which recovery would be impossible. As apologist William Arndt says on page 26 in *Bible Difficulties,* "If we take everything miraculous out of the Bible, how little will there be left."

Without the miracle of the Resurrection, for example, Christianity would collapse. As Paul said in 1 Cor. 15:14 and 15:17 (RSV), "If Christ has not been raised, then our preaching is in vain and your faith is in vain. . . . If Christ has not been raised, your faith is futile and you are still in your sins." Apologist Harold Lindsell was quite correct when he said on page 204 of *The Battle for the Bible,* "Once we discard miracles, we automatically open the door that leads to a denial of the virgin birth and the bodily resurrection of Jesus Christ from the dead." Apologist Robert Mounce is equally on target when he says on page 15 of *Answers to Questions About the Bible,* "The Christian faith is openly supernaturalistic."

Parenthetically, we might note that in so far as miracles are concerned, one of the most famous, the virgin birth, was eclipsed by several events in the Old Testament. As Muhammad Ata ur-Rahim says on page 20 of *Jesus, A Prophet of Islam,* "The birth of Adam was the greatest miracle, as he was born without a father or mother. The birth of Eve too was a greater miracle than the birth of Jesus, inasmuch as she was born without a mother." Rahim could also have noted that Adam and Eve came into the world as full-grown adults, which is considerably more spectacular than the virgin birth.

Although some of the most incredible biblical statements lie within the category of the miraculous, apologists vigorously contend that *scriptural* accounts of supernatural events are unlike those that one can expect to encounter elsewhere. They are somehow more realistic, more plausible, more feasible. On page 62 in *Know Why You Believe* apologist Paul Little says, "Biblical miracles, in contrast to miracle stories in pagan literature and those in other religions, were not capricious or fantastic."

Biblical miracles were not fantastic? Is Little serious? Sticks turning into snakes and people rising from the dead are not fantastic? If a woman turning into a pillar of salt is not fantastic, what is? If the sun standing still is not incredible, what is?

Following in Little's footsteps, apologists McDowell and Stewart state on page 74 in *Answers to Tough Questions,* "Admittedly, there are many stories from our Lord's day among the Greeks and Romans which are so fanciful and ridiculous that they are not worthy of serious consideration. This is in complete contrast to the biblical miracles, which never offer a mindless display of the supernatural."

Biblical miracles are not fanciful and ridiculous? Don't be absurd! Of course they are! They are as preposterous as any supernatural events presented in ancient literature. One rarely finds a candid assessment of miracles by Christian fundamentalists, but on pages 83 and 84 of *Beyond the Basics* apologist David DeWitt states,

> William Nolen, M.D., did a survey of the "healing" ministry of Kathryn Kuhlman. He writes, "In talking to these people, I tried to be as honest, understanding, and objective as possible, but I couldn't dispense with my medical knowledge and my common sense. I listened carefully to everything they told me and followed up every lead that might have led to a confirmation of a miracle. I was led to an inescapable conclusion: Of the patients who had returned to Minneapolis to reaffirm the cures claimed at the miracle service, not one had, in fact, been miraculously cured of anything."

DeWitt continues by saying,

> I, too, am prepared to state categorically that I have never, ever seen any healing that was contrary to nature. I have pursued this subject with doctors and theologians and have never found anyone who could show me a supernatural event of any

kind. I have, of course, heard a multitude of stories and read many books and articles that claim supernatural miracles. But none of those authors or conversationalists were ever able to show me one. I am sure many of my Christian friends consider me to be extremely limited and unfortunate. I would simply say that I have heard these stories for years, and I have not heard a new type of story in a long time. I have investigated every type of story and have yet to find anything appearing to be supernaturally of God.

Such honesty is rarely encountered in the Christian fundamentalist community!

The most common defense of biblical miracles, or miracles in general for that matter, is well stated on page 27 of *A Defense of Biblical Infallibility* by Clark Pinnock, who states, "Empirical science cannot contest the validity of a miracle for the simple reason the event cannot be repeated for experiment today. The evidence for a miracle, as for any historical event, is the testimony of those who witnessed it. . . . Science which denies the possibility of miracles is both unbiblical and unhistorical."

Pinnock fails to realize that the burden of proof lies on him who alleges. Those who deny the existence of miracles are under no obligation to prove anything, while those who affirm their existence must prove everything. That the burden of proof lies on him who alleges is axiomatic to all rational thought. But proof is something believers in miracles just can't provide. Scientists do not necesarily contest the existence of miracles. But miracles aren't factored into scientific calculations because they aren't demonstrable. Miracles can't be duplicated and tangible evidence for their existence is not forthcoming. The only thing defenders of miracles can produce is the testimony of witnesses claiming to have encountered supernatural events. Of course, witnesses alone to a unique occurrence are insufficient evidence of their validity. If they were sufficient, any crackpot, wild-eyed, crazy event could be proved to have really happened simply because someone said so. If a group of people claimed to have seen Elvis Presley, for example, that would have to be true until skeptics proved otherwise.

Those who say Jesus rose from the grave must substantiate their belief, while those who believe otherwise are under no obligation to prove anything. The Achilles heel for belief in miracles is also the death blow for a belief in God and the supernatural in general. The burden of proof lies on him who alleges, not others. And because the existence of God can no more be demonstrated than the existence of supernatural occurrences in general, both must remain in the realm of imagination. As Thomas Paine says on page 81 of volume 9 of his *Works,* "All the tales of miracles, with which the Old and New Testament are filled, are fit only for impostors to preach and fools to believe." David Hume was also on the mark when he said, "The Christian religion not only was at first attended with miracles, but even at this day cannot be believed by any reasonable person without one."

One of the most prevalent and crucial of all mistakes made by believers in miracles resides in their propensity to look upon supernatural events as harbingers of a divine message, a divine messenger, or a higher power. Believers in miracles view them as proof or evidence of a superior strength or force that should be taken into account.

This point is made many times by biblical apologists. On page 5 in volume 1 of *Answering Christianity's Most Troubling Questions* apologist Richard Sisson says, "There are several ways God has set the Bible apart from all spurious religious literature. First, the human authors of Scripture did not simply share opinions. They claimed to be God's spokesmen, and they substantiated their claims with *mighty deeds*. Those mighty deeds, miracles in many cases, became a significant credential (see Acts 2:22, 2:43, 5:12)." On page 75 in *Answers to Tough Questions* apologists McDowell and Stewart say, "The miracles of Jesus . . . were meant to be objective signs to the people that He was the promised Messiah, since one of the credentials of the Messiah would be signs and miracles." On page 257 in *Basic Theology* Charles Ryrie says, "By the miracles which verified to the people of His day that Jesus was a true Prophet." And on page 66 in *Dr. Rice, Here Is My Question* apologist John R. Rice says, "Certainly the miracles prove that Jesus came from God."

In reality, miracles do nothing of the sort and the Bible itself says they are not to be taken as signs of deity, godliness, the messiahship, or prophetic capabilities. Believers like Sisson, McDowell, Stewart, and Ryrie are plagued by an inability to either admit or realize that the Bible repeatedly says supernatural events are not to be used to prove anything. Such events are not reliable evidence and should not be used to substantiate statements, beliefs, or credentials. Unlike the others, Rice was apparently aware of the biblical difficulties associated with his earlier pronouncement, so he hastened to add a modification on the same page:

> In John 5:36 please note that Jesus did not say that His works proved His deity. They simply proved "the Father hath sent me" which He said. And we must not add more than Jesus said. Any prophet who came from God working miracles, like Elijah or Elisha or Moses or Paul, could very properly have said the same thing. Miracles proved they were from God but they did not prove deity, for many others besides Jesus have had the power to work miracles.

Although Rice tried to render his response more palatable from a biblical perspective, he failed miserably. Miracles not only don't prove deity, they don't prove their source is the messiah or from God either. Remember, the pharaoh's magicians did miracles and one would hardly say they were from God. Exod. 8:6–7 says, "Aaron stretched out his hand over the waters of Egypt; and the frogs came up, and covered the land of Egypt. And the magicians did so with their enchantments, and brought up frogs upon the land of Egypt." Exod. 7:10–

11 says the pharaoh's magicians turned their rods into serpents and Exod. 7:21–22 says they turned the river into blood.

So the ability to do miracles does not establish one's credentials as an agent of God. In fact, on several occasions the Bible specifically states that those who perform miracles are not divine agents and are not to be trusted. Sisson, McDowell, Stewart, Ryrie, and Rice all fail to take into account some very important verses in this regard. Matt. 24:23–24 and Mark 13:21–22 say, "If any man shall say unto you, Lo, here is Christ or there; believe it not. For there shall arise false Christs, and false prophets, and shall shew great signs and wonders; insomuch that, if it were possible, they shall deceive the very elect." These verses clearly show that those who perform miracles are not to be trusted and those who claim to be a Christ because they can perform miracles and prophesy are not to be trusted either. And that would include Jesus of Nazareth. How do apologists know he was the real McCoy?

In addition, 2 Thess. 2:8–9 in the New International Version states, "Then the lawless one will be revealed. . . . The coming of the lawless one will be in accordance with the work of Satan displayed in all kinds of counterfeit miracles, signs and wonders, and in every sort of evil that deceives." This brings into doubt the whole question of what miracles convey. Clearly Satan and his agents can perform miracles to entrap people; so one can never be sure that those who perform miracles are not agents of Satan seeking to lead people astray. In the same vein, Rev. 16:14 says, "For they are the spirits of devils, working miracles" and shows that workers of miracles could very easily be the Devil's agents.

False prophets are also able to perform miracles and deceive God's people. In fact, they are used by God to test the convictions of true believers. Deut. 13:1–3 says,

> If there arise among you a prophet, or a dreamer of dreams, and giveth thee a sign or a wonder, And the sign or wonder come to pass whereof he spake unto thee, saying, Let us go after other gods, which thou hast not known, and let us serve them; thou shalt not hearken unto the words of that prophet, or that dreamer of dreams: for the Lord your God proveth you, to know whether ye love the Lord your God with all your heart and with all your soul.

In other words, you are being tested and by heeding the words of any prophet, you can never be positive you are not following the kind of false prophet condemned by God by going after other gods.

Rev. 19:20 provides further corroboration of the dangers involved in believing a prophet because he can perform miracles. It states, "The beast was taken, and with him the false prophet that wrought miracles." So any believer relying upon miracles to establish the truth of statements made by Jesus, Peter, Paul, the Apostles, the prophets, or the patriarchs, or to establish the credentials of any key figure, is treading on thin ice, indeed.

The conflict between the Bible and miracles on the one hand and science and reason on the other is well summarized in the story of an eight-year-old lad who was asked by his mother what he had learned at Sunday School. "Well," he said, "our teacher told us about God sending Moses behind the enemy lines to rescue the Israelites from the Egyptians. When they came to the Red Sea, Moses called for the engineers to build a pontoon bridge. After they had all crossed, they all looked back and saw the Egyptian tanks coming. Moses radioed headquarters on his walkie-talkie to send bombers to blow up the bridge and saved the Israelites." "Bobby!" exclaimed his mother, "Is that really the way your teacher told you that story?" "Uh, not exactly, Mom," Bobby said, "But if I told it her way, you'd never believe it."

Is it any wonder that one of the heroes of the American Revolution, Ethan Allen of Green Mountain Boy fame, said, "In those parts of the world where learning and science have prevailed, miracles have ceased; but in those parts of it that are barbarous and ignorant, miracles are still in vogue."

Before concluding the subject of miracles one cannot help but ask: What did Jesus Christ do that makes him stand out in the crowd, that sets him apart from the rest of humanity? What did he do that was so spectacular or proved he was the messiah? Some will no doubt say that he performed miracles. Well, so did many others and they did so before him. Some will say that he rose from the dead. Well, so did many others and they also rose before him. Some will say that he led and taught an exemplary life, when that applies to thousands who lived before him. Some will say that Jesus alone fulfilled the Old Testament messianic prophecies, but we have presented more than enough data to prove the opposite. Some will say that he voluntarily died for the sins of humanity, when that is merely an assertion based on nothing concrete. People can claim anything, and do, but that's not proof. Finally, no doubt some will claim that Jesus was God, incarnate. But a tremendous amount of evidence presented in previous chapters proves that a belief of that kind is far from reality. Jesus obviously couldn't be God when he made statements such as: "For my Father is greater than I" in John 14:28, and "Why callest thou me good? there is none good but one, that is, God," found in Mark 10:18.

Conclusion

In conclusion, we can see that the Bible is light years from being a fountain of wisdom and truth. More than enough comments are readily available to convince all but the most dogmatic proponents that Scripture contains a veritable cornucopia of false and misleading statements, teaches an inane reliance upon ineffective prayer, projects upon believers an unrealistic aura of perfection, promises a degree of power to the faithful that borders on the omnipotent, and fosters a belief in miracles that is not only risky but in direct defiance of biblical warnings. One can readily understand the intelligence exhibited by Thomas Paine when he said on pages 271 and 272 of his *Works,*

> If we found in any other book pretending to give a system of religion, the falsehoods, falsifications, contradictions, and absurdities, which are to be met with on almost every page of the Old and New Testament, all the priests of the present day, who supposed themselves capable, would triumphantly show their skill in criticism, and cry it down as a most glaring imposition. But since the books in question belong to their own trade and profession, they, or at least many of them, seek to stifle every inquiry into them and abuse those who have the honesty and courage to seek to inquire.

Robert Ingersoll encapsulated the entire arena of false teachings, miracles, prayer, temporal power, and perfection when he said on page 285 of volume 1 of his *Works,* "Take from the church the miraculous, the supernatural, the incomprehensible, the unreasonable, the impossible, the unknowable, and the absurd, and nothing but a vacuum will remain."

13

Social Issues I

Abortion, Alcohol, Anti-Semitism, Cannibalism, Children, Communism, Death Penalty, Divorce, Gambling

If there is any aspect of biblical teachings upon which millions of religious laymen place tremendous importance, it lies in the realm of social issues and related biblical pronouncements. How the Bible views abortion, anti-Semitism, gambling, homosexuality, divorce and other social topics is of crucial importance to the lives of millions. What is conveniently omitted from the equation, however, is the extent to which the average person is kept ignorant of the multiple problems, contradictions, and inconsistencies that accompany the biblical stance on each issue.

This chapter as well as that which follows will try to rectify this oversight by analyzing each topic individually. Rather than assigning a degree of significance to one subject over another, as would be implied in any order of consideration we deemed appropriate, we've opted for the more neutral approach of simply taking issues in alphabetical order.

Abortion

Contrary to the claims of biblicists, abortion is not prohibited by any biblical verse or any series of connected verses. The main text that is repeatedly cited by apologists in this regard is Exod. 21:22-23, which says, "If men strive, and hurt a woman with child, so that her fruit depart from her, and yet no mischief

251

follow: he [the perpetrator] shall be surely punished, according as the woman's husband will lay upon him; and he shall pay as the judges determine. And if any mischief follow, then thou shalt give life for life."

Fundamentalist John R. Rice, whom Jerry Falwell described as his mentor, alleged on page 8 of his book *Abortion* that, "Only in the case of Exod. 21:22–25 does the Bible specifically mention retaliation for the death or injury of an unborn child." Unfortunately for apologists, reliance upon these verses is inadequate for several reasons:

First, mankind is no longer under the Old Law according to biblicists and Exodus 21 is an example of that law.

Second, and even more important, careful reading of the words will show that they do not prohibit abortion. In fact, they aren't even discussing abortion. Notice what is said: If two men are fighting and hurt a pregnant woman such that a miscarriage occurs, "yet no mischief follows: he shall surely be punished." In other words, the man who caused the miscarriage will be punished and forced to pay by the woman's husband and a judge, for what he did to the woman, not for what he did to the fetus.

Third, the last line of the verse says, "If any mischief follow, then thou shalt give life for life." If any mischief *to the woman, not the fetus,* follows, then the offender will be killed. The key word is "if." "If" any mischief follows. The mischief has already occurred, if the *miscarriage* was the main concern. Obviously, subsequent mischief to the woman is the only concern, since the fetus is gone. In truth, Exod. 21:22–23 has nothing to do with abortion. It's actually saying that if two men are fighting and a pregnant woman is injured in the process and has a miscarriage, but suffers no other injury, the offender should be punished by the woman's husband. On the other hand, if the woman incurred "mischief," which appears to be her death, then the injuring party must die.

Although there are no verses in the Bible clearly in opposition to abortion, is there any strategy by which biblicists can use the Bible to oppose abortion? Yes, there is, but two hurdles must first be surmounted. They must not only find verses in opposition to the killing of human beings in general but also find verses saying the fetus is a human being throughout the nine-month gestation period. If the fetus is a human being for the entire nine months and the killing of humans is wrong, then biblical opposition to abortion can be demonstrated.

If we believe that the prohibitions against killing in Rev. 21:8 ("murderers . . . shall have their part in the lake which burneth with fire and brimstone"), 1 John 3:15 ("And ye know that no murderer hath eternal life abiding in him"), Gen. 9:6 ("Whoever sheds the blood of man, by man shall his blood be shed"), and Exod. 21:12 ("He that smiteth a man, so that he die, shall be surely put to death"), as well as the Sixth Commandment against killing, are operative, referring to the killing of human beings, one can reasonably conclude the first hurdle has been scaled.

The second obstacle, however, is considerably more formidable. Apologists must not only employ verses showing that which lives in the womb is a human being, but that it is a human being *throughout the entire nine-month period.* Having laid down the requirements, we can now analyze the most commonly used antiabortion texts. Exod. 23:7 says, "Keep thee far from a false matter; and the innocent and righteous slay thou not." Deut. 27:25 says, "Cursed be he that taketh reward to slay an innocent person," and 2 Kings 24:4 says, "And also for the innocent blood that he shed: for he filled Jerusalem with innocent blood which the Lord would not pardon." These three verses are inapplicable to abortion because they assume the very point in dispute, i.e., that the fetus is a human being. A fetus would have to be a human being in order to be innocent. Everyone would agree that the slaying of innocent people is wrong. But apologists are obligated to prove that fetuses are "people" according to the Bible before claiming the Bible prohibits abortion. Humanity precedes innocence.

Unfortunately for apologists, all three of the following verses show that even *newborns* are by no means innocent and deal a fatal blow to the whole "age of accountability" concept. Ps. 58:3 says, "The wicked are estranged from the womb: they go astray *as soon as they be born,* speaking lies"; Job 14:4 says, "Who can bring a clean thing out of an unclean? not one"; and Job 15:14 says, "What is man, that he should be clean? and he which is born of a woman, that he should be righteous?" One could also argue that Ps. 51:5 which says, "I was shapen in iniquity: and in sin did my mother conceive me" shows that the fetus is not innocent. It's hard to conceive of one being shapen in sin and iniquity while remaining pure and innocent.

Ruth 4:13 ("Boaz took Ruth, and she was his wife: and when he went in unto her, the Lord gave her conception, and she bare a son"), Gen. 29:32 ("Leah conceived, and bare a son"), and Gen. 30:22–23 ("God hearkened to her, and opened her womb. And she conceived, and bare a son") are used by abortion opponents in a deceptive attempt to ignore the nine-month gestation period by equating conception with birth. Apologists conveniently ignore the fact that all three verses say a son emerged at birth, but none says he was a son at conception or during the nine months of gestation.

As can readily be seen from what has been covered so far, the point at which a human being comes onto the scene is a key question, not only in the biblical but also the scientific and legal community. Does humanity begin at conception, at birth, or at some point during the nine intervening months? Isa. 49:5, ("Now, saith the Lord that formed me from the womb to be his servant"), Isa. 49:1, ("The Lord hath called me from the womb; from the bowels of my mother hath he made mention of my name"), and Eccles. 11:5 ("As you do not know how the spirit comes to the bones in the womb of a woman") (RSV) are used by anti-abortionists to prove that fetuses become human beings at some point during gestation, but they do not prove that point coincides with conception.

Whether formed "from" the womb (i.e., after leaving) or "in" the womb, the fact remains that these verses are not saying the fetus becomes a full-fledged human being at conception.

Biblicists also rely upon Ps. 139:13–16 (RSV), which says, "For thou didst form my inward parts, thou didst knit me together in my mother's womb . . . my frame was not hidden from thee, when I was being made in secret. . . . Thy eyes beheld my unformed substance." These comments are used to prove the fetus is a human being, but apologists fail to realize these verses could only be used to prove the fetus formed at conception becomes a human being at some point during the nine months. They don't prove a fetus is a human being at conception. How could one be a human being at conception, if one is knit together, formed, and made in secret during the pregnancy?

Matt. 1:18 says, "When as his mother Mary was espoused to Joseph, before they came together, she was found with child of the Holy Ghost," and Gen. 25:21–24 says, "Rebekah his [Isaac's] wife conceived. And the children struggled together within her. . . . And the Lord said unto her, Two nations are in thy womb, and two manner of people shall be separated from thy bowels, and the one people shall be stronger than the other people. . . . And when her days to be delivered were fulfilled, behold there were twins in her womb." These are the strongest anti-abortion verses discussed so far because they clearly show the fetus is a child at some indefinite point during the gestation period, according to the Bible.

That point is actually fixed when Luke 1:41 ("It came to pass that, when Elizabeth heard the salutation of Mary, the babe leaped in her [Elizabeth's] womb.") and Luke 1:44 ("As soon as the voice of thy salutation sounded in mine ears, the babe leaped in my womb for joy") are combined with Luke 1:36 which says, "Behold, thy cousin Elizabeth, she hath also conceived a son in her old age: and this is the sixth month with her, who was called barren." Biblicists can now reasonably allege that the Bible teaches that the fetus is a human being by the sixth month of pregnancy.

From this, as well as all other verses discussed so far, we can conclude the following with reference to the biblical stance on abortion. Our biblically-oriented friends can use the Bible to prove the fetus is a human being not only at birth but by the 6th month of gestation. But they can't use the Bible to clearly prove the fetus is a human being at conception or during the 1st and 2nd trimesters, and that's when nearly all abortions occur.

Anti-abortionists have one final verse that could be interpreted as the strongest part of their case yet. Jer. 1:4–5 says, "Then the word of the Lord came to me saying, Before I formed thee in the belly I knew thee; and before thou came forth out of the womb I sanctified thee, and I ordained thee a prophet unto the nations." This verse appears to be the only verse in the entire Bible seeming to say that someone is not only a human being at conception but prior to same.

Unfortunately for biblicists, the key phrase, "Before I formed thee in the belly, I knew thee," is ambiguous. Does it mean the speaker did not yet exist but God had already planned what he would be prior to conception, or does it mean that he already existed and God knew who he was? If anti-abortionists opt for the latter, they'll open a whole can of worms they'd do well to keep contained.

Second, God is speaking to Jeremiah alone. Upon what basis do they assume this applies to all of humanity?

And finally, retreat to a verse of this nature means that apologists have abandoned any attempt to prove from the Bible that the fetus is a human being during the first six months of gestation. Instead, they are saying the fetus is a human being before conception, spiritually speaking, which is much less demonstrable.

In closing, something should be said in regard to the woman involved in the abortion issue. After all, she *is* of crucial importance to the whole process. Robert Ingersoll definitely expressed the view of millions when he said on page 505 of volume 4 of his *Works*, "Science must make woman the owner, the mistress of herself. Science, the only possible savior of mankind, must put it in the power of woman to decide for herself whether she will or will not become a mother." For millions in favor of legalized abortion, the issue is based more on a woman's right to choose than a biblically based argument having to do with when a human being comes onto the scene.

Alcohol

The second topic in our alphabetical listing is alcohol. Probably no chemical in the history of mankind has been more involved with the destruction of human life than alcohol. Throughout the ages groups of one sort or another have risen to fight its pernicious influence and religiously oriented bodies have been no exception. Biblicists have viewed themselves as being in the forefront of the abstinence movement via such organizations as Alcoholics Anonymous and the Womens' Christian Temperance Union, which was instrumental in ushering in Prohibition.

Although one need not exhibit much wisdom to see why people should be encouraged to shun alcohol, an exceptional degree of insight is needed to see how the Bible can be of assistance in this regard. Only by the selective use of verses can one invoke the Bible as an anti-alcohol source. Because intoxicating drinks are a sociological problem of the first magnitude, an exhaustive biblical discussion of the issue is in order. All of the verses in opposition to its consumption will be listed first, followed by all those advocating its employment.

Both categories can be subdivided into verses that are more and less forceful. Verses most in favor of the teetotalist position are Hab. 2:5 (RSV), "Moreover, wine is treacherous; the arrogant man shall not abide"; Rom. 14:21, "It is good neither to eat flesh (even that of Jesus Christ?], nor to drink wine, nor any thing whereby thy brother stumbleth"; Prov. 20:1, "Wine is a mocker, strong drink is raging: and whosoever is deceived thereby is not wise"; 1 Tim. 3:2-3), "A bishop then must be blameless, the husband of one wife, vigilant, sober . . . not given to wine . . ."; Titus 1:7-8, "For a bishop must be blameless, as the steward of God; . . . not given to wine . . . sober, just, holy, temperate"; Lev. 10:9, "Do not drink wine nor strong drink, thou nor thy sons with thee, when ye go into the tabernacle of the congregation lest ye die: it shall be a statute for ever throughout your generations"; and Prov. 23:29-32, "Who has woe? Who has sorrow? Who has strife? Who has complaining? Who has wounds without cause? Who has redness of eyes? Those who tarry long over wine, those who try mixed wine. Do not look at wine when it is red, when it sparkles in the cup and goes down smoothly. At the last it bites like a serpent, and stings like an adder."

Verses opposing the consumption of alcohol with less definitiveness are Eph. 5:18, "Be not drunk with wine, wherein is excess"; 1 Cor. 6:10, "Nor thieves, nor covetous, nor drunkards . . . shall inherit the kingdom of God"; Hosea 4:11, "Whoredom and wine and new wine take away the heart"; Luke 1:15 "He shall be great in the sight of the Lord, and shall drink neither wine nor strong drink . . . ," Isa. 28:7 (RSV) "These also reel with wine and stagger with strong drink; the priest and the prophet reel with strong drink, they are confused with wine, they stagger with strong drink; they err in vision, they stumble in giving judgment"; Ps. 60:3 (RSV), "Thou hast made thy people suffer hard things; thou hast given us wine to drink that made us reel"; Dan. 1:8 (RSV) "Daniel resolved that he would not defile himself with the king's rich food, or with the wine which he drank"; 1 Pet. 4:3, "We walked in lasciviousness, lusts, excess of wine, revellings, banquetings, and abominable idolatries"; Hos. 3:1, "Then said the Lord unto me, Go yet, love . . . an adulteress, according to the love of the Lord toward the children of Israel, who look to other gods, and love flagons of wine," and Num. 6:2-4, "When either man or woman shall separate themselves to vow a vow of a Nazarite. . . . He shall separate himself from wine and strong drink, and shall drink no vinegar of wine, or vinegar of strong drink, neither shall he drink any liquor of grapes, nor eat moist grapes, or dried. All the days of his separation shall he eat nothing that is made of the vine tree." The weakness inherent in some of the latter citations lies in the fact that they appear to oppose drunkenness and excess rather than drinking per se.

On the other side of the coin are those verses that advocate indulging in drink, and they too can be divided into stronger and weaker comments. Among the stronger are 1 Tim. 5:23, "Drink no longer water, but use a little wine for thy stomach's sake and thine often infirmities"; Prov. 31:6-7, "Give strong drink unto him that is ready to perish, and wine unto those that be of heavy heart. Let him drink and forget his poverty, and remember his misery no more"; Eccles.

9:7, "Go thy way, eat thy bread with joy, and drink thy wine with a merry heart; for God now accepteth thy works"; Jer. 13:12, "Thus saith the God of Israel, Every bottle shall be filled with wine"; Isa. 55:1 (RSV), "Every one who thirsts, come to the waters; and he who has no money come buy and eat! Come, buy wine and milk"; Joel 2:19, "The Lord will answer and say unto his people, Behold, I will send you corn, and wine, and oil, and ye shall be satisfied therewith"; Amos 9:14, "I will bring again the captivity of my people of Israel . . . and they shall plant vineyards, and drink the wine thereof"; Deut. 14:25–26 (RSV), "You shall turn it into money . . . and go to the place which the Lord your God chooses, and spend the money for whatever you desire, oxen, or sheep, or wine or strong drink, whatever your appetite craves"; Gen. 27:28, "God give thee of the dew of heaven, and the fatness of the earth, and plenty of corn and wine"; Isa. 25:6 (RSV), "On this mountain the Lord of hosts will make for all peoples a feast of fat things, a feast of wine"; 1 Tim. 3:8, "Likewise must the deacons be grave, not doubletongued, not given to much wine"; and Titus 2:3, "Not given to much wine."

One can easily see from these verses that the following comment by Morris and Clark on page 225 of *The Bible Has the Answer* is utterly inaccurate and flies in the face of clear biblical precepts: "It is significant that nowhere does the Bible actually endorse the drinking of wine or other intoxicating drinks. On the contrary, there are numerous warnings against it." Morris and Clark compound their nonsense by making the mistake of quoting Eph. 5:18 to prove their point. The verse says, "Be not drunk with wine, wherein is excess; but be filled with the Spirit." They fail to note that this verse does not condemn drinking but only being drunk.

Finally, there are verses that support drinking but with less assertiveness. Prime examples are Ps. 104:15, "Wine that maketh glad the heart of man"; Num. 28:7, "In the holy place shalt thou cause the strong wine to be poured unto the Lord for a drink offering"; Eccle 5:18, "Behold that which I have seen: it is good and comely for one to eat and to drink"; Judg. 9:13, "The vine said unto them, Should I leave my wine, which cheereth God and man . . . ?"; Deut. 7:13, "He will love you, bless you; he will also bless your grain and your wine"; Gen. 14:18, "Melchizedek King of Salem brought forth bread and wine: and he was the priest of the most high God"; Zech. 9:17, "Corn shall make the young men cheerful, and new wine the maids"; Joel 3:18, "In that day the mountains shall drip sweet wine, and the hills shall flow with milk, and all the stream beds of Judah shall flow with water"; and Num. 6:20, "After that the Nazarite may drink wine."

Judging from all of the above, one can easily see that the Bible simultaneously condemns and condones the drinking of alcoholic beverages. Christians have always had difficulty with this subject not only because of the myriad verses in support of drinking but the acts of their savior, himself. Everyone knows that Jesus changed water into wine and believers are hard-pressed to justify his behavior. The common apologetic response has been that the water was not changed into wine but into unfermented grape juice.

Fortunately, there are fundamentalists willing to admit the inadequacy of this explanation. One of these, David O'Brien, was asked the following question on page 365 of *Today's Handbook for Solving Bible Difficulties:* "If the Bible teaches that drinking is a sin, why did Jesus turn water into wine, and why did Paul tell Timothy to drink wine for his stomach?" O'Brien responded by saying,

> I've read all the arguments about unfermented grape juice and how fermentation doesn't take place naturally in the climate of Palestine, and I have to tell you—they're based more on wishful thinking than on linguistic study or scientific understanding. Jesus turned the water into real wine. I know this makes some believers nervous. I know it makes some hostile. "How can I counsel alcoholics not to drink if you're telling them drinking isn't a sin?" they ask me. I wish the Bible did teach that drinking is a sin, but it doesn't. It contains numerous warnings against the *abuse* of alcohol, but nowhere does it say it's a sin. And we are not free to make the Bible say what it doesn't say just to make our decisions easier. For me there's a very profound principle at work here.

On the next page O'Brien lays down his very important 37th principle in this regard, namely,

> Don't bend and twist the meaning of the biblical text to avoid an unpleasant conclusion. If we convolute the meaning of a text to avoid a conclusion that we find unpleasant, we might as well give up the doctrine of inerrancy. If we reject the clear meaning for an interpretation that is more palatable, we render such a doctrine irrelevant. We have good reason, of course, for our strong feelings about alcohol. In our day alcohol is used as a means to an end. The societal pressure to drink to excess is monumental. . . . Christians in my situation have an even stronger reason for avoiding alcohol. I'm the son of an alcoholic. . . . But despite all this, the Bible does not say that drinking of alcohol is a sin. . . . Did the overseer at the banquet think mere grape juice would dull the wedding guests' taste buds? Did Paul warn against the overindulgence of grape juice (Ephesians 5:18)? Did Noah drink too much grape juice (Genesis 9:21)? Is grape juice a mocker (Proverbs 20:1)? Did Jeremiah liken himself to a man overtaken by grape juice (Jeremiah 23:9)?

This kind of honest analysis rarely emanates from the fundamentalist community and is about as good a summary of this problem as one could devise. O'Brien has nailed truth to the wall for all to see. The conclusion is obvious. When the biblical text said wine it meant wine, not grape juice.

Based upon all of the foregoing verses, we can see that the Bible's teachings on the consumption of alcohol are inconsistent and contradictory. The oft-quoted remark, "You can prove anything you want from the Bible," is borne out by this subject better than most. If one seeks a verse in favor of drinking, it's available; if one seeks the opposite, it's there, too. If someone chooses to attack from the outside the biblical stance on war, injustice, slavery, brutality, morality, and many other topics, biblicists have plenty of verses available to support whatever position expediency dictates. Because of the extremely contradictory nature of biblical pronouncements, the Bible is made to order for external assaults and brickbats thrown from a distance.

But when one goes within the Book to compare verse with verse and simply asks, for example, "Should I drink or shouldn't I?" he finds no consistent response; he's left hanging. Because the overwhelming majority of the people do not know the Book very well and are not aware of its inconsistencies and contradictions, they are satisfied with whatever answer apologists provide and easily given the impression the Bible is the wisest of all volumes.

Failure to take cognizance of this fact has been one of the greatest mistakes of freethought advocates throughout history. The latter have concentrated far too much upon the external approach at the expense of internal dilemmas. One should not focus primarily upon extrabiblical information to the exclusion of that which is internal. There is more than enough information within the Book to refute its validity. The Bible is its own worst enemy. It just isn't prudent to concentrate on externals, although they should be included.

Anti-Semitism

A third major social issue covered by biblical teachings relates to Jews and their role in the formation of Christianity. One does not have to read very far into the Book of John, the Book of Acts, or the writings of Paul to see comments that easily buttress anti-Semitism. Examples abound in the Book of John, especially. Three verses that depict Jews as the persecutors of Jesus are John 5:16 ("Therefore did the Jews persecute Jesus, and sought to slay him, because he had done these things on the sabbath day"), John 5:18 ("The Jews sought the more to kill him, because he not only had broken the sabbath, but said also that God was his Father, making himself equal to God"), and John 7:1 ("After these things Jesus walked in Galilee: for he would not walk in Jewry; because the Jews sought to kill him").

These three verses alone are sufficient to create hatred of Jews in the minds of Christians. But they are only part of a larger picture. In John 8:52 the Jews directly accuse Jesus of "having" a devil and according to John 18:35 the Jews are responsible for delivering Jesus to Pilate to be executed. Lastly, John 19:1–23 indicates that, along with the Roman soldiers, some Jews were responsible for the crucifixion of Jesus.

One can easily see from these verses and others in the Book of John that the author looked upon Jews as the main enemy of Jesus and the primary force behind his demise. Most important of all, in John 8:44 Jesus himself attacks the Jews by saying, "Ye are of your father the devil, and the lusts of your father ye will do." Imagine saying that the Jews are "of your father the Devil"! If that is not made to order for the production of anti-Semitism and Nazi thought, nothing is!

Other verses also contribute to the anti-Semitic onslaught. Not to be outdone, Paul adds to the hammering by saying in 1 Thess. 2:15 that the Jews killed both the Lord Jesus and their own prophets. According to Acts 9:23 and 13:50 the Jews are accused of persecuting Paul and his followers: "After many days were fulfilled, the Jews took counsel to kill him [Paul]" and "The Jews stirred up the devout and honorable women, and the chief men of the city, and raised persecution against Paul and Barnabas, and expelled them." Even Peter enters the anti-Semitic foray by accusing the Jews of crucifying Jesus (Acts 4:10 and 5:30).

A fact of immense importance in regard to this whole matter, which apologists seek to keep under wraps as much as possible, is that all statements alleging the Jews killed Jesus are directly contradictory to what Jesus, himself, predicted would occur. In Matt. 20:19 and Mark 10:33–34 Jesus said of himself, "They shall condemn him to death, and shall deliver him to the Gentiles: And they shall mock him, and shall scourge him, and shall spit upon him, and shall kill him." Jesus clearly predicted he would be killed by the Gentiles, not the Jews, even though several verses blame the Jews. Although biblical support for their position is readily available, many of those who say that the Jews killed Jesus are apparently unaware of the fact that they are also saying Jesus was a false prophet.

In summary, one can say without fear of exaggeration that the Book of John and the Book of Acts are anti-Semitic in tone and the Jews are implicated in just about every wrong deed described therein.

Cannibalism

People occasionally ask if the Bible supports cannibalism in any form and the answer, succinctly stated, is yes. The following enumeration covers virtually every relevant biblical comment in this regard and shows that the key verses fall into two broad categories: those in which God or Jesus commands or condones cannibalistic activity, and those in which activities of this nature are merely related.

One can justifiably accuse the Bible of advocating cannibalism in light of the former, but not the latter. Merely relating instances of cannibalism, rape, incest, or other atrocious behavior doesn't mean such activities are being fostered, proposed, or condoned by the Bible.

Among the former are such verses as: Lev. 26:29 ("Ye shall eat the flesh of your sons, and the flesh of your daughters shall ye eat"); Jer. 19:9 ("I will cause them to eat the flesh of their sons and the flesh of their daughters, and they shall eat every one the flesh of his friend"); Isa. 49:26 ("I will make your oppressors eat their own flesh, and they shall be drunk with their own blood as with wine"); and Ezek. 5:10 ("Fathers shall eat their sons in the midst of thee, and sons shall eat their fathers").

In addition, there are a number of statements by Jesus that some Christians have chosen to spiritualize for expediency's sake, while others provide a literal interpretation. In John 6:53–54 Jesus says, "Verily, verily, I say unto ye, Except you eat the flesh of the Son of man, and drink his blood, ye shall have no life in you. Whosoever eateth my flesh, and drinketh my blood, hath eternal life; and I will raise him up at the last day." Matt. 26:26–28, Luke 22:19–20, Mark 14:22–24, and 1 Cor. 11:24–26 say, "As they were eating, Jesus took bread, and blessed it, and brake it, and gave it to the disciples, and said, Take, eat: this is my body. And he took the cup, and gave thanks, and gave it to them, saying, Drink ye all of it; For this is my blood." And in John 6:56–57 Jesus says, "He that eateth my flesh, and drinketh my blood, dwelleth in me and I in him. . . . So he that eateth me, even he shall live by me." So, clearly cannibalism is an inseparable part of the Eucharist and is promoted by Jesus.

On the other side of the coin are verses that merely relate or predict cannibalistic activity: 2 Kings 6:28–29, "So we boiled my son, and did eat him. And I said unto her on the next day, Give thy son, that we may eat him and she hath hid her son"; Lam. 4:10 (RSV), "The hands of compassionate women have boiled their own children; they became their food"); Zech. 11:9 (RSV), "What is to die, let it die; what is to be destroyed, let it be destroyed; and let those that are left devour the flesh of one another"); Isa. 9:20 (RSV), "They snatch of the right, but are still hungry, and they devour on the left, but are not satisfied; each devours his neighbor's flesh"); and Deut. 28:53–57 (RSV), "You shall eat the offspring of your own body, the flesh of your sons and daughters. . . . The man who is the most tender and delicately bred among you will grudge food to his brother, to the wife of his bosom . . . so that he will not give to any of them any of the flesh of his children whom he is eating. . . . The most tender and delicately bred woman among you . . . will grudge to the husband of her bosom . . . her children whom she bears, because she will eat them secretly."

One can easily see from all of the above that the Bible not only relates instances of cannibalism, but openly advocates and commands cannibalistic activity in several instances. How utterly disgusting! And this comes from the supposedly Good Book.

Children

Punishment of children is one thing; child abuse is another. Unfortunately, many biblical verses can be easily used to justify the former by means of the latter. Prov. 23:13–14 says, "Withhold not correction from the child: for if thou beat him with the rod, he shall not die. Thou shalt beat him with the rod, and shalt deliver his soul from hell." Prov. 22:15 (RSV) says, "Folly is bound up in the heart of a child, but the rod of discipline drives it far from him." Prov. 20:30 (RSV) says, "Blows that wound cleanse away evil; strokes make clean the innermost parts." Prov. 13:24 (RSV) says, "He who spares the rod hates his son, but he who loves him is diligent to discipline him." Prov. 19:18 says, "Chasten thy son while there is hope, and let not thy soul spare for his crying." Prov. 29:15 (RSV) says, "The rod and reproof give wisdom, but a child left to himself brings shame to his mother." Prov. 26:3 says, "A whip for the horse, a bridle for the ass, and a rod for the fool's back" children are often foolish, of course. And Deut. 21:18–21 (RSV) says,

> If a man has a stubborn and rebellious son, who will not obey the voice of his father or the voice of his mother, and, though they chastise him, will not give heed to them, then his father and his mother shall take hold of him and bring him out to the elders of his city . . . and they shall say to the elders of his city, "This our son is stubborn and rebellious, he will not obey our voice; he is a glutton and a drunkard. Then all the men of the city shall stone him to death with stones; so you shall purge the evil from your midst.

Clearly these verses could be cited by any unreasonable parent to justify reprehensible corporal punishment. Although worthy of severe condemnation, stubbornness, rebellion, gluttony, and drunkenness are not capital offenses in any system of real justice.

Then there are verses that demean and degrade children by looking upon them as little more than objects to be punished for the misdeeds of others. Exod. 20:5 says, "I the Lord thy God am a jealous God, visiting the iniquity of the fathers upon the children unto the third and fourth generation of them that hate me." Lev. 26:22 says, "I will also send wild beasts among you, which shall rob you of your children." Hos. 13:16 says, "Samaria shall become desolate: for she hath rebelled against her God: they shall fall by the sword; their infants shall be dashed in pieces, and their women with child shall be ripped up." Isa. 13:16–18 (RSV) says, "Their infants will be dashed in pieces before their eyes; their houses will be plundered and their wives ravished. . . . Their bows will slaughter the young men; they will have no mercy on the fruit of the womb; their eyes will not pity children."

Is it any wonder the Bible has functioned as a major obstacle to the welfare and advancement of children? What it purports to teach "to" children bears little resemblance to its preferred treatment "of" children.

Communism

Although most biblicists are strongly opposed to communism, their prized book has some decidedly communistic teachings. The Book of Acts is most relevant in this regard. Acts 2:44–45 says, "All that believed were together, and had all things common; And sold their possessions and goods, and parted them to all men, as every man had need." And Acts 4:34–37 says, "Neither was there any among them that lacked: for as many as were possessors of lands or houses sold them, and brought the prices of the things that were sold, And laid them down at the apostles' feet: and distribution was made unto every man according as he had need."

In 2 Thess. 3:10–12 Paul made a statement with which Lenin would concur. He said, "For even when we were with you, this we commanded you, that if any would not work, neither should he eat. For we hear that there are some which walk among you disorderly, working not at all, but are busybodies. . . . Them that are such we command and exhort by our Lord Jesus Christ, that with quietness they work, and eat their own bread." Paul made a similar comment in Eph. 4:28 (RSV): "Let the thief no longer steal, but rather let him labor, doing honest work with his hands, so that he may be able to give to those in need."

Having all things in common, distributing according to need, withholding food because of idleness, and requiring honest labor from all concerned are central to the message of the *Communist Manifesto,* even when not explicitly stated.

Death Penalty

Within Christianity has arisen a movement known as Reconstructionism, which seeks to solve the ills of society by returning to a strict interpretation of the old Law. As incredible as it may sound, its adherents seek to return to an era in which "an eye for an eye, and a tooth for a tooth" literally reigned supreme. Their philosophy borders is reminiscent of the Middle Ages and the Ayatollah's Iran. You don't have to look at all of the old Law to visualize the injustice that would reign supreme if it were to be instituted. A mere perusal of the old Law's restrictions and penalties pertaining to capital crimes is enough to convince the most obstinate observer that this is not the way to proceed. Before anyone makes the mistake of jumping on this bandwagon to mayhem, he would do well to note just the violations for which one must be executed in the Old Testament. It is crucial to note that these maxims are no more sensible now than when first passed thousands of years ago. A few are reasonable, but most range from dubious to preposterous.

There are at least thirty-four reasons for which you can be executed in the Old Testament. Num. 15:32-35 says, "While the children of Israel were in the wilderness, they found a man that gathered sticks upon the sabbath day. . . . And the Lord said to Moses, The man shall be surely put to death, all the congregation shall stone him with stones outside the camp." For merely failing to keep the Sabbath this was a severe penalty, indeed. Exod. 31:14-15 requires the death penalty for doing any work upon the sabbath. Exod. 19:12 in the RSV says, "Take heed that you do not go up into the mountain or touch the border of it; whoever touches the mountain shall be put to death." Imagine executing somebody because he had the temerity to touch a mountain! According to Num. 3:38, any stranger who comes near the congregation's tabernacle is to be put to death. He doesn't have to do anything to it. Merely approaching it is sufficient. Another lesson in keeping your distance is found in Num. 3:10 (RSV), which says, "You shall appoint Aaron and his sons, and they shall attend to their priesthood; but if any one else comes near, he shall be put to death."

According to the old Law, in certain instances you don't have to do anything other than say the wrong words. Physical acts are not required. Exod. 21:17 and Lev. 20:9 (RSV) say, "Whoever curses his father or his mother shall be put to death." Even general cursing can get you killed. Lev. 24:14 (RSV) says, "Bring out of the camp him who cursed; and let all who heard him lay their hands upon his head, and let all the congregation stone him." If everyone on earth who curses were to be killed, that would all but decimate the world's population.

According to Exod. 21:15, "He that smiteth his father, or his mother, shall be surely put to death." Although striking one's parents is more grievous than cursing them, it is by no means deserving of death. Deut. 21:18-21 even goes so far as to require all the men of the city to stone a son to death who is viewed as stubborn and rebellious by his parents. If this rule were ever enacted, carnage would reign supreme throughout the youth of this nation. Additional injustice is clearly evident in the fact that sons need only be viewed as stubborn and rebellious. That doesn't necessarily mean they are.

One of the most negative aspects of biblical commandments pertains to the large number of sex acts for which the old Law has no tolerance whatever— for which capital punishment is deemed appropriate. Apparently some of the Old Testament authors had psychological hangups with this topic because they allowed very little deviation from the accepted path. Exod. 22:19 (RSV) says, "Whoever lies with a beast shall be put to death." Deut. 22:20-21 requires capital punishment for any female who is found not to be a virgin on her wedding day. Several verses prohibit sexual conduct that is condemned in modern society, but no sane community would have a death penalty attached. For example, Lev. 20:10 (RSV) says, "If a man commits adultery with the wife of his neighbor, both the adulterer and the adulteress shall be put to death." Lev. 20:11 (RSV) mandates, "The man who lies with his father's wife has uncovered his father's nakedness; both of them shall be put to death, their blood is upon them." It's worthy of note that one would be hard pressed to see how his father's nakedness was uncovered, rather than that of his father's wife, since the son did not lie with his father. Lev. 20:12 (RSV) prescribes, "If a man lies with his daughter-in-law, both of them shall be put to death; they have committed incest, their blood is upon them." A reasonable man would conclude that their blood is upon the executioner rather than themselves, because the punishment is too stringent for the crime. In addition, sex with an in-law is usually not incestuous.

Lev. 20:14 prohibits any sexual contact between a man and his mother-in-law and death by fire is to be administered to all violators. For many married men, the act itself would be a fate comparable to death. Lev. 20:13 condemns homosexuality and specifically states that any male who lies with another male as with a woman has committed an abomination and should be killed. Lev. 21:9 not only designates who should be killed for a specific sex act but prescribes the manner of implementation. It states that any daughter of any priest who becomes a whore is to be burned with fire.

According to Exod. 21:29, you are to be executed if your ox gores someone to death and has been accustomed to goring in the past. If Lev. 20:27 were enacted we would be required to execute any man or woman who is a medium or wizard. That would include a large number of people who are presently engaged in horoscopes, séances, fortunetelling, and New Age activities. In fact, we would have to kill those women who now claim to be witches if we were to take Exod. 22:18 seriously.

A particularly ridiculous statute is located in Deut. 22:23–24 (RSV), which says, "If there is a betrothed virgin, and a man meets her in the city and lies with her, then you shall bring them both out to the gate of that city, and you shall stone them to death with stones, the young woman because she did not cry for help though she was in the city." This ruling is not only absurd but completely oblivious to extenuating circumstances, a common affliction of many biblical maxims. Maybe the man had a knife at the woman's throat; maybe she was so terrified she couldn't speak; maybe she was gagged; maybe she was deaf and dumb; maybe she was drugged or intoxicated; maybe she was too young to know the wickedness of the deed or that the perpetrator was not to be trusted; maybe she was ordered to obey by some superior; maybe her IQ was much too low to understand what was occurring; maybe she had been taught to accept such behavior; maybe she had been sexually abused on a regular basis as a child and had grown to accept such behavior; maybe she had laryngitis. As with any crime, there could be any number of extenuating circumstances that the mechanical application of rigid rules by inflexible judges could never adequately incorporate.

One of the greatest failings of Old and New Testament law is that no account is made of all the factors surrounding any reprehensible act. You did it and that's all that counts; that's all we want to know. Where you came from, your background, your upbringing, your environment, your parentage, the number and severity of your prior transgressions, your comprehension, your physical composition, and many other mitigating considerations are not to be factored in. A fundamental principle of Scripture in nearly every instance is that your act is either good or bad. There is no in between, no shades of gray, no extenuating circumstances, and for that reason justice is to be dispensed in a perfunctory manner. That is one of the major shortcomings of the Old Law in general.

Finally, among the most ridiculous pronouncements in the Old Testament, especially the Book of Leviticus, are a liberal assortment of *religious* prohibitions with a death penalty attached. According to Exod. 22:20 and Deut. 17:2-5, you are to be killed if you sacrifice to any god, except the Lord only, and you are to be killed if you worship any other god. Lev. 24:16 clearly states that anyone who blasphemes the name of the Lord shall be put to death. Deut. 17:12 requires the same penalty for showing contempt for the Lord's priests or judges. Deut. 13:2 and 5-10 decree death for telling people to go after other gods, and Deut. 18:20 says all false prophets are to be killed.

In summary, one can easily see that the Old Testament requires death for a wide variety of acts that by no means merit capital punishment. In fact, one should not be punished at all for committing some of these acts. Of the more than thirty-four deeds that merit capital punishment according to the Old Testament, only three could be considered worthy of extreme punishment. Exod. 21:16 requires execution for kidnapping, Exod. 21:12-14 has the same penalty for premeditated murder, and Num. 35:30-31 mandates capital punishment for any murder witnessed by more than one person.

Other reasons for which capital punishment is to be applied according to the Old Testament could be mentioned, but the message is clear. If society were to adopt the code of conduct demanded by the Old Testament, executions would become commonplace, and injustice would reign supreme.

Divorce

Some of the restrictions Jesus attached to divorce are more stringent than those of the old Law and, fortunately, are all but ignored by modern society. The tough laws of the Old Testament occasionally seem rather mild when placed beside measures demanded by Jesus. Deut. 24:1-2 says, "When a man hath taken a wife, and married her, and it come to pass that she find no favor in his eyes, because he hath found some uncleanness in her; then let him write her a bill of divorcement . . . and when she is departed out of his house, she may go and be another man's wife." This is a reasonably intelligent maxim, although it would be even more rational were it not so one-sided. The rule says that if a man finds some uncleanness in his wife, he may divorce her and she is free to go and marry another man. It would be considerably more balanced if a woman who found some uncleanness in her husband were allowed to do likewise. But, alas, equality of the sexes is a concept at odds with the biblical scheme of things.

Despite major shortcomings the old Law does make some allowances in this regard, while Jesus lays down some rules that almost no one in today's society takes seriously, not even organizations that technically prohibit divorce, such as the Catholic Church. In Luke 16:18 Jesus says, "Whosoever putteth away his wife, and marrieth another, committeth adultery: and whosoever marrieth her that is put away from her husband committeth adultery." That is, if you divorce your wife and marry another you have committed adultery, and if you marry someone who has been divorced, you have committed adultery.

Left unclear is the status of someone who divorces but never remarries. They have not committed adultery, but have they violated a prohibition against divorce? The same problem is left unanswered by Jesus in Mark 10:11–12, where he says, "Whosoever shall put away his wife and marry another, committeth adultery against her. And if a woman shall put away her husband, and be married to another, she committeth adultery." Again we see a clear condemnation of remarriage after divorce, but no clear condemnation of divorce itself. The question appears to be answered by Matt. 5:32, where Jesus says, "whosoever shall put away his wife, saving for the cause of fornication, causeth her to commit adultery." But, alas, this is no answer either, because the man who divorces his wife for any reason other than her fornication causes her to commit adultery, while no stigma is directly attached to him. And if we turn to Matt. 19:9 ("Whosoever shall put away his wife, except it be for fornication, and shall marry another, committeth adultery") for an answer, we remain in the dark because it allows a man to both divorce and remarry if his wife is guilty of fornication. So, in essence, those who divorce and remarry are repeatedly condemned, except in the case of the woman's fornication, while no clear-cut condemnation of divorce exists as long as no remarriage is involved.

That would appear to settle the issue. But wait a minute. What about Matt. 19:6 and Mark 10:9 (RSV), which say, "So they are no longer two but one flesh. What therefore God has joined together, let no man put asunder." What at first appeared to be some rather lenient requirements with respect to divorce alone are now seen to be even tighter than those to be found in the Old Testament. Whereas the earlier verses seem to have allowed divorce as long as the participants did not remarry, Matt. 19:6 and Mark 10:9 obviate any possibility of divorce whatever.

In effect, Jesus has three positions in the world of marital difficulties. According to his position in Luke 16:18 and Mark 10:11–12, you are *not* condemned for obtaining a divorce but only for remarrying. The second position which is exemplified by Matt. 19:9, allows you to divorce *and* remarry without committing adultery, so long as the divorce is a result of your wife's fornication. The third and most restrictive position, found in Matt. 19:6 and Mark 10:9, prohibits divorce for any reason and appears to settle the issue once and for all. There are to be *no* exceptions or mitigating circumstances. Regardless of what the real position of Jesus may be, the question is moot because the absolute prohibitions of Matt. 19:6 and Mark 10:9 are compelling.

One can only guess at the number of Christians who have ignored these teachings, and is it any wonder in view of their leader's inconsistency? Paul opted for the absolute prohibition by saying in 1 Cor. 7:10, "Unto the married I command, yet not I, but the Lord, Let not the wife depart from her husband." A command from the Lord would appear to be rather final. And Paul was even more emphatic when he said in Rom. 7:2-3, "For the woman which hath a husband is bound by the law to her husband so long as he liveth . . . So then if, while her husband liveth, she be married to another man, she shall be called an adulteress." The first part melds Paul with the third position of Jesus, while the second part would appear to place him in the tradition of Jesus' first position.

So, if you are looking for consistency with respect to the biblical stance on divorce, expect to search in vain and be disappointed. The only definitive answer that seems viable is that two verses, Matt. 19:6 and Mark 10:9, prohibit any form of divorce whatever and, thus, overrule all other formulas. Regardless of what all others may allege, these two passages say divorce is prohibited, period, and that should settle the matter conclusively.

Gambling

Our ninth and final topic in this chapter, gambling, is also of immense importance to society's evolution and deserves critical analysis. As is true of alcohol, it is hard to see how biblicists can oppose gambling when so many biblical verses show it was commanded by God or performed by his spokesmen and chosen people with apparent impunity. Divine condonation is evident in Joshua 14:2 ("By lot was their inheritance, as the Lord commanded by the hand of Moses."), Joshua 21:8 ("The Israelites granted to the Levites these cities and their pastures by lot, as the Lord had commanded through Moses"), and Num. 26:52 and 55–56 ("The Lord spake to Moses saying . . . the Land shall be divided by lot: according to the names of the tribes of their fathers they shall inherit. According to the lot shall possession thereof be divided between many and few"). In each instance, God ordered crucial disputes to be settled by the drawing of lots.

Although not directly ordered by God, gambling, or the casting of lots, was also performed by God's chosen in Josh. 18:10, "Joshua cast lots for them in Shiloh before the Lord"; Josh. 18:6, "That I may cast lots for you here before the Lord our God"; Josh. 18:8, "That I may here cast lots for you before the Lord in Shiloh"; Josh. 19:51, "Divided for an inheritance by lot in Shiloh before the Lord"; 1 Sam. 14:42 (RSV), "Then Saul said, 'Cast the lot between me and my son Jonathan.' And Jonathan was taken"; Acts 1:26 (RSV), "They cast lots for them, and the lot fell on Matthias and he was enrolled with the eleven apostles"; 1 Chron. 24:5 (LB), "All tasks were assigned to the various groups by coin toss so that there would be no preference"; 1 Chron. 24:30–31 (LB), "These were the descendants of Levi . . . they were assigned to their duties by coin-toss without distinction as to age or rank. It was done in the presence of King David . . . and the leaders of the priests and Levites"; 1 Chron. 25:8 (RSV),, "They cast lots for their duties, small and great, teacher and pupil alike"; 1 Chron. 26:13–14; Neh. 10:34; Judges 20:9; and 1 Sam. 10:20–21. Even Proverbs 18:18 (LB) ("A coin toss ends arguments and settles disputes between powerful opponents") implicitly advocates gambling as a way to settle conflicts.

Despite all evidence to the contrary, apologists try to depict the Bible as an opponent of gambling. The following rationalization is rather typical of that which emerges from the pen of most biblicists. When asked if he felt Christians should participate in gambling games and what he thought about bingo being played in a church, fundamentalist M. R. DeHaan said on page 243 in *508 Answers to Bible Questions,*

> Not only is gambling absolutely contrary to the Word of God, because it puts faith in chance and fate rather than in the providence of God, but even our civil authorities who do not go by the Bible, outlaw gambling and think it is evil. Every state in the Union has certain laws against gambling, and, even though they are not always enforced, it is the general consensus even among authorities that gambling is an evil. It is seeking to profit by the loss of someone else which is equivalent to stealing. I do not know how anyone can find any argument, either in reason, logic, decency or in the Bible in regard to this practice.

How many mistakes can one man make in such a short paragraph! *First,* as we have already shown, gambling was not only widely practiced in the Bible but often carried out in compliance with God's instructions.

Second, one can't help but notice that DeHaan failed to provide one citation for his allegation that the Bible is unalterably opposed to gambling.

Third, as far as civil authorities outlawing gambling is concerned, the explosion of state lotteries has pretty much put the quietus to that supporting argument.

Fourth, and most important of all, DeHaan's allegation that gambling is equivalent to stealing is a blockbuster. That would mean all stock and bond markets, commodity exchanges, and insurance policies would be nothing more than another name for stealing, because each one involves making a profit through the loss of others. Indeed, DeHaan's comments are a veritable indictment of world capitalism. One may not be able to find an argument based on reason, logic, or decency for the legitimacy of gambling, but he should have no problem finding biblical support.

Conclusion

That completes our analysis of the biblical approach to nine major social issues and clearly shows that the Bible's position with respect to abortion, alcohol, anti-Semitism, cannibalism, children, communism, the death penalty, divorce, and gambling is either ambiguous or reprehensible. Additional social issues will be discussed with similar documentation in the next chapter.

14

Social Issues II

Homosexuality, Human Sacrifice, Intellectualism, Intolerance, Lending, Nationalism, Polygamy, Poverty, Profanity, Self-Degradation

This chapter will continue the previous chapter's alphabetical discussion of major social issues that are addressed in one way or another by Scripture. Many important contradictions and inconsistencies accompany the biblical treatment of many social problems and that which follows will provide additional confirmation of that fact.

Homosexuality

One of the most controversial biblical teachings pertains to whether or not the Bible condemns or condones homosexuality. Homosexuals and sympathetic ministers have repeatedly tried to employ biblical precepts in their ongoing dispute with biblicists of a more traditional orientation to prove that the Bible supports, or at least does not condemn, homosexuality. But one need only read the Book to see that their efforts are in vain. There is no sense in arguing with the obvious.

Numerous Bible verses condemn homosexual activities. Lev. 18:22 says, "Thou shalt not lie with mankind, as with womankind: it is an abomination." Lev. 20:13 says, "If a man also lie with mankind, as he lieth with a woman, both of them have committed an abomination: they shall surely be put to death." Judg. 21:11

271

says, "Ye shall utterly destroy every male, and every woman that has lain by man." The text of 1 Kings 14:24 says, "There were also sodomites in the land: and they did according to all the abominations of the nations which the Lord cast out before the children of Israel," and 1 Kings 15:12 says, "He took away the sodomites out of the land." Deut. 23:17 declares, "There shall be no whore of the daughters of Israel, nor a sodomite of the sons of Israel." Clearly homosexuality, usually referred to as sodomy, is condemned in the Old Testament.

Of course, homosexuals can always contend these prohibitions are from the old Law and, since we are no longer governed by the old Law, they are no longer applicable. However, that can be dismissed by citing some equally convincing *New Testament* verses: Rom. 1:26–27 says, "For this cause God gave them up unto vile affections: for even their women did change the natural use into that which is against nature: And likewise also the men, leaving the natural use of the woman ["natural use" is clearly a degrading phrase, since women are not to be used], burned in their lust toward one another; men with men working that which is unseemly." The text of 1 Cor. 6:9–10 (ML) declares, "Be not misled; neither profligates, nor idolaters, nor adulterers, nor partakers of homosexuality . . . will inherit the kingdom of God." The text of 1 Tim. 1:9–10 (NASB) says, "The law is not made for a righteous man, but for those who are lawless and rebellious, for the ungodly and sinners . . . and immoral men and homosexuals."). The New Testament is by no means out of step with the Old Testament.

The gay community could possibly cite instances in which major biblical figures engaged in activities that could be interpreted as homosexual in nature. For instance, in 2 Sam. 1:26, David says, "I am distressed for thee, my brother Jonathan: very pleasant hast thou been unto me: thy love to me was wonderful, passing the love of women." Paul told his followers to greet one another with a holy kiss in Rom. 16:16, 2 Cor. 13:12, 1 Thess. 5:26, and 1 Pet. 5:14. But these verses are ambiguous regarding physical love and cannot really be used to substantiate strong biblical support for homosexuality. There is virtually no possibility they could withstand the strain of rigorous cross-examination.

Is there, then, any approach homosexuals could take to counter the claims of strict constructionists? Yes, there is. They could always say the Bible is just plain wrong and that settles the matter. After all, the Bible not only allows, but promotes, slavery and the subordination of women, which are utterly reprehensible. The biblical stance on homosexuality could be cited as just another instance of an inaccurate and misguided doctrine.

Human Sacrifice

Human sacrifice is one of the most repulsive, indeed barbarous, acts in which human beings can engage. It is not only a wanton case of murder, nearly always masquerading under the guise of religion and service to god, but a dehumanizing practice that can only result in the degeneration of all participants. Unfortunately, the Bible not only describes instances of human sacrifice, but relates instances in which God Almighty both condones and promotes this horrible activity. In Exod. 22:29–30 God is quoted as saying, "Thou shalt not delay to offer the first of thy ripe fruits, and of thy liquors: the firstborn of thy sons shalt thou give unto me. Likewise shalt thou do with thine oxen, and with thy sheep." We all know what happened to oxen and sheep on a regular basis in the Old Testament. God is shown to be just as vicious in Ezek. 20:26 (RSV), which says, "I defiled them through their very gifts in making them offer by fire all their first-born, that I might horrify them; I did it that they might know that I am the Lord." For a god of love, he certainly has a bizarre means of expressing it.

In fact, when you get down to basics, many Christians are apparently unable to realize that their own theology of salvation rests upon a human sacrifice. On page 295 in volume 9 of *The Life and Works of Thomas Paine* Paine poignantly notes,

> Christian authors exclaim against the practice of offering up human sacrifices, which, they say, is done in some countries; and those authors make those exclamations without ever reflecting on the fact that their own doctrine of salvation is founded on a human sacrifice. They are saved, they say, by the blood of Christ. The Christian religion begins with a dream and ends with a murder.

So, in essence, human sacrifice is clearly an inseparable part of the biblical message.

Intellectualism

ANTI-INTELLECTUALISM

One of the most insidious of all biblical teachings is that the intellect is not to be relied upon as the final arbiter of one's decisions. Faith in Jesus, theological insights, and spiritual gifts are to replace knowledge, disputation, and philosophy as the ultimate source of truth and knowledge. In effect, faith is to replace proof, hope is to replace work, and trust is to replace evidence. People are to put their trust in forces and beings beyond their control, rather than in their own talents and abilities.

This debilitating approach to life's challenges can only lead to self-effacement and low self-esteem. The pronounced tendency of the Bible to denounce intellect, thought, and what the New Testament refers to as human wisdom (as if another kind existed) is exemplified in such verses as: Heb. 11:1 (RSV), "Now faith is the assurance of things hoped for, the conviction [evidence—KJV] of things not seen"; Eccles. 6:8, "What hath the wise more than the fool"; 1 Cor. 1:22–23 (RSV), "Jews demand signs and Greeks seek wisdom, but we preach Christ crucified, a stumbling block to Jews and folly to Gentiles"; 1 Cor. 4:10 (RSV), "We are fools for Christ's sake, but you are wise in Christ"; 1 Cor. 2:1–2 (RSV), "I [Paul] did not come proclaiming to you the testimony of God in lofty words or wisdom. For I decided to know nothing among you except Jesus Christ and him crucified"; 1 Cor. 3:18–19 (RSV), "Let no one deceive himself. If any one among you thinks that he is wise in this age, let him become a fool that he may become wise. For the wisdom of this world is folly with God."

Imagine adhering to a philosophy in which one of its prime propagandists openly advocates becoming a fool. But to continue our listing: 1 Cor. 1:19–21 (RSV), "It is written, I will destroy the wisdom of the wise, and the cleverness of the clever I will thwart. Where is the wise man? Where is the scribe? Where is the debater of this age? Has not God made foolish the wisdom of the world? For since, in the wisdom of God, the world did not know God through wisdom"; 1 Cor. 2:13–14 (RSV), "We impart this in words not taught by human wisdom but taught by the Spirit, interpreting spiritual truths to those who possess the Spirit. The unspiritual man does not receive the gifts of the Spirit of God, for they are folly to him, and he is not able to understand them because they are spiritually discerned"; 1 Cor. 2:4 (RSV), "And my speech and my message were not in plausible words of wisdom"; and finally, Eccles. 1:18, "In much wisdom is much grief: and he that increaseth knowledge increaseth sorrow."

The debilitating aspect of Christianity is all too evident in most of these verses. Those adopting the anti-intellectual stance propounded would be open to all the vicissitudes life has to offer. Like lambs to the slaughter, they would be easy pickings for those of a more rational but unscrupulous outlook. Anyone with a modicum of intelligence knows that greater knowledge is far more likely to decrease than increase sorrow.

Our listing should also include: 1 Cor. 1:17, "For Christ sent me not to baptize, but to preach the gospel: not with wisdom of words"; 1 Cor. 4:4, "For I know nothing by myself"; 1 Cor. 1:25–27 (RSV), "For the foolishness of God is wiser than men. . . . not many of you were wise according to worldly standards . . . but God chose what is foolishness in the world to shame the wise"; 1 Cor. 8:1–2 (RSV), "Knowledge puffs up, but love builds up. If any one imagines that he knows something, he does not yet know as he ought to know"); 1 Cor. 2:6–7 (RSV), "Yet among the mature we do impart wisdom, although it is not a wisdom of this age or of the rulers of this age, who are doomed to pass away. But we impart a secret and hidden wisdom of God"; and Col. 2:8 (RSV), "See to it that no one makes a prey of you by philosophy and empty deceit, according to human tradition, according to the elemental spirits of the universe, and not according to Christ."

The message Paul repeatedly propounds is that one should ignore what evidence, experimentation, and reality teach; listen to what the Bible in general and Jesus in particular say. In other words, believe biblical pronouncements and Jesus rather than your lying eyes and ears. This is nothing less than a prescription for disaster. Anyone who ignores wisdom, the wisdom of this world, the wisdom of the wise, philosophy, and knowledge, as Paul calls them, does so at his own peril. Is it any wonder people have been maimed and died because they shunned adequate medical attention, engaged in prayer overdose, relied on miracles, played with serpents, drank deadly potions, plucked out their eyes, and otherwise followed biblical mandates?

Central to any sensible society is the belief that truth is to be discovered through the interchange of ideas in an open forum. Yet Christians are repeatedly admonished to elude those of another persuasion and avoid the exchange of ideas through dialogue. They are told to flee nonbiblical ideas because they are not only wrong and lead believers astray but are possessed by those with less than honorable motives.

Christian beliefs are not to be questioned or doubted and dogmatic sentiments are clearly evident in such verses as Rom. 16:17-18 (RSV), which says, "I appeal to you, brethren, to take note of those who created dissensions and difficulties, in opposition to the doctrine which you have been taught; avoid them. For such persons do not serve our Lord Christ, but their own appetites, and by fair and flattering words they deceive the hearts of the simple-minded." By "simple minded" one can only assume Paul is referring to his own followers, and who is in a better position to know?

Similar verses are: 2 Tim. 2:16-17 (RSV), "Avoid such godless chatter, for it will lead people into more and more ungodliness, and their talk will eat its way like gangrene"; 1 Tim. 6:20, "O Timothy, keep that which is committed to thy trust, avoiding profane and vain babblings, and the oppositions of science falsely so called"; 2 Tim. 2:14 (RSV), "Remind them of this, and charge them before the Lord to avoid disputing about words, which does no good, but only ruins the hearers"; Titus 3:9-10 (RSV), "But avoid stupid controversies, genealogies, dissensions, and quarrels over the law, for they are unprofitable and futile. As for a man who is factious, after admonishing him once or twice, have nothing more to do with him"; Rom. 14:1 (RSV), "As for the man who is weak in faith, welcome him, but not for disputes over opinions"; 1 Tim. 6:3-5 (RSV), "If any one teaches otherwise and does not agree with the sound words of our Lord Jesus Christ and the teaching which accords with godliness, he is puffed up with conceit, he knows nothing; he has a morbid craving for controversy and for disputes about words, which produce envy, dissension, slander, base suspicions, and wrangling among men"; Col. 2:4 (RSV), "I say this in order that no one may delude you with beguiling speech"; and finally 2 Tim. 2:23-25 (RSV), "Have nothing to do with stupid, senseless controversies, you know that they breed quarrels.

And the Lord's servant must not be quarrelsome but kindly to every one, an apt teacher, forbearing, correcting his opponents with gentleness."

How one corrects one's opponents with gentleness, after having been repeatedly told to avoid the opposition entirely, is rather hard to fathom. A comment by Robert Ingersoll on page 260 of volume 2 in his *Works* is particularly apropos: "In the Old Testament no one is told to reason with a heretic, and not one word is said about relying upon argument, upon education, or upon intellectual development—nothing except simple brute force."

Imagine giving your followers the impression that all those who lack faith in Christianity in general and Jesus in particular are unreasonable and wicked! Who would be open to dialogue with anyone so portrayed? But that is the import of: 2 Thess. 3:2, "That we may be delivered from unreasonable and wicked men: for all men have not faith"; 1 John 2:22, "Who is a liar but he that denieth that Jesus is the Christ? He is antichrist, that denieth the Father and the Son"; and 2 John 7, "Many deceivers are entered into the world, who confess not that Jesus Christ is come in the flesh. This is a deceiver and an antichrist." Additional relevant verses are Heb. 13:9 and 2 John 9–11. On page 141 in *Answers to Tough Questions* McDowell and Stewart allege, "Christianity is sensible; it is reasonable. . . . Today people picture Christian faith as a blind leap into the dark, when it actually is a step towards the light."

If Christianity is a step toward light, then it is the light of hell, as the previous verses have shown. Christianity is neither sensible nor reasonable and has little to do with the shedding of light on anything. It is by no means accidental that Christianity was nurtured, grew, and flourished during what has come to be known as the Dark Ages. The Bible corroborates Robert Ingersoll, who says on page 606 in volume 8 of his *Works,* "When religion becomes scientific, it ceases to be religion and becomes science. Religion is not intellectual—it is emotional. It does not appeal to reason. The founder of a religion has always said, 'Let him that has ears to hear, hear!' No founder has said: 'Let him that has brains to think, think!' " And on page 133 of volume 9 in *The Life and Works of Thomas Paine,* Paine says, "As you can make no appeal to reason in support of an unreasonable religion, you then . . . bring yourselves off by telling people they must not believe in reason but in *revelation.*" And Voltaire said, "The truths of religion are never so well understood as by those who have lost the power of reason."

Because of closed-minded verses, including those already cited, some believers avoid all contact or ideological interaction with freethought advocates. That is unfortunate, because closed and indoctrinated minds are among those most difficult to penetrate. Influencing someone who flatly rejects openness to critical ideas and mistakenly assumes everything in the freethought inventory is erroneous is quite difficult, to say the least. A person so inclined believes the Bible in spite of reason and proof, not because of them. People of this persuasion are as hard to affect as those who have fallen into a purely metaphysical ideology entirely divorced from reality, reason, and proof. The latter are all but impossible to reach and are often found in the back rooms of psychiatric hospitals. Sigmund Freud said, "Religion is comparable to a childhood neurosis." And Havelock Ellis was probably as poignant as anyone when he said, "The whole religious complexion of the modern world is due to the absence from Jerusalem of a lunatic asylum."

The opposite of reason is faith, a concept biblicists readily admit lies at the core of Christianity and about which many notable individuals have made some poignant comments. H. L. Mencken, for example, said of religion that it is "an illogical belief in the occurrence of the improbable." On page 244 in *Science and Christian Tradition* Thomas Huxley said, "The profound psychological truth, that men constantly feel certain about things for which they strongly hope, but have no evidence, in the legal or logical sense of the word; he calls this feeling 'faith.' " Ben Franklin said that, "The way to see by Faith is to shut the Eye to Reason."

In closing this subject, we could do no better than quote Ambrose Bierce, who probably encapsulated the concept as well as anyone when he defined faith as "belief without evidence in what is told by one who speaks without knowledge, of things without parallel."

PRO-INTELLECTUALISM

Although the Bible is essentially anti-intellectual, oddly enough a lesser but distinct element of pro-intellectualism is evident in a few biblical comments. The Bible occasionally reverses itself by urging believers to engage in dialogue and debate with the opposition. These verses are useful to rational people when biblicists refuse to interact intellectually because of the anti-intellectual philosophy propounded by "God's Word." All freethought advocates should have these verses readily available for those occasions in which biblicists in general and Christians in particular refuse to discuss the Bible's dilemmas.

Prime examples of pro-intellectual passages in the Bible are Isa. 1:18, "Come now, and let us reason together, saith the Lord"; 2 Cor. 10:5 (RSV), "We destroy arguments and every proud obstacle to the knowledge of God"; 2 Tim. 4:2 (RSV), "Preach the word, be urgent in season and out of season, convince, rebuke, and exhort, be unfailing in patience and teaching"; James 3:17 (RSV), "But the wisdom from above is first pure, then peaceable, gentle, open to reason"; Acts 17:17, "Therefore disputed he [Paul] in the synagogue with the Jews and with the devout persons and in the market daily with them that met with him"; Acts 19:9, "He [Paul] departed from them, and separated the disciples, disputing daily in the school"; and 2 Tim. 2:24–25 (RSV), "The Lord's servant must not be quarrelsome but . . . correcting his opponents with gentleness." It would be wise for those with a rational bent to have the following verses readily available in their immediate memory portfolio for those occasions in which biblicists seek to flee to

more comfortable terrain: Jude 3, "Ye should earnestly contend for the faith";
1 Peter 3:15 (RSV), "Always be prepared to make a defense to any one who
calls you to account for the hope that is in you"; and 1 Thess. 5:21, "Prove
all things; hold fast that which is good."

Other relevant verses that tend to foster dialogue and debate are: Acts 18:4,
"He [Paul] reasoned in the synagogue every sabbath, and persuaded the Jews
and the Greeks"; Acts 18:19, "He [Paul] . . . entered into the synagogue, and
reasoned with the Jews"; Acts 17:2 ("Paul, as was his manner, went in to them,
and three Sabbath days, reasoned with them out of the Scriptures"; 1 Tim. 6:12,
"Fight the good fight of faith"; Titus 1:9 (RSV), "He [a bishop] must hold firm
to the sure word as taught, so that he may be able to give instruction in sound
doctrine and also to confute those who contradict it"; Titus 1:13, "Rebuke them
sharply that they may be sound in the faith"; 2 Tim. 1:7 (RSV), "God did not
give us a spirit of timidity but a spirit of power and love and self-control"; Eccle.
7:25, Acts 15:39, 1 Cor. 4:13, Col. 4:6, 2 Tim. 4:5, Titus 2:15, and Acts 24:25.
One can't help but note the number of times believers are urged to use reason
by a book that is not only decidedly irrational and superstitious but a strong
proponent of closed-mindedness.

Finally, don't forget to mention Prov. 15:10, "He who hateth reproof will
die"); Prov. 12:1 (RSV), "Whoever loves discipline loves knowledge, But he who
hates reproof is stupid"; and Prov. 14:15, "The simple believeth every word: but
the prudent man looketh well to his going." Don't forget to cite them to those
who dislike being told they have been suckered, intellectually conned, and even
victimized by religious hucksters.

Intolerance

We can now move to a topic closely related to anti-intellectualism—intolerance.
One of the hallmarks of nearly all religions is the degree to which they cannot
bear the presence of other beliefs. And Christianity is no exception in this regard.
Although apologists try to put the best face forward on Christianity's inherent
narrow-mindedness, the facts speak for themselves. Rarely do Christians admit
to intolerance but occasionally a rare bird steps forward. Just such an apologist
is David DeWitt, who, when asked if Christians are too narrow-minded, said
on page 20 of *Answering the Tough Ones,*

> People are often quick to recognize that Christianity is intolerant of other beliefs.
> That's true. But the reason is that Christianity emphasizes objective truth. That
> is, it is based on real history—real people, places, and events. Christianity is
> basically news, not views. Truth is narrow by definition. Tolerance in personal
> opinions is a virtue, but tolerance when dealing with facts is ridiculous.

Well, there you have Christian intolerance in all its unabashed candor. You bet they're intolerant. When it comes to facts as Christians see them, there's no other way to go. If only more biblicists were as frank! The excesses to which this can lead were well noted by Samuel Taylor Coleridge, who said, "He who begins by loving Christianity better than Truth, will proceed by loving his sect or church better than Christianity, and end in loving himself better than all."

The intolerance practiced by unrestrained Christians is exemplified in a story told by Robert Ingersoll on page 379 in volume 2 of his *Works.* "There was an Old Spaniard on his deathbed who sent for a priest, and the priest told him that he would have to forgive his enemies before he died. He said, 'I have none.' 'What! no enemies?' cried the priest. 'Not one,' said the dying man; 'I killed the last one three months ago.' "

Lending

The next topic—lending at interest—is distinctly at odds with what the biblical God expects of moral human beings and, for obvious reasons, scriptural teachings in this regard are less publicized. After all, if you were a minister, priest, or rabbi heavily dependent upon the largess of wealthy parishioners, would you decry the very activity by which your contributors obtained the funds being donated to the church coffers? Hardly! Any clergyman who preached or emphasized that part of the Bible would be looking for other employment in short order. The fact that the Bible denounces this activity is irrelevant. Politics are going to prevail over biblical teachings. As is true in so much of life, when money comes in the door, truth goes out the window.

The following verses clearly show that creditors are condemned by the God of the Bible. Ezek. 18:5–17 (RSV) says,

> If a man is righteous and does what is lawful and right, if he . . . does not lend at interest or take any increase . . . is careful to observe my ordinances— he is righteous, he shall surely live, says the Lord God. . . . If he . . . lends at interest, and takes increase, shall he then live? He shall not live. He has done all these abominable things; he shall surely die; his blood shall be upon him- self. But if this man begets a son who . . . withholds his hand from iniquity, takes no interest or increase, he shall not die for his father's iniquity; he shall surely live.

In the same vein, Ps. 15:2–5 (RSV) says, "He who walks blamelessly . . . does not put out his money at interest, and does not take a bribe against the innocent. He who does these things shall never be moved." Interestingly enough, the latter comment puts lending at interest in the same category as bribery. Exod. 22:25

(RSV) says, "If you lend money to any of my people with you who is poor, you shall not be to him as a creditor, and you shall not exact interest from him." Denunciation of lending money at interest is also evident in Deut. 23:19–20 (RSV), which says, "You shall not lend upon interest to your brother, interest on money, interest on victuals, interest on anything that is lent for interest. To a foreigner you may lend upon interest, but to your brother you shall not lend upon interest." If extracting interest is acceptable, as many apologists allege, then why does the old Law restrict it to foreigners only?

Nationalism

One of the prime sources of war, aggression, exploitation and corruption in world history has been nationalism. Millions of people have given their lives to this negative force in world development. And, as one might suspect, the Bible has been one of its strongest and earliest proponents. Foreign nations and people of foreign extraction or ethnicity are often denigrated in Scripture. Three books that are particularly egregious in this regard are Nehemiah, Ezra, and Ezekiel.

Prime verses promoting dislike or distrust of foreigners are: Neh. 13:3 (RSV), "When the people heard the law, they separated from Israel all those of foreign descent"; Neh. 9:2 (NIV), "Those of Israelite descent had separated themselves from all foreigners"; Neh. 13:27 (NIV), "Must we hear now that you too are doing all this terrible wickedness and are being unfaithful to our God by marrying foreign women?"; and Neh. 13:30 (NIV), "So I purified the priests and the Levites of everything foreign."

Verses of this kind are hardly calculated to foster international love, respect, and camaraderie. Not to be outdone are: Isa. 1:7 (NIV), "Your country is desolate, your cities burned with fire; your fields are being stripped by foreigners right before you"; Ezek. 11:9 (NIV), "I will drive you out of the city and hand you over to foreigners and inflict punishment on you"; Ezek. 28:7–10 (NIV), "I am going to bring foreigners against you, the most ruthless of nations; they will draw their swords. . . . They will bring you down to the pit, and you will die a violent death in the heart of the seas. . . . You will die the death of the uncircumcised at the hands of foreigners"; Ezek. 30:12 (NIV), "By the hand of foreigners I will lay waste the land and everything in it"; and Ezek. 44:7–9 (NIV), "In addition to all your other detestable practices, you brought foreigners . . . into my sanctuary. . . . No foreigner . . . is to enter my sanctuary, not even the foreigners who live among the Israelites."

More citations are available but the point has been made. The Bible is a prime source for nationalistic rivalries, suspicions, distrust, competition, and fears. One would be hard pressed to find biblical verses that generate trust, cohesion, empathy, and brotherhood between nationalities. From the very beginning of the biblical narrative the Israelites were set apart as God's chosen people, while the attitude toward all others varies from avoidance to abhorrence. The Bible is not written in such a way that it helps bring nations, nationalities, and ethnic groups together. Quite the contrary, from the conflicts between the Israelites and other ethnic groups onward, the story never changed. The Amorites, the Jebusites, the Hivites, the Philistines, and many others were always cast in the role of the bad guys, while Israel was God's chosen nation. If that's not calculated to create an aura of national superiority, nothing is. One can readily understand why Christians, who claim to have inherited the Israelite legacy, consider themselves superior to all others.

Polygamy

Polygamy is widely condemned as repugnant, if not immoral. The admission of Utah into the Union was held in abeyance until the Mormons officially repudiated the practice. Utah became a state in 1896 only after the policy had been changed by clerical/political leaders. In defense of their position Mormons repeatedly invoked the Bible and, unfortunately for biblicists opposed to polygamy, the Bible not only fails to condemn the practice but lends considerable support to its legitimacy. Many Old Testament patriarchal heroes had multiple wives. Biblical backing for Mormon behavior is easy to find, although Mark Twain is reported to have denied its legitimacy to a Mormon. The Mormon claimed polygamy was perfectly moral and he defied Twain to cite any passage of Scripture which forbade it. "Well," said Twain, "how about that passage that tells us no man can serve two masters at the same time?" On a more serious note, key figures and verses in this regard are Judg. 8:30, which says, "Gideon had threescore and ten sons of his body begotten: for he had many wives"; 1 Kings 11:3, which says of Solomon, "He had seven hundred wives, princesses, and three hundred concubines"; Gen. 31:17, which says, "Jacob rose up, and set his sons and his wives upon camels"; Gen. 36:6, which says, "Esau took his wives, and his sons, and his daughters"; and 2 Chron. 11:21, which says, "Rehoboam loved Maachah the daughter of Abraham above all his wives and his concubines."

Undoubtedly the most prominent polygamist is the Old Testament patriarch, David. He is crucial to this discussion not only because a number of verses show he had numerous wives, including 2 Sam. 5:13 ("David took him more concubines and wives out of Jerusalem") and 1 Chron. 14:3 ("David took more wives at Jerusalem"), but also because a wide assortment of verses show he was the essence of moral rectitude. The text of 1 Sam. 25:28 says, "Because my lord [David] fighteth the battles of the Lord, and evil hath not been found in thee all thy days"; 2 Sam. 19:27 says, "But my lord the king [David] is an angel of God"; 1 Kings 15:3 says, "His [Abijam's] heart was not perfect with the Lord his God, as was the heart of David his father"; and Acts 13:22 says, "I [God] have found David the son of Jesse, a man after mine own heart which shall fulfil all my will." One could also relate 1 Kings 9:4, 11:4, 11:6 and 15:11 and Neh. 12:36. If David was an angel of God in whom evil had not been found *all the days of his life,* if his heart was perfect with the Lord and he was a man after God's own heart, it is virtually impossible to make a serious biblically based argument for the condemnation of polygamy.

David lived after the Old Law in general and the Ten Commandments in particular were enacted, so there is little reason to believe his marital behavior violated God's laws. After all, Scripture clearly states in 1 Kings 15:5 that David did that which was right in the eyes of the Lord, and turned not aside from anything that God commanded him *all the days of his life,* except in the matter of Uriah the Hittite. Deut. 21:15–16 not only fails to condemn polygamy but actually provides rules by which the sons of one's wives are to be treated.

Even if New Testament maxims in opposition to polygamy could be produced, they would be all but worthless, since they would only prove God had changed his mind in regard to what was moral. While moral in the Old Testament, polygamy would have become immoral in the New. In effect, morals would be changing over time and biblicists would be obligated to reconcile this with Mal. 3:6, "I am the Lord, I change not") and "situation ethics," which they deplore. The only verse that seems to forestall polygamy, Deut. 17:17 ("Neither shall he multiply wives to himself") appears to be applicable only to one individual in a particular situation.

In conclusion, if you are opposed to polygamy, don't expect much support from the Bible.

Poverty

Besides the periodic sexual revelations of prominent televangelists such as Jim Bakker and Jimmy Swaggart, one of the most revealing displays of Christian hypocrisy lies in the arena of wealth and poverty. One does not have to read very far into the New Testament to see that a true Christian would have to be as poor as the homeless to satisfy Scripture. The importance of adherence to a vow of poverty is constantly repeated by Scripture and there can be no debate about the meaning of the text. What is required of all true Christians is abundantly evident and the "reading out of context" defense won't save the day.

Lavish cathedrals, private jets, expensive automobiles, luxurious homes, costly clothes, and the finest cuisine are only some of the items possessed by many Christian leaders today, proving beyond any doubt that many have departed dramatically from New Testament teachings and have no intention of returning to them. It is far less painful to ignore and rationalize than accept and follow.

How many people would be willing to jettison six- or seven-figure incomes just to satisfy biblical verses that denounce the accumulation of wealth? Not many, and Christians are no exception. The meaning and intent of the following verses are abundantly clear, although experience shows that the strength of wealth's lure is even clearer and more powerful.

In Luke 14:33 (RSV) Jesus says, "Whoever of you does not renounce all that he has cannot be my disciple." That is about as clear as one can be. If you want to be a disciple of Jesus, then you'll have to surrender all material possessions, as he did. In Matt. 19:21 (RSV) Jesus says, "If you would be perfect, go, sell what you possess, and give to the poor, and you will have treasure in heaven: and come, follow me." When the rich young ruler in Mark 10:17–22 (RSV) asked what he had to do in order to inherit eternal life, he was told by Jesus that he had to follow the commandments Jesus listed. When the young ruler replied that he had observed them from his youth, Jesus said, "You lack one thing; go, sell what you have, and give to the poor, and you will have treasure in heaven."

Now let's be serious! Except for some monks, nuns, and other ascetic troglodytes, does anyone know of any Christians who have given up all they have in order to follow Jesus? Of course not! But that is clearly required. In Mark 8:34 (RSV), Jesus said, "If any man would come after me, let him deny himself and take up his cross and follow me." Notice that Jesus says *any* man, not just those he is addressing at that particular time. Look at the lifestyles of the rich and famous such as Billy Graham, Jimmy Swaggart, Oral Roberts, Jerry Falwell, Rev. Schuller, Rev. Ike, Cardinal O'Connor, Pope John Paul, and many others and ask yourself, What are they denying themselves? The answer is nothing. They get the best of everything, the finest life has to offer, although they are quite secretive about revealing the amount to the public. By and large, and for obvious reasons, their private lives are kept under wraps.

These propagandists should tremble in terror when they read verses like Matt. 19:23–24 (RSV), which says, "It will be hard for a rich man to enter the kingdom of heaven. Again I tell you, it is easier for a camel to go through the eye of a needle than for a rich man to enter the kingdom of God." Mark 10:23 says, "Looking around, Jesus said to His disciples; 'How difficult it is for these possessing wealth to enter the kingdom of God.' " Matt. 6:19 (RSV) says, "Do not lay up for yourselves treasures on earth, where moth and rust consume and where thieves break in and steal, but lay up for yourselves treasures in heaven." Most Christians are accumulating treasures as fast as possible and those at the apex of the religious pyramid are among the most successful.

Christians are told repeatedly not only to avoid the accumulation and retention of wealth but to give away whatever they possess. Luke 12:33–34 (RSV) says, "Sell your possessions and give alms . . . for where your treasure is, there will your heart be also." Luke 11:41 (RSV) says, "But give for alms those things which are within," and Luke 3:11 (RSV) says, "He who has two coats, let him share with him who has none; and he who has food, let him do likewise." According to Matt 5:42 (RSV), you are to "give to him that begs from you, and do not refuse him who would borrow from you." Matt. 5:40 says, "If you are sued in court and have your coat taken away, you should give the victor your other coat also." After all, didn't Jesus allegedly say it's more blessed to give than to receive?

With millions of homeless currently on the streets of America, many Christians have exposed their true feelings to fellow human beings by ignoring the clear instructions laid down in 1 John 3:17-18, which says, "Whoever possesses the world's resources and notices that his brother is in need and then locks his heart against him, how is the love of God within him." How many Christians really agree with Paul, who said, "For Jesus's sake I have suffered the loss of all things, and count them as refuse, in order that I may gain Christ." One does not have to look long or hard to see that Christians in general and Christianity's leaders in particular have thumbed their noses en masse at this requirement. They have no intention, whatever, of giving away all they have accumulated, regardless of what the New Testament says. Personal pain and sacrifice may be required to follow Christ, but they simply aren't in the cards.

Christian evangelists and proselytizers traverse most of the world and for them Jesus told his missionaries in Matt. 10:9-10 (RSV), "Take no gold, nor silver, nor copper in your belts, no bag for your journey, nor two tunics, nor sandals, nor a staff; for the laborer deserves his food." Jesus told them their needs should be taken care of en route. Given the supplies and entourage that accompany them, the organizers of modern crusades have, in effect told Jesus where to get off on this particular pronouncement.

Perhaps the most damaging verses for the mass of humanity are not those that admonish people to give away or avoid the accumulation of wealth, which few heed anyway, but those that lead people to believe that all of their wants and needs will be provided without any effort on their part. Verses that give people the impression that their fate is being looked after by some supreme, beneficent being are the most dangerous for several reasons. *First,* most people are doing everything feasible to accumulate as much wealth as possible and because few are succeeding, many are inclined to accept their fate rather than work for a change. *Second,* most people are not particularly energetic and this verse is ideal for those who wish to sit back and do nothing. *And lastly,* most people believe that some beneficent force rules the universe and, for this reason, are inclined to uncritically accept the teachings found in Matt. 6:25-34 (Modern Language) which says,

I tell you therefore, do not worry about your living—what you are to eat or drink, or about your body, what you are to wear. Is not the life more important than its nourishment and the body than its clothing? Look at the birds of the air, how they neither sow nor reap nor gather into barns, but your heavenly Father feeds them. Are you not more valuable than they? Furthermore, who of you is able through worrying to add one moment to life's course? And why worry about clothes? Observe carefully how the field lilies grow. They neither toil nor spin, but I tell you that even Solomon in all his splendor was never dressed like one of these. But if God so clothes the grass of the field that exists today and is thrown into the furnace tomorrow, will He not more surely clothe you of little faith? Do not, then, be anxious saying, "What shall we eat?" or "What shall we drink?" or "What are we to wear?" For on all these things pagans center their interest while your heavenly Father knows that you need them all. But seek first His kingdom and His righteousness and all these things will be added to you. Do not worry therefore.

One would be hard-pressed to find a passage more at variance with reality and more detrimental to the advancement of the world's people in their never-ending quest to improve their living standards. Indeed, these verses are diametrically opposed to what nearly every child is taught from infancy: namely, you should work hard, study, prepare, and plan if you expect to succeed in life, and woe be to him who expects to get something for nothing. If there is anything people, especially poor people, should not be taught, it is that they should sit back, relax and turn their future over to fate and the elements. This has been far too pervasive in world history and detrimental to the lives of billions.

Anyone who expects to improve his or her condition had better plan on doing the job alone. If you are expecting some kind of beneficent supreme being to bail you out, forget it. There is no solid evidence that some sort of God agreed to become the world's babysitter by taking humanity to raise. In fact, those who have sought assistance the most are precisely those who have received it the least, while those who have taken destiny into their own hands have fared the best.

In summary, then, insofar as wealth is concerned nearly all Christians have chosen a lifestyle decidedly at odds with clear biblical mandates.

Profanity

If there is any area in which the Bible should excel, it is in the promotion of common decency and propriety. After all, isn't the Bible the source from which all wisdom flows? Does it not provide the model for proper conduct and speech? At least that's the billing, and you would expect compliance. But, alas, like so much that is advertised in the media, the Bible is a long way from being the best source of proper speech. Indeed, much of the book should not be read in polite society and many of its comments belong in the expletive-deleted column. If people are going to censor books, films, and magazines, and that is strongly recommended by the Bible's most rigid adherents, they had better start with the

Bible that lies on the dining room table or stands in the hall bookcase, because some of the Bible is utterly disgusting.

At this point we enter what could be described as the trash television version of biblical analysis, because Scripture is liberally sprinkled with statements that are more appropriate for scandal magazines and scurrilous television than a medium for the propagation of morality and ethical behavior. If Scripture is correct when it says in Prov. 15:26 "The words of the pure are pleasant words," then the Bible can no longer be deemed pure. You would never know the Bible is pure from that which follows. Before embarking upon a presentation of relevant biblical verses, one should realize from the outset that that which follows emanates from Scripture, not its opponents. It's their trash, not ours.

The first and most obvious aspect of biblical degeneracy revolves around those verses which are nothing more than filth and should be treated as such. Prime examples are 2 Kings 18:27, which says, "Hath he not sent me to the men which sit on the wall, that they may eat their own dung, and drink their own piss with you," and Deut. 23:1–2, which says, "He that is wounded in the stones, or hath his privy member cut off, shall not enter into the congregation of the Lord. A bastard shall not enter into the congregation of the Lord." It does not require a great deal of wisdom to know what stones and privy member are referring to, nor does it require much insight to suspect that words were altered in translation in order to provide more civil terminology. Incidentally, I read 2 Kings 18:27 on a 50,000 watt radio talk show several years ago and was promptly censored by the station.

Additional examples of explicit biblical verbiage are: Song of Sol. 8:10, "I am a wall and my breasts like towers"; Prov. 5:19, "Let her breasts satisfy thee at all times; and be thou ravished always with her love"; and Song of Sol. 5:4, "My beloved put in his hand by the hole of the door, and my bowels were moved for him." One can safely assume the hole of the door is not referring to a keyhole in a lock. This is the kind of language you would expect to hear in locker rooms or street gangs. Biblical authors seemed to have had an infatuation with the word "breasts." Additional relevant verses in this regard are: Song of Sol. 1:13, "A bundle of myrrh is my well beloved unto me; he shall lie all night betwixt my breasts"; Song of Sol. 4:5, "Thy two breasts are like two young roes that are twins, which feed among the lilies"; Ezek. 23:3, "There were their breasts pressed, and there they bruised the teats of their virginity"; Ezek. 23:34, "Thou shalt . . . pluck off thine own breasts: for I have spoken it, saith the Lord God"; Song of Sol. 7:3, "Thy two breasts are like two young roes that are twins"; Song of Sol. 8:8, "We have a little sister, and she has no breasts"; and Song of Sol. 7:7–8, "This thy stature is like to a palm tree, and thy breasts to clusters of grapes . . . now also thy breasts shall be as clusters of the vine"; Ps. 22:9, "Thou didst make me hope when I was upon my mother's breasts"; Job 21:24, "His breasts are full of milk; and his bones are moistened with marrow"; Isa. 66:11, "That ye may suck, and be satisfied with the breasts of her consolation." This kind of interest in the upper anatomy of women resembles that found in topless bars and strip joints.

Another prime example of biblical uncouthness and incivility is found in the number of times in which males are referred to as those who urinate against the wall. This is evident in 1 Sam. 25:34, "Surely there had not been left unto Nabal by the morning light any that pisseth against the wall"; 1 Kings 16:11, "He left him not one that pisseth against a wall, neither of his kinsfolk, nor of his friends"; and 2 Kings 9:8, "I will cut off from Ahab him that pisseth against the wall." It's interesting to note that these references to pissing against the wall are only found in the King James Version. All of the modern versions have opted for the more expedient approach of cleaning up the language by simply referring to men in general.

Besides breasts and piss the Bible has an exceptional interest in testicles. Verses in which they play a prominent role are: Lev. 21:18–20, "He shall not approach: a blind man, or a lame . . . or a man that is brokenfooted, or . . . hath his stones broken"; Job 40:17, "He moveth his tail like a cedar: the sinews of his stones are wrapped together"; and Deut. 23:1, "He that is wounded in the stones."

The God of the Bible also has an inordinate interest in dung or human feces. This fetish is evident in Ezek. 4:12 ("And thou shalt bake it with dung that cometh out of man, in their sight"), Ezek. 4:15 ("I have given thee cow's dung for man's dung, and thou shalt prepare thy bread therewith"), and 1 Kings 14:10 ("I will bring evil upon the house of Jeroboam, and will cut off from Jeroboam him that pisseth against the wall . . . and will take away the remnant of the house of Jeroboam, as a man taketh away dung, till it all be gone"). God's preoccupation with dung reaches a climax in Mal. 2:3, which says, "Behold, I [God] will corrupt your seed, and spread dung upon your faces, even the dung of your solemn feasts." Does anyone know of someone who has spread dung on the faces of others? Doesn't that make you want to cringe! Just form a mental image of an almighty perfect being spreading dung on the faces of people!

God is not only portrayed as a being overly concerned with breasts, piss, testicles, and human feces but a pervert preoccupied with the sexual organs of women. That is clear by reading Isa. 3:17 ("The Lord will smite with a scab the crown of the head of the daughters of Zion, and the Lord will discover their secret parts") and Nahum 3:5 ("I am against thee, saith the Lord of hosts; and I will discover thy skirts upon thy face, and I will show the nations thy nakedness, and thy kingdoms thy shame").

One of the most disgusting of all passages, Ezek. 23:19–21 says, "She increased her harlotry . . . and doted upon her paramours, whose members were like those of asses, and whose issue was like that of horses. Thus you longed for the lewdness of your youth, when the Egyptians handled your bosom and pressed your young breasts." One need not translate harlot, paramours, members, issue, bosom, and breasts for any reasonably informed individual. The general tenor is all too clear and explanations are neither necessary nor proper.

Many Christians are never told that several verses refer to a disgusting ritual in which people put their hand on the male genitalia while swearing an oath. Three verses clearly falling into this category are Gen. 24:2 ("Abraham said unto his eldest servant of his house, that ruled over all that he had, Put I pray thee, thy hand under my thigh"), Gen. 47:29 ("He called his son Joseph, and said unto him, If now I have not found grace in thy sight, put I pray thee, thy hand under my thigh, and deal kindly and truly with me"), and Gen. 24:9 ("The servant put his hand under the thigh of Abraham his master, and sware to him concerning that matter").

Nearly every religion has used a phallic symbol in one form or another and the Judeo-Christian tradition is no exception. Apparently Zipporah, the wife of Moses, looked upon the penis as part of a religious rite when in Exod. 4:25 she "took a sharp stone, and cut off the foreskin of her son, and cast it at his [Moses'] feet, and said, Surely a bloody husband art thou to me."

We might conclude our litany of biblical profanities, obscenities, immoralities, and perversities by citing a list provided by Harry Barnes on pages 174 and 175 of his work entitled *Twilight of Christianity.* He notes that daughters have sexual intercourse with their father in Gen. 19:30–38; Amnon rapes his sister in 2 Sam. 13:12–14; Absalom violates his father's concubines in 2 Sam. 16:22; Rachel rents her husband to Leah in Gen. 30:15–16; Abraham fornicates with a maidservant in Gen. 16:3; Judah lies with his daughter-in-law in Gen. 38:14–18; a woman is abused all night in Judg. 19:25; Reuben commits incest in Gen. 35:22; Onan "spills his seed" in Gen. 38:8–10; Abraham lends his wife to the pharaoh in Gen. 12:15–19; two sisters lose their virginity in Ezek. 23:3–21; and Potiphar's wife attempts to seduce Joseph. As disconcerting as it may be to responsible individuals, people are still sending their children to Sunday School to read a book from which this garbage has not been expunged?

Probably no biblical information has been more discussed in freethought circles than the scandalous stories pervading the Old Testament. Even when the Bible is *not* advocating or condoning the atrocious behavior about which it speaks, the Book is to be condemned for addressing such activities in a decidedly gratuitous and egregious manner. In many instances, no real purpose is accomplished by using language that is odious and abominable or relating disgusting events. Some of these events are all but impossible, and there was no need to refer to them other than to satisfy the author's perverse interest in the sexually bizarre. Deut. 25:11–12, for instance, says, "When men strive together one with another, and the wife of the one draweth near for to deliver her husband out of the hand of him that smiteth him, and putteth her hand, and takes him by the secrets: Then thou shalt cut off her hand." Has anyone ever seen or heard of an instance in which two men were fighting and the wife of one interfered by reaching in and grabbing the penis or testicles of the other? Let's be realistic. Relating an account of this nature says more about the sick interests of the biblical author than any moral law being outlined.

That can also be said of the events in 2 Sam. 16:22 which says, "Absalom went in unto his father's concubines in the sight of all Israel." What ruler in history, no matter how degenerate, ever had intercourse with concubines in full view of his entire population? An event of this nature has little to do with the real world, although it *does* say a great deal about the character of one of the Old Testament's authors. It is no defense to say that the Bible deals with real life when events of this kind have little to do with reality. Going to the bathroom, sitting on toilets, having bowel movements, and using urinals are a part of real life too, but there are civil and uncivil ways to discuss them. One should have no problem discussing these topics while excluding terminology more in tune with locker rooms and street gangs than polite society.

Some passages can warm you up just by reading them. The text of 1 Kings 1:2 says, "Let there be sought for my lord the king a young virgin: and let her stand before the king, and let her cherish him, and let her lie in thy bosom, that my lord the king may get heat." It's safe to say that the king is not the only one who is going to get heat with passages like this.

Following his anthology of scriptural obscenities, Harry Barnes judiciously commented on page 175, "It is obvious that if the Boston judge who presided over the case of Theodore Dreiser's *American Tragedy* were to adopt the same attitude with regard to the Bible, every bookseller in Boston would be held liable for a jail sentence in offering the Bible for sale in his bookshop."

In summary, it's safe to conclude that any reference to the Bible as the "Good Book" is without substance and wholly unwarranted.

Self-Degradation

One of the most serious social ills in modern society is mental illness brought on, in large part, by the fact that millions of people have low self-esteem and a low self-concept. People who are taught by the Bible and other media to look upon themselves as little more than pieces of dung, to quote Martin Luther, often live out the image imbued. When people are repeatedly told in hundreds of biblical verses that they are depraved, degenerate, hopeless, lazy, ignorant, and helpless; when they are repeatedly demeaned, degraded, and debased, they will much more easily fall into a feeling of hopelessness and despair when conditions do not develop as they desire.

Is it any wonder that mental illness is so closely associated with those raised in an environment in which humanity is viewed negatively rather than positively and in which frustration is all persuasive? A negative outlook on everything other than the next world is poisonous to normal living. In conditions of that kind people will tend to look upon themselves as the source of all failure when, in reality, much of that which occurs is beyond their control. Nearly every factor of real significance in a person's life is beyond his influence. People have nothing to say about who their parents are, the environment in which they are reared, the intelligence they receive at birth, their genetic composition, their childhood associates, their physical condition, the country in which they are born, the teachers they have in school and so on ad infinitum. In fact, the degree to which people can control their destiny is amazingly restricted, when all factors are taken into account. All the time the powers-that-be are telling you how free you are, that's exactly what you aren't. No wonder people are so beset with difficulties and self-denigrating. No wonder anti-social behavior is so all-pervasive. How can people respect others when they don't even respect themselves?

15

Prophecies

Nonexistent, Unfulfilled, False, Jesus' False Prophecies, Book of Revelation

If there is any area toward which defenders of Scripture gravitate when asked to prove the Bible is the inerrant word of a supreme being, it is prophetic accuracy, a subject that is near and dear to the hearts of biblicists. The latter contend the book must be God's Word because only a book written by the hand of God could be so correct in predicting future events. At least that's the theory. And by manufacturing, twisting, distorting, and perverting hundreds of verses, biblicists have successfully sold this con game to millions of people. By one of the greatest flimflams in history, they have been able to convince millions that the Bible has a perfect record of prognostication and is therefore divinely inspired.

What the biblicists fail to reveal, of course, is the large number of inaccurate forecasts. The Bible's prophetic capability has more holes than a sieve and its reliability is far closer to 1 percent than 100 percent. The Bible's poor record demonstrates the truth found in Eccle. 6:12, "Who can tell a man what shall be after him under the sun?" Certainly not Scripture. Apparently the Bible's authors decided to ignore a warning in their own book.

Prophecy is a topic freethinkers generally avoid because of the amount of imprecision, vagueness, and uncertainty that prevails throughout. If there is any arena in which the Bible allows biblicists to let their imaginations run wild, this is it. The entire subject reeks with glittering generalities and nebulous meanderings supported by tortured interpretations and perverted verses. Apologist Hal Lindsey notes on page 13 of *The Late Great Planet Earth*, "Astrologers

291

frequently guard their trade by predicting in generalities." That applies perfectly to his Christian compatriots presenting biblical prophecy.

Some of the more candid apologists readily concede that problems permeate this topic throughout. On pages 70 and 71 in *Scripture Twisting* fundamentalist James Sire says,

> There is nothing in Scripture more difficult to treat with certainty than the inter-
> pretation of predictive prophecy, especially those prophecies in both the Old and
> New Testaments which were not fulfilled by the time of the New Testament
> era and interpreted as such by New Testament authors. . . . Christians themselves
> disagree markedly on specific meanings of specific passages.

On page 3 of *A Survey of Bible Prophecy* apologist Ludwigson says, "In modern times, wide differences of opinion have arisen as to the exact meaning of what is called the 'inspiration' of the Scriptures. But in no area have these diversities been so many, and so pronounced, as in the area of Biblical prophecy, especially those prophecies which point to events still in the future."

And after discussing millennialism, postmillennialism, premillennialism and a Pre-, Mid-, or Post-tribulational Rapture, apologist Ryrie cogently states on page 493 of *Basic Theology*, "Back and forth the discussion of the words goes. What can we conclude? Simply that the words themselves are inconclusive." All too often that's about as accurate an analysis as any.

A second major problem with prophetic activity, besides vagueness, is that biblicists often claim modern events are the fulfillment of biblical truths, while ignoring the obvious fact that the same events have been occurring on a regular basis ever since the prediction was made. One biblicist, Tim Weber, was honest enough to admit as much when he said on page 43 of *The Future Explored*,

> so many silly mistakes about predicting the end. Too many believers today contend
> that Jesus' coming is at hand because they can point to wars and the threat
> of wars, earthquakes and famines, the persecution of Christians in different parts
> of the world, and so on. The truth is that *every* generation from the early church
> on could make the same claims! There have always been wars and calamities
> in the world. In fact, natural disasters in the past make some of ours look like
> minor inconveniences. An earthquake in China during the 16th century killed
> over 800,000 people. An epidemic of the plague took the lives of over 75 million
> people in fourteenth-century Europe, while a famine in 1878 caused the starvation
> deaths of nearly 10 million Chinese. Clearly then, no single generation has cornered
> the market on wars, famines, or earthquakes.

A third problem with predicting the future is that many biblical verses clearly show that prophets are not to be believed or taken seriously. For understandable reasons, Christians have ignored these comments en masse. Some of the most obvious examples are: Hosea 9:7 (RSV), "The prophet is a fool, the man of the spirit is mad, because of your great iniquity and great hatred"; Mic. 3:5, "Thus saith the Lord concerning the prophets that make my people err"; and Zech. 13:2, "I will cause the prophets and the unclean spirit to pass out of the land." With verses like these, as well as the following, it's a wonder that anyone takes biblical prophecy seriously.

Likewise, Lam. 2:14 (RSV) says, "Your prophets have seen for you false and deceptive visions; they have not exposed your iniquity to restore your fortunes, but have seen for you oracles false and misleading"; 1 Kings 22:23 says, "The Lord hath put a lying spirit in the mouth of all these thy prophets, and the Lord hath spoken evil concerning thee"; Mic. 3:11 (NIV) says, "Her leaders judge for a price, her priests teach for a bribe, and her prophets tell fortunes for money. Yet they lean upon the Lord and say, 'Is not the Lord among us? No disaster will come upon us' "; Isa. 28:7 (RSV) says, "The priest and the prophet reel with strong drink, they are confused with wine, they stagger with strong drink; they err in vision, they stumble in giving judgment"; and Jer. 23:11 (RSV) says, "Both prophet and priest are ungodly; even in my house I have found their wickedness." After reading verses like these, even true believers should be inclined to flee to the hills when a prophet approaches, because they could never be sure he's legitimate.

Having noted that prophetic comments are often vague, prophetic events are often historically repetitious, and Scripture often describes prophetic figures as untrustworthy, we can now analyze those biblical prophecies that are specific enough to be exposed as fraudulent. Generally speaking, prophetic failures can be grouped into three broad categories: First, those that were incorrectly fulfilled, i.e., fulfilled in a manner different from that predicted; second, those that have never occurred, a group too large to discuss in toto; and third, New Testament references to nonexistent Old Testament prophecies. Our critique will begin with the third category because it's the smallest and most easily covered.

Nonexistent Prophecies

First, Mark 1:2 in the Revised Standard Version says, "As it is written in Isaiah the prophet, 'Behold, I send my messenger before thy face, who shall prepare thy way.' " The problem with this prophecy lies in the fact that there is no such comment in Isaiah. It doesn't exist. Isaiah said nothing of the sort.

Second, Matt. 2:23 says, "He [Joseph] came and dwelt in a city called Nazareth, that it might be fulfilled which was spoken by the prophets, He shall be called a Nazarene." The phrase, "He shall be called a Nazarene," does not exist in the Old Testament. There is no such prophecy and Jesus was never called a Nazarene.

And *third,* Matt. 27:9-10 says, "Then was fulfilled that which was spoken by Jeremy the prophet, saying, And they took the 30 pieces of silver, the price of him that was valued, whom they of the children of Israel did value; And gave them for the potter's field, as the Lord appointed me." The problem with this citation is that no such statement resides in the Book of Jeremiah. Jer. 32:8–9 does not apply because Matthew says 30 pieces of silver were involved, while Jeremiah says 17; Jeremiah says one man alone bought the field, while Matthew says "they" bought it; and Matthew is discussing blood money that *was not* approved by God, while the money in Jeremiah *was* approved by God.

Incorrectly Fulfilled Prophecies

The second category of prophetic comments is far larger and composed of those predictions which were incorrectly fulfilled or fulfilled in a manner different from that which was forecast. Many of the most prominent examples are:

First, Gen. 2:17 says, "But of the tree of the knowledge of good and evil, thou shalt not eat of it: for in the day that thou eatest thereof thou shalt surely die." As we all know, Adam ate the fruit but did not die that day. In fact, he lived to be 930 years old, according to Gen. 5:5. So the prophecy failed. If a spiritual, as opposed to a physical, death was intended, as apologists allege, then why wouldn't this also be true of what Nathan told David in 2 Sam. 12:14? David had sinned against God and Nathan said in 2 Sam. 12:14, "Because by this deed thou hast given great occasion to the enemies of the Lord . . . the child also that is born to thee shall surely die"—and verse 12:18 clearly shows David's child died physically, not spiritually, shortly thereafter.

Apologists who have little concern for intellectual integrity, especially when dealing with predictions of this kind, mistakenly ignore the advice offered by one of their own, William Arndt, who said on page 133 of *Bible Difficulties,* "It must be remembered that a deviation from the literal sense is not justified unless the Scriptures themselves prescribe such a course." If only more apologists would follow this advice!

A *second* inaccurate prophecy is found in Gen. 28:13, where God says to Jacob, "I am the Lord God of Abraham thy father, and the God of Isaac: the land whereon thou liest, to thee will I give it, and to thy seed." Jacob never received the promised land.

Third, in Gen. 35:10 God said to Jacob, "Thy name is Jacob; thy name shall not be called any more Jacob, but Israel shall be thy name: and he called his name Israel." Yet, just eleven chapters later, in Gen. 46:2, the text says, "God spoke unto Israel in the visions of the night, and said, Jacob, Jacob. And Jacob said, Here am I."

Fourth, Deut. 23:3 predicts, "An Ammonite or Moabite shall not enter into the congregation of the Lord, even to their tenth generation shall they not enter into the congregation of the Lord for ever." But we find in Ruth 1:4, 1:22, 4:13, and 4:17 that Ruth, a Moabite, not only entered the congregation of the Lord within ten generations but gave birth to ancestors of David and Jesus.

Fifth, in Jon. 3:4 Jonah cried, "Yet forty days, and Nineveh shall be overthrown!" But Jon. 3:10 (RSV) shows the prophecy materialized in a manner precisely opposite to that which was predicted. It states, "When God saw what they did, how they turned from their evil way, God repented of the evil which he said he would do to them, and he did not do it." It is no defense to say that they turned from their evil ways and, therefore, God was justified in changing his mind, because the conditions under which Jonah had made his prophecy had changed. If he had been a true prophet, Jonah would have seen this change coming. Even more important, the prophecy was not conditional. Jonah flatly stated Nineveh would be overthrown in forty days and that did not occur.

Sixth, Isa. 52:1 says, "Put on thy beautiful garments, O Jerusalem, the holy city: for henceforth there shall no more come into thee the uncircumcised and the unclean." Anyone even remotely familiar with Jerusalem today knows that the uncircumcised and the unclean have never stopped traveling through Jerusalem.

Seventh, in 2 Chron. 1:12, God said to Solomon, "Wisdom and knowledge is granted unto thee; and I will give thee riches, and wealth, and honour, such as none of the kings have had that have been before thee, neither shall there any after thee have the like." This prophecy is decidedly false because there were several kings in his day, and scores since who could have thrown away the value of Palestine without missing the amount. The wealth of Solomon has been exceeded by many kings and is comparatively small by today's standards.

Eighth, in 1 Thess. 4:16–17 Paul stated, "The Lord himself shall descend from heaven with a shout, with the voice of the archangel, and with the trump of God: And the dead in Christ shall rise first: Then *we* which are alive and remain shall be caught up together with them in the cloud to meet the Lord in the air: And so shall *we* ever be with the Lord." Paul shared the delusion taught by Jesus that he would be snatched up bodily into heaven with other saints then living and never taste death. The use of "we" clearly proves as much. It is difficult to deny that Paul was certain that the end of the world was coming in the lifetime of his contemporaries.

Ninth, Gen. 15:16 predicts, "In the fourth generation they [Abraham's descendants] shall come hither again." God told Abraham that his descendants would return from Egypt in the fourth generation. Yet, if Abraham is included, it actually occurred during the sixth generation. The generations were: Abraham and Isaac, Levi in Exod. 1:2, Kohath in Exod. 6:16, Amram in Exod. 6:18, and Moses in Exod. 6:20.

Tenth, Jer. 34:4–5 predicted that Zedekiah would experience a peaceful death by saying, "Hear the word of the Lord, O Zedekiah king of Judah: Thus saith the Lord of thee, Thou shalt not die by the sword; But thou shalt die in peace."

But Jer. 52:10–11 shows that Zedekiah died in something less than a peaceful manner, "The king of Babylon slew the sons of Zedekiah before his eyes: . . . Then he put out the eyes of Zedekiah; and the king of Babylon bound him in chains, and carried him to Babylon, and put him in prison till the day of his death." If that is a peaceful death, deliver us from violent ones.

Eleventh, Another one of these peaceful death predictions that never came to fruition is found in 2 Kings 22:20, which says, "I will gather thee [Josiah] unto thy fathers, and thou shalt be gathered into thy grave in peace."

The prophetess Huldah predicted that Josiah would die in peace. Yet, 2 Kings 23:29–30 shows that Josiah was killed at Megiddo by the king of Egypt, buried in Jerusalem, and replaced by his son, Jehoahaz. One could hardly call this a peaceful death!

Twelfth, Jer. 42:17 in the RSV says, "All the men who set their faces to go to Egypt to live there [as did the Jews] shall die by the sword, by famine, and by pestilence; they shall have no remnant or survivor from the evil which I will bring upon them." Yet Jews established a cultural center in Alexandria, Egypt, in the first century and have continued to live there ever since.

Thirteenth, a significant number of verses predict the permanent destruction of Tyre. Ezek. 26:14 says, "Thou [the city of Tyre] shalt be built no more"; Ezek. 26:21 says, "I will make thee a terror, and thou shalt be no more: though thou be sought for, yet shalt thou never be found again"; and Ezek. 27:36 says, "The merchants among the people shall hiss at thee, thou shalt be a terror, and never shalt be any more." Tyre is supposed to be destroyed and never rebuilt, but several verses show that Tyre existed throughout New Testament times and still exists today. Mark 7:24 says, "He arose and went into the borders of Tyre and Sidon." Acts 12:20 says, "Herod was highly displeased with them of Tyre and Sidon." One could also consult Mark 7:31, Acts 21:3 and 7, Matt. 15:21, and Mark 3:8 to see that Tyre never disappeared.

Fourteenth, Joshua 8:28 says, "Joshua burnt Ai, and made it a heap for ever, even a desolation to this day," even though people live in Ai now and have lived in that city ever since the prophecy was made.

Fifteenth, the destruction of Babylon and the permanent removal of all of its inhabitants was predicted in Jer. 50:39–40 and Isa. 13:19–22 which says, "Babylon . . . shall be as when God overthrew Sodom and Gomorrah. It shall never be inhabited, neither shall it be dwelt in from generation to generation: neither shall the Arabian pitch tent there; neither shall the shepherds make their fold there. But wild beasts of the desert shall lie there; . . . and satyrs shall dance there. . . . and her time is near to come, and her days shall not be prolonged."

It is important to note that: (a) There has never been any time since Isaiah that Babylon was uninhabited. People lived there during New Testament times, according to Matt. 1:11, 12, and 17; Acts 7:43; and 1 Pet. 5:13; and a few continue doing so today; (b) Arabians still visit there; (c) Shepherds still make their fold there; and (d) Babylon has never been known for its dancing satyrs.

Sixteenth, another depopulation prediction is found in Jer. 49:33, which says, "Hazor shall be a dwelling for dragons, and a desolation for ever; there shall no man abide there, nor any son of man dwell in it." People have never stopped living in Hazor and continue to do so.

Seventeenth, Jer. 33:17 says, "David shall never want a man to sit upon the throne of the house of Israel," and Ps. 89:3-4 says, "I have sworn to David my servant, Thy seed will I establish for ever, and build up thy throne to all generations." God promised there would always be a Davidic king, but the Davidic line ended with Zedekiah and no king returned to the Davidic throne for 450 years. Moreover, what descendant of David is now ruling in the Middle East?

Eighteenth, in Isa. 7:1-7 (RSV), God told Isaiah to promise Ahaz, the king of Judah, that his enemies, Rezin and Pekah, would not harm him. The text states,

> in the days of Ahaz . . . king of Judah, Rezin the king of Syria and Pekah the king of Israel came up to Jerusalem to wage war against it, but they could not conquer it . . . and the Lord said to Isaiah, Go forth to meet Ahaz . . . and say to him, "Take heed, be quiet, do not fear, and do not let your heart be faint because of these two smoldering stumps of firebrands . . . saying, Let us go up against Judah and terrify it, and let us conquer it for ourselves. . . . It shall not stand and it shall not come to pass."

Yet Ahaz and his forces were slaughtered by Rezin and Pekah, according to 2 Chron. 28:5-6, which says, "The Lord his God delivered him [Ahaz] into the hand of the king of Syria; and they smote him . . . and he was also delivered into the hand of the king of Israel, who smote him with a great slaughter. For Pekah . . . slew in Judah one hundred and twenty thousand in one day." Clearly God's promise to Ahaz failed.

Nineteenth, Ezek. 29:15 says Egypt "shall be the basest of the kingdoms; neither shall it exalt itself any more above the nations: for I will diminish them, that they shall no more rule over the nations." Yet, Egypt has never been the basest of kingdoms and in the 1820s Egypt conquered and ruled the Sudan, another nation.

Twentieth, Deut. 28:43-44 says, "The stranger that is within thee [that is, the Jews] shall get up above thee very high; and thou shalt come down very low. He shall lend to thee, and thou shalt not lend to him: he shall be the head, and thou shalt be the tail." According to this prophecy Jews would be borrowers and not lenders. If Jews had always been debtors instead of great creditors throughout history, Christians would hail this as a fantastic prophecy instead of the failure it is.

Twenty-first, Deut. 15:6 says of Israel, "Thou shalt lend to many nations, but thou shalt not borrow." As a prophecy this clearly failed. Today, Israel borrows heavily from the United States and has sought billions of dollars in loan guarantees.

Twenty-second, one of the Bible's more comprehensive prophecies is found in several related verses. Gen. 12:3 says, "In thee [Abraham] shall all families of the earth be blessed." Gen. 22:18 and 26:4 say, "In thy seed shall all the nations of the earth be blessed." And Gen. 28:14 says, "In thee [Jacob] and in thy seed shall all the families of the earth be blessed."

The total inaccuracy of these predictions lies in the fact that all of the nations of the earth have not been blessed through Abraham, Jacob, or their descendants, the Jews. Christians claim that Christ fulfilled this prophecy by giving Christianity to the world (note, for instance, Acts 3:25-26 and Gal. 3:8-9). But this assumes Christianity has been a blessing, whereas history shows much to the contrary. Even supposing, for argument's sake, that Christianity is a blessing, the prophecy remains unfulfilled. The Chinese, the Hindus, the Jews, the Muslims and, in fact, most of humanity, does not accept Jesus as their savior. The intrafamily strife that Jesus promised in several verses, and the national and religious strife that have arisen from Christianity throughout the centuries, can hardly be described as a blessing on all nations and all families, whatever benefits it may have conferred on some.

Twenty-third, one of the more disappointing promises by God is found in Exod. 3:7-8, which says, "The Lord said, I have surely seen the affliction of my people which are in Egypt. . . . I am come down . . . to bring them up out of that land into a good land and large, unto a land flowing with milk and honey." Anyone acquainted with the Eastern Mediterranean knows that Palestine was neither a good land nor a large one. Far from being a land which might poetically be described as flowing with milk and honey, it is, and was within historic times, a barren and desolate land in the main. In size it was a little larger than tiny Wales. Of course the Jews were infatuated with their own land, but this is no reason why other people should accept their patriotic illusions as fact.

Twenty-fourth, one of the earliest false prophecies surfaces in Gen. 4:12, which says, "When thou [Cain] tillest the ground, it shall not henceforth yield unto thee her strength, a fugitive and a vagabond shalt thou be in the earth." But Gen. 4:16-17 says, "Cain went out from the presence of the Lord, and dwelt in the land of Nod . . . and he builded a city." Instead of becoming a vagabond as was forecast, Cain took a wife, built a city, established a line of descendants and seems to have led a settled life.

Twenty-fifth, in Gen. 17:15-16 God said to Abraham, "As for Sarai thy wife . . . I will bless her . . . and she shall be a mother of nations," and in Gen. 17:4 God said to Abraham, "Thou shall be the father of many nations." What nations? Apparently the only nations descended from Sarah and Abraham were the Jews, the Ishmaelites, the Midianites, and the Edomites.

Twenty-sixth, according to Gen. 15:13 God told Abraham that his descendants would be a stranger in a land that was not theirs, serve its inhabitants, and be afflicted for 400 years. One need only read Exod. 12:40 to see that the sojourning of the children of Israel in Egypt was for 430 years, not 400 years as forecast.

Twenty-seventh, Gen. 46:4 says, "I [God] will go down with thee [Jacob] into Egypt; and I will also surely bring thee up again: and Joseph shall put his hand upon thine eyes." According to Hebrew the phrase "and Joseph" should have been translated as "then Joseph." In other words, the prophecy was that Jacob would return to Israel from Egypt while still alive. Yet one need only read Gen. 47:28–30 and 50:2–6, which say, "Jacob lived in the land of Egypt 17 years . . . and he called his son Joseph, and said unto him . . . bury me not I pray thee, in Egypt," and "Joseph commanded his servants the physicians to embalm his father . . . and the Egyptians mourned for him three score and ten days" to see that Jacob died in Egypt before his entry into Israel.

Twenty-eighth, Deut. 33:23 says, "And of Naphtali he said, O Naphtali, satisfied with favor and full with the blessing of the Lord: possess thou the west and the south." In truth, Naphtali received a district in the north of Palestine but none in the south or the west (see *Westminster Historical Map of Bible Lands,* plate 4, or *Standard Bible Atlas,* map 4).

Twenty-ninth, David, the man after God's own heart according to Scripture, predicted in 1 Sam. 27:1, "I shall now perish one day by the hand of Saul." But one need only read 1 Kings 2:10 which says, "David slept with his fathers and was buried in the city of David" to see that David did *not* die by the hand of Saul. In fact, Saul died much earlier than David, according to 1 Sam. 31:5–6 and 2 Sam. 1:1.

Thirtieth, one of the most crucial of all prophecies is found in Jer. 22:30, which says, "Thus saith the Lord, Write ye this man [Coniah] childless, a man that shall not prosper in his days: for no man of his seed shall prosper, sitting upon the throne of David, and ruling any more in Judah." In other words, no descendant of Coniah will ever sit on the throne of David. Under the name of Jeconias, Coniah is listed in Matt. 1:11 as an ancestor of Jesus, who, according to Luke 1:32, *must* sit on the throne of David. Jesus is precluded from becoming an heir to the throne of David because he descended from Coniah and if he ever sits upon the throne of David as Luke 1:32 *requires,* the prophecy in Jer. 22:30 will be proven false.

Thirty-first, in John 5:25 Jesus says, "I say unto you, The hour is coming, and now is, when the dead shall hear the voice of the Son of God: and they that hear shall live." Notice the verse says, "And now is," which shows that the dead were to hear Jesus' voice and live at that time. Yet none of this prophecy came to fruition.

Thirty-second, one of the more pathetic comments made by God is found in Acts 18:9–10, in which God promises Paul complete protection by saying,

"Then spake the Lord to Paul in the night by a vision, Be not afraid, but speak, and hold not thy peace: For I am with thee, and no man shall set on thee to hurt thee." But Acts 21:32 says, "When they saw the chief captain and the soldiers, they left beating of Paul," and Acts 23:2 says, "The high priest Ananias commanded them that stood by Paul to smite him on the mouth." That hardly sounds like Paul was enjoying the protection promised by God. Paul laments his own beatings in 2 Cor. 11:23–25: "I am more; in labors more abundant, in stripes above measure, in prisons more frequent, in deaths oft. Of the Jews five times received I forty stripes save one. Thrice was I beaten with rods, once was I stoned." If that's an example of God's protection, deliver me.

Thirty-third, in Amos 7:11 Amos says, "Jeroboam shall die by the sword, and Israel shall surely be led away captive out of their own land." But 2 Kings 14:29 says, "Jeroboam slept with his fathers, even with the kings of Israel; and Zachariah his son reigned in his stead," clearly implying that he did not die by the sword. "Slept" is not the biblical word used for those who die by the sword.

Thirty-fourth, in citing an Old Testament prediction the speaker in John 7:52 said, "Search and look: for out of Galilee ariseth no prophet." Yet several of the most distinguished Jewish prophets, such as Jonah, Nahum, Hosea, and Elijah, were from Galilee.

Thirty-fifth, Gen. 49:13 predicts, "Zebulun shall dwell at the shore of the sea; he shall become a haven for ships, and his border shall be at Sidon." Two aspects of this prophecy are false. The borders of Zebulun never extended to the sea and never reached to the city of Sidon.

Thirty-sixth, one would be hard-pressed to reconcile the forecast in Gen. 8:22 (RSV), "While the earth remains, seedtime and harvest, and cold and heat, and summer and winter, and day and night shall not cease," with Gen. 41:54, which says, "The seven years of dearth began to come, according as Joseph had said: and the dearth was in all lands," and with Gen. 41:56, which says, "The famine was over all the face of the earth." If seedtime and harvest were not to cease, then how could there have been famine over all the earth?

Thirty-seventh, according to Jer. 22:18–19, the Lord said that Jehoiakim, son of Josiah, king of Judah, would be buried with the burial of an ass, drawn and cast forth beyond the gates of Jerusalem. And Jer. 36:30 says, "His dead body shall be cast out in the day to the heat, and in the night to the frost." But 2 Kings 24:6 shows that, "Jehoiakim slept with his fathers." If the prophecy was fulfilled as predicted in Jeremiah, it's hardly likely that the compilers of Kings would have misled readers by using language implying the opposite occurred.

Thirty-eighth, as a spokesman for God in Amos 7:14 and 17, Amos told Amaziah that his wife would be a harlot in the city and his sons and daughters would fall by the sword and he would die in a polluted land. Yet Amaziah's son Uzziah succeeded him on the throne and died a leper; so he could not have been a child who was slain by the sword. In addition, 2 Kings 14:19 says Amaziah was slain in Lachish in Judah, which was no more polluted than any other territory in the age of the prophets.

Thirty-ninth, Amos 8:9 says, "It shall come to pass in that day, saith the Lord God, that I will cause the sun to go down at noon, and I will darken the earth in the clear day." This is supposedly a prediction of events that were to accompany the Crucifixion as related in Matt. 27:45, which says, "Now from the sixth hour [noon] there was darkness over all the land unto the ninth hour." Defenders of the Bible constantly accuse their attackers of taking verses out of context, but that is a tactic upon which they repeatedly rely and Amos 8:9 provides a good example of it. The biblicists neglected to read the verse after Amos 8:9, which says, "I will bring up sackcloth upon all loins, and baldness upon every head," and shows other events were to occur simultaneously. When did all loins wear sackcloth or all heads exhibit baldness?

Fortieth, Ezek. 29:16 in the Living Bible says, "Israel will no longer expect any help from Egypt. Whenever she thinks of asking for it, then she will remember her sin in seeking it before." Recent agreements between Israel and Egypt destroyed the validity of this prophecy.

Forty-first, one of the Bible's more flamboyant prophecies is found in Jer. 50:39–40 (RSV), which says, "Wild beasts shall dwell with hyenas in Babylon, and ostriches shall dwell in her; she shall be peopled no more forever, nor inhabited for all generations. As when God overthrew Sodom and Gomorrah and their neighbor cities, says the Lord, so no man shall dwell there, and no son of man shall sojourn in her." Anyone acquainted with the Middle East knows that hyenas and ostriches have never been dominant inhabitants of Babylon. Indeed, were it not for zoos in the area their presence would never be noticed.

Forty-second, in 1 Sam. 2:27–34 God reprimands Eli and his sons for their terrible behavior and tells them he will no longer allow their family to be priests. Then God says, "I will raise me up a faithful priest [Samuel] who shall do according to that which is in mine heart and in my mind: and I will build him a sure house; and he shall walk before mine anointed for ever." Although Samuel was the faithful priest set up to replace Eli, he had no sure house built up, and his sons were almost as bad as Eli's as shown in 1 Sam. 8:1–3, which says, "It came to pass, when Samuel was old, that he made his sons judges over Israel. . . . And his sons walked not in his ways, but turned aside after lucre, and took bribes, and perverted judgment." Moreover, neither Samuel nor his descendants walked before God's anointed forever, unless "forever" means a very short time.

Forty-third, in Josh. 17:17–18 Joshua spoke to the house of Ephraim and Manasseh and said, "Thou art a great people, and hast great power . . . for thou shalt drive out the Canaanites, though they have iron chariots, and though they be strong." But Judg. 1:27–29 declares, "Neither did Manasseh drive out the inhabitants of Beth-shean and her towns, nor Taanach. . . . but the Canaanites would dwell in that land. . . . Neither did Ephraim drive out the Canaanites that dwelt in Gezer; but the Canaanites dwelt in Gezer among them." This prophecy failed completely as the Canaanites proved to be immovable before the onslaught of Manasseh and Ephraim.

Forty-fourth, one of the more complex, as well as most discussed, inaccurate prophecies is found in Ezek. 26:7–12, which says,

> Thus saith the Lord God; Behold, I will bring upon Tyrus Nebuchadrezzar king of Babylon, a king of kings, from the north, with horses, and with chariots, and with horsemen, and companies, and much people. He shall slay with the sword thy daughters in the field: and he shall make a fort against thee, and cast a mount against thee. . . . And he shall set engines of war against thy walls, and with his axes he shall break down thy towers . . . thy walls shall shake at the noise of the horsemen. . . . With the hoofs of his horses shall he tread down all thy streets: he shall slay thy people by the sword, and thy strong garrisons shall go down to the ground. And they shall make a spoil of thy riches, and make a prey of thy merchandise: and they shall break down thy walls, and destroy thy pleasant houses.

By now the picture is clear. Tyre is to be destroyed and plundered by Nebuchadrezzar. At least, that's what is supposed to occur. But what actually happens is clearly related eleven chapters later, in Ezek. 29:18–20 (RSV), which says,

> Nebuchadrezzar king of Babylon made his army labour hard against Tyre; every head was made bald and every shoulder was rubbed bare; yet neither he nor his army got anything from Tyre to pay for the labour that he had performed against it. Therefore thus says the Lord God: Behold, I will give the land of Egypt to Nebuchadrezzar king of Babylon; and he shall carry off its wealth and despoil it and plunder it; and it shall be the wages for his army. I have given him the land of Egypt as his recompense for which he labored.

So, Nebuchadrezzar did not take Tyre or make a spoil of its riches. Because the town was on an island, as shown by Ezek. 27:4 ("Thy borders are in the midst of the seas") his thirteen-year siege failed. No historian, either Greek or Phoenician, mentions Tyre being taken, plundered, or destroyed by Nebuchadrezzar. God promised Nebuchadrezzar Egypt as compensation, but this he never received either.

Forty-fifth, and finally, Ezek. 30:4–16 yields another protracted prophecy that deserves an itemized analysis. It says,

> The sword shall come upon Egypt, and great pain shall be in Ethiopia, when the slain shall fall in Egypt, and they shall take away her multitude, and her foundations shall be broken down. Ethiopia, and Libya, and Lydia, and all the mingled people . . . shall fall with them by the sword. . . . And they shall know

that I am the Lord, when I have set a fire in Egypt, and when all her helpers shall be destroyed. . . . Thus saith the Lord God; I will also make the multitude of Egypt to cease by the hand of Nebuchadrezzar king of Babylon. He and his people with him, the terrible of the nations, shall be brought to destroy the land: and they shall draw their swords against Egypt, and fill the land with the slain. And I will make the rivers dry. . . . and there shall be no more a prince of the land of Egypt: and I will put a fear in the land of Egypt. . . . And I will set fire in Egypt.

Six verses later the text contributes to the mayhem by saying,

Thus saith the Lord God; Behold, I am against the pharaoh king of Egypt, and I will break his arms. . . . And I will scatter the Egyptians among the nations and will disperse them through the countries. And I will strengthen the arms of the king of Babylon, and put my sword in his hand. . . . I shall put my sword into the hand of the king of Babylon, and he shall stretch it out upon the land of Egypt. And I will scatter the Egyptians among the nations.

That Egypt was to be destroyed and scattered by the king of Babylon is all too obvious from these predictions. But history shows that: (a) The multitudes of Egypt have never been taken away or scattered among other countries; (b) Ethiopia, Libya, Lydia, and Egypt have never fallen to a common destroyer; (c) A large conflagration never occurred in Egypt; (d) Nebuchadrezzar never destroyed the land of Egypt; (e) A prince continued to rule in Egypt long after Nebuchadrezzar died; (f) The rivers of Egypt were never made dry (What *rivers* are in Egypt other than the Nile?); and (g) None of the evils that Ezekiel said Nebuchadrezzar would bring upon Egypt ever occurred. Alexander the Great actually conquered Egypt 240 years later.

So, to close out our second category, we can safely say that any contemporary prognosticator with a batting average comparable to that of the Bible would be classified as a charlatan in the tradition of psychics, mystics, mediums, seers, soothsayers, clairvoyants, spiritualists, crystal gazers, palmists, and fortune-tellers.

False Prophecies

The third and final category of prophecies are those that have never materialized. Some biblicists, such as those in the Church of Christ, contend that all the prophecies in the Old Testament have already been fulfilled. If so, one cannot help but ask when the following, which have little or no possibility of being fulfilled, occurred:

First, Gen. 15:18 says, "The Lord made a covenant with Abram saying, Unto thy seed have I given this land, from the river of Egypt to the great river, the river Euphrates." Although it could be argued that Israelite territory extended to the Nile as a result of the Six Day War, it is questionable whether it ever will extend to the Euphrates.

Second, Isa. 17:1 says, "The burden of Damascus . . . is taken away from being a city, and it shall be a ruinous heap." Yet, the *Encyclopaedia Britannica* says Damascus, which is one of the oldest cities in the world, has been continuously inhabited and is the only city in Palestine that has never been completely destroyed. Never has it been a ruinous heap.

Third, according to Isa. 19:18, "Five cities in the land of Egypt will speak the language of Canaan, swear to the Lord of hosts, and one shall be called the city of destruction." To this day no five cities in the land of Egypt have never learned to speak Hebrew or any other language from Canaan, and none has been nicknamed the city of destruction.

Fourth, Isa. 20:4 says, "So shall the king of Assyria lead away the Egyptians prisoners, and the Ethiopians captives, young and old, naked and barefoot, even with their buttocks uncovered to the shame of Egypt." When did Assyrians capture Egyptians and Ethiopians and lead them away with their buttocks uncovered?

Fifth, Isa. 65:20 makes this incredible statement: "No more shall there be in it an infant that lives but a few days . . . for the child shall die a hundred years old." When has everyone without exception lived to be at least a hundred years old?

Sixth, Ezek. 29:9–12, along with verses 30:23, 30:26, 32:9–12 and 32:20, says,

> The land of Egypt shall be desolate and waste . . . and I will make the land of Egypt utterly waste and desolate, from the tower of Syene even unto the border of Ethiopia. No foot of man shall pass through it, nor foot of beast shall pass through it, neither shall it be inhabited forty years. And I will make the land of Egypt desolate in the midst of the countries that are desolate, and her cities among the cities that are laid waste shall be desolate forty years: and I will scatter the Egyptians among the nations, and I will disperse them through the countries.

The problem with all these predictions is that (a) Egypt has never been desolate and waste from Syene to Ethiopia; (b) Men and beasts have never failed to pass through Egypt; (c) There has never in history been a forty-year period—in fact, not even a single day—in which Egypt was uninhabited; (d) Egypt has never been surrounded by countries that are desolate; (e) Egypt's cities have never been desolate forty years; and (f) Egyptians have never been scattered among other nations. How's that for prophetic reliability?!

Seventh, Joel 3:17 says, "Then shall Jerusalem be holy, and there shall no strangers pass through her any more." It goes without saying that strangers and visitors have always passed through Jerusalem and continue to do so.

Eighth, one of the most absurd prophecies is found in Zeph. 3:13, which says, "The remnant of Israel shall not do iniquity, nor speak lies; neither shall a deceitful tongue be found in their mouth." Whoever heard of any large body of people entering a period in which they no longer did iniquity, spoke lies, or practiced deceit? The remnant of Israel, nor of any other nation, has never stopped doing iniquity or speaking lies and never will.

Ninth, Zech. 10:11 (RSV) says, "They shall pass through the sea of Egypt; and the waves of the sea shall be smitten, and all the depths of the Nile dried up." The Nile has never dried up and there is no reason it ever should.

Tenth, Zech. 14:11 says, "But Jerusalem shall be safely inhabited." The state of the Middle East today and for the past several centuries leaves his prophecy wildly unrealized.

Eleventh, Jer. 9:11 says, "I will make Jerusalem heaps, and a den of dragons; I will make the cities of Judah desolate, without an inhabitant." Jerusalem has never been a den of dragons and Judah has never been uninhabited. Neither has ever been a ruinous heap.

Twelfth, Isa. 13:10 says, "For the stars of heaven and the constellation thereof shall not give their light: the sun shall be darkened in its going forth, and the moon shall not cause her light to shine." And Isa. 60:19–20 says, "The sun shall be no more thy light by day; neither for brightness shall the moon give light unto thee. . . . The sun shall no more go down; neither shall the moon withdraw itself." When for goodness sake have the sun, moon, and stars ever failed to emit their light? May fate save us if they ever do.

Thirteenth, Isa. 30:26 says, "The light of the moon shall be as the light of the sun, and the light of the sun shall be sevenfold, as the light of seven days." Mankind is yet to witness such brightness and may the elements have compassion on us if we ever do.

Fourteenth, Isa. 19:8 (RSV) says, "The fishermen will mourn and lament, all who cast hook in the Nile; and they will languish who spread nets upon the water." At no time in the Nile's history has it been emptied of fish or unproductive for fishermen, although as with most polluted bodies of water, it is becoming less productive.

Fifteenth, Isa. 34:8–10 (RSV) says, "The streams of Edom shall be turned into pitch, and her soil into brimstone; her land shall become burning pitch. Night and day it shall not be quenched; its smoke shall go up for ever. From generation to generation it shall lie waste; none shall pass through it for ever and ever."

Needless to say, this is another litany of outlandish prognostications that have never materialized. Obvious problems contained therein are (a) The streams of Edom have never turned to pitch; (b) Edom's soil has never turned to brimstone; (c) Edom's land has never become burning pitch, that continues to burn forever; (d) Edom does not lie in waste; and (e) people continue to pass through Edom every day.

Sixteenth, God promised in Jer. 32:37 that, "He would gather the banished tribes out of all countries, whither he had driven them in his anger and bring them again to this place and cause them to dwell safely." The banished tribes have never returned and dwelt safely. In fact, even today many are returning to Israel only to leave later because the area is neither safe nor secure.

Seventeenth, in the same tradition God says to the Israelites in Hos. 2:18 (RSV), "I will abolish the bow, the sword, and war from the land; and I will make you lie down in safety." The Israelites have never dwelt in safety and with the Middle East as armed as it is today there is little possibility of them doing so. Actually, Middle East weaponry is more abundant and further from abolition than ever.

Eighteenth, Joel 2:27–28 says, "My people shall never be ashamed. And it shall come to pass afterward, that I will pour out my spirit upon all flesh; and your sons and your daughters shall prophesy, your old men shall dream dreams, your young men shall see visions." Christians say this was fulfilled on the day of Pentecost and subsequently. But God did not by any means pour out his spirit upon "all flesh." Nor are the Jews so hardened as never to have been ashamed amidst their poverty and afflictions.

Nineteenth, Zech. 14:8 (RSV) says, "On that day living waters shall flow out from Jerusalem, half of them to the eastern sea and half of them to the western sea; it shall continue in summer and winter." Not only have no waters ever flowed in any direction from Jerusalem to a sea, but one can't help but wonder what seas are intended.

Twentieth, 2 Sam. 7:10 (RSV) says, "I will appoint a place for my people Israel, and will plant them, that they may dwell in their own place, and be disturbed no more; and violent men shall afflict them no more, as formerly." Jews are still scattered over the world and violent men still disturb and afflict them in every land, including modern Israel.

Twenty-first, Isa. 65:17 and 25 say, God will "create new heavens and a new earth; and the former shall not be remembered, nor come into mind. . . . The wolf and the lamb shall feed together, and the lion shall eat straw like the bullock; and dust shall be the serpent's meat." When have the wolf and lamb fed together? When has the lion eaten straw like the bullock? When has the serpent eaten dust? These extravagant predictions regarding peace and tranquility are interpreted in whatever manner is deemed most expedient, but have plainly never been literally true.

Twenty-second, in the Modern Language Version Ezekiel 12:23 says, "For the days are drawing near, and the fulfillment of every vision shall soon come to pass." After more than 2,000 years, the wait continues.

Twenty-third, another one of the extravagant claims by Isaiah is found in verse 60:12, which says, "For the nation and kingdom that will not serve thee [the Hebrews] shall perish; yea, those nations shall be utterly wasted." Nations never subjugated by the Jews continue to flourish. If this poetical expression of ancient Jewish national hopes is perverted into a reference to Christ or his Church, then it may be pointed out that many nations have advanced and are advancing without Christ.

Twenty-fourth, Jer. 8:17 says, "I will send serpents, and cockatrices, among you, which will not be charmed, and they shall bite you, saith the Lord." This prophecy could never be fulfilled because cockatrices are mythical creatures.

Twenty-fifth and lastly, in Luke 1:32–33 an angel said God would give Jesus the throne of his father David and he would reign over the house of Jacob forever. Since Jesus has never received the throne of David or reigned over the house of Jacob (the Jews), who indeed have rejected him, expediency dictates that this prophecy be interpreted in a spiritual or figurative sense. Even then, however, it remains unfulfilled, for the Jews still reject the Gospel. Jesus does not reign over them except in the contrived sense that he reigns over everything as God.

The obvious conclusion to be drawn from all of the above is that many biblical prophecies have never been fulfilled and those who allege otherwise are mistaken. In far too many cases, the biblical record of predictive reliability ranges from poor to pitiful, from paltry to pathetic.

Jesus' False Prophecies

Any discussion of prophetic fallacies within the Bible would not be complete without noting the large number of errors by the one being who is supposed to be perfection personified. The one person who is allegedly more truthful, more moral, more reliable, more accurate than all others is precisely the one who made the largest number of *inaccurate* prophecies. I am referring to no less a figure than Jesus Christ, our alleged redeemer, the very man who has a prophetic record that can only be described as dismal. Because most of Jesus' mistakes have been duly noted in previous chapters, we will only relate those that should be memorized by all objective analysts of Christianity:

First, in John 13:38 Jesus said to Peter, "The cock shall not crow, till thou hast denied me thrice." Mark 14:66–68, of course, reveals that the cock actually crowed after the first denial, not the third.

Second, in Matt. 12:40 Jesus said, "For as Jonas was three days and three nights in the whale's belly, so shall the Son of man be three days and three nights in the heart of the earth." In other words, just as Jonah was in the whale for three days and three nights Jesus was to be buried for three days and three nights. But Jesus was killed and buried sometime on a Friday afternoon and raised sometime on the following Saturday night or Sunday morning. You don't need to be a statistical genius to see that from Friday afternoon to Sunday morning is not three days and three nights. To be technical, it is barely a day and a half.

Third, in Mark 8:31 Jesus said, "The Son of man must suffer many things . . . and be killed, and after three days rise again."

Note carefully! It says "after" three days he would rise again. Jesus died and was buried on a Friday evening and rose sometime during Saturday night or Sunday morning. *After* three days means that he should actually have arisen after three full days had passed which would have delayed the resurrection until Monday afternoon at the earliest.

Fourth, in Matt. 16:28 Jesus made one of those classic predictions that has haunted his supporters ever since, forcing them to concoct an endless number of rationalizations to explain its failure. Jesus said, "Verily I say unto you, There be some standing here, which shall not taste of death, till they see the Son of man coming in his kingdom." And in Mark 9:1 he said, "Some of them that stand here which shall not taste of death, till they have seen the kingdom of God come with power."

These prophecies clearly show that Christ's coming was to occur during the lifetime of then-existing persons. Yet when did the Kingdom of God come with power? The text of 2 Peter 3:8, which says, "Be not ignorant of this one thing, that one day is with the Lord as a thousand years, and a thousand years as one day," cannot be used as an escape hatch because Jesus repeatedly stated that his contemporaries would see his return. All of Jesus' contemporaries passed away, and dozens of generations after them, yet we still await the kingdom of God's arrival.

Fifth, another prophecy that has tied supporters of Jesus into knots is found in Mark 13:30–31, which says, "Verily I say unto you, that this generation shall not pass, till all these things be done. Heaven and earth shall pass away: but my words shall not pass away." Jesus made this statement after listing a wide assortment of events that were to occur. Yet no one has seen the Son of man coming in the clouds of heaven with power and great glory, nor has he sent his angels to gather the elect from all parts of the world. Moreover, the sun has not become darkened; the moon has not failed to reflect light, and the stars have not "fallen" from heaven. Nearly two thousand years have passed and this prophecy remains unfulfilled, although Jesus strongly stated it would be fulfilled in the lifetime of his generation. On page 46 in *The Future Explored* apologist Tim Weber addressed this very issue and made some frank admissions. After dispensing with some minor biblical criticisms he said, "Those verses aren't too difficult, but those which follow have caused Bible scholars all kinds of trouble."

He then quotes Mark 13:30–31 and says,

In these verses, the problem lies in the meaning of "this generation" and once again "these things." Normally, one would take "this generation" to refer to those living in Jesus' day and "these things" to refer to the same things as in the previous verse. But you can see the problem: if we go along with that interpretation, then Jesus was obviously mistaken. The coming of the Son of Man did not occur during the lifetime of those hearing the prophecy on the Mount of Olives. . . . There have been many attempts to deal with this problem. As we might expect, liberal scholars claim there is no problem at all: Jesus was mistaken. He thought the end would occur within a few years, but obviously blew it. Conservative scholars, on the other hand, have offered a number of other interpretations. Many evangelicals argue that "this generation" should be translated "this race." Thus Jesus is saying that the human race (or Israel as some contend) will not pass away before his *Parousia*. The Greek allows some justification for this translation, but it doesn't seem to make much sense. Is it really necessary for Jesus to predict that someone will be alive at the time of His appearing?

Another more recent evangelical interpretation contends that "this generation" refers to the last generation before Christ's return, whenever it may be. . . . His contention is, therefore, that within a generation of the founding of modern Israel, the Second Coming will occur. Since Israel was established in 1948 and a biblical generation is roughly 40 years (Psalms 95:10), we should expect the Second Coming by 1987 at the outside.

Since 1987 has come and gone, we can now toss another theory onto the scrap heap.

Sixth, in Matt. 17:11–13 Jesus says, "Elias truly shall first come, and restore all things. But I say unto you, That Elias is come already. . . . Then the disciples understood that he spoke to them of John the Baptist." If John the Baptist is Elias as Jesus alleges, then the obvious question becomes: What did John the Baptist restore? The answer is . . . nothing.

Seventh, in Luke 23:43 Jesus said to the thief on the cross, "To day shalt thou be with me in paradise." But how could they have been together in paradise that day if Jesus was to lay in the tomb three days?

Eighth and lastly, Matt. 20:19, Mark 10:33–34, and Luke 18:32–33 clearly show that Jesus predicted he would be killed by the Gentiles. But it is equally clear in John 19:14–18 that he was killed by the Jews. So Jews and Gentiles are both responsible.

These are only some of the examples one could relate to show that the prophetic capabilities of Jesus are far closer to those of crystal ball enthusiasts than perfection. A more extensive list is available in chapter 6.

Book of Revelation

And finally, any discussion of the Bible's predictive accuracy would also not be complete without a brief analysis of the biblical book that is associated with prophetic accuracy more than any other, the Book of Revelation. As far as prophecy is concerned, no book is cited more often by apologists. Biblicists neglect to mention,

however, that the book is employed by so many because it is understood by
so few. In fact, the Book of Revelation is so vague, so nebulous, so fantastic,
that one theory is as good as another in interpreting it. Anyone who has read
the book of Revelation can understand why Martin Luther said on pages 398–
400 of volume 35 of his *Works,*

> I miss more than one thing in this book and it makes me consider it to be
> neither apostolic nor prophetic . . . they are supposed to be blessed who keep
> what is written in this book; and yet no one knows what that is, to say nothing
> of keeping it. This is just the same as if we did not have the book at all. . . . My
> Spirit cannot accommodate itself to this book. . . . Christ is neither taught nor
> known in it. . . . Many have tried their hands at it, but until this very day they
> have attained no certainty. Some have even brewed it into many stupid things
> out of their own heads. Because its interpretation is uncertain and its meaning
> hidden, we have let it alone until now, especially because some of the ancient
> fathers held that it was not the work of St. John the Apostle.

Luther should have noted that his analysis is applicable to more than the
Book of Revelation. On page 190 in *Answers to Questions About the Bible* apologist
Robert Mounce denounces commentaries on the Book of Revelation and in-
advertently provides a good critique of nearly all commentaries on biblical prophecies by saying,

> commentaries on Revelation . . . tend to force a larger interpretive pattern onto
> the book. Most of the basic questions seem to have been settled ahead of time
> and the role of the commentator is to demonstrate how all the individual verses
> support his predetermined thesis. It is interesting to note how writers in the opening
> chapters use such qualifying phrases as "it seems to me" or "it is probably true,"
> but by the time they arrive at the last chapters have so convinced themselves
> that they are emboldened to say, "there is no doubt that" or "it has been established
> that" in reference to passages as ambiguous as those in chapter one!

Conclusion

What better way to conclude our extensive analysis of biblical prophecy and the
inaccuracy of same than by relating the following observation by Thomas Paine
found on pages 129 and 130 in *The Age of Reason*? What he said relative to
the Book of Isaiah is applicable to more of the Bible than apologists would ever
be willing to admit. He stated,

> Whoever will take the trouble of reading the book ascribed to Isaiah, will find
> it one of the most wild and disorderly compositions ever put together; it has

neither beginning, middle, nor end; and, except for a short historical part, and a few sketches of history in the first two or three chapters, is one continued, incoherent, bombastical rant, full of extravagant metaphor, without application, and destitute of meaning; a school-boy would scarcely have been excusable for writing such stuff; it is . . . prose run mad.

In light of everything noted so far, one would hope that at least one biblical vision will eventually come true. Zech. 13:4 (RSV) says, "On that day every prophet will be ashamed of his vision when he prophesies; he will not put on a hairy mantle in order to deceive, but he will say, 'I am no prophet.' "

It is too bad so many Christians completely ignore the advice given in Jer. 23:16, which says, "Thus saith the Lord of hosts, Hearken not unto the words of the prophets that prophesy unto you: they make you vain: they speak a vision of their own heart, and not out of the mouth of the Lord." One can readily understand from all the above why Jer. 14:14–15 (RSV) says, "The Lord said to me: 'The prophets are prophesying lies in my name; I did not send them, nor did I command them or speak to them. They are prophesying to you a lying vision, worthless divination, and the deceit of their own minds. . . . I did not send them."

If that doesn't correctly describe the reliability of biblical prophecy, nothing will.

16

Salvation

Faith, Works, Grace, Whim, Predestination, Universalism, Annihilationism, Heaven

A subject of great importance to all Christians is salvation and the alleged afterlife. Because belief in the reality of a world to come is central to Christianity, how one obtains access to this realm of perfection is critical to millions of Christians. After all, if there's nothing to look forward to, then all is for nought. And if there *is* something far better in a world beyond death, then what could be more important than knowing what must be done in order to receive the ultimate reward?

The basic problem, however, is that even if one were to accept the Bible as God's word and believe that heaven awaited those who gained entrance, one could never know for sure what must be done in order to reach heaven. The Bible is just too vague, too nebulous, too contradictory for even those who seek to follow its advice. This is because Scripture clearly outlines no less than *five* different methods by which one can be saved and the requisite procedures for each, while failing to mention that the different methods are often either mutually exclusive, divergent, or contradictory. If one is true, then the others fall by the wayside and vice versa. The five methods are works, faith, predistination, whim, and universalism.

Whether people are saved by faith, works, predestination, universalism or whim has been one of the most prominent issues throughout the history of biblical disputation. Each provides a means by which a loyal Christian can attain heaven; each can be supported by numerous biblical verses; and each diverges from the other. True believers are forced to take destiny into their own hands and choose from among the options available. Before one can decide, however, he must not only be shown the verses in support of each path, but the many problems that accompany them. Rest assured all have considerable biblical backing and the most effective way to prove they are defensible is to cite the appropriate verses.

Faith

On page 176 in *508 Answers to Bible Questions* apologist M. R. DeHaan aptly says of faith, "I realize that these theological matters are not always easy to understand, but we have to receive a great many things in the Word of God by faith, and faith begins where reason ends." DeHaan is one of the few biblicists honest enough to admit that faith and reason are in different realms; one is the absence of the other; faith picks up where reason leaves off. If only more apologists were as candid as DeHaan! On page 20 in *The Light of Reason,* volume 1, Shmuel Golding is even more frank, correctly observing, "Christianity is nothing if not a religion of faith. Faith is a virgin giving birth to a child. Faith is that child sharing a trinity with the God of creation. Faith is a resurrection that no one saw. Faith is a 'coming soon' which has never happened after 2,000 years of waiting. But the fundamentalist is not a reasonable fellow. He finds that his ignorance is bliss."

With these pertinent observations in mind, let's now begin with faith, because that path to a golden afterlife takes precedence over all others according to most biblicists and nearly all fundamentalists. Many verses can be used in support of this position and the following are prime examples: John 14:6, "I am the way, the truth, and the life: no man cometh unto the Father, but by me"; John 3:18, "He that believeth on him is not condemned; but he that *believeth not* is condemned already"; John 3:36, "He that believeth on the Son hath everlasting life and he that believeth not the Son shall not see life; but the wrath of God abideth on him"; 1 John 5:12, "He that hath the Son hath life; and he that hath not the Son of God hath not life"; Acts 16:30-31, "What must I do to be saved? And they said, 'Believe on the Lord Jesus Christ, and thou shalt be saved, and thy house' " (notice it says "What *must* I do); John 8:24, "Ye shall die in your sins: for if ye believe not that I am he, ye shall die in your sins"; Mark 16:16, "He that believeth and is baptized shall be saved; but he that believeth not shall be damned"; and 1 Cor. 3:11 (RSV), "No other foundation can any one lay than that which is laid, which is Jesus Christ."

One should carefully note that these verses are emphatic because each not only says you are saved by faith, but that *only* by faith in Jesus are you saved. Faith is not just *a* route to salvation; it's the *only* route.

Many other verses note the central role of faith in salvation. John 3:16 says, "God so loved the world, that he gave his only begotten Son, that whosoever believeth in him should not perish, but have everlasting life." John 6:28-29 says,

"What shall we do, that we might work the works of God? Jesus answered. . . . This is the work of God, that ye believe on him whom he hath sent." John 6:47 says, "I say unto you, He that believeth on me hath everlasting life." Acts 4:12 says, "Neither is there salvation in any other: for there is none other name under heaven given among men, whereby we must be saved." Acts 13:39 says, "By him all that believe are justified from all things." Notice the reference to *belief* and being justified from *all* things! Rom. 5:1 says, "Therefore being justified by faith, we have peace with God through our Lord Jesus Christ." Gal. 3:11 says, "For, The just shall live by faith." The text of 2 Tim. 3:15 says, "The holy Scriptures, which are able to make thee wise unto salvation through faith which is in Christ Jesus." Heb. 11:6 says, "But without faith it is impossible to please him: for he that cometh to God must believe that he is, and that he is a rewarder of them that diligently seek him"), And lastly, Eph. 2:8-9 says, "By grace are ye saved through faith; and that not of yourselves: it is the gift of God . . . lest any man should boast."

So we can clearly see that more than enough verses exist to prove that you are saved by faith or belief and several verses contend you are saved by belief alone.

Works

However, a large number of verses can just as easily be used to prove that salvation comes through good works. It isn't what you believe that matters; it's what you do, how you conduct your life that counts. The most important verses in this regard are Micah 6:8, "What doeth the Lord require of thee, but to do justly, and to love mercy, and to walk humbly with thy God"; Deut. 10:12-13, "Now Israel, what doeth the Lord thy God require of thee, but to fear the Lord thy God, to walk in all his ways, and to love him, and to serve the Lord thy God with all thy heart and with all thy soul, To keep the commandments of the Lord, and his statutes, which I command thee this day for thy good?"; Eccles. 12:13, "Fear God and keep his commandments: for this is the whole duty of man." These are clear enough. All that is required is good deeds. Notice that nothing is said about believing in anything.

In Matt. 19:16-18, a man asks Jesus, "Good Master, what good thing shall I do, that I may have eternal life?" Jesus responds by saying, "If thou wilt enter into life, keep the commandments." The man asks which commandments those were. And Jesus says "Thou shalt do no murder, Thou shalt not commit adultery, Thou shalt not steal, Thou shalt not bear false witness, Honor thy father and thy mother, and Love thy neighbor as thyself." Notice that Jesus told the man to follow only five of the Ten Commandments and added a requirement that isn't even a commandment (Loving thy neighbor as thyself). Jesus omitted five commandments, and, most important, said nothing about believing in anything.

In Mark 10:17–19 the same account is related but Jesus gratuitously adds a different additional commandment: Defraud not.

When the same account is related a third time in Luke 18:18–22, Jesus says the additional obligation expected of one who has followed the commandments is to sell all that he has and give the money to the poor in order to have treasure in heaven. Again, nothing is said about believing in anything.

To move on, Ps. 62:12 says, "For thou renderest to every man according to his work." Luke 19:8–9 says, "Zacchaeus stood, and said to the Lord; Behold, Lord, the half of my goods I give to the poor; and if I have taken any thing from any man by false accusations, I restore him fourfold. And Jesus said unto him, This day is salvation come to this house." Ps. 15:1–3 (RSV) says, "O Lord, who shall sojourn in thy tent? Who shall dwell on thy holy hill? He who walks blamelessly, and does what is right, and speaks truth from his heart; who does not slander with his tongue, and does no evil to his friend, nor takes up a reproach against his neighbor." John 5:28–29 is quite strong and says, "Marvel not at this: for the hour is coming in which all that are in the graves shall hear his voice, And shall come forth; they that have done good, unto the resurrection of life; and they that have done evil the resurrection of damnation."

Notice the dual reference to the word "done."

James 2:21 says, "Was not Abraham our father justified by works?" James 2:25 says, "Was not Rahab the harlot justified by works when she had received the messengers?" Matt. 7:24 says, "Whosoever heareth these sayings of mine, and doeth them, I will liken him unto a wise man, which built his house upon a rock." Gen. 4:7 (RSV) says, "If you do [Notice it says *do*] well, will you not be accepted?" Ezek. 18:4–9 says, "The soul that sinneth, it shall die. But if a man be just, and do that which is lawful and right . . . hath walked in my statutes, and hath kept my judgments, to deal truly; he is just, he shall surely live." Matt. 16:27 says, "The Son of Man shall come . . . and then he shall reward every man according to his works." And finally, Luke 1:25–28 says,

> Behold, a certain lawyer stood up, and tempted him saying, Master, what must I do to inherit eternal life? Jesus said unto him, What is written in the law? How do you read it? And he answered, Thou shalt love the lord thy God with all thy heart, and with all thy soul, and with all thy strength, and with all thy mind; and thy neighbor as thyself. And Jesus said unto him, Thou hast answered right: this do [Again notice the word "do"], and you shall live.

This passage, like those preceding it, clearly shows that salvation is obtained by good deeds and belief is not a factor. Nothing is said about believing in anything.

Apologists Boa and Moody express the view of all those who rely upon faith as the only route to salvation when they say on page 177 of *I'm Glad You Asked,* "Any system of salvation by works clearly conflicts with the Bible." But, as we have already seen, precisely the opposite is true. Works are pivotal.

Some apologists will allege that all of the verses in support of works as the road to salvation were uttered prior to the death of Jesus on the cross and that salvation before the cross was, indeed, obtained by works. However, after the cross the requirement was shifted to faith.

This stance simply won't withstand the light of scrutiny, because all of the following comments were uttered *after the cross* and clearly show that events on the cross changed nothing: In 2 Cor. 5:10, "We must all appear before the judgment seat of Christ; that every one may receive the things done in his body, according to what he hath done, whether it be good or bad"; in 1 Cor. 7:19 (NIV), "Circumcision is nothing and uncircumcision is nothing. Keeping God's commands is what counts"; in 1 Cor. 9:24, "Know ye not that they which run in a race run all, but one receives the prize? So run that ye may obtain"; in Acts 10:35, "In every nation he that feareth him, and worketh righteousness, is accepted with him"; in Rev. 22:14, "Blessed are they that do his commandments, that they may have right to the tree of life, and may enter in through the gates into the city"); in Rev. 22:12, "My reward is with me, to give every man according as his work shall be"; in 2 Peter 1:10, "If ye do these things, ye shall never fall"; in Rom. 2:5–6, "The righteous judgment of God; Who will render to every man according to his deeds"; in Rom. 2:13, "For not the hearers of the law are just before God but the doers of the law shall be justified."

An exceptionally strong statement in support of works is James 1:27, which says, "Pure religion and undefiled before God and the Father is this, To visit the fatherless and widows in their affliction, and to keep himself unspotted from the world."

Finally, Rev. 20:12–15 says, "I saw the dead, small and great, stand before God; and the books were opened . . . and the dead were judged out of those things which were written in the books, according to their works [Notice it does not say faith] . . . and they were judged every man according to their works . . . and whosoever was not found written in the book of life was cast into the lake of fire."

Clearly salvation by works was just as important after the cross as before. For adherents in faith to contend otherwise is a weak argument, indeed. Not only is it important to note that all of these comments were made after the cross, but that Paul, the very architect of faith itself, made some of them. Other important verses in this regard are Luke 14:13–14, 14:23–24, and 18:29–30, Matt. 7:21 and 10:42, John 6:27, 2 Cor. 6:17, and James 1:25.

In fact, when all is said and done believers in faith alone should note that several verses clearly prove faith without works is useless. The following verses imply, if anything, that works can survive without faith, but not vice versa. James

2:24 says, "You see then how that by works a man is justified, and not by faith only." James 2:17 and 2:20 are about as clear as any verses when they say, respectively, "Even so faith, if it has not works, is dead, being alone," and "Faith without works is dead." James 2:26 says, "As the body without spirit is dead, so faith without works is dead also." And James 2:14 says, "What doth it profit, my brethren, though a man say he hath faith, and have not works? can faith save him?"

The Book of James is the death knell for the arguments of those who contend that you are saved by faith alone. No wonder that quintessential apostle of faith only, Martin Luther, called the Book of James an epistle of straw. It runs directly counter to a cardinal teaching of Protestantism.

Grace

Although the fundamentalist wing of Christianity contends that faith alone is the sole means by which to obtain salvation, many verses show that a third path known as grace, a euphemism for whim or caprice, is the correct route. God simply looks down and chooses whom he wishes to save based on no other criteria than capriciousness. This is the import of the comment found on page 73 of *Essential Christianity,* in which the apologist Walter Martin says, "We must understand, then, that faith and works can never in themselves (or together, for that matter) save anyone. It is sovereign grace *alone* that forms the basis for eternal salvation."

Verses in support of salvation by grace are: John 6:44 ("No man can come to me, except the Father which hath sent me draw him"); 1 Cor. 12:18 ("God set the members every one of them in the body, as it hath pleased him"); Rom. 9:16 ("It is not of him that willeth, nor of him that runneth, but of God that showeth mercy"); John 3:27 ("A man can receive nothing, except it be given him from heaven"); Titus 3:5 ("Not by works of righteousness which we have done, but according to his mercy he saved us, by the washing of regeneration, and renewing of the Holy Ghost"); Isa. 43:25 ("I [God], am he who blots out the transgressions for my own sake, and thy sins I will not remember"); Acts 15:11; Acts 22:14; Jer. 30:21; Rom. 3:24, 6:23, 11:5, and 11:6; Eph. 2:5; and Ps. 86:13. More than enough evidence can be produced to buttress biblical support for belief in salvation by grace alone. Is it any wonder Christians turn themselves over to fate and allow the elements to direct their destiny? Why be concerned if salvation is out of one's hands, regardless?

Faith-alone adherents repeatedly and erroneously tell the world that Christianity differs from all other religions because of its stress upon salvation by faith rather than works. For corroboration, we might note the following comment on page 175 in *I'm Glad You Asked* by apologists Boa and Moody, "Ten of the 11 major religions of the world teach salvation by good deeds. Christianity stands alone with its emphasis on grace rather than works for salvation." On page 60 of *The Bible Has the Answer* apologists Morris and Clark similarly state, "Every religion, with the exception of genuine Christianity, is a religion of salvation through both faith and works."

In addition, apologists repeatedly tell others that salvation is a gift, pure and simple, that there is *absolutely nothing* one can do to earn salvation. It is freely given by the grace of God and is not the result of anything one does or can do. At least that is what they say: it is an *unearned,* an *unmerited gift* wholly unobtainable by works. On page 132 of *The Liberation of Planet Earth* apologist Hal Lindsey says that grace means "to freely give something to someone which he can in no possible way deserve or merit or earn."

Apologetic writings, especially those encased in a fundamentalist perspective, are mistakenly replete with three messages in this regard:

The *first* is that salvation is *not earned* but obtained wholly without works or merit on our part. On page 160 in *Answers to Questions About the Bible* apologist Mounce says, "That there is nothing that man can do to *merit* forgiveness is the clear teaching of the Scripture." On page 144 in *The Bible Has the Answer* Morris and Clark say, "If salvation is really the gift of God's grace . . . as the Bible teaches, then how can there be a price one has to pay to earn it?" And on page 53 in the same book Morris and Clark say, "There are numerous other false ideas about salvation that are prevalent, but all of them . . . consist in man's doing something which he feels will help earn his salvation."

The *second* message is that salvation is an unearned free gift. This can be found on page 144 in Morris and Clark's book, where they say, "One of the clearest emphases of the gospel is that salvation is a free gift (Eph. 2:8-9, Rom. 6:23) attained not by works of any kind." And on page 202 of *I'm Glad You Asked* Boa and Moody say, "Inherent in the idea of a gift is that it must be received from the giver, and this is true of the gift of salvation."

The *third* message is that salvation comes from God's mercy, his grace. As John R. Rice says on page 281 of *Dr. Rice, Here Is My Question,* "Oh, if people would only get the idea out of their heads that salvation is by man's doing good instead of the grace of God!" On page 156 in *Answers to Questions About the Bible* Mounce says, "Grace is unmerited favor."

On pages 63 and 68 in *Answering Christianity's Most Puzzling Questions,* volume 1, Sisson, says, "Grace is irritating because there is absolutely nothing meritorious about receiving what we do not deserve . . . God saves people by His grace alone . . . grace means enjoying favor when we deserve God's wrath. In 40 years the Lord has taught me . . . I can do absolutely nothing to save myself."

On page 77 in *False Doctrines Answered* John R. Rice says, "Men must be saved by the grace of God, without human merit, by simple faith in the atoning work of Jesus Christ." On page 133 in *Does the Bible Contradict Itself?* Arndt says, "Man must be saved, if he is to be saved at all, by grace and not by anything he has achieved or earned."

And finally, on pages 72–73 and 78–79 in *Essential Christianity* apologist Walter Martin says,

> In a real sense this is all quite analogous to the Biblical doctrine of grace, which has been accurately defined as the unmerited favor of God . . . faith and works can never in themselves (or together for that matter) save anyone. It is sovereign grace *alone* that forms the basis for eternal salvation. . . . Note carefully that if we could earn our salvation in any way [notice he says, "in any way"] then grace would be annulled, for then it is no longer the *gift* of God but a *debt* which God owes to us. . . . the absolute sovereignty of grace is one of the unshakable foundations of essential Christianity.

The fatal flaw permeating the previous comments and observations, however, lies in the fact that *salvation is not a free gift* at all. It is earned; it is merited. There's nothing free about it. Even in Christianity it must be earned. You must take an affirmative act, i.e., accept Jesus as your Lord and Savior, or face condemnation. One merits salvation when he accepts Jesus. In fact, salvation can't be denied if one commits himself to Christ.

Biblicists fail to realize that faith, itself, is a work. You must do something, i.e., believe, in order to be saved. Salvation is *not* a gift and if you don't fulfill the necessary requirement, you can't be saved. In John 14:6, 3:18, and 3:36, and in 1 John 5:12, all quoted earlier, Jesus clearly said he was the *only* way. Also note Acts 4:12 and 1 Cor. 3:11: you must do something to be saved; you must *believe*; that's salvation by works.

In effect, Christianity, like *all* other major religions, requires salvation by works. What you do *does* determine where you go. The only difference lies in the fact that Christianity requires a particular form of work, i.e., belief or faith. If you don't go out of your way to get it, you're lost. Thinking, believing, remembering, and other mental processes require effort. If work is not involved, then millions of employees are taking money under false pretenses.

In fact, apologists, themselves, admit faith is a work. On page 257 in *Dr. Rice Here Is My Question* Rice says, "Faith is not *feeling*; faith is *doing*," and on page 79 in *Essential Christianity* Walter Martin says, "Paul goes on to point out that a man's faith in Christ is counted by God as the supreme work of righteousness." Note well that Martin says that faith is a work.

Even the Bible admits faith is a work in 1 Thess. 1:3 ("Remembering without ceasing your work of faith and labor of love"); 2 Thess. 1:11 ("And the work of faith with power"); John 6:29 ("This is the work of God, that ye believe on him"); and Gal. 5:6 ("But faith which worketh by love").

Faith is as much a work as physical deeds, because both require people to take an affirmative act. Consequently, salvation is not a free gift. It is earned or achieved, is based on merit, is not based on grace or God's mercy, and *has* a price attached. God is obligated to pay a debt to all those who fulfill the requirement of believing. Although most biblicists say there is nothing you can do to merit salvation, in reality, precisely the opposite is true. There is not only something you can do; there is something you *must* do.

Whim

Ultimately, the only alternative to salvation by works is salvation by whim, in which God, alone, determines who will be saved. This really *is* salvation by grace spoken of by the biblicists, because this kind of salvation is truly a gift. People are required to do absolutely nothing. Beliefs, behavior, Jesus, morality, faith, and works are irrelevant and immaterial. God simply chooses and salvation really does become a free gift. If you must do anything to receive something, if a price is attached, then it is no longer a gift. Only when based on God's whim is salvation truly provided gratis.

All religions, including Christianity, believe in salvation by works or salvation by whim. No third alternative is available. You either earn salvation or you don't. And if you don't, then you freely receive that which others are denied. You receive God's grace, which is nothing more than a euphemism for bias and partiality. Salvation by grace exhibits one of the more blatant biblical contradictions because it is clearly antithetical to Rom. 2:11 ("For there is no respect of persons with God,") Eph. 6:9 ("Your Master also is in heaven; neither is there respect of persons with him") and other verses that deny God plays favorites.

Predestination

DESCRIBED

Having discussed faith, works, grace, and whim, we now come to one of the strongest beliefs by which one can be saved according to the Bible—predestination. One of the most prominent figures in modern church history, John Calvin, is strongly associated with this concept, but it is a belief that is repugnant to most of Christendom.

Most biblicists allege that God knows what will occur prior to an event but leaves man free to make the choice. In other words, men are free to choose what God already knows will happen. However, Calvin and others of his stripe stress biblical pronouncements that throw a monkey wrench into this whole scenario.

God doesn't just know ahead of time; he determines it; he fixes it; he plans it; it is his idea. In reality, Calvin viewed free will as a myth. In doing so he highlighted one of the most serious and blatant contradictions in biblical theology—free will versus determinism. As fundamentalist professor Charles Ryrie says on page 311 of *Basic Theology,* "No human mind will ever harmonize sovereignty and free will, but ignoring or downplaying one or the other in the interests of a supposed harmony will solve nothing."

Calvin's opponents rightly observed that the abolition of free will destroys moral responsibility. Thomas Paine took note of the problems this generates by saying on page 208 in volume 9 of his *Life and Works,* "Another set of preachers tell their congregations that God predestinated and selected from all eternity, a certain number to be saved, and a certain number to be damned eternally. If this were true, *the day of Judgment* is past: *their preaching* is in vain, and they had better work at some useful calling for their livelihood. This doctrine . . . has a direct tendency to demoralize mankind."

Unfortunately for Calvin's Christian opponents, literally scores of verses substantiate his position. The following enumeration is rather lengthy: Eph. 1:4–5, "According as he hath chosen us in him before the foundation of the world. . . . Having predestinated us unto the adoption of children by Jesus Christ himself, according to the good pleasure of his will"; Rom. 8:29–30, "Whom he did foreknow, he also did predestinate to be conformed to the image of his Son. . . . Moreover whom he did predestinate, them he also called"; Eph. 1:11, "In whom also we have obtained an inheritance, being predestinated according to the purpose of him who worketh all things after the counsel of his [Notice it does not say "our"] own will"; Acts 13:48, "When the Gentiles heard this, they were glad, and glorified the word of the Lord; and as many as were ordained to eternal life believed"; Eph. 2:10, "We are his workmanship, created in Christ Jesus unto good works, which God hath before ordained that we should walk in them"; Psalms 139:16 (NIV), "Your eyes saw my unformed body. All the days ordained for me were written in your book before one of them came to be"; 1 Thess. 5:9 (RSV), "For God has not destined us for wrath, but to obtain salvation through our Lord Jesus Christ"; Prov. 16:9, "A man's heart deviseth his way: but the Lord directeth his steps"; Job 23:14, "He will carry out what he has planned for me, and of many such matters He is mindful"; 1 Cor. 7:17 (RSV), "Let every one lead the life which the Lord has assigned to him, and in which God has called him"; Prov. 20:24, "Man's goings are of the Lord; how can a man then understand his own way?"; John 6:44, "No man can come to me, except the Father which hath sent me draw him"; Prov. 19:21 (NIV), "Many are the plans in a man's heart, but it is the Lord's purpose that prevails."

Further, Prov. 16:33, "The lot is cast into the lap; but the whole disposing thereof is of the Lord"; Job 14:5 (NIV), "Man's days are determined; you have decreed the number of his months and have set limits he cannot exceed"; Acts

17:26 (NIV), "From one man he made every nation of men, that they should inhabit the whole earth; and he determined the times set for them and the exact places where they should live"; Acts 2:47, "The Lord added to the church daily such as should be saved"; Psalms 37:23, "The steps of a good man are ordered by the Lord"; Dan. 11:36, "That which is determined shall be done"; Matt. 20:23 (NIV), "Jesus said to them, 'You will indeed drink from my cup, but to sit at my right or left is not for me to grant. These places belong to those for whom they have been prepared by my Father' "; Acts 4:28 (NIV), "They [Herod, Pilate, the Gentiles, and the people of Israel] did what your power and will had decided beforehand should happen"; Rev. 17:8, "Whose names were not written in the book of life from the foundation of the world"; 2 Tim. 1:9, "Who hath saved us, and called us with an holy calling, not according to our works, but according to his own purpose and grace, which was given us in Christ Jesus before the world began"; Matt. 25:34 (RSV), "Then the King will say to those at his right hand, 'Come, O blessed of my Father, inherit the kingdom prepared for you from the foundation of the world' "; 1 Pet. 2:8, "A stone of stumbling and a rock of offense, even to them which stumble at the word, being disobedient: whereunto also they were appointed"; and Jer. 1:4–5, Jude 4, 1 Pet. 1:20, Rev. 13:8, and Rev. 20:15.

The list is lengthy, but it makes the point. Predestination is of critical importance to Christian theology because of its impact on concepts such as heaven, hell, sin, salvation, faith, works, rewards, the Atonement, the Devil, the Decalogue, the Crucifixion, and so much else. As far as Christian theology is concerned, predestination is alive and well and no amount of rationalization can prove otherwise.

REFERENCED

In addition to the verses already mentioned several terms clearly strengthen the deterministic aspect of biblical teachings. Each is employed repeatedly and shows that God selects many, if not all, of those to be saved or brought within the realm of God's people.

First are the *elect,* those picked by God. If they are selected by him, then their salvation is determined more by God's acts than their own deeds or beliefs. Prime examples of relevant verses are: Matt. 24:31, "He shall send his angels with a great sound of a trumpet, and they shall gather together his elect from the four winds, from one end of heaven to the other"; 1 Thess. 1:4, "Knowing, brethren beloved, your election of God"; Isa. 45:4, "For Jacob my servant's sake, and Israel mine elect"; Isa. 65:9, "Mine elect shall inherit it, and my servants shall dwell there"; Mark 13:20, "But for the elect's sake, whom he hath chosen, he hath shortened the days"; Luke 18:7, "Shall not God avenge his own elect"; Rom. 8:33, "Who shall lay any thing to the charge of God's elect?"; Col. 3:12,

"Put on therefore, as the elect of God, holy and beloved"; Matt. 24:24, "If it were possible, they shall deceive the very elect"; Mark 13:22, "To seduce, if it were possible, even the elect"; and Mark 13:27, Rom. 11:7, Isa. 42:1, Isa. 65:22, 2 Tim. 2:10, and Matt. 24:22.

Second are the *chosen,* who, like the elect, are singled out for preferential treatment. Key verses are: 2 Thess. 2:13, "We are bound to give thanks alway to God for you, brethren beloved of the Lord, because God has from the beginning chosen you to salvation"; John 15:16, "Ye have not chosen me, but I have chosen you, and ordained you"; Matt. 20:16 and 22:14, "So the last shall be first, and the first last: for many shall be called but few chosen"; Deut. 10:15 (NIV), "Yet the Lord set his affection on your forefathers and loved them, and he chose you, their descendants, above all the nations, as it is today"; Ps. 33:12, "Blessed is the nation whose God is the Lord; and the people whom he hath chosen for his own inheritance"; Ps. 135:4, "The Lord hath chosen Jacob unto himself, and Israel for his peculiar treasure"; John 15:19, "I have chosen you out of the world, therefore the world hateth you"; Acts 22:14, "The God of our fathers hath chosen thee, that thou shouldest know his will, and see the Just One, and shouldest hear the voice of his mouth"; Rom. 11:5 (NIV), "At the present time there is a remnant chosen by grace"; Isa. 44:1-2, "Yet now hear, O Jacob my servant, and Israel whom I have chosen. . . . Fear not, O Jacob, my servant; and thou, Jesurun, whom I have chosen"; Ps. 65:4, "Blessed is the man whom thou choosest, and causest to approach unto thee, that he may dwell in thy courts"; Titus 1:1, "From Paul, the slave of God and the messenger of Jesus Christ. I have been sent to bring faith to those God has chosen"; 1 Pet. 1:1-2, "Peter, an apostle of Jesus Christ . . . chosen and destined by God the Father"; and Deut. 7:7 and Acts 10:41.

Third, are the *called,* who also are selected above others. Key verses in this regard are: 1 Cor. 1:26, "Ye see your calling, brethren, how that not many wise men after the flesh, not many mighty, not many noble, are called"; Acts 2:39, "The promise is unto you, and to your children, and to all that are afar off, even as many as the Lord our God shall call"; Gal. 1:15, "It pleased God, who separated me from my mother's womb, and called me by his grace"; 1 Thess. 2:12, "That you would walk worthy of God, who hath called you unto his kingdom and glory"; Heb. 9:15, "They which are called might receive the promise of eternal inheritance"; 1 Pet. 5:10, "The God of all grace, who hath called us to his eternal glory by Christ Jesus"; Rom. 1:6, "Among whom are ye also the called of Jesus Christ"; 2 Tim. 1:9, "Who hath saved us, and called us with an holy calling, not according to our works, but according to his own purpose and grace, which was given to us in Christ Jesus before the world began"; 1 Cor. 1:24, "Unto them which are called, both Jews and Greeks"; and 1 Cor. 7:20, 1 Cor. 7:24, 1 Pet. 3:9, and 2 Pet. 1:10.

Fourth and last are the *given,* those whom God singled out for special consideration by giving them to Jesus for salvation. Special verses are: John 6:37, "All that the Father giveth me shall come to me: and him that cometh to me I will in no wise cast out"; John 17:2, "Thou hast given him power over all flesh, that he should give eternal life to as many as thou hast given him"; John 6:65, "He [Jesus] said, no man can come to me, except it were given unto him of my Father"; John 17:9, "I pray for them: I pray not for the world, but for them which thou hast given me: for they are thine"; John 17:11–12, "Holy Father, keep through thine own name those whom thou has given me, that they be one as we are. . . . those that thou gavest me I have kept"; John 17:24, "Whom thou hast given me"); and John 17:6 (NIV), "I have revealed you to those whom you gave me out of the world. They were yours; you gave them to me and they have obeyed your word."

Words like *elect, chosen, called,* and *given* show that God, in effect, either predestines many to salvation or strongly influences the outcome. Certainly anyone given to Jesus by God is provided a decided advantage. In essence, God is not only playing favorites but materially, if not decisively, determining the outcome.

Whether they be the elect, the called, the chosen, or the given, the hands of predestination are unmistakable throughout. To the extent that God determines the players and their roles, it is out of man's control. And to the extent it is out of his control, man becomes little more than a participant in a play whose scenario has already been written and whose music has already been choreographed. Even more important, man cannot justifiably be held responsible for his behavior or sent to Hell because of misdeeds over which he has no control.

IMPLIED

And finally, we come to some verses that just exude an aura of predestination by their very wording. Excellent examples are: Luke 10:20, "But rather rejoice, because your names are written in heaven"; Acts 2:23 (NV), "This man was handed over to you by God's set purpose and foreknowledge"; 1 Cor. 12:18 (NIV), "In fact God has arranged the parts in the body, every one of them, just as he wanted them to be"; 1 Cor. 2:7 (NIV), "We speak of God's secret wisdom, a wisdom that has been hidden and that God destined for our glory before time began"; Luke 22:22, "Truly the Son of man goeth, as it was determined"; and Rom. 9:18, "Therefore hath he mercy on whom he will have mercy, and whom he will he hardeneth." Interested observers should also note Heb. 12:22–23, 1 Sam. 12:22, Ps. 86:13, and Dan. 5:23.

In summary, then, Scripture clearly shows that predestination is an inseparable part of biblical theology and all but ransacks the faith and/or works advocates.

Apologists have wrestled with the problem of free will versus determinism for centuries. If ever there was a dilemma that can only be described as a hopeless muddle, this is it, and many apologetic writings reflect as much. In defining "Foresight Election," Charles Ryrie says on page 310 in *Basic Theology,* writes,

> This view holds that God elects on the basis of foreseen faith. By election we mean that sovereign act of God in grace whereby He chose in Christ Jesus for salvation all those whom He foreknew would accept Him. . . . It is probably true to say that a great majority of evangelicals consciously or unconsciously hold this concept of election. . . . This makes foreknowledge foresight without any pretemporal elective action on God's part.

This is the kind of theological doubletalk that makes religion so erroneous, deceptive, and worthless. All Ryrie is saying is that God chose to be saved those he knew ahead of time would accept Jesus, which makes no sense whatever. If God chose them to be saved, then their later acceptance of Jesus had nothing to do with free will. It was already determined. Ryrie is trying to have predestination without predestination.

On page 314 in the same book Ryrie's comments become even more muddled when he says, "To be sure, election assures that those chosen will be saved, but it alone does not save them. People are saved through faith in the substitutionary death of Christ. . . . Election, the death of Christ, testimony of His death, and personal faith are all necessary in the salvation of an individual. Election alone does not save."

Nonsense! Of course election alone saves. If an individual is elected, he's automatically saved. That's axiomatic. How could someone be elected and simultaneously be lost? It is a contradiction in terms. If a person is lost, then he was not elected.

On page 315 Ryrie further struggles with this problem by providing the following illustrations. He says, "Does God know the day you are going to die? The answer is yes. He does. Question: could you die a day sooner? The answer is no. Question: why do you eat? Answer: to live. . . . Suppose I do not eat? Then I will die. Would that be the day God planned that I should die? These are questions that do not need to be asked or answered. Just eat." Yes, they do need to be asked and answered, because they go to the heart of this gobbledygook. Ryrie seeks to evade the problem and proceed to other matters, because he knows no answer exists.

Finally, on the same page, Ryrie states, "Does God know who are elect? Of course, He elected them. Can any of them be lost? No. Then why pray and witness? Because that is how they will be saved." How can this be true? That's not how they will be saved. They were already saved. Ryrie goes on, "Will any of them fail to believe? No. Then why do they have to believe? Because that is the only way they can be saved, and unless they do believe they will not be saved." Again, more gobbledygook. If your salvation has already been fixed then what you believe is irrelevant.

Ryrie concludes in the only way he can after constructing this monstrous pile of muddle: "Do not let your mind ask the theoretical and useless questions." In other words, don't think. Just listen and believe and above all do not dwell on this problem. It's a good source for tangled thought processes and migraine headaches. But, then, didn't Ryrie admit earlier that faith takes off where reason ends?

On page 254 in *Dr. Rice Here Is My Question* Rice was asked to explain predestination and immediately leaped into the mire by saying, "Predestination is taught in Romans 8:28–29, and simply means that God knows ahead of time who will trust Him." Wrong, wrong, wrong! God does *not* just know something ahead of time. He determines it. He fixes it. It is his idea. That is a big difference. On page 141 in *The Bible Has the Answer* apologists Morris and Clark clearly show the Bible does not have the answer by saying,

It is not contradictory therefore, but rather complementary, to hold that man determines his own decisions and actions and yet also to recognize that God in some inscrutable way has foreordained those very things. Although admitting we cannot really understand this paradox, we accept both aspects of it by faith and then act accordingly, trusting God to make it all clear in eternity.

Talk about blind, unquestioning adherence to a blatant contradiction, this is it! Again we see faith as that realm beyond reason into which people wander at their own peril. "Paradox" is merely a euphemism for a massive contradiction. Every time Christians admit they have no adequate reply, we are told God will provide an answer in the great beyond.

Apologist Barry Wood only adds to the miasma by saying on page 116 in *Questions Non-Christians Ask,* "Everything Paul says about predestination applies only to those who are already saved. The Bible nowhere says the lost person is predestined to go to hell or heaven." Utterly false! Obviously, everyone *must* be predestined either to heaven or hell, since there is no third option. And unless everyone is predestined to go to heaven, some must be predestined for hell. Moreover, can Wood provide scriptural support for his allegation that predestination only applies to those who are saved?

On page 117 he says, "How do you leave room for man's free will to accept or reject God's call? We must admit this a difficult thing to understand. Just read Romans 9 through 11 and see if Paul understands it. He didn't! He was left with a paradox."

I say, don't be elusive. It is not difficult to understand; it is impossible to understand and that is why Paul's position is paradoxical.

And Wood concludes by saying on page 119, "I know this is a mind bender."

That's an understatement if ever there was one. Every contradiction is a mind bender, and this is one of the bendiest.

The clearest admission of all, however, is found on page 281 of *Today's Handbook for Solving Bible Difficulties,* in which Christian spokesman David O'Brien says,

> Using one of the basic rules of interpretation, the clearest, simplest reading of Romans 9 is that God predestines and those who are predestined play no active part in the Divine decree. As a lifelong Arminian, it grieves me to admit this, but that's the simplest reading of the text. Read in this way, Paul is presenting a picture of God making such decisions that please Him, for reasons that only He can know or understand, and carrying out those decisions without the consent, cooperation, or resistance of the people involved.

All O'Brien is saying is that the behavior of everything and everybody was fixed from the beginning and people are only acting out a predetermined scenario written by God. If that isn't injustice in action and a blatant refutation of the declaration in Deut. 32:4, that God is just, I don't know what is.

Universalism

The fifth and final road to salvation is one of the more interesting biblical teachings, and fundamentalists detest with all the vigor of a segregationist expounding on the need for separation of the races. It is the concept of universalism, i.e., the belief that *everyone* is going to be saved, regardless, with no exceptions. Apologists deny that this concept has any biblical basis and seek to avoid the topic and all relevant verses as much as possible. But, unfortunately, for them, universalist salvation cannot be shoved under the rug. Although universalism is subject to criticism, (what biblical concept isn't!), there are at least eighteen verses that lend impressive, if not convincing, credence thereto.

Those most often cited by universalists are: John 12:32, "I, if I [Jesus] be be lifted up from the earth, will draw all men unto me"; 1 Tim. 4:10, "We trust in the living God, who is the Saviour of all men, specially of those that believe" (notice Jesus says he is the savior of *all* men, *especially* those who believe, not *just* those who believe); 1 Cor. 15:22, "As in Adam all die, even so in Christ shall all be made alive"; Mark 3:28, "Verily I say unto you, All sins shall be forgiven unto the sons of men, and blasphemies wherewith soever they shall blaspheme"; Rom. 5:18, "Therefore as by the offense of one judgment came upon all men to condemnation; even so by the righteousness of one the free gift came upon all men unto justification of life"; Rom. 11:32 (RSV), "For God has consigned all to disobedience, that he may have mercy upon all"; 1 John 2:2, "He is the propitiation for our sins; and not for ours only, but also for the sins of the whole world"; and John 1:29, "Behold the Lamb of God, which taketh away the sin of the world."

Other relevant verses of less potency are: John 1:9, "That was the true Light, which lighteth every man that cometh into the world"; 1 Tim. 2:4, "Who will have all men to be saved, and to come unto the knowledge of the truth"; Titus 2:11, "For the grace of God that bringeth salvation hath appeared to all men"; Heb. 2:9, "But we see Jesus, who was made a little lower than the angels for the suffering of death, crowned with glory and honor; that he by the grace of God should taste death for every man"; 2 Cor. 5:19, "To wit, that God was in Christ, reconciling the world unto himself, not imputing their trespasses unto them; and hath committed unto us the word of reconciliation"; Eph. 1:10, "That in the dispensation of the fulness of times he might gather together in one all things in Christ, both which are in heaven, and which are on earth; even in him"; Acts 3:21, "Whom the heaven must receive until the times of restitution of all things, which God hath spoken by the mouth of all his holy prophets since the world began"; Col. 1:19-20, "It pleased the Father that in him should all fulness dwell; And having made peace through the blood of his cross, by him to reconcile all things unto himself"; 2 Peter 3:9, "The Lord is not slack concerning his promise, as some men count slackness; but is long suffering to us-ward, not willing that any should perish but that all should come to repentance"; and Phil. 2:10.

With verses such as these, is it any wonder that universalism has always had adherents within the Christian community?

Other verses say we are saved by "calling on the name of the Lord" (Acts 2:21, Joel 2:32, Rom. 10:13), "hoping" (Rom. 8:24), "fearing the Lord" (Acts 10:35), and "eating Jesus" (John 6:50-51, 53-54, and 57-58). These verses only add to the muddle of how we are saved.

Annihilationism

A final outcome that can be easily supported by biblical verses, but does not belong among the five means by which one can be saved, is annihilationism, the belief that there is no salvation for anyone to begin with. In this understanding of the afterlife, there is no sense in worrying about works versus faith versus predestination versus grace versus universalism, because no one is going anywhere, except to oblivion. This is probably the most definitive view of all and was relegated to the end of our monologue because no means to salvation are provided for anyone.

The most powerful verses in support of annihilationism are the found in Eccles. Verse 9:5 says, "For the living know that they shall die; but the dead know not any thing, neither have they any more a reward: for the memory of them is forgotten." Even more strongly, verses 3:19–21 declare,

> For that which befalleth the sons of men befalleth beasts; even one thing befalleth them: as one dieth, so dieth the other; yea they all have one breath; so that a man hath no preeminence above a beast: for all is vanity. All go to one place; all are of the dust, and all turn to dust again. Who knoweth whether the spirit of man goeth upward and the spirit of the beast goeth downward to the earth?

That is about as definitive as one can be. If this passage is true, then every road to salvation is useless. If man has no preeminence, then all efforts to improve one's standing in a world to come are for nought. On page 343 in *Dr. Rice, Here Is My Question* Rice is asked if animals have an afterlife. He answers, "I believe the Bible is clear that animals do not have an immortal soul in the same sense that people do. They are not made in the image of God. They have no life after death. There is nothing in the Bible about animals being redeemed."

In this Rice conveniently ignores Eccles. 3:19–21, which considers man to be no better off in this respect. Animals are going wherever humanity is going, and if animals have no life after death, then neither does man. The passage clearly states man has no preeminence and all the earth's creatures go to one place. If animals only go down into the dust, but man can go to heaven, then man does have preeminence over the beasts. That would mean there were two places, not one, and "one thing does not befall them all."

Another relevant verse is Ps. 88:10, which says, "Wilt thou shew wonders to the dead? shall the dead arise and praise thee?"

So annihilationism can be supported biblically and all but destroys any hope of salvation for anyone. It all but negates the entire subject of salvation and renders all relevant commentaries moot.

Heaven

Finally we come to a topic that is near and dear to the hearts of all Christians. From a biblical and theological perspective what is the most important goal of nearly every believer? Why so much concern about salvation or being saved? To what end are their efforts directed; what's it all for? In a nutshell, it's to save souls from hell and for heaven. Jesus is only a means to that end; he is not the end in itself. The overriding purpose is to ferry people into that realm of eternal bliss known as heaven. As far as theology is concerned, all the preaching, all the writing, all the time, effort, and money are geared toward that one overarching, all-encompassing aspiration. But, unfortunately, very few of heaven's pursuers have seriously considered the biblical problems and ramifications associated with this concept. They just haven't thought it through.

Biblically speaking, seven verses and a parable attribute qualities to heaven that range from unacceptable to loathsome. Why would anyone want to cross its threshold in light of Rev. 12:7, which says, "There was war in heaven; Michael and his angels fought against the dragon; and the dragon fought and his angels." Heaven is supposed to be a perfect place, yet this account declares that it experienced a war. How could there have been a war in a perfect place and if it happened before, why couldn't it occur again? Why would anyone want to enter a region for eternity in which war can occur, when that is precisely what most people are trying to avoid?

Further, everyone in heaven must be perfect, so how could a war have occurred? On page 177 in *I'm Glad You Asked* Boa and Moody state,

> A system that demands less than perfection must allow some evil, and, therefore, must ask God to approve of this evil. If God allowed imperfect people into heaven, then heaven would no longer be perfect. Heaven is without suffering and sin, not just a place where there is minimal suffering and sin . . . for heaven would soon look like earth if imperfect people were allowed in.

Very true, so how could a war have happened in heaven? Other verses are equally critical: Rev. 19:14 says, "The armies which were in heaven followed him upon white horses." Again, we have the incongruity of war in heaven. Matt. 11:12 says, "From the days of John the Baptist until now the kingdom of heaven suffereth violence and the violent take it by force." Suffering and violence in a perfect place? Matt. 11:11 says, "He that is least in the Kingdom of heaven is greater than he." How can heaven, the perfect place, have inequality and levels of status? Matt. 16:19 says, "I will give unto thee the keys of the kingdom of heaven: and whatsoever thou shalt bind on earth shall be bound in heaven." How could people be bound or restrained in a perfect place of freedom? But, then again, perhaps it isn't that free? Matt. 24:35 says, "Heaven and earth shall pass away, but my words shall not pass away." Heaven will pass away? Why seek a place that will eventually vanish and how can one spend eternity there? To forestall the back-to-the-Greek defense and reliance upon the assertion that the word "Heaven" is only referring to the sky above, we should note that the word in this verse comes from the Greek word *ouranos* which is the only word used for "heaven" in all the Gospels.

Matt. 13:33 and Luke 13:20–21 say, "The Kingdom of heaven is like unto leaven, which a woman took, and hid in three measures of meal, till the whole was leavened." How can heaven be utopian when it is comparable to leaven, considered a contaminant in numerous other places in the Bible: 1 Cor. 5:8 ("Let us keep the feast, not with old leaven, neither with the leaven of malice and wickedness; but with the unleavened bread of sincerity and truth"); Lev. 10:12 ("Moses spake unto Aaron. . . . Take the meat offering that remaineth of the offerings of the Lord made by fire, and eat it without leaven . . . for it must be holy"); 1 Cor. 5:6 (RSV) ("Your boasting is not good. Do you not know that a little leaven leavens the whole lump?"); Luke 12:1 ("He began to say unto his disciples first of all, Beware ye of the leaven of the Pharisees, which is hypocrisy"); and Mark 8:15. So clearly, leaven is a nefarious addition, a pollutant, a corruption, and for heaven to be compared to leaven diminishes its attraction immensely.

Lastly, we have a parable in Matt. 20:1-16 (RSV) that demonstrates that heaven is the antithesis of justice in action. Briefly stated, the parable is as follows: Early one morning an estate owner went out and hired some workers for his field at a certain wage [one denarius] per day. Three, six, nine, and eleven hours later he hired additional workers. Yet everyone received the same amount of money that evening. In Matt. 20:1 Jesus equated this arrangement with heaven. Those who worked the entire day protested and Jesus related the dialogue that occurred. "On receiving it they grumbled at the householder, saying, 'These last worked only one hour, and you have made them equal to us who have borne the burden of the day and the scorching heat.' But he replied to one of them, 'Friend, I am doing you no wrong; did you not agree with me for a denarius? Take what belongs to you, and go; I choose to give to this last as I give to you. Am I not allowed to do what I choose with what belongs to me?' " If that is heaven, Christians are pursuing the kind of environment that's all too prevalent on earth today. I'm tempted to say, heaven help them. But obviously that is no answer. Like war, it is precisely the kind of condition nearly everyone is trying to avoid. For Jesus to quote the landowner (God) as saying, "Friend I am doing you no wrong" is enough to create a total rejection of both Jesus and heaven.

These are only a few of the many questions that must be addressed by those who take heaven seriously and seek to provide a rationale. Questions of this nature are of immense import because millions of people are literally staking their lives on its existence. Everything they do and say is done with an eye on that final arena, the expected reward. Believers should realize that problems as potent as any found throughout the Bible accompany the whole concept.

Conclusion

All of the foregoing clearly proves that not only is the biblical road to salvation vague and conflicting but that which faces those who travel its circuitous path is restrictive, iniquitous, and capricious.

17

Biblical History I

Old and New Testament Fallacies, Jesus' Trial and Execution, Population, Liberalism, Forty

Anyone acquainted with the Bible knows that the Book is saturated with historical figures and events. Indeed, in many respects they comprise the very core of its narrative. But what believers are rarely shown by apologetic scholars and other spokesmen for Christianity are the numerous historical inaccuracies permeating Scripture from beginning to end. This area of difficulty alone is sufficient to dethrone the Bible as an answer to mankind's problems. There are more than enough historical mistakes to prove beyond any doubt that the Bible is far from inerrant and couldn't possibly be the word of a perfect being. Historical problems, inconsistencies, improbabilities, and contradictions comprise a significant part of Scripture and related extrabiblical information. Arranged in order from Genesis to Revelation, the following examples are more than sufficient to substantiate the Bible's historical *un*reliability.

Old Testament Fallacies

First, if Noah was 500 years old when he begat Shem, as Gen. 5:32 says and 600 years old at the time of the Flood as Gen. 7:6 says, then Shem had to have been 100 years old at the time of the Flood and 102 years old when he begat Arphaxad two years after the Flood. Yet Gen. 11:10 says Shem was 100 years old, not 102, when he became the father of Arphaxad two years after the flood.

333

Second, according to Gen. 11:1 and 11:6 there was one world language when the Tower of Babel was created. Yet, one chapter earlier, in Gen. 10:5 (NIV), we are told, "The maritime peoples spread out into their territories by their clans within their nations, each with its own language."

How could languages have been created at the Tower of Babel in Gen. 11 when Gen. 10:5 shows a variety of languages existed before the tower appeared?

Third, if Abraham's father, Terah, was 70 years old when Abraham was born, as Gen. 11:26 says, and Abraham left Haran at age 75 after his father died, as Gen. 12:4 and Acts 7:4 say, then Terah could not have lived beyond the age of 145, i.e., 70 + 75. Yet Gen. 11:32 says Terah lived to be 205 and died in Haran. To state the same problem another way, if Terah was 70 years old when Abraham was born and Terah died at age 205, then Abraham was 135 years old when Terah died. Yet, Abraham was only 75 years old when he left Haran *after* the death of his father. In essence, we are supposed to believe that Abraham was only 75 years old after having lived 135 years.

Fourth, Exod. 1:15–16 (RSV) says, "The king of Egypt said to the Hebrew midwives, one of whom was named Shiphrah and the other Puah, 'When you serve as midwife to the Hebrew women, and see them upon the birthstool, if it is a son, you shall kill him; but if it is a daughter, she shall live.' " Would the pharaoh have entrusted the execution of a command on which he thought the safety of his kingdom depended to *Hebrew* slaves, especially when it involved harsh measures against the Hebrew people?

Fifth, Exod. 12:40 says the children of Israel lived in Egypt for 430 years. However, when read in conjunction with Ex. 6:18 and 6:20 the following problems emerge. Kohath, Jacob's grandson, who went down into Egypt with Jacob, lived 133 years. Kohath's son was Amram, who lived 137 years. According to Ex. 7:7 Amram's son was Moses, who was 80 years old when the Israelites left Egypt. This would mean the Israelites could not have been in Egypt longer than 350 years (133 years for Kohath + 137 years for Amram + 80 years for Moses). Even if Kohath had been born the day the Israelites entered Egypt, the Hebrews could not have been in Egypt longer than 350, years which is in direct conflict with the 430 years claimed in Exod. 12:40.

Sixth, Num. 14:33 says, "Your children shall wander in the wilderness for 40 years." Does "wander" mean "be lost"? If so, how could hundreds of thousands of people be lost for forty years in an area only four hundred miles wide as its widest part?

Seventh, Josh. 10:12–14 (NIV) says,

On the day the Lord gave the Amorites over to Israel, Joshua said to the Lord in the presence of Israel: O sun, stand still over Gibeon, O moon, over the Valley of Aijalon. So the sun stood still, and the moon stopped, till the nation avenged itself on its enemies. . . . The sun stopped in the middle of the sky and delayed going down about a full day. There has never been a day like it before or since, a day when the Lord listened to a man.

To add idiocy to nonsense 2 Kings 20:11 (NIV) says, "Then the prophet Isaiah called upon the Lord, and the Lord made the shadow go back the 10 steps it had gone down on the stairway of Ahaz." Naturally the sudden arrest of the earth's motion, much less a reversal of its direction, would have caused a worldwide catastrophe of the first magnitude. The sun has never stopped its apparent forward motion or appeared to reverse direction, and the Bible is only propagating as history what belongs in the realm of mythology.

Eighth, one of the more intriguing bits of historical fabrication concerns the Amalekites. According to 1 Sam. 15:7-8, Saul smote the Amalekites and "'utterly destroyed them." In Isa. 27 we find these same Amalekites destroyed by David. Passing on to Isa. 30 we learn that the Amalekites were once again wiped out, with the exception of four hundred young men "which rode on camels and fled." And finally, in the days of Hezekiah, this much-lived people were once more exterminated "positively" and for the last time, according to G. W Foote, editor of *Freethinker* magazine. The Amalekites just wouldn't stay dead. Apparently more than just cats have nine lives.

Ninth, 2 Sam. 5:6-7 (NIV) says, "The king [David] and his men marched to Jerusalem to attack the Jebusites, who lived there. The Jebusites said to David, 'You will not get in here; even the blind and the lame can ward you off.' They thought, 'David cannot get in here.' Nevertheless, David captured the fortress of Zion, the City of David [Jerusalem]."

These verses clearly leave the impression that David could not, and did not, enter Jerusalem until the events in 2 Samuel 5. Yet, back in 1 Sam. 17:54 we find that, "David took the Philistine's head and brought it to Jerusalem."

How could David have taken Goliath's head to Jerusalem in 1 Samuel, when it was a still a Jebusite city from which David was excluded as late as 2 Samuel 5? The duel between David and Goliath and the subsequent entry of David into Jerusalem with Goliath's head, as related in 1 Samuel, is said to have occurred in 1062 B.C., while the conquest and initial occupancy of Jerusalem by the Israelites related in 2 Samuel occurred in 1047 B.C., fifteen years later.

Tenth, regarding the house that Solomon built for the lord, 1 Kings 5:15-16 (NIV) says, "Solomon had 70,000 carriers and 80,000 stonecutters in the hills, as well as 3,300 foremen who supervised the project and directed the workmen"; 1 Kings 6:2 (RSV) says, "The house which Solomon built for the Lord was 60 cubits long, 20 cubits wide, and 30 cubits high," and 1 Kings 6:38 (RSV) says, "he was 7 years in building it."

Imagine. It took 153,300 men 7 years to build a house that was 96 by 32 by 48 feet. The elephant labored and bore a mouse.

Eleventh, 1 Kings 6:1 says, "The four hundred and eightieth year after the

Israelites came out of Egypt was the fourth year of Solomon's reign over Israel."
Yet Acts 13:17–20 (NIV) says that God "led them out of that country and endured
their conduct forty years in the desert. He overthrew seven nations in Canaan
and gave their land to his people as their inheritance. All of this took about
450 years. After this, God gave them judges until the time of Samuel the prophet."
If there were 450 years from the time the Israelites left Egypt until rule by
judges began, and there were 480 years between the time they left Egypt until
the fourth year of Solomon's reign as 1 Kings 6:1 says, then the judges, Saul
and David, both of whom lived before Solomon, could only have ruled for a
total of 26 years (480 years minus 450 years minus the 4 years used by Judge
Solomon). Yet 2 Sam. 5:4 shows that David, alone, ruled for 40 years.

Twelfth, 1 Kings 10:14 (NIV) says, "The weight of the gold that Solomon
received yearly was 666 talents, not including the revenues from merchants and
traders and from all the Arabian kings and the governors of the land."

A talent of gold is worth a little over $30,000 in 1994 dollars. Just picture
that! Solomon, the chief of a petty, barren district of Asia Minor without significant
arts, manufacturing, or civilization received $20,000,000 ($30,000 × 666 talents)
per year. Yet the Roman emperor of the time received only $22,000,000 per year
from all of his Asiatic provinces.

Thirteenth, 1 Kings 16:23 (RSV) says, "In the 31st year of Asa king of Judah,
Omri began to reign over Israel, and reigned for 12 years." This conflicts with
1 Kings 16:28–29 (RSV), which says, "Omri slept with his fathers . . . and Ahab
his son reigned in his stead. In the 38th year of Asa king of Judah, Ahab the
son of Omri began to reign over Israel."

How could Omri have reigned twelve years, if he ruled from the thirty-first
to the thirty-eighth year of Asa's rule? That's seven years, not twelve. Or stated
another way, how could Ahab have taken over from his father Omri in the thirty-
eighth year of Asa's rule, when Omri didn't give up his rule until the forty-third
year of Asa's rule? After all, 31 + 12 = 43.

Fourteenth, according to 2 Kings 15:19, "Pul the King of Assyria came against
the land." Assyria never had a king named Pul. Scholar John Remsburg says
the king who reigned in Assyria at that particular time was Iva-bish.

Fifteenth, 2 Kings 18:1 (NIV) says, "In the third year of Hoshea . . . king
of Israel, Hezekiah . . . king of Judah began to reign." That seems simple enough
until we read verse 13, which says, "In the fourteenth year of King Hezekiah's
reign, Sennacherib King of Assyria attacked all the fortified cities of Judah and
captured them."

The problem is that the third year of Hoshea was no later than 728 B.C.
The fourteenth year of Hezekiah's reign, therefore, would be around 714 B.C.,
14 years later. But Sennacherib did not come to the throne of Nineveh until
705 B.C. and, according to his own *Annals,* the invasion of Judah took place

in 701 B.C. Therefore, the invasion by Sennacherib must have occurred in the twenty-seventh year of Hezekiah's reign, not the fourteenth.

Sixteenth, 2 Kings 19:35 says, "It came to pass that night, that an angel of the Lord went out, and smote in the camp of the Assyrians an hundred fourscore and five thousand [185,000]: and when they arose early in the morning, behold they were all dead corpses." This is incredible history. An army of 185,000 men is killed by an angel. Then its members *arise* the next morning to find that each of them is dead. Each of its members realizes he is dead.

Seventeenth, 1 Chron. 22:14 (RSV) says, "With great pains I [David] have provided for the house of the Lord 100,000 talents of gold, a million talents of silver."

By today's standards the gold collected by David amounted to $3 billion and the silver amounted to $2 billion. In effect, we are supposed to believe that David, who ruled a small area at the eastern end of the Mediterranean, gathered more bullion than was possessed by the Roman Empire at the height of its power.

Eighteenth, 2 Chron. 2:12 says, "Huram said moreover, Blessed be the Lord God of Israel that made heaven and earth." Huram, king of Tyre, was not a Jew. Would he have said that the God of Israel made heaven and earth?

Nineteenth, 2 Chron. 7:5 (RSV) says, "King Solomon offered as a sacrifice 22,000 oxen and 120,000 sheep." These numbers are nothing short of incredible in light of the fact that these animals were killed within one week. That would have required the continual killing and burning of five oxen and twenty-four sheep every minute for the entire seven days, assuming the average of twelve hours per day of daylight were allotted for work.

Twentieth, 2 Chron. 21:20 (RSV) says, "He [Jehoram] was 32 years old when he began to reign, and he reigned 8 years in Jerusalem; and he departed with no one's regret. They buried him in the city of David." Obviously Jehoram must have left the throne at age forty (32 + 8 = 40). But incredibly, 2 Chron. 22:1–2 says, "The inhabitants of Jerusalem made Ahaziah his youngest son king in his stead. . . . Ahaziah was 42 years old when he began to reign." If Jehoram began to reign at age thirty-two and ruled eight years, then he died at age forty. Yet his son took over at age forty-two. How could a son be two years older than his father? How could a forty-two-year-old son take over from his forty-year-old father?

Twenty-first, Ezra 1:2 says, "Thus saith Cyrus king of Persia, The Lord God of heaven hath given me all the kingdoms of the earth." When did Cyrus rule all the world or even all the known world for that matter?

Twenty-second, Isa. 44:14 says, "He planteth an ash, and the rain doth nourish it." Not in Western Asia. Ash trees do not grow there. Some commentators think a pine was meant.

Twenty-third, Isa. 44:28 says, "He [Cyrus] is my [God's] shepherd and shall perform all my pleasure: even saying to Jerusalem, Thou shalt be built; and to the temple, Thy foundation shall be laid".

How could Isaiah have written this, since he died around 698 B.C., and Cyrus's decree in favor of the Jews returning to Jerusalem, described here, did not occur until 536 B.C., 162 years later? Biblicists will say this is merely an accurate prophecy, while some knowledgeable authorities say the story was written long after the event.

Twenty-fourth, Dan. 5:30-31 (RSV) says, "That very night Belshazzar the Chaldean king was slain. And Darius the Mede received the kingdom [the Chaldean kingdom of Babylon] being about 62 years old." The difficulties here are: (a) Belshazzar was not the king of Babylon or the Chaldean Empire. Nabonidus was the king of Babylon when the Chaldean Empire expired. Belshazzar was his son; (b) Darius never took the kingdom nor was he ever king of Babylon; (c) There is no reference to Darius the Mede in any ancient document currently known; and (d) profane history says it was Cyrus the Persian who conquered the Babylonian empire.

Twenty-fifth, Dan. 5:2 (NIV) says, "While Belshazzar was drinking his wine, he gave orders to bring in the gold and silver goblets that Nebuchadnezzar his father had taken from the temple." Nebuchadnezzar was not the father of Belshazzar. Unlike the KJV, the Modern Language Version admits as much by calling Nebuchadnezzar his grandfather.

Twenty-sixth and lastly, one of the more renowned historical problems arises when we compare. Exod. 12:40, which says the children of Israel lived in Egypt 430 years, to Gal. 3:16-17 (NIV), which says, "The promises were spoken to Abraham and to his seed. . . . What I mean is this: The law, introduced 430 years later, does not set aside the covenant previously established by God and thus do away with the promise."

This means Israel got the Law 430 years after Abraham got the Covenant. If what Paul says in Galatians is true, then Abraham must have gotten the Covenant on the day the Israelites entered Egypt and the Israelites must have gotten the Law on the day they left Egypt, *or* Abraham got the Covenant before they entered Egypt and the Israelites got the Law while they lived in Egypt, which clearly violates the historical scenario in the Book of Exodus. How could the Israelites have been in Egypt for 430 years, as related in Exod. 12:40, if the Law was given 430 years after the Covenant was given to Abraham?

In summary, the Old Testament is clearly plagued by historical problems of immense importance.

New Testament Fallacies

The New Testament is also amply supplied with historical inaccuracies.

First, Matt. 2:1 (RSV) says, "When Jesus was born in Bethlehem of Judea in the days of Herod the king." There was no such person as Herod the King because the Jews were under the control of Roman emperors who ruled by governors or tetrarchs, not kings.

Second, Matt. 2:16 (NIV) says, "When Herod realized that he had been outwitted by the Magi, he was furious, and he gave orders to kill all the boys in Bethlehem and its vicinity who were 2 years old and under." This verse raises three problems: (a) Josephus devoted nearly forty chapters to the life of Herod and relates every important event in his life. He detested Herod and dwelled on his crimes and errors. Yet he never mentioned this massacre and appears to have known nothing about it; (b) No ancient historian recalls this massacre; and (c), Herod already had full-grown sons to succeed him. Why would a ruler fear being supplanted by the babe of an obscure Nazarene carpenter?

Third, Matt. 2:22 (RSV) says, "When he [Joseph] heard that Archelaus reigned over Judea in place of his father Herod, he was afraid to go there, and being warned in a dream he withdrew to the district of Galilee." The problem with this is that a son of Herod also reigned in Galilee; so how could he have been more secure there than in Judea?

Fourth, Matt. 8:32 (RSV) says, "He [Jesus] said to them [the devils], Go. So they came out and went into the swine." These swine are as imaginary as the devils mentioned, since the keeping of swine was prohibited in ancient Judea and Galilee. The French philosopher Voltaire wanted to know how swine could have been there to start with.

Fifth, Matt. 23:35 says, "That upon you [the Pharisees and scribes] may come all the righteous blood shed upon the earth, from the blood of righteous Abel unto the blood of Zacharias son of Barachias, whom ye slew between the temple and the altar."

This verse is fraught with problems.

(a) How could the Pharisees and scribes be responsible for Abel's death and those of his immediate righteous successors, since he lived long before they did?

(b) The Zacharias mentioned was actually killed in Jerusalem in A.D. 69. Jesus is accusing people of killing a man who was yet to die. He was the same Zacharias Barouchos who, according to Josephus, was slain in the temple a short time before the destruction of Jerusalem in A.D. 70. There is no other man known to history to whom this passage could apply, according to several scholars.

(c) Several apologists seek to resolve the problem by contending Zacharias is actually the Zechariah of Old Testament fame. The problem with this lies in the fact that the accusation of Jesus was intended to cover all the time from the first offense to the last. If this is referring to the Zechariah of 2 Chron. 24:20, then that would mean no righteous blood was shed from his day to that of Jesus, 850 years later. After all, the passage refers to all the righteous blood shed upon the earth from Abel to Zecharias. What about the righteous blood shed *after* Zecharias? Since all the righteous blood shed between Zechariah and the Pharisees of Jesus' day would be excluded, all of the time from the first offense to the last would *not* be covered.

Sixth, Matt. 27:38 says, "Then there were two thieves crucified with him, one on the right hand, and the other on the left." Thieves were not crucified. Theft was not even a capital offense in the Roman Empire, being contrary to both Jewish and Roman law.

Seventh, Matt. 27:51–53 says, "The veil of the temple was rent in twain from the top to the bottom; and the earth did quake, and the rocks rent; and the graves were opened; and many bodies of the saints which slept arose, and came out of the graves after his resurrection, and went into the holy city, and appeared unto many." As incredible as these events are, no historian of antiquity mentions them. In addition, how could there be "saints" before the church created canonization and set up the saint calendar? Jews had no saints.

Eighth, Mark 1:4 (RSV) says, "John the baptizer appeared in the wilderness, preaching a baptism of repentance." The only extrabiblical evidence of John the Baptist's existence is a passage in *The Antiquities* of the historian Josephus (book 18, chapter 5, section 2), which appears to be an interpolation (a forgery). Herod had put away his wife, who was the daughter of Aretas. In response, Aretas defeated Herod, who appealed to the Roman emperor Tiberius for help. Tiberius sent Vitellius, a Syrian governor. Then follows an account of John the Baptist. From that, the narrative returns to Vitellius, saying that he prepared to make war with Aretas. How the passage on John the Baptist relates to the narrative one can only guess and for that reason it appears to be spurious.

Ninth, Mark 7:31 says, "He came unto the sea of Galilee, through the midst of the coasts of Decapolis." This statement was made by Mark when there were no coasts of Decapolis. The name was not known before the reign of Emperor Nero.

Tenth, Mark 14:3 states, "And being in Bethany in the house of Simon the leper, as he sat at meat."

This is highly improbable, since lepers could not legally live in the cities.

Eleventh, Mark 15:33 says, "When the sixth hour was come, there was darkness over the whole land until the ninth hour." There is no mention of this event by any secular historian of that period.

Twelfth, Mark 15:46 (NIV) says, "So Joseph [of Arimathea] bought some linen cloth, took down the body, wrapped it in the linen, and placed it in a tomb cut out of rock." This account is rejected by many critics because a member of the Sanhedrin wouldn't desecrate the Passover by making a purchase of linen that day as occurred in this instance.

Thirteenth, Luke 2:46 states of the child Jesus, "It came to pass, that after three days they found him in the temple, sitting in the midst of the doctors, both hearing them, and asking them questions." Not until the time of Gamaliel in the middle of the first century A.D. was a child allowed to sit in the presence of rabbis.

Fourteenth, Luke 23:12 (RSV) states, "Herod and Pilate became friends with each other that very day, for before they had been at enmity with each other."

Pilate and Herod were enemies to the day of Pilate's recall by Rome. Herod was continually plotting to unite his Galilee with Pilate's Judea, which Herod's father had promised him.

Fifteenth, Luke 23:33 says, "When they were come to the place, which is called Calvary, there they crucified him." If Jesus had been tried, convicted, and executed by the Jews, he would not have been crucified, but stoned. Jews never used crucifixion.

Sixteenth, John 2:20 (NIV) says, "The Jews replied, 'It has taken 46 years to build this temple.' " In book 15, chapter 11, section 6 of *The Jewish Antiquities* Josephus gives a full account of the building of the temple and says it took one and a half years. Herod built it between 19 and 17 B.C.

Seventeenth, John 11:49 (NIV) says, "One of them, named Caiaphas, who was high priest that year." This language implies that the high priest was appointed annually, whereas the office was occupied for life or until removal. Caiaphas had been high priest for many years.

Eighteenth, John 11:51–52 (RSV) says, "He [Caiaphas] did not say this of his own accord, but being high priest that year he prophesied that Jesus should die for the nation." Jews knew that prophesying was not a privilege or part of the high priest's office. A high priest did not assume the role of prophet, much less would he have uttered the prophecy ascribed to Caiaphas. It would have been foreign to the Jewish mind and for even one person to have been put to death to save all of Israel would have been murder.

Nineteenth, John 13:38 says, "Verily, verily, I, Jesus, say unto thee, The cock shall not crow, till thou hast denied me thrice."

Scholar English says cocks were not allowed in Jerusalem at that time.

Twentieth, according to John 19:6 Pilate said to them, "Take him, and crucify him: for I find no fault in him." The highest court of a country pronounced a man innocent and then condemned him to death! That's highly unlikely.

Twenty-first, John 19:31 says, "The Jews therefore . . . besought Pilate that their legs [Jesus' and the thieves'] might be broken, and that they might be taken away."

This punishment, known as crucifragium, was a distinct mode of execution and was never combined with crucifixion. Moreover, neither method was ever employed to punish theft.

Twenty-second, after the Resurrection, John 20:9 says, "as yet they knew not the Scripture." What Scripture? When this was written there was no Scripture about the death and resurrection, nor would there be for a hundred years.

Twenty-third, Acts 3:21 says, "Which God hath spoken by the mouth of all his holy prophets since the world began." What prophets were living when the world began?

Twenty-fourth, in Acts 5:36 (NIV) Gamaliel gives a speech before the Jewish council and says, "Some time ago Theudas appeared, claiming to be somebody, and about 400 men rallied to him. He was killed, all his followers were dispersed, and it all came to nothing."

Josephus says the revolt by Theudas referred to by Gamaliel occurred when Fadus was procurator of Judea, in A.D. 45 or 46. Yet Gamaliel made this speech earlier than A.D. 36. Many feel he spoke in A.D. 29. Thus, the author of Acts makes Gamaliel speak of an event as if it had already occurred which, in reality, did not happen until approximately sixteen years later.

Twenty-fifth, Acts 7:14–16 (NIV) says, "After this, Joseph [while in Egypt] sent for his father Jacob and his whole family, 75 in all. Then Jacob went down to Egypt, where he and our fathers died. Their bodies were brought back to Shechem and placed in the tomb that Abraham had bought from the sons of Hamor at Shechem for a certain sum of money." On pages 269 and 270 in *The Jew and the Christian Missionary* Gerald Sigal all but destroyed the validity of these verses by making the following points:

(a) Jacob's family that went down into Egypt, inclusive of Joseph and his sons, numbered 70 persons, not 75 (Gen. 46:27, Exod. 1:5, and Deut. 10:22).

(b) Jacob was not buried in the city of Shechem, but in the cave of Machpelah, which is located near the city of Hebron (Gen. 23:19, Gen. 49:29–30 and Gen. 50:13).

(c) The Hebrew Scriptures do not give any indication that the forefathers of the tribes of Israel were buried in Shechem. Only Joseph is said to have been buried there (Josh. 24:32).

(d) Abraham did not buy a tomb in Shechem. He bought the cave of Machpelah, which he used as a burial place, and which, as previously stated, is located near the city of Hebron (Gen. 23:19).

(e) The cave of Machpelah was not bought from the sons of Hamor, but from Ephron the Hittite (Gen. 23:17–18 and Gen. 50:13).

(f) It was Jacob, not Abraham, who purchased a piece of land near Shechem from the sons of Hamor. Gen. 33:19 and Josh. 24:32 show that the author of Acts confused the two purchases.

Twenty-sixth, one of the more involved passages is Luke 3:1–2, which says, "Now in the 15th year of the reign of Tiberius Caesar, Pontius Pilate being governor of Judea, and Herod being tetrarch of Galilee, . . . Lysanias the tetrarch of Abilene, Annas and Caiaphas being the high priests, the word of God came unto John the son of Zacharias in the wilderness."

Fundamental problems with these verses are: (a) How could John have gotten the word of God during the reign of Lysanias in Abilene when Lysanias had been dead for thirty-four years when John's contemporary, Jesus, was born? Lysanias was put to death at the instigation of Cleopatra sixty years before Jesus began his ministry, according to Josephus, in book 15, chapter, 4, section 1 of his *Jewish Antiquities*; (b) At the time mentioned by Luke the territory of Abila or Abilene was no longer a tetrarchy; and (c) Two people never held the office of high priest jointly, as is claimed for Annas and Caiaphas. It would have been the same as having two popes.

Twenty-seventh and lastly, another of the more involved historical problems arises from Luke 2:1-2, which says, "And it came to pass in those days, that there went out a decree from Caesar Augustus, that all the world should be taxed. (And this taxing was first made when Cyrenius was governor of Syria.)"

Basic problems with this are:

(a) History says nothing about a taxing (census) ever being taken of the whole Roman world. The KJV says, "All the world should be taxed"; yet no such decree was issued by Augustus. He not only never issued a general decree but never attempted a uniform assessment. Taxes were done province by province.

(b) When Jesus was born, the governor of Syria was not Cyrenius. Cyrenius did not become governor of Syria until nearly ten years after the death of Herod and Matt. 2:1 says Jesus was born during the reign of Herod: "Now when Jesus was born in Bethlehem of Judaea in the days of Herod the king."

(c) If Jesus was born during the reign of Herod as Matthew says, Joseph, whether a resident of Judea or of Galilee, could not have been taxed by Augustus in any event, since neither province was then a part of Roman Syria. Both provinces belonged to Herod's kingdom and Herod's subjects were not taxed by the Romans.

(d) Cyrenius made a census in Palestine but this occurred ten years after the death of Herod, during whose reign Jesus was born. On pages 87 and 88 in *Bible Difficulties* Arndt makes the following admission,

> We now come to the charge that Luke became guilty of an error in ascribing the governorship of Syria at the time of the birth of Jesus to Cyrenius. That we are here facing a difficulty is undeniable. . . . The list of Roman governors of Syria for the last years of the reign of Herod the Great (and it will be remembered that Jesus was born while Herod was still living) does not include Cyrenius. . . . Since Herod died in 4 B.C., Jesus must have been born about 6 to 4 B.C. . . . Cyrenius was not governor when the Savior appeared.

Well, it's good to know that at least one apologist is willing to face reality.

Jesus' Trial and Execution

Now we come to a biblical scenario that is exceptionally rich in contradictory data. Freethought literature has long noted the multitude of New Testament historical problems associated with Jesus' trial and subsequent events.

First, Mark 14:65 states, "Some began to spit on him, and to cover his face, and to buffet him, and to say unto him, Prophesy: and the servants did strike him with the palms of their hands." Every person acquainted with the Jewish history of that age knows this turmoil would not have been permitted. In the Sanhedrin and Roman courts, law, dignity, and decorum prevailed throughout.

Second, we read in Mark 14:61, "Art thou the Christ, the Son of the Blessed?" No Jew, especially a priest, would use the expression, "Christ, Son of the Blessed," or imply that the messiah was divine or blessed above others. That was not the Jewish view of the messiah.

Third, Mark 14:54 says, "Peter followed Jesus afar off, even into the palace of the high priest." No trial was ever held at the residence or palace of the high priest. All meetings of the Sanhedrin were held in the hall adjoining the temple. A trial at any other place would have been illegal.

Fourth, according to Mark 15:21, "They compelled one Simon, a Cyrenian, who passed by, coming out of the country, the father of Alexander and Rufus, to bear his cross." For Simon to have been compelled to carry the cross of Jesus is highly improbable, since in executions of this kind the criminal was always required to carry the instrument of crucifixion himself as a mark of disgrace.

Fifth, Mark 15:42 states, "When the even was come, because it was the preparation, that is the day before the sabbath." The sabbath began at sunset on the day that Jesus is declared to have been crucified. Jewish law would not permit a dead body to be exposed on the sabbath. Since crucifixion is a lingering death often lasting several days, it is unlikely the Jews would have demanded that punishment commence on Friday when they knew Jesus would not have been taken down for many hours, if not days, including all or part of the sabbath.

Sixth, we read in Luke 22:15 that Jesus "said unto them, With desire I have desired to eat the passover with you before I suffer." The Synoptic gospels, Matthew, Mark, and Luke, say that the trial was held during the feast of the Passover. Yet that wouldn't be possible since no trials were held by the Jews during this feast.

Seventh, John 18:39 (RSV) says, "You have a custom that I [Pilate] should release one man for you at the Passover; will you have me release for you the King of the Jews?" And Mark 15:6 says, "Now at that feast [Pilate] released unto them one prisoner, whomsoever they desired." There is no historical authority or precedent whatever for this alleged custom. No Roman government could have safely adopted it.

Eighth, Luke 22:66–67 says, "As soon as it was day, the elders of the people and the chief priests and the scribes came together, and led him into their council, saying, Art thou the Christ? tell us."

Several problems accompany these verses:

(a) Jesus is being questioned by the Sanhedrin, a Jewish court. Yet Jewish courts did not question a prisoner. He could not even plead guilty, according to some authorities.

(b) According to the Synoptics, Jesus apparently had no lawyer. The Jewish scholar Maimonides said this would have been against Jewish law.

(c) According to the Synoptics the trial lasted only a few hours. Yet Jewish law required at least two days for a capital offense—one day for the prosecution, one day for the defense.

(d) The Synoptics say that the trial was held on Friday, the day before the Sabbath. But no trial for a capital offense was ever allowed to begin on the day before the Sabbath.

(e) By having Jesus appear before Annas, Caiaphas, Pilate, and Herod, the authorities subjected him to four legal proceedings, if not trials, in one day, which would have been illegal.

(f) And lastly, according to Luke, the trial might have occurred during the day, while Matthew and Mark say it started during the night. The trial could not have been held during the night, as Matthew and Mark allege, because Jewish law prohibited the opening of a trial at night. The Sanhedrin could not hold a session before 6 A.M. or after 3 P.M.

Ninth, John 19:1-3 states, "Pilate therefore took Jesus, and scourged him. And the soldiers platted a crown of thorns, and put it on his head, and they put on him a purple robe, and said, Hail, King of the Jews! and they smote him with their hands."

Jesus is said to have suffered indignities at the hands of a Roman court. But every lawyer knows Roman courts were models of decorum for a thousand years. Scourging was often inflicted by the Romans before execution, but never before conviction and sentencing.

Tenth, John 19:12 says, "Pilate sought to release him: but the Jews cried out, saying, If thou let this man go, thou art not Caesar's friend." John 19:16 says, "Then he delivered him [Jesus] unto them to be crucified."

Between the Pilate of the New Testament and the Pilate of history there is little in common. The New Testament Pilate is subservient to the Jews, acceding to their every wish. The real Pilate hated Jews and his cruelty toward them provoked his recall. The New Testament declares that Pilate desired to release Jesus but did not because of Jewish opposition. Who ruled Judea, Pilate or the Jews? If we are to believe the evangelists, the Romans ruled Judea, while the Jews ruled the Romans.

Eleventh and lastly, a well-known courtroom scene is found in Mark 14:61-64, which says, "The high priest asked him [Jesus], and said unto him. Art thou the Christ, the Son of the Blessed? And Jesus said, I am: and ye shall see the Son of man sitting on the right hand of power. . . . Then the high priest rent his clothes, and saith, What need we any further witnesses? Ye have heard the blasphemy: what think ye? And they all condemned him to be guilty of death."

Several difficulties accompany this sequence of events:

(a) Jesus, it was charged, had declared himself to be the son of God. This, if true, would not have constituted blasphemy. It was no offense against the law for a man to claim that he was the son of God. All men, especially all good men, were recognized as the sons of God. In *The Jew and the Christian Missionary,* on page 233 Gerald Sigal says,

> In the final analysis, whether the evidence represented fact or fancy is not important. What is most significant is that nothing attributed by the witnesses to Jesus would have been considered blasphemous by a Jewish court. Perhaps his claim was foolish and pretentious, but it was not one justifying his condemnation to death.

Even if Jesus had been proven guilty of blasphemy, he could not have been put to death, for blasphemy had ceased to be a capital offense. And is it reasonable to suppose that the Romans would have condemned a man to death for an offense against a religion which they regarded as one of the vilest of superstitions?

(b) Jesus had a trial before the Sanhedrin also in Matt. 26:57–68 and Luke 22:54–71. But at about this time (A.D. 30) the Sanhedrin ceased to have jurisdiction over capital offenses. After its jurisdiction ceased Jesus could not have been tried before it, and before its jurisdiction ceased, he would not have had a subsequent trial before a political figure such as Pilate.

In summary, anywhere from fourteen to twenty-seven legal infractions are recorded in the biblical accounts of Jesus' trial. The meeting was held at night, in the residence of the High Priest, during Passover, and under circumstances that precluded a quorum of twenty-three. No defense witnesses were called, condemnation and execution occurred on the same day, and the penalty, crucifixion, did not match the crime, blasphemy.

Population

A final aspect of biblical historical problems concerns the degree to which several numbers and population statistics are either incredible, impractical, or inaccurate. Prime examples include:

First, Gen. 46:27 (NIV) states, "The members of Jacob's family which went to Egypt, were 70 in all." This flies in the face of Exod. 38:26, which says, "From everyone who had crossed over to those counted, 22 years old or more, a total of 603,550 men." In other words, over six hundred thousand men above the age of twenty-two crossed the Red Sea with Moses. For each man one can safely assume there was at least one woman and three children, which would have totalled more than three million people.

One of Jacob's sons who went down into Egypt with him was named Levi (Exod. 1:1-2, Gen. 34:25) and Levi was the father of Kohath (Gen. 46:11, Exod. 6:16, 1 Chron. 6:1). Kohath was the father of Amram (Exod. 6:18, Num. 26:58, 1 Chron. 6:2), who was the father of Moses (Num. 26:59, 1 Chron. 6:3, 23:13), who led the Exodus. This would mean seventy people went down into Egypt in Gen. 46 and approximately three million people emerged only four generations later. The sons of Jacob had approximately five sons each. If all of Jacob's grandsons also had had five sons each and so on, and nobody had died, which is impossible, there would have been nowhere near six hundred thousand males by the time the Exodus occurred. Any rational increase in these numbers would not change the totals very much, even if all of the seventy who went down into Egypt were Jacob's grandsons and each had had five sons. Biblical scholar Joseph Wheless says that for three million people to have left four generations later, each of the fifty-five males of the first generation would have to have had forty children (twenty boys and twenty girls) and so on each generation.

It is especially difficult to see how the Israelites increased to three million in light of Deut. 7:7, which says, "The Lord did not set his love upon you, nor choose you, because ye were more in number than any people; for ye were the fewest of all people." Today's rabbis are fully alive to this reductio ad absurdum, and to retrieve the situation some have supposed that a number of servants accompanied Joseph's kinsmen on their journey into Egypt. Unfortunately for apologetic rabbis, these servants are nowhere mentioned in Scripture, but even if we were to allow the claim, the rate of multiplication is still fanciful.

Second, Exod. 12:51 adds to this problem by saying, "It came to pass the selfsame day, that the Lord did bring the children of Israel out of the land of Egypt by their armies."

If, in fact, three million Israelites left in one day, "the selfsame day," we are faced with the following problems:

(a) It would have taken several days, if not weeks, for the message to have reached the people in the outlying districts and even more time for people to have assembled and departed. Imagine contacting and assembling two million to three million people in one night in that day and age!

(b) Before they left Egypt, Exod. 12:35-36 says, the Israelites did according to the word of Moses: "They borrowed from the Egyptians jewels of silver, and jewels of gold, and raiment: and the Lord gave the people favor in the sight of the Egyptians, so that they lent unto them such things as they required. And they spoiled the Egyptians." Assuming it took one hour to mobilize and eight hours to collect the things mentioned in Exod. 12:35-36, the Israelites would have had fifteen hours left to leave Egypt. That would have required them to move at more than sixty miles per hour, according to one source.

(c) If the Israelits had marched in close order with fifty abreast and only a yard interval between ranks, an exodus of three million people would have been 48,284 ranks forming a column twenty-eight miles long.

Third, when we compare Lev. 8:3-4, in which God says to Moses, "Gather thou all the congregation together unto the door of the tabernacle of the congregation. And Moses did as the Lord commanded him; and the assembly was gathered together unto the door of the tabernacle of the congregation," with Exod. 27:18, which states, "The length of the court shall be an hundred cubits, and the breadth fifty every where," a major problem immediately surfaces.

Gathering over 600,000 men in front of a tent in a court with dimensions of only 150 feet by 75 feet is all but impossible—a crowd that size would comprise a mass about the size of a square with each side a fourth of a mile long. When we note that Leviticus says all the congregation was gathered, not just the men of the congregation, the problem grows to astronomical proportions.

Fourth, Deut. 1:1 declares, "These be the words which Moses spake to all Israel." How could one man have spoken to, and been heard by, more than six hundred thousand people, let alone three million in that era?

Fifth, Num. 11:31-32 (NIV) says, "A wind went out from the Lord and drove quail in from the sea. It brought them down all around the camp to about 3 feet above the ground, as far as a day's walk in any direction. All that day and night and all the next the day the people went out and gathered quail. No one gathered less than 10 homers. Then they spread them out all around the camp."

This rain of quail food presents some major difficulties besides the fact that quail don't live out at sea.

(a) A homer is about 10 bushels, so the least gathered by anyone was 100 bushels. Estimating 120 quail to the bushel gives 12,000 quail to each person, a rather large accumulation to say the least.

(b) According to the *Jewish Encyclopedia,* a biblical day's journey is 44,815 meters or 27.8 miles. The area covered by the quail would be about 4,400 square miles (all three feet high). If each quail had consumed 27 square inches, there would be 29 trillion quail or 12,000,000 quails per Jew. More than a cubic mile of quail would be involved. This would be enough quail to fill forty million railroad box cars, forming a train about 350,000 miles long, long enough to reach around the earth fourteen times at the equator.

Sixth, another historical problem is evident in Deut. 2:14 (NIV), in which Moses says, "Thirty-eight years passed from the time we left Kadesh Barnea until we crossed the Zered Valley. By then, that entire generation of fighting men had perished from the camp, as the Lord had sworn to them." We are supposed to believe that all of Moses' 603,550 fighting men died within thirty-eight years after they left Egypt and only Moses survived. He had to have survived since he is the alleged source of this verse.

Seventh, in Deut. 5:3 Moses says, "The Lord made not this covenant [the covenant at Sinai] with our fathers, but with us [the Israelites] even us, who are all of us here alive this day." Moses made this statement thirty-eight years after the covenant was made at Sinai and after thousands of Israelites had wandered in the wilderness for the same period; yet not one person out of 2,500,000 Exodites had died. Naturally this implies the opposite of the "entire generation of fighting men had perished."

Eighth, Deut. 7:1 (NIV) says, "When the Lord your God brings you [the Israelites] into the land you are entering to possess and drives out before you many nations—the Hittites, Girgashites, Amorites, Canaanites, Perizzites, Hivites and Jebusites, seven nations larger and stronger than you—and when the Lord your God has delivered them over to you and you have defeated them, then you must destroy them totally."

If this verse is added to Deut. 7:7 (NIV), which says, "The Lord did not set his affection on you and choose you because you were more numerous than other peoples, for you were the fewest of all peoples," we face an absurdity. If each of the seven nations had more constituents than the three million Israelites, then the Israelites defeated a combined population of at least twenty-one million people, a force seven or eight times its size.

In addition to the military logistics of such a campaign, one should consider the agricultural and other difficulties raised by the contention that Palestine, an area that currently supports no more than five million people, could sustain many more people in ancient times.

Ninth, an historical absurdity emerges when we combine Josh. 6:3–4 (NIV), which says, "March around the city [Jericho] once with all the armed men. Do this for 6 days," with Josh. 6:15 (NIV), which says, "On the 7th day they got up at daybreak and marched around the city 7 times in the same manner, except that on that day they circled the city 7 times".

There were over 600,000 men in the Israelite army according to Num. 26:2 and 51, and many observers ask how that many men could have gone around a city seven times in one day in that era.

Tenth, a population problem diametrically opposed to what we have discussed so far becomes obvious when we read 1 Kings 20:15 (NIV), which says, "So Ahab summoned the young officers of the provincial commanders, 232 men. Then he assembled the rest of the Israelites, 7,000 in all." How could the Israelites have been the chosen people, when they went from over three million people during the Exodus to seven thousand in the days of Ahab?

Eleventh, 2 Chron. 13:3 says, "Abijah set the battle in array with an army of valiant men of war, even 400,000 chosen men; Jeroboam also set the battle in array against him with 800,000 chosen men, being mighty men of valour."

All of these soldiers were Jews. All lived in Palestine, a poor miserable little country about a fourth the size of New York. Yet this little country put 1,200,000 soldiers in the field. This would have required a population of 10 to 12 million people in Palestine which would have been absurd for a country that could have barely supported 2,000,000.

Twelfth, 2 Chron. 13:17 says, "There fell down slain of Israel 500,000 chosen men."

If this is correct, it ranks as one of the greatest massacres in history. At Gettysburg, the greatest battle of the American Civil War, the Confederacy lost fewer than five thousand men, a hundredth the number of slain Israelites.

Thirteenth and lastly, 2 Chron. 17:14–18 says, "Their enrollment by families was as follows: . . . Adnah the commander, with 300,000 fighting men; next, Jehohanan the commander, with 280,000, next, Amasiah . . . with 200,000. From Benjamin: Eliada, a valiant soldier, with 200,000 men . . . next, Jehozabad with 180,000 men armed for battle." Totalling 1,160,000, these were the men who served the king, besides those he stationed in the fortified cities throughout Judah. How on earth could they have possibly assembled an army of 1,160,000 men in that area?

In summary, then, from a numerical perspective biblical history has more than its share of incredulities. Far too often mythology supplanted reality.

Liberalism

The liberal wing of Christianity seeks to escape many dubious accounts in biblical history by conceding they are mythological or fictitious. Liberals readily admit many events are unrealistic but contend Christians are under no obligation to believe in the fanciful as long as the essential teachings of the Bible remain unaffected. From their perspective, it is the central message that counts, not a multitude of historical details. Essentially this argument resembles the one used in reference to inerrancy. What difference does it make if biblical details are inaccurate as long as its central message is true? What they fail to realize, of course, is that facts are r ·1cial to the entire issue. They go to the heart of the matter. How do you know what in a work is true when you begin to admit that certain parts are false. Where do you draw the line? To preserve their intellectual integrity, biblical liberals deny inerrancy. In doing so, however, they merely ignore the problem confronted head-on by biblical fundamentalists: truth must generally be seamless.

Lawyers build cases on facts and details. That's the meat and potatoes of their business. And that's no less true of historians and historical accounts. As Charles Ryrie says on page 92 in *Basic Theology,* "The Bible cannot be inaccurate in matters of history and accurate in doctrine."

Many Old Testament historical accounts that are lightly tossed off as mythological by the liberal wing of Christianity go to the very crux of the Book's credibility. Conservatives claim they must be true, no matter how absurd, because Jesus said they occurred. They say that anyone who says they are fanciful is not only saying Jesus is a liar but ruling out any possibility of Jesus being God.

What are these events? Well, in Luke 17:26–27 (NIV), Jesus says, "Just as it was in the days of Noah, so also will it be in the days of the Son of Man. People were eating, drinking . . . up to the day Noah entered the Ark. Then the flood came and destroyed them all." These verses, along with Matt. 24:37–39, clearly show that Jesus believed in a real flood and a real Noah.

Matt. 12:40 (RSV) quotes Jesus as saying, "For as Jonah was three days and three nights in the belly of the whale," clearly showing that Jesus considered the story of Jonah and the whale to be fact. Jesus also believed that Lot's wife had in fact turned into a pillar of salt, because he says in Luke 17:32, "Remember Lot's wife." In Luke 20:37 Jesus says, "Now that the dead are raised; even Moses shewed at the burning bush," demonstrating his belief in that story.

When Jesus said in Luke 17:29, "The same day that Lot went out of Sodom it rained fire and brimstone from heaven, and destroyed them all," he demonstrated his belief in the raining of fire and brimstone. John 6:49 shows Jesus believed the Israelites ate manna in the wilderness. And, as important as any, Matt. 19:4 and Mark 10:6 clearly show that Jesus felt there was a real Adam and Eve. He did not look upon these people as fictitious or mere symbols. On page 87 in *Basic Theology* Ryrie states,

> Jesus used historical incidents in the Old Testament in a manner which evidenced His total confidence in their factual historicity. He acknowledged that Adam and Eve were created by God, that they were two living human beings, not merely symbols of mankind and womankind, and that they acted in specific ways (Matt. 19:3–5, Mark 10:6–8). He verified events connected with the flood of Noah's day; namely that there was an ark and that the Flood destroyed everyone who was not in that ark (Matt. 24:38–39, Luke 17:28–29). On two different occasions, He authenticated God's destruction of Sodom, and the historicity of Lot and his wife (Matt. 10:15, Luke 17:28–29). He accepted as true the story of Jonah and the great fish (Matt. 12:40) and acknowledged the historicity of Isaiah, Elijah, Daniel, Abel, Zechariah, Abiathar, David, Moses, Abraham, Isaac, and Jacob. Christ did not merely *allude* to these stories, but He *authenticated* the events in them as factual history to be completely trusted.

The point is that Christian liberalism will not stand the strain. If you believe these biblical events are mythological or fictitious, then you cannot be a Christian and believe that Jesus was God incarnate.

Forty

Lastly, we can't help but note in passing the frequency with which the number forty recurs in biblical history. Moses was forty years in Egypt, forty years in Midian, and forty years in the desert of Sinai. Othniel judged Israel for forty years. Barak gave Israel peace for forty years as did Gideon. The Philistines oppressed Israel for forty years and Saul, David, and Solomon reigned forty years each. It rained forty days and forty nights at the time of the Flood and Moses fasted forty days and nights, as did Jesus. And according to Acts there was an interval of forty days between the Resurrection and the Ascension. This unlikely recurrence of the number forty at so many critical junctures in the history of the Israelites and of Jesus clearly indicates that in the Bible we are dealing with mythology and numerology, not historical reality.

Conclusion

The obvious conclusion to be garnered from all of the above is that biblical history is utterly saturated with inaccuracies, inconsistencies, improbabilities, impossibilities, contradictions, mythology, and folklore. For correct information relative to the events of the early Judeo-Christian era, the Bible is certainly not to be trusted, quoted, promoted, or propagated.

18

Biblical History II

Creation Accounts Conflict, Self-Contradictions of Accounts, Genesis Problems, Moses and the Pentateuch

The historical biblical topic that has generated about as much controversy as any throughout the ages has been the ideological stance taken by the Book of Genesis with respect to the formation of the universe in general and the earth in particular. Few subjects have attracted more attention, and in many respects the battle continues unabated.

In a previous chapter we covered rather extensively the battle between science and the myth of creation as related in the Bible, but less well-known is the conflict between the two accounts of creation within the Book of Genesis itself. One need only read the first three chapters of the Bible to see that there is a vast difference between the first account of creation given in Gen. 1:1–2:3 and the second account, which begins at Gen. 2:4 and goes well into the third chapter. The two accounts conflict on many major points and no amount of apologetic rationalization can reconcile what biblicists refer to as the Elohistic and Jehovistic versions.

The two creation accounts disagree with one another in numerous instances and are also internally inconsistent. Major examples of disagreements between the accounts include:

Creation Accounts Conflict

First, in the first account Gen. 1:25 says, "God made the beasts of the earth" and in Gen 1:27 state, "God created man in his own image." But in the second account Gen. 2:7 says, "God formed man of the dust of the ground" and Gen 2:19 states, "God formed every beast of the field, and every fowl of the air; and brought them unto Adam." In other words, according to the first account man was created *after* the beasts, while the second account says he was created *before* the beasts. Man *had* to have been created before the beasts in the latter instance; otherwise, how could they have been brought to him?

Second, Gen. 1:21 says, "God created . . . every winged fowl" and five verses later declares, "God created Man in his own image." However, in the second account Gen. 2:7 says, "God formed man of the dust of the ground" and twelve verses later declares, "God formed . . . every fowl of the air." In the first creation God made the fowl, then man; in the second he made man and then the fowl.

Third, Gen. 1:12–13 says, "The earth brought forth . . . the fruit tree on the 3rd day" and verses 1:27 and 1:31 say, "God created man in his own image on the 6th day." In the second account, however, Gen. 2:7 says, "God formed man out of the dust of the ground," and verse 2:9 says, "Out of the ground the Lord God made to grow every tree that is . . . good for food." Succinctly stated, in the first creation God made the fruit trees on the third day and created man three days later, while in the second account God made man before the fruit trees.

Fourth, Gen. 1:20 says, "Let the waters bring forth abundantly . . . fowl that may fly," but Gen. 2:19 says, "Out of the ground the Lord God formed every . . . fowl of the air."

According to the first creation all winged fowl were created out of the *waters,* while the second account says every fowl of the air was created out of the *ground.*

Fifth, Gen. 1:21 and 1:23 show that God created every fowl on the fifth day and made the beasts of the earth on the sixth day. But Gen. 2:19 says, "Out of the ground the Lord God formed every beast of the field and every fowl of the air."

In essence, according to the first creation account fowl were created on the fifth day and beasts on the sixth, but under the second creation account fowl and beasts were formed simultaneously in one creative act.

Sixth, Gen. 1:29 says, "God said, 'Behold I have given you . . . every tree, in which is the fruit of a tree yielding seed; to you it shall be for meat,' " while Gen. 2:17 says, "Of the tree of the knowledge of good and evil, thou shalt not eat of it."

In the first account Adam may eat from *any* fruit tree; while in the second he may *not* eat the fruit of all trees.

Seventh, in the first creation account Gen. 1:27 says, "God created man in his own image." But in the second account, Gen. 3:5 says, "God doth know that in the day you eat thereof, then your eyes shall be opened, and ye shall be as gods, knowing good and evil," and 3:22 says, "The Lord God said, Behold, man has become as one of us, to know good and evil." In the first creation man is made in the image of God; while in the second that likeness is acquired by learning of good and evil.

Eighth, Gen. 1:27 says, "God created man in his own image, in the image of God created he him; male and female created he them." But Gen. 2:20–22 differs significantly by saying, "But for Adam there was not found a help mate for him," and then goes on to explain that woman was made from one of Adam's ribs.

In the first creation man and woman appeared on earth together; in the second, man came first and later his rib was taken to make a woman.

Ninth, Gen. 1:2 says, "The earth was without form, and void. . . . And the Spirit of God moved upon the face of the waters," and Gen. 1:9–10 says, "God said, 'Let the waters under the heaven be gathered together unto one place, and let the dry land appear': and it was so. And God called the dry land Earth; and the gathering together of the waters he called Seas." All of this occurred on the third day according to the thirteenth verse.

But Gen. 2:4–6 in the second account states, "In the day that the Lord God made the earth . . . the Lord God had not caused it to rain upon the earth. . . . There went up a mist from the earth and watered the whole face of the ground."

In the first creation account the earth was first covered with water and land did not appear until later. In the second creation account there was no water at first. The earth was dry land and was later watered by a mist.

Tenth, Gen. 1:11 (RSV) in the first account says, "God said, 'Let the earth bring forth grass, the herb yielding seed, and the fruit tree yielding fruit after his kind . . . upon the earth." Yet Gen. 2:4–5 in the second account says, "In the day that the Lord God made the earth and the heavens, And every plant of the field before it was in the earth, and every herb of the field before it grew."

In the first creation plants were created *from* the earth, they were a product *of* the earth. In the second creation the phrase, "before it was in the earth," indicates that plants were created before they had contact with the earth. The plants were created *away* from the earth and then transported *to* the earth.

Eleventh, two additional inconsistencies are worthy of note. Gen. 1:28 says, "God blessed them, and God said to them, 'Be fruitful and multiply . . . and have dominion over . . . every living thing that moveth upon the earth.' " That appears to clash with Gen. 2:15, which says, "The Lord God took man and put him into the garden of Eden to dress and to keep it." Under the first creation God gave man and woman dominion—rule—over all things and ordered them to subdue the earth. Under the second creation man and woman were confined to the Garden of Eden and essentially ordered to care for it—this is not exactly "dominion."

Twelfth and finally: In the first account God is always called "God"; in the second he is always called "Lord God."

In summary, then, the evidence clearly supports the contention that the two accounts of Genesis clash on important issues and are by no means consistent.

FIRST ACCOUNT PROBLEMS

Besides contradictions and inconsistencies between the two accounts, each contradicts itself and science. Noteworthy in the First Account are:

First, Gen. 1:4–5 says that on the first day, "God saw the light, that it was good: and God divided the light from the darkness. And God called the light Day and the darkness he called Night." But Gen. 1:14–16 and 19 say God said the following on the *fourth* day: " 'Let there be lights in the firmament of the heaven to divide the day from the night. . . .' And God made two great lights; the greater light to rule the day, and the lesser light to rule the night." The obvious question this generates is: Why would God need to divide the day from the night on the fourth day, when it had already been done on the first day?

Second, another clash within the first account comes to the fore when we compare Gen. 1:1, which says God created the heaven and the earth *on the first day,* with Gen. 1:16 and 19 which say, "God made two great lights; the greater light to rule the day, and the lesser light to rule the night" *on the fourth day.* According to indisputable science, the earth was created *after* the sun, not *before.* Yet, this part of Genesis says the sun was created three days *after* the earth.

Third, Gen. 1:12–13 says, "The earth brought forth grass . . . and the tree yielding fruit" on the third day. This clashes with Gen. 1:21 and 1:23, which say, "God created great whales, and every living creature that moveth, which the waters brought forth abundantly" on the fifth day. There are few reputable scientists who would say that the earth was covered with fruit-bearing trees before animal life appeared in the seas.

Fourth, a problem of greater importance than apologists would like to admit is found in Gen. 1:28, which says, "God blessed them, and said to Adam and Eve, Be fruitful, and multiply, and replenish the earth." "Replenish" means that men or people must have existed before Adam. How could the earth be *re*plenished unless it had been plenished before Adam and Eve? How do you *re*plenish something that has never been plenished to start with? Although a significant amount of discussion has surrounded what has come to be known as the Pre-Adamic peoples, there is no biblical support for their existence.

Fifth, Gen. 2:2 creates a rather interesting dilemma by saying, "On the 7th day God ended his work . . . and he rested on the 7th day." If God ended his work *on* the seventh day, then he must have been *working* on the seventh day.

Unless he was working on the seventh day, he could not have *stopped* working on the seventh day. Therefore, God worked on all seven days, which would include the sabbath. God broke his own commandment not to work on the sabbath. And why would an omnipotent being need to rest to begin with?

Sixth, a variation on a problem that *Biblical Errancy* has presented many times is created by Gen. 1:31 which says, "God saw everything that he had made, and, behold, it was very good." How could evil have entered a world in which everything was good, yea perfect, when the work of creation was completed?

Seventh, Gen. 1:26 and 1:27 conflict with one another, even though they are sequential. They state, "God said, 'Let us make man in our image, after our likeness. . . . So God created man in his own image, in the image of God created he him; male and female created he them." The question is: Is God one or several? Which is applicable—"his" or "our," "he," or "us"?

Eighth, and finally, according to Gen. 1:26 God said, "Let us make man in our image, after our likeness'" which flies directly in the face of Isa. 40:25, which says, "To whom then will ye *liken me,* or shall I be equal? saith the Holy One." If man has been made in God's image, it is safe to say he has been likened to God.

SECOND ACCOUNT PROBLEMS

The second account is not without internal problems either. *First,* one of the most obvious begins to emerge when Gen. 2:17, which says, "Of the knowledge of good and evil, thou shalt not eat of it: for in the day that thou eat thereof thou shalt surely die" is compared to Gen. 3:4, which says, "The serpent said unto the woman, Ye shall not surely die," and Gen. 5:5, which says, "All the days that Adam lived were 930: and he died." Adam ate the forbidden fruit but he did not die. In effect, the serpent told the truth and God didn't. If the meaning was that a spiritual death would ensue, as many biblicists allege, then they should explain why the same word is used quite literally in 2 Sam. 12:13–14 (NIV), which says, "David said to Nathan, 'I have sinned against the Lord.' Nathan replied, 'The Lord has taken away your sin. You are not going to die. But because by doing this you have made the enemies of the Lord show utter contempt, the son born to you will die.' " And indeed verse 12:18 relates that David's child did die on the seventh day. Clearly a spiritual death was not intended and there is no reason to believe that a literal death was not the meaning of God's warning in Gen. 2:17 as well.

Second, we know from Deut. 32:4 that God is a rock and his work is perfect, but Gen. 3:6 (NIV) says, "When the woman [Eve] saw that the fruit of the tree was good for food and pleasing to the eye, and also desirable for gaining wisdom, she took some and ate it. She also gave some to her husband, who was with her, and he ate it." As was discussed earlier, if God's work is perfect and part of his work is Adam and Eve, then they were perfect also. How, then, could they have sinned?

Third, Gen. 3:4–5 says, "The serpent said unto the woman . . . For God doth know that in the day you eat thereof, then your eyes shall be opened, and ye shall be as gods, knowing good and evil." And in Gen. 3:22 God says, "Man has become as one of us, to know good and evil." In essence, in Gen. 3:22 God is saying the serpent told the truth when he said that man would learn good and evil, and Christians must reconcile this with John 8:44 (NIV), which says the Devil is incapable of telling the truth. It states, "The devil . . . was a murderer from the beginning, not holding to the truth, for there is no truth in him. When he lies, he speaks his native language, for he is a liar and the father of lies."

Fourth and lastly, Gen. 3:8–9 says, "Adam and his wife hid themselves from the presence of the Lord God . . . and the Lord God called unto Adam and said unto him, Where art thou?" Yet in Job 34:22 we are told, "There is no darkness . . . where the workers of iniquity may hide themselves." The only conclusion to be drawn from this is that either the workers of iniquity can, in fact, hide themselves, or God is practicing deception.

Incidentally, in this passage Eve is referred to as Adam's wife. But no verse or verses show that they ever went through any form of marriage ritual or ceremony. The fact that she emerged from Adam's rib no more proves they were husband and wife than the birth of a son from his mother's womb proves *they* are husband and wife. In fact, genetically they are closer to being brother and sister!

Genesis Problems

As we have seen, numerous contradictions exist within and between the two accounts of creation in Genesis. Each not only disagrees with the other but itself as well. In addition, there are some significant general problems that need to be addressed and a lesser number of questions that are just plain bothersome. Verses within the former are the following:

First, Gen. 2:2 says, "On the seventh day God ended his work which he had made; and he rested on the seventh day from all his work which he had made." What makes God masculine? How could God be masculine unless he had the physical attributes and/or organs of a male? To conceive of God having male genitalia or, even more important, to think of him using them as nature intended borders on the bizarre.

Second, Gen. 1:2 says, "The earth was without form, and void." How could something material exist without some kind of form?

Third, Gen. 4:14–15 says, "It shall come to pass, that every one that findeth me [Cain] shall slay me. And the Lord said unto Cain, Therefore whosoever slayeth you, vengeance shall be taken on him sevenfold." Since the only people in existence at that time, other than Cain himself, were Adam and Eve, who was it that God thought might slay Cain? Abel had already been slain by Cain.

Fourth, Gen. 4:16 states, "Cain went out from the presence of the Lord, and dwelt in the land of Nod." How do you leave or escape the presence of an omnipresent God? That's an utter absurdity. God is by definition everywhere.

Fifth, Gen. 4:17 says, "Cain knew his wife; and she conceived and bare Enoch; and he [Cain] builded a city." A question that has been asked by millions, even millions of Christians, over the years is: Where did Cain get his wife? If she is his sister, as some biblicists allege, then we are all products of incest. And how could one man build a city?

Verses within the first two chapters of the Bible that give rise to lesser quandaries include:

First, Gen. 2:17 says, "Of the tree of the knowledge of good and evil, thou shalt not eat of it." Why would God prevent man from knowing good from evil? According to Christians, one of the most critically redeeming features of the Bible is the importance it places upon distinguishing good from evil. Gen. 2:17 runs counter to the alleged entire tenor of the Book.

Second, Gen. 4:9 says, "And the Lord said unto Cain, Where is Abel thy brother?" Why would an all-knowing God ask questions when he already knows the answers? Either God does not know all or he is being deceptive.

Third, after Cain killed Abel we find the following in Gen. 4:12 and 15, "A vagabond shalt thou [Cain] be in the earth. . . . And the Lord said unto him, Therefore whosoever slays Cain, vengeance shall be taken on him sevenfold. And the Lord set a mark upon Cain, lest any finding him should kill him." How on earth could God be the epitome of justice and rectitude when he not only failed to punish Cain for killing Abel but promised him protection from potential slayers?

Fourth and lastly, Gen. 1:1 says, "In the beginning God created the heaven and the earth."

If the only places in which things can exist are heaven, hell, and earth, where was God when he created heaven and earth? Surely not in hell. It is no defense to say that heaven only refers to the skies above, because the heaven referred to in Gen. 1:1 comes from the same Hebrew word that is used throughout the Old Testament in reference to God's abode.

In summary, one can safely conclude from all of the above that the Book of Genesis is plagued by a wide assortment of contradictions and incongruities that obviate any possibility of it being the word of a perfect, supreme being.

Moses and the Pentateuch

A second historical problem of immense significance concerns the whole issue of whether or not Moses wrote the Pentateuch—the first five books in the Bible. Christians, especially those of a more fundamentalist persuasion, firmly contend that Moses authored the books of Genesis, Exodus, Leviticus, Numbers, and Deuteronomy. They base their belief not only upon historical information but upon statements by Jesus to the effect that Moses wrote the Law, i.e., the Pentateuch. In John 7:19 Jesus says, "Did not Moses give you the law, and yet none of you keepeth the law"; in John 1:17 Jesus says, "For the law was given by Moses"; and in John 5:46–47 Jesus says, "For had ye believed Moses, ye would have believed me: for he wrote of me. But if ye believe not his writings, how shall ye believe my words?"

The man who picked up where Moses left off, Joshua, says in Josh. 8:32, "There in the presence of the Israelites, Joshua copied on stones the law of Moses, which he [Moses] had written." The New Testament Sadducees said in Mark 12:19 (NIV), " 'Moses wrote for us.' " Even Paul got into the act by saying in Rom. 10:5 (RSV), "Moses writes that the man who practices the righteousness which is based on the law shall live by it."

So Moses wrote the Pentateuch according to biblical figures and many biblicists.

Before anyone quickly concludes this topic is of secondary importance, however, he would do well to read the words of apologist M. R. DeHaan, who says the following on pages 41 and 42 of his work *Genesis and Evolution,*

> But there is even a more serious implication, a clever subtle attack upon the *authority* and *truthfulness* of Jesus Christ. Prove that Moses did *not* write the books of the Pentateuch and you prove that Jesus was totally mistaken and not the infallible Son of God he claimed to be. Upon your faith in Moses as the writer of the five books attributed to him rests also your faith in Jesus as the Son of God. You cannot believe in Jesus Christ without believing what Moses wrote. You see, there is much more involved in denying the books of Moses than most people suppose. If this seems like an extreme statement, consider these words of Jesus, for Jesus quoted more frequently from the writings of Moses than any other part of the Old Testament. Jesus believed, taught, and asserted that the books of Moses were authentic, binding, and as genuine as He Himself. Listen to Jesus in Mark 12:26, ". . . have ye not read in the book of Moses, how in the bush God spoke unto him (Moses) saying, I am the God of Abraham, and the God of Isaac, and the God of Jacob?" Here Jesus vouches for the authenticity of Moses' record concerning the burning bush, quoting from Exod. 3:6. Or listen to Jesus after His resurrection as He converses with the travelers on the road to Emmaus in Luke 24:27: "And beginning at Moses and all the prophets, he expounded unto them in all the Scriptures the things concerning himself." The disciples recognized the books of Moses and accepted them, for

when they had met Jesus, Philip and Nathanael exclaimed in John 1:45: ". . . We have found him, of whom Moses in the law and the prophets did write. . . ." In John 3:14–15 Jesus risks his reputation as Saviour upon the authority of Moses, and says: "And as Moses lifted up the serpent in the wilderness, even so must the Son of man be lifted up: That whosoever believeth in him should not perish, but have eternal life." As Moses—so Christ. If Moses' authority is questionable, so is Jesus'. But now listen to the all-conclusive, incontrovertible words of Christ as to the authority of the record of Moses: "You diligently study the Scriptures because you think that by them you possess eternal life. These are the Scriptures that *testify about me.* But do not think I will accuse you before the Father. Your accuser is Moses, on whom your hopes are set. If you believed Moses, you would believe me, for he wrote about me. But since you do not believe what he wrote, how are you going to believe what I say?" We see then that Jesus endorsed the writings of Moses. He attached to them as much authority as to His own words. Since Jesus endorses the authority of Moses, He stakes His own claims of authority upon this fact.

On pages 93 and 94 in *More Evidence that Demands a Verdict* apologist Josh McDowell summarizes the Judeo-Christian view of the Mosaic authorship rather succinctly:

These OT verses record that the Torah or "the Law," was from Moses: Joshua 8:32 speaks of "the law of Moses, which he had written." The following verses . . . refer to an actual *written* 'law of Moses,' not simply an oral tradition: Josh. 8:31 and 8:34, 1 Kings 2:3, Ezra 3:2, Ezra 6:18, Neh. 8:1, Neh 13:1 . . . [and many others]. The New Testament writers also held that the Torah or "the Law" came from Moses.

McDowell then proceeds to list other New Testament verses that support Mosaic authorship: Luke 2:22, John 1:45, Mark 7:10, Mark 12:26, John 7:23, and Acts 3:22. So believing Moses wrote the Torah is very important.

But just as these verses and others are cited to prove Moses *was* the author of the first five books of the Bible, substantial evidence exists to prove he was *not.* There are far too many internal difficulties to take Mosaic authorship seriously. Moses could not have been the writer of the Pentateuch because of the large number of verses excluding the possibility of his authorship. The following are prime examples:

First, Gen. 12:6 says, "Abram passed through the land unto the place of Sichem . . . and the Canaanite was then in the land." And Gen. 13:7 says, "The Canaanite and Perizzite dwelled then in the land." Both verses state that the Canaanites were *then* in the land of Canaan when Abraham arrived and clearly imply that they were *not* there when these verses were being written. The work of expelling the Canaanites did not begin until the days of Joshua, after Moses died, and did not end until the days of David. Since Gen. 12:6 and Gen. 13:7 could not have been written until *after* the Canaanites had left the land, which was 450 years after the death of Moses, Moses could not have been the author of the passages.

Second, Gen. 36:31 says, "These are the kings that reigned in the land of Edom, before there reigned any king over the children of Israel." This passage could *only* have been written after the first king, Saul, began to reign over the Israelites, and thus could not have been written by Moses who lived long *before* Saul. A key passage in this regard is 1 Sam. 10:24–25.

Third, Gen. 49:10 says, "The sceptre shall not depart from Judah, nor a lawgiver from between his feet, until Shiloh come." These words could not have been written until Judah received the sceptre, which was not until David ascended the throne nearly four hundred years *after* the death of Moses.

Fourth, Exod. 11:3 states, "The man Moses was very great in the land of Egypt." People are usually spoken of as great only after their death, and Moses would hardly have made a comment of this nature about himself.

Fifth, Exod. 16:35 says, "The children of Israel did eat manna 40 years, until they came . . . unto the borders of the land of Canaan." Moses died in the wilderness before the Israelites crossed over into the land of Canaan. How could he have known what would happen after they crossed over? How could he have known they would stop eating manna after they entered Canaan? Besides, according to Joshua 5:12 the Israelites were still eating manna after they had crossed the Jordan River, when they were camped at Gilgal in Canaan.

Sixth, Exod. 23:19 (NIV) says, "Bring the best of the first fruits of your soil to the house of the Lord your God." This could not have been written before the time of Solomon, for God had no house prior to the erection of the temple by Solomon 447 years after the death of Moses. When David offered to build a house to God, God forbade it and said that he had never lived in a house since the Israelites had left Egypt—2 Sam. 7:6 clearly states, "I [God] have not dwelt in any house since the time that I brought up the children of Israel out of Egypt, even to this day, but have walked in a tent and in a tabernacle."

Seventh, Lev. 18:28 (NIV) says, "If you defile the land, it will vomit you out as it vomited out the nations that were before you." How could Moses have written this since he never saw the promised land and the other nations were not driven or vomited out until David's time?

Eighth, Num. 15:32 (RSV) says, "While the people of Israel were in the wilderness, they found a man gathering sticks upon the sabbath day." How could Moses have written this since it implies the Israelites were no longer in the wilderness? "Were" in the wilderness proves this verse was written *after* they had left the wilderness, and Moses could not have been the source since he died *in* the wilderness.

Ninth, Num. 15:32–34 (RSV) says, "While the people of Israel were in the wilderness, they found a man gathering sticks upon the sabbath day. And those who found him gathering sticks brought him to Moses and Aaron, and to all the congregation. They put him in custody, because it had not been made plain what should be done to him." How could it not be plain what they had to do? Moses himself received a law in Exod. 31:15 that said anyone who did any work on the sabbath should be put to death. Moses could not have written Num. 15 because he would have known this.

Tenth, Moses i s often referred to in the third person, which shows the Pentateuch is a biography, not an autobiography. Relevant verses are Num. 1:1 ("The Lord spake unto Moses in the wilderness of Sinai"); Num. 2:1 ("The Lord spake unto Moses"); and Deut. 33:1 ("This is the blessing, wherewith Moses the man of God blessed the children of Israel before his death"). Pronouns like I, me, myself, or mine are never employed by this writer, as would be the case if Moses were the author.

Eleventh, Deut. 4:38 (NIV) says, "to drive out before you nations greater and stronger than you and to bring you into their land to give it to you for your inheritance, as it is today." This verse must have been written after Moses died, since the Israelites did not possess the land as an inheritance until *after* his demise.

Twelfth, Deut. 15:22 says, "Thou shalt eat it within thy gates." The phrase "within thy gates" occurs in the Pentateuch about twenty-five times and refers to the gates of Palestinian cities, which the Israelites did not inhabit until *after* the death of Moses.

Thirteenth, Deut. 28:68 (NIV) says, "The Lord will send you back in ships to Egypt on a journey I said you should never make again. There you will offer yourselves for sale to your enemies as male and female slaves, but no one will buy you." How could Moses have written this when he said earlier in Deut. 17:16, that, "You shall never return that way [toward Egypt] again." Are the Israelites going back to Egypt or aren't they? Deut. 28:68 says the Lord will send them back to Egypt; whereas Moses said they would *never* return to Egypt.

Fourteenth, Deut. 33:1 (NIV) states, "This is the blessing that Moses the man of God pronounced on the Israelites before his death." In this verse Moses is not only spoken of in the third person and in laudatory terms, but his death is referred to as an event already accomplished. The verse all but devastates any belief in Moses as the source.

Fifteenth, Exod. 30:13 and 30:24 say, "This they shall give . . . half a shekel after the shekel of the sanctuary." Robert Ingersoll notes that Moses could not have written these verses since there was no such thing as a "shekel of the sanctuary" until long after Moses lived.

Sixteenth, biblicists should carefully note that Josh. 8:31 and Neh. 8:1 refer to *the book* of the law of Moses. They attribute to Moses only *one* book, if any, not five.

Seventeenth, 1 Kings 2:3 says, "Keep the charge of the Lord thy God, to walk in his ways, to keep his statutes, and his commandments, and his judgments, and his testimonies, as it is written in the law of Moses." On page 114 in *A Survey of the Old Testament* apologist Gleason Archer defends the Mosaic authorship concept by quoting "in the book of the law of Moses" from Josh. 8:31, 1 Kings 2:3, and 2 Kings 14:6 and later asserting, "The authorship of the Torah is always attributed personally to Moses." Apparently Archer missed a very simple point. These verses refer to things being "in" the law of Moses, but nowhere do they say they were written "by" Moses. "Written in the Law of Moses" does not mean Moses did the writing himself. Moreover, although the verse refers to the laws and commandments of God being in the law of Moses, that would not necessarily mean Moses wrote the entire Pentateuch.

Eighteenth, Exod. 20:10 states, "The seventh day is the sabbath of the Lord thy God: in it thou shalt not do any work, thou, nor thy son . . . nor thy stranger that is within thy gates." How could Moses have written this, when it implies the author was in Palestine? The word "gates" is not applicable to prior wanderings in the wilderness, when Moses lived, but only to the period following his demise. The Israelites had no cities with gates when Moses lived.

Nineteenth, Deut. 2:12 (NIV) says, "Horites used to live in Seir, but the descendants of Esau drove them out. They destroyed the Horites from before them and settled in their place, just as Israel did in the land the Lord gave them as their possession." How could Moses have written this, when the words presuppose a time when the Israelites were already in possession of Canaan, having expelled its former inhabitants? That happened *after* the death of Moses.

Twentieth, Gen. 10:5 says, "By these were the isles of the Gentiles divided in their lands." There were no Gentiles until after the Jews became a nation and that occurred when Israel split off from Judah and became an independent kingdom under Rehoboam, the son of Solomon. The Jews had no distinctive religion until after the days of Solomon, which was long after Moses.

Twenty-first, Gen. 23:2 states, "Sarah died in Kirjath-arba; the same is Hebron in the land of Canaan." Moses could not have written this because the city was not called Hebron, a modern name, until Caleb received it after the division of the land and named it Hebron after one of his sons. As Joshua 14:13–15 states, "Joshua blessed him, and gave unto Caleb . . . Hebron for an inheritance. . . . And the name of Hebron before was Kirjath-arba."

Twenty-second, Exod. 24:13 says, "Moses rose up, and his minister Joshua." These don't sound like words Moses would have written.

Twenty-third, Gen. 14:14 says, "When Abram heard that his brother was taken captive, he armed his trained servants . . . and pursued them unto Dan." Deut. 34:1 says, "The Lord shewed him [Moses] all the land of Gilead, unto Dan." The problem with these two verses is that there was no place known as Dan until years after Moses lived. Dan was built after the death of Samson, who died 350 years after the death of Moses. The city was originally called Laish.

This is clearly shown in Judg. 18:29, which says, "They called the name of the city Dan, after the name of Dan their father . . . howbeit, the name of the city was Laish at first."

Twenty-fourth, Gen. 40:15 says, "I was stolen away out of the land of the Hebrews." Moses could not have written this verse since there were no "Hebrews" in the days of Joseph or of Moses. The word "Hebrews" could not be applied to the Jews until they possessed Canaan late in Joshua's time.

Twenty-fifth, one of the more potent anti-Mosaic authorship verses is Num. 12:3, which says, "The man Moses was very meek, above all the men which were upon the face of the earth." If Moses wrote this, then he could not have been very meek. The verse itself refutes meekness. Moreover, one would hardly call Moses meek when he said in Num. 31:17, "Kill every male among the little ones, and kill every woman that has known man by lying with him."

Those words more closely resemble those of a tyrant than a man possessed by humility.

Twenty-sixth, Deut. 34:10 states, "There arose not a prophet since in Israel like unto Moses, whom the Lord knew face to face." This verse not only demonstrates an amazing lack of meekness on the part of Moses, in clear violation of Num. 12:3, but appears to have been written *after* Moses died. In addition, it is difficult to see how Moses could truthfully say he saw God face to face, if he also wrote Exod. 33:20, which says, "Thou canst not see my [God's] face: for no man shall see me and live."

Twenty-seventh, after all is said and done, undoubtedly the most powerful argument against Mosaic authorship of the Pentateuch comes from Deut. 34:5–6, which says, "So Moses the servant of the Lord died there in the land of Moab. . . . And they buried him in a valley . . . but no man knoweth of his sepulchre unto this day."

Let us be sensible. How could a man have described his own death and burial? Some scholars seek to escape this dilemma by alleging that Joshua wrote the last part of Deuteronomy. Unfortunately for them, this would therefore include Deut. 34:9, which says, "Joshua the son of Nun was full of the Spirit of Wisdom." It is difficult to see how Joshua could have authored this in light of the fact that if he was full of the spirit of wisdom he certainly was not filled with the spirit of modesty.

Just as important is the fact that by attributing the final verses of Deuteronomy to Joshua, apologists are conceding that Moses did not write some of the Pentateuch. While addressing this very issue on page 22 in *Answers to Tough Questions,* Josh McDowell says,

> Though orthodox Christians and Jews alike argue that Moses wrote the first five books of the Old Testament, some people deny his authorship of the fifth book, Deuteronomy. They do this partly on the grounds that chapter 34 contains

the account of Moses' death. Since no one can write an account of his own death, they argue, doesn't this mean the Book of Deuteronomy had to have been written later than the time of Moses? . . . A plausible explanation is to assume that it was written after the death of Moses, by Joshua.

McDowell conveniently neglects to provide so much as a shred of evidence that Joshua was the author. Following this kind of rationale, one could just as easily attribute it to Eleazar, Aaron's son, Achan, a contemporary of Joshua, or any one of a number of other post-Mosaic figures.

Another evangelical scholar who is also willing to admit that Moses did not write the last chapter of Deuteronomy is Gleason Archer, who says on page 263 of *A Survey of the Old Testament Introduction*, "Chapter 34 is demonstrably post-Mosaic, since it contains a short account of Moses' decease."

Other evidence of an even more technical nature proving Moses did not write the Pentateuch could be presented but the point has been made. The evidence is overwhelming, regardless of what Jesus, Joshua, Paul or the Sadducees may say to the contrary. Defenders of Christianity are on the horns of a dilemma. If they succumb to the facts and concede Moses could not have written the Pentateuch, they bring the veracity and divinity of Jesus into question. If they choose to man the barricades at all costs, they are fighting a battle that can only result in defeat and further erode their credibility. The most determined biblicist can see that there is no way Moses could have written the Torah. Even Josh McDowell, one of today's staunchest apologists, made the following inadvertent admission on page 21 in *Answers to Tough Questions,* "In the past 50 years archeological finds have vindicated many of the Old Testament claims supporting the probability of Mosaic authorship." Notice that McDowell qualifies his comment with the word "probability." He did not say "certainty"; he said "probability."

Besides the fact that data strongly demonstrate that there is no possibility of Moses having written the Pentateuch, the dearth of information relative to his existence indicates that he was a mythological figure. Even some fundamentalist scholars don't deny that Moses was probably a fictitious character. On page 9 in *Biblical Criticism* apologist R. K. Harrison states,

The main problem faced by historical criticism in this and other areas seems to be a lack of contemporary objective data associated with specific biblical personages and events. This situation is particularly acute in the case of Moses, for whom no secular corroborative information is extant. . . . From the standpoint of external evidence, therefore, the historicity of Moses is very hard to demonstrate.

Before concluding our discussion of Moses and the Pentateuch, some general observations are in order.

First, we should note that Moses nowhere claims to have written the Pentateuch nor does the Bible impute the Torah to him. Only the "Law" is attributed to Moses and that is only *part* of the Torah. On page 82 in *The Abingdon Bible Handbook* Garrett-Evangelical Theological Seminary professor Edward Blair says,

> The Pentateuch nowhere clearly claims that Moses was the author of the whole of it. Passages that refer to Moses' writing down "all the words of the Lord," "this law," and the like . . . refer only to certain parts which seem to be included in the whole. . . . It is obvious that certain statements in the Pentateuch imply a time of writing later than Moses (e.g., Gen. 12:6, 13:7, 36:31, Deut. 34:6).

And on page 355 in the same book Blair states, "Nothing that can be attributed with certainty to Moses is now present in the Pentateuch."

Second, the books are written in the third person and the author never says "I did," except in speeches.

Third, the books of the Pentateuch are never ascribed to Moses in the inscriptions of Hebrew manuscripts or in printed copies of the Hebrew Bible, nor are they referred to as the "Books of Moses" in the Septuagint or the Vulgate. This only occurs in modern translations.

Fourth, there is no important difference between the language of the Pentateuch allegedly written by Moses and that of books written shortly before the Judaic return from the Babylonian Captivity a thousand years later. If there had been no change in a language in a thousand years, that would have presented an unparalleled event in human history.

Fifth and lastly, the great repetition in the Pentateuch tends to prove there were several authors. Subjects are often introduced as if they had not been referred to before and show different peculiarities of language. Many liberal theologians and scholars are not only willing to admit that more than one author penned the Book of Genesis, for example, but actively propound the multiauthorship position. On pages 10–12 in *The Bible, the Quran, and Science* Maurice Bucaille summarizes the situation rather well by stating,

> One can easily imagine how difficult it was to combat a legend [that Moses wrote the Pentateuch] that was strengthened by Jesus himself who, as we have seen, supported it in the New Testament. It is to Jean Astruc, Louis XV's doctor, that we owe the decisive argument. By publishing in 1753 his *Conjectures on the original writings which it appears Moses used to compose the Book of Genesis* Astruc placed the accent on a plurality of sources. He was probably not the first to have noticed it, but he did however have the courage to make public an observation of prime importance: two texts, each denoted by the way in which God was named, either Yahweh or Elohim, were present side by side in Genesis. The latter therefore contained two juxtaposed texts. The scholar Eichorn made the same discovery for the other four books; then Ilgen noticed that one of

the texts isolated by Astruc, the one where God is named Elohim, was itself divided into two. The Pentateuch literally fell apart. The nineteenth century saw an even more minute search into the sources. In 1854 four sources were recognized, called the Yahvist version, the Elohist version, the Deuteronomist version, and the Priestly or Sacerdotal version. It was even possible to date them. (1) The Yahvist version was placed in the ninth century B.C. (written in Judah). (2) The Elohist version was probably a little more recent (written in Israel). (3) The Deuteronomist version was from the eighth century B.C. for some scholars and from the time of Josiah for others. (4) The Sacerdotal or Priestly version came from the period of exile or after the exile; sixth century B.C. It can be seen that the arrangement of the text of the Pentateuch spans at least three centuries. . . . The multiplicity of sources brings with it numerous disagreements and repetitions. Father de Vaux gives examples of this overlapping of traditions in the case of the Flood, the kidnapping of Joseph, his adventures in Egypt, disagreement on names relating to the same character, and differing descriptions of important events. Thus the Pentateuch is shown to be formed from various traditions brought together more or less skillfully by its authors. . . . The latter allowed improbabilities and disagreements to appear in the texts, however, which led modern man to the objective study of the sources.

Conclusion

In summary, Moses did not write the Pentateuch and all arguments to the contrary are doomed to failure. In fact, there is virtually no extrabiblical information that the man, Moses, is any more than a figment of mythology.

19

Sabbath

Saturday, Sunday, The Change

Except for Jesus Christ, probably no biblical topic receives more attention than the Ten Commandments. From one end of Christendom to the other the Ten Commandments are constantly projected as basic maxims for Christian attitudes and behavior. Yet one of the most important commandments is violated on a regular basis by the overwhelming majority of those claiming to adhere to Christian principles. In Exod. 20:8–11 (RSV), the Fourth Commandment clearly states, "Remember the sabbath day, to keep it holy. Six days you shall labor, and do all your work; but the seventh day is a sabbath to the Lord your God; in it you shall not do any work, you, or your son, or your daughter . . . therefore the Lord blessed the sabbath day and hallowed it."

Except for some sabbatarian groups, such as the Seventh-Day Adventists, biblicists do not even go to church on the correct day. Saturday, not Sunday, is the sabbath, and there is no substantive biblical support for calling Sunday—the first day of the week—the sabbath. No valid biblical reason exists for shifting the sabbath from Saturday to Sunday, which occurred sometime during the post-Apostolic period. Why the switch was made is a matter of speculation and of little concern to us. The fact that the alteration is in direct conflict with the Fourth Commandment and cannot be biblically substantiated is what matters.

Saturday

Arguments to the effect that Saturday rather than another day, such as Sunday, should be honored as the sabbath are clearly persuasive. Among the most potent are:

First, many verses clearly state that God made the seventh day, not the first day or just any day, the sabbath. Exod. 31:15 says, "Six days may work be done; but in the seventh is the sabbath of rest, holy to the Lord"; Exod. 20:9–10 says, "Six days shalt thou labour, and do all thy work: But the seventh day is the sabbath of the Lord thy God"; Exod. 16:26 says, "Six days you shall gather it; but on the seventh day, which is the sabbath"; Deut. 5:14 says, "The seventh day is the sabbath of the Lord thy God"; and Lev. 23:3 states, "Six days shall work be done: but the seventh day is the sabbath of rest." Clearly the seventh day, and no other, is the sabbath.

Second, The basis for biblical designation of the seventh day as the sabbath is the example of God himself; many verses allege that God rested from creating on the seventh day, not the first. Gen. 2:2–3 says, "On the seventh day God ended his work which he had made; and he rested on the seventh day from all his work which he had made. And God blessed the seventh day"; Exod. 20:11 says, "In six days the Lord made heaven and earth, the sea, and all that in them is, and rested the seventh day, wherefore the Lord blessed the sabbath day, and hallowed it"; Exod. 31:17 says, "in six days the Lord made heaven and earth, and on the seventh day he rested"; Heb. 4:4 says, "God rested on the seventh day from all His works"; and Exod. 34:21, Lev. 23:8, and Deut. 16:8 make the same point.

The sabbath was created as a memorial to God resting on the seventh day of creation and it could not be changed to the first day unless the whole process of creation was repeated. In the Fourth Commandment God specifically said the seventh day was to be kept holy. Why would the keeping of the sabbath have been placed in the Ten Commandments, if it wasn't as important as the others and could be changed? The Ten Commandments were written on two tablets of stone, according to Deut. 5:22, and by the finger of God according to Exod. 31:18. How many biblical laws were deemed to be of such importance as to be permanently engraved in stone?

Third, in addition to the Fourth Commandment, many other verses clearly show that God specifically decreed that the sabbath was to be honored. Ezek. 20:20 says, "Hallow my sabbaths; and they shall be a sign between me and you"; Isa. 56:2 states, "Blessed is the man that doeth this, and the son of man that layeth hold on it; who keepeth the sabbath from polluting it"; Isa. 58:13–14 contends that, "If you do not tramp upon the Sabbath by doing your business on My holy day, but call the Sabbath an enjoyment, in order that the Lord might be sacredly honored . . . then you shall find your delight in the Lord, and I will nourish you"; and Exod. 31:14 contends, "You shall keep the sabbath therefore; for it is holy unto you: every one that defileth it shall surely be put to death." So the sabbath was to be honored.

Fourth, Jesus himself clearly honored the sabbath, as is shown by Matt. 24:20, which says, "But pray ye that your flight be not in the winter, neither on the sabbath day," and by Luke 4:16, which says, "As his custom was, he [Jesus] went into the synagogue on the sabbath day, and stood up to read."

Fifth, Acts 13:44, 16:13, 17:1–4, 18:4, and 18:11 show that Paul also honored the sabbath. Contrary to popular belief, the apostolic church continued to observe the seventh-day sabbath after the death and resurrection of Christ. In fact, the Book of Acts records eighty-four sabbaths on which Paul and his associates held religious services. On the other hand, not one word in the entire Bible authorizes the keeping of any other day except Saturday.

Paul preached on the sabbath, as is shown by Acts 13:14–16 (RSV), which says, "On the sabbath they [Paul and his company] went into the synagogue and sat down. After reading of the law and the prophets . . . Paul stood up . . . and said." Acts 13:42 (RSV) says, "People begged that these things might be told to them the next sabbath," and shows that the Gentiles asked that the same words be preached to them the next sabbath. If the sabbath had been changed, why did Paul's followers ask him to preach the following Saturday rather than on the next day, Sunday? As the anonymous author from the Bible Advocate Press of a pamphlet entitled "Should the Seventh Day Sabbath be Observed" said on page 13, "The Gentiles besought that these words might be preached to them the next sabbath. Did you catch that? There were Gentiles present, as well as Jews. And they specifically asked Paul to preach the same sermon to them again the next Sabbath."

Sixth, another reason showing that Saturday rather than Sunday should be honored as the sabbath is that Jews and Christians all agreed on the appropriate day and never argued over the sabbath in the first century. In all the charges against Paul, the Jews never accused him of violating the sabbath.

Seventh, Isa. 56:6–7 (RSV) states, "Foreigners who join themselves to the Lord . . . everyone who keeps the sabbath, and does not profane it, . . . these I will bring to my holy mountain and make them joyful." The passage shows that God promised a special blessing on all Gentiles who would keep the sabbath. He never promised a blessing on anyone who kept another day holy.

Eighth, Luke 23:53-56 says, "He [Joseph of Arimathea] took it [Jesus' body] down. . . . And that day was the preparation; and the sabbath drew on. And the women . . . followed after. . . . And they returned, and prepared spices and ointments: and rested the sabbath day according to the commandment." These verses show that Christ's followers kept the sabbath even after his death because of the biblical Commandment.

Ninth, Jer. 17:24–25 (NIV) says, "If you are careful to obey me, declares the Lord, and bring no load through the gates of this city on the Sabbath, but keep the Sabbath day holy by not doing any work on it, then kings who sit on David's throne will come through the gates of this city with their officials . . . and this city Jerusalem will be inhabited forever." And Jer. 17:27 (NIV) says, "If you do not obey me to keep the Sabbath day holy by not carrying any load as you come through the gates of Jerusalem on the Sabbath day, then I will kindle an unquenchable fire in the gates of Jerusalem that will consume her fortresses." God promised that Jerusalem would stand forever if the Jews kept the sabbath, and it would be destroyed if they did not.

Tenth, Isa. 66:23 (RSV) says, "From new moon to new moon, and from sabbath to sabbath, all flesh shall come to worship before me, says the Lord." In effect, God is contending that the sabbath will remain a day of worship for eons to come.

Eleventh and lastly, there is a substantial amount of evidence to prove that no valid reason exists for honoring Sunday, the first day of the week:

a. Sunday is never called sacred, the sabbath, the Lord's Day, or holy anywhere in the Bible.

b. The only remark in the entire Old Testament about the first day of the week is in Gen. 1:5, which says, "The evening and the morning were the first day."

c. There is no record in all of Scripture that God ever transferred His blessing from the sabbath to another day of the week. Nowhere in all of Scripture do we find a command to keep any other day in place of the seventh day sabbath or that the sacredness God gave to the seventh day was moved to the first.

d. Sunday was never viewed as a memorial of anything. Nowhere in Scripture does God ever say the first day was in honor of anything or that it was ever a part of God's law. There is not one occurrence where God ever pronounced anything on the first day of the week. The first day was always called just that— the first day—and nothing else.

e. By saying that, "God divided the light from the darkness. and God called the light Day, and the darkness he called Night. And the evening and the morning were the first day," Gen. 1:4-5 shows God actually worked, rather than rested, on the first day of the week.

f. Exod. 20:8-10 ("Remember the sabbath day, to keep it holy. Six days shalt thou labour, and do all thy work: But the seventh day is the sabbath of the Lord thy God: in it thou shalt not do any work"), Exod. 23:12 ("Six days thou shalt do thy work, and on the seventh day thou shalt rest"), and Exod. 34:21 are specific commands by God for us to work on the first day of the week.

g. Jesus never honored the first day. Instead, he rested on the sabbath by lying in the tomb and not rising until Sunday, the first work day, and he never had anything to say about the first day of the week. Like God, he never gave one instance in which he kept the first day as a day of rest or said anything about sanctifying the first day.

h. Paul never made any attempt to meet with the Gentiles on the first day of the week and he never said he kept Sunday holy or tried to do so.

i. The apostles never rested on the first day and never said that it was sacred.

j. None of the patriarchs of the Old Testament ever kept the first day of the week or mentioned it.

In fact, the first day of the week is mentioned only eight times in the entire New Testament and *none* of them justifies transferring the sabbath from Saturday to Sunday. Only one of the eight verses involves any sort of religious gathering and the word "Sunday" never appears once. The sabbath is mentioned fifty-nine times in the New Testament and always with respect, whereas, Sunday is never referred to with sacredness or sanctity. Because the first day of the week is rarely mentioned in the New Testament, each reference warrants the following itemized analysis:

First, Matt. 28:1 refers to "the end of the sabbath, as it began to dawn toward the first day of the week," which says only that the sabbath ends before the first day begins. No sanctity is attached to Sunday in this verse and nothing is changed. The verse clearly states the sabbath has ended before the first day begins and clearly shows that the first day couldn't be the sabbath.

Second, Mark 16:1-2 says, "When the sabbath was past. . . . And very early in the morning the first day of the week, they came unto the sepulcher at the rising of the sun." The verse in another reference to when the women arrived at the tomb. Again, nothing is altered. Like Matt. 28:1 this verse clearly states that the sabbath is past before the first day begins. Therefore, the first day could not be the sabbath.

Third, Mark 16:9 says, "When Jesus was risen early the first day of the week," in no way implying that the sabbath is to be changed. Nothing in the verse in question hallows Sunday or says God made it holy. Nothing commands us to observe it. Nothing sets it apart as a memorial of the Resurrection or for any other purpose. There is no command or example of rest on this day. Moreover, two of the oldest Greek manuscripts of the New Testament, Alpha and Beta, along with many other manuscripts and patristic witnesses, do not contain Mark 16:9-20, which has led many scholars to conclude that these verses aren't even part of the original gospels.

Fourth, Luke 24:1 says, "Upon the first day of the week, very early in the morning, they came unto the sepulcher." This verse changes nothing and places no religious significance on the first day of the week.

Fifth, John 20:1 says, "The first day of the week cometh Mary Magdalene early, when it was yet dark." This is nothing more than the simple record of an early morning arrival. No religious significance is given to the first day of the week here and nothing is changed.

Sixth, the gathering of the disciples in the upper room on the Sunday of Christ's resurrection as recorded in John 20:19 was the result of "fear of the Jews." It says, "Then the same day at evening, being the first day of the week, when the doors were shut where the disciples were assembled for fear of the Jews, came Jesus and stood in the midst." The disciples assembled in order to hide, not to worship. They weren't gathered in honor of the Resurrection because Mark 16:11–14 and Luke 24:37, 24:39, and 24:41 show they did not yet believe it had occurred. Moreover, there is nothing in the passage doing away with the obligation of keeping the seventh day holy. There is no scriptural basis for concluding this event was of such significance that Sunday should be made the sabbath. Nothing in the text calls this day "the sabbath" or the "Lord's Day" or gives it a sacred title. Nothing sets it apart or makes it holy. No authority for changing a command of God comes into play.

Seventh, Acts 20:7 says, "Upon the first day of the week, when the disciples came together to break bread, Paul preached to them . . . and continued his speech until midnight."

No real force is present in this verse because it says Paul and his missionary company held a gathering on the first day of the week at night. Even if they had held communion services that night, this would in no way have made it a holy day. A religious meeting does not make a day sacred. The breaking of bread in Acts 20:11 did not make a day sacred. In Luke 22 Jesus broke bread during the Last Supper, on a Thursday night, and Acts 2:43 and 46 prove his disciples continued doing so *every day of the week* by saying, "Many wonders and signs were done by the apostles. . . . And they, continuing daily with one accord in the temple, and breaking bread from house to house."

In addition, Acts 20:7 does not say the disciples held communion on the first day of every week. Although it provides clear proof the disciples heard a sermon on Sunday, there is no proof they heard one every Sunday or did not also hear them as usual on Saturdays. If the meeting referred to in Acts 20:7 began during the day on Sunday and continued into the night, the next morning would have been the second day of the week, Monday. If the meeting began at the start of the first day of the week, which would be Saturday night (biblical days start at dusk), it would have continued until Sunday morning. In either case, nothing is said about making the day sacred and part of both meetings would have occurred on a day other than Sunday.

Eighth and finally, 1 Cor. 16:2 (NIV) says, "On the first day of every week, each one of you should set aside a sum of money in keeping with his income, saving it up, so that when I come no collections will have to be made."

This verse contains no suggestion of a day of worship or a religious service. Neither is it a command to hold religious meetings on the first day of the week. To conclude that it indicates that the apostolic church recognized Sunday as a day of religious worship (complete with plate passing) is to assume more than the biblical writer wrote. Yes, it speaks of a collection. But for whom, for what? Not for the preacher, not for evangelism—apparently for the saints. This passage does not say to drop a coin in the collection plate at a church service. It says, "Let every one of you lay by him in store." Lay by! Store up! Store up by oneself at home. Not lay by at church, but at home. This is the only time Paul mentioned the first day and it had no connection with a weekly collection at a church service. Paul taught Christians to do their secular business at home on the first day of the week. Instructing people to set aside some wealth each Sunday or delivering a sermon on a Sunday evening hardly warrants changing the sabbath.

The obvious conclusion to be drawn from all eight references to the first day of the week is that none of them changed the sabbath from Saturday to Sunday and none of them bestowed any special status upon Sunday. After viewing all eight passages, the anonymous author of a Christian pamphlet from the Bible Advocate Press entitled "The First Day of the Week in the Bible" correctly concludes on page 14, "One fact should be clear: none gives scriptural authority to the notion that Sunday has replaced *the* Sabbath as the day of rest and worship."

Sunday

Having completed a comprehensive, biblically based exposition of why the sabbath was never changed from Saturday to Sunday, we can now focus on the major weaknesses in Christian apologetic responses to sabbatarians. Numerous citations have already shown that the seventh day of the week, Saturday, is the sabbath, not Sunday, and there is no valid reason for paying homage to Sunday rather than Saturday. But, as is to be expected, Christians have concocted a wide variety of excuses to justify what can only be described as a blatant violation of a cardinal biblical teaching—the Fourth Commandment. They have devised a rather lengthy list of rationalizations, justifications, obfuscations, and prevarications to prove the day of worship was altered ages ago. The importance of this topic is shown in the fact that if millions can violate one of the Ten Commandments on a regular basis with impunity, then there is no limit as far as biblical teachings in general are concerned. Because Christians heatedly deny Sunday observance involves any kind of Fourth Commandment transgression, the following critique of their arguments is presented.

The *first* argument used by Christian apologists—that the Sabbath was for the Jews only—is disproven by the following points:

a. By saying, "He [Jesus] said unto them, The sabbath was made for man, and not man for the sabbath," Mark 2:27 proves the sabbath was made for all mankind, not a particular group such as the Hebrews. The sabbath is not Jewish.

b. The seventh day sabbath was given as a sacred legacy to mankind two thousand years before the first Jew existed. It was given to humanity by God on the seventh day of Creation Week, long before Jews were a separate group. On page 52 in the pamphlet, "Saturday, Sunday and Salvation," Dwight Herbert correctly states, "The text does not say that the Sabbath was given to the children of Israel *only*. It says the Sabbath is a sign that God is willing and able to "sanctify" His people. . . . Are the Jews the only people to be sanctified? Are they the only people of God? Obviously not."

c. The Bible never calls the Scriptural sabbath "Jewish" but always the "Sabbath of the Lord thy God." God allegedly rules everyone. "Thy" is a general reference.

d. God calls the "sabbath," "my sabbaths." They are his and do not belong to a particular group. There are no Jewish sabbaths or Gentile sabbaths, as is demonstrated by Ezek. 20:20–21, which says, "hallow my sabbaths . . . they polluted my sabbaths."

e. If the sabbath was given only to the Jews, then why isn't this true of all other Old Testament laws as well, since they all came through Hebraic writers and Jewish leadership. If the sabbath commandment only applies to the Jews, then the other nine commandments should only apply to them as well.

f. In Acts 7:38 Stephen says Moses was in the congregation in the desert with our fathers and the angel who spoke to him on Mount Sinai, and he received living words "to give unto us." The phrase "to give unto us" proves the sabbath was not given to the Jews only, because Stephen was speaking to Gentiles as well as Jews.

g. In Gen. 26:5 God said, "Abraham obeyed my voice, my charge . . . my commandments, my statutes, and my laws" and shows that Abraham was keeping God's commandments long before his descendants reached Mt. Sinai. The sabbath was to be held in high esteem long before the Israelites received the Ten Commandments on Sinai, which would tend to prove it applied to everyone, not just the Israelites. The Fourth Commandment clearly states, "Remember the sabbath." The word "remember" shows that sabbath observance already existed when God wrote the law in stone at Sinai. On page 5 in the pamphlet "Should the Seventh Day Sabbath be Observed?" the anonymous author representing the Bible Advocate Press aptly states, "Many, today, believe that the Sabbath was 'Jewish'—that it was a part of the ceremonial 'law of Moses' and therefore should not be observed by Christians. But the sabbath existed long before the time of Moses. We have shown that it was established by God at creation—over 2,000 years before Moses was born."

The *second* argument used by Christian apologists is that *the law was nailed to the cross,* so we don't need to keep the sabbath. The apologists love to cite Col. 2:14 ("Blotting out the handwriting of ordinances that was against us, which was contrary to us, and took it out of the way, nailing it to the cross"), Eph. 2:15 ("Having abolished in his flesh the enmity, even the law of commandments contained in ordinances"), and Col. 2:16–17 ("Let no man therefore judge you in meat, or in drink, or in respect of an holy day or of the new moon, or of the sabbath days: which are the shadow of things to come").

Several problems accompany this argument: a. If the law was nailed to the cross, then the Ten Commandments went along for the ride, because they are part of the Law, too;

b. Why would Jesus say in John 15:10 that he kept his father's commandments, if the Ten Commandments were to be nailed to the cross?

c. In Matt. 5:17 Jesus said, "Think not that I am come to destroy the law, or the prophets: I am not come to destroy but to fulfill."

In order to evade the obvious implication of this verse, some theology schools allege that "fulfill" means to abolish. How foolish can one be! They would have us believe that the verse should read, "Jesus came not to destroy the law but to abolish the law," which makes no sense whatever. Obviously "fulfill" does not mean to abolish.

A *third* argument used by Sunday supporters is that the sabbath can be kept on any day of the week as long as one day is set aside each week. The problems with this rationalization are:

a. There is no scriptural support for it. Exod. 20:9–10 says, "Six days shalt thou labor, and do all thy work: But the seventh day is the sabbath of the Lord thy God: in it thou shalt not do any work." This passage and many like it is obviously speaking of the seventh day, not any day out of seven.

b. Christians rely heavily upon Rom. 14:5–6 (NIV), which states, "One man considers one day more sacred than another; another man considers every day alike. Each one should be fully convinced in his own mind. He who regards one day as special, does so to the Lord. He who eats meat, eats to the Lord, for he gives thanks to God; and he who abstains, does so to the Lord and gives thanks to God."

Unfortunately, the contention that it really doesn't matter which day of the week a person observes as his weekly "day of worship," as long as he does it "to the Lord," cannot stand much scrutiny. If one can consider any day as the sabbath, then there isn't really a sabbath day at all. By allowing anyone to determine for himself when the sabbath should be honored, Paul, in effect, rewrote that part of the Old Testament that clearly and repeatedly says Saturday is the sabbath. If an individual can pick any day of the week as his sabbath, then how is he honoring the sabbath? All he is doing is honoring a sabbath or, to be more precise, honoring a day that he chooses to call the sabbath. On page 10 in "Saturday, Sunday and Salvation" apologist Dwight Herbert was asked if it really mattered which day was kept as long as one day in seven was honored. He responded by saying, "This reasoning would be plausible if God had said in the fourth commandment "a seventh day" or even "every seventh day," but God used the definite article *the:* Remember *the* seventh day is the sabbath of the Lord thy

God. . . . The definite article *the* limits the Sabbath to only one day of the week, namely, the seventh."

On the front page of a pamphlet entitled "Letter from Rome," published by Trail Guides, we have the following:

> I could understand a Bible Christian arguing from Col. 2:16, that we ought to make no difference between Saturday, Sunday, and every other day of the week; that under the Christian dispensation all such distinctions of days were done away with; one day was as good and as holy as another; there were to be no Sabbaths, no holy days at all. But not one syllable does it say about the obligation of the Sabbath being transferred from one day to another.

The *fourth* argument used by apologists is that the first day is to be kept as the sabbath rather than the seventh because it honors the Resurrection. This explanation is fatally flawed for several reasons:

a. Jesus never told others to change the sabbath to Sunday in honor of his resurrection.

b. There is no scriptural support for this. As the anonymous author from the Bible Advocate Press in the pamphlet entitled "The First Day of the Week in the Bible" says on page 7, "Nowhere in Scripture is there the slightest hint that the weekday upon which Christ rose from the dead was to be regarded as a day of rest and worship." And on page 15 in "Saturday, Sunday and Salvation" Herbert says, "Nowhere in the Bible is there a command to change the Sabbath from Saturday to Sunday in commemoration of Christ's resurrection."

c. The Crucifixion is as important as the Resurrection, if not more so. So why wasn't the sabbath transferred to Friday? After all, Jesus came to sacrifice himself for humanity and that occurred on Friday, not Sunday. Those who wish to abandon a clear command to keep the seventh day sacred by opting for another day would do well to keep Friday holy in honor of Calvary.

On the front of a Trail Guides pamphlet entitled "Questions and Answers About the Bible Sabbath—Pt. 2" an anonymous author makes the following correct observation: "Frankly, the resurrection of Christ is in no way as important as is Calvary. Those who wish to abandon a clear command of God to keep the Seventh day for another day, would do well to keep Friday holy in honor of Calvary."

d. If the Resurrection of Jesus on Sunday caused the sabbath to be changed to Sunday, then why did Paul and the disciples continue to look upon Saturday as the sabbath even *after* the Resurrection?

A *fifth* argument used by apologists to justify changing the Sabbath to Sunday is that the first sabbath lasted many ages; so we can't keep it today. This tactic is also fraught with problems.

a. If days were thousands or millions of years in length, why would God command us to keep a day holy, when that would have been impossible?

b. There is no scriptural support for the assertion that the first sabbath lasted many ages.

c. If each day of Creation Week was thousands or millions of years long, then the sixth day upon which Adam was created was thousands or millions of years in length. The sixth day was followed by the seventh day which was also thousands or millions of years long. *Following* the seventh day Adam fell into sin, which would mean he lived throughout the entire thousands or millions of years of that seventh day. But this could not be true, since we know Adam lived to be only 930 years old, according to Gen. 5:3–5. On page 37 in "Saturday, Sunday and Salvation" Herbert also notes, "Each day of creation was divided into nearly equal parts—a dark portion and a light portion. If each part was millions of years in length, no sense can be made of the story. How could green plants live through millions of years of darkness? According to record, each plant reproduced its kind. Without light all plant life would have been dead after several months." In reality, the word "day" in the opening chapters of Genesis refers to a literal twenty-four-hour day as we know it, not a period encompassing thousands or millions of years.

A *sixth* argument used by apologists is that *Jesus changed the sabbath from Saturday to Sunday.* But verses such as John 1:3 ("All things were made by him; and without him was not any thing made that was made"), Col. 1:16 ("For by him were all things created, that are in heaven, and that are in earth, visible and invisible"), and Heb. 1:2 ("Hath in these last days spoken unto us by his Son, whom he hath appointed heir of all things, by whom also he made the worlds") show that Jesus created everything, including the sabbath. Are we to believe he changed his mind and decided to pick another day? And where is scriptural support for this?

A *seventh* argument used by those who defend Sunday-worship is that *the disciples* changed the sabbath to Sunday. The difficulties with this are: (a) There is no scriptural support for it; (b) The disciples would have had no more right to change the sabbath than anyone else. As is stated on the front of the anonymously authored Bible Advocate Press pamphlet entitled "Letter from Rome," "You will tell me that Saturday was the Jewish Sabbath, but that the Christian Sabbath has been changed to Sunday. Changed! By whom? Who has authority to change an express Commandment of Almighty God?"; and (c) Luke 23:56 ("They returned, and prepared spices and ointments: and rested on the sabbath day according to the commandment") and Acts 13:14–16, 13:42–46, 16:12–15, and 17:1–4 show that Paul *and the disciples* faithfully kept the sabbath after the Resurrection and never changed it to Sunday.

An *eighth* argument used by Sunday defenders is that the Bible sabbath is the seventh day, but Sunday is the real "Lord's day." Rev. 1:10 says, "I was in the Spirit on the Lord's Day." Somehow these few, vague words are thought to justify changing the sabbath from Saturday to Sunday. This ruse has several holes.

a. We are told about the "Lord's Day" in Rev. 1:10, but are never told what day it is. No specific day is mentioned. Why assume Sunday is under discussion? Rev. 1:10 does not mention the first day of the week or Sunday. As Herbert says on page 21 of "Saturday, Sunday and Salvation," "Notice, however, that the text does not tell us which day was the Lord's day."

b. Nowhere in Scripture is the first day of the week called the Lord's day. As the author of "The First Day of the Week in the Bible" says on page 12, "No Scripture connects the Lord with the first day of the week."

c. Rev. 1:10 says nothing about changing the sabbath from Saturday to Sunday. It is not mentioned, referenced, implied, or hinted at.

d. The Lord's Day is the day of the Lord is Lord of, and in Mark 2:28 Jesus Christ said he was Lord of the sabbath, not Sunday.

e. The seventh day sabbath was called the sabbath of the Lord in Exod. 20:10 ("The seventh day is the sabbath of the Lord thy God"), Lev. 23:3 ("The seventh day is . . . the sabbath of the Lord"), and Deut. 5:14 ("The seventh day is the sabbath of the Lord thy God").

It was called the day "unto the Lord" in Exod. 16:23 ("Tomorrow is the rest of the holy sabbath unto the Lord"), Exod. 16:25 ("For to day is a sabbath unto the Lord"), Exod. 31:15 and Exod. 35:2.

And it was called "His holy day" in Isa. 58:13 ("If thou turn away thy foot from the sabbath, from doing thy pleasure on my holy day; and call the sabbath a delight, the holy of the Lord"). All of this proves that if any day is the Lord's Day it is Saturday, not Sunday.

f. The "Lord's Day" could very easily be the final day of the Lord, the day of his manifest judgment of the world. Many people feel that Rev. 1:10 is not referring to any particular day of the week but to the period mentioned in more than thirty prophecies as the "day of the Lord." It is speaking of the coming plagues climaxing in the coming of Christ and the millennium.

A *ninth* argument used by some Sunday worshipers is that *every* day is holy. There is no scriptural support for this either, and if all days are holy then no days are holy, or more holy than others, and the principle of sabbath observance disappears.

A *tenth* contention used by Sunday adherents is that the sabbath can't be kept because we don't know what day it is. It has been lost in history. Two problems are immediately apparent with this explanation: a) There is no scriptural support for it, and b) the Jews have been keeping the sabbath for thousands of years and know when it occurs. On page 12 in "Saturday, Sunday and Salvation" Herbert was asked how he could be so sure which day was the seventh, when the calendar has been changed so many times. He aptly said, "No question about it—the calendar has been changed. But not the weekly cycle!"

An *eleventh* contention made by Sunday supporters is that Sunday is the Christian sabbath, not the Jewish sabbath. The problems with this are that (a) there is no scriptural support for it—indeed, the very idea of two different sabbaths verges on blasphemy—and (b) Sunday was never the sabbath of the Christians in the Bible or early Christian history. Sunday was not called the sabbath until the 1600s.

A *twelfth* argument used by Sunday adherents is that Jesus' first appearance to his disciples after his Resurrection was on Sunday, and the outpouring of the Holy Spirit on the church first occurred on a Sunday Pentecost. This is one of the points made by apologist Gleason Archer on pages 116–21 in *The Encyclopedia of Bible Difficulties.* Unfortunately, Archer failed to explain why the fact that Jesus first appeared to his disciples on Sunday or the Holy Spirit first fell on the church on Sunday would be of such significance as to overrule God's commandment that the seventh day was to be the sabbath. They are rather weak reeds to lean on, especially when Archer admits on page 117, "After Pentecost it seems that the Christian community continued to celebrate the 7th day Sabbath as before, by gathering with other Jews (both converted and unconverted) for the reading of the Torah, for preaching, and for prayer."

A *thirteenth* and final contention often used by Christians is that the sabbath was made for God and not for man. They cite Exod. 20:10 ("The seventh day is the sabbath of the Lord thy God") as proof. These Christians appear to be unaware that their assertion is directly contrary to Jesus' teaching in Mark 2:27, that the sabbath was made for man, and not man for the sabbath.

In summary, the evidence is overwhelmingly in favor of those opposed to Sunday observance.

Several years ago a sabbatarian Christian offered a substantial reward to any person who could supply "ONE Bible TEXT to prove *any* of the following statements": (a) Sunday, or the first day, is the Lord's Day; (b) Sunday, or the first day, has been blessed and sanctified; (c) Christ observed Sunday, or the first day, as the Sabbath day; (d) The apostles kept Sunday, or the first day, as the Sabbath day; (e) Sunday, or the first day, commemorates the Resurrection; (f) We should not work on Sunday or the first day; (g) Sunday is the Christian sabbath; (h) Sunday is the new day of worship; (i) Christ declared Sunday to be holy; (j) The seventh day Sabbath was made for the Jews only.

The Change

The man who offered the reward prefaced his remarks with the correct observation that the Catholic Church is responsible for the change to Sunday. The anonymous Trail Guides author of the pamphlet entitled "Who Changed the Bible Sabbath" says on page 3 that Sunday observance "is a law of the holy Catholic Church alone. The Bible says, 'Remember the Sabbath day to keep it holy.' The Catholic Church says: 'No. By my divine power I abolish the Sabbath day and command you to keep holy the first day of the week.' As a result, the Christian world bows down in reverent obedience to the command of the Catholic Church."

On page 13 of "The Change of the Sabbath" a Bible Advocate Press author says, "Roman Catholics have always been very free to admit that the change from Sabbath to Sunday was their work. In this they are perfectly consistent for they believe that their church has the authority from God to establish such observances."

The following two passages from Catholics themselves state their position in all its radiant splendor. On the front page of a pamphlet entitled "Catholicism Speaks" we have, "Question: Have you any other way of proving that the church has power to institute festivals of precept? Answer: Had she not such power she could not have done that in which all modern religionists agree with her:—She could not have substituted the observance of Sunday, the first day of the week, for the observance of Saturday, the seventh day of the week, a change for which there is no Scriptural authority."

And on the second page of the same pamphlet Monsignor Louis Segur says, "It is worth while to remember that the observance of Sunday . . . not only has no foundation in the Bible, but it is in flagrant contradiction with its letter, which commands rest on the Sabbath, which is Saturday. It was the Catholic Church which, by the authority of Jesus Christ, has transferred this rest to Sunday in remembrance of the resurrection of our Lord. Thus the observance of Sunday by the Protestants is the homage they pay, in spite of themselves, to the authority of the Catholic Church."

On pages 149 and 150 of *False Doctrines Answered* Protestant fundamentalist John R. Rice concedes the same point after some preparatory comments.

It is clear that the Sabbath of the Ten Commandments is Saturday, the seventh day of the week. Yet for generations people have been speaking of Sunday, the first day of the week, as "the Christian Sabbath." Sunday school has been called "the Sabbath school." If asked to explain why they observe Sunday as a Sabbath instead of Saturday as commanded in the Ten Commandments, most preachers and Bible teachers simply say that when Jesus rose from the dead the Sabbath was changed from Saturday to Sunday. Since Christ rose upon the first day of the week, they say, therefore the apostles and other NT Christians changed the Sabbath day from Saturday to Sunday. However, there is no record in the New Testament of the Sabbath being changed from Saturday to Sunday. Acts 20:7 tells how the Christians at Troas met upon the first day of the week to break bread. In 1 Cor. 16:2 Paul commanded Christians to lay by them in store money for the collection for the poor saints at Jerusalem. But neither of those Scriptures nor any other Scriptures command New Testament Christians to observe Sunday as a Sabbath. There is no biblical evidence for saying that the Sabbath was changed from Saturday to Sunday by the apostles or by Jesus after His resurrection. In saying so, we have followed the example of the Roman Catholics.

The only rational conclusion to be drawn from all of the above is that most Christians are violating the Fourth Commandment on a regular basis. For them to condemn others for violating any of the Ten Commandments seems rather ridiculous in light of the fact that they are routinely violating the Fourth Commandment. When all is said and done, the basic questions remain. *Where does the Bible specifically and clearly change the sabbath to Sunday? And what are Christians doing to prove that they love, honor, and obey the Fourth Commandment?*

20

Paul

Contradictions, Misquotations, Nonquotes, Ill-Conceived Comments, Misinterpretations, False Prophecies

Except for Jesus Christ, no individual in the entire Bible is treated by Christians with as much respect and awe as Paul, originally known as Saul of Tarsus. Paul is showered with all the reverence and adulation of a demigod and his words are accepted as those from a figure with divine attributes. If, in fact, Paul wrote the Epistles, as Christians allege, then no figure in history, with the possible exception of Jesus, contributed more to the formulation of biblical theology and had greater influence on the development of Christianity in general and the New Testament in particular.

What has been kept out of the limelight, however, is the incredibly large number of mistakes, inaccuracies, and erroneous comments that can be laid at Paul's doorstep. Gerald Sigal touched on this issue when he said on page 272 in *The Jew and the Christian Missionary,* "There is a general lack of respect for the integrity of the Scriptures in the Pauline method. In his overriding desire to convert the masses to his beliefs, Paul is guided by the dubious assumption that the end justifies the means. . . . Since Paul did not hesitate to use deceit in his conversion process, it did not matter to him that he distorted the Scriptures."

Paul's tendency to operate by expediency was quite pronounced and no discussion of devious activity with respect to biblical figures and no critique of the Bible would be complete without an extensive analysis of Paul's inadequacies, which, generally speaking, can be grouped under five broad headings: (a) statements in which Paul *contradicts* both other parts of Scripture and himself; (b) Paul's *misquotations* of biblical verses; (c) Paul's accurate quotations corrupted by *misinterpretations* (d) Paul's inaccurate, misleading or *ill-conceived* comments; and (e) Paul's *nonquotes,* his citations of nonexistent Old Testament verses. For purposes of discussion we will stipulate the common apologetic belief that Paul wrote the entire New Testament except for the Gospels, The Book of Acts, and all books following Hebrews.

Contradictions

Prime examples of Paul's contradictions are:

First, Deut. 24:16 says, "The fathers shall not be put to death for the children, neither shall the children be put to death for the fathers: every man shall be put to death for his own sin." But in 1 Cor. 15:3 Paul says, "Christ died for our sins according to the Scriptures," and in 1 Cor. 15:22 Paul says, "As in Adam all die, even so in Christ shall all be made alive." If every man is to be put to death for his own sin, then how can Paul justifiably say all must die for what Adam did and Jesus died for what all do?

Second, in Heb. 12:23 Paul says God is the judge of all, while in 1 Cor. 6:2 he says the saints shall judge the world.

So who is to judge, God or the saints?

Third, Eccles. 7:9 says, "Be not hasty in thy spirit to be angry; for anger resteth in the bosom of fools." Prov. 16:32 and Prov. 22:24 say the same. But in Eph. 4:26 Paul tells people to, "Be ye angry . . . let not the sun go down upon your wrath" and all but ignores Ecclesiastes.

Fourth, in Gen. 32:30 Jacob says, "I have seen God face to face, and my life is preserved." Ex. 33:11, Isa. 6:1, and 6:5, and Amos 7:7–8 also say that God was seen by people. Yet Paul says in 1 Tim. 6:16, "God alone has immortality . . . whom no man has ever seen or can see"; in Col. 1:15, "Who is the image of the invisible God"; and in 1 Tim. 1:17, "Now unto the King eternal, immortal, invisible."

So, was God seen or wasn't he?

Fifth, Rom. 2:11 says, "There is no respect of persons with God," and Eph. 6:9 says, "Knowing that your Master also is in heaven; neither is there respect of persons with him." These clash with Rom. 1:16, which says the gospel "is the power of God unto salvation to every one that believeth; to the Jew first, and also to the Greek" and Rom. 9:13, which says, "Jacob have I loved, but Esau have I hated."

If God does not play favorites, as Paul asserts, then why is the Jew first, and why is Jacob loved while Esau is hated? And why do the following verses also show that some are given preference over others: Deut. 14:2, "Thou art an holy people unto the Lord thy God and the Lord has chosen thee to be a peculiar people unto himself, above all the nations that are upon the earth," and Deut. 7:14, "Thou shalt be blessed above all people."

We are told by Paul that God does not play favorites when these verses, as well as many others, clearly prove otherwise.

Sixth, Paul says in Heb. 9:27, "It is appointed unto men once to die, but after this the judgment." But this conflicts with Paul's comments in 1 Cor. 15:51 ("We shall not all sleep, but we shall all be changed"); Heb. 11:5 ("By faith Enoch was translated that he should not see death, and was not found, because God had translated him"); and 1 Thess. 4:16–17 ("The dead in Christ shall rise first: Then we which are alive and remain shall be caught up together with them in the clouds, to meet the Lord in the air: and so shall we ever be with the Lord").

Paul alleges in Hebrews that all men must die but says the opposite in Corinthians, Thessalonians, and elsewhere. He tells us all men must die even though the Bible has examples of people who did not in Gen. 5:24 ("Enoch walked with God: and he was not; for God took him"), and 2 Kings 2:11 ("Elijah went up by a whirlwind into heaven").

Seventh, in Gen. 2:18 (RSV) the Lord says, "It is not good that the man should be alone; I will make him a helper fit for him." Obviously Paul disagrees with the Lord because he says in 1 Cor. 7:27, "Art thou loosed from a wife? seek not a wife," and in 1 Cor. 7:7–8 he says, "I would that all men were even as I myself [that is, single] . . . I say therefore to the unmarried and widows. It is good for them if they abide even as I."

Eighth, in 1 Cor. 9:24 Paul says that of all those who run in a race only one receives the prize, and then tells us to run that we may obtain the prize. Yet, in Rom. 9:16 Paul says that it is not a matter of he who wills or he who runs, but of God who shows mercy. So, does human effort (running) matter or doesn't it?

Ninth, in Rom. 5:12–19 Paul repeatedly states that we are all sinners because of Adam's sin; yet Ezek. 18:20 and Deut. 24:16 contend, respectively, "The soul that sins it shall die. The son shall *not* bear the iniquity of the father, neither shall the father bear the iniquity of the son," and "The fathers shall *not* be put to death for the children, neither shall the children be put to death for the fathers: every man shall be put to death for his own sin." Of course, if we are all sinners because of Adam, then obviously the son shall bear the iniquity of the father.

Tenth, We are told by Paul in Rom. 13:9, "Thou shalt not covet," but in 1 Cor. 12:31 he tells us to "covet earnestly the best gifts."

So are we or are we not to covet?

Eleventh, in 1 Cor. 7:23 Paul tells us not to become slaves of men, but in Col. 3:22 he orders slaves to obey their earthly masters in everything. Are we to accept slavery or not?

Twelfth, in Gal. 6:2 Paul says we are to "Bear ye one another's burdens, and so fulfil the law of Christ." But three verses later Paul says that each man is to bear his own load.

So, who carries our load, we or they?

Thirteenth, Eccles. 1:4 says, "One generation passeth away, and another generation cometh, but earth abideth forever." But in Heb. 1:10–11 Paul says, "Thou, Lord, didst found the earth in the beginning, and the heavens are the work of thy hands; they will perish, but thou remainest."

How can the earth perish, when the Old Testament contends it will abide forever?

Fourteenth, in Heb. 11:27 (RSV) Paul tells us that, "By faith he [Moses] left Egypt, not being afraid of the anger of the king." If that is true then how does Paul explain Exod. 2:14–15, which relates a conversation between a Hebrew and Moses: "And he said, Who made thee a prince and a judge over us? intendest thou to kill me, as you killedst the Egyptian? And Moses feared and said, Surely this thing is known. Now when Pharaoh heard this thing, he sought to slay Moses. But Moses fled from the face of Pharaoh and dwelt in the land of Midian." If Moses was not afraid, as Paul contends, then why did he flee from the Pharaoh and why does the text say "Moses feared"?

Fifteenth, in 1 Cor. 15:50 Paul assures us that, "Flesh and blood cannot inherit the kingdom of God; neither doeth corruption inherit incorruption." If so, then how does Paul explain the fact that "Elijah went up by a whirlwind into heaven" (2 Kings 2:11), and "Enoch walked with God; and he was not; for God took him" (Gen. 5:24)? Both were corrupt flesh and blood individuals who entered the Kingdom of God. Elijah and Enoch must be corrupt because, as Rom. 3:23 says, "All have sinned and come short of the glory of God."

Sixteenth, Paul says in 2 Cor. 10:18 (RSV), "It is not the man who commends himself that is accepted, but the man whom the Lord commends." Then Paul has the audacity to say in just the next chapter, in verses 11:5–6, "I suppose I was not a whit behind the very chiefest apostles. But though I be rude in speech, yet not in knowledge," and in the very next chapter in verse 12:11, "I ought to have been commended of you; for in nothing am I behind the very chiefest apostles."

How could Paul be accepted or viewed as a proper role model in light of such braggadocio? In 2 Cor. 11:18 he adds to his immodesty by saying, "Seeing that many glory after the flesh, I will glory also."

Seventeenth, Paul's comment about God in 1 Tim. 6:16 ("Who only hath immortality, dwelling in the light which no man can approach unto") is at odds with several Old Testament verses, such as 1 Kings 8:12 ("Then spake Solomon, The Lord said that he would dwell in thick darkness"), Psalms 97:2 ("Clouds and darkness are around about him [God]"), and Psalms 18:11 ("He made darkness his secret place; his pavilion round about him were dark waters").

How can God dwell in light as Paul contends, when the Old Testament repeatedly says he was in darkness and dark waters?

Eighteenth, in Rom. 12:14 Paul says, "Bless them which persecute you: bless, and curse not." Yet 2 Tim. 4:14 shows that when Alexander the coppersmith did evil to him, Paul asked the Lord to reward him according to his works. Paul preached forgiveness but sought the opposite for his detractors.

Nineteenth, in an act of self-denigration, Paul says in 1 Cor. 15:9 (RSV), "I am the least of the apostles, unfit to be called an apostle, because I persecuted the church of God." But in 2 Cor. 11:5 (RSV) he says, "I think that I am not in the least inferior to these superlative apostles."

So does he look upon himself as unfit to be an apostle or equal to those of highest rank?

Twentieth, Prov. 27:2 tells us, "Let another man praise thee, and not thine own mouth; a stranger and not thine own lips." But Paul ignores God's admonition by saying in 2 Cor. 11:17-18 (RSV), "Since many boast of worldly things, I too will boast," and in 2 Cor. 12:11 he says, "You have made me act like a fool, boasting like this. . . . There isn't a single thing these other marvelous fellows have that I don't have too." Clearly Paul chose to ignore the lesson to be learned from Proverbs 27.

Twenty-first, in 1 Tim. 5:23 Paul says, "Drink no longer water, but use a little wine for thy stomach's sake and thine often infirmities." But in Romans 14:21 he reverses direction and says, "It is good neither to eat flesh, nor to drink wine." Centuries earlier an ancient author wrote in Prov. 20:1, "Wine is a mocker, strong drink is raging; and whosoever is deceived thereby is not wise."

So the obvious question becomes: Are we to drink alcoholic beverages or aren't we? Paul provides no consistency.

Twenty-second, in Rom. 7:18 Paul says, "I know that in me (that is in my flesh) dwelleth no good thing," even though he says in Gal. 2:20, "I am crucified with Christ: nevertheless I live; yet not I, but Christ liveth in me." Imagine that! Paul said no good thing dwells within him, even though he has Christ within. But then, perhaps, he's telling the truth. After all, who knows Jesus better, Paul or the average Christian?

Twenty-third, in Gal. 3:16-17 Paul says the promises made to Abraham and his seed by God were followed 430 years later by the advent of the Law. How could the Law have been given to Moses 430 years after the promise was made to Abraham, when the enslavement of the Israelites in Egypt alone lasted 430 years, according to Exod. 12:40, or at least 400 years, according to Gen. 15:13?

Twenty-fourth, in Acts 13:20 Paul said that after the Israelites destroyed the seven nations of Canaan they were ruled by judges for 450 years until Samuel the prophet appeared. But one need only read 1 Kings 6:1 to see that that is impossible. It says the 480th year after they came out of Egypt was the fourth year of Solomon's reign over Israel. If there were 476 years between the time the Israelites left Egypt until the *first* year of Solomon's reign, and judges ruled for 450 of these years, then Saul and David, both of whom ruled before Solomon, could only have ruled for a total of twenty-six years. Yet 2 Sam. 5:4 says David alone ruled forty years.

Twenty-fifth, one would be hard-pressed to reconcile Numbers 23:21, which says, "He [God] has not seen iniquity in Jacob, neither has he seen perverseness in Israel," with Paul's comment in Rom. 10:21 that, "To Israel he saith, All day long I have stretched forth my hands unto a disobedient and gainsaying people." We are supposed to believe that Israel exhibits no perverseness, even though God complains "all day long" about its constant disobedience.

Twenty-sixth, in Acts 24:15, Paul says, "I have hope toward God . . . that there shall be a resurrection of the dead, both of the just and the unjust," while in 1 Cor. 15:52 he says, "In a moment . . . the dead shall be raised incorruptible, and we shall be changed." First Paul *hopes* there will be a resurrection of the dead, then he is *sure* there will be such a resurrection.

So which is the real Paul?

Twenty-seventh, Psalms 145:15–16 says, "The eyes of all wait upon thee [that is, God]; and thou givest them their meat in due season. Thou openest thine hand, and satisfiest the desire of every living thing." But this clashes with Paul's comment in Rom. 8:22 that, "We know the whole creation groaneth and travaileth in pain together until now." How could God be satisfying the desire of every living thing, when Paul says the whole creation groans in pain?

Twenty-eighth, how could Paul's comment in Rom. 2:13 ("Not the hearers of the law are just before God, but the doers of the law shall be justified") be correct when Paul says in the next chapter, Rom. 3:20, that, "By the deeds of the law there shall no flesh be justified in his sight." Will the doers of the law be justified or not? You'll never know from Paul.

Twenty-ninth, in 2 Tim. 3:16 Paul says, "All Scripture is given by inspiration of God, and is profitable for doctrine, for reproof, for correction, for instruction in righteousness." Likewise in 1 Cor. 14:37 Paul states, "The things that I write to you are the commandments of the Lord." But in 2 Cor. 11:17 Paul contends that what he speaks is "not after the Lord, but as it were foolishly, in the confidence of boasting." The texts of 1 Cor. 7:6, 7:12, and 7:25 also contain Pauline injuctions that the author notes are not "of the Lord." The point is, if all Scripture, including the writings of Paul, emanate from God and are divinely inspired, how can Paul occasionally say he is *not* speaking for God?

Thirtieth, in Heb. 6:18 Paul says, "It was impossible for God to lie," and in Titus 1:2 he says God cannot lie. How can Paul be telling the truth when 1 Kings 22:23 says, "The Lord has put a lying spirit in the mouth of all these thy prophets." Jer. 20:7, Ezek. 14:9, Jer. 4:10, and Jer. 15:18 all say the Lord fostered deception. Paul himself noted in 2 Thess. 2:11 that God sent people "strong delusion, that they should believe a lie."

Thirty-first, in 1 Cor. 10:1-2 (NIV) Paul makes one of his more misleading observations by saying, "I do not want you to be ignorant of the fact, brothers, that our forefathers were all under the cloud and that they all passed through the sea. They were all baptized into Moses in the cloud and in the sea." One need only read Exodus chapters 19–20 and 28–29 to see that Paul should be more concerned with his own ignorance than that of others. The cloud was *before* and *behind* his forefathers, they were not *in* or *under* it. And none of the forefathers were baptized; none touched the sea. If anybody was "baptized," it was the Egyptians.

Thirty-second, Paul lays down the maxim in Rom. 2:6 that God "will render to every man according to his deeds," and in 1 Cor. 3:8 he notes, "Every man shall receive his own reward according to his own labour." If that is true, then Paul needs to explain to his followers the meaning of Josh. 24:13, which says, "I [God] have given you a land for which ye did not labour, and cities which ye built not, and ye dwell in them; of the vineyards and oliveyards which ye planted not do ye eat." If God only rewards men according to their deeds and labor, then Josh. 24:13 and several other verses are examples of prevarication in action.

Thirty-third, in Acts 20:26 Paul says he is pure from the blood of all men. If that is true then how does he justify his comments in Acts 22:4 (NIV), "I persecuted the followers of this Way to their death, arresting both men and women and throwing them into prison"; Acts 26:10, "Many of the saints did I shut up in prison, having received authority from the chief priests; and when they were put to death, I gave my voice against them"; and Acts 22:20, "When the blood of thy martyr Stephen was shed, I [Paul] also was standing by, and consenting to his death, and kept the raiment of them that slew him." And how does Paul explain observations by others found in such verses as Acts 9:21, "Isn't this Paul who destroyed them which called on his name in Jerusalem" and Acts 9:1, "Saul [Paul] was still breathing out murderous threats against the Lord's disciples." Many other verses could also be cited to show that Paul was far from pure from the blood of others.

Thirty-fourth, in Acts 20:22 (NIV) Paul says, "Compelled by the Spirit I am going to Jerusalem, not knowing what will happen to me there." But in Acts 21:4 (NIV), he says, "Finding the disciples there, we stayed with them seven days. Through the Spirit they urged Paul not to go on to Jerusalem." Paul says the spirit compelled him to go on to Jerusalem, while the same spirit told others to tell him otherwise.

Thirty-fifth, in 1 Cor. 11:14 Paul says, "Doth not even nature itself teach you, that, if a man have long hair, it is a shame unto him?" If long hair is a shame as Paul alleged, then why was it associated with holiness in such Old Testament verses as Judges 13:5 and 1 Sam. 1:11? Num. 6:5 says, "He shall be holy and shall let the locks of the hair of his head grow." In addition, one can't help but note that every contemporary picture and statue of Jesus shows him with long hair, usually accompanied by facial hair.

Thirty-sixth, 1 Cor. 14:33, 2 Thess. 3:16, and Rom. 15:33 say, "God is not the author of confusion, but of peace." How can these observations by Paul be true when Psalms 144:1 says, "The Lord teaches my hands to war, and my fingers to fight," and Exod. 15:3 says, "The Lord is a man of war."

Thirty-seventh, in 1 Cor. 3:16–17 (RSV) Paul says, "Do you not know that you are God's temple and that God's Spirit dwells in you? If any one destroys God's temple, God will destroy him." If God destroys those who destroy God's temples, as Paul claims, then why hasn't God destroyed himself? After all, we are told in Num. 16:35, 1 Sam. 2:6, and Psalms 135:10 that God killed people. Or is this another example of God being above and beyond morality? Do as I say, not as I do.

Thirty-eighth, Exod. 1:22 says, "The pharaoh charged all his people, saying, Every son that is born you shall cast into the river." And in Exod. 2:2 the mother of Moses "conceived, and bare a son: and when she saw that he was a goodly child, she hid him three months." If these comments in Exodus are true, then the following observation by Paul in Heb. 11:23 must be false: "By faith Moses, when he was born, was hid three months by his parents, because they saw he was a proper child; and they were not afraid of the king's commandment." If Moses' mother was not afraid, then why did she hide Moses?

Thirty-ninth, in Rom. 2:6 Paul says, "Who will render to every man according to his deeds." In 1 Cor. 3:8 he says, "Every man shall receive his own reward according to his own labour." And in 2 Cor. 11:15 he says the end of people will be "according to their works." But in Rom. 3:28 ("We conclude that a man is justified by faith without the deeds of the law") and Gal. 2:16 ("Knowing that a man is not justified by the works of the law, but by the faith of Jesus Christ") Paul clearly says that faith is the main element determining one's destiny. Paul repeatedly states that one's ultimate reward and salvation are based on works and good deeds, while simultaneously contending they are based on faith. So which is the final arbiter, and will the real Paul please stand up?

Fortieth, Paul can't even come to a definite conclusion as to whether or not the old Law should be followed. Rom. 2:13 ("The doers of the law shall be justified"), Rom. 3:31 ("Do we then make void the law through faith? God forbid: yea, we establish the law"), and Rom. 7:1 ("Know ye not, brethren . . . how that the law hath dominion over a man as long as he liveth?") prove that those who do the law shall be justified. Yet, in Gal. 3:13 Paul says, "Christ hath redeemed us from the curse of the law," and in Rom. 7:4 he says, "Wherefore, my brethren, ye also are become dead to the law by the body of Christ." A multitude of verses on both sides of the equation clearly expose the utterly inconsistent position Paul held on this topic.

Forty-first, several problems accompany Paul's conversion on the road to Damascus and also vitiate his veracity:

a. Acts 9:7 says, "The men which journeyed with him *stood* speechless, hearing a voice, but seeing no man." In other words, the men with Paul were standing.

But in relating the same account in Acts 26:14 ("When we were all *fallen* to the earth, I *heard* a voice speaking unto me") Paul says the men fell to the ground. In Acts 22:9 Paul submits another version of what happened by saying, "They that were with me saw indeed the light, and were afraid; but they *heard not* the voice of him that spake to me." In the latter instance, he says that the men with him did not hear a voice. So what really occurred is anyone's guess.

b. Another problem surfaces in 1 Cor. 9:1, in which Paul says, "Am I not an apostle? am I not free? have I not seen Jesus Christ our Lord?" But what actually occurred in Paul's encounter with Jesus on the road to Damascus is related in Acts 9:4 and 9:8-9, which say Paul "fell to the earth and heard a voice saying unto him; Saul, Saul, why persecutest thou me? . . . And Saul arose from the earth; and when his eyes were opened, he saw no man: but they led him by the hand, and brought him into Damascus. And he was there three days without sight." Acts 9:4-9, 22:7-9, and 26:14-15 discuss the same events. Despite Paul's claim in 1 Cor. 9:1 ("Have I not seen Jesus Christ our Lord?"), in none of them does the narrative say Paul saw Jesus. Indeed, Paul had his eyes open briefly and only *heard* Jesus.

Forty-second, undoubtedly one of the most preposterous of Paul's comments is found in 2 Cor. 3:17, "Where the Spirit of the Lord is, there is liberty." A similar piece of nonsense is found in Gal. 3:28, "There is neither Jew nor Greek, there is neither bond nor free, there is neither male nor female: for ye are all one in Christ Jesus." The amount of biblical material that could be cited from previous chapters and many issues of *Biblical Errancy* to demonstrate the contrary is overwhelming. In no way does the Bible support the abolition of slavery or the equality of women and minority groups. The Bible is decidedly class-conscious by nature.

Forty-third, Eccles. 3:19-21 (RSV) says, "The fate of the sons of men and the fate of beasts is the same; as one dies so dies the other . . . man has no advantage over the beasts. . . . All go to one place; all are from the dust, and all turn to dust again. Who knows whether the spirit of man goes upward and the spirit of the beast goes down to the earth?" Paul would be hard-pressed, indeed, to reconcile that declaration with his comment in 1 Cor. 15:52-53 that, "The trumpet shall sound, and the dead shall be raised incorruptible . . . and the mortal must put on immortality." Believing man will be raised incorruptible, Paul obviously thinks humanity does have an advantage over the beasts.

Forty-fourth, in Heb. 11:17 Paul says, "By faith Abraham, when he was tried, offered up Isaac . . . offered up his only begotten son." Gen. 16:16 and 21:15 show that Abraham had two sons, Isaac and Ishmael, and Ishmael was fourteen years older than Isaac. So Paul must have lied when he said Abraham offered up his only begotten son. Isaac was not his only son, nor even his only son at that time, because Ishmael was fourteen years older.

Forty-fifth, we are told in Rom. 2:11 that there is no respect of persons with God; yet we find the following comments by Paul in Eph. 3:4–5 and Col. 1:26, respectively: "When ye read, ye may understand my knowledge in the mystery of Christ which in other ages was not made known unto the sons of men, as it is now revealed unto his holy apostles and prophets," and "even the mystery which hath been hid from ages and from generations, but now is made manifest to his saints." If God does not play favorites as Paul alleges in Romans, then why was the mystery kept from earlier generations?

Forty-sixth and finally, Paul is contradictory with respect to whether *all* meats can be eaten. In Acts 15:28–29 he says, "It seemed good to the Holy Ghost, and to us, to lay upon you no greater burden than these necessary things; That ye abstain from meats offered to idols and from blood." This passage suggests that readers can eat all meats except those offered to idols. But in 1 Cor. 10:25 (RSV) Paul says, "Eat whatever is sold in the meat market without raising any question on the ground of conscience." And two verses later Paul says, "If one of the unbelievers invites you to dinner . . . eat whatever is set before you without raising any question on the ground of conscience." Similarly liberal attitudes toward diet are expressed in 1 Cor. 8:8 and Col. 2:16.

So, in Acts Paul says everything can be eaten except that which has been offered to idols, but later says in 1 Corinthians that everything can be eaten with no restrictions, whatever.

The obvious conclusion to be drawn from all the information presented in this section is that Paul frequently contradicts both himself and Scripture.

Misquotations

Almost no bounds exist with respect to Paul's propensity to extract from the Old Testament and the Gospels the meanings he desires. Given Paul's celebrated intellect, the following misquotations testify to what can only be called the man's notable lack of integrity:

First, one of the great misquotes of Paul is found in Acts 20:35, where he says, "Ye ought to support the weak and to remember the words of the Lord Jesus, how he said, It is more blessed to give than to receive." Nowhere in the New Testament did Jesus ever make such a statement. Paul's oratory got away from him.

Second, in 1 Cor. 3:19–20 ("It is written. . . . The Lord knoweth the thoughts of the wise, that they are vain") Paul misquotes Psalms 94:11 ("The Lord knoweth the thoughts of man, that they are vanity"). Surely not all men are wise. Wisdom and men are not synonymous. Paul seems to be narrowing the focus of the Old Testament passage for rhetorical and possibly even populist effect.

Third, Rom. 15:12 says, "Esaias [Isaiah] saith, There shall be a root of Jesse, and he shall rise to reign over the Gentiles; in him shall the Gentiles trust." But

Paul is misquoting Isa. 11:10, which actually says, "In that day there shall be a root of Jesse, which shall stand for an ensign of the people; to it shall the Gentiles seek."

The problem is that Isaiah does *not* say the root of Jesse shall reign or rule over the Gentiles. He merely states that he will act as a standard or banner for the people. The proof of this is that in the second line Isaiah refers to "it"—the standard or banner—not "him," the root of Jesse, as Paul would have it.

Fourth, in 1 Cor. 2:9 Paul says, "It is written, Eye hath not seen, nor ear heard, neither have entered into the heart of man, the things which God has prepared for them that love him." Here Paul is misquoting Isa. 64:4 (RSV): "From of old no one has heard or perceived by the ear, no eye has seen a God besides thee, who works for those who wait for him." The essential points are that (a) Nowhere in Isa. 64:4 does it say, "Neither have entered into the heart of man"; (b) Isa. 64:4 says, "No eye has seen a God besides thee," which Paul omits; and (c) Paul states, "The things which God hath prepared for them that love him," although Isa. 64:4 does not state, or even imply, that there is a reward prepared for those who love God. It merely states that God will work for those who wait for him.

Fifth, in Eph. 4:8 ("Wherefore Jesus saith, When he ascended up on high, he led captivity captive, and gave gifts unto men") Paul misquotes Psalms 68:18 ("Thou hast ascended on high, thou hast led captivity captive: thou hast received gifts for men.") Paul errs because (a) Psalms 68:18 says "received gifts" not "gave gifts"; (b) Psalms 68:18 says "thou," not "he"; (c) Jesus never led captivity captive, led others to a high mount, or gave gifts to men. To the contrary, the Devil led him to a high mount; and (d) there's a big difference between "giving gifts to men" and "receiving gifts for men."

Sixth, in Rom. 3:4 ("It is written, That thou mightest be justified in thy sayings, and mightest overcome when thou art judged") Paul misquotes Psalms 51:4 ("Thou mightest be justified when thou speakest, and be clear when thou judgest"). The differences are: (a) Psalms 51:4 says "judge" not "art judged," and (b) Psalms 51:4 says, "and be clear" or "blameless," not "and might overcome" or "prevail."

Seventh, in Heb. 10:7 ("Then said I, Lo I come [in the volume of the book it is written of me] to do thy will, O God") Paul distorts Psalms 40:7–8 ("Then said I, Lo, I come [in the volume of the book it is written of me] . . . I delight to do thy will, O my God: yea, thy law is within my heart"). Paul leaves out the last phrase, "thy law is within my heart," because that would have shown God's will *is* the Law. If Paul had quoted the full verse, he would have been stressing the importance of upholding the old Law; but Paul minimized the old Law, so he understandably omitted the last verse.

Eighth, in 1 Cor. 15:54–55 Paul says, "Then shall be brought to pass the saying that is written, Death is swallowed up in victory. O death, where is thy sting? O grave, where is thy victory?" Unfortunately he misquotes Isa. 25:8 (RSV), "He will swallow up death for ever," and Hos. 13:14, "O death, I will be thy plagues; O grave, I will be thy destruction." The discrepancies are: (a) Isaiah says death will be swallowed up "for ever" not "in victory"; (b) Hosea says "thy plagues" not "thy sting"; (c) Hosea was *not* written in interrogatory form; and (d) Hosea says, "thy destruction" not "thy victory." It is difficult to see how Paul's words could be accurately derived from Isaiah and Hosea.

Ninth, in Heb. 10:36–37 Paul says, "Ye might receive thy promise. For yet a little while, and he that shall come will come, and will not tarry." Paul perverts a "promise" made in Hab. 2:3: "The vision is yet for an appointed time, but at the end it shall speak, and not lie: though it tarry, wait for it; because it will surely come, it will not tarry."

The difficulty is that Habbakuk says nothing about "he." The "it" in the verse is a vision, not Jesus, and has nothing to do with the arrival of any individual. Habbakuk is referring to the maturation of a vision he has.

Tenth, in Rom. 11:26–27 Paul says, "So all Israel shall be saved: as it is written, There shall come out of Sion the Deliverer, and shall turn away ungodliness from Jacob, For this is the covenant unto them, when I shall take away their sins." Here Paul misquotes and misuses Isa. 59:20–21: "The Redeemer shall come to Zion, and unto them that turn from transgression in Jacob, saith the Lord. As for me, this is my covenant with them, saith the Lord."

Paul's distortions lie in the facts that: (a) Isa. 59:20 says "to" Zion, not "out of" Zion; (b) the phrase "when I shall take away their sins" is not in Isaiah 59. Paul created that ex nihilo, from nothing; (c) nowhere does Isaiah use the words "saved" or "salvation" as Paul uses them; and (d) Isaiah says the Redeemer shall come "to them that turn from transgression in Jacob." It does not say the Deliverer "shall turn away ungodliness from Jacob." In other words, he will come to those who turned from transgression on their own volition. It does not say he will turn away the ungodliness.

Eleventh, in Rom. 10:6–8 (NIV) Paul says, "The righteousness that is by faith says: 'Do not say in your heart, "Who will ascend into heaven?" (that is, to bring Christ down) or "Who will descend into the deep?" ' (that is, to bring Christ up from the dead). But what does it say? 'The word is near you; it is in your mouth and in your heart,' that is, the word of faith we are proclaiming." [Parenthetical material is in the original.]

Here Paul claims scriptural authority ("The righteousness by faith says") but in fact he is misusing the authority of Deut. 30:12–14, which is part of a long speech by God (related by Moses) about the rewards, or dire punishments, of keeping or falling away from God's commandments. Speaking of those commandments, God allegedly says, "It is not in heaven, that thou shouldest say, Who shall go up for us to heaven, and bring it unto us, that we may hear it, and do it? Neither is it beyond the sea, that thou shouldest say, Who shall go over the sea for us, and bring it unto us, that we may hear it, and do it? But the word is very nigh unto thee, in thy mouth, and in thy heart, that thou mayest do it."

The dissimilarities are many: (a) Deuteronomy says nothing about "faith"; (b) Deuteronomy is referring to seeking "it" and doing "it" (commandments), not seeking "him" or doing "him"; (c) Deuteronomy does not even imply Christ or Jesus, let alone mention him; and (d) Deuteronomy is referring to penitence and is not about believing in or bringing down Jesus from heaven or up from the dead; and (e) all Moses is saying in Deuteronomy is that the commandments, not Jesus or the word of faith, are close by and one need not make extraordinary efforts to find them.

Twelfth, in Rom. 9:33 Paul says, "It is written, Behold, I lay in Sion a stumbling-stone and a rock of offense: and whosoever believeth on him shall not be ashamed." This is an erroneous reproduction of two verses, Isa. 28:16: "Thus saith the Lord God, Behold, I lay in Zion for a foundation a stone, a tried stone, a precious corner stone, a sure foundation: he that believeth shall not make haste"; and Isa. 8:14: "He shall be for a sanctuary; but for a stone of stumbling and for a rock of offense to both houses of Israel."

The differences are: (a) Isaiah says nothing about "on him" or being "ashamed"; (b) The stumbling stone and rock of offense referred to in Isa. 8:14 are speaking of God himself; and (c) Isa. 28:16 says the stone God will lay is a precious corner stone, a sure foundation, not a stumblingstone or a rock of offense as related in Isa. 8:14.

Paul deceptively combines two unrelated verses and alters the text in the process. Obvious problems with his rendition are: (a) Isaiah says, "He that believeth shall not make haste." Again, it never uses the phrase "he that believeth *on him*": (b) Isaiah says "make haste" not "be confounded": and (c) Isaiah never implies the stone is "elect" or "chief" among many.

Incidentally, Peter also distorted Isa. 28:16 in 1 Peter 2:6: "It is contained in the Scripture, Behold, I lay in Sion a chief corner stone, elect, precious: and he that believeth on him shall not be confounded."

The conclusion to be drawn from all of the above is that Paul is by no means a reliable source for Old Testament citations. Quite the contrary, misquotations were his stock in trade.

Nonquotes

Paul also generated a sizable number of quotations of *nonexistent* Old Testament statements—*nonquotes*. He makes comments as if they were recitations of Old Testament verses when, in fact, they are nowhere to be found. For example:

First, in Rom. 10:11 Paul says, "Scripture saith, Whosoever believeth on him shall not be ashamed." No such statement exists in Scripture. Contrary to the belief of some, Isa. 28:16, Jer. 17:7, and Joel 2:32 do not apply.

Second, in 2 Tim. 3:8 ("Jannes and Jambres withstood Moses") Paul refers to two individuals who are never mentioned in the Old Testament, and there is no evidence that they are the Pharaoh's sorcerers mentioned in Exod. 7:11, as some allege.

Third, Paul says in 1 Tim. 1:18, "This charge I commit unto thee, son Timothy, according to the prophecies which went before on thee." Unfortunately, there are no Old Testament prophecies pertaining to, or referring to, Timothy.

Fourth, Paul comments in Eph. 5:14 (RSV), "It is said, Awake, O sleeper, and arise from the dead, and Christ shall give you light." This may be said somewhere, but not in the Old Testament. It is nowhere to be found in Scripture and, contrary to the beliefs of some, Isa. 60:1 and 26:19 do not apply.

Fifth, Paul comments in 1 Cor. 15:4–6, "He [Jesus] rose again the third day according to the Scriptures: and he was seen of Cephas [Peter], then of the twelve: After that, he was seen of above five hundred brethren at once." This claim is unsubstantiated because: (a) No gospel says that Peter saw Jesus before the twelve; (b) No gospel states that Peter was the first person to see Jesus alive after the Resurrection, although Paul implies as much; and (c) No gospel states that five hundred people saw Jesus at one time after the Resurrection. Five hundred people *never at any time* stated they saw Jesus. *Paul* says five hundred saw Jesus, and we only have his word for it, the same Paul who admits he operates by expediency as will be shown later.

Sixth, in Heb. 10:5–6 Paul quotes Jesus as having said when he came into the world, "Sacrifice and offering thou wouldest not, but a body hast thou prepared me; In burnt offerings and sacrifices for sin thou hast had no pleasure." Unfortunately, Paul misquotes and misapplies Psalms 40:6, which says, "Sacrifice and offering thou didst not desire; mine ears hast thou opened: burnt offering and sin offering hast thou not required."

The problems are:

a. "A body hast thou prepared me" is not in Psalms 40:6. Paul created it.

b. "Mine ears hast thou opened" is in Psalms 40:6 but Paul omitted it.

c. Psalms 40:6 was said by the same person who subsequently uttered Psalms 40:12 ("mine iniquities have taken hold upon me, so that I am not able to look up; they are more than the hairs of mine head").

How could this have been Jesus, since the speaker confesses to having committed many iniquities? Paul took Psalms 40:6 out of context and used it for his own devices.

d. Nowhere in the New Testament did Jesus say what Paul attributed to him in Heb. 10:5–6.

Seventh and lastly, Paul alleges in Rom. 2:24 that, "The name of God is blasphemed among the Gentiles through you [Jews who do not keep the Law], as it is written." But nowhere does the Old Testament say that the name of God is blasphemed among the Gentiles through you (Jews not keep the law) including Isa. 52:5 and 2 Sam. 12:14. The former says it is God's people who are blaspheming, while the latter attributes it to David.

In summary then, the evidence clearly shows that Paul not only misquoted the Old Testament but created quotations out of thin air.

Ill-Conceived Comments

The fourth major category encompassing Paul's literary failings involves ill-conceived comments, of which there is an abundant supply.

First, in 1 Thess. 2:3 (NIV) Paul says, "The appeal we make does not spring from error or impure motives, nor are we trying to trick you." Yet, in 2 Cor. 12:16 (NIV) he says, "Yet, crafty fellow that I am, I caught you by trickery!" So, is Paul a trickster or isn't he?

Second, Paul, like Jesus, often ignored his own advice. For example, in Rom. 12:14 he says, "Bless them which persecute you: bless and curse not." Yet in Acts 23:3 he denounces someone by saying, "God shall smite thee, thou whited wall."

Third, in Col. 1:23 (RSV) Paul says, "From the hope of the gospel which you heard, which has been preached to every creature under heaven, and of which I, Paul, became a minister." Apparently Paul was infected with a degree of megalomania. At no time has every living person heard the gospel and certainly not in the middle of the first century. Indeed, millions of people have come and gone without having had any contact with the Bible whatever.

Fourth, in 1 Cor. 2:8 Paul says, "Which none of the princes of this world knew; for had they known it, they would not have crucified the Lord of glory." What princes crucified Jesus? He was killed by a mob and some soldiers.

Fifth, in Gal. 1:19 Paul said, "Other of the apostles saw I none, save James the Lord's brother." Where does any gospel say Jesus had an apostolic brother by the name of James?

Sixth, in 1 Cor. 10:8 Paul refers to a plague described in the Book of Numbers ("And fell in one day 23,000"). Yet Num. 25:9 clearly says the number was 24,000, not 23,000, and shows Paul erred by 1,000.

Seventh, in Heb. 4:2 Paul says, "For unto us was the gospel preached, as well as unto them." The gospel was never preached to Paul. He simply converted after a vision and began preaching.

Eighth, Paul's comment in 1 Cor. 15:4-5 ("He was buried and that he rose again the third day according to the Scriptures: And that he was seen of Cephas, then of the twelve") clashes with Matt. 27:5 ("Judas cast down the pieces of silver in the temple, and went and hanged himself"). Jesus could not have been seen by the twelve after the Resurrection, unless Judas came back to life. Judas was dead after the Resurrection and only eleven apostles remained. Judas' replacement, Matthias, was not elected until after the Ascension.

Ninth, in 1 Cor. 15:36 (RSV) Paul says, "You foolish man! What you sow does not come to life unless it dies." The organic processes constituting physical life do not cease in grain that grows up into wheat. If they ceased, wheat would not grow from wheat seeds (grain). In order to be correct Paul should have said that what you sow does not come to life if it dies, not *unless* it dies.

Tenth, in Heb. 11:26 Paul says Moses "considered abuse suffered for the Christ greater wealth than the treasures of Egypt." How and when was Moses punished or subjected to suffering because of a belief in Jesus or the Christ? Where is that in Scripture? Paul is concocting his own script.

Eleventh, in Heb. 11:35 (RSV) Paul says, "Some [of the prophets] were tortured, refusing to accept release, that they might rise again to a better life." Nowhere does the Old Testament say that people suffered torture because they expected a resurrection. From whence Paul garnered this concept, we can only speculate.

Twelfth, in Gal. 3:13 Paul says, "Christ hath redeemed us from the curse of the law, being made a curse for us: for it is written, Cursed is every one that hangeth on a tree." According to Paul's reasoning, it would appear anyone who was ever crucified or hung on a tree could be a savior.

Thirteenth, in Heb. 6:1 Paul says, "Leaving the principles of the doctrine of Christ let us go on unto perfection." The conclusion to be drawn from this observation is that Christ's doctrine is not perfection but only a step in that direction.

Fourteenth, Rom. 5:13 ("Until the law sin was in the world; but sin is not imputed when there is no law") and Rom. 4:15 ("Where no law is, there is no transgression") are examples of doubletalk. If sin was not imputable to people before the Law and there was no transgression, then how could sin have been in the world? How could sin have been imputable to no one? If sin was in the world, then it must have been imputable; otherwise, how could it have existed?

Fifteenth, in 1 Cor. 12:24–27 (RSV) Paul says, "God has so composed the body [of Christ] . . . , that there may be no discord in the body, but that the members may have the same care for one another. If one member suffers, all suffer together; if one member is honored, all rejoice together. Now you are the body of Christ and individually members of it." Religious conflicts between Christians throughout the ages and the existence of over 1,500 Christian denominations demonstrate the inaccuracy of this assertion.

Sixteenth, in Heb. 2:4 Paul made another major mistake by saying, "God also bearing them witness, both with signs and wonders, and with divers miracles." Verses such as Mark 13:21–22 and Rev. 13:11, 13–14, 16:14, and 19:20 show that God's presence is *not* substantiated by the presence of miracles. One need only read Exod. 7:11–12 and 8:7 and 2 Thess. 2:8–9 to see that many biblical figures, both good and bad, performed miracles. Matt. 24:23–24 and Deut. 13:1–

3 specifically state that miracles are *not* to be used as a test for God's presence. Even the Devil performs miracles.

Seventeenth, in Col. 1:15 Paul says, "Who [Jesus] is the image of the invisible God, the firstborn of every creature." The problems with this are: (a) If Jesus and God are equal and eternal, how could either be born? and (b) In no sense could Jesus be considered the firstborn, either as a man or as a God. As a God he could never have been born and as a man he lived after untold numbers had already been born.

Eighteenth, in Heb. 1:2 Paul muddies the waters mightily by saying, "[God] Hath in these last days spoken unto us by his Son, whom he hath appointed heir of all things, by whom also he made the worlds." An heir is appointed for a time when the appointer dies or is incapacitated. In effect, Paul is saying God will die or become incapacitated and Jesus will fall heir to his kingdom, which are impossible. God clearly said in Isa. 48:12, "I am the first, I also am the last," which means he is without beginning or end; he is eternal.

Nineteenth, while talking about the Levitical priesthood in Heb. 7:11 Paul erroneously states that "under it the people received the law." Actually, in the form of the Ten Commandments and other rules, the Law was given to the Israelites before the Levitical priesthood emerged. The priesthood and Temple service were switched from the responsibility of the firstborn Israelites to the tribe of Levi *after* the Israelites worshiped the golden calf, which the Levites refused to do, and *after* the Law had arrived on the scene.

Twentieth, Paul creates some erroneous history when he says in Gal. 4:22–24, "It is written, that Abraham had two sons, the one by a bondmaid [Hagar], the other by a freewoman [Sarah] . . . for these are the two covenants; the one from Mount Sinai, which gendereth to bondage, which is Agar [Hagar]." The Law was given from Sinai to the descendants of the freewoman, Sarah, through Isaac and not to the descendants of the bondwoman, Hagar, through Ishmael.

Twenty-first, in Heb. 7:2–3 Paul says Melchizedek was "without father, without mother, without descent, having neither beginning of days, nor end of life, but made like unto the Son of God; abideth a priest continually." Although Gen. 14:18 implies Melchizedek was only a priest, Paul attributes qualities to him that are possessed only by Jesus. And since Jesus is God, Melchizedek must be little short of divine too; otherwise, he is not "like the Son of God," as Paul claims.

Twenty-second, in Heb. 11:13 (RSV) Paul, the alleged messenger of God, accuses God of breaking his promise to Abraham. Paul says, "These all died in faith, not having received what was promised [by God], but having seen it and greeted it from afar." In effect, Paul is accusing God of lying.

Twenty-third, in 1 Cor. 10:24 Paul says, "Let no man seek his own, but every man another's wealth." This verse speaks for itself.

Twenty-fourth, Paul shows his allegiance to expediency and opportunism by being a religious chameleon. In 1 Cor. 9:20–23 he says, "Unto the Jews, I became as a Jew, that I might gain the Jews, to them that are under the law, as under the law, that I might gain them that are under the law; To them that are without law, as without law . . . that I might gain them that are without law. To the weak became I as weak, that I might gain the weak: I am made all things to all men, that I might by all means save some. And this I do for the gospel's sake." How's that for pure opportunism?

Twenty-fifth, in 1 Cor. 10:23 Paul says, "All things are lawful for me, but all things are not expedient: all things are lawful for me, but all things edify not." In effect, the allegedly moral Paul looks upon himself as a law unto himself. And to think a recent president was accused of considering himself above the law and operating on expediency!

Twenty-sixth, in Gal. 2:11–12 (NIV) Paul reprimands Peter by saying, "When Peter came to Antioch, I opposed him to his face, because he was clearly in the wrong. Before certain men came from James, he used to eat with the Gentiles. But when they arrived, he began to draw back and separate himself from the Gentiles because he was afraid of those who belonged to the circumcision group." Paul accuses Peter of acting expediently, yet in 1 Cor. 9:22, Paul admits he is "all things to all men."

Twenty-seventh, in Acts 26:23 Paul says, "That Christ should suffer and . . . be the first that should rise from the dead." Jesus certainly wasn't the first to rise from the dead as anyone who is acquainted with the Old Testament or the Gospels knows all too well. See 1 Sam. 28:7–15, 1 Kings 17:17–22, 2 Kings 4:32–35 and 13:21, Matt. 9:18–25 and 27:52–53, Luke 7:11–15, and John 11:43–44.

Twenty-eighth, in several verses Paul openly admits he spoke foolishly, which is more than his followers are willing to concede. Key verses in this regard are: 2 Cor. 11:17 ("What I am saying I say not with the Lord's authority, but as a fool, in this boastful confidence"); 2 Cor. 11:21 ("I speak foolishly"); 2 Cor. 11:23 ("I speak as a fool); 2 Cor. 11:1 (RSV) ("I wish you would bear with me in a little foolishness. Do bear with me!"); and 2 Cor. 12:11 ("I am become a fool in glorying").

Twenty-ninth, in 2 Cor. 11:8–9 Paul says, "I robbed other churches, taking wages of them, to do you service." This verse speaks for itself. Comments are unnecessary.

Thirtieth, in Eph. 2:8–9 Paul makes one of his most quoted statements. "For by grace are ye saved through faith; and that not of yourselves: it is the gift of God: not of works, lest any man should boast."

Unfortunately Paul erred. The act of accepting by faith is a work itself. You must take an affirmative act in order to be saved; being saved by faith not a mere gift. If you don't act, you get only condemnation.

Thirty-first, in Acts 9:5, on the road to Damascus, Paul says "Who art thou, Lord? And the Lord said, I am Jesus whom thou persecutest."

The obvious question that would be asked by any objective observer in this situation is: Why would Paul ask who is speaking, when he called the speaker "Lord"? He must have known who was speaking. If not, why did he call him lord? How could he not have known?

Thirty-second, in Gal. 5:3 (NIV) Paul says, "Again I declare to every man who lets himself be circumcised that he is obligated to obey the whole law." Luke 2:21, Phil 3:5, and Acts 16:3 show that Jesus, Paul, and Timothy, respectively, were all circumcised and obligated to keep the whole Law. Yet, although Jesus and Paul were key New Testament figures, they ignored significant parts of it.

Thirty-third, in Heb. 10:5–10 (NIV) Paul says,

> When Christ came into the world, he said: Sacrifice and offering you did not desire, but a body you prepared for me. . . . Sacrifices and offerings, burnt offerings and sin offerings you did not desire, nor were you pleased with them. . . . Then he said, Here I am, I have come to do your will. He sets aside the first to establish the second. And by that will, we have been made holy through the sacrifice of the body of Jesus Christ once and for all.

Paul quotes Psalms 40:6, which clearly says that God does not want sacrifices to him. And yet he also quotes Jesus as alleging that one final sacrifice is needed. There are no bounds to Paul's ability to extract from the Old Testament the sense he desires. He goes so far as to find a demonstration of the necessity of the sacrifice of Christ in a passage in Psalms that clearly affirms that God does *not* desire sacrifice, but obedience to his will.

Thirty-fourth, Paul's cunning and deception are further exposed by his comments while on trial before the Sanhedrin. Realizing that some of his accusers were Sadducees and the others were Pharisees, he calls out in Acts 23:6–8 (NIV), "My brothers, I am a Pharisee, the son of a Pharisee. I stand on trial because of my hope in the resurrection of the dead. When he said this, a dispute broke out between the Pharisees and the Sadducees, and the assembly was divided. The Sadducees say that there is no resurrection, and that there are neither angels nor spirits, but the Pharisees acknowledge them all." In Acts 24:21 Paul reaffirms the same charge even though Acts 21:28 and 24:5 prove the actual charges were quite different, and Paul lied in order to foment division in the courtroom and derail his accusers.

Thirty-fifth and lastly, contrary to Gal. 1:18, in which Paul says, "After three years I went up to Jerusalem to see Peter, and abode with him 15 days," three different New Testament accounts found in Acts 9, 22, and 26 state that Paul went to Jerusalem shortly after he left Damascus, not three years later.

So, in essence, another obvious conclusion to be drawn from Paul's comments is that he was more interested in propagating a philosophy than propounding the truth.

Misinterpretations

The final major category of Paul's failings involves misinterpretations of biblical verses and is about as convoluted as any. The following examples demonstrate that even when quoting accurately Paul often misconstrued Old Testament verses.

First, Paul erred gravely by incorrectly applying "seed" to Jesus in Gal. 3:16, which says, "To Abraham and his seed were the promises made. He said not, And to seeds, as of many; but as of one, And to thy seed, which is Christ." The problems with this are:

a. "Seed" in the Old Testament was never used in the singular, as Gen. 13:15–16, 15:5, 15:13, 26:4, and 32:12 clearly show. It is plural and always referred to descendants.

b. If "seed" is referring to Jesus alone, then Gen. 12:7 would mean God gave Jesus, the creator of heaven and earth, the land of Canaan as an inheritance; Gen. 13:16 and 22:17 would mean Jesus was as numberless as the dust of the earth; Gen. 15:13 would mean Jesus and a nation of Christs would serve Egypt four hundred years, and Gen. 17:9–10 would mean the covenant of circumcision was established with Jesus. All these readings are, of course, absurd.

c. Why would God make a promise to Jesus to begin with, since Jesus is coexistent and coequal with God?

Second, in Heb. 12:21 Paul says, "So terrible was the sight, that Moses said, I exceedingly fear and quake." Paul is allegedly referring to the fear Moses had when he stood at the base of an untouchable mountain and witnessed blazing fire, gloom, darkness, and trumpets sounding. Yet Paul is quoting Deut. 9:19, "I was afraid of the anger and hot displeasure, wherewith the Lord was wroth against you to destroy you," in which Moses is actually referring to the fear he had at the Lord's anger when God found the Israelites worshipping the golden calf. Again, we have another instance in which Paul used the Old Testament for his own ends.

Third, in Gal. 3:13 Paul says, "Christ hath redeemed us from the curse of the law, being made a curse for us: for it is written, Cursed is every one that hangeth on a tree." Paul used Deut. 21:22–23 for his own purposes, because it says, "If a man has committed a sin worthy of death, and he be to be put to death, and thou hangeth him on a tree: his body shall not remain all night upon the tree, but thou shalt in any wise bury him that day, for he that is hanged is accursed of God." Paul's distortions are: (a) Deut. 21:22 is referring to a sinful man and that could not be Jesus, since he is supposedly sinless; (b) Jesus was not hanged; and (c) Jesus did not die on a tree.

Fourth, in Heb. 10:30 (NIV) Paul falsely accuses God of saying "It is mine to avenge; I will repay," which comes from Deut. 32:35, when Moses was the real source.

Fifth and lastly, Paul says in Acts 13:30–33 (NIV), "God raised him [Jesus] from the dead, and for many days he was seen by those who had traveled with him from Galilee to Jerusalem. They are now his witnesses to our people. We tell you the good news: What God promised our fathers he has fulfilled for us, their children, by raising up Jesus. As it is written in the second Psalms: You are my Son; today I have become your Father."

Where does Psalms 2 say or imply that in some distant day God will raise Jesus of Nazareth, Joseph's son, from the dead? The second Psalms does not promise that (a) anyone will rise from the dead; (b) he who is the Son of God must rise from the dead; (c) Jesus of Nazareth is the son of God; or (d) anyone risen from the dead shall be the son of God. In truth, the psalmsist in Psalms 2:7, David, is speaking of himself, not Jesus.

False Prophecies

To close our critique of the Apostle Paul who, interestingly enough, was not even one of the twelve apostles, we could do no better than highlight some of his false prophecies.

In 1 Thess. 4:15 Paul says, "we which are alive and remain unto the coming of the Lord shall not prevent them which are asleep." And in 1 Thess. 4:17 Paul says, "We which are alive and remain shall be caught up together with them in the clouds, to meet the Lord in the air; and so shall we ever be with the Lord." Both verses prove beyond any reasonable doubt that Paul was certain the end of the world was coming in the lifetime of his contemporaries. He expected to be snatched up bodily into heaven with the other saints then living and, like them, never taste death. As Frank Morison says on page 139 of his famous work, *Who Moved the Stone?*, "Paul believed that Jesus of Nazareth would return in glory to the earth, and he clearly expected it in his own lifetime. . . . It was a belief which commended itself to vast numbers of people during the first fifty years of the Christian era, and St. Paul shared it." Yet Paul and his contemporaries never witnessed the return of Jesus, and they were never taken up into the air.

And lastly, Heb. 1:2 ("In these last days"), 1 Cor. 7:29 ("The time is short") and Heb. 10:37 ("Yet a little while, and he that shall come will come, and will not tarry") clearly show that Paul taught others that Christ's coming and the end of the world were close at hand. After two thousand years, it is safe to say that Paul was deluded.

Conclusion

The only realistic conclusion to be drawn from our extensive and detailed commentary on Paul's credibility and reliability is that he is one of the most deceitful, hypocritical, duplicitous, opportunistic, and inaccurate charlatans to have ever emerged on the world scene. If there is anything for which Paul is *not* qualified, it is sainthood.

21

Accommodations

Misquotations, Nonquotes, Misinterpretations, Ignored Teachings

One of the most egregious violations of intellectual integrity by the founders of Christianity is shown in their gross distortions of the Old Testament for purposes of propaganda and indoctrination. In their never-ending quest for religious legitimacy and status, they did not hesitate to twist, distort, pervert, and concoct Old Testament verses in any manner deemed expedient. Here, as much as anywhere else in the Bible, the true colors of the creators of Christianity come through in all their radiant splendor. Examples of their perfidious display of propagandistic propensities are abundantly evident to anyone with a reasonably critical eye.

Generally speaking, they fall into three broad categories: *misquotations* (a deliberate misquotation of Old Testament passages), *nonquotes* (quoting nonexistent Old Testament passages), and *misinterpretations* (correctly quoting Old Testament passages while distorting their intended meaning).

Misquotations

First, is Matt. 3:3, which declares, "This is he that was spoken of by the prophet Esaias, saying, 'The voice of one crying in the wilderness, Prepare you the way of the Lord, make his paths straight.' " This is an inaccurate translation of Isa. 40:3 (RSV), "A voice cries: In the wilderness prepare the way of the Lord, make straight in the desert a highway for our God." The differences are: (a) nothing is said in Isaiah about one crying in the wilderness; (b) the present tense verb

407

"cries" shows Isaiah is not making a prophecy but only speaking of a contemporary; and (c) Matthew has "paths" (plural), while Isaiah has "a highway" (singular).

Second, Matt. 4:10, "Saith Jesus unto him, Get thee hence, Satan: for it is written, Thou shalt worship the Lord thy God, and him only shalt thou serve," is a major distortion of Deut. 6:13, which says, "Thou shalt fear the Lord thy God, and serve him, and shalt swear by his name." Nowhere does Deut. 6:13 say thou shalt serve God only.

Third, Matt. 11:10 says, "This is he, of whom it is written, Behold, I send my messenger before thy face, which shall prepare thy way before thee." This is a misquote of Mal. 3:1, "Behold, I will send my messenger, and he shall prepare the way before me." Several conflicts are evident in Matt 11:10: (a) the Old Testament says "thy way before me," not "the way before thee"; (b) Mal. 3:1 says "will send" (future tense) rather than "send" (present tense); (c) many biblical antecedents are conjectural and there is little reason to believe Malachi is referring to Jesus or John the Baptist; (d) Jesus created the phrase "before thy face," which does not exist in Malachi; and (e) the coming of Jesus was always spoken of as a time of joy and happiness. Yet the coming of the Lord in Malachi, especially Mal. 4:1 ("Behold, the day cometh, that shall burn as an oven; and all the proud, yea, and all that do wickedly, shall be stubble") and Mal. 4:5 ("I will send you Elijah the prophet before coming of the great and terrible day of the Lord") is a scene of fear and terror like the day of judgment. How, then, could the scene in Malachi be referring to the birth of Jesus, as some allege? Evidence suggests that Mal. 3:1 is not a prognostication of John the Baptist or Jesus.

Fourth, Matt. 12:17–21 says,

> That it might be fulfilled which was spoken by Esaias the prophet, saying, Behold my servant, whom I have chosen; my beloved, in whom my soul is well pleased: I will put my spirit upon him, and he shall show judgment to the Gentiles. He shall not strive nor cry; neither shall any man hear his voice in the streets. A bruised reed shall he not break, and smoking flax shall he not quench, till he send forth judgment unto victory. And in his name shall the Gentiles trust.

Matthew's quotation represents an attempt to apply Isa. 42:1–4 to Jesus. That passage says,

> Behold my servant, whom I uphold; mine elect, in whom my soul delighteth; I have put my spirit upon him: he shall bring forth judgment to the Gentiles. He shall not cry, nor lift up, nor cause his voice to be heard in the street. A bruised reed shall he not break, and the smoking flax shall he not quench: he shall bring forth judgment unto truth. He shall not fail nor be discouraged, till he have set judgment in the earth, and the isles shall wait for his law.

Matthew's quotation is a major distortion of Isaiah for many reasons: (a) Isaiah says "have put" (past tense) rather than "will put" (future tense); (b) "not strive" is not in Isaiah; (c) "nor lift up" is in Isaiah but not Matthew; (d) "streets" in Matthew is "street" in Isaiah; (e) "victory" in Matthew is "truth" in Isaiah; (f) there is no conditional "till" in Isaiah; (g) "in his name shall the Gentiles trust" is not in Isaiah; and (h) apparently because reality could no longer be ignored, Matthew omitted, "He shall not fail nor be discouraged, till he has set judgment in the earth, and the isles shall wait for his law."

Fifth, Matt. 13:35, "That it might be fulfilled which was spoken by the prophet saying, I will open my mouth in parables; I will utter things which have been kept secret from the foundation of the world," is an inaccurate portrayal of Psalms 78:2–3: "I will open my mouth in a parable: I will utter dark sayings of old: Which we have heard and known, and our fathers have told us."

The contrasts are: (a) Psalms 78 says nothing about "things which have been kept secret since the world began" but only of dark sayings of old. These sayings refer to old sayings, not things which have been kept secret; (b) the phrase, "which we have heard and known, and our fathers have told us," which can be found in Psalms 78, is the opposite of "secret" in Matt. 13; and (c) Psalms 78 says "a parable," while Matthew says "parables."

Sixth, Luke 4:17–21 says,

> There was delivered unto him [Jesus] the book of the prophet Esaias [Isaiah]. And when he had opened the book, he found the place where it was written; The Spirit of the Lord is upon me, because he hath anointed me to preach the gospel to the poor; he hath sent me to heal the brokenhearted, to preach deliverance to the captives, and recovering of sight to the blind, to set at liberty them that are bruised. To preach the acceptable year of the Lord. And he closed the book, and he gave it again to the minister, and sat down. . . . And he began to say to them, This day is the Scripture fulfilled in your ears.

In Luke 4 Jesus used Isa. 61:1–2 for his own ends. It actually says,

> The spirit of the Lord God is upon me; because the Lord hath anointed me to preach good tidings unto the meek; he hath sent me to bind up the brokenhearted, to proclaim liberty to the captives, and the opening of the prison to them that are bound; To proclaim the acceptable year of the Lord, and the day of vengeance of our God; to comfort all that mourn.

The problems are: (a) Isaiah says nothing about healing the blind; (b) Isaiah says "opening of the prison to them that are bound," not "to set at liberty them that are bruised"; (c) Jesus omitted the part about proclaiming "the day of vengeance of our God" which is located in Isaiah; and (d) the statement in Isaiah was made by Isaiah concerning himself, long before Jesus was born. It cannot be twisted into proving that Jesus was anointed. Actually, Jesus is quoting a statement by Isaiah that he (Isaiah) has been appointed by God to tell the exiled, broken, downtrodden, afflicted, captive Jews that the day is coming when they shall be saved, eat the riches of the Gentiles, and have eternal joy.

Seventh, John 19:37 ("Scripture saith, They shall look on him whom they pierced") is an incorrect representation of Zech. 12:10 ("They shall look upon me whom they have pierced, and they shall mourn for him, as one mourneth for his only son"). The variances are:

a. Why say "as one mourns for his only son" when Jesus is a son of the house of David?

b. Would it make sense to have the house of David responsible for the death of Jesus when that is the house from which Jesus arose? Would his own house kill him?

c. Zech. 12:11 says in regard to the same individual, "In that day shall there be a great mourning in Jerusalem." But there was very little mourning for Jesus on the day he died.

d. If correctly translated the word "pierced" should be "blasphemed." Both words, "blasphemed" and "pierced," come from the same Hebrew root (note, for example, Lev. 24:11).

e. the statement in Zechariah has nothing to do with Jesus. Zechariah is saying that God will make Judah and Jerusalem so powerful in the future that those nations who attack them will be destroyed. Then the people of Jerusalem will look with compassion and mourning on those they have pierced and killed.

Eighth, Acts 1:20 ("It is written in the Book of Psalms, Let his habitation be desolate, and let no man dwell therein") is a distortion of Psalms 69:25 ("Let their habitation be desolate; and let none dwell in their tents"). Psalms 69:25 says, "their" habitation and "their" tents. At no time does it refer to one person or "his." Psalms 69:25 is actually an appeal by David to God for aid in David's struggle with his enemies and has no reference to Judas, as is implied in Acts.

Ninth, Acts 2:16–17, "This is that which was spoken by the prophet Joel; and it shall come to pass in the last days, saith God," is a perversion of Joel 2:28, which says, "It shall come to pass afterward, that I will pour, etc."

Joel says merely "afterward." He says nothing about "the last days."

Tenth, Rom. 3:4, "It is written, That thou mightest be justified in thy sayings, and mightest overcome when thou art judged," perverts Psalms 51:4 which says, "That thou mightest be justified when thou speakest, and be clear when thou judgest." Psalms 51:4 says "judge," not "art judged." There is a big difference between judging and being judged.

Eleventh, Rom. 9:33 says, "It is written, Behold, I lay in Sion a stumblingstone and a rock of offense: and whosoever believeth on him shall not be ashamed." This is an erroneous reproduction of Isa. 28:16, which says, "Thus saith the Lord God, Behold, I lay in Zion for a foundation a stone, a tried stone, a precious corner stone, a sure foundation: he that believes shall not make haste," and Isa. 8:14, "He shall be for a sanctuary; but for a stone of stumbling and for a rock of offense to both houses of Israel."

The differences are: (a) Isaiah says nothing about "on him" or being "ashamed"; (b) the stumbling stone and rock of offense referred to in Isa. 8:14 are speaking of God himself; and (c) Isa. 28:16 says the stone God will lay is a precious corner stone, a sure foundation, not a stumblingstone or a rock of offense, as is related in Isa. 8:14. Paul deceptively combines two unrelated verses and alters the text in the process.

The text of 1 Peter 2:6, "It is contained in the Scripture, Behold, I lay in Sion a chief corner stone, elect, precious: and he that believeth on him shall not be confounded," is also a distortion of Isa. 28:16. Obvious problems are: (a) Isaiah says, "He that believes shall not make haste." Again, it never uses the phrase "he that believes on him"; (b) Isaiah says "make haste" not "be confounded"; and (c) Isaiah never implies the stone is "elect" or "chief" among many.

Twelfth, Rom. 15:12, "Esaias saith, There shall be a root of Jesse, and he that shall rise to reign over the Gentiles; in him shall the Gentiles trust," does not accurately reproduce Isa. 11:10, which says, "In that day there shall be a root of Jesse, which shall stand for an ensign of the people; to it shall the Gentiles seek." Isa. 11:10 does not state that the root of Jesse shall reign or rule over the Gentiles but merely states that he will act as a standard or banner for the people. And even more important, Isaiah says "to it" not "to him" shall the Gentiles gravitate.

Thirteenth, in 1 Cor. 3:20 ("The Lord knoweth the thoughts of the wise, that they are vain") Paul misquotes Psalms 94:11 ("The Lord knoweth the thoughts of man, that they are vanity"). Psalms 94 says "man," not "the wise." Most assuredly, all men are not wise. Wisdom and men are by no means identical.

Fourteenth, 1 Cor. 15:54–55 says, "Then shall be brought to pass the saying that is written, Death is swallowed up in victory. O death, where is thy sting? O grave, where is thy victory?" This is a perversion of both Isa. 25:8 ("He will swallow up death for ever") and Hosea 13:14 ("O death, I will be thy plagues; O grave, I will be thy destruction"). The conflicts are: (a) Isaiah says death will be swallowed up "for ever," in the RSV, MT, NIV, NAB, ASV, JB, ML, and LB, not "in victory"; (b) Hosea says "thy plagues" not "thy sting"; (c) Hosea says "thy destruction" not "thy victory"; and (d) Hosea was not written in interrogatory form.

Fifteenth, Ephesians 4:8 says, "Wherefore he saith, 'When he ascended up on high, he led captivity captive, and gave gifts unto men.' " This does not correctly reproduce Psalms 68:18 which says, "Thou hast ascended on high, thou hast led captivity captive: thou hast received gifts for men."

The variances are: (a) Psalms 68:18 says "received gifts," not "gave gifts"; (b) Psalms 68:18 says "thou," not "he"; (c) Jesus never led captivity captive or led others to a high mount; (d) what gifts did Jesus give to men?; and (e) there is a tremendous difference between "giving gifts to men" and "receiving gifts for men."

Sixteenth and finally, 1 Peter 2:22, "Who did no sin, neither was guile found in his mouth," misquotes Isa. 53:9, which says, "Because he had done no violence, neither was any deceit in his mouth." Isaiah says "no violence," not "no sin." Isaiah never said the person or persons to whom he was referring were sinless. Sin and violence are not identical. Knowing Jesus' behavior toward the money-changers, perhaps Peter realized that the phrase, "he hath done no violence," was inapplicable.

Nonquotes

Major examples of New Testament references to nonexistent Old Testament verses are the following:

First, Matt. 2:23, "He [Joseph] came and dwelt in a city called Nazareth, that it might be fulfilled which was spoken by the prophets, He [Jesus] shall be called a Nazarene") does not refer to any Old Testament passage:

a. Judg. 13:5 ("For the child shall be a Nazarite"), which many apologists invoke, is irrelevant because a Nazarite was not an inhabitant of Nazareth. Nazarite means "dedicated" or "consecrated" and refers to an Israelite who consecrated himself or herself and took a vow of separation and self-imposed abstinence for the purpose of some special service (see *The New Compact Bible Dictionary,* page 391).

b. Acts 24:5 ("A ringleader of the sect of the Nazarenes") shows the Nazarenes are a specific sect and not residents of Nazareth.

c. Judg. 13:5-7 and 13:16-17 clearly show that Samson is the Nazarite referred to.

Second, Matt. 12:5 says, "Have ye not read in the law, how that on the sabbath days the priests in the temple profane the sabbath, and are blameless?" Nowhere does the Old Testament state that priests in the temple profaned the sabbath and were considered blameless.

Third, Matt. 23:35 says, "That upon you may come all the righteous blood shed upon the earth, from the blood of righteous Abel unto the blood of Zacharias son of Barachias, whom ye slew between the temple and the altar."

In the first place, the name Barachias is not in the Old Testament. Secondly, the Old Testament Zacharias is the son of Jehoida, not Barachias, as is shown in 2 Chron. 24:20-22.

Fourth, following a description of the events surrounding the arrest and betrayal of Jesus, Matt. 26:56 says, "All this was done, that the Scriptures of the prophets might be fulfilled." What Scriptures? What prophets? No quotation from the Old Testament is provided nor is the name of any biblical author mentioned.

Fifth, Mark 1:2 (RSV) says, "It is written in Isaiah the prophet, 'Behold, I send my messenger before thy face, who shall prepare thy way.' " No such statement exists in Isaiah.

Sixth, Mark 9:13 says, "I say unto you, That Elias is indeed come, and they have done unto him whatsoever they listed, as it is written of him." There are no Old Testament predictions of things that were to happen to Elias.

Seventh, Luke 24:46 says, "It is written, thus it behoved Christ to suffer, and to rise from the dead the third day." Nothing is written in the Old Testament about Christ rising from the dead, especially on the third day.

Hosea 6:1-2 says, "Come, and let us return unto the Lord; for he hath torn, and he will heal us; he hath smitten, and he will bind us up. After two days will he revive us: in the third day he will raise us up, and we shall live in his sight." But this passage is inapplicable to Luke 24 for several reasons: (a) it is referring to several beings as is demonstrated by the repeated use of the word "us"; (b) the Lord never tore and smote Jesus, as is stated in Hosea 6:1; (c) Verse 6:2 in Hosea ("After two days will he revive us: in the third day he will raise us up") was not quoted, probably because it says *he will revive us*; it does not say *he will be revived.* And nowhere does the New Testament say Jesus was revived after *two* days; and (d) Verse 6:3 (RSV) says, "Let us press on to know the Lord." How could Jesus learn anything additional about the Lord, when he allegedly is the Lord?

Eighth, John 1:45 says, "We have found him, of whom Moses in the law, and the prophets did write, Jesus of Nazareth, the son of Joseph." As was shown in a previous chapter, Moses did not write the Law or the Torah. Therefore, he could not have written about Jesus of Nazareth. In fact, none of the Old Testament prophets wrote of Jesus. Incidentally, how Jesus could be called the son of Joseph when Matt. 1:18 says, "She was found with child of the Holy Ghost," has always been bothersome.

Ninth, John 7:38, which supposedly reproduces part of the Old Testament, says, "He that believeth on me, as the Scripture hath said, out of his belly shall flow rivers of living water." But commonly invoked verses such as Isa. 44:3, Isa. 55:1, Ezek. 47:1, and Isa. 58:11 are inapplicable.

Tenth, John 20:9 says, "As yet they knew not the Scripture, that he must rise again from the dead." This verse is inapplicable to Jesus because there is no Old Testament statement to the effect that he must rise from the dead, nor is there a suggestion anywhere of Jesus rising *again* from the dead. "Again" means that he rose from the dead more than once and since Jesus allegedly rose only once, it is inapplicable to him regardless.

Eleventh, Acts 20:35 says, "Ye ought to support the weak, and to remember the words of the Lord Jesus, how he said, 'It is more blessed to give than to receive.' " At no time did Jesus ever say, "It is more blessed to give than to receive" and Matt. 10:8 ("Freely ye have received, freely give") has no relevance, since neither giving nor receiving is considered to be more blessed than the other.

Twelfth, while listing the injustices suffered in the Old Testament by his ancestors, Paul says in Heb. 11:35 (RSV), "Some were tortured, refusing to accept release, that they might rise again to a better life." Yet nowhere does the Old Testament say that people suffered torture because they expected to rise again to a better life.

Thirteenth and lastly: James 4:5 says, "Do ye think that the Scripture saith in vain, The spirit that dwelleth in us lusteth to envy?" No such statement can be found in the Old Testament, although apologists occasionally allude to Gen. 6:5, Gen. 6:11, Gen. 8:21, Prov. 21:10, and Eccles. 4:4.

That concludes our listing of nonquotes and clearly demonstrates that New Testament writers often let their imaginations do their walking through Old Testament pages.

Misinterpretations

Prime examples of New Testament misinterpretations of Old Testament quotes include:

First, Matt. 1:21-23 says, "She shall bring forth a son, and thou shalt call his name Jesus: for he shall save his people from their sins. Now all this was done, that it might be fulfilled which was spoken of the Lord by the prophet saying, 'Behold, a virgin shall be with child, and shall bring forth a son, and they shall call his name, Emmanuel,' which being interpreted is, God with us." This is misinterpreting a prophecy found in Isa. 7:14 which says, "The Lord himself shall give you a sign; Behold, a virgin shall conceive, and bear a son, and shall call his name Immanuel."

The main problems are: (a) Jesus could not be the Immanuel referred to, since Immanuel means "God is with us," whereas, Joshua, the word "Jesus," means "Yahweh is salvation"; (b) Jesus was never called Immanuel. In fact, Matt. 1:21 itself says he would be called Jesus; (c) referring to the same child, Isa. 7:16, says, "For before the child shall know to refuse the evil, and choose the good." How could this be Jesus, since he would not need to learn good from bad? This is another example of biblicists taking a verse out of context; and (d) the passage says Jesus will save "his people," whereas, the mission of Jesus was to save *all* people.

Second, Matt. 2:14-15 says, "When he [Joseph] arose, he took the young child and his mother by night, and departed into Egypt. And was there until the death of Herod: that it might be fulfilled which was spoken of the Lord by the prophet, saying, Out of Egypt have I called my son." Matthew has misinterpreted Hosea 11:1-3 (RSV), which says, "When Israel was a child, I loved him, and out of Egypt I called my son. The more I called them, the more they went from me; they kept sacrificing to the Baals, and burning incense to idols. Yet it was I who taught Ephraim to walk." The divergences are:

a. The use of "them" and "they" shows that Hosea was clearly referring to a *group* of people, Israel to be exact, not Jesus. The use of "Israel" and "Ephraim" in Hosea provides additional evidence that Israel is the topic of conversation. Matthew chose to omit most of Hosea 11:1–3 for obvious reasons.

b. Jesus never sacrificed to Baal or burned incense to idols.

c. In Exod. 4:22–23 God called Israel, not Jesus, his son by saying, "Thus saith the Lord, Israel is my son, even my firstborn." Exod. 4:22 proves beyond any reasonable doubt that Israel is the son referred to.

d. "Called" is a past-tense verb showing that Hosea is referring to a group living long before Jesus.

Third, Matt. 2:17–18 says, "Then was fulfilled that which was spoken by Jeremy the prophet, saying, 'In Rama was there a voice heard, lamentation, and weeping, and great mourning, Rachel weeping for her children, and would not be comforted, because they are not.' " This supposedly comes from Jer. 31:15–17, which says, "Thus saith the Lord; A voice was heard in Ramah, lamentation, and bitter weeping; Rachel weeping for her children refused to be comforted for her children, because they were not. Thus saith the Lord; Refrain thy voice from weeping . . . and they shall come again from the land of the enemy . . . thy children shall come again to their own border."

But Matthew is not alluding to Jeremiah 31 for several reasons:

a. Jeremiah is referring to some Israelites who are crying because they have been taken captive out of Israel and their children are dying. His statement has nothing to do with Jesus.

b. "Was heard" shows that Jeremiah was speaking of an event that had already occurred. He quotes Yahweh as speaking in the past tense.

c. How were the children Herod killed going to return from the land of the enemy? By saying "they are not" Matthew is referring to children who are deceased. In saying, "Thy children shall come again to their own border," Jeremiah is referring to children who are still living.

d. There is nothing in the verse justifying its applicability to the children killed by Herod.

e. Why wasn't Leah, rather than Rachel, depicted as the grieving mother, since it was from her that Herod's victims were descended? Leah, rather than Rachel, was the female ancestor of the inhabitants of Bethlehem.

Jeremiah 31:15–17 is actually predicting that the Israelite children taken captive to Babylon will return to Israel.

Fourth, Matt. 8:17, "That it might be fulfilled which was spoken by Esaias the prophet, saying, 'Himself took our infirmities, and bare our sicknesses,' " is supposedly a reproduction of Isa. 53:4, which says, "Surely he hath borne our griefs, and carried our sorrows: yet we did esteem him stricken, smitten of God, and afflicted." The obvious dissimilarities to be noted are: (a) When did Jesus bare the diseases he cured?; (b) When was Jesus smitten by God?; and (c), "hath borne" and "smitten" are past tense verbs showing that an event prior to the time of Isaiah is under discussion.

Fifth, Matt. 27:35, "That it might be fulfilled which was spoken by the prophet, They parted my garments among them, and upon my vesture did they cast lots," was supposedly taken from Psalms 22:18, "They part my garments among them, and cast lots upon my vesture." Apologists conveniently ignore the fact that: (a) Psalms 22 uses present tense verbs and is referring to events contemporaneous with the author; (b) the writer of Psalms 22 is not prophesying anything; and (c) the writer of Psalms 22 is actually speaking of himself, not Jesus or anyone else.

Sixth, Acts 1:16 says, "Men and brethren, this Scripture must needs have been fulfilled, which the Holy Ghost by the mouth of David spake before concerning Judas, which was guide to them that took Jesus." In the first place, David never said anything about Judas. Psalms 41:9, to which the author of Acts is referring, says, "Yea, mine own familiar friend, in whom I trusted, which did eat of my bread, hath lifted up his heal against me." This passage is decidedly inapplicable because the same speaker says just five verses earlier, in Psalms 41:4, "I said, Lord, be merciful to me: heal my soul; for I have sinned against thee." If Jesus is the speaker in Psalms 41:9, then he is also the sinner in Psalms 41:4. But the Bible repeatedly states in such verses as 1 John 3:5 and 1 Peter 2:22 that Jesus is sinless. This is nothing more than another instance of Christians taking a verse out of context and using it for their own ends.

Seventh, Matt. 27:5–10 says,

He [Judas] cast down the pieces of silver in the temple, and departed, and went and hanged himself. And the chief priests took the silver pieces, and said, "It is not lawful to put them into the treasury, because it is the price of blood." And they took counsel, and bought with them the potter's field, to bury strangers in. Wherefore that field was called, The field of blood, unto this day. Then was fulfilled that which was spoken by Jeremy the prophet, saying, "And they took the thirty pieces of silver, the price of him that was valued, whom they of the children of Israel did value; And gave them for the potter's field, as the Lord appointed me."

Although supposedly taken from the Book of Jeremiah, this quote is nowhere to be found in Jeremiah. Some apologists have conceded as much and alleged it is actually to be found in the Book of Zechariah. Zechariah 11:12–13 says, "I said unto them, If ye think good, give me my price; and if not, forbear. So they weighed for my price thirty pieces of silver. And the Lord said to me, Cast it unto the potter: A goodly price that I was prised at of them. And I took the thirty pieces of silver, and cast them to the potter in the house of the Lord."

But Zechariah is wholly inappropriate for several reasons: (a) in Zechariah the thirty pieces of silver were called a goodly price, while in Matthew the thirty pieces were the price of blood; (b) in Zechariah the deal was approved by the Lord, while in Matthew it was condemned by Him; (c) in Zechariah the money was given to the potter in the house of the Lord; while in Matthew the money was refused admittance to the treasury, and the priests used it to buy a potter's field; (d) in Zechariah, "I," that is, one man, gave the thirty pieces to a potter; while, in Matthew "they," a group, took the thirty pieces of silver and gave them for a potter's field; (e) Zechariah nowhere mentions a field; and (f) "to the potter" in the King James Version of Zechariah should have been translated "into the treasury," as was done in the Revised Standard Version. Thus, it would have no relation to the potter mentioned in Matthew.

Eighth, Acts 2:30 says, "God had sworn with an oath to him [David], that of the fruit of his loins, according to the flesh, he would raise *up Christ* to sit on his throne." This is supposedly taken from Psalms 132:11–12, which says, "The Lord hath sworn in truth unto David; he will not turn from it; Of the fruit of thy body will I set upon thy throne. If thy children will keep my covenant and my testimony that I shall teach them, their children shall also sit upon thy throne for evermore."

For tactical reasons apologists fail to note that according to Psalms 132 all of David's descendants who keep God's covenant will sit upon David's throne, not just one man. There is no hint whatsoever that only one man received the promise. Even if one person were under discussion, why assume Jesus of Nazareth is the specific person under discussion? Psalms does not mention Christ.

Ninth, Acts 13:30–33 says,

> God raised him [Jesus] from the dead: And he was seen many days of them which came up with him from Galilee to Jerusalem, who are his witnesses unto the people. And we declare unto you glad tidings, how that the promise which was made to the fathers, God hath fulfilled the same to us their children, in that he hath raised up Jesus again; as it is also written in the second psalm (2:7): Thou art my Son, this day have I begotten thee.

Anyone who has read it can't help but ask where Psalms 2:7 says that in some distant day Jesus of Nazareth, Joseph's son, will be raised from the dead? Nowhere does Psalms 2 contend that: (a) anyone will rise from the dead; (b) he who is the Son of God must rise from the dead; (c) Jesus will rise *again* from the dead; (d) Jesus of Nazareth is the son of God; and (e) anyone risen from the dead shall be the son of God.

Tenth, Gal. 3:13 ("Christ hath redeemed us from the curse of the law, being made a curse for us: for it is written, Cursed is every one that hangeth on a tree") was taken from Deut. 21:22–23, which says, "If a man have committed a sin worthy of death, and he be put to death, and thou hang him on a tree: his body shall not remain all night upon the tree, but thou shalt in any wise bury him that day; (for he that is hanged is accursed of God)."

Paul uses Deut. 21:22–23 to serve his own ends because: (a) Deut. 21:22 is talking about a sinful man, which would exclude Jesus because he is sinless, according to 1 Peter 2:22, and (b) Jesus was not hanged, nor did he die on a tree. Incidentally, it is difficult to see how in good conscience Paul could call Jesus "accursed of God."

Eleventh, Gal. 3:16 says, "To Abraham and his seed were the promises made. He saith not, And to seeds, as of many; but as of one, And to thy seed, which is Christ." Paul tries to give the impression that the seed referred to, and the one who received the promise, was Christ. This is a blatant distortion of the Old Testament for many reasons:

a. The word "seed" in the Old Testament always refers to many people, not one person. One need only read Gen. 13:15–16, Gen. 15:5, Gen. 15:13, Gen. 26:4, and Gen. 32:12 to see that seed always refers to descendants, plural.

b. Gen. 12:7 ("The Lord appeared unto Abram, and said, unto thy seed will I give this land") would mean God would give Jesus, the creator of heaven and earth, the land of Canaan as an inheritance. How absurd! Moreover, Jesus never received the land.

c. The following verses would make Jesus "numberless." Gen. 13:16 says, "I will make thy seed as the dust of the earth, so that if a man can number the dust of the earth, then shall thy seed also be numbered," and Gen. 22:17 says, "I will multiply thy seed as the stars of the heaven, and as the sand which is upon the sea shore."

d. Gen. 15:13 says, "He said unto Abram, Know of a surety that thy seed shall be a stranger in a land that is not theirs, and shall serve them; and they shall afflict them for four hundred years." This would mean that Jesus would serve Egypt for four hundred years and be afflicted for four hundred years. Yet, he lived only thirty-three years and was never in Egypt, much less afflicted there. "Theirs" and "them" clearly show that many persons, not one, are referred to.

e. Gen. 17:9–10 says, "God said to Abraham. . . . This is my covenant, which ye shall keep, between me and you and thy seed after thee; Every man child among you shall be circumcised." If Jesus were the "seed" referred to in this case, it would mean the covenant of circumcision between God and Abraham was continued by Jesus. Are we to believe God continued a covenant with Jesus? How could a covenant exist between God and Jesus, since Jesus is coexistent and coequal with God; he's one of the Trinity?

Twelfth and lastly, Heb. 1:5, "I [God] will be to him [supposedly Jesus] a Father, and he shall be to me a Son," was deceptively taken from 2 Sam. 7:14,

"I will be his father, and he shall be my son." The verses are clearly unrelated: (a) Paul omitted the last half of the passage, which says, "If he commit iniquity, I will chasten him with the rod of men, and with the stripes of the children of men." Because Jesus could not commit iniquity, the verse must be referring to a mere mortal. Certainly God would not beat Jesus with a rod and cause stripes to be put on him. Would God even threaten to chasten Jesus with stripes? And (b) in 2 Sam. 7:14 God is saying he will call Solomon, not Jesus, his son.

In sum and substance, an incredible amount of evidence exists to prove that New Testament writers misquoted, misinterpreted, twisted, distorted, perverted, misapplied, and misunderstood a tremendous number of Old Testament verses. They even went so far as to manufacture Old Testament verses. Anyone seeking objective scholarship in the field of biblical apologetics has embarked upon a journey into the realm of myth and fantasy in which people operate on expediency and pursue the nonexistent. Nothing is so biased as someone whose heart precedes his head, whose desire precedes his discretion, and whose wish precedes his wisdom.

Ignored Teachings

For hundreds of years biblicists have been lecturing people on the importance of adhering to the Bible's teachings on ethics, manners, and morality. They quote Jesus and Paul profusely with a liberal sprinkling of Old Testament moralisms. The problem with their approach lies not only in an oft-noted failure to practice what they preach, but an equally pronounced tendency to ignore what the Bible, itself, preaches. Biblicists practice what can only be described as "selective adherence." What they like, they expound; what they don't like, they ignore, even though the validity or strength of one is no less powerful than that of the other. That which is palatable and acceptable is supposedly applicable to all, while that which is obnoxious, inconvenient, or self-denying is only applicable to those addressed long ago. Biblical moralists enjoy quoting the Ten Commandments, the Sermon on the Mount, and many of Paul's preachings, for example, but don't even pretend to heed other, equally valid maxims.

The following sections expose the selectivity of apologetic compliance.

POVERTY

First, a true follower of Jesus would have to be extremely poor—as poor as the homeless. The Bible makes this abundantly clear with numerous verses, like Luke 14:33 ("None of you can be my disciple unless he gives up everything he has"), Matt. 19:21 ("If you want to be perfect, go and sell all you have and give the money to the poor and you will have riches in heaven"), Luke 12:33 ("Sell your possessions and give alms"), Luke 11:41 ("Give what is in your cups and plates to the poor, and everything will be clean for you"), Matt. 6:19–21 ("Lay not up for yourselves treasures upon earth, where moth and rust doth corrupt. . . . But lay up for yourselves treasures in heaven. . . . For where your treasure is, there will your heart be also"), Mark 10:23 ("How shall they that have riches enter into the kingdom of God"), Matt. 19:23–24 ("I tell you, it is easier for a camel to go through the eye of a needle than for a rich man to enter the kingdom of God"), and Luke 18:22 ("A certain ruler told Jesus that he had obeyed all the commandments from his youth up. But, Jesus said, Yet lackest thou one thing: sell all that thou hast, and distribute unto the poor, and thou shalt have treasure in heaven: and come, follow me").

Paul says in Phil. 3:8 (RSV), "For his sake I have suffered the loss of all things and count them as refuse, in order that I may gain Christ." Imagine Billy Graham, Oral Roberts, Jerry Falwell, Jimmy Swaggart, Rex Humbard, Rev. Ike, Robert Schuller, and thousands of other wealthy religious propagandists heeding such pronouncements. To say this is out of the question is an understatement. It is much easier and far less painful to explain away clear-cut obligations than surrender great wealth because of biblical injunctions. The lavish personal wealth of many Christian leaders bears witness to their complete avoidance of these teachings. Luke 3:11 (RSV) says, "Who has two coats, let him share with him who has none; and he who has food, let him do likewise." One can only speculate as to the number of coats the evangelists have in their closets.

Jesus says in Matt. 5:42, "Give to him that asketh thee, and from him that would borrow of thee turn not thou away." Asking any affluent Christian leader or any Christian denomination for a sizable portion of his or its wealth would be an exercise in futility. How many biblicists attempt to obey the biblical precept in Luke 6:29–30 (RSV): "From him who takes away your coat do not withhold even your shirt. Give to every one who begs from you; and of him who takes away your goods do not ask them again"? They also ignore Matt. 5:40, which says, "If any man sues you in court, and takes away your coat, let him have thy cloak also." However, apologists don't mind quoting the previous verse, Matt. 5:39, which tells us to turn the other cheek, because in that verse the focus is on attitudes rather than concrete results; no direct physical denial is involved. Turning one's cheek is far less painful and tangible than surrendering dollars. It is much more nebulous and subject to interpretation and evasion.

In Matt. 10:9–10 Jesus commissioned his twelve apostles to, "Provide neither gold, nor silver, nor brass in your purses, nor scrip for your journey, neither two coats, neither shoes, nor yet staves, for the workman is worthy of his meat." If these were morally correct procedures for Christians two thousand years ago, then they should be obligatory for today's disciples. But one need only view the entourage and wealth accompanying any well-known contemporary evangelist on his periodic forays into the hinterlands to see the inconsistency involved. Early Christian groups even practiced a form of communal ownership of property. Acts

2:44–45 says, "All that believed were together, and had all things common; and sold their possessions and goods and parted them to all men, as every man had need." Yet except for a few isolated communities, today's biblicists preach the opposite.

Biblical precepts clearly show that it is not enough to avoid the accumulation of wealth. Christians should actively seek to eliminate whatever property may come their way. In so far as wealth and property are concerned, Christian monks, ascetics, and some Amish and Mennonite factions, for example, are far closer to biblical teachings than any of the well-known clergymen and denominations of today. While engaged in dialogue with a fundamentalist minister years ago, I noted that his Lincoln Continental parked nearby was wholly inconsistent with biblical tenets. After offering the usual apologetic rationalizations, (e.g., I lead a frugal life and the Bible does not require the avoidance of wealth), he denounced my motives and left. None of his defenses was biblically sustainable.

DIVORCE

Another topic well supplied with verses at odds with current Christian practices is divorce. A true follower of Jesus cannot divorce someone, according to Matt. 19:6 (RSV) ("They are no longer two but one flesh. What therefore God has joined together, let not man put asunder"). However, Matt. 5:32 allows an exception in case of wifely adultery: "Whosoever shall put away his wife saving for the cause of fornication, causeth her to commit adultery." Nor should a Christian marry someone who is already divorced, according to Matt. 5:32 ("Whosoever shall marry her that is divorced committeth adultery"). The Bible also says in Mark 10:11 that anyone who obtains a divorce and marries another is an adulterer.

According to Christ's teachings, therefore, one should never obtain a divorce, except from an adulterous spouse; one should never marry a divorced person; and whoever obtains a divorce and marries another is committing adultery. On top of everything else, Matt. 19:6 obviates divorce for any reason whatever and thus renders all other instructions mute. One can only estimate the number of Christians who have ignored these maxims.

PUBLIC PRAYER

A third biblical teaching that is ignored by Christians on a routine basis pertains to prayer in public education. Current attempts to put prayer into the schools run directly counter to biblical teachings. In one of his few comments on the manner in which one should pray, Jesus said prayer should be a private affair devoid of public display. That is the core of Matt. 6:5–6 (RSV), which says, "When you pray you must not be like the hypocrites; for they love to stand and pray in the synagogues and at the street corners, that they may be seen by men. Truly, I say to you they have received their reward. But when you pray, go into your room and shut the door and pray to your Father who is in secret." Biblicists violate this obligation on a regular basis and have no intention of correcting their behavior.

It is interesting to note that Paul's maxim in 1 Cor. 11:4 that men should pray with their heads uncovered is generally followed, because removing one's hat isn't particularly inconvenient. On the other hand, his tenet in 1 Cor. 11:5–15 that women must keep their head covered with a veil during prayer *is* quite inconvenient and, for this reason, has either been rationalized away or ignored, even though it is no less binding than any other New Testament precept.

ADDITIONAL IGNORED TEACHINGS

Additional biblical teachings that are often ignored by the Bible's proponents can generally be divided into those that liberals ignore, those which conservatives ignore, and those that both ignore. Although the points that follow are, like the labels "liberal" and "conservative," generally broad and gray on the edges, the underlying principles remain salient.

Among the tenets that many liberals evade is 1 Cor. 11:14, which forbids men to have long hair. Long-haired individuals are usually of a more liberal persuasion, although exceptions definitely exist. While gazing at contemporary pictures and statues of a long-haired Jesus, one can't help but wonder what his image-makers were thinking.

Another tenet found in 1 Cor. 14:34 ("Let your women keep silence in the churches: for it is not permitted unto them to speak") clearly prohibits women from being ministers or otherwise speaking in church. In no way would Paul support the current movement to ordain women.

And a third tenet prohibits men and women from wearing each other's clothing. Deut. 22:5 says, "The woman shall not wear that which pertaineth to a man, neither shall a man put on a woman's garment: for all that do so are abomination unto the Lord." Until recent years pants were viewed in this country as a man's garment and opponents of changes in female dress quoted this verse repeatedly. One can debate what is long hair or man's clothing, but every group of Christians has had a definition and liberals have nearly always been the first to deviate.

There are also a number of maxims that conservatives and fundamentalists are the first to shun. Rightists are usually stronger advocates of military involvement and capital punishment than liberals are and, thus, the first to ignore 1 Cor. 3:16–17, which says, "Don't you know that you are God's temple and that God's Spirit lives in you? If anyone destroys God's temple, God will destroy him; for God's temple is sacred, and you are that temple." In Matt. 26:52 Jesus says believers are to put up their swords because all those who take up the sword will die by the sword. The degree to which Christians, especially conservative Christians, have eschewed this maxim has no limits.

Some religious conservatives and many Roman Catholics also practice repetitious and monotonous prayer in violation of Matt. 6:7, which says, "When ye pray, use not vain repetitions, as the heathen do: for they think that they shall be heard for their much speaking."

A number of instructions are ignored by liberals and fundamentalists alike. Christians, for example, are not supposed to take their disputes before non-Christian courts or judges, according to 1 Cor. 6:1. Christian women are supposed to dress discreetly without braided hair, gold, pearls, or costly attire, according to 1 Tim. 2:9 and 1 Peter 3:3. Without any doubt, violations of these rules are too numerous to mention.

Several teachings are not only routinely violated by all concerned but would be difficult to follow in any event. For example, according to Matt. 7:1 and Luke 6:37, biblicists are not to judge others, despite the fact that judges, juries, voters, employers, teachers, and many other professionals are constantly making judgments of others.

Followers of Jesus are supposed to hate their parents, according to Luke 14:26: "If any man come to me, and hate not his father, and mother, and wife, and children, and brethren, and sisters, yea, and his own life also, he cannot be my disciple." And according to the rule laid down in Matt. 5:39 believers are not to oppose evil when hit on one cheek but are to turn the other also. If this were followed, one might just as well abolish all law enforcement.

Matt. 23:9 says, "Call no man your father upon the earth, for one is your Father, which is in heaven." Not only is this rule ignored, but Catholicism uses "father" as a specific title for priests.

Christians are not supposed to plan or prepare because God will provide. That is the central message of one of the most preposterous passages in the entire Bible, Matt. 6:25–34, which says, "Take no thought for your life, what ye shall eat, or what ye shall drink; nor yet for your body, what ye shall put on. . . . Behold the fowls of the air: for they sow not, neither do they reap, nor gather into barns; yet your heavenly Father feedeth them. Are ye not much better than they?" If that isn't the ultimate in religious indoctrination, nothing is.

And finally, Jesus, who clearly is of greater importance than Paul, said the old Law was to remain in force until heaven and earth passed away and all is accomplished. He then proceeded to condemn not only Paul but nearly all present-day Christians by saying in Matt. 5:18–19 (RSV) that, "Whoever then relaxes one of the least of these commandments and teaches men so, shall be called least in the kingdom of heaven." Because heaven and earth continue to exist and many prophecies remain unfulfilled, biblicists should still be following the old Law. Christians in general and Paul in particular are headed toward heaven's wrath, according to this logic.

One of the clearest expressions of selective adherence to biblical precepts by the Book's proponents is shown in their approach to the Old Testament. They leap in and out of the old Law like porpoises in a ship's wake. If they like it, they quote it; if they don't, they won't. Christians have not hesitated to use Old Testament maxims found alongside passages that are rejected. In fact, some have been given great importance, despite the fact that distinctions between that which is acceptable and that which isn't are wholly arbitrary. If one is going to utilize the Old Law, then he must obey all of its precepts, not just those that are palatable. One can't pick and choose without valid, objective standards for making distinctions. Just as the rules quoted earlier are almost universally rejected, those which follow are widely accepted and regularly employed to regulate human behavior. Among scores of verses they enjoy and employ are those that teach the following: (a) contact with mediums and wizards is forbidden according to Lev. 19:31, Lev. 20:6, and Deut. 18:10–12; (b) infanticide is prohibited according to Deut. 12:31 and Lev. 18:21; (c) people are not to worship celestial bodies such as the sun, the moon, and the stars, according to Deut. 4:19; (d) Lev. 27:30–32 says people should tithe by giving a tenth of their income to the Lord, which biblicists equate with the church; (e) Lev. 18:22, Lev. 20:13, and Gen. 19:5 say homosexuality is immoral and should be prohibited; (f) Lev. 19:28 outlaws tattoos and marks on one's body; and (g) killers are to be executed according to Gen. 9:6, Exod. 21:12, and other verses.

A crucial issue lingering behind all of the above is: What about all of the Old Testament laws that are conveniently ignored but of equal weight. Biblicists act as if the following did not exist: Deut. 23:19–20 says money can *not* be lent at interest to your brother, only to foreigners. Deut. 14:8 says eating pork is forbidden. Num. 5:28–29 says trials for adultery are to be by ordeal. Lev. 19:27 says beards can't be rounded. Deut 24:5 says a newly married man cannot go to war or be charged with business for one year. Deut. 25:1–3 says a guilty man can be beaten with as many as forty blows. Lev. 19:19 and Deut. 22:11 say garments composed of wool and linen cannot be worn. Punishment shall be administered on the basis of an eye for an eye according to Deut. 19:21. Deut. 15:6 says your nation can lend to other nations but not borrow from them.

Exod. 22:18 says, "Thou shalt not suffer a witch to live" and is one of the most notorious of all verses found in the old Law. Not long ago it was cited profusely and brought devastation to the lives of thousands. Deut. 15:1–3 says debtor brothers shall be released from their obligation every seven years.

Exod. 22:2–3 says, "When a burglar is caught breaking in and is fatally beaten, there shall be no charge of manslaughter, unless it happened after dawn, in which case there is manslaughter." One can readily understand why this rule is not quoted, since the time of day would have little relevance to whether or not a killing was manslaughter. Justice and Old Testament teachings are often at odds.

Exod. 22:25 (RSV) says, "If you lend money to any of my people with you who is poor, you shall not be to him as a creditor, and you shall not exact interest from him." And Lev. 25:35–37 (RSV) says, "If your brother becomes poor and cannot maintain himself with you, you shall maintain him. . . . Take no interest from him or increase, but fear your God. . . . You shall not lend to him your money at interest, nor give him your food for profit." Adherence to these rules would all but abolish capitalism.

Exod. 22:29–30 says, "Thou shalt not delay to offer the first of thy ripe fruits, and of thy liquors: the firstborn of thy sons shalt thou give to me. Likewise shalt thou do with thine oxen, and with thy sheep: seven days it shall be with his dam; on the eighth day thou shalt give it to me." Bible verses advocating child sacrifice are systematically ignored and no longer quoted for obvious reasons.

Deut. 22:8 (RSV) says, "When you build a new house, you shall make a parapet for your roof, that you may not bring the guilt of blood upon your house, if any one fall from it." One would be hard-pressed to find home builders who add parapets to house roofs for reasons of safety pursuant to an Old Testament maxim.

Deut. 22:12 (RSV) states, "You shall make yourself tassels on the four corners of your cloak with which you cover yourself." Few people urge others to put four tassels on the corners of their cloak.

And Deut. 23:24–25 (RSV) says, "When you go into your neighbor's vineyard, you may eat your fill of grapes, as many as you wish, but you shall not put any in your vessel. When you go into your neighbor's standing grain, you may pluck the ears with your hand, but you shall not put a sickle to your neighbor's standing grain." One can understand why biblicists don't quote this regulation very often, either. What right does anyone have to take his neighbor's property at will? Because the owner's acquiescence does not seem to be needed, God appears to be condoning theft.

Biblicists employ verses at will and even go so far as to twist some into saying that which is desired. For example, fundamentalists and evangelicals vigorously oppose abortion but have been hard-pressed to find biblical statements to corroborate their position. In their determination they have been forced to rely upon an exceedingly weak section found in Exod. 21:22–24 stating that if two men are fighting and one injures a pregnant woman in the process, he shall repay her according to the degree of injury inflicted upon *her,* not the fetus.

And finally, if biblicists are going to quote the Old Law with respect to executing murderers, then why don't they quote Old Testament verses that require capital punishment for a wide variety of acts other than murder? The following acts warrant execution, according to the Bible: striking your father or your mother, cursing your father or mother, cursing in general, failing to observe the sabbath, gathering sticks on the sabbath, committing adultery, lying with your father's wife, lying with your daughter-in-law, having relations with a wife and her mother, not being a virgin on your wedding day, lying with a beast, committing homosexual acts, being a medium or wizard, being a witch, sacrificing to other gods, blaspheming the name of the Lord, coming near the priesthood, being a false prophet, drinking strong drinks while in the tabernacle, and allowing your ox to gore someone.

The many maxims listed on the last few pages are God's rules. Imagine living in that era! All of these maxims are part of the Old Covenant and of equal import. Why quote the Ten Commandments and rules against infanticide, for example, while ignoring equally valid tenets? A believer's obligation to any one tenet is no more than his obligation to all. If Christians have stepped into the shoes of the Israelites and become, in effect, the new Chosen People, as they allege, then they should inherit not only the privileges of that office but the duties as well. Understandably, they want the former but not the latter.

Conclusion

In summary, then, biblicists teach, preach, and attempt to reach others with many Old Testament moralisms and obligations, but are not adverse to selectively using those that best suit their interests. Old Testament verses that are liked are expounded no end, while those that are distasteful are consigned to oblivion. If "sin is the transgression of the law," as 1 John 3:4 says, then Christians should be following all of the old Law, not just bits and pieces. The only honest conclusion one can draw from all of the above is that hypocrisy and expediency, not faith and obedience, are the true hallmarks of Christian conformity to biblical precepts. Distasteful tenets are routinely and widely ignored.

22

Conflicts

Jesus vs. Paul, Peter vs. the Old Testament, Peter vs. the New Testament, Peter vs. Paul, Peter vs. Jesus, Peter vs. Peter

Although Jesus, Peter, and Paul are the three most important figures in the New Testament, the degree to which their teachings clash is a sight to behold. Peter disagrees with Jesus and Paul on many points, while the latter two often contradict one another. As on television's "To Tell the Truth," one can't help but ask, "Will the true voice of Christianity please stand up?"

Jesus vs. Paul

Paul claims to speak for Jesus in Rom. 9:1 ("I say the truth in Christ, I lie not") and 2 Cor. 11:10 ("The truth of Christ is in me"), but in fact Paul says a great deal that contradicts Jesus' teachings. Excellent examples are the following:

First, Jesus says, "Go not into the way of the Gentiles" (Matt. 10:5), "I am not sent but unto the lost sheep of the house of Israel" (Matt. 15:24), and "Salvation is of the Jews" (John 4:22). But Paul says, "The Lord has commanded us, saying, I have set you to be a light for the Gentiles, that you may bring salvation to the uttermost parts of the earth" (Acts 13:47), "Henceforth, I [Paul] will go unto the Gentiles" (Acts 18:6), and "I should be the minister of Jesus Christ to the Gentiles" (Rom. 15:16). Jesus told his followers not to go to the Gentiles and Paul said precisely the opposite.

Second, Jesus tells his followers in Matt. 15:24, "I am not sent but unto the lost sheep of the house of Israel." And in Matt. 10:5–6 he says, "Go not into the way of the Gentiles, and into any city of the Samaritans enter ye not: But go rather to the lost sheep of the house of Israel." Paul, on the other hand, says in Rom. 10:12, "There is no difference between the Jew and the Greek: for the same Lord over all is rich unto all that call upon him." In Rom. 1:16 he says, "I am not ashamed of the gospel of Christ: for it is the power of God unto salvation to every one that believeth; to the Jew first, and also to the Greek." And in Rom. 3:22 Paul states, "The righteousness of God which is by faith in Jesus Christ unto all and all them that believe: for there is no difference." In essence, Jesus told his followers to go only to the Jews, while Paul said there was no difference between Jews and Greeks. Moreover, one need only read Acts 15:3 to see that Paul and Barnabas ignored Jesus' travel restrictions by passing through Phoenicia and Samaria declaring the conversion of the Gentiles.

Third, Jesus says in Matt 5:17–19,

Think not that I am come to destroy the law, or the prophets: I am not come to destroy but to fulfil. For verily I say to you, Till heaven and earth pass, one jot or one tittle shall in no wise pass from the law, till all be fulfilled. Whosoever therefore shall break one of these least commandments and shall teach men so, he shall be called least in the kingdom of heaven.

Likewise Matt. 23:27–3 Jesus declares, "The scribes and the Pharisees sit in Moses' seat: All therefore whatsoever they bid you observe, that observe and do." But in Rom. 7:4 Paul says, "My brethren, ye also are become dead to the law by the body of Christ" and in Gal. 3:13 he says, "Christ hath redeemed us from the curse of the law."

Jesus says the law would stand till heaven and earth passed, while Paul says it was a curse to be viewed as dead. On page 144 in *Does the Bible Contradict Itself* apologist William Arndt takes note of the clash on the law between Jesus and Paul by saying, "Paul says that the Jewish laws concerning days, and months, and seasons, and years are no longer binding. Jesus says that not a single letter of the Law dare be ignored. Does not that constitute a conflict between Paul and our Lord? Of course, Arndt follows this up by trying to prove no conflict exists.

Fourth, in Matt. 28:19 Jesus says, "Go ye therefore, and teach all nations, baptizing them in the name of the Father and of the Son, and of the Holy Ghost." Yet, we find Paul saying in 1 Cor. 1:17, "Christ sent me not to baptize, but to preach the gospel."

So, to baptize or not to baptize, that is the question.

Fifth, in Matt 5:22 Jesus says, "Whosoever shall say, Thou fool, shall be in danger of hell fire." But in 1 Cor. 15:36 Paul says, "Thou fool, that which thou sowest is not quickened, except it die." In Gal. 3:1 Paul says, "O foolish Galatians, who hath bewitched you." And in 1 Cor. 4:10 he says, "We are fools for Christ's sake." Apparently Paul doesn't feel "fool" is a dangerous word or hell-fire is a place to be feared.

Sixth, Paul says in Gal. 2:20, "I live by the faith of the Son of God, who loved me, and gave himself for me." And in Gal. 1:4 he says Jesus "gave himself for our sins." Paul also stresses this in Eph 5:2 and 5:25. Yet in Matt. 27:46 Jesus says, "My God, my God, why hast thou forsaken me?" And in Matt. 26:39 Jesus says, "O my Father, if it be possible, let this cup pass from me." If Jesus gladly sacrificed himself for humanity, as millions are taught, you would never know it from his utterances. They certainly aren't the words of someone who is dying willingly for anyone.

Seventh, in Eph 6:2 Paul says, "Honour thy father and mother; which is the first commandment," but in Luke 14:26 Jesus states, "If any man come to me, and hate not his father, and mother, and wife, and children, and brethren, and sisters, yea and his own life also, he cannot be my disciple." Now there's a clash!

Eighth, in 1 Tim. 2:8 Paul ignores a prior command of Jesus by saying, "I will therefore that men pray everywhere lifting up holy hands," because Jesus had said in Matt. 6:5–6, "When thou prayest, thou shalt not be as the hypocrites are: for they love to pray standing in the synagogues and in the corners of the streets, that they may be seen of men. . . . But you, when thou prayest, enter into thy closet and when thou hast shut thy door, pray to the Father which seeth in secret." Those clamoring for prayer in the schools had better quote Paul, not Jesus.

Ninth, it is difficult to reconcile Jesus' comment in Matt. 28:18, "All power is given unto me in heaven and in earth" with Paul's comment in 2 Thess. 2:9 (RSV), "The coming of the lawless one by the activity of Satan will be with all power and with pretended signs and wonders." Who, then, has all power, Jesus or the lawless one? Perhaps they are the same or, then again, maybe both have all power and both are gods.

Tenth, in Col. 2:3 Paul says that all the treasures of wisdom and knowledge are hidden in Jesus, whereas a far more modest Jesus said in Mark 13:32, "Of that day and that hour knoweth no man, no not the angels which are in heaven, neither the Son." Obviously Jesus didn't feel he was as omniscient as did Paul.

Eleventh, in Acts 13:39 Paul contends that by Jesus "all that believe are justified from all things, from which you could not be justified by the law of Moses." In Matt. 12:32 Jesus differs markedly on this point by saying, "Whosoever speaketh against the Holy Ghost, it shall not be forgiven him neither in this world, neither in the world to come." And in Mark 3:29 he says, "He that shall blaspheme against the Holy Ghost hast never forgiveness, but is in danger of eternal damnation." Contrary to Paul, Jesus holds that you can never be justified from all things, if you have blasphemed the Holy Ghost. The latter is unforgivable.

Twelfth, in Luke 18:14 Jesus specifically says that "Every one that exalteth himself shall be abased; and he that humbleth himself shall be exalted." Paul completely ignores his advice by engaging in braggadocio in 2 Cor. 11:5, "I suppose I was not a whit behind the very chiefest apostles"; 2 Cor. 12:11, "I ought to have been commended of you: for in nothing am I behind the very chiefest apostles"; and 2 Cor. 11:17-18, "I speak it not after the Lord, but as it were foolishly, in this confidence of boasting. Seeing that many glory after the flesh, I will glory also." Apparently Paul did not feel that being abased was something to be feared either, since he boasted and bragged on several occasions.

Thirteenth, the nonsense of the Trinity comes to the fore when we compare Paul's comments in Phil 2:6 ("Who, being in the form of God, thought it not robbery to be equal with God") and Col. 2:9 ("In him dwelleth all of the fulness of the Godhead bodily"), with Jesus' specific denials of trinitarian connections in John 14:28 ("My Father is greater than I") and John 20:17 ("I ascend unto my Father, and your Father; and *to my God,* and your God"). Paul may consider Jesus to be God's equal, but Jesus clearly does not.

Fourteenth, Paul's comment in Heb. 6:18 ("It was impossible for God to lie") flies in the face of Jesus' comment in Matt. 19:26 that, "With men this is impossible; but with God all things are possible." How can all things be possible for God, as Jesus asserts, if it is impossible for God to lie, as Paul claims?

Fifteenth, in Matt. 19:21 Jesus alleges that, "If thou wilt be perfect, go and sell that thou hast, and give to the poor, and thou shalt have treasure in heaven." But Paul later states in Gal. 6:5 that "every man shall bear his own burden." One can't help but ask why people would be obligated to aid the poor if every man is supposed to bear his own burden.

Sixteenth, in Rom. 12:14 Paul says, "Bless them which persecute you: bless and curse not." Clearly this did not have a high priority with Jesus who says, "Ye fools and blind" in Matt. 23:17; "Woe unto you, scribes and Pharisees, hypocrites! for ye are like unto whited sepulchres" in Matt. 23:27; and "Ye serpents, ye generation of vipers" in Matt. 23:33. Paul laid down a maxim which Jesus had cast aside years earlier.

Seventeenth, interestingly enough, Jesus gave similar advice that Paul chooses to ignore. In Matt. 5:44 Jesus stated, "I say unto you, Love your enemies, bless them that curse you, do good to them that hate you." And in Luke 6:27-29 he says, "Love your enemies, do good to them which hate you, bless them that curse you. . . . And unto him that smiteth thee on the one cheek offer also the other." Contrary to Jesus' advice, Paul felt there were times when enemies should be reviled rather than blessed. Acts 23:2-4 (NIV) states, "At this the high priest Ananias ordered those standing near Paul to strike him on the mouth. Then Paul said to him, God will strike you, you whitewashed wall! You sit there to judge me according to the law, yet you yourself violate the law by commanding that I be struck. Those who were standing near Paul said, You dare to insult God's high priest?"

Eighteenth, in 1 Tim. 6:16 Paul says only Jesus has immortality, even though Jesus says in John 3:16, "God so loved the world, that he gave his only begotten Son, that whosoever believeth in him should not perish, but have everlasting life." Paul said only Jesus had immortality, while Jesus said others have everlasting life as well. If Paul had said only Jesus could provide immortality to others, there would have been no problem. But he said only Jesus *has* immortality. How can only Jesus be immortal when everyone is immortal, whether willingly or not, according to Christian beliefs? Whether in heaven, hell, purgatory, or limbo, immortality is inescapable.

Nineteenth, in Matt. 11:30 Jesus says, "My yoke is easy, and my burden is light." Yet in 2 Tim. 3:12 Paul says, "all that will live godly in Christ Jesus shall suffer persecution," and in Heb. 12:6 he states, "Whom the Lord loveth he chasteneth, and scourgeth every son whom he receiveth." Persecution and scourging hardly sound like the concomitants of an easy yoke and a light burden. If persecution, chastening, and scourging are light burdens, one can only shudder at the prospect of what would be deemed a heavy load.

Twentieth, Paul says in Titus 3:2 that we are "to speak evil of no man, to be not brawlers, but gentle, shewing all meekness unto all men." By going into the temple and overthrowing the tables of the money changers, Jesus clearly showed he felt that discarding meekness and becoming a brawler were sometimes warranted.

Twenty-first, in 1 Cor. 6:9-10 Paul asks, "Know ye not that the unrighteous shall not inherit the kingdom of God? Be not deceived: neither fornicators, nor idolaters, nor adulterers, nor effeminate, nor abusers of themselves with mankind . . . shall inherit the kingdom of God." Jesus, on the other hand, says in Matt. 21:31, "The publicans and harlots go into the kingdom of God before you." Whether or not harlots will enter the kingdom of God appears to be a matter of dispute. Paul specifically denied fornicators and adulters would enter heaven, despite the fact that Jesus said harlots would gain admittance even before others.

Twenty-second, in Matt. 15:11 Jesus contends that, "Nothing from without a man, that enters into him can defile him." Yet Paul says in Titus 1:7, "A bishop must be blameless . . . not given to wine." He also decries the use of wine in 1 Tim. 3:3, 1 Tim. 3:8, and Rom. 14:21. If nothing entering a man from the outside can defile a man, then why prohibit the consumption of wine?

Twenty-third, in Luke 12:4 Jesus states, "Be not afraid of them that kill the body, and after that have no more that they can do." And in Matt. 5:39 he says, "I say unto you, That ye resist not evil." Acts 14:5-6, on the other hand, shows that, "When there was an assault made by both of the Gentiles and also of the Jews with their rulers, to use them [Paul and Barnabas] despitefully, and to stone them, They were aware of it, and fled into Lystra and Derbe." Being fearful and not wanting to risk life and limb, Paul and Barnabas ignored the advice of Jesus and resisted evil by fleeing.

Twenty-fourth, in Matt. 19:21 Jesus states, "If thou wilt be perfect, go and sell that thou hast and give to the poor, and thou shalt have treasure in heaven." Yet in 1 Thess. 4:10–12 Paul says, "We beseech you brethren, that ye . . . may walk honestly toward them that are without, and that ye may have lack of nothing." How can one lack nothing, if he sells all he has and gives to the poor?

Twenty-fifth, while describing Jesus in Eph. 2:14–17 Paul states, "He is our peace. . . . Having abolished in his flesh the enmity . . . so making peace . . . and came and preached peace to you." This clashes dramatically with Jesus' comments in Matt. 10:34 ("Think not that I am come to send peace on earth, I came not to send peace, but a sword"); Luke 12:51 ("Suppose ye that I am come to give peace on earth? I tell you, Nay; but rather division"); and Luke 22:36 ("He that hath no sword, let him sell his garment and buy one"). If Jesus was as peaceful as Paul would have us believe, you would never know it from his verbal admonitions and treatment of the moneychangers.

Twenty-sixth, in Rom. 13:4 Paul says one's ruler "beareth not the sword in vain: for he is the minister of God," even though Jesus says in Matt. 26:52, "Put up again thy sword into his place, for all they that take the sword shall perish with the sword." How could sword-swinging rulers be God's ministers, when Jesus says that all who take up the sword shall perish with it?

Twenty-seventh, despite the fact that Jesus says in Matt. 23:10 (RSV), "Neither be called masters, for you have one master, the Christ," Paul says in Eph. 6:5, "Servants, be obedient to them that are your masters according to the flesh . . . as unto Christ." Jesus says he is our only master, while Paul told servants to obey their masters as if they were obeying Christ himself. How many masters are there? Jesus says one, himself, while Paul says many.

Twenty-eighth, in Acts 20:35 Paul says, "Remember the words of the Lord Jesus, how he said, 'It is more blessed to give than to receive.' " Nowhere in Scripture does Jesus make this statement.

Twenty-ninth, the trinitarian dilemma comes to the fore in John 10:30 when Jesus says, "I and my Father are one" but in Rom. 8:34 Paul says, "It is Christ . . . who is even at the right hand of God." If Jesus and God are one, as Jesus claims, then how could Jesus sit beside God, as Paul asserts? That would require two beings.

Thirtieth, in Matt. 7:1–2 Jesus says, "Judge not, that ye be not judged. For with what judgment ye judge, ye shall be judged." Paul, on the other hand, says in 1 Cor. 5:12 (RSV), "Is it not those inside the church whom you are to judge?" and in 1 Cor. 2:15 (RSV) he says, "The spiritual man judges all things, but is himself to be judged by no one."

Paul not only ignores Jesus' advice by telling men to judge, but makes some judgments of his own, such as that found in 1 Cor. 5:3, "I verily, as absent in body, but present in spirit, have judged already."

Thirty-first, in 2 Cor. 5:10 Paul states, "We must all appear before the judgment seat of Christ." Yet Jesus clearly says, "Ye judge after the flesh; I judge no man" (John 8:15); "Who made me judge and a divider over you?" (Luke 12:14); and "I came not to judge the world, but to save the world" (John 12:47). Somebody should have told Paul that Jesus had already renounced the job or maybe Paul just decided to ignore Christ's teaching.

Thirty-second, Jesus states in John 5:22 that, "The Father judgeth no man, but hath committed all judgment unto the Son." But Paul says in 1 Cor. 6:2 (RSV), "Do you not know that the saints will judge the world?"

Who, then, will judge the world, the Son or the Saints?

Thirty-third, the judging problem is further compounded when we compare Paul's comment in Heb. 12:23, that God was the judge of all, with Jesus' comments in John 5:22 ("The Father judgeth no man, but hath committed all judgment unto the Son") and John 9:39 (RSV) ("For judgment I came into this world, that those who do not see may see"). God was to do all judging according to Paul, while Jesus assigned the task to himself, specifically.

Thirty-fourth, in Matt. 24:24 and elsewhere Jesus states that, "There shall arise false Christs, and false prophets, and shall shew great signs and wonders; insomuch that if it were possible, they shall deceive the very elect." In other words, false prophets and false Christs can do miracles. Yet Paul says in Heb. 2:4, "God also bearing them witness, both with signs and wonders, and with diverse miracles." And in 2 Cor. 12:12 he says, "Truly the signs of an apostle were wrought among you in all patience, in signs, and wonders, and mighty deeds."

Jesus clearly states that the ability to do signs and miracles was not to be used to prove someone represented God, but Paul preaches the opposite. Oddly enough, in 2 Thess. 2:8–9 Paul discredits his own assertions in Hebrews and 2 Corinthians by alleging that the forces of Satan *could* do miracles.

Thirty-fifth, in Matt. 16:27 Jesus says, "The Son of man shall come in the glory of his Father with his angels; and reward every man according to his works." Paul, however, says in Rom. 3:20 that, "By the deeds of the law there shall no flesh be justified in his sight." Jesus says you shall be rewarded according to your works, while Paul contends that adherence to the law justifies no one. Faith saves, not works. What, then, happens to the man who leads a virtually immaculate life but has no faith? According to Paul he is condemned to eternal punishment, while Jesus promises a reward commensurate with the number of his good deeds. And what happens to a man who leads the a despicable life but accepts Jesus minutes before execution for his crimes? According to Paul he is saved, while Jesus says hell awaits his arrival.

Thirty-sixth, in Mark 8:31 Jesus says he would be killed, and after three days rise again; yet, Paul says in 1 Cor. 15:4 that Jesus "was buried, that he was raised again on the third day according to the Scriptures." So the question becomes, did Jesus rise "on" or "after" the third day?

Thirty-seventh, Paul says in Heb. 13:14, "Here have we no continuing city, but we seek one to come." How does Paul square that with Jesus' comment in Matt. 5:5 that the meek shall inherit the earth? That would be quite an accomplishment! We have no continuing city with this world, but the meek are going to inherit it!

Thirty-eighth, in Matt. 6:25–28 and 33–34 Jesus teaches,

> Take no thought for your life, what ye shall eat, or what ye shall drink; nor yet for your body. . . . Behold the fowls of the air: for they sow not, neither do they reap, nor gather into barns; yet your heavenly Father feedeth them. . . . Consider the lilies of the field, how they grow; they toil not, neither do they spin. . . . But seek ye first the kingdom of God, and his righteousness; and all these things shall be added to you. Take therefore no thought for the morrow: for the morrow shall take thought for the things of itself.

Paul, on the other hand, says in 1 Cor. 3:8, "Every man shall receive his own reward according to his own labour" and in 2 Thess. 3:10 he says, "This we commanded you, that if any would not work, neither should he eat." So, we have Jesus telling us to forget about labor and planning, God will provide; while Paul tells us that each person will be rewarded according to the amount of labor exerted, and no one will be rewarded who does not produce accordingly.

Thirty-ninth, although Jesus says in Matt. 5:34–35, "I say unto you, Swear not at all, neither by heaven; for it is God's throne: Nor by the earth," Paul says in Heb. 7:21, "The Lord sware and will not repent." In effect, Paul attributes comments to God that are condemned by Jesus.

Fortieth, in Heb. 10:5–7 (NIV) Paul claims that Jesus said to God, "Sacrifice and offering you did not desire, but a body you prepared for me; with burnt offerings and sin offerings you were not pleased. Then I said, Here I am—it is written about me in the scroll—I have come to do your will, O God." Nowhere in the Gospels does Jesus make a statement of this kind. Part of it is from Psalms 40:6–7, which could not have been said by Jesus, since a subsequent verse, Psalms 40:12, states, "Mine iniquities have taken hold upon me . . . they are more than the hairs of mine head." The person who said the latter also spoke in Psalms 40:6–7. Would Jesus have more iniquities than the hairs of his head?

So, in summarizing all of the above, one can understand why Maurice Bucaille says on page 52 of *The Bible, the Quran, and Science,* "Paul is considered the most controversial figure in Christianity. He was considered to be a *traitor* to Jesus' thought by the latter's family and by the apostles who had stayed in Jerusalem in the circle around James. Paul created Christianity at the expense of those whom Jesus had gathered around him to spread his teachings." Christianity could much more accurately be called Paulianity than Christianity.

Peter vs. the Old Testament

Having noted the numerous conflicts between Jesus and Paul we can now turn to a third individual of immense biblical importance—Peter. If there is anyone who seems to have disagreements with just about everything and everybody it is Peter. He clashes with the Old Testament, the New Testament, Jesus, Paul, and even himself on occasion. His comments are deserving of special consideration and our analysis of his one-man crusade will begin by noting the number of times he diverged from Old Testament teachings.

CONTRADICTIONS

Some of the most prominent examples of *contradictions* between Peter and the Old Testament are:

First, Acts 10:34 says, "Peter opened his mouth, and said, 'Of a truth I perceive that God is no respecter of persons.' " In effect, Peter says God does not play favorites, even though evidence to the contrary is overwhelming. God does have his pets, as can be seen by Deut. 14:2 ("Thou art an holy people unto the Lord thy God, and the Lord hath chosen thee to be a peculiar people unto himself, above all the nations that are upon the face of the earth"); Deut. 7:6 ("The Lord thy God hath chosen thee to be a special people to himself, above all people that are upon the face of the earth"); Deut. 7:14 ("Thou shalt be blessed above all people"); and 1 Chron. 17:22 ("Thy people Israel didst thou make thine own people for ever; and thou, Lord, becamest their God"). Verses such as 1 Sam. 12:22, Isa. 51:16, and Exod. 2:25, also clearly show that the biblical God plays favorites.

Second, in 2 Peter 3:10–11 Peter says, "The heavens shall pass away with a great noise, and the elements shall melt with fervent heat, the earth also and the works that are therein shall be burned up . . . all these things shall be dissolved." This clashes with Eccles. 1:4 ("One generation passeth away, and another generation cometh, but the earth abideth for ever"; Psalms 104:5, "Who laid the foundations of the earth, that it should not be removed for ever"; and Deut. 4:40, "That thou mayest prolong thy dᵃys upon the earth, which the Lord thy God giveth thee, for ever").

On the one hand, we are told the earth will be burned up, while on the other, it is to abide forever.

Third, in 1 Peter 3:18 Peter says, "Christ also hath once suffered for sins, the just for the unjust, that he might bring us to God." This runs contrary to the entire spirit of Deut. 24:16, which says, "The fathers shall not be put to death for the children, neither shall the children be put to death for the fathers: every man shall be put to death for his own sin." If God decreed that every man should be put to death for his own sins, then why would he accept the sacrifice of Jesus for the acts of others? Although a magnanimous act it has nothing to do with justice.

Fourth, in Acts 1:24 ("Thou, Lord, which knowest the hearts of all men") Peter claims that God knows what lies in the hearts of all men. But that runs counter to Old Testament verses showing that God does not know all: Deut. 8:2, "Thou shalt remember all the way which the Lord thy God led thee these forty years in the wilderness, to humble thee, and to prove thee, to know what was in thine heart, whether thou wouldest keep his commandments or no"; Deut. 13:3, "The Lord your God proveth you, to know whether ye love the Lord your God with all your heart and with all your soul"; and Gen. 18:21, "I [God] will go down now, and see whether they have done altogether according to the cry of it, which is come unto me; and if not, I will know."

In at least 3 instances an omniscient being does not know all and seeks to learn something.

Fifth, in many verses Jeremiah repeatedly said Babylon was to be destroyed forever and never be reinhabited. Prime examples are Jer. 51:26 ("Thou [Babylon] shalt be a desolate for ever, saith the Lord"); Jer. 51:62 ("None shall remain in it, neither man nor beast, but that it shall be desolate for ever"); and Jer. 51:64 ("Thus shall Babylon sink, and shall not rise from the evil that I will bring upon her"). Yet Peter says there was a church and people at Babylon as late as the apostolic period, according to 1 Peter 5:13 which says, "The church that is at Babylon."

Sixth, in 1 Peter 2:22 Peter says Jesus did no sin and guile was not found in his mouth, despite the fact the numerous false, misleading, and erroneous statements by Jesus that are well documented in a previous chapter and in issues 24, 25, 27, and 28 of *Biblical Errancy.*

Seventh, in Acts 2:22 Peter says, "Men of Israel, hear these words; Jesus of Nazareth, a man approved of God among you by miracles and wonders and signs, which God did by him in the midst of you, as ye yourselves also know." If the ability to do miracles proves one is approved of God as Peter alleges, then the Pharaoh's magicians must also be approved of God, because Exod. 7:11–12 says, "Then Pharaoh also called the wise men and the sorcerers: now the magicians of Egypt, they also did in like manner with their enchantments. For they cast down every man his rod, and they became serpents." and Exod. 8:7 says, "The magicians did so with their enchantments, and brought up frogs upon the land of Egypt."

Eighth, 2 Peter 2:4 says, "God spared not the angels that sinned, but cast them down to hell, and delivered them into chains of darkness, to be reserved unto judgment." This conflicts with Job 1:6–7, which says, "There was a day when the sons of God came to present themselves before the Lord, and Satan came also among them. And the Lord said unto Satan, Whence comest thou? Then Satan answered the Lord, and said, From going to and fro in the earth, and from walking up and down in it."

Peter says Satan was one of the angels that sinned and was among those cast down into hell into the chains of darkness to be reserved unto judgment, but Job alleges Satan presented himself before God after walking back and forth over the earth. If the Devil was to be kept restrained in the chains of darkness until the judgment, how could he have been walking back and forth on earth?

Ninth, in Acts 3:22 Peter says, "Moses truly said unto the fathers, A prophet shall the Lord your God raise up to you of your brethren, like unto me." Jesus was supposedly the prophet that was "like unto Moses." But if Jesus was really "like unto Moses," then he could not have been God incarnate, since Moses was not God incarnate nor did he ever claim to be such. Moreover, Jesus could not have been the prophet referred to by Moses, since he failed to meet the requirements outlined in Deut. 18:22, "When a prophet speaketh in the name of the Lord, if the thing follow not, nor come to pass, that is the thing which the Lord hath not spoken, but the prophet hath spoken it presumptuously." One is not a prophet from God if what he predicts fails to materialize, and since much of what Jesus prophesied failed to come to pass, as was noted in a previous chapter and issue 28 of *Biblical Errancy,* he could not have been the prophet mentioned by Moses.

Tenth, in Acts 3:21 Peter says, "Which God hath spoken by the mouth of all his prophets *since the world began.*" What prophets existed and spoke for God when the world began?

Eleventh and finally, in 2 Peter 3:9 Peter says, "The Lord is not slack concerning his promise, as some men count slackness; but is long-suffering toward us, not willing that any should perish, but that all should come to repentance." This does not agree with Prov. 16:4 (RSV), which says, "The Lord has made everything for its purpose, even the wicked for the day of trouble." Peter says the Lord wants all to come to repentance even though he intentionally created wicked people, according to Proverbs. Why would God create something that is wicked so everything would come to him in repentance? Why create a problem you want to abolish?

MISQUOTATIONS

Peter also misquotes a number of Old Testament verses:

First, 1 Peter 2:6 says, "It is contained in the Scripture, Behold I lay in Sion a chief corner stone, elect, precious: And he that believeth on him shall not be confounded." In trying to quote Isa. 28:16 ("Thus saith the Lord God, Behold, I lay in Zion for a foundation a stone, a tried stone, a precious corner stone, a sure foundation: he that believeth shall not make haste"), Peter twists Isaiah in several respects: (a) Isaiah says, "He that believeth shall not make haste." It never uses the phrase "believeth on him"; (b) Isaiah says "make haste" not "be confounded"; and (c) Isaiah never implies the stone (which Christians believe to be Jesus) is "elect."

Second, Acts 1:20 says, "It is written in the book of Psalms, Let his habitation be desolate, and let no man dwell therein." Here Peter sought to duplicate Psalms 69:25, which says, "Let their habitation be desolate; and let none dwell in their tents."

The problem is that Psalms 69:25 says "their" habitation and "their" tents. At no time does it refer to one person or "his." The psalm is actually an appeal by David to God for aid in David's struggle with his enemies.

Third, Acts 2:16–17, "This is that which was spoken by the prophet Joel; and it shall come to pass in the last days, saith God") is a poor duplication of Joel 2:28, which says, "It shall come to pass afterward, that I will pour." Joel says "afterward," not "in the last days."

Fourth, Acts 1:20 says, "It is written in the book of Psalms, Let his [allegedly Judas'] habitation be desolate, and let no man dwell therein: and his bishopric let another take." This is supposed to reproduce Psalms 109:8 ("Let his days be few; and let another take his office"), which is allegedly a Davidic prophecy about Judas.

Unfortunately, there are several problems with this comparison: (a) Psalms 109:8 says nothing about a bishopric. Office and bishopric are not necessarily the same; (b) While Peter is referring to the subject's habitation being desolate, the psalmist is referring to his days being few. They are not identical, since one could have many days and still conclude with a desolate habitation; and (c) the psalmist, David, is referring to his enemies, not Judas. David is saying he hopes his enemies are punished. The context of Psalms 109:8 shows it is not a Davidic prophecy about Judas.

Fifth and lastly, in 1 Peter 2:22 ("Who did no sin, neither was guile found in his mouth"), Peter misuses Isa. 53:9 ("Because he had done no violence, neither was any deceit in his mouth." Isaiah says "no violence," instead of "no sin." Sin and violence are not the same. Apparently Peter realized that "he hath done no violence" could not be applied to Jesus because of the latter's treatment of the moneychangers at the temple.

MISINTERPRETATIONS

And finally, we have instances in which Peter *misinterprets* Old Testament verses.

First, in Acts 1:16 Peter says, "Men and brethren, this Scripture must needs have been fulfilled, which the Holy Ghost by the mouth of David spake before concerning Judas, which was guide to them that took Jesus." To begin with,

David never said anything about Judas. A verse such as Psalms 41:9, "Yea, mine own familiar friend, in whom I trusted, which did eat of my bread, hath lifted up his heel against me," does not apply because the speaker in Psalms 41:9 said five verses earlier, in Psalms 41:4, "I said, Lord, be merciful unto me: heal my soul; for I have sinned against thee." If Jesus is the speaker in Psalms 41:9, then he is also the sinner in Psalms 41:4. Yet the Bible states that Jesus was sinless in 1 John 3:5 ("In him is no sin") and 1 Peter 2:22 ("Who did no sin").

Second, 1 Peter 2:8 ("A stone of stumbling, and a rock of offense, even to them which stumble at the word, being disobedient") does not adequately reproduce Isa. 8:14 ("He shall be for a sanctuary; and a stone of stumbling and a rock of offense to both houses of Israel"): (a) The verse preceding Isa. 8:14, Isa. 8:13 ("Sanctify the Lord of hosts himself; and let him be your fear, and let him be your dread") shows that the "he" in Isa. 8:14 is referring to God, not Jesus, and (b) Isa. 8:14 says he is a rock of offense to both houses of Israel only, not to all those who are disobedient, as would be true of Jesus' mission.

Third, Peter's comment in Acts 2:27, "Because thou wilt not leave my soul in hell, neither wilt thou suffer thine Holy One to see corruption," reproduces Psalms 16:10, "For thou wilt not leave my soul in hell; neither wilt thou suffer thine Holy One to see corruption."

Although Peter correctly quotsd Psalms 16:10, he misapplies the statement to Jesus because: (a) "Holy One" was translated from a Hebrew word meaning holy ones or saints (plural), not Holy One (singular). The plural shows it refers to the pious generally; and (b) "corruption" comes from a Hebrew word meaning "grave," not corruption. Correctly translated the verse should have been, "Wilt not suffer thy saints to see destruction or disintegration."

Fourth, in Acts 2:30, "God had sworn with an oath to him [David], that of the fruit of his loins, according to the flesh, he would raise up Christ to sit on his throne," Peter misrepresents Psalms 132:11–12, which says, "The Lord hath sworn in truth unto David; he will not turn from it; Of the fruit of thy body will I set upon thy throne. If thy children will keep my covenant and my testimony that I shall teach them, their children shall also sit upon thy throne for evermore." Conflicts are evident in that (a) the psalmist alleges *all* of David's descendants who keep God's covenant will sit upon David's throne. There is no hint whatsoever that only one man received the promise; and (b) the psalmist does not mention Christ or Jesus.

Fifth and lastly, 1 Peter 1:11 declares, "The Spirit of Christ which was in them [prophets] did signify, when it testified beforehand the sufferings of Christ, and the glory that should follow." And Acts 3:18 says, "Those things, which God before had shewed by the mouth of all his prophets, that Christ should suffer, Jesus has so fulfilled."

Such are Peter's comments concerning the suffering Jesus. Isaiah 53 speaks of a suffering servant, which Peter is interpreting as the suffering Jesus. But for a wide variety of reasons mentioned in a previous chapter and issue 30 of *Biblical Errancy,* the suffering servant of Old Testament fame could not be Jesus.

In summary, several verses clearly demonstrate that Peter was not above misinterpreting the Old Testament when he felt the need.

Peter vs. the New Testament

Peter also made a sizable number of statements that conflict with New Testament teachings. Good examples are:

First, Peter distorts biblical history in Acts 4:26–27, which says, "The kings of the earth stood up, and the rulers were gathered together against the Lord, and against his Christ. For of a truth against the holy child Jesus, whom thou hast anointed, both Herod, and Pontius Pilate, with the Gentiles, and the people of Israel, were gathered together." Peter's error is clearly exposed by Matt. 27:24, which says, "When Pilate saw that he could prevail nothing, but that rather a tumult was made, he took water, and washed his hands before the multitude, saying I am innocent of the blood of this just person." Peter alleges in Acts that Pilate and Herod were against Christ, while Matthew clearly shows that Pilate was not only not against Jesus but considered him an innocent and just person.

Second, Peter's comment in Acts 5:30 ("The God of our fathers raised up Jesus, whom ye slew and hanged on a tree") conflicts with the events related in Matt. 27:40 ("If thou be the Son of God, come down from the cross"). Peter and Matthew disagree on the particulars of the Crucifixion. Did Jesus die on a tree or a cross? Was he hanged or crucified? And was he slain *before* being hanged, as Acts implies, or was he alive and conversant while being crucified as Matthew implies?

Third, Acts 2:4 says, "They were all [including the Apostles] filled with the Holy Ghost." Yet John 20:22 says that when Jesus "had said this, he breathed on them [including the Apostles], and saith unto them, Receive ye the Holy Ghost." Acts 2:4 says the apostles, among others, were all filled with the Holy Ghost, even though they had already received the Holy Ghost via Jesus, according to John 20:22. If they lost the Holy Ghost, which later returned, then they temporarily lost the assurance of salvation which fundamentalists claim is impossible.

Fourth, Acts 1:18 says, "This man [Judas] purchased a field with the reward of iniquity; and falling headlong, he burst asunder in the midst, and all his bowels gushed out." This does not agree with Matt. 27:3–7, which says, ("Then Judas, which had betrayed him [Jesus], when he saw that he was condemned, repented himself, and brought again the thirty pieces of silver to the chief priests and elders. Saying, I have sinned in that I have betrayed innocent blood. And they said, What is that to us? . . . And he cast down the pieces of silver in the temple, and departed, and went and hanged himself. And the chief priests, took the silver pieces, and said, It is not lawful to put them into the treasury, because it is the price of blood. And they took counsel, and bought with them the potter's field, to bury strangers in."

Peter's account of what occurred with respect to Judas' betrayal in Acts differs from Matthew's in several respects: (a) Peter says Judas used the thirty pieces of silver to purchase a field, while Matthew says he threw the money on the temple floor and left; (b) Peter says Judas purchased a field with the thirty pieces of silver, but Matthew says the priests used the money to purchase a potter's field; and (c) Peter says Judas burst open in the middle and all his bowels gushed out, while Matthew says he died by hanging himself.

Fifth, to conclude the issue of how Judas died, we might note that Peter says in Acts 1:18–19, "And falling headlong, he burst asunder in the midst, and all his bowels gushed out. And it was known unto all the dwellers at Jerusalem; insomuch as that field is called in their proper tongue, Aceldama, that is to say, The field of blood." But Matt. 27:6–8 says, "The chief priests took the silver pieces, and said, It is not lawful to put them into the treasury, because it is the price of blood. And they took counsel, and bought with them, the potter's field, to bury strangers in. Wherefore that field was called, the field of blood."

Peter says the field was called "the field of blood" because the blood of Judas was poured on it; while Matthew says it was called "the field of blood" because it was bought with blood money.

Before ending our analysis of Peter's conflicts with the New Testament, a couple of his comments in the Book of Acts that generate unique problems of their own should be noted:

First, in Acts 2:36 Peter said, "Let all the house of Israel know assuredly, that God hath made that same Jesus, whom ye have crucified, both Lord and Christ." How could God have made Jesus both Lord and Christ, when that would have meant he was neither at one time?

And *second,* in Acts 2:31 Peter says, "He [David] seeing this before spoke of the resurrection of Christ that his soul was not left in hell, neither did his flesh see corruption." "Left" in hell means the soul of Jesus was there at one time. How could the soul of a perfect being ever have been in hell?

Peter vs. Paul

Peter also clashed with Paul on several issues. Good examples are:

First, Peter makes an outlandish statement in Acts 10:34 ("I perceive that God is no respecter of persons"). Paul, on the other hand, concedes that God *does* play favorites, as is shown by his indirect admissions in Rom. 1:16 ("I am not ashamed of the gospel of Christ: for it is the power of God unto salvation to everyone that believeth; to the Jew first, and also to the Greek"); Rom. 2:10 ("Glory, honour, and peace to every man that worketh good, to the Jew first, and also to the Gentile"); and Col. 1:26 ("Even the mystery which hath been hid from ages and from generations, but now is made manifest to his saints"). In effect, Paul disagrees with Peter's belief that God is impartial and plays no favorites.

Second, the signs and miracles problem resurfaces through a comparison of Peter's comment in Acts 2:22 ("Men of Israel, hear these words; Jesus of Nazareth, a man approved of God among you by miracles and wonders and signs, which God did by him in the midst of you") with Paul's utterance in 2 Thess. 2:9 ("Even him, whose coming is after the working of Satan with all power and signs and lying wonders"). Paul clearly notes that the ability to do signs and wonders can *not* be used to prove one is approved by God as Peter alleges, unless Satan is approved by God. From Paul's perspective Satan and his agents can do signs and wonders as well.

Third, upon no point do Paul and Peter clash more directly than that created by a comparison of Paul's comment in 2 Cor. 3:17 ("Where the Spirit of the Lord is, there is liberty") with Peter's admonition to slaves in 1 Peter 2:18 that servants, a euphemism for slaves, should "be subject to your masters with all fear; not only to the good and gentle, but also to the froward [overbearing]." Telling people to willingly submit to their masters, regardless of the latter's behavior, fosters anything but a spirit of liberty.

Fourth, a final clash between Peter and Paul materializes when Peter's comment in Acts 15:7, "Men and brethren, ye know how that a good while ago God made choice among us, that the Gentiles by my mouth should hear the word of the gospel, and believe," is compared with Paul's comment in Gal. 2:7–8 (RSV) that, "They saw that I had been entrusted with the gospel to the uncircumcised, just as Peter had been entrusted with the gospel to the circumcised." Peter and Paul can't even agree on who is to take the message to whom. Peter feels his duty is to take the message to the Gentiles, while Paul considers that it is his duty and that Peter's obligation is to go to the circumcised, that is, the Jews. Apparently both preferred speaking to Gentiles rather than Jews. Perhaps this is because the former were easier to persuade.

In summary, Peter and Paul clearly had more than one ideological disagreement.

Peter vs. Jesus

One of Peter's most distinguishing characteristics is the degree to which he, like Paul, clashed with Jesus on significant topics. Prime illustrations are:

First, Jesus says in John 8:15, "Ye judge after the flesh; I judge no man."

This is in direct opposition to what Peter says in Acts 10:42: "He [Jesus] commanded us [his followers] . . . to testify that it is he which was ordained of God to be the Judge of the quick and the dead."

So, will Jesus judge or won't he? You'll never know from these two.

Second, on the issue of peace, Peter, like Paul, describes Jesus in a manner markedly different from that which Jesus applies to himself. Peter says in Acts 10:36 (NIV), "This is the message God sent to the people of Israel, telling the good news of peace through Jesus Christ, who is Lord of all." This is in dramatic opposition to the words of Jesus in Matt. 10:34, "Think not that I am come to send peace on earth, I came not to send peace, but a sword." Jesus just wouldn't accept the peacemaker role that others feel he represented.

Third, Peter follows in Paul's footsteps by disagreeing with Jesus on the question of servility in 1 Peter 2:18: "Servants, be subject to your masters with all fear; not only to the good and gentle, but to the froward [overbearing]," while Jesus contends in Matt. 4:10 that, "It is written, Thou shalt worship the Lord thy God, and him only shalt thou serve."

Fourth, in Acts 2:38 Peter says, "Repent, and be baptized every one of you in the name of Jesus Christ for the remission of sins." And in Acts 10:48 Peter "commanded them to be baptized in the name of the Lord." However, in Matt. 28:19 Jesus says, "Go ye therefore, and teach all nations, baptizing them in the name of the Father, and of the Son, and of the Holy Ghost." So the question becomes one of deciding if people are to be baptized in the name of Jesus, in the name of the Lord, or in the name of the Father, the Son, and the Holy Ghost. You would think they could at least get the ritual down pat.

Fifth, like Paul, Peter disagrees with Jesus on the question of adherence to the law. Peter says in Acts 15:8–10 (RSV), "God . . . bore witness to them [the Gentiles] giving them the Holy Spirit just as he did to us; and he made no distinction between us and them, but cleansed their hearts by faith. Now therefore why do you make a trial of God by putting a yoke [being circumcised and following the old Law] upon the neck of the disciples which neither our fathers nor we have been able to bear?" Peter felt adherence to the law and circumcision were no longer necessary.

But, as noted earlier in Paul's disputes with Jesus, Jesus had a far different view. Luke 16:17 ("It is easier for heaven and earth to pass, than one tittle of the law to fail") and Matt. 5:18 ("I say unto you, Till heaven and earth pass, one jot or one tittle shall in no wise pass from the law, till all be fulfilled") clearly show that Jesus advocated strict adherence to the Law.

In essence, Jesus said the Old Law would never fail till all be fulfilled, while Peter and Paul considered compliance with its provisions by all gentile converts to be an unnecessary yoke.

Sixth, Peter split with Jesus and Paul on another major issue. In Acts 2:22 ("You men of Israel, hear these words: Jesus of Nazareth, a man approved of

God among you by miracles and wonders and signs, which God did by him in the midst of you") Peter contends that the capacity to do miracles and wonders proved a person was from God. Jesus, on the other hand, states in Matt. 24:23–24 that the ability to do miracles does *not* prove one is approved by God. Jesus and Paul were in concert on this point because both contended false christs and false prophets can perform miracles as well.

In addition, Peter said signs were given to his generation despite the fact that Jesus said in Mark 8:12, "Why doth this generation seek after a sign? Verily I say unto you, There shall no sign be given to this generation."

Seventh, Peter says in 1 Peter 3:22 that Jesus has gone into heaven and is on the right hand of God. Yet, Jesus claims in John 10:30 that he and the Father were one. How can two beings be one, i.e., identical, while sitting beside one another?

Eighth, in John 10:27–29 Jesus says, "My sheep hear my voice, and I know them, and they follow me: And I give unto them eternal life; and they shall never perish, neither shall any man pluck them out of my hand. My Father, which gave them me, is greater than all; and no man is able to pluck them out of my Father's hand." From the perspective of Jesus, salvation is irreversible. Once saved, always saved.

But Peter holds a dramatically different view. In 2 Peter 2:20–22 he says,

> If after they have escaped the pollutions of the world through the knowledge of the Lord and Savior Jesus Christ, they are again entangled therein, and overcome, the latter end is worse with them than the beginning. For it had been better for them not to have known the way of righteousness, than after they have known it, to turn from the holy commandment delivered unto them. But it is happened unto them according to the true proverb, The dog is turned to his own vomit again; and the sow that was washed, to her wallowing in the mire.

As far as Peter is concerned, the "sheep" *can* be plucked out of the Father's hand and those who have knowledge of Jesus *can* return to the "pollutions of the world." People *can* accept Jesus and later reject him. In other words, people can lose their salvation.

Ninth, Peter, like Paul, felt the gospel message should be taken to everyone, regardless. This is evident from comments by Peter in Acts 10:28 ("God hath shewed me that I should not call any man common or unclean"); Acts 15:7 (NIV) ("Brothers, you know that some time ago God made a choice among you that the Gentiles might hear from my lips the message of the gospel and believe"); and Acts 10:34–35 (NIV) ("I now realize how true it is that God does not show favoritism but accepts men from every nation who fear him and do what is right"). But in Matt. 10:5 ("Go not into the way of the Gentiles, and into the city of the Samaritans enter ye not") and Matt. 15:26 ("It is not meet to take the children's bread, and cast it to dogs") Jesus clearly shows that he looks upon some people as unclean and unworthy of his message.

Being more realistic than Jesus, Peter and Paul eventually realized that the message would have to be modified dramatically in order to be marketable. A major alteration would be required if Christianity was going to survive. It would have to be carried to far more people than just Jews—as far as nearly all Jews were concerned, too much about Jesus did not fit the Judaic concept of the messiah or the events that were to accompany his arrival.

Tenth and finally: Peter says in 2 Peter 3:9, "The Lord is not . . . willing that any should perish, but that all should come to repentance." If that is true, then why was Isaiah's comment in Isa. 6:10 repeated by Jesus in John 12:40 (NIV), "He [the Lord] has blinded their eyes and deadened their hearts, so they can neither see with their eyes, nor understand with their hearts, nor turn—and I would heal them." As far as Jesus is concerned, God most assuredly does blind the eyes of many and demonstrates a marked willingness to allow them to perish. If God isn't willing that all people perish, then why would he blind their eyes and deaden their hearts to his message?

In any event, the message to be garnered from the prior textual conflicts is that Peter clashed with mankind's alleged savior on many key issues.

Peter vs. Peter

Perhaps most egregiously, Peter did not always even agree with himself. Some noteworthy examples are: In 1 Peter 1:17 Peter says he thinks that "God is no respecter of persons," but one chapter later, in 1 Peter 2:9 (NIV), Peter says, "You are a chosen people, a royal priesthood, a holy nation, a people belonging to God, that you may declare the praises of him who called you out of darkness into his wonderful light. Once you were not a people, but now you are the people of God." God called them out of darkness to be his chosen people and that isn't playing favorites? If he isn't choosing favorites, why didn't he call everybody? Don't all people belong to God ("God is no respecter of persons") or does that only apply to just a chosen few?

And finally, it is hard to reconcile Peter's comment in 2 Peter 2:4, "God spared not the angels that sinned, but cast them down to hell, and delivered them into chains of darkness, to be reserved unto judgment," with his assertion in 1 Peter 5:8 that one should "be sober, be vigilant because your adversary the devil, as a roaring lion, walketh about, seeking whom he may devour." How could the devil be walking around seeking whom to devour when he is chained in hell until judgment?

Conclusion

In essence, the most important lesson to be learned from all of the above is that the major New Testament biblical figures not only disagreed with one another on many crucial issues but also diverged significantly from the Old Testament. Anyone who seeks consistency in that which is taught by Jesus, Peter and Paul has embarked upon a journey of disillusionment. The most important founders of Christianity are hopelessly at odds with one another on numerous issues and no amount of apologetic rationalization, justification, and obfuscation can hide this overarching fact. No one concerned with being realistic could possibly trust individuals who are as loose with the facts and cavalier with the truth as those who founded Christianity. Imagine trying to work in accord with men who can't even agree with one another! In the words of today's adolescent, they just couldn't get their act together.

23

New Testament Service to the Elite

Acceptance and Submission, Rejection of Wealth, Expectation of Reward, Closed-mindedness, Human Nature, Fostering Slavery

In the arsenal of the power elite (to borrow from C. Wright Mills) lie many ideological control mechanisms—the press, radio, television, educational institutions—each maintained in such a manner as to perpetuate those ideas the elite deems important. Yet, only one of these institutions has, for all practical purposes, been above reproach. Criticism of the press, radio, television, and other media is considered acceptable, while criticism directed toward Christianity in general and the Bible in particular has been considered anathema. For too long the grievous effect of biblical teachings upon millions of people has been either ignored or treated lightly. But Scripture should be no more immune from exposure than any other instrument of the power elite.

The negative and regressive essence of the New Testament in particular has often been looked upon as a temporary deviation from an otherwise correct path and not indicative of Christianity and the Bible as a whole. Few beliefs are more in conflict with reality. Statements, teachings, and concepts within the New Testament, combined with two thousand years of Christian history, prove beyond any doubt that the Bible has been effectively employed to the advantage of dominant groups with tragic effects upon the history of humanity.

Many individuals will doubtless view such a contention as sacrilegious, irresponsible, and erroneous, while others will see it as oversimplified, distorted, or deceptive. A few will probably contend the New Testament is being misinterpreted and phrases are being taken out of context. The latter response would have some validity if most of the New Testament were as mystical and esoteric as the Book of Revelation. It would be difficult to know what was intended, since one interpretation would be as plausible as another. But much of the New Testament, on the contrary, is quite vivid. Clarity is provided through simplicity of speech and repetition in slightly altered form. The attitude the New Testament would have people adopt toward many important aspects of life is all too clear. This can be illustrated by numerous quotes and parables extracted from a modern English version of the New Testament entitled *Good News for Modern Man* and its successor, *Today's English Version* (TEV), published by the American Bible Society of New York. Unless people are aware of the extent to which their lives are manipulated by a minority, they can easily be victimized because of the New Testament's influence.

Superficially, the Bible propagates humility, peace, love, and brotherhood. These are repeated themes as subsequent quotes will show. In reality, however, these themes are a blueprint for bondage. Appearances would lead most individuals to believe that any work teaching the importance of love, peace, and humility is contributing to the creation of a better world. But exteriors are often deceiving. Deception lies in the fact that a society of peace, love, and brotherhood will never emerge until people obtain greater control of their lives, which can never occur as long as they direct peace, love, brotherhood, and humility towards their leaders. In other words, peace, love, and brotherhood can sometimes only be established by practicing the exact opposite for a period of time.

Most people look upon creating peace and brotherhood by initiating dissension as self-defeating and contradictory. They erroneously believe that society is composed of one big amorphous mass of people who are failing to exercise sufficient self-control, brotherly love, and peaceful intent toward their neighbors. They fail to see that society is in fact often composed of basically two groups, the stronger of which, a minority, manages society and foments disunity among the other group, the majority, as one means by which to dominate it. The material aspects of society exercise the greatest influence upon people and are directed by the minority in such a manner as to keep them divided. Since the minority's interests are served by dividing and factionalizing, there will be no peace, love, brotherhood, and humility throughout the land (despite the most extensive teaching and preaching to the contrary) as long as such a minority exercises disproportionate control. Preaching love toward all only serves to maintain the existing—often exploitive— state of affairs. Christians are taught that love and mercy should guide their relationships with others; yet, without distinction as to rulers and ruled, this can only lead to entrapment. In effect, preaching brotherly love perpetuates its opposite.

Acceptance and Submission

The New Testament is replete with statements that preach support for the elite under the guise of love, peace, and humility. Excellent examples are: Matt. 5:44 ("Love your enemies . . . and pray for them which despitefully use you"); Luke 6:35 (LB) ("Love your enemies! Do good to them!"); 1 Cor. 4:6 (TEV) ("None of you should be proud of one person and despise another"); and Gal. 5:14 (TEV) ("For the whole law is summed up in one commandment: Love your neighbor as you love yourself").

The New Testament urges individuals to love their opponents, obey their masters, serve them faithfully, and respect their leadership. Prominent verses are Col. 3:22 (TEV) ("Slaves, obey your human masters in all things, not only when they are watching you because you want to gain their approval; but do it with a sincere heart because of your reverence for the Lord"); 1 Tim. 6:1–2 (TEV) ("Those who are slaves must consider their masters worthy of all respect, so that no one will speak evil of the name of God and our teaching. Slaves belonging to Christian masters must not despise them, for they are their brothers. Instead they are to serve them even better, because those who benefit from their work are believers whom they love"); and 1 Peter 2:18–20 (TEV) ("You servants must submit yourselves to your masters and show them complete respect, not only to those who are kind and considerate, but also to those who are harsh. God will bless you for this, if you endure the pain of undeserved suffering because you are conscious of his will. For what credit is there in enduring the beatings you deserve for having done wrong? But if you endure suffering even when you have done right, God will bless you for it").

In each instance, serving one's master faithfully is linked to serving the Lord faithfully. Employment of the Bible to strengthen the hand of those on top is unmistakable. Additional statements buttressing the status quo by urging patient endurance on the part of the beleaguered are Phil. 2:14 (TEV) ("Do everything without complaining or arguing"); Phil. 4:11–12 (TEV) ("I have learned to be satisfied with what I have . . . so that anywhere, at any time, I am content, whether I am full or hungry, whether I have too much or too little"); and 1 Peter 4:1 (TEV) ("Since Christ suffered physically, you too must strengthen yourselves with the same way of thinking").

Believers are repeatedly told to remain peaceful and reject physical responses to provocations. Prime verses are Matt. 5:9 (TEV) ("Happy are those who work for peace: God will call them his children!"); Rom. 12:18 (TEV) ("Do everything possible on your part, to live at peace with everybody"); Rom. 14:19 (TEV) ("So then, we must always aim at those things that bring peace"); and Heb. 12:14 ("Try to be at peace with everyone").

Such teachings aid the elite by enabling them to rule more efficiently and thoroughly. Those in charge understandably deplore activism not out of any humanitarian motives but because they do not want the pyramid upset. Peace to the elite is the maintenance of the status quo with itself at the apex. Fully cognizant of the fact that peaceful intent directed toward the minority is of far greater significance than that directed toward friends, relatives, and acquaintances, the New Testament aids the elite by urging believers to be at peace with all men. Like love, mercy, obedience, and faithful service, peace toward all without distinguishing rulers and ruled is entrapment.

Shunning civil disturbances is a central theme of the New Testament. The crowd that called for Christ's death in Luke 23:13-25 also called for the release of Barabbas, a convicted rioter. Believers can easily infer from this that those favoring activism are anti-Christ. Is it accidental that as a peaceful Jesus is turned over to his enemies a convicted rioter is released from prison? As one is released, the other is enchained. Christ and an insurgent are set in contrast to one another.

Believers must remain peaceful even when wronged. And since the dominant minority is far more responsible for injustices done to the population at large than any other individual or group, in this respect the New Testament clearly renders aid to the former. Relevant verses are Matt. 5:39 (TEV) ("I tell you: do not take revenge on someone who wrongs you. If anyone slaps you on the right cheek, let him slap your left cheek too"); Luke 6:27-29 (TEV) ("Love your enemies, do good to those who hate you, bless those who curse you and pray for those who mistreat you"); Matt. 6:14 (TEV) ("If you forgive others the wrongs they have done to you, your father in heaven will also forgive you"); Luke 11:4 (TEV) ("We forgive everyone who does us wrong"); and Matt. 18:21-22 (TEV) ("Then Peter came to Jesus and asked, 'Lord, if my brother keeps on sinning against me, how many times do I have to forgive him? Seven times?' 'No, not seven times,' answered Jesus, 'but seventy times seven' ").

If people are to accept their condition, obey orders, and labor diligently, they must possess a relatively low opinion of their own importance, capabilities, and merits. They must be convinced that their lowly status is in accord with the natural order of life and that humility is a virtue. *Be humble* is definitely a recurring message of the New Testament as the following comments show: Rom. 12:16 (TEV) ("Do not be proud, but accept humble duties. Do not think of yourself as wise"); John 13:16 (TEV) ("No slave is greater than his master, and no messenger is greater than the one who sent him"); Luke 17:9-10 (TEV) ("The servant does not deserve thanks for obeying orders, does he? It is the same with you; when you have done all you have been told to do say, 'We are ordinary servants; we have only done our duty' "); and Mark 9:35 (TEV) ("Whoever wants to be first must place himself last of all and be the servant of all").

Believers are told not only to be humble but to refrain from *all* criticism and judgment of others. Matt. 7:1 ("Do not judge others: so that God will not judge you"); Rom. 14:13 (TEV) ("So let us stop judging one another"); and James 5:9 (TEV) ("Do not complain against one another, my brothers, so that God will not judge you"). The word "others" includes people within society at large as well as the influential minority. Teaching people not to criticize the ruling minority obviously aids those in control. On the other hand, if a noncritical attitude toward fellow members of the ruled majority were emphasized, New Testament teachings would appear to be working against the interests of the rulers. However, such an observation is erroneous because so many materially divisive aspects of society are present that stressing the importance of criticizing one's neighbors isn't needed. It would only create perpetual social disruption and be counter-productive. Division along racial, national, ethnic, occupational, and sexual lines is fostered by the minority, yet not so much animosity that the movement of society comes to a halt. The brink is never far away.

Believers are not even to consider themselves worthy of criticizing others, as the following verses show: James 4:12 (TEV) ("Who do you think you are to judge your fellow man"); Matt. 10:24–25 (TEV) ("No pupil is greater than his teacher; no slave is greater than his master. So a pupil should be satisfied to become like his teacher, and a slave like his master"); and Matt. 7:4–5 (TEV) ("How dare you say to your brother, 'Please, let me take that speck out of your eye,' when you have a log in your own eye? You hypocrite! First take the log out of your own eye, and then you will be able to see clearly to take the speck out of your brother's eye").

The importance of being humble, accepting one's menial status and possessing a lowly opinion of one's own ability to criticize is also taught through the use of parables. When Jesus saw several guests choosing the best places at a table he said in Luke 14:8–11 (TEV),

> When someone invites you to a wedding feast, do not sit down in the best place. It could happen that someone more important than you has been invited, and your host, who invited both of you, would have to come and say to you, 'Let him have this place.' Then you would be embarrassed and have to sit in the lowest place. Instead, when you are invited, go and sit in the lowest place, so that your host will come to you and say, 'Come on up, my friend, to a better place.' This will bring you honor in the presence of all the other guests. For everyone who makes himself great will be humbled, and everyone who humbles himself will be made great.

Jesus is not only promoting class distinctions by stating that some people are more important than others, but also advising people to accept their lowly status under the mistaken assumption that they will later experience the exhilaration of ascending through the ranks. In reality, few succeed by being offered higher positions because of subservient behavior. Believers are being insidiously taught that if they voluntarily accept their lowly position, honors and promotions are the ultimate reward. This philosophy has been propagated by ruling classes for centuries.

Those in power exercise far more influence and control over the average individual's life than do his companions, relatives, fellow employees, and neighbors. The powerful regulate what he sees, hears, and believes; they dominate his ideological environment; they control his material conditions and are far more responsible for his status and well-being than immediate acquaintances. So the attitude an individual has toward those of the dominant group is of infinitely greater importance than his approach toward others of his social class. If the average individual's philosophy is one of maintaining peace, love, mercy, and humility, regardless of the consequences, the result is a foregone conclusion. No amount of injustice, poverty, or degradation is going to shake his resolve to submit to those primarily responsible for his condition. He will be as pliable as putty, as meek as a lamb. As Matt. 5:5 (TEV) says, "Happy are those who are humble." What more could the minority desire? They would have created the perfect citizen—a being unwilling to resist no matter how severe the subjugation. Snared in New Testament teachings and not really understanding the overall situation, this individual would honestly believe that the most intelligent means by which to create a world of love, peace, and brotherhood would be through the immediate institution of these ideas in one's daily affairs. He would be convinced that only the immediate creation of love and humility toward one's fellow man is the answer, without drawing any distinction between rulers and ruled.

Christians are not only directed to be peaceful, humble, loving and obedient but also to work hard and acknowledge the alleged importance of their master's role. Several parables corroborate these contentions quite well. Although supposedly a description of the joy attending the arrival of Jesus, the story of the servants found in Matt. 25:14-29 (TEV) is actually a subtle means by which to encourage more ingenuity on the part of laborers serving employers. Before leaving on a trip an owner gave the equivalent of $5,000 to one servant, $2,000 to another and $1,000 to a third. While the master was away, the servant with $5,000 increased his amount to $10,000 through investment, and the servant who received $2,000 also doubled his amount. But the servant who received $1,000 hid his money in the ground. When the master returned, accounts were settled. The servant who earned $5,000 was called a good and faithful servant by the master and put in charge of large amounts. The servant who earned $2,000 was treated in the same manner. But the servant who hid the money in the ground was labeled a bad and lazy servant for not having increased his amount. His $1,000 was taken from him and given to the servant with $10,000. The servant stated, "You reap harvests where you did not plant, and you gather crops where you did not scatter seed." The servant who hid the $1,000 was punished not only for failing to increase the funds entrusted to his care but also for verbally challenging the master's right to any portion of the crop because the latter contributed no labor.

Although unsaid, the moral of the story is that servants failing to increase the master's wealth or disputing the master's appropriation of servant-created wealth should be punished.

The parable of the tenants in the vineyard in Matt. 21:33–44 (TEV) also seeks to justify the master's role and behavior. A landowner planted a vineyard, put a fence around it, dug a hole for the winepress, and built a tower. Then he rented the vineyard to tenants and left home on a trip. When harvest time arrived he sent his slaves to obtain his share from the tenants. Those sent were killed or mistreated, and subsequent slaves who were dispatched received comparable treatment. Finally, the landowner sent his son, who was also killed, supposedly to obtain his possessions. After studying the event, Jesus asks, "Now, when the owner of the vineyard comes, what will he do to those tenants?" His companions reply, "He will certainly kill those evil men." Jesus agrees and adds, "And rent the vineyard out to other tenants, who will give him his share of the harvest at the right time." Then Jesus quotes Scripture as to the importance of the master by saying, "The stone [the master] which the builders rejected as worthless turned out to be the most important of all," and closes with a warning to anyone who might dare to question the master's value by saying, "So I tell you, the Kingdom of God will be taken away from you and be given to a people who will produce the proper fruits."

In other words, subservience to a master is equated with the Kingdom of God. Whoever falls on this stone will be broken to pieces; and if the stone falls on someone it will crush him to dust. The entire story is presented from the master's perspective. The impressions conveyed are that: owners do the primary labor, tenants are unreasonably brutal and owners aren't, tenants try to seize property and owners don't, owners deserve part of the produce even when they contribute no labor, owners are just trying to earn an honest and reasonable living despite all adversity, and whoever objects to this arrangement should be rightfully punished. Obviously this teaching, as well as a similar story in Luke 20:9–18 (TEV), aids those in control. Those who resist or attempt to seize property ("his property will be ours" in Luke 20:14) are depicted as brutal and irrational, while Christ's utterance, "Give him his share," in Matt. 21:41, implies that the master's gains in this situation are justified.

Another parable supporting the master is that of the workers in the vineyard, found in Matt. 20:1–18. Again, the narrative is supposedly describing the kingdom of heaven. Early one morning an owner hired some men to labor in a vineyard at the wage of a silver coin a day. At nine o'clock, twelve o'clock, three o'clock, and five o'clock he hired more men, all for the same wage. When evening came he told his foreman to pay the men beginning with those who were hired last and ending with those who were hired first. Everyone was to be paid a silver coin. Those hired first thought they would receive more but did not. They took their money and started grumbling, wanting to know why they were not paid more. The owner replied that they were not cheated because they agreed to do a day's work for a silver coin. He ordered them to leave, said he should be able to do as he wished with his money, and asked if they were jealous because of his generosity. The lesson conveyed is that once having committed themselves workers should accept wages that they find to be unjust. Even when wronged workers should honor their commitments. In other words, the right of owners to dispose of property as they so desire and the sacredness of contracts are more important than justice. Property rights are superior to justice is the message.

People are also taught to consider wealth differentials as quite natural and unworthy of concern. Inequities are to be expected, according to Matt. 13:12 (TEV), "For the person who has something will be given more, so that he will have more than enough; but the person who has nothing will have taken away from him even the little he has." After all, doesn't Matt. 26:11 say, "You will always have the poor people with you"? Again the status quo is strengthened through the elimination of opposition and criticism.

New Testament authors even go so far as to depict those well off as just average citizens worthy of sympathy and respect. Could it be accidental that after Jesus was killed and the tumult subsided the only person to offer him a decent burial was an affluent man named Joseph? The implication of this story, found in Matt. 27:57–60, is that only people of substance can be relied upon after others, like Judas, emerge as betrayers. In Mark 12:41 (TEV) the narrative states Jesus was sitting near the Temple treasury and noticed that, "Many rich men dropped in a lot of money." Accounts of this nature create a favorable impression in the minds of believers toward those well off.

A similar theme is found in Mark 2:13–17 (TEV) where Jesus is eating with tax collectors, who are arms of the dominant group. When asked why he associated with these individuals, Jesus replied, "People who are well do not need a doctor, but only those who are sick. I have not come to call respectable people, but outcasts." The impression conveyed by this story is that tax collectors are not expropriators fully cognizant of their actions, but sick people who know not what they do and deserve more sympathy than condemnation. Pity, not opposition, should be directed towards the tax collector, who is to be viewed as a sick man needing aid, not a parasite. No doubt that aid is a less defensive, less alert citizenry. By describing the tax collector in a manner calculated to generate a degree of respectability and empathy, the New Testament is aiding him and those he serves.

The death of Jesus in Luke 23:13–25 (TEV) is attributed not to the government, as represented by Pontius Pilate, but to a crowd of citizens whom Pilate could not dissuade. Jews are later blamed for the act. After Jesus is nailed to the cross Luke 35 says, "The people stood there watching, while the Jewish leaders made fun of him." By accusing Jews of the execution, the New Testament has not only set Christians against Jews for centuries, and aided the minority in their consistent policy of divide and rule, but also, through Pilate's defense of Christ's innocence lent dignity and credibility to the dominant group itself.

The story of Zacchaeus found in Luke 19:1–10 (TEV) also creates a feeling of benevolence toward the elite. As Jesus was passing through the town of Jericho a tax collector by the name of Zacchaeus came out to see him but could not see over the crowd because he was so little. Portraying the tax collector as diminuitive quickly creates compassion in the mind of the reader. Unable to see, Zacchaeus ran ahead of the crowd and climbed a tree to see Jesus pass, implying that, even with difficulties the worst of people is seeking the Christian path. As Jesus passes he says, "Hurry down, Zacchaeus, because I must stay in your house today." The fact that Jesus chose to stay with Zacchaeus, a tax collector, and not someone acceptable to the majority, is crucial. Later Zacchaeus says to Jesus, "Listen, sir! I will give half my belongings to the poor; and if I have cheated anyone, I will pay him back four times as much." And when Jesus responds by saying, "Salvation has come to this house today; for this man, also, is a descendant of Abraham," the final touch of sympathy, empathy, and respectability is provided the tax collector. Believers have been subconsciously taught that if Jesus can forgive the abuses of a dominant few, so can they. The message is that members of the elite are really "good guys at heart."

Christ's followers are not only instructed to view with compassion and obediently serve, but also to uncritically support the prevailing political apparatus allied to those in control.

Key verses in this regard are 1 Peter 2:13–14 (TEV), "For the sake of the Lord submit yourselves to every human authority: to the Emperor, who is the supreme authority, and to the governors"; Titus 3:1 (TEV), "Remind your people to submit to rulers and authorities, to obey them"; and above all, Rom. 13:1–5 (TEV),

> Everyone must obey the state authorities, because no authority exists without God's permission, and the existing authorities have been put there by God. Whoever opposes the existing authority opposes what God has ordered; and anyone who does so will bring judgment on himself. For rulers are not to be feared by those who do good, but by those who do evil. Would you like to be unafraid of the man in authority? Then do what is good, and he will praise you, because he is God's servant working for your own good. But if you do evil, then be afraid of him, because his power to punish is real. He is God's servant and carries out God's punishment on those who do evil. For this reason you must obey the authorities—not just because of God's punishment, but also as a matter of conscience.

Since political leaders are being portrayed as God's agents and those on top determine what is proper and orderly, the Bible here is obviously being used to buttress the state.

Scripture further aids the elite and its governmental supporters by requiring believers to obediently pay taxes and fines, as the following verses demonstrate: Romans 13:6–7 (TEV), "That is also why you pay taxes, because the authorities are working for God when they fulfill their duties. Pay, then, what you owe them; pay them your personal and property taxes, and show respect and honor for them all"; Matt. 22:21 (TEV), "Pay to the Emperor what belongs to the Emperor, and pay to God what belongs to God"; and Matt. 5:25–26 (TEV), "If someone brings a lawsuit against you and takes you to court, settle the dispute with him while there is time, before you get to court. Once you are there, he will turn you over to the judge, who will hand you over to the police, and you will be put in jail. There you will stay, I tell you, until you pay the last penny of your fine." Naturally, those who bring lawsuits, especially in ancient times, were nearly always the affluent.

Everything considered, if Christians actually behaved as the New Testament directed, it is highly improbable that the Roman government would ever have thrown them to the lions. Either the story is myth or exceptional circumstances prevailed.

Rejection of Wealth

Before people will willingly accept deprivation and submission, they must be convinced their physical needs are of no consequence or of considerably less importance than that which supposedly comes later. As long as they remain primarily concerned with procuring adequate food, clothing, shelter, and other necessities of life, people's thoughts will essentially remain on this world and not what allegedly follows. The elite know it is immensely more difficult to take advantage of people who place great importance upon the material condition of their environment and the eradication of deprivation than to abuse those to whom everyday living conditions are of little consequence. It is beneficial to a ruling elite to have for the common religion a theology in which believers are repeatedly told to shun goods, surrender their possessions, and forego any attempt to improve themselves materially. In earlier quotes Christians were told to work hard and support the overall arrangement. When these two instructions are combined it becomes apparent that Christians are being taught to labor diligently while renouncing that which they produce. To say instructions of this kind favor those on top is to utter a tautology.

An essential factor in the equation is rejection of possessions and material improvements. Persuading people to repudiate those aspects of life necessary for a decent, productive, beautiful, meaningful existence for the unsubstantiated promise of eternal happiness, is a formidable assignment, indeed, even for the New Testament. This consideration undoubtedly accounts in large measure for the great emphasis placed upon rejecting this world. Relevant verses in this regard are: Col. 3:2 (TEV) ("Keep your minds fixed on things there, not on things here on earth"); Phil. 3:8 (TEV) ("For his [Jesus] sake I have thrown everything away; I consider it all as mere garbage"); 1 John 2:15–16 (TEV) ("Do not love the world or anything that belongs to the world. If you love the world, you do not love the Father. Everything that belongs to the world . . . none of this comes from the Father"); Luke 12:33–34 (TEV) ("Sell all your belongings and give the money to the poor. Provide for yourselves purses that don't wear out, and save your riches in heaven. . . . For your heart will always be where your riches are"); and 1 Tim. 6:7–10 ("What did we bring into the world? Nothing! What can we take out of the world? Nothing! So then, if we have food and clothes, that should be enough for us").

In Luke 12:16–21 (TEV) Jesus tells a parable about a man who decided to store his abundant harvest in new and bigger barns and live a life of ease and luxury off his stored grain and other goods. Then God appeared to him and said, "You fool! This very night you will have to give up your life; then who will get all these things you have kept for yourself?" The moral of the fable is that worldly goods are of little worth and provide no long-term security. Eventually they will have to be surrendered to others.

The negative aspect of such teachings lies in the fact that there is nothing wrong with loving material enhancement and a more affluent environment, so long as they are not obtained at the expense of others and are not seen as ends in themselves but as a means to enrich, improve, and ennoble life in general. Any effort to improve one's material status involves love to some degree. Why would improvement be sought if no element of love were involved? In effect, the New Testament is surreptitiously teaching people not to compete with those in control for material goods.

Believers are not only taught to eschew belongings but to give away that which they possess, two admonitions which would effectively rule them out as competitors. Prime verses are Luke 18:22 (TEV) ("Sell all you have and give the money to the poor"); Matt. 5:40 (TEV) ("And if someone takes you to court to sue you for your shirt, let him have your coat as well"); Matt. 19:21 (TEV) ("If you want to be perfect, go and sell all you have and give the money to the poor, and you will have riches in heaven"); and Luke 14:33 (TEV) ("None of you can be my disciple unless he gives up everything he has"). Again, the humanitarian facade of biblical teachings conceals a sinister motive and a tragic result. Benevolence toward the poor is an innocuous approach to the poverty problem. But when directed toward other aspects of society, which is unavoidable as long as Christians are taught to view philanthropy per se as a virtue, without regard to differences in influence, disparities will continue. Charity toward all that is devoid of power considerations is a self-defeating proposition. As long as the elite is not bothered, conditions will endure, and as long as they endure donations to the poor will be far outweighed by forces creating differentials.

Expectation of Reward

Teaching people to remain peaceful, surrender their possessions, allow themselves to be taken advantage of without protest, deny their ability to accurately criticize, sympathize with the elite, be eternally patient, and all but reject this world and everything in it is quite difficult to say the least. Such instructions contrast sharply with reasonable instincts, such as the will to survive and rational conclusions to be drawn from daily living. Naturally a submissive philosophy is going to be spurned by many people, since an individual could expect to be victimized at every opportunity. It is merely a senseless form of self-denial and self-effacement that can only benefit those who know better, those who understand how things operate, those whom Scripture serves. In the passage, "Offer yourselves as a living sacrifice to God" (in Rom. 12:1, TEV), the word "God" could easily be replaced by "the elite."

Knowing that many people who accept the New Testament's teachings will suffer because of their incompatibility with reality and to forestall the possibility of rejection, New Testament authors promise infinite rewards in the next world for those who believe and endure. Key verses are Luke 6:35 (TEV) ("Love your enemies and do good to them; lend and expect nothing back. You will then have a great reward"); 2 Tim. 2:12 (TEV) ("If we continue to endure, we shall also rule with him"); Rom. 8:18 (TEV) ("I consider that what we suffer at this present time cannot be compared at all with the glory that is going to be revealed to us"); Mark 10:29-30 (TEV) ("Anyone who leaves home or brothers or sisters or mother or father or children or fields for me, and for the gospel . . . in the age to come he will receive eternal life"); and John 11:25-26 (TEV) ("Whoever believes in me will live, even though he dies; and whoever lives and believes in me will never die").

And the poor will receive preferential treatment in the distribution of rewards according to James 2:5-6 (TEV) ("God chose the poor people of this world to be rich in faith and to possess the Kingdom which he promised to those who love him"); James 1:9-10 (TEV) ("The Christian who is poor must be glad when God lifts him up, and the rich Christian must be glad when God brings him down. For the rich will pass away like the flower of a wild plant"); and Matt. 19:30 (TEV) ("Many who now are first will be last, and many who now are last will be first").

In the parable of the great feast in Luke 14:16-24 (TEV) Jesus further pacifies and placates the poor with promised rewards. The story concerns a man who is going to give a feast. He invites many well-to-do people, but all give various reasons for not being able to attend. The man becomes furious and orders his servants to invite the poor, the crippled, and the lame in the streets and alleys. The parable closes with the man saying, "None of those men who were invited . . . will taste my dinner." In other words, God may invite the rich to heaven but only the downtrodden will arrive.

God will aid and support the burdened believer according to Luke 1:52–53 (TEV), "He brought down mighty kings from their thrones, and lifted up the lowly. He has filled the hungry with good things, and sent the rich away with empty hands," and Luke 4:18 (TEV), "To set free the oppressed."

And the rich will receive their just desserts according to Luke 6:24–25 (TEV) ("How terrible for you who are rich now; you have had your easy life! How terrible for you who are full now; you will go hungry! How terrible for you who laugh now; you will mourn and weep!"); James 1:11 (TEV) ("The sun rises with its blazing heat and burns the plant; its flower falls off, and its beauty is destroyed. In the same way the rich man will be destroyed while he goes about his business"); James 5:1 (TEV) ("And now, you rich people listen to me! Weep and wail over the miseries that are coming upon you!"); and Matt. 19:23–24 (TEV) ("It will be very hard for rich people to enter the Kingdom of heaven. I repeat: it is much harder for a rich person to enter the Kingdom of God than for a camel to go through the eye of a needle").

But the parable of Lazarus in Luke 16:19–25 (TEV) is probably the most effective piece of mass mollification. There was a wealthy man who lived in luxury and a poor man named Lazarus who was full of sores and begged at the rich man's door. Lazarus died and was taken to a feast in heaven but when the rich man died he was put in great pain and suffering in hell. The rich man called out to heaven for pity and received the following reply. "Remember, my son, that in your lifetime you were given all the good things, while Lazarus got all the bad things. But now he is enjoying himself here, while you are in pain." That teachings such as these fortify the status quo and strengthen the more well-to-do by causing people to endure their lowly state is all too obvious.

Just as tranquilizing as the promise of rewards for allowing themselves to be milked (disguised under the euphemism of following in Christ's path) is the teaching that believers are to welcome their suffering as a challenge or test. New Testament authors approached the problems of poverty and subjugation in a very ingenious manner. If the believer's condition improves, he is told to look upon this as a gift from God and he is to remain humble. If his environment worsens, he is to view this as a challenge; his faith is being increasingly tested as conditions deteriorate. If he endures, all the greater will be the reward. So, no matter what happens the believer is caught in a web of pacification. Few acts would be of greater benefit to those in control than to convince people that misery is bliss and worsening conditions should generate ever greater happiness and contentment.

Excellent relevant verses are: Rom. 5:3 (TEV) ("We also boast of our troubles, because we know that trouble produces endurance, endurance brings God's approval, and his approval creates hope"); James 1:12 (TEV) ("Happy is the person who remains faithful under trials; because when he succeeds in passing such a test, he will receive as his reward the life which God has promised to those who love him"); James 1:2–4 (TEV) ("Consider yourselves fortunate when all kinds of trials come your way, for you know that when your faith succeeds in facing such trials, the result is the ability to endure. Make sure that your endurance carries you all the way without failing, so that you may be perfect and complete, lacking nothing"); 1 Peter 1:6–7 (TEV) ("Be glad about this, even though it may now be necessary for you to be sad for a while because of the many kinds of trials you suffer. Their purpose is to prove that your faith is genuine . . . your faith . . . must also be tested that it may endure"); and 1 Peter 4:12–13 (TEV) ("My dear friends, do not be surprised at the painful test you are suffering, as though something unusual were happening to you. Rather be glad that you are sharing Christ's sufferings").

In every instance, tragedy is depicted as triumph. Regardless of what happens to the believer, a subdued individual will emerge. In reality, misery does not exist as some sort of divine test, but is the byproduct of demonstrable societal forces and inequitable activities.

Because irrationality and a noticeable absence of valid evidence permeates the New Testament, faith must necessarily be a hallmark of Christian theology. Literally scores of statements are made without a shred of evidence. The promises contained in the Sermon on the Mount are good examples. No matter what conditions tend to prove, and regardless of how many statements are unsubstantiated, believers are asked to uncritically accept New Testament "truths" on faith alone. Followers who will just listen and believe, regardless of what reality says to the contrary, are what New Testament authors seek to create. Don't think, analyze and criticize; just listen, absorb, and believe, this is the message. The following verses demonstrate this quite well: Heb. 11:1 (TEV) ("To have faith is to be sure of the things we hope for, to be certain of the things we cannot see"); John 9:36 (TEV) ("Tell me who he is, sir, so I can believe in him!"); Mark 10:15 and Luke 18:17 (TEV) ("I assure you that whoever does not receive the Kingdom of God like a child will never enter it"); 1 Tim. 1:13 (TEV) ("I did not yet have faith and so did not know what I was doing"); and Heb. 11:6 (TEV) ("No one can please God without faith").

On one occasion in John 20:24–29 (TEV) a disciple named Thomas would not believe that Jesus appeared before the others until he saw the scars of the nails in Christ's hands. When later they were shown and Thomas believed, Christ said, "How happy are those who believe without seeing me!" Just as rational men do not accept misery as happiness, they do not accept unsubstantiated allegations based on faith. An irrational philosophy of total reliance upon and submission to fate is bound to create and perpetuate pain, suffering, and disappointment and motivate most observers to seek a more sensible approach.

Cognizant of this fact, New Testament authors again portrayed that which is ridiculous as a test or challenge. They again managed to twist reality in such a manner as to use damaging evidence for their own ends. Previously believers were told to view misery as a welcomed physical test; now they are told to view blind, irrational faith as a sort of mental test. An illustrative verse in this regard is Rom. 8:24–25 (TEV), which says, "For it was by hope that we were saved; but if we see what we hope for, then it is not really hope. For who hopes for something that he sees? But if we hope for what we do not see, we wait for it with patience."

People are taught to conclude that the failure of faith or prayers to alleviate their pain and suffering or provide for their daily needs is not attributable to the fact that reliance upon them is useless, inane, and debilitating, but to the fact that they have been insufficiently employed. Not less, but more dependence upon prayer and faith is propounded. That is the essential message of Col. 4:2 (TEV) ("Be persistent in prayer") and James 5:13–15 (TEV) ("Is anyone among you in trouble? He should pray. . . . This prayer, made in faith will heal the sick person; the Lord will restore him to health"). Believe and somehow, "Whatever is now covered up will be uncovered and every secret will be made known" (Matt. 10:26 TEV).

In Luke 18:1–8 (TEV) Jesus tells a parable about a fearless judge who was continually bothered by a widow pleading for her rights. Finally the judge says, "Even though I don't fear God or respect man, yet because of all the trouble this widow is giving me, I will see to it that she gets her rights. If I don't, she will keep on coming and finally wear me out!" The moral of the story is that God will eventually answer the prayers of those who are sufficiently persistent. This is analogous to telling a drinker that his headache from overindulgence will disappear if drinking is resumed. Problems are not solved by increased injections of that which originally contributed to the difficulties. Dependence upon prayer, as opposed to human energy and ingenuity, divorces man from the real world, creates unhealthy feelings of inadequacy, directs efforts into ineffective channels, and allows problems to increase to the point of being overwhelming. The negative side of prayer far exceeds the positive.

Anytime faith comes in the window, planning goes out the door, and Christianity is no exception in this regard. Believers are constantly urged to shun planning because God will supposedly provide. Turn your life over to fate (which, it so happens, a few can influence far more than others), or to God, is the overriding message of Matt. 6:26–34 (TEV):

> Look at the birds flying around: they do not plant seeds, gather a harvest, and put in barns; yet your Father in heaven takes care of them! Aren't you worth much more than birds? Can any of you live a bit longer by worrying about it? And why worry about clothes? Look how the wild flowers grow: they do

not work or make clothes for themselves. . . . It is God who clothes the wild grass—grass that is here today and gone tomorrow, burned up in the oven. Won't he be all the more sure to clothe you? What little faith you have! So do not start worrying: 'Where will my food come from? or my drink? or my clothes? (These are the things the pagans are always concerned about.) Your Father in heaven knows that you need all these things. Instead, be concerned above everything else with the Kingdom of God and with what he requires of you, and he will provide you with all these other things. So do not worry about tomorrow; it will have enough worries of its own. There is no need to add to the troubles each day brings.

Similarly Matt. 7:7 (TEV) says, "Ask and you will receive; seek, and you will find; knock, and the door will be opened to you."

With the large number of extravagant claims and requests in the New Testament, one can readily understand why nearly every imaginable inducement to accept it is tendered. No gun is left unfired, no trap unset. *Anything* will be made available upon request, as can be seen from Matt. 21:22 (TEV) ("If you believe, you will receive whatever you ask for in prayer"); Mark 11:24 (TEV) ("When you pray and ask for something, believe that you have received it, and you will be given whatever you ask for"); John 14:14 (TEV) ("If you ask me for anything in my name, I will do it"); and John 15:7 (TEV) ("If you remain in me, and my words remain in you, then you will ask for anything you wish, and you shall have it").

Protection and aid will always be provided according to Rom. 8:31 (TEV) ("If God is for us, who can be against us"); 1 Cor. 3:16–17 (TEV) ("Surely you know that you are God's temple, and that God's Spirit lives in you! So if anyone destroys God's temple, God will destroy him"); Luke 1:71 (TEV) ("He promised through his holy prophets long ago that he would save us from our enemies, and from the power of all those who hate us"); and 2 Thess. 3:3 (TEV) ("He will strengthen you and keep you safe from the Evil One").

And powers more potent than those of superman will be conferred according to Matt. 17:20 (TEV) ("I assure you that if you have faith as big as a mustard seed, you can say to this hill, 'Go from here to there!' and it will go. You could do anything!"); Luke 17:6 (TEV) ("If you had faith as big as a mustard seed, you could say to this mulberry tree, 'Pull yourself up by the roots and plant yourself in the sea' and it would obey you"); Matt. 21:21 (TEV) ("I assure you that if you believe and do not doubt, you will be able to do what I have done to this fig tree. And not only this, you will even be able to say to this hill, 'Get up and throw yourself in the sea' and it will"); and Mark 9:23 (TEV) ("Everything is possible for the person who has faith").

From immortality to owning the universe, nothing is out of reach for the true believer. Those who feel the hour is too early to become a Christian are warned to be ready now in such verses as Matt. 24:44 (TEV) ("The Son of Man will come at an hour when you are not expecting him"); Mark 13:35-37 (TEV) ("Watch, then, because you do not know when the master of the house is coming—it might be in the evening, or at midnight, or before dawn, or at sunrise. If he comes suddenly, he must not find you asleep. What I say to you, then, I say to all: Watch!"); 1 Thess. 5:2-3 (TEV) ("The Day of the Lord will come as a thief comes at night. When people say, 'Everything is quiet and safe,' then suddenly destruction will hit them!"); and 2 Peter 3:10 (TEV) ("But the Day of the Lord will come like a thief").

Those who feel the hour is past because of prior behavior are promised forgiveness in a series of parables. In the parable of two sons, found in Matt. 21:28-32 (TEV), a father asks his older son to work in the vineyard and he refuses but later goes. The younger son immediately agrees but never complies. Jesus asks who was the better person and his audience replies, "The older one." Jesus says, "I tell you the tax collectors and the prostitutes are going into the Kingdom of God ahead of you. For John the Baptist came to you showing you the right path to take, and you would not believe him; but the tax collectors and the prostitutes believed him." The moral of the story is that those who behave improperly initially, but later change, will be forgiven.

In another parable, found in Luke 7:36-48 (TEV), a sinful woman slavishly cleans Christ's feet while he visits the home of Simon the Pharisee. Jesus forgives her sins saying, "Do you Simon see this woman? I came into your home, and you gave me no water for my feet, but she has washed my feet with her tears and dried them with her hair. You did not welcome me with a kiss, but she has not stopped kissing my feet since I came. You provided no oil for my head, but she has covered my feet with perfume." In other words, those who slavishly serve Christian theology will be saved regardless of prior behavior.

"It's never too late" is also the conclusion to be drawn from the parable of the prodigal son, found in Luke 15:11-32. A young boy leaves home, goes elsewhere to live, leads a corrupt life, finds conditions are worse, returns home, begs for forgiveness from his father, who represents God, and is pardoned.

In many instances, especially where New Testament teachings are highly dubious, out-and-out terror is employed. Skeptics, rationalists, and other thoughtful critics are threatened with a whole gamut of cruel and unusual punishments if they fail to succumb. Recourse to terrorism is found in Matt. 7:26, 10:15, 10:28, 10:39, and elsewhere.

Miracles are also extensively utilized as fearsome reinforcement mechanisms. In a large number of instances, one kind of miracle or another follows various messages, especially highly questionable ones. Prominent examples are Matt. 1:18, 4:2, 4:24, and 8:3. After nearly every teaching session Christ's powers are reaffirmed by the performance of a miracle or miracles. If the latter were not extensively utilized, Jesus would appear to be little more than an average citizen expressing personal opinions. Accounts of miracles create submission, humility, awe, slavishness, and fear in the mind of the recipient. The alleged existence of miracles is used in a manner similar to that of Spanish conquistadors employing firepower to frighten and intimidate New World natives. Teach, intimidate; teach, intimidate; teach, intimidate; this is the cycle. The miraculous act of curing the sick is the beneficent facade; intimidation is the reality. The fear of an alleged omnipotent God, generated by biblical teachings, is not a temporary aberration from the Christian path but an inseparable part of the whole philosophy. Of this there can be no doubt. God is to be feared as can be seen from Luke 12:5 (TEV), "I will show you whom to fear: fear God, who, after killing, has the authority to throw into hell."

A final method by which people are persuaded to accept biblical teachings involves the use of spirits and other supernatural phenomena that are liberally sprinkled throughout the New Testament. Discussions of angels, ghosts, demons, Satan, an archangel, visions, evil spirits, apparitions, and other beings are used to overawe people and cause them to accept Christian ideology out of fear for their own security. Even though the existence of supernatural beings is never proven, the very act of discussing their presence is intimidating. The supernatural is found in Matt. 1:18, 3:16, 4:5, and elsewhere.

Closed-Mindedness

Any philosophy, theory, or ideology that is based essentially on faith, irrationality, and blind obedience to unsubstantiated allegations, propositions, and promises is bound to be highly vulnerable to criticism and attack. The contentions of people who rely more on faith than reason, belief than proof, compliance than criticism, superstition than science will always be subject to refutation and disproof.

Key elements in the New Testament's response to this problem are solidification and isolation. Adherents are to be made so determined in their faith that no amount of contradictory evidence will loosen their resolve. The attitude the New Testament seeks to create is, "I don't care what evidence exists to prove that various phenomena or precepts in the New Testament are fraudulent and the work is essentially an indoctrinating tool wielded by a dominant group, if the Bible says it, then it must be true." Once this outlook is inculcated, the door has slammed shut to any further dialogue. Reasoning is no longer of any use, Jesus has taken over.

Solidification works best through isolation. Believers are warned to refrain from argumentation and disputation with critics and nonbelievers. The latter are to be considered misguided and that's that. Don't listen to them is the message of Col. 2:4 (TEV) ("Do not let anyone deceive you with false arguments, no matter how good they seem to be"); 1 Tim. 6:20–21 (TEV) ("Avoid the profane

talk and foolish arguments of what some people wrongly call 'Knowledge' ");
2 Tim. 2:23-24 (TEV) ("But keep away from foolish and ignorant arguments;
you know that they end up in quarrels. The Lord's servant must not quarrel");
and Titus 3:9-10 (TEV) ("But avoid stupid arguments, long lists of ancestors,
quarrels, and fights about the Law. They are useless and worthless. Give at least
two warnings to the person who causes divisions, and then have nothing more
to do with him").

Even the most rational, logical, peaceful, thoroughly researched discussions
are to be avoided because they supposedly create nothing more than quarrels
and fights. This has been the time-honored approach of demagogues for centuries—
indoctrinate and isolate, isolate and indoctrinate. The real reason arguments are
to be shunned is that Christian teachings cannot withstand rational analysis and
believers are liable to be swayed by it.

It is strictly taboo for believers to criticize or test what they are told according
to Matt. 4:7 (TEV) ("Do not put the Lord your God to the test") and Rom.
9:20 (TEV) ("But who are you my friend, to talk back to God? A clay pot does
not ask the man who made it, 'Why did you make me like this?' ").

Mark 11:27-33 (TEV) relates a story in which Jesus is asked, "What right
do you have to do these things? Who gave you such a right?" Jesus replies that
if they will answer his question, he will answer theirs. His question is too difficult
for them to respond and he closes by saying, "Neither will I tell you, then, by
what right I do these things." In other words, don't question Christ's authority.
He isn't obligated to reply. Testing is not needed, since by some mysterious process
the alleged truth of Christianity will be shown to believers. Luke 7:35 (TEV)
says, "God's wisdom, however, is shown to be true by all who accept it," and
1 John 2:27 (TEV) says, "As long as his Spirit remains in you, you do not need
anyone to teach you. For his Spirit teaches you about everything, and what he
teaches is true, not false."

As far as scriptural teachings are concerned, it is virtually impossible for
a critic, analyst, or observer to be honest, sincere, and well-meaning. The New
Testament depicts him as a cunning, deceitful, hypocritical trickster consciously
or unconsciously leading unwary Christians down the rose-lined path to destruction.
Proving the contrary is ruled out *ab initio,* from the beginning. Here, more than
anywhere else, the New Testament propounds the ultimate in closed-mindedness.
To cast suspicion on all those who present another approach to life or question
the accuracy of biblical beliefs by depicting them as false prophets and deceivers
is the ultimate in misrepresentation. Although not directly stated, the New Testament
has given its adherents the impression that any and all critics are hypocritical
frauds misleading the unwary.

The following verses bear this out: Matt. 7:15 (TEV) ("Be on your guard
against false prophets; they come to you looking like sheep on the outside, but
on the inside they are really like wild wolves"); Matt. 24:11 (TEV) ("Then many

false prophets will appear and fool many people"); Matt. 24:24–26 (TEV) ("False Messiahs and false prophets will appear; they will perform great miracles and wonders in order to deceive even God's chosen people, if possible"); 2 Peter 2:1–3 (TEV) ("False prophets appeared in the past among the people, and in the same way false teachers will appear among you. They will bring in destructive, untrue doctrines"); and 1 Tim. 6:3–4 (TEV) ("Whoever teaches a different doctrine and does not agree with the true words of our Lord Jesus Christ and with the teaching of our religion is swollen with pride and knows nothing. He has an unhealthy desire to argue and quarrel about words").

When the amount of facts, data, and evidence tending to invalidate Christian beliefs becomes overwhelming, the ultimate isolator is employed. Believers are assured they possess a secret truth incomprehensible to outsiders. Although a mountain of evidence may exist to prove that following Jesus involves a deceptive, masochistic form of self-torture that only benefits those in charge, biblicists are told to ignore reality and view critics as hopeless devil-agents incapable of understanding their higher "truth." In essence, the New Testament's message is, "Forget what reality says, listen to what I say. Are you going to believe me or your lying eyes?"

Relevant verses are: 1 Cor. 2:6–7 (TEV) ("Yet I do proclaim a message of wisdom to those who are spiritually mature. But it is not the wisdom that belongs to this world, or to the powers that rule this world. . . . The wisdom I proclaim is God's secret wisdom, hidden from mankind"); 1 Cor. 2:13–14 (TEV) ("So then, we do not speak in words taught by human wisdom. . . . Whoever does not have the Spirit cannot receive the gifts that come from God's Spirit. Such a person really does not understand them; they are nonsense to him, because their value can be judged only on a spiritual basis"); 1 Cor. 1:20–21 (TEV) ("God has shown that this world's wisdom is foolishness! For God in his wisdom made it impossible for men to know him by means of their own wisdom. Instead, by means of the so-called 'foolish' message we preach, God decided to save those who believe"); 1 Cor. 1:27 (TEV) ("God purposely chose what the world considers nonsense in order to shame the wise, and he chose what the world considers weak in order to shame the powerful"); 1 Cor. 3:18–20 (TEV) ("If anyone among you thinks that he is wise by this world's standards, he should become a fool, in order to be really wise. For what this world considers to be wisdom is nonsense in God's sight. . . . God traps the wise in their cleverness. . . . The Lord knows that the thoughts of the wise are worthless"); and 1 Cor. 4:10 (TEV) ("For Christ's sake we are fools; but you are wise in union with Christ!").

Again the New Testament manages to turn ominous defeat into partial victory. Contradictory data is portrayed as a test of the believer's faith. The more out-of-tune with reality Christianity becomes, the greater the test and ultimate reward. Teaching an individual to "become a fool in order to become wise" ranks with the ultimate in indoctrination. If this isn't a black-is-white approach, what is?

The lengths to which the elite will go to generate support are truly awesome.

Much of the New Testament is devoted to urging those who have succumbed to spreading the philosophy ("Go, then, to all peoples everywhere and make them my disciples"—Matt. 28:19 TEV); act as dedicated soldiers ("Take your part in suffering, as a loyal soldier of Christ Jesus"—2 Tim. 2:3 TEV); be active ("Faith without actions is dead"—James 2:26 TEV); teach the young (Luke 5:36–38); accept scorn and ridicule ("Everyone who wants to live a godly life in union with Christ Jesus will be persecuted"—2 Tim. 3:12 TEV), and voluntarily die if necessary ("Then you will be arrested and handed over to be punished and be put to death"—Matt. 24:9 TEV).

Human Nature

Before concluding the issue of behavioral control, special consideration should be given to the fact that the New Testament's authors blame an alleged human nature for the ills that plague mankind, rather than an arrangement that favors a few at the expense of many. Some sort of psychological makeup in men whose existence is never proven, whose nature is never exposed, whose composition is never defined, whose cause is never revealed, rather than conditions, is supposedly responsible for humanity's problems. The reasoning in this regard is relatively simple. Since man made society and his environment, since he is responsible for the existing arrangement, then whatever ills and evils exist are ultimately caused by man and not external conditions. Man makes his environment more than the environment makes man; thus, evil must originate in man.

Human nature is evil is the message in such verses as Mark 7:20–23 (TEV) ("It is what comes out of a person that makes him unclean. For from the inside, from a person's heart, come the evil ideas which lead him to do immoral things, to rob, kill, commit adultery, be greedy, and do all sorts of evil things; deceit, indecency, jealousy, slander, pride, and folly—all these evil things come from inside a person and make him unclean"); Mark 7:18–19 (TEV) ("Don't you understand? Nothing that goes into a person from the outside can really make him unclean, because it does not go into his heart but into his stomach"); and Mark 7:15 (RSV) ("There is nothing outside a man which by going into him can defile him; but the things which come out of a man are what defile him").

So human nature is the villain according to New Testament teachings, and from it spring mankind's problems. The fallacy of this reasoning lies in the fact that it doesn't start from an awareness of the crucial importance of material conditions to man's maturation. The problems plaguing people are the unintentional and unavoidable byproducts of society's composition and are not the result of an alleged human nature. People are created first and only later become creators.

How they develop determines what they later produce, not vice versa. In reality, material conditions make man more than man makes material conditions. Biblicists have put the wagon before the donkey.

Fostering Slavery

If not salvation, what, then, has Jesus' death on the cross meant for humanity? What does Christianity mean if not peace, love and brotherhood? For hundreds of millions of trusting beings it has engendered bondage, bondage to an ideology that is the very antithesis of that which it purports to represent. Masked as mankind's friend it actually serves a privileged few. Billed as a purveyor of peace and love, it buttresses an arrangement which negates peace and love from the beginning. Supposedly an answer to humanity's problems, it does little more than urge followers to seek aid and succor from a nebulous other-world, while leaving their disadvantageous position undisturbed. Almost *never* does the New Testament advise followers to object when unjustly treated, seek equality instead of subservience, seek justice instead of submission, seek involvement rather than escape, seek improvement rather than acceptance, seek self-respect rather than self-debasement, seek proof rather than faith, seek decent conditions instead of abject poverty, seek labor and planning instead of hope and prayer, seek sexual equality instead of male supremacy, seek liberation instead of enslavement, or seek man's failings in external factors instead of innate corruption.

Christianity, the Bible, and Jesus are all euphemisms for a covert, insidious form of slavery. The behavior of an ideal Christian would be comparable to that of a slave or sheep. In fact, Jesus, himself, makes this comparison repeatedly, since denial of its validity would be ridiculous in light of all the above and the following admissions: John 10:7 (TEV) ("So Jesus said again: 'I am telling you the truth, I am the gate for the sheep' "); John 21:15 (TEV) ("Jesus said to him, 'Take care of my lambs' "); Hebrews 13:20 (TEV) ("Our Lord Jesus, who is the Great Shepherd of the sheep."); 1 Cor. 7:22 (TEV) ("A free man who has been called by Christ is his slave"); Gal. 6:17 (TEV) ("I am the slave of Jesus"); 1 Peter 2:16 (TEV) ("Live as God's slaves"); and Romans 6:22 (TEV) ("Slaves of God").

Christians have been rightly called men enchained, as can be seen in 2 Cor. 2:14 (TEV) ("Led by God as prisoners in Christ's victory procession") and Eph. 3:1 (TEV) ("For this reason I, Paul, the prisoner of Christ Jesus"). And once Christ was so degrading and revealing as to compare converting human beings with catching fish. In Luke 5:9–10 (TEV) Simon and others with him were amazed at the large number of fish they had caught. . . . Jesus said to Simon, "Don't be afraid; from now on you will be catching men."

Even though Christians are repeatedly referred to as sheep and slaves, Scripture proclaims in 2 Cor. 3:17 (KJV) that, "Where the Spirit of the Lord is, there is liberty." It would be difficult to imagine a statement more at variance with reality. Few utterances in the entire Bible are more erroneous. A dominant theme of the entire New Testament is that individuals should totally and unquestioningly surrender themselves to Jesus without hesitation or qualms, while discounting all information that tends to prove the imprudence of such an act. The New Testament equates this with freedom.

Slavery in following Christ, being a slave of Christ, is freedom, according to the New Testament. *Webster's Dictionary* defines freedom as the "liberation from slavery" and if Webster is correct, then any form of slavery automatically obviates freedom. Contradictions of this nature should not be surprising, however, since allegations that violate every form of rational thought permeate the New Testament. Any work contending that misery is to be welcomed as a test of one's faith, that lack of valid evidence for its teachings is to be viewed as a welcome challenge to one's beliefs, and that the remedy for ineffective prayer is more prayer, can understandably allege that slavery is freedom. It's nothing more than the logical conclusion of a black-is-white philosophy.

Unfortunately, many persons have already succumbed to biblical teachings and of those tragic individuals who doggedly believe, despite all information demonstrating the Bible's value to a minority alone, one can only conclude by quoting the author of Gal. 6:14 (TEV), who wrote one of the most revealing comments in the entire book: "For by means of his cross the world is dead to me, and I am dead to the world." How true that is!

24

Aside: Other Holy Books

The Book of Mormon, The Koran

The Book of Mormon

Some topics are so relevant to the Bible or of such importance that their omission would be a significant oversight. The Book of Mormon is a good example. Because many view it as comparable in weight to the Bible and much of it duplicates Scripture, an abbreviated exposure of its contents is in order.

The Mormon religion was founded in 1830 by one Joseph Smith in upstate New York. The event was one of a great many religious changes occurring in early nineteenth-century America during a period of religious revival known as the "Great Awakening."

The Book of Mormon is supposedly the translation of gold plates received by Smith from an angel. The book tells the story of a group of Hebrews who came to America around 600 B.C. They eventually split into two groups, one of which , the Lamanites, fell away from their biblical beliefs and eventually became the ancestors of American Indians (that speculated origin for Native Americas was popular at the time), the other of which, the Nephites, developed a civilization which was visited by Jesus after the Ascension, and was eventually destroyed by the Lamanites. This history was written on the gold plates and buried for the intervening centuries until dug up by the angel Moroni and shown to Smith, who, of course, returned them, making any study of original sources for the Book of Mormon impossible.

Points one might want to make when Mormons come to call are the following:
First, according to Alma 7:9–10 Jesus is supposed to have been born in

Jerusalem, not Bethlehem. It says, "For behold, the kingdom of heaven is at hand, and the Son of God cometh upon the face of the earth. And behold, he shall be born of Mary, at Jerusalem." That this is a blatant case of an inaccurate prophecy goes without saying.

Second, according to Moriah 26:23, God created sin. It says, "For it is I that takes upon me the sins of the world; for it is I that hath created them." If so, why shouldn't God be punished like everyone else?

Third, the list of the twelve disciples in the Book of Mormon in no way resembles that of the Bible. Third Nephi 9:4 states, "Behold Nephi and his brother whom he had raised from the dead, whose name was Timothy, and also his son, whose name was Jonas, and also Mathoni, and Mathonihah, his brother, and Kumen, and Kumenonhi, and Jeremiah, and Shemnon, and Jonas, and Zedekiah, and Isaiah—now these are the names of the disciples whom Jesus had chosen." Well, will the true disciples please stand up!

Fourth, while the Bible promotes the subservience of women and the existence of slavery, the Book of Mormon buttresses racism. Alma 3:6 says, "The skins of the Lamanites were dark, according to the mark which was set upon their fathers, which was a curse upon them because of their transgression and their rebellion." And 2 Nephi 5:21-23 says, "As they were white, and exceedingly fair and delightsome to come upon." And 3 Nephi 2:15-16 states, "Their curse was taken from them, and their skin became white like unto the Nephites; And their daughters became exceedingly fair." And Jacob 3:8 says, "O my brethren, I fear that unless you shall repent of your sins that their skins will be whiter than yours, when you shall be brought with them before the throne of God."

Obviously white-skinned people are viewed as good people, while those in black are cursed sinners. On page 218 in *The Kingdom of the Cults* apologist Walter Martin correctly states, "Mormonism, then, is clearly a religion with a shameful history of white supremacist doctrines and practices."

Fifth, most interesting is the fact that Christians condemn polygamy, which the Bible does not denounce, except possibly in Deut. 17:17, while Mormons practice polygamy which the Book of Mormon *does* denounce, in no uncertain terms: Mormons are well known for having many wives both then and now; yet their *Book of Mormon* says in Jacob 2:24, "Behold, David and Solomon truly had many wives and concubines, which thing was abominable before me, saith the Lord." Ether 10:5 in the same book says, "Riplakish did not do that which was right in the sight of the Lord, for he did have many wives and concubines." And Jacob 2:27-28 says, "For there shall not any man among you have more than one wife; and concubines he shall have none; For I, the Lord God, delight in the chastity of women. And whoredoms are an abomination before me." Interested parties should also read Mosiah 11:2 and Jacob 1:15. Obviously many Mormons have chosen to ignore their own book and the clear commands of God contained within it.

Sixth, anti-Semitism is also a significant factor in the Book of Mormon. The text of 2 Nephi 10:3 states, "Wherefore, as I said unto you, it must needs be expedient that Christ . . . should come among the Jews, among those who are the more wicked part of the world; and they shall crucify him . . . and there is none other nation on earth that would crucify their God." And 2 Nephi 25:2 says, "For I, Nephi, have not taught them many things concerning the manner of the Jews; for their works were works of darkness, and their doings were doings of abominations." One should also note the sentiments expressed in Jacob 4:14.

Seventh and lastly, like the Bible, the Book of Mormon contradicts itself with respect to how one is saved. Is it by faith or works? The text of 3 Nephi 11:33-34 says, "Whoso believeth in me, and is baptized, the same shall be saved; and they are they who shall inherit the Kingdom of God. And whoso believeth not in me, and is not baptized, shall be damned." And Ether 4:18 states, "He that believeth and is baptized shall be saved; but he that believeth not shall be damned."

On the other hand, Mosiah 12:33 says, "if you keep the commandments of God you shall be saved," and Nephi 22:31 says, "If you shall be obedient to the commandments, and endure to the end, you shall be saved."

So what do you do with those who believe in Jesus but ignore the commandments or those who adhere closely to the commandments but do not believe in Jesus? For some reason both Mormons and fundamentalists can't seem to visualize a person who practices one while ignoring the other. Why can't you have faith without works or works without faith? Why must they be inseparable?

In addition to ill-advised textual comments, anyone familiar with the Bible and the Book of Mormon can't help but notice the extent to which the latter has duplicated the former's material. Whoever wrote the Book of Mormon was one of the greatest plagiarists of all time. On page 187 in *The Kingdom of the Cults* apologist Walter Martin correctly observes, "According to a careful survey of the Book of Mormon, it contains at least 25,000 words from the King James Bible. In fact, verbatim quotations, some of considerable length, have caused the Mormons no end of embarrassment for many years."

Finally, issue 23 of *Biblical Errancy* listed some problems within the Book of Mormon, prompting correspondence between E. M. T., a Mormon who sent us a critical letter commenting on our analysis of his prized piece of literature, and myself. The following is a summary of that interesting correspondence.

E. M. T. begins by saying,

Issue #23 of *Biblical Errancy* says the Book of Mormon ". . . is viewed by many as comparable in weight to the Bible. . . ." This is technically not true. Joseph Smith taught that the Bible was the Word of God only as it was translated correctly. He placed no such qualification on the Book of Mormon. He called it the most perfect book ever translated from ancient records. However, that does not mean that certain passages cannot be changed. In fact, anti-Mormons gleefully point out the large number of changes that have been made in it.

Apparently E. M. T. doesn't realize that he missed the point. Nearly all biblicists, not just Joseph Smith, believe the Bible is the word of God only to the extent that it is translated correctly. You'd get very little disagreement on that point. E. M. T. said the Book of Mormon was translated from ancient records so, to be logical and consistent, Joseph Smith must consider it to be God's word only to the extent that it is translated correctly. How does that differ from the typical Christian view of the Bible? The fact that he views it as, "The most perfect book ever translated from ancient records" is of no consequence, because that is precisely the view many biblicists have of the King James Version of the Bible.

E. M. T. continues by relating *Biblical Errancy*'s contention that Alma 7:9–10 says Jesus was supposed to have been born in Jerusalem, not Bethlehem, and alleging that we failed to quote the passage in full. According to E. M. T. we should have added the following words: "He shall be born of Mary, at Jerusalem which is the land of our forefathers, she being a virgin." E. M. T. claims Joseph Smith knew as well as any Bible student that Jesus was born in Bethlehem not Jerusalem. If he was just concocting a book that he wanted to foist off as being from God, he surely wouldn't have put in "Jerusalem." The famous gold plates were referring to a geographical area, not a city, when they said, "The land of our forefathers," a land that included Bethlehem. E. M. T. fails to realize that the words in question were omitted because they weren't germane to the issue. If Jerusalem did refer to both a land, in 1 Nephi 7:2, Alma 21:1, and 3 Nephi 20:29, and a city, in Alma 21:24, 3 Nephi 9:7, and 1 Nephi 1:4, E. M. T. would only have leaped from one problem to another. Where on earth is the "land" of Jerusalem? If E. M. T. could provide so much as one *reputable* biblical atlas or scholarly work that delineates a "land" of Jerusalem, a land that also encompasses Bethlehem, we would extract his argument from the dust bin in which it now resides.

Next, E. M. T. attacked our comment that the list of the twelve disciples in the Book of Mormon in no way resembles that of the Bible. He candidly admits that Jesus named different apostles when he came to the Americas. He asks how on earth would Peter, James, John, and others serve their missions in the Old World and the New World at the same time? E. M. T. fails to realize that the list of names found in 3 Nephi 19:4 makes no allusion to the New World or a second list of twelve apostles. From whence comes the second list of twelve apostles is a matter of pure conjecture. There is certainly no biblical list of another twelve. Moreover, if there is a second group of twelve apostles, then there was a second Last Supper as well, because that is what appears to be occurring in the previous chapter of 3 Nephi.

Moving from the Book of Nephi in the Book of Mormon, E. M. T. attacked the assertion that Mormonism promotes racism by saying he does not believe that God curses people by giving them a black skin. Later, he states that he hopes his church will change and believes it is doing so, which is only a backhanded admission that it currently is, in fact, racist. E. M. T. contends that when the Scriptures of the Church were revised in 1982 one passage which said the Lamanites would become "white and delightsome" has been changed to read "pure and delightsome." He also asks us to note that the church dropped its barring of black people from full church participation on Sept. 30, 1978, which is only another way of admitting that the church was racist, as the Book of Mormon requires. On page 218 in *The Kingdom of the Cults* Walter Martin makes the following poignant observation in this regard:

> The Book of Moses records the fact that Cain, the first murderer, was the progenitor of the Negro race, his black skin being the result of a curse by God. On this basis the Mormons for years avoided and ignored blacks in their missionary work, believing that pre-existent souls, which were considered less than valiant in the "war in heaven" between Christ and Satan, were punished by being assigned to black bodies during their mortality. Until 1978 they were denied all the "blessings" and "privileges" of the priesthood, but a revelation of convenience gave them full access to these glories and neatly removed the last major obstacle to the Mormon "evangelization" of Africa and the rest of the world.

E. M. T. fails to comprehend that it is not a matter of what you believe, but what the book says. And the Book of Mormon clearly promotes racism with such statements as, "The skins of the Lamanites were dark, according to the mark which was set upon their fathers, which was a curse upon them because of their transgression and their rebellion" (Alma 3:6). If E. M. T. does not feel the LDS church is promoting racism, then why did he say, "I can only hope the church will change"? Any abandonment of racist policies by the LDS church is in opposition to the Book of Mormon's teachings, not because of them. Mormon leaders are engaging in the same kind of dishonest revisionism with reference to the Book of Mormon that biblicists employ with respect to the Bible. When a problem becomes unbearable they simply rewrite the script. If Mormon leaders no longer bar black people from full participation, then all they have done is vitiate the very book upon which they place so much reliance.

E. M. T. also believes that the Book of Mormon is not anti-Semitic, but is only referring to those Jews who were evil. As far as Jews as a whole are concerned, he feels the Mormon church recognizes them as a special people of God. The text of 2 Nephi 10:3 clearly shows the error of E. M. T.'s ways by stating, "Wherefore, as I said unto you, it must needs be expedient that Christ . . . should come among the Jews, among those who are the more wicked part of the world; and they shall crucify him . . . and there is none other nation on earth that would crucify their God." E. M. T. fails to note that the word "nation," and the contrast created between Jews and the rest of the world, show that the entire Jewish community is included. There is nothing in this verse or the others quoted in the issue 23 of *Biblical Errancy* that would lead one to believe only evil Jews were intended.

In essence, any objective critique of the Book of Mormon will demonstrate beyond any reasonable doubt that the book is racist, anti-Semitic, historically unreliable, and plagued by a multitude of problems that obviate any possibility of it being the divine word of a perfect being. It is just another volume in a long series of bogus writings propagated by people involved in a conspiracy to con the mass of humanity. Like the Bible, the sooner the Book of Mormon is relegated to the realm of superstition, mythology, and folklore the better.

The Quran

Islam is often touted as more realistic, truthful and compassionate than Christianity, and for those reasons is increasingly advocated as an alternative religious belief system. Muslims have always been evangelists, and in recent decades they have been making strong efforts to work their way into American society in particular. In the process they have spread an immense amount of propaganda that is far more deceptive than accurate. Their most important writing, the Quran (or Koran), the supposedly contemporary record by his associates of the sayings of Mohammed, is a historical rival to the Bible and for that reason merits some consideration in any discussion of religious history and the Bible.

Our analysis will only focus on those Quranic comments that clearly show that the Quran is not a viable alternative to Scripture, is flawed throughout, and is no more the word of a beneficent, perfect, supreme being than the Bible. One is as false as the other. Having studied the Quran from cover to cover, one cannot help but note that it is even more boring than the Bible. It is a veritable miasma of imprecise allusions, vague generalizations, and constant repetitions. It could act as a good antidote for insomnia. The incessant use of pronouns with indeterminate antecedents is unworthy of any writing claiming to be the word of a divine being. Indeed, the constant use of "us" and "we" when referring to God, himself, could easily lead one to believe that Muslims are trinitarians. True, the Quran has fewer contradictions than the Bible, but that arises more out of a propensity for less specificity, more generalities, greater symbolism, fewer topics, infrequent prophecies, and more repetition, than any adherence to consistency.

In his voluminous translation and commentary *The Holy Quran*, Muslim A. Yusuf Ali concedes on page xxx that, "The same things are repeated over and over again in the Quran." Because Ali is acutely aware of the fact that the

Quran is much more chaotic and dissonant than Muslims would like to admit or others to know, he also concedes on page xxi that,

> A stranger to the Quran, on his first approach to it, is baffled when he does not find the enunciation of its theme or its division into chapters and sections or separate treatment of different topics and separate instructions for different aspects of life arranged in a serial order. On the contrary, there is something with which he has not been familiar before and which does not conform to his conception of a book.

Yes, there certainly is. And that something is a tremendous amount of disorganization and metaphysical meandering. Ali's confession continues on the same page,

> The same subject is repeated in different ways and one topic follows the other without any apparent connection. . . . The speaker and the addressees, and the direction of the address change without any notice. . . . That is why the unwary reader is baffled and puzzled when he finds all these things contrary to his preconceived conception of a book. He begins to feel that the Quran is a book without any order or inter-connection between its verses or continuity of its subject, or that it deals with miscellaneous topics in an incoherent manner.

Of course, all of the above is pure rationalization, reminiscent of that employed by biblical apologists. The real reason objective readers feel that the Quran is a book without any order or systematic connection is that the book is in fact without order or systematic connection, and that's a pretty good reason.

For the sake of simplicity and coherence, we will address those issues of most interest to freethinkers that expose the Quran for the fraud that it is. For purposes of simplification we should note that while the Bible is divided into book, chapter, and verse the Quran is divided into suras and ayats. There are 114 suras and thousands of ayats. The denotation 3:67, for example, would indicate sura 3, ayat 67. The crucial messages that clearly emerge from Quranic statements include:

First, the Quran propagates a message of intolerance, brutality, and barbarity toward non-Muslims. Sura 5:51 says, "Take not the Jews and the Christians for your friends and protectors: They are but friends and protectors of each other." Not only does this passage display a contempt for Jews and Christians but an appalling ignorance of historical events. All too often Jews and Christians have barely been able to stomach one another's presence.

Sura 5:33 says, "The punishment of those who wage war against God and His Apostle, and strive with might and main for mischief through the land is execution, or crucifixion, or the cutting off of hands and feet from opposite sides." Intolerance of this magnitude exceeds that of the New Testament, because the latter never goes so far as to advocate the execution of all those who oppose the key figures of Christianity.

Sura 9:36 says, "Fight the pagans"; sura 33:61 says, "Wherever they are found, they shall be seized and slain without mercy"; and sura 9:5 says, "Fight and slay the Pagans wherever you find them and seize them." Believers in the Quran are urged to be no more open-minded than Old Testament Hebrews.

A clear and present danger to non-Muslims would arise in the United States if strict believers in the Quran were to assume positions of national importance. Iran's Ayatollah Khomeini is much more representative of Quranic Islam than liberal Muslims and Muslim public relations agents who appear in the media. Sura 16:118 says, "To the Jews We prohibited such things as We have mentioned to thee before." And 26:55–58 says, "These Israelites are but a small band. . . . So we expelled them from gardens, springs, treasures, and every kind of honorable position." The intolerance exhibited by these verses resembles the Christian treatment of Jews during the Spanish rule of Ferdinand and Isabella, the age of the Spanish Inquisition.

Corporal punishment is promoted in the Quran. Sura 5:38 says, "As to the thief, male or female, cut off his or her hands." And sura 8:12 says, "I will instill terror into the hearts of the Unbelievers: smite you above their necks and smite all their finger tips off them."

As you can see, tolerance, humaneness, and restraint are not the Quran's strong points. While discussing unbelievers the Quran says in sura 4:89, "They but wish you would reject Faith, as they do, and thus be on the same footing as they. . . . But if they turn renegades, seize them and slay them wherever you find them." This is also the message of sura 4:91. If Muslims ever gained control of this country and obeyed the Quran, one can only shudder at what would occur.

Second, Muslims must have some degree of paranoia if they really believe sura 4:101, which says, "For the Unbelievers are unto you open enemies. . . . The unbelievers wish . . . to assault you in a single rush."

Third, all too often Quranic legal procedures are unjust and brutal. Sura 24:2–4 says, "The woman and the man guilty of adultery or fornication are to be flogged with a hundred stripes: let not compassion move you in their case." It further states that a man guilty of adultery or fornication can only marry an adulteress or an unbeliever.

Fourth, the Quranic attitude toward divorce is strange. Sura 2:229 says only two divorces are permissible and 65:1 lays down the absurd rule that when a prophet divorces a woman the latter is not to be expelled from her house unless she is guilty of some lewdness. What kind of divorce exists when both parties must continue living together?

Fifth, sura 4:3 says, "Marry women of your choice, two, three, or four." The Quran supports the disgusting practice of polygamy in which a man gathers wives like a bull gathers cows.

Sixth, the Quran reeks with sexism and male chauvinism, and no amount of apologetic palaver can prove otherwise. Sura 2:228 says, "Women shall have rights similar to the rights against them, according to what is equitable; But men have a degree of advantage over them." How's that for doubletalk! Women shall have equal rights, but men will have an advantage over them.

Sura 4:11 says, "God directs you as regards your children's inheritance: to the male, a portion equal to that of two females." Sura 4:176 says, "If there are brothers and sisters, they share, the male having twice the share of the female."

One can't help but notice the degree to which Islam and Christianity are in agreement on the importance of keeping women in subjugation. Clearly the Quran puts no stock whatever in equality between the sexes. No wonder women in Muslim-dominated countries are forced to go around in black sheets like mobile prisoners with everything covered but their eyeballs. In *The Glorious Koran* Marmaduke Pickthall expounds the Muslim view of Quranic teaching in this regard on page 79 and only makes matters worse: "Men are in charge of women, because Allah hath made the one of them to excel the other, and because they spend of their property for the support of women. So good women are obedient. . . . As for those from whom ye fear rebellion, admonish them and banish them to beds apart, and beat them. Then if they obey you, seek not a way against them." Talk about male supremacy! Men are in charge because Allah wills it and you can *beat women* when you merely *fear* rebellion. It doesn't have to actually occur.

Seventh, like the Bible, the Quran supports slavery: sura 24:32, "Marry those among you who are single, or the virtuous ones among your slaves, male or female"); sura 24:33, "If any of your slaves ask for a deed in writing to enable them to earn their freedom for a certain sum, give them such a deed"; and sura 4:92, "If one kills a Believer, it is ordained that he should free a believing slave."

Eighth, sura 5:18 says, "Both the Jews and Christians say: 'We are sons of God, and His beloved.' Why then does He punish them for their sins?" For Muslims to allege others are being particularly punished for their sins is hardly worthy of serious consideration in light of the fact that agony, ignorance, superstition, deprivation, regression, disease, and misery flourish in Muslim-dominated areas of the world.

Ninth, Muslims are as superstitious as Christians. Sura 19:29-30 says, "But Mary pointed to the babe. The wise men said: 'How can we talk to one who is a child in the cradle?' Jesus said: 'I am indeed a servant of God: He hath given me a revelation and made me a prophet.' " Imagine a baby speaking in the cradle right after birth! Quranic miracles resemble those in the New Testament.

Tenth, Muslims contend the Quran is scientifically precise, even though, according to sura 15:16, they believe in signs of the zodiac: "It is We Who have set out the zodiacal signs in the Heavens."

An interesting scientific inaccuracy in sura 29:41 says, "The flimsiest of houses is the Spider's house." In reality, pound for pound the silk composition of a spider's home makes it anything but the flimsiest of houses.

Eleventh, suras 19:97 and 44:58 say, "So have We made the Quran easy in thine own tongue." Suras 54:17, 54:22, 54:32, and 54:40 say, "We have indeed made the Quran easy to understand and remember." In fact, it's neither. One need only read the Book to see that. And sura 73:20 says, "Read you, therefore, of the Quran as much as may be easy for you," which for many can't be much. If there is anything the Quran is not, it is easy to read. How can one statement be so utterly false?

Sura 28:2 says, "These are Verses of the Book that makes things clear," and sura 43:2 says, "By the Book that makes things clear." If there is anything the Quran does *not* do it is make things clear.

Twelfth, Islam, like Christianity, degrades its supreme being, God, by alleging that he plays favorites. Sura 16:71 says, "God has bestowed His gifts of sustenance more freely on some of you than others." Gifts are not earned but given according to preference.

Thirteenth and lastly, we can't help but quote sura 25:30, which says, "Truly my people took this Quran for just foolish nonsense." Now why on earth would somebody do that?

Conclusion

A close reading of the Quran leads to the unavoidable conclusion that Islam in general and the Quran in particular deserve no more respect than Christianity and the Bible. Both are composed of superstitions, contradictions, hypocrisy, intolerance, brutality, inaccuracies and deception. A more comprehensive listing of Quranic failings can be found in issues 105, 106, and 107 of *Biblical Errancy*.

25

The Philosophy of *Biblical Errancy*

Cause for Concern, Tactics, Apologetic Defenses, Strategy, What's Needed, Procedures, A Personal Note

Much of this chapter emerged from a speech given in Chicago years ago and, like that speech, will focus on the most effective strategy and tactics by which to combat religious superstition in general and the Bible in particular. The purpose of this encyclopedia is to offset the entirely one-sided presentation of the Bible that is usually foisted on the public. One need only watch television or listen to radio to see that people are hearing all of the pros and none of the cons, all of the positives and none of the negatives. Naturally this is even more the case in churches, Sunday schools, and other religious forums. People have a right to know the truth; that's their prerogative. They have a right to hear reality and that's not being provided. Afterwards, if they still wish to remain in the maze of religious superstition through which they wander, that's their option, their error to make.

But to have a nation of 250,000,000 people in which tens of millions are hearing a totally biased presentation of anything, especially the Bible, is unwise if not dangerous. Unfortunately, many people put abortion, education, divorce, politics, and other topics into a biblical context and approach events from a biblical perspective. So it is imperative that the Book be exposed and confronted head on. A kind of Sunday School in reverse telling people all of the things they should have heard on Sunday morning but didn't is greatly, if not urgently, needed.

Cause for Concern

At this juncture some people will no doubt ask, So what? If people want to believe that superstitious medieval nonsense, let them. That's their mistake not mine. Answering this question thoroughly would require a separate chapter, but one need not cover all the gory details to illuminate the general situation. Biblicists absorbing the propaganda they are fed will eventually infect everyone in the nation, if for no other reason than the number of people involved. Believers in the Bible have potent political power and to shuffle them off to an isolated corner isn't realistic. An antisocial mentality with the following prominent features will emanate from those adhering closest to biblical teachings.

First, they will contend, for instance, that a better world is coming, so why work to improve this one? They won't be involved in the improvement of social conditions or participate in such projects as VISTA and the Job Corps. Even donations of money to missionary programs in foreign countries will be done more out of an urge to ingratiate themselves with others so the latter can be indoctrinated than out of a real concern for the welfare of fellow human beings. Their strategy is both subtle and insidious, if not unscrupulous.

Second, strong believers in the Bible are not going to be concerned with the environment or the physical rape, pillage, and plunder of the planet. After all, why be concerned if you are only going to live here for approximately eighty to ninety years? One former Christian recently told me that, in contrast to how he felt before, the fate of the whales has now become important to him.

Third, people who rely on the Bible are going to depend on prayer and outside forces to cope with life's vicissitudes, rather than their own efforts, which will make them easy to manipulate, especially by those pretending to lead them to the promised land.

Fourth, they won't oppose wars with real conviction and might even welcome them for several reasons: (a) To most Christians death is nothing more than a sleep in which you are waiting for a day to arise. So there is no real loss in dying. Since you can't really be destroyed regardless of what happens on the battlefield, why be concerned with war or the nuclear threat? (b) Since you're going to a better world, why be concerned about your fate in this one? And (c) why try to fight the tide of history since Armageddon is inevitable, regardless?

Fifth, they will oppose sexual equality and support the subordination of women. According to the Bible: a woman was the prime cause of original sin, women are less clean than men, and women are to be subservient to men. Paul's position on the role of women is especially demeaning and sexist. His male chauvinistic teachings can't help but damage the image Christian women have of themselves.

Sixth, of great importance is the fact that religious people are going to believe that giving to "God's representatives," people such as Jerry Falwell, Robert Schuller, Pat Robertson, and Billy Graham, is equivalent to giving to God himself. Buying their way into heaven is the unspoken motive and accounts in large measure for the fact that many churches and clergymen reek with affluence.

Seventh, believers are going to feel their antisocial behavior can be exonerated by bequeathing wealth to the church, repenting, confessing, accepting Jesus, fasting, abstaining, and fulfilling rituals. For many of them church-going will be a way to cleanse their record and conscience on Sunday for their bad deeds committed during the week, which will then allow them to continue as before the following week. People will seriously feel that confession, or something akin to same, will purify their account. Such concepts could foster antisocial behavior as easily as could the fundamentalist belief that good deeds are irrelevant to salvation. Once saved always saved.

Eighth, they will rely upon supposed experts to interpret Scripture for them, fail to view events objectively, be willingly subservient rather than independent, and see the world through the eyes of those who find them easy to persuade and manipulate.

Ninth, believing themselves to possess constant, eternal truths, they won't be open to change and new ideas, even though any qualified scientist knows nothing is so permanent as change.

Tenth, because of their belief in original sin, they will view people as inherently corrupt and associate with others on a basis of hypocrisy. While outwardly smiling and exhibiting all of the expected social graces, inwardly, they will look upon people as pieces of dung, to quote Martin Luther, fit only to be altered and remolded as deemed preferable.

Eleventh, as is often noted in freethought literature, adherents to Jesus will feel they have the truth, the whole truth, and nothing but the truth. The inevitable byproduct of their philosophy will be intolerance, with all the accompanying war and conflict.

Twelfth, those entrapped in the Judeo-Christian tradition will tend to view themselves as superior to others and chosen by God to carry his message. Because of the importance God laid upon the Jews at the expense of all others, biblicists will strongly believe in national superiority and adopt the national myopia so clearly evident in Old Testament authors.

Thirteenth, not being inclined to marry outside their religion, ethnic group, or nationality, they will adhere to a narrow, provincial outlook that will generate endless isolation and mistrust of those in other groups. Their minds will be closed to foreign ideas, regardless of validity or merit.

Fourteenth, those well schooled in scripture will emphasize genealogies, family ancestry, and family relations more than personal accomplishments and social relationships within the community at large. The narrow, clannish, ethnic mentality that will arise can only lead to conflict and judgments based on concepts such as bad blood and good stock.

Fifteenth, as outlined in Matthew, they will view antisocial behavior as the result of things from within rather than without. Conditions will *not* be seen as responsible for bad behavior; instead, internal factors will be viewed as the prime determinant. People of this persuasion fail to realize that if the latter were true, then most criminal activity would not arise from the poorer sections of society. Unbeknownst to them, people so indoctrinated are really saying that those who live in higher crime areas are inherently bad; something is wrong with them, personally, rather than their environment. But most antisocial behavior has far more to do with the conditions in which people are raised than anything innate. Affluent people have far more at stake and are less inclined to engage in antisocial behavior out of pure self-interest, if for no other reason.

Sixteenth, those placing their trust in the Bible will tend to rely upon saviors and redeemers, somebody who will lead them to the promised land, instead of their own wisdom and capabilities.

Seventeenth, because of concepts such as heaven and hell and rewards and punishments, people will be inclined to behave appropriately because they expect personal satisfaction rather than because it is the right thing to do. Good deeds and proper social behavior will arise more out of self interest than a real commitment to decency. The entire New Testament is closely involved with rewards, rewards, and more rewards. In truth, people should do the right thing simply because it *is* the right thing to do, not because they expect some kind of kickback or payoff.

Eighteenth, people who rely heavily upon biblical precepts will be more prone to accept and endure mistreatment and injustice than fight back.

Nineteenth, they will not be inclined to plan and labor but accept whatever fate has to offer, which can only lead to the detriment of all concerned.

Twentieth, because of statements in the Book of John and the Book of Acts, as well as comments by Peter and Paul, an anti-Semitic attitude will be hard to avoid.

Twenty-first, anyone taking the Bible seriously will have superstitious, mythological views on many subjects, which can only act as a terrible retardant on scientific advancement. For example, the concept of evolution—basic to every branch of the life sciences—is regarded by many Bible believers as anti-biblical nonsense.

Twenty-second, those who take Scripture seriously and believe miracles and supernatural intervention will deliver them from adversity will be more inclined to accept and endure than act and alter.

Twenty-third, because of the importance placed on the old Law, especially the Ten Commandments, the mechanical application of stringent laws with little or no consideration for mitigating circumstances, reminiscent of the ayatollahs in Iran, will be carried over into modern society.

And *lastly,* because of verses such as those found in Psalms, Christians will tend to sit back and relax, believing that corrupt people will get theirs in the end. As far as they are concerned, the outcome has been written on the wind by God, so to speak, and there is no need to act or be concerned. God will do it all.

In short, there are more than enough reasons for opposing all efforts to propagate the Bible.

Tactics

The question now becomes one of defining those tactics that should be employed by more rational minds to counteract people who place reliance upon the Bible. Radio and television are an especially effective means by which to combat the opposition because of the large number of biblicists who often listen to these media. One should seek to reach the maximum number of people possible and the media reach far more than speaking engagements or publications. Today's citizenry is oriented toward audio/visual messages and a radio or television audience of more than a hundred thousand people is quite common. Many will be affected, whether knowingly or not. So the question now becomes one of delineating the most reliable tactics to employ during media appearances. What follows are those stratagems that have been found to be most productive over the years:

First, and very important, ask the right questions. That is absolutely crucial. Even the order of the questions is important. If your initial points aren't effective or are easily countered, biblicists are going to look elsewhere. They'll not only lose interest in the subject but respect for your capabilities. Many adherents to the Bible look upon biblical encounters as comparable to preventing a breach. Remember the Dutchman who stuck his finger in the dike? Christians, especially fundamentalists, feel that if one point gets through, the whole dam will go. So they will fight very hard in the early stages.

Second, focus on absolutes. Concentrate on biblical statements containing words such as "only," "all," "each," "never," "every," and "none." Comments of an absolutist nature close the door and allow no escape. All that is required to doom the opposition is the identification of one or two exceptions.

Third, although important, a number of topics should be relegated to the back burner. Good examples are: the Babylonian influence on the formation of the canon, the history of church atrocities and bad popes, pagan influences on early Christianity, the similarity of beliefs between Christianity and other religions, dating the books of the Bible, determining who wrote what when, historical disproofs of biblical history, the theological beliefs of America's founding fathers, the history of the Canon's formation, and the creation vs. evolution controversy. These subjects should be given a secondary status for several reasons:

a. Biblicists won't recognize outside data of this nature and will simply say, "I don't care what you have, if it says the Bible is false, it's wrong, and that's that. The Bible is God's Word and they aren't." Even though a mountain of scientific and historical data may be submitted, they won't allow it to supersede scriptural pronouncements. This view is aptly expressed on page 103 of *All About the Bible* by apologist Sidney Collett, who says, "I prefer to take the word of the Lord Jesus before all the scientific men who ever lived." On page 39 of *The Bible, the Quran, and Science* Maurice Bucaille comments on this: "If science is useful [to biblicists] in confirming the Biblical description, it is invoked, but if it invalidates the latter, reference is not permitted."

b. To dwell on historical matters will only cause biblicists to trot out historians whose data proves the opposite. The problem with historical argumentation is that ultimately the issue comes down to whom you want to believe, because none of us were there. You have to accept the historian's word for it.

c. The main reason for avoiding these subjects is that they simply don't carry weight with the public. The average Christian doesn't recognize them as topics of real substance, but prefers to talk about Jesus, the Resurrection, and the requirements for salvation. He is far more concerned about his own welfare than anything else. As a result, freethinkers should stay almost entirely within the Bible and simply compare one part of the Book with another because Scripture is its own worst enemy: biblicists won't have something outside the Bible telling them the Bible is false; they will have the Bible telling them the Bible is false. And that is much more difficult to minimize or avoid. When something in Mark is saying the exact opposite of that which can be found in John, when Exodus is saying Deuteronomy is lying, biblicists are on the horns of a dilemma. They are much more likely to wrestle with problems of that nature than most of the usual antireligious argumentation on the market. They are problems that will haunt them long after an encounter has ended. Biblicists will mull these arguments over for a while, assuming they have any real concern for truth.

Fourth, in any biblical discussion start with simple problems rather than those of a more complex nature. The easier things are to comprehend, the less chance people will become lost. Focus on problems the average person with no in-depth training can understand. The following are good examples, especially when confronting people with some knowledge of the Book: Num. 23:19 says God doesn't repent but Exod. 32:14 clearly says he does. Exod. 33:20 says no man has seen God's face and lived, while in Gen. 32:30 a man says, "I have seen God face to face and my life is preserved." Solomon had *forty thousand* stalls for horses, according to 1 Kings 4:26, while 2 Chron. 9:25 says it was *four thousand* stalls. The text of 2 Sam. 10:18 has two contradictions in one verse. It says David slew the men of *seven hundred* chariots and forty thousand *horsemen*, while 1 Chron. 19:18 says it was *seven thousand* chariots, not seven hundred, and forty thousand *footmen*, not horsemen. Tactically, it is very important to dwell on chapter and verse, get in there among them, and don't run from the Book.

Undoubtedly one of the biggest sources of biblical problems lies in the fact that the Bible is horribly repetitious. Deuteronomy repeats a lot of Exodus;

Chronicles repeats much of Samuel and Kings; Proverbs is repetitious, and the Gospels follow in lockstep. And in all this repeating the Book constantly relates data that are out of synchronization. Christians could have eliminated everything that was repetitious and inconsistent, but they haven't had much coordination over the years and have allowed things to continue.

A good problem with which to agitate a radio audience is Rom. 3:23 ("All have sinned, and come short of the glory of God"). *All* means all; that's what it says. But Gen. 6:9 says, "Noah was a just man and *perfect* in his generations" and Job 1:1 and 1:8 say the same about Job. The obvious question is: If these men were perfect, how, then, can all be sinners? Biblicists will usually play with the word "perfect" and contend Gen. 6:9 doesn't say Noah is perfect; it says he was "blameless" or "complete." Authors of newer versions of the Bible try to escape the problem by revamping the wording. When Christians can't solve a problem and all else has failed, they often opt for the simple expedient of rewriting the script and this instance is no exception.

Another good example of script alteration is the "kill" or "murder" situation in the Sixth Commandment, which usually is translated as, "Thou shalt not kill." This creates a problem for Christian soldiers and other believers. How could any army or police force be successful if its members took "Thou shalt not kill" literally? Consequently, in many modern versions "kill" has been changed to "murder," for expediency's sake.

In regard to the rewriting of scripture, Maurice Bucaille makes the following poignant comment on page 9 of *The Bible, The Quran, and Science*: "These men manipulated the texts to please themselves, according to the circumstances they were in and the necessities they had to meet."

Fifth and lastly, a very important tactic is to focus on problems that require little more than reason, logic, and common sense. One doesn't have to be well-versed in Scripture or a biblical scholar to see many dead ends. Christians say, for instance, that you must have Jesus to be saved. That's an absolute rock-bottom requirement. What, then, do you do about fetuses that die in the womb and babies that die in infancy? What do you do about people with low IQs, the mentally ill, or those in the New World before the missionaries arrived? There is no means by which these categories of human beings could have accepted Jesus or accept Jesus, so they must be condemned to hell. But since they couldn't accept him and must enter hell, how could God be just, as is asserted in Deut. 32:4? This problem involves millions of people, because tens of millions of fetuses have died in the womb and hundreds of millions of people have lived in ancient and foreign cultures over the centuries. By saying people become human beings at conception rather than birth, fundamentalists exacerbated the injustice and intensified their problem by adding billions to the list of those wronged by being given no access to salvation.

Other problems of this kind are: Why are we punished for Adam's sin? After all, he ate the forbidden fruit, we didn't; it's his problem not ours, especially in light of Deut. 24:16, which says the children shall not be punished for the sins of their fathers. Moreover, why are women punished for what Eve did? That's her problem not theirs. Where is the justice? If Adam was created by God, then Adam had to have been perfect. How, then, could he have sinned? Defenders say, "He had free will." But regardless of how much free will he had, if he chose to sin then he wasn't perfect. If someone says he is perfect and seconds later sins, what better evidence could be produced to prove he isn't perfect? He has rebutted his own assertion.

To add to the maelstrom, we are being punished for Adam; that's wrong. Jesus is being punished for us, and that's wrong. Yet, it is all corrected by the death of Jesus on the cross. In essence, two wrongs do make a right, according to Christian theology. In addition, Jesus supposedly died on the cross for our sins and for that reason many Christians have a disgusting statue of a man being executed in their children's bedrooms. The theory is that Jesus stepped into our shoes and took our place. The problem is that no court in the land would accept an arrangement of this kind. If you were sentenced to death and your son voluntarily stepped forward and said, "I'll sit in the electric chair for my father," no judge in the nation would agree. For Jesus to die in our place is a magnanimous gesture, but it has nothing to do with justice. Any God who would accede to an arrangement of that kind just wants blood and doesn't really care who dies as long as someone pays. When our supposed savior was on the Cross he said, "My God, my God, why hast thou forsaken me?" How could he be our savior when he couldn't even save himself? Those aren't the words of a savior voluntarily dying for our sins but the words of a man who can think of a hundred places he'd rather be. He's not up there saving you or me; he's trying to save his own skin.

Another key problem is how God can talk to God. When Jesus was on the Cross he said, "Forgive them Father, they know not what they do." The obvious question is: To whom was he speaking? The common response is that he was speaking to God. But I thought Jesus was God! And they'll say, yes he is. But wait a minute! You have God talking to God. How can God talk to God? That's two Gods. How can God out there somewhere talk to God here on earth if there is only one God? Incidentally, Jews and Muslims also have an antitrinitarian stance because they view the trinitarian concept as blasphemous. The whole idea that a man could be God is both heretical and absurd from their perspective. One need only read sura 5:72–75 in the Quran to see that trinitarians are condemned to hell according to Islam.

Another very important pillar in Christianity's foundation is the Resurrection. Paul said in 1 Cor. 15 that without the Resurrection our faith is in vain. Christianity rises or falls on its existence. If Jesus didn't rise, there is no validity whatever to Christianity. Yet one need only cite all of the problems surrounding the Resurrection that were related in chapter 5, or in issue 2 of *Biblical Errancy,* to remove a crucial support in Christianity's edifice.

The point that probably strikes home more than any other, however, emerges from a recitation of God's deeds in the Old Testament. We are constantly told the Bible is God's word. But before anyone takes a claim of this nature seriously, he should be read a list of the repulsive deeds committed by God somewhere in the Bible. At this point the list of God's deeds related in chapter 9 or in issues 115 through 120 of *Biblical Errancy* should be read and followed by asking, "Now can you imagine anyone, any person, saying, 'Yes that's my book, that represents me, that's the way I am,' " especially a supposedly perfect being. Is there any individual in history with a worse record? In fact, to go even further, can biblicists cite one good, decent act committed by God in the entire Old Testament that would make you want to hug him around the neck, kiss him on the cheek, and say, "Good job, well done, I'm proud of you." Satan clearly comes out of the Bible looking much better than God. You'd almost think the Bible was written by Satan about God.

After about an hour or so of discourse with the Bible's believers, the latter will usually digress from the topic at hand and ask the following questions of an effective opponent: Who are you? Where did you come from? Why are you doing this? What do you hope to gain? and, of course, the everpresent, Are you saved? In too many instances, they seek to leave the Book, close its covers, and discuss their questions. That's sad because it exposes the extent to which they have been indoctrinated. The rationalizations of even the most intelligent believers begin to collapse when confronted by people aware of the Bible's shortcomings and able to present their case effectively.

Apologetic Defenses

In any encounter with the Bible's defenders, knowing the apologetic arguments beforehand is very important, because a few biblicists are knowledgeable and can handle themselves better than most. Freethinkers must not only know their material but also be aware of the arguments most often used by the opposition. So be prepared for the following defenses:

First, you are taking verses out of context. If this ruse has been invoked once, it has been used a million times. Freethinkers are supposedly extracting one verse, while ignoring all those in the immediate vicinity. Not true, is the only sane reply! One need only go to Proverbs, for example, to see that there is no context in many instances. The narrative is just a series of unrelated statements that leap from topic to topic. One need only read the verses verbatim to see that nothing is being taken out of context. That's a grossly unfair and inaccurate criticism in hundreds of instances. Many conflicts between the books of Samuel, Kings, and Chronicles, to cite other examples, involve nothing more than numbers and figures that are not open to interpretation or the contextual argument. If anyone is taking anything out of context it is the biblicists who find dozens of prophecies of Jesus in the Old Testamet by selectively quoting and isolating certain passages.

Second, another argument one can expect to hear is the "copyist" defense. Biblicists will concede the Book has contradictions but contend that that is because somebody incorrectly copied the original manuscripts. On page 15 in *All About the Bible* apologist Sidney Collett says,

> But in spite of all this painful care, mistakes did creep in, as the documents now in existence show; for this work of copying was after all human. Perhaps one of the most striking cases of a copyist's error is found in the age of Ahaziah, 2 Kings 8:26 stating that he was 22 years old when he began to reign, while 2 Chron. 22:2 says he was 42. Now none of the original documents in our possession help us in this at all, so that it is evidently due to an error of a very early copyist.

What "original documents"? How does Collett know there were documents of this kind? And where are these original documents that are now in our possession? No doubt hundreds of scholars would like to have that question answered. On page 94 in *I'm Glad you Asked* apologists Kenneth Boa and Larry Moody say, "Errors have crept into the biblical *text* through scribal mistakes and modernization. For example, 1 Kings 4:26 states that Solomon had 40,000 stalls of horses for his chariots, but 2 Chron. 9:25 says that the figure is 4,000. The exaggerated figure in 1 Kings is a common scribal error due to similarity in numerical notation. (Also compare 2 Sam. 10:18 with 1 Chron. 19:18.)"

But how do Boa and Moody know that that is true, since everyone agrees we have no copies of the originals? Anything we have, any translation, be it the KJV, the RSV, the NASB, the NIV, or any other, is merely a book composed by a group of people looking at a collection of documents that purport to be accurate representations of original documents that no longer exist. We have thousands of documents and no valid way of knowing not only which ones have copyist errors and which don't, but also what the errors are. In too many cases estimates, "guesstimates," and votes have determined the outcome.

Third, another common argument is that freethinkers are unqualified to criticize because they don't know Greek and Hebrew. Biblicists claim you have to know these languages in order to understand the original meaning. In truth, you don't have to be a scholar in either language. On page 20 in a work entitled *Bible Difficulties* fundamentalist William Arndt admitted as much when he said, "With the various revised versions at hand, with an analytical concordance, with reliable commentaries, and with the help of dictionaries of the Bible language, the reader need not know Greek or Hebrew to verify the original meaning of a given passage. He has in his mother tongue the means whereby he may determine the correctness of most of the obscure translations."

One does not need to know these languages to ask questions like most of those already posed. Of equal importance is the fact that scholars don't even agree on how verses should be translated. You could be the world's greatest Greek or Hebrew scholar and still have experts dispute your interpretations. So who is correct? If scholars agreed, there wouldn't be so many versions on the market with major differences.

Fourth, another defense one can expect to face is the "natural man" argument. The text of 1 Cor. 2:14 says, "The natural man receiveth not the things of the Spirit of God for they are foolishness unto him: neither can he know them, because they are spiritually discerned." In other words, until you adopt a particular mindset, a certain mentality, you won't be *able* to see that the Bible is true. All biblicists are saying with this circular argument is that if you accept it as true, you'll see it's true, and if you see it's true, you'll accept it as true.

Fifth, a related defense, as circular as the "natural man" argument, is the "let Scripture interpret Scripture" ploy, according to which you can only interpret the Bible accurately by seeing the overall themes of the Bible. But this defense is nothing more than a self-fulfilling strategy of picking and choosing passages that support a preconceived notion while ignoring and rationalizing away those that don't.

Sixth, another oft-invoked defense falls under the label of what is known as Pascal's Wager: You'd better believe it; you never know, it might be true; don't take any chances; be on the safe side. It goes without saying that anyone who believed something for that reason, and that reason alone, would be a hypocrite of the first magnitude. But even more importantly, you'd have to believe thousands of religions simultaneously just to be "on the safe side," because you could never be sure which one taught the truth. Why focus only on Christianity unless, of course, you have already been influenced?

Many beliefs of different religions are diametrically opposed. How, for example, could I be a Muslim and a Christian simultaneously, when one of them says that you must be a trinitarian and the other says that trinitarians are guilty of blasphemy and condemned? Because a dichotomy is present and one excludes the other, a gamble is unavoidable. All Christians are gambling not only with respect to which denomination is correct but with respect to whether or not it is wise even to be a Christian.

Seventh, another widespread defense is that critics are overusing the literal approach. "You have to realize there are symbolic meanings and metaphors" is the common refrain. This defense is usually employed when the common sense interpretation of the natural meaning of the words creates an obvious inaccuracy or absurdity. Although a valid defense in a few instances, it is nearly always employed by biblicists for no other reason than to escape a mess.

Eighth, another prominent defense one can expect to hear is: That's what it says but that's not what it means. To that one can't help but ask: If that's not what it means, then why was it translated that way? Advocates of this tactic are actually saying they could have constructed a more appropriate version of the text than a panel of experts and, in so far as the text under consideration is concerned, the latter are incompetent. In effect, adherents to this defense are contending they know Greek and Hebrew better than a distinguished group of scholars. Virtally every version of the Bible on the market was composed by a group of Greek and Hebrew translators who examined a wide variety of manuscripts and chose the wording they deemed most suitable. For this defense to merit serious consideration it would have to emanate from someone who was not only exceedingly adept in the art of translating but extremely well versed in Greek and/or Hebrew. And unfortunately, those who rely upon this defense most are often anything but well-versed in such knowledge.

Ninth, another common rebuttal is that the culture of that era accounts for scientific fallacies and behavioral shortcomings in the Bible, especially the Old Testament. Despite apologetic adherence to an immutable Decalogue, the slaughtering of innocent babies and other atrocious acts are somehow acceptable and scientific observations need not be precise in what is deemed to be the perfect book. In reality, in all too many instances, cultural context can neither mitigate nor justify the abrogation of scientific absolutes and moral imperatives which have prevailed from the beginning. This defense is little more than a disingenuous contrivance that is often discomforting even for its proponents.

A *tenth* and final argument often relied upon is that of pettiness. Pettiness is a matter of opinion, and what is petty to some is justifiably serious to others. Effective lawyers often use details deemed "petty" by their opposition.

Ironically, apologist Richard Sisson provides as poignant a comment on these apologetic defenses as anyone when he says on pages 55 and 56 in volume 2 of *Answering Christianity's Most Puzzling Questions,* "People do strange things when they are cornered by facts. When evidence cannot be denied, men who care nothing for the truth simply become illogical. Minds become willfully ignorant and emotions turn hostile." His observations are both relevant and cogent for deeds so prevalent.

In summary, the freethinker should spend a significant amount of time in bookstores and libraries reading apologetic works. One should prepare as would a general going into battle. Anyone who intends to fire something over should know what could return in response. All teams in sports send out scouts to evaluate the opposition; businesses buy and analyze their opponents' products, and all nations spy on one another constantly. Each knows he must discover what resides in the other's arsenal before competition is a realistic option. Those who go on the air without having done their homework can expect to be hit with unfamiliar arguments, thrown off track, and even unnerved to some extent. So, knowing what lies in the opponent's inventory prior to an encounter is both prudent and wise. That's not to say the opposition won't score some points. At one time or another every freethinker has not fared as well as he would have liked. But the secret to ultimate success is to do your research, be prepared, return to the fray, and don't quit.

Strategy

The following outline describes the best overall strategy for the freethought movement in general.

First, proselytization is a must. Freethinkers must go on the offensive and not expect biblicists to come calling. Why would people come to sanity when they are already convinced they have the truth? They must be shown the error of their ways before they will be open to other views. As of now this is certainly not being done. There is no reason to expect believers in the Bible to appear on our doorstep for quick conversions when they have been indoctrinated to believe that freethinkers are satanic agents. That is a major roadblock to all dialogue. You cannot build a parallel road and say, "Look at my road; isn't it better than your road? Why don't you travel down my road instead of yours?" You haven't shown your opponents what is wrong with their road, so why should they take yours? Freethought groups have only been picking up people who have rejected religion in general and the Bible in particular for their own personal reasons, not as a result of being persuaded or shown the error of their theological ways. All too often freethought organizations have been little more than psychological support groups providing a service comparable to that rendered former alcoholics by Alcoholics Anonymous.

Second, you must reeducate people by telling them what they should have heard from the beginning but didn't; that is, you must teach a kind of Sunday School in Reverse.

Third, you must build bridges, not walls, and eschew put-downs. Try to avoid damaging peoples' self-image or self-respect. The idea is to persuade and convert, not embark upon an ego trip to humiliate. To demean, degrade, or embarrass will do little to create sympathy, empathy, or liberality.

Fourth, generally speaking, avoid humor. Jokes are entertaining but will cause biblicists to assume you haven't seriously considered the topic and don't understand the full implications. If you'd only thought it through, you'd see it's true.

Fifth, don't use profanity and dress indecently. Do nothing that would confirm the image some people have of the Bible's opponents.

Sixth, return to the topic repeatedly; give people time to ponder your points, and return later with more problems. Unfortunately, members of the freethought movement will occasionally say, "Well, I met a Christian, presented many of my best arguments, and watched him ignore everything and walk away." What an inept analysis of the situation! Surely they don't expect positive results on such short notice! Having failed to convert someone in thirty minutes from beliefs held for thirty years, they become discouraged. That is by no means the real world. People must be deprogrammed as they were programmed. And how were they indoctrinated? By going to church and Sunday School week after week after week. People must be given information, be given time to mull it over, be given more information, and be given even more time to think. That is why it's so important for freethinkers to have weekly radio and television programs. Making a single appearance, submitting some concepts, and walking off victoriously into the sunset is more appropriate for the plot of B-grade movies than reality.

Seventh, people must be led from the Bible by a long, slow, gradual process of many revelations. That's how most freethinkers evolved. None experienced a miraculous change overnight. Nearly every atheist or freethinker came out of a religious background of one sort or another by means of a protracted and thorough transformation.

Eighth, and very important, freethinkers must enter the Bible and know its contents; that is crucial. A lot of studying is involved. You can't stand at a distance and throw rocks. For discussion purposes only, you must at first assume that such things as the Resurrection, Salvation, the Messiah, Judgment Day, and the like are plausible and then reveal the logical problems accompanying each concept. Freethinkers who say, for instance, that the Resurrection is nonsense, that when you are dead you're dead and that's that, or contend that salvation is a myth, won't get very far.

Ninth, put vague topics on the back burner, and none is more vague than eschatology. Biblicists love to talk about what happens after death and where the world is going. In Christian circles today eschatology is quite the rage and futuristic books are being published in abundance. The subject is very imprecise and no books in the Bible are more nebulous than Daniel and Revelation. Even Martin Luther rejected the latter because of its imprecision, and because he felt Christ and the Holy Spirit aren't in it. In essence, freethinkers should know when they are entering an arena that has a myriad of escape hatches and back doors because of verses that can be easily symbolized or spiritualized. Eschatology is one of the best because of its multitude of fire escapes.

And *tenth,* don't spend time debating atheism, agnostism, or humanism. Anyone who identifies himself as such is going to spend the rest of the encounter defending his own beliefs, while the Bible will remain unscathed. Once you allow the conversation to be sidetracked, your interrogators will start asking questions like: "How do you explain design in the world?" or "How was the universe created?" and so on. They will resurrect all of the old arguments that have been heard so often. You won't be exposing their ideas; instead, they will be attacking yours and you'll remain on the defensive throughout. Seizing the offensive is very important, because that is where success resides; don't expect to prevail on the defensive. Constantly return to their philosophy, not yours.

Another danger in discussing atheism, agnosticism, or humanism is the subtle manner in which the burden of proof can be shifted onto the shoulders of the critic when it properly lies on the shoulders of he who alleges. If somebody asserts there is a God, don't contend there is or isn't. Ask for proof; after all, he brought up the idea. Don't allow your opponent to challenge you to prove there isn't a God. That would be analogous to somebody telling me people live inside the planet Jupiter and saying, "If you doubt it's true, prove they don't." What he is really saying is that until I prove they don't live there, they do, in fact, live there. That makes it true.

The Achilles' heel of all religious, superstitious thought is that the burden of proof lies on him who alleges. Those who concoct an idea must prove its existence. Listeners or debaters are under no requirement to prove its nonexistence. If a theory is to be accepted as true until someone can prove otherwise, then every crackpot, weirdo, hair-brained, screwball idea is valid until disproven. How could anyone prove beings do not live inside the planet Jupiter, for example? No one has the means by which to prove the idea is absurd. More importantly, however, no one is under an obligation to do so. Proponents of an idea, on the other hand, *are* required to prove they do. That's the essence of science, something apologist Donald Guthrie insidiously tries to undermine on page 97 of *Biblical Criticism* by referring to science as destructive criticism and superstition as constructive criticism. He states, "Destructive criticism begins with the assumption that nothing is valid until proved true, which a priori rules out the possibility of treating such a basic Christian event as the resurrection of Jesus as historical. Constructive criticism takes the opposite view and regards as valid the claims of the NT until they can be proved false."

Talk about standing reality on its head! Teachings of this kind show why religion is so dangerous to rational thought and should be kept from youthful minds. Assertions must be demonstrable and independently verifiable by different people. That is basic to science and rational thought.

In addition, if the burden of proof can be shifted to those who reject any given idea, by the time sufficient information has appeared to prove it is preposterous, many more asinine beliefs will have come out of the woodwork, only to place mankind in a never-ending treadmill of tracking down phantasms.

Those in opposition to the Bible should focus on pretested questions and have a battery of zingers ready for encounters. After providing your opening arguments on the radio, for example, discuss what interests callers, because they usually have a stable of topics that "turn them on." Don't belabor what strikes your fancy when it's clearly of little interest to others. Having an ability to sense what is activating the audience is very important. Teachers instruct first-graders differently than they do seniors, and that applies to critiquing the Bible as well. Methods and content must vary dramatically and be tailored to the audience. Being able to empathize and know when points are poignant are very important. It's also crucial to realize that activities of this nature involve more than a debate with fundamentalists. People are on a broad spectrum of opinion about the Bible that ranges all the way from fundamentalist to atheist and everyone is constantly evolving. Many points appropriate for Christian liberals carry little weight with conservatives and vice versa. For that reason arguments should be directed primarily toward fundamentalists because that will affect the entire spectrum. Exposing the Bible's inadequacies influences everyone to some degree. All will tend to gravitate to the religious left.

If arguments are tailored only to liberals, millions of conservatives will remain unaffected. Moreover, liberals tend to agree with freethinkers on many important topics. From their perspective, for example, each of the six creation days is referring to millions of years, not a literal day; Jonah wasn't swallowed by a whale or a fish, and a stick did not turn into a snake. Many of them reject as mythological almost as many events of this nature as do freethinkers, so an argument in opposition to miracles is not going to carry much clout with liberals. A more effective approach would be to say, for instance: "Wait a minute! You don't believe in Noah and the Flood; you don't believe Lot's wife turned into a pillar of salt; you don't believe Jonah was swallowed by a whale; you don't believe Adam and Eve were real people? Then you don't believe Jesus, because he said these events occurred. If you say they didn't occur, then you are saying Jesus is a liar and, thus, he couldn't be God. You're no Christian." That's a valid technique to use against liberals, as fundamentalists know well enough. Zeroing-in on conservatives is also preferable because they are the most vocal opponents of reason and liberals are so divergent in their views that refutation of some can leave many untouched.

Knowing who is reachable is very important. For those who seek conversions, debates with hardened fundamentalists like Jerry Falwell and Pat Robertson are all but fruitless, since they have not only a belief system but also financial empires at stake. One must be realistic. Instead, one should converse with biblicists of this kind before an audience that is reasonably open-minded and composed of a broad spectrum of religious views. By showing what's wrong with the beliefs of prominent fundamentalists, their followers or viewers will be influenced. In this particular instance, changing your opponent is not nearly as important as exposing the error of his ways before others. The main focus should be on the audience. Talk to the hard core only when you know people less firm in their views are listening.

A major problem with people in the freethought movement is that they are too satisfied with fending off religionists. Christians will appear at the door, for example, start a conversation, proselytize, leave some literature, and walk away. The freethought person will then reflect, "Whew, I got out of that one; he didn't change me; I won that exchange." Oh no he didn't. He lost! He lost because Christians are far more numerous than freethinkers and the latter can only gain by increasing their numbers at the expense of the former. Those freethinkers who actively engage propagandists brought to their doors for deliverance and direct them down the road to rationality achieve victory. Merely fending Christians off and keeping them at bay is not victory but defeat. Just because they failed to convert you does not mean you won by any means. With numbers what they are, freethinkers are in trouble if they don't expand their population vis-à-vis their opposition.

Encounters with biblicists, especially on the air, resemble court trials. The Bible is the defendant; the apologist is the defense lawyer; the critic is the prosecutor; the moderator is the judge, and the audience is the jury. Occasionally you'll have trouble on the air if your host is biased. Media people must be closely watched, as some are tricky. Sometimes, for instance, they will seek to set the agenda by determining the line of discussion ahead of time, which is comparable to asking the prosecutor before the trial what he's going to ask the defendant. Don't tip your hand or allow the line of discussion to be set by others. Unsympathetic people seek to channel the discussion to where the Bible is less vulnerable. So, know where the Bible is weakest and go there.

Another tactic that wouldn't be allowed in a court of law is interruption after the first question. Courts allow prosecutors to present their cases without interruption and an opponent of the Bible should be accorded no less. Then, if people want to criticize, that's acceptable. But a critic of the Bible should at least be allowed to state his case. Many hosts don't allow that. You present one point and are immediately pounced upon. All appearances should be tape recorded for reasons that will be explained later.

And finally, some crucial requests need to be addressed to the producer before appearances on the radio.

First, ask for a tape recording of your appearance.

Second, ask to have your name, address, and phone number broadcast.

Third, ask to be allowed to tell people that a free sample of your materials will be provided to anyone who writes.

Fourth, ask to be allowed to choose the opening questions.

And *lastly,* ask to know if someone is going to be on as your opponent. Not long ago I appeared on a California radio station and wasn't told I would be debating the founder of the Pensacola Bible Institute until five minutes before air time. I'd already read one of his books and would like to have known he was going to be on so I could have questioned him about its contents.

One of the few Christian programs in the United States with any intellectual content is John Ankerberg's television show. The program is one-sided, of course, but at least makes a pretense of scholarship and objectivity. When going on programs of this kind freethinkers should not debate two people simultaneously. Debating a Christian professor while also confronting the moderator, as is common practice, is to be involved in a two on one exchange in which you're allocated one-third of the time. Winning is very difficult when your opponents have two-thirds of the resources and you are restricted to one-third. You should also not be asked to debate half the audience simultaneously. Anybody who has confronted several people at once knows the difficulties associated with discussing different topics concurrently.

What's Needed?

The question now becomes one of deciding what needs to be done. This is of tremendous importance and merits special emphasis. Freethinkers should create a national organization of knowledgeable experts to write literature, give speeches, and appear on the media. It should be a think tank composed of individuals who know the book as well as believers and have a full-time paid staff. A tremendous amount of study and research will be required to accomplish its purpose. Unfortunately, Christians already have organizations of this kind. The Christian Research Institute, the Research and Education Foundation, and the "John Ankerberg Show," to name only a few, were all created for one basic purpose—to eradicate the opposition, figuratively speaking, and gain converts. They usually concentrate on the cults (Mormons, Jehovah's Witnesses, and Moonies) and similar groups because millions of people are involved in them. But if freethought organizations and publications grew to sizable proportions and became a real threat, biblicists would shift their focus and produce more information in opposition to secularists. A good example of the type of literature one could expect is a book that emerged several years ago entitled *The New Atheism,* which attacked me, Gordon Stein, Paul Kurtz, Madalyn O'Hair and some other advocates of freethought. Stein and I wrote responses in our respective publications. Biblicists pay people to attack the opposition and we need point men as well. We need institutes, courses, seminars, and relevant literature.

Fortunately, freethinkers who know the Bible and every issue of *Biblical Errancy* will be well-prepared to confront the opposition. *Biblical Errancy* is the most comprehensive refutation of the Bible in the English-speaking world, and could be the definitive source for critics of the Bible. Other people have produced similar information but no one, including Robert Ingersoll and Thomas Paine, ever created anything approaching the volume of *Biblical Errancy.* An antireligious enterprise of this nature will require a lot of time, energy, and "sticktuitiveness." One can expect a long, protracted struggle with no allowance for short attention spans or sunshine patriots. It's going to be more like Valley Forge in the winter than Acapulco in the summer. But a very satisfying sense of accomplishment will surely emerge.

In response to this strategy many will no doubt say, "You mean I have to do all that? You mean I have to read, study, research, and so forth?" No, not necessarily. Some people just can't bring themselves to read the Bible, especially the King James Version, with all those "thee's," "thou's," and "begat's" of Elizabethan English. To them it's a bore, and, frankly, I'm sympathetic. I can think of a hundred books I'd rather read than the Bible. The plot is often thin. It's repetitious and often about as exciting as reading a dictionary. But it must be mastered. Because of its numerous supporters, Scripture can't be avoided. For those who can't bring themselves to master its intricacies, other activities are available. Productive efforts would include such things as:

a. Calling colleges and other institutions to arrange appearances for *Biblical Errancy* spokespersons.

b. Calling radio stations that have Christian mouthpieces and asking if they feel an obligation to provide balance; then volunteering our panel of experts.

c. Providing funds and other physical services such as lodging and transportation for traveling freethought spokespersons.

d. Circulating public access tapes.

e. Asking eight to ten well-chosen questions.

f. Arranging speaking engagements.

g. Distributing anti-Bible literature, especially that produced by *Biblical Errancy,* at conventions and assemblies.

h. Sending letters to the editors of newspapers.

i. Reeducating those who come to your door. Don't be content with merely shooing them away. Don't let Mormons and Jehovah's Witnesses escape. After all, a poor misguided soul has been brought to your door for salvation from benightedness and this could very well be one of the few times he or she will ever be exposed to the Bible's inadequacies. At our home they are invited in and happily seated. After about forty-five minutes, though, they nearly always seek sanctuary elsewhere. As they start for the door I always suggest another meeting, and, although they sometimes agree, a repeat engagement rarely occurs. Pursuit is usually ineffective.

The freethought organization that is so badly needed should meet periodically so members can compare notes on what works and what doesn't. In order to discuss the most effective tactics to employ, every appearance by freethought spokespersons should be recorded. The whole encounter resembles a football game. You go to the locker room, play the tapes, and see what needs to be changed. Then you go out, play another game, come back, and view your tapes again. Self-criticism is a must and the subtle Judeo-Christian influences all of us carry to one degree or another must be screened. Most freethought people come from religious backgrounds and have not left their past as much as they think. Reservations dwell within. One can readily understand the concerns of an Ohio woman who recently stated she was afraid she would backslide and reenter the Christian ideological swamp if she started talking to biblicists.

Opposition, counterattacks, and censorship are to be expected. Censorship is especially insidious and surreptitious. After appearing on the radio I'm often told a return engagement is a distinct possibility, but it rarely occurs because of opposition from clergymen, station management, sponsors, hosts, callers, and other influential figures. I've had people admit as much during subsequent contacts. Free speech is not as prominent as we are led to believe and this becomes increasingly obvious as one's presentation becomes more powerful, more accurate, more poignant, more cogent, and more relevant. Although I'm sometimes brought on the media as an interesting diversion or sideshow, those responsible quickly learn they have a major problem on their hands. When all is said and done, however, conditions are by no means hopeless, because a broad spectrum of believers in varying stages of evolution and open-mindedness are seeking answers.

Procedures

For those who wish to approach biblicism proficiently and duplicate our process, the following are good procedures to use:

First, buy the *Layman's Parallel Bible,* which has four versions—the King James, the Revised Standard, the Modern Language, and the Living Bible—in parallel columns. Then proceed as follows. Read the King James Version. If you can't understand it, read the Revised Standard Version; it's newer and not quite as difficult. If you still don't understand the text, read the Modern Language Version. And if you still don't understand, read the Living Bible. It's a pathetic paraphrase with many inaccuracies, but easy to read. Go through the entire Bible in this manner. Buy a red pen with which to mark contradictions and other problems. Internal problems are noted on the pages to the left and external problems are noted on the pages to the right. Avoid Christian commentaries. Don't be swayed as to what is being said or what commentators allege is intended. Just read it cold.

Second, buy *Strong's Exhaustive Concordance,* because some kind of comprehensive index is a must. The location of every word in the King James Version of the Bible is provided. All you need to do is remember any word in any verse and the book will cite every verse in which it appears. Another key resource is a historical atlas of biblical lands that will help trace, for instance, the migration of the Israelites during the Exodus.

Third, contact Christians; go to their meetings and ask questions. Several years ago I participated in a Seventh-Day Adventist seminar on the Books of Daniel and Revelation and everyone present was of a fundamentalist mentality, except myself. I asked questions every week and after about the fifth or sixth week, you could have heard a feather drop when I spoke. The participants were afraid something was going to come out of my mouth they hadn't considered or didn't want to hear. The minister teaching the course tried to persuade me to join his church and stated privately several times that his church would send me to an all-expense-paid seminary if I would accept Jesus and work for his denomination. Those whom they can't refute they occasionally co-opt. Be willing to go to any meetings Christians sponsor *as long as questions are permitted throughout.* Don't waste time listening to one-sided sermons. The only strategy of greater potency would be either force or control of peoples' education from birth.

Conclusion

If you really delve into the Bible you will see that it is a maze, a mass, a veritable labyrinth of contradictions, inconsistencies, inaccuracies, poor mathematics, bad science, erroneous geography, false prophecies, immoral comments, degenerate heroes, and a multitude of other problems too numerous to mention. It may be somebody's word but it certainly isn't the product of a perfect, divine being. The Bible has more holes in it than a backdoor screen. In a society dominated by the Book's influence, all freethinkers should do what Adam and Eve did when they were expelled from the Garden of Eden. They went out and raised Cain.

A Personal Note

On a more personal note, people have often asked me why I would devote so much energy to analyzing the Bible. Why do you spend so much time reading a book you don't believe in anyway? they ask. Why do you waste your time? If the Book is not what it claims to be, then why do you care what it says? If people want to believe the Bible is divinely inspired, then why not leave them alone?

The answer to these questions is relatively simple. I spend so much time exposing the Bible because it needs to be done, that's why. Millions of people are receiving a totally unbalanced presentation of the Book. A far more accurate portrayal is badly needed, and since no one is filling that role to any meaningful degree, I feel an obligation to fill the void.

The Bible adversely affects millions of people in thousands of ways and it is crucial that both the Book's inadequacies and its negative teachings be exposed. Suffice to say, the Bible is a contradictory, deceptive, inaccurate, superstitious, debilitating, hallucinatory conglomeration of mythology and folklore that keeps its adherents in a detached stupor masquerading as a valid depiction of reality. Time is never wasted when it is devoted to altering the false opinions and beliefs of millions of my fellow citizens who vote and otherwise influence my environment.

502   THE ENCYCLOPEDIA OF BIBLICAL ERRANCY

If no attempt were made to change the beliefs of these people, they would continue as before and that could only inure to the detriment of millions, including myself. To leave them alone, as some suggest, would only be another way of accepting the status quo with the religious crowd on top. No thanks! Nearly all questions of this nature are little more than subtle attempts to discourage us from doing anything and are posed by those who would like nothing better than for our program to fade into the sunset.

Bibliography

Quoted Extrabiblical Sources

Ali, A. Yusuf. *The Holy Quran,* 2d ed. American Trust Publications, 1977.

Ankerberg, John, Dr. John Weldon, and Dr. Walter C. Kaiser, Jr. *The Case for Jesus the Messiah.* Harvest House Publishers Inc., 1989.

Archer, Gleason. *Encyclopedia of Bible Difficulties.* Zondervan Publishing House, 1982.

Archer Jr., Gleason L. *A Survey of Old Testament Introduction,* rev. ed. Moody Press, 1985.

Arndt, W. *Bible Difficulties.* Concordia Publishing House, 1971.

———, *Does the Bible Contradict Itself?,* 5th ed. rev. Concordia Publishing House, 1955.

Ata ur-Rahim, Mohammad. *Jesus: A Prophet of Islam.* MWH London Publishers, 1979.

Barnes. *The Twilight of Christianity.* Vanguard Press, 1929.

Bible Advocate Press, "The Change of the Sabbath," undated booklet.

Bible Advocate Press, "The First Day of the Week in the Bible," undated booklet.

Bible Advocate Press, "Should the Seventh Day Sabbath Be Observed?," undated booklet.

Blaiklock, E. M. *Jesus Christ, Man or Myth?* Thomas Nelson Publishers, 1984.

Blair, Edward P. *Abingdon Bible Handbook.* Parthenon Press, 1975.

Boa, Kenneth, and Larry Moody, *I'm Glad You Asked.* SP Publications, 1982.

Boice, James Montgomery, *Does Inerrancy Matter?* International Council on Biblical Inerrancy, 1979.

Bucaille, Maurice. *The Bible, the Quran and Science.* North American Trust Publication, 1979.

Callahan, John D. *Science and Christianity,* 1985.

Campbell, Patrick. *The Mythical Jesus,* 3d ed. Waverley Publishing Co. Ltd., 1965.

Collett, Sidney. *All About the Bible.* Fleming H. Revell Co.

Colquhoun, Frank. *Hard Questions.* Inter-Varsity Press, 1976.

DeHaan, M. R. *508 Answers to Bible Questions.* Zondervan Publishing House, 1982.

———. *Genesis and Evolution.* Zondervan Publishing House, 1978.

DeWitt, David A. *Answering the Tough Ones.* Moody Press, 1980.

———. *Beyond the Basics.* Moody Press, 1983.

Geisler, Norman. *The Battle for the Resurrection.* Thomas Nelson Publishers, 1989.

Geisler, Norman, and William Nix. *A General Introduction to the Bible.* Moody Press, 1983.

Geismar, Maxwell. *Mark Twain and the 3 R's.* Bobbs-Merrill, 1973.

Golding, Schmuel, *The Light of Reason,* 2 vols. Jerusalem Institute of Biblical Polemics, 1988.

Gromacki, Robert. *The Virgin Birth Doctrine of Deity.* Baker Book House, 1981.

Haley, John, *Alleged Discrepancies in the Bible.* Baker Book House, 1983.

Harrison, R. K., Waltke, B. K. Guthrie, and G. D. Fee. *Biblical Criticism.* Zondervan Publishing House, 1978.

Herbert, Dwight. *Saturday, Sunday and Salvation.* Pacific Press Publishing Association, 1980.

Ingersoll, Robert. *The Works of Robert G. Ingersoll,* 12 vols. Ingersoll Publishers, 1900.

Jefferson, Thomas, *The Writings of Thomas Jefferson,* 20 vols. Thomas Jefferson Memorial Association, 1903.

Johnson, Carl G. *So the Bible Is Full of Contradictions.* New Hope Press, 1983.

Kaplan, Aryeh. *The Real Messiah.* National Conference of Synagogue Youth/ Union of Orthodox Jewish Congregations of America, 1976.

Kennedy, D. James. *Why I Believe.* Word Inc., 1980.

Lawlor, George L. *Almah . . . Virgin or Young Woman?* Regular Baptist Press, 1973.

Lindsell, Harold. *The Battle for the Bible.* Zondervan Publishing House, 1981.

Lindsey, Hal. *The Late Great Planet Earth.* Zondervan Publishing House, 1971.

———. *The Liberation of Planet Earth.* Zondervan Corporation, 1981.

Little, Paul E. *Know Why You Believe.* Inter-Varsity Press, 1971.

Ludwigson, R. *A Survey of Bible Prophecy.* Zondervan Publishing House, 1975.

Luther, Martin. *Luther's Works,* 55 vols. Concordia Publishing House and Muhlenberg Press, 1960.

Martin, Walter. *Essential Christianity.* Regal Books, 1980.

———. *The Kingdom of the Cults.* Bethany House Publishers, 1985.

McCabe, Joseph. *Did Jesus Ever Live?*, in *The Myth of the Resurrection and Other Essays*. Amherst, N.Y.: Prometheus Books, 1993.

McDowell, Josh. *Evidence for Faith: Practical Apologetics*. Word Inc., 1975.

———. *Evidence That Demands a Verdict*, rev. ed. Here's Life Publishers Inc., 1979.

———. *More Evidence That Demands a Verdict*. Campus Crusade for Christ, 1975.

McDowell, Josh, and Donald Stewart. *Answers to Tough Questions Skeptics Ask About the Christian Faith*. Here's Life Publishers Inc., 1980.

———. *Reasons Skeptics Should Consider Christianity*. Here's Life Publishers, 1981.

Morey, Robert A. *A Christian Handbook for Defending the Faith*, 2d ed. Presbyterian and Reformed Publishing Co., 1981.

Morison, Frank. *Who Moved the Stone?* Faber and Faber, 1971.

Morris, Henry M., and Martin Clark. *The Bible Has the Answer*. Creation-Life Publishers, 1980.

Mounce, Robert H. *Answers to Questions About the Bible*. Baker Book House, 1979.

O'Brien, David E. *Today's Handbook for Solving Bible Difficulties*. Bethany House Publishers, 1990.

Ott, Ludwig. *Fundamentals of Catholic Dogma*. Tan Books and Publishers, Inc., 1974.

Paine, Thomas. *The Age of Reason*. G. P. Putnam's Sons, Knickerbocker Press, 1890.

———. *The Life and Works of Thomas Paine*, 10 vols. Thomas Paine National Historical Association, 1925.

———. *The Theological Works of Thomas Paine*. J. P. Mendum Investigator Office, 1875.

Pentecost, J. Dwight. *Things to Come, A Study in Biblical Eschatology*. Zondervan Publishing House, 1964.

Pickthall, Marmaduke. *The Glorious Quran*, 2d ed. World Islamic Publications, 1981.

Pinnock, Clark H. *A Defense of Biblical Infallibility*. Presbyterian & Reformed Publishing Co., 1967.

Rice, John R. *Abortion*. Sword of the Lord Publishers, 1975.

———. *Dr. Rice, Here Is My Question*. Sword of the Lord Publishers, 1962.

———. *False Doctrines Answered*. Sword of the Lord Publishers, 1970.

Rowland, Dunbar. *Jefferson Davis*, 10 vols. J. J. Little and Ives Co., 1923.

Ruckman, Peter. *Problem Texts*. Pensacola Bible Institute Press, 1980.

Ryrie, Charles C. *Basic Theology*. SP Publications, 1986.

———. *What You Should Know About Inerrancy*. Moody Bible Institute, 1981.

Sigal, Gerald. *The Jew and the Christian Missionary*. KTAV Publishing House, 1981.

Sire, James. *Scripture Twisting*. Intervarsity Press, 1980.

Sisson, Richard. *Answering Christianity's Most Puzzling Question,* vols. 1 and 2. Moody Press, 1982.

Sproul, R. C. *Knowing Scripture*. Intervarsity Press, 1977.

———. *Reason to Believe*. Zondervan Publishing House, 1978.

Stewart, Donald. *99 Questions People Ask Most About the Bible*. Tyndale House Publishers, 1987.

———. *101 Questions People Ask Most About Jesus*. Tyndale House Publishers, 1987.

Trail Guides. "Catholicism Speaks," undated pamphlet.

———. "Letter from Rome," undated pamphlet.

———. "Questions and Answers About the Bible Sabbath," parts 1 and 2, undated pamphlet.

———. "Who Changed the Bible Sabbath?", undated pamphlet.

Ward, Norman. *Perfected or Perverted*. Which Bible? Society.

Weber, Timothy P. *The Future Explored*. SP Publications, 1978.

Wenham, John. *Easter Enigma*. Zondervan Publishing House, 1984.

Wood, Barry. *Questions Non-Christians Ask*. Fleming H. Revell Co., 1977.

General Index

Index of Verse Citations

THE BOOK OF MORMON

THE QURAN